Contents

PAGE 2

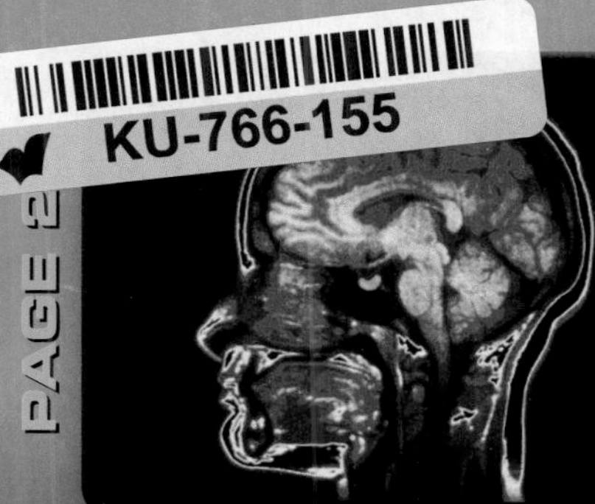

The pituitary gland is the 'master' gland.

PAGE 63

He can hold his drink!

PAGE 128

Experiments that go with a bang.

PAGE 184

What's lurking in your food?

PAGE 281

From Galileo to Hubble.

Welcome to Collins GCSE Science!

This book aims to give you a fascinating insight into contemporary science that is relevant and useful to you, right now today. We have written it to convey the excitement of Biology, Chemistry and Physics, and hope it will help you to carry a knowledge and understanding of science and scientific thinking with you throughout life.

USING THIS BOOK

What you should know

There is a lot of science out there. The good news is that GCSE science builds upon what you have already learned. Key ideas are taken further and you will meet a few new ones. We've summarised what you should know for each main section: biology, chemistry and physics.

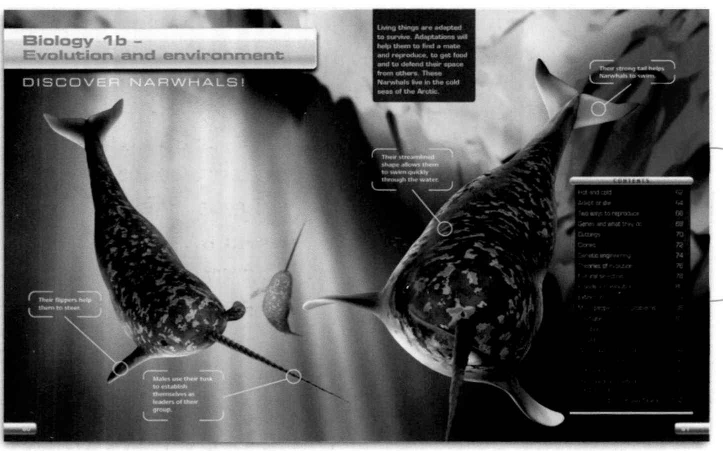

Unit opener

There are six units: two biology, two chemistry and two physics. Each begins with an image showing just some of the exciting science you will learn about. Also listed on this page are the spreads you will work through in the unit.

Main content

Each of the six units is made up of approximately 20 double page spreads. These tell you all you need to know. As you read through a spread you will start with some basic ideas and be guided to a more detailed understanding of the science. There are also questions for you to check your progress.

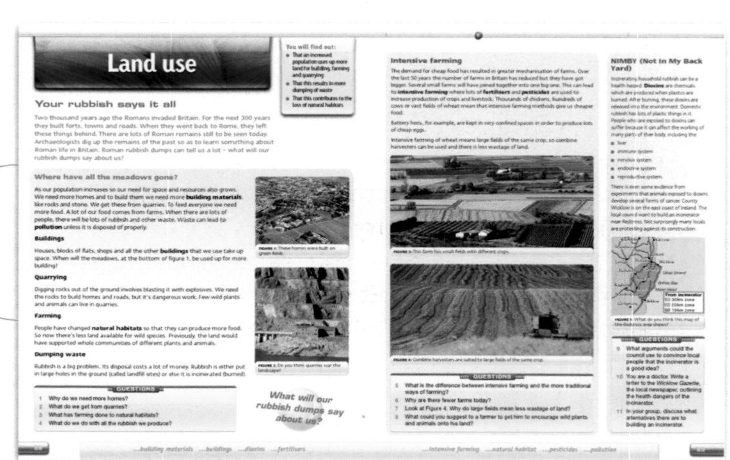

Coll...

...A GCSE

sc...ce

...R AQA GCSE
...CIENCE A+B

Ken Gadd SERIES EDITOR
Mary Jones
Aleks Jedrosz
Emma Poole
Rob King
Louise Petheram
Charles Golabek
Edmund Walsh

William Collins' dream of knowledge for all began with the publication of his first book in 1819. A self-educated mill worker, he not only enriched millions of lives, but also founded a flourishing publishing house. Today, staying true to this spirit, Collins books are packed with inspiration, innovation and a practical expertise. They place you at the centre of a world of possibility and give you exactly what you need to explore it.

Collins. Freedom to teach.

Published by Collins
An imprint of HarperCollinsPublishers
77–85 Fulham Palace Road
Hammersmith
London
W6 8JB

Browse the complete Collins catalogue at
www.collinseducation.com

10 9 8 7 6
ISBN-13 978 0 00 721449 5
ISBN-10 0 00 721449 9

British Library Cataloguing in Publication Data. A Catalogue record for this publication is available from the British Library.

Commissioned by Kate Haywood and Cassandra Birmingham; Publishing Manager: Michael Cotter; Project Editor: Penny Fowler; Project management, editing, page make-up and picture research by Hart McLeod, Cambridge; Page make-up by eMC Design; Additional editor: Anita Clark; Internal design by JPD; Cover design by John Fordham; Cover artwork by Bob Lea; Exam questions written by Dr Martin Barker, Lesley Owen and Karen Nicola Thomas; Glossary written by Gareth Price; Illustrations by Peters and Zabransky, Rory Walker, Bob Lea, Pete Smith (Beehive Illustration), Roger Wade-Walker and Angela Knowles (Specs Art); Production by Natasha Buckland; Printed and bound in Hong Kong by Printing Express Ltd

Acknowledgements

The authors and publishers are grateful to the following for permission to reproduce photographs. Whilst every effort has been made to trace the copyright holders, in cases where this has been unsuccessful or if any have been inadvertently overlooked, the Publishers will be pleased to make the necessary arrangements at the first opportunity.
p3ScottCamazine/SciencePhotoLibrary,KellyCline/istock.com,PeterGuttman/Corbis,NASA/ESA/STScI/SPL,OscarAlonsoAlgote/istock.com;p6tlScottCamazine/SPL,trBSIPVEM/SPL,blMaximilianStockLtd/SPL,brDanielBrunner/istock.com;p7tlBrockMay/SPL,trMehauKulyk/SPL,blCarolynA.McKeone/SPL,brRichardMelloul/Sygma/Corbis;p8/9backgroundAlfredPasieka/SPL;p8tlBryanThompson/istock.com,trVasileTiplea/istock.com,blWayneStadler/istock.com,brEricCoia/istock.com;p9tlRogerHarris/SPL,trNOTKNOWN,blMikeAgliolo/SPL,brJoyPowers/istock.com;p10/11backgroundJoeTucciarone/SPL;p10trAndreaLeone/istock.com,brFrankWright/istock.com;p11tlAndyButlerEyeUbiquitous/Corbis,trJoaoSaraiva/istock.com,blGeorgeArgyropoulos/istock;p12/13backgroundRogerHarris/SPL;p14.1AfloFotoAgency/OxfordScientificFilms;p15.6MalcolmRomain/istock.com;p16.1ScottCamazine/Alamy;p17.5CNRI/SPL;p18.1DavidReed/Corbis;p20.1AIRIO/RexFeatures;p21.4ConeyIJay/SPL,.5britishcolumbiaphotos.com/Alamy;p22.1ScottCamazine/SPL;p24.1BubblesPhotolibrary/Alamy;p25.2PascalGoetgheluck/SPL,.3JamesKingHolmes/SPL;p26.1DrArthurTucker/SPL;p27.3MargaretSmeaton/istock.com,.4TonyMcConnell/SPL;p28.1DexImage/Alamy,.2Gusto/SPL;p29.5Haslin/CorbisSygma;p30.1Reuters/Corbis,.2Reuters/Corbis;p31.3JeremyHorner/Corbis,.4WendyStone/Corbis,.5DavidMunns/SPL;p32.1TNTMagazine/Alamy;p33.4GJLP/SPL,.5SteveHorrell/SPL;p36.1GeorgeB.Diebold/Corbis,.2ComstockImages/Alamy;p37ig3StevieGrand/SPL;p38.1PaulFievez/BIPs/GettyImages,.2GeoffTompkinson/SPL;p39.3BSIP,AuscapeFerrero/SPL;p40.1DerekCroucher/Corbis,.2TimPage/Corbis;p41.3AndrewWong/Reuters/Corbis;p42.1Shout/Alamy,.2OttoLang/Corbis;p43.4RandyFaris/Corbis;p44.1PeterMenzel/SPL;p46.1DrJeremyBurgess/SPL,.2EyeofScience/SPL;p47.3SPL,.4JeanLoupCharmet/SPL,.5SPL;p48.1Dr;PMarazzi/SPL,.2SPL;p49.4SPL,.6Bettmann/Corbis;p50.1JeanLoupCharmet/SPL,.2JohnDurham/SPL;p51.3DrJeremyBurgess/SPL,.4Will&DeniMcIntyre/SPL;p52.1GaryParker/SPL,.3BiomedicalImagingUnit,SouthamptonGeneralHospital/SPL;p53.4CDC/JamesGathany/SPL,.5KevinFoy/Alamy;p54.1GettyImages,.2RoyaltyFree/Corbis;p55.4SPL;p56.12005JIC,.2SPL;p62.1leftDanGuravich/Corbis,rightReuters/Corbis,.22005JIC,.3WolfgangKaehler/Corbis;p63.4MichaelS.Yamashita/Corbis,.6PeterGuttman/Corbis,.7AdamJones/SPL;p64.1W.PerryConway/Corbis,.2ClaudeNuridsany&MariePerennou/SPL;p65.3leftNeilMillerPapilio/Corbis,rightWilliamErvin/SPL,.4DavidT.Roberts/SPL,.5bothMichael&PatriciaFogden/Corbis;p66.1JerryIrwin/SPL,.2Michael;PGadomski/SPL;p67.4bothChristianDarkin/SPL,.6Bluestone/SPL;p68.1AlfredPasieka/SPL;p69.4Will&DeniMcIntyre/SPL,.5MarkBurnett/SPL,.6JamesKingHolmes/SPL,.7JamesKingHolmes/SPL;p70.1SunnivaHarte/PhotoLibrary;p71.3OwenFranken/Corbis,.4SPL;p72.1JohnHoward/SPL,.2JimRichardson/Corbis;p73.4MauroFermariello/SPL,.5WinfredWisniewskiFrankLanePictureAgency/Corbis;p74.1MauroFermariello/SPL,.2BillBarksdale/AGStock/SPL;p75.3IanBoddy/SPL,.5VolkerSteger/SPL,.6VolkerSteger/SPL;p76.2Bettmann/Corbis;p77.4NikWheeler/Corbis;p78.1DavidAubrey/SPL;p79.3&4MichaelW.Tweedie/SPL,.5JimZipp/SPL;p80.1KajR.Svensson/SPL,.2KevinCurtis/SPL;p81.3NASA/SPL;p84.1D.VanRavenswaay/SPL,.2DrJeremyBurgess/SPL,.3SheilaTerry/SPL;p85.4RebeccaCairnsWicks,.5GeorgeBernard/SPL;p86.1BernardBison/CorbisSygma,.2SimonFraser/SPL,.3MartinBond/SPL;p87.5RobertBrook/SPL;p88.1LondonAerialPhotoLibrary/Corbis,.2PeterHulmeEcoscence/Corbis;p89.3PeterBowater/SPL,.4ChrisSattlberger/SPL;p90.1SimonFraser/SPL;p91.3NASA/SPL;p92.1DavidWeintraub/SPL,.2Bettmann/Corbis;p93.4Carl&AnnPurcell/Corbis,.5bothDrJeremyBurgess/SPL,.6ChrisButler/SPL;p94.3SimonFraser/SPL;p95.4bothAlfredPasieka/SPL,.5AdamHartDavis/SPL;p96.1SPL,.2allC.Gourlay&BrianCoakleyusedwithkindpermission;p98.1AndersRyman/Corbis;p99.4ScottCamazine/SPL;p100.1Magellan/NASAJPL/RogerRessmeyer/Corbis;p101.5PatrickWard/Corbis,.6JeremyHorner/Corbis;p102.1DrArthurTucker/SPL;p103.22005JIC;p104.12005JIC..2FrankGuergens/istock.com;p108/109backgroundSteveTaylor/GettyImages;p110.1Mica/Alamy,.2AndrewLambertPhotography/SPL;p111.4SPL;p112.1CharlesD.Winters/SPL;p114.1JoeMcDonald/BruceColemanInc./Alamy,.2AndrewLambertPhotography/SPL;p116.1MarkWallis/istock.com,.2BrianProirier/istock.com,.3ScottSpencer/istock.com;p117.6SteveGeer/istock.com;p118.1TheManitobaMuseum,Winnipeg,Manitoba,Canada,usedwithkindpermission,.2PamJeffreys/istock.com;p119.3JustinKase/Alamy,.4AndrewLambertPhotography/SPL;p120.1MarkStroeier/istock.com,.2MarkThomas/SPL;p122.2BiophotoAssociates/SPL;p124.1PaulLaragy/istock.com,.2LiCat/istock.com,.3DanVanOss/istock.com;p125.5leftSalem/istock.com,centreMilesSherrill/istock.com,rightHelleBro/istock.com;p126.1SimonFraser,.2KyleMaass/istock.com,.3SamanthaGrandy/istock.com;p127.4AravindTeki/istock.com;p128.1OscarAlonsoAlgote/istock.com;p129.5CharlesD.Winters/SPL,.62005JIC,.7istock;p130/131backgroundPeterCade/GettyImages;p130RogerBamber/Alamy;p131NicRandall/Alamy;p132.12005JIC,.3DavidCrockett/istock.com;p134.2leftStanLivingston/istock.com,rightLizVanSteenburgh/istock.com,bottomLorenaMartinez/istock.com,.3RobertBrook/SPL;p135.4ZoeYau/istock,.5JonahManning/istock.com;p136.1DoD/CNP/Corbis,.3SPL;p137.4JoseManuelSanchisCalvete/Corbis;p138.12005JIC,.2GillesGlod/istock.com;p139.5HughMacDougall/istock.com,.6PaulCowan/istock.com;p140.1Images/Alamy,.2KimKulish/Corbis;p142.1NASA/SPL,.22005JIC;p143.3SheilaTerry/SPL,.4PaulThompsonEyeUbiquitous/Corbis;p144.1AlaskaStockLLC/Alamy,.2LagunaDesign/SPL,insetKennethEward/Biografx/SPL;p146.1Reuters/Corbis;p148.1DuncanWalker/istock.com;p149.2CalebZahnd/istock.com,.3JackSullivan/Alamy;p150.1JoshuaSowin/istock.com,.2LesaSweet/istock.com;p151.32005JIC,.4PamelaHodson/istock.com;p1522005JIC;p158.1fountainofuselessinfo/istock.com;p160.1JoeGough/istock;p161.2PamRoth/istock;p162.1Prof.DavodHall/SPL;p163.2RaynaJanuska/istock.com,.3YoussoufCader/istock;p164.1MartynF.Chillmaid/SPL;p165.2JoyFera/istock.com,.3KissBotond/istocm.com;p166.1RobertFried/Alamy,.2BSIP/SPL,.3PaulTopp/istock.com;p167.4FlinnScientific,usedwithkindpermission,.5KennethC.Zirkel/istock.com;p168.1LisaMcDonald/istock.com,.2AlanCollins/istock.com;p169.3AndrewLambertPhotography/SPL,.42005JIC,.5CraigSmith/istock.com;p170.1JamesMargolis/istock,.2PaulCowan/istock.com;p171.3JerryMason/SPL,.5MonikaAdamczyk/istock.com;p172.1RobertBrook/SPL,.2MaximilianStockLtd/SPL;p173.3JonMcIntosh/istock.com,.4JamesKingHolmes/SPL;p174.1MarkEvans/istock.com,.3TomLewis/istock.com;p175.4JaimieD.Travis/istock.com,.6FoodandDrugAdministration/SPL;p176.1istock.com,.2JoseCarlosPiresPereira/istock.com;p177.5AndrewLambertPhotography/SPL;p180.1SamanthaGrandy/istock.com;p181.4CNRI/SPL;p182.1RachelBlaser/istock.com,.2JohnShepherd/istock.com;p183.3ColinCuthbert/SPL;p184.1KellyCline/istock.com,.2AndrewLambertPhtotography/SPL;p186.1TomVanSant/GeosphereProject,SantaMonica/SPL;p188.1BryanBusovicki/istock.com,.2TrulsSlevigen/istock.com;p189.4ArielLux/istock.com;p190.1Corbis;p191.3SpaceImaging/SPL;p192.1ElizabethShoemaker/istock.com,.2TonyMcConnell/SPL;p193.4DavidWoods/Corbis;p194.12005JIC;p195.3ChrisBjornberg/SPL;p196.1VeraBogaerts/istock.com,.2ThomasBlaser/istock.com;p197.3MichaelMarten/SPL;p198.1BrianDouglass/istock.com,.2JoyFera/istock.com,.3HorstGossmann/istock.com;p202/203backgroundHiroyukiMatsumoto/GettyImages;p204.1SteveGeer/istock.com,.2AndrzejPuchta/istock.com;p205.4MattMatthews/istock.com;p206.12005JIC;p207.5GertjanHooijer/istock.com;p208.1istock.com;p209.5TomMarvin/istock.com;p210.1SergeyKashkin/istock.com;p211.5ScottWaite/istock.com;p212.1KrzysztofNieciecki/istock.com;p215.3MarkSykes/Alamy,.4USDepartmentofEnergy/SPL;p216.1DavidWeintraub/SPL;p217.7FordMotorCompanyLimited,usedwithkindpermission;p218.1MaximilianStockLtd/SPL,.22005JIC;p220.1LawrenceManning/Corbis,.2AnssiRuuska/istock.com;p222.1RobertMinnes/istock.com;p223.5LuisLotax/istock.com;p226.1MartinBond/SPL,.3GBPhotostock/istock.com;p228.1GideonMendel/Corbis;p229.42005JIC,.5VolkerSteger/SPL:;p230.1MichaelDonne/SPL,.22005JIC,.32005JIC;p231.4RobertKyllo/istock.com;p232.1CoverSpot/Alamy;p233.3VStock/Alamy,.5DavidMartynHughes/Alamy;p234.1ValeryLarson/istock.com,.22005JIC,.32005JIC;p235.42005JIC;p236.1LindaBair/istock.com;p238.1YvesGrau/istock.com;p239.42005JIC;p240.12005JIC,.2ScottCressman/istock.com;p241.6CreditUSDept.ofEnergy/SPL;p242.1MartinBond/SPL,.2JoeGough/istock.com,.3FrancoiseSauze/SPL;p243.4BMPix/istock.com,.5EricCoia/istock.com;p244.1SimonFraser/SPL,.2OliverCannell/istock.com,.3MauricGapponi/istock.com;p245.4MartinBond/SPL;p246JIC;p250/251backgroundDetlevVanRavenswaay/SPL;p252.2TedKinsman/SPL;p253.3HowardSayer/Alamy,.4PhilippePsaila/SPL,.5R.Maisonneuve,PubliphotoDiffusion/SPL;p258.2/SPL;p260.1BSIP,Giral/SPL,.2AntoniaReeve/SPL;p261.4ColinCuthbert/SPL;p262.1JulianBaum/SPL,.2JimVarney/SPL;p263.4LowellGeorgia/Corbis;p265.4DrKFRSchiller/SPL;p266.1Underwood&Underwood/Corbis;p268.1STR/AP/EMPICS;p269.4MartinDohrn/SPL;p270.1GeraldFrench/Corbis,.2HankMorgan/SPL;p271.5WillMcIntyre/SPL;p277.3ISM/SPL,.5CordeliaMolloy/SPL;p278.1RoyaltyFree/Corbis,.2JimDowdalls/SPL;p279.3USDepartmentofEnergy/SPL,.4Reuters/Corbis;p280.1SheilaTerry/SPL,.2MikeMorley/istock.com,.3DavidParker/SPL;p281.5NASA/ESA/STScI/SPL,.6ChrisButler/SPL;p282.12005JIC,.22005JIC;p283.3DetlevVanRavenswaay/SPL,.5NASA/SPL;p284.2RoyalObservatory,Edinburgh/AAO/SPL;p285.3JerryLodriguss/SPL;p286.2GeorgeArgyropoulos/istock.com;p287.4DaleDarby/SPL,.5Sanford/Agliolo/Corbis;p288.2MarkGarlick/SPL,.3RoyalObservatory,Edinburgh/SPL;p290.1DetlevVanRavenswaay/SPL;p291.2DavidA.Hardy/SPL,.3NASAGSFC/SPL;p292.1ChrisButler/SPL;p293.2Dept.ofPhysics,ImperialCollege/SPL;p2942005JIC,AlbertLozano/istock;p298ImageStateRoyaltyFree/Alamy;p299.1Lisegagne/istock.com,.2KosPictureSource/Alamy,.32005JIC;p300.1AdamSmith/GettyImages,.2TekImages/SPL;p302HemeraTechnologies/Alamy;p303.1JIC,.2ChrisGeorge/Alamy;p304.1AndrewLambertPhotography/SPL,.2DynamicGraphicsGroup/ItStockFree/Alamy;p309GeorgeRanalli/SPL;p310DrJeremyBurgess/SPL;p311DrKariLounatmaa/SPL,DrJeremyBurgess/SPL.

The Publishers would also like to thank: The Random House Group Ltd. for permission to reproduce an extract from Rubbish! by Richard Girling, published by Eden Project Books.

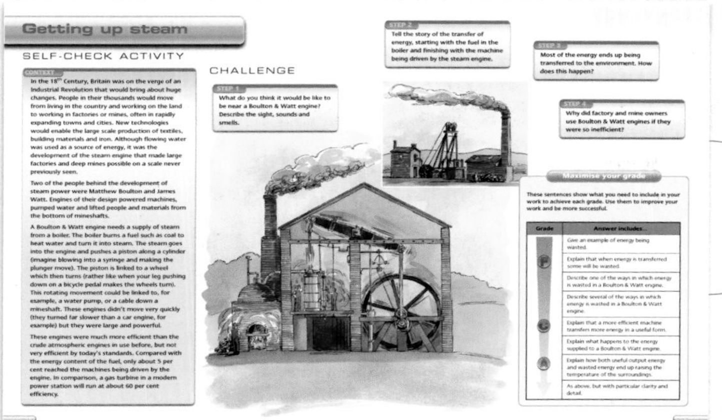

Mid-unit assessment

These give you opportunities to see how you are getting on. There are assessments for you to learn from. Each gives you a mini-case study to read, think about and then answer some questions.

Unit summary

Key facts and ideas, and the links between them, are summarised in spider diagrams. A really useful way of revising is to make your own concept maps. The diagrams are a good starting point for doing this. There is a quiz for you to try and an activity as well.

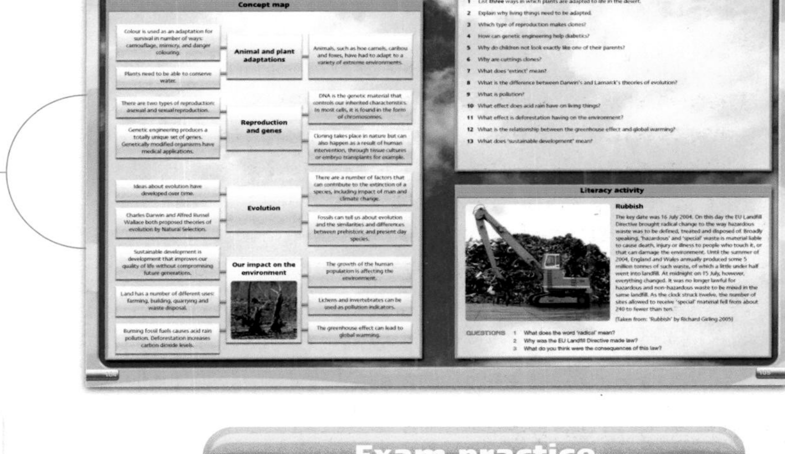

Exam practice

Once you've learned the science you have to show in an exam what you know and can do. Exam technique helps. It's important to be clear about what the examiner is looking for. It's also important to give your answer as clearly as possible. So we've provided you with some practice questions.

How Science Works

Scientists make observations and measurements. They try to make sense of these data and use them to develop scientific ideas. They design and carry out investigations. We've given you some things to think about. Hopefully it will give you an insight into the thinking behind the doing.

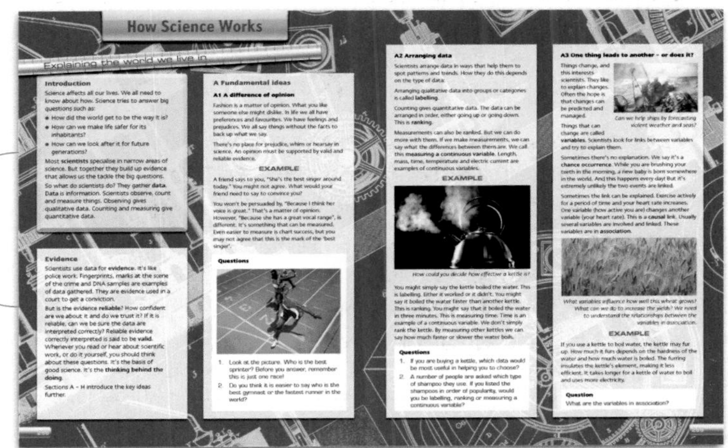

Cells, tissues, organs and systems

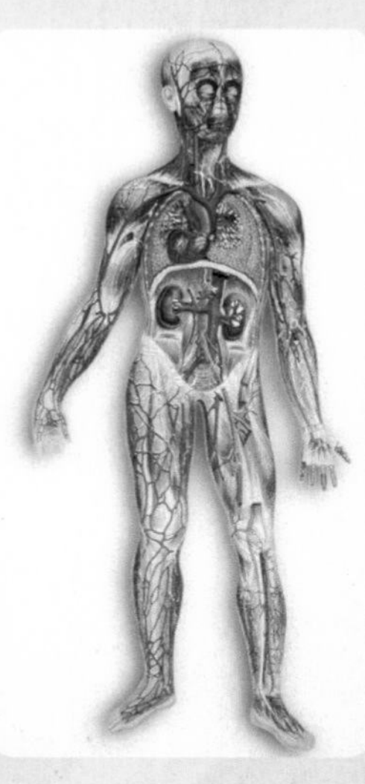

All living things are made of cells. There are many different kinds of cells, each one adapted for a particular function.

Cells group together to form tissues, and tissues group together to form organs. The heart, brain and stomach are examples of organs. Groups of organs that are involved in the same tasks form body systems. So, for example, the heart and the arteries are part of the blood system.

1 Name one specialised cell. What is its function? How is it adapted for this function?

2 Give one example of an organ not mentioned here. What body system is it part of?

Human reproduction

A new life begins when a sperm fuses with an egg, forming a zygote. The zygote develops into a fetus and then into an embryo, in the mother's uterus.

On average, an egg is released each month from a woman's ovaries. The lining of the uterus grows thicker, ready to receive the egg if it is fertilised. If it is not, then the lining breaks down and is lost from the body during menstruation.

3 Name the part of a man's body where sperm are made, and the part of a woman's body where eggs are made.

4 What is the name for the organ in the uterus that allows the mother's and embryo's blood to come very closely together and exchange substances?

Food and energy

A balanced diet contains some of each main nutrient type – carbohydrates, fats, proteins, minerals, vitamins, fibre (roughage) and water.

As food passes through the digestive system, large molecules are broken down to small ones. The small molecules are absorbed through the walls of the intestine. They go into the blood, and are carried around the body to every cell.

Cells get the energy they need by combining glucose with oxygen. This is called aerobic respiration. Oxygen diffuses into the blood from the air spaces in the lungs, while carbon dioxide diffuses in the other direction.

5 Name one mineral and one vitamin, and say why we need them.

6 Write down the word equation for aerobic respiration.

Keeping healthy

A good diet is a good start for being healthy. So is taking some kind of exercise that you enjoy.

Smoking does great damage to the lungs and heart. It often causes cancer. Alcohol is a drug that affects the activity of the brain. It slows down your response times and makes it likely that you will make bad decisions.

Although some bacteria are useful to us, some can cause infectious diseases. So can viruses. The body has its own natural protection against them, most importantly our white blood cells. We can also use antibiotics to kill bacteria in the body. Immunisation can protect against some infectious diseases.

7 What is the addictive substance in tobacco smoke?

8 Name one disease caused by a virus, and one caused by a bacterium.

Adaptations

All living things are adapted. This lets them interact with their environment and survive in their natural habitat. Habitats range from the very cold to the very hot. This means that living things will be adapted in different ways.

9 What does "survival" mean?

10 Name a habitat. Describe how a plant or animal is adapted to surviving there.

Reproduction and genes

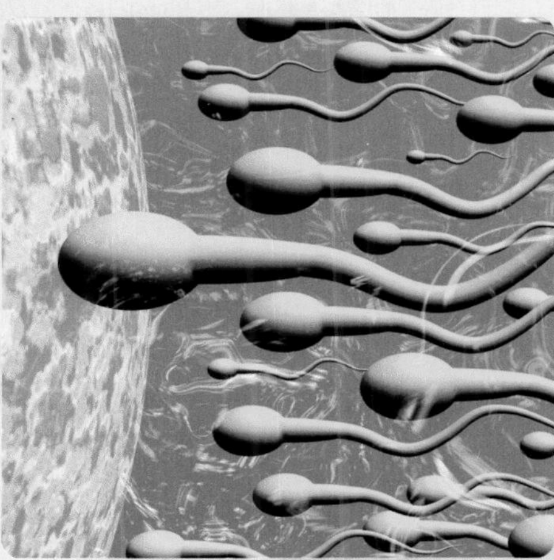

Living things need to reproduce. Eggs and sperms contain information that is inherited by the offspring. A fetus, or embryo, is the developing offspring. Not all characteristics are inherited; some develop as a result of the environment.

11 Why do living things need to reproduce?

12 What happens when the embryo has finished developing?

Evolution and extinction

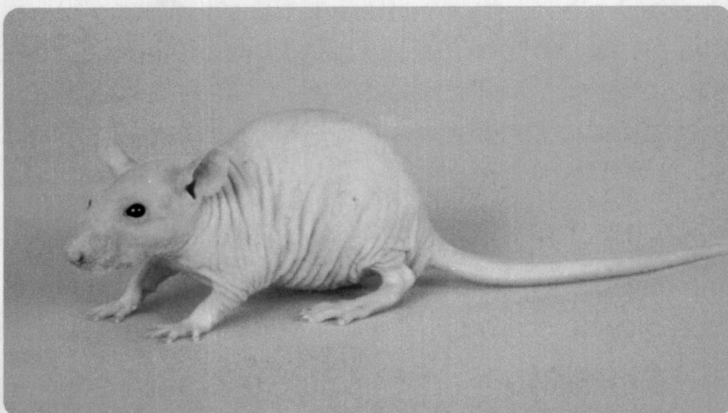

Living things show variation. Offspring of the same parents will not be identical, they will show variation. Some of this variation will be inherited and the rest will be as the result of environmental influences. Selective breeding can result in new varieties of living things.

13 What does it mean when we say that living things show variation?

14 What does selective breeding mean?

Our environment

Living things, and the environment, need protection from the damaging effects of human activity. This includes burning fossil fuels and the use of toxic materials on the land. Fossil fuels were made from prehistoric plants and animals. This took millions of years. When oil, coal and natural gas are burned, acid rain is produced.

Fertilisers, herbicides and pesticides are toxic substances. They are used by farmers but sometimes they can accumulate in food chains and food webs.

15 How do toxic chemicals affect food chains?

16 What is meant by sustainable development?

Atoms

Materials can be classified as solids, liquids or gases, but they are all made up of tiny particles called atoms. Elements are made of just one type of atom. There are only about one hundred different elements. Atoms can join together to form molecules. A molecule of oxygen is made when two oxygen atoms join together. When atoms of two or more different elements join together, a compound is formed. The compound carbon dioxide is made when carbon and oxygen atoms are joined.

1 What is the difference between a compound and a mixture?

2 What type of atoms would be found in a molecule of sulfur dioxide?

Limestone

Limestone is a sedimentary rock. All limestones contain the compound calcium carbonate but their exact composition varies depending on how the limestone was originally formed. Powdered limestone can be used to neutralise acidic soils.

When limestone is heated, a chemical reaction takes place. However, the total mass before the reaction is always the same as the total mass after the reaction. This is because there must still be the same number of atoms; they are just arranged in a different way.

3 If a limestone rock is a brown colour what does this tell us about where it was formed?

4 Why do we powder limestone before we use it to neutralise soils?

Useful metals

Metals like copper and iron are very useful materials. They are hard and strong and can be used to make objects like cars or boats. Metals are also good conductors of heat and electricity. A few metals, like gold can be found as nuggets in nature. These metals are very unreactive.

Most metals can only be found as part of a compound. Ores contain high concentrations of metal compounds. Metals can be extracted from these ores. Different methods are used to extract the metal depending on how reactive the metal is.

5 Would you expect the metal sodium to be found as a pure nugget or as part of a compound? Why?

6 Metals are good conductors of electricity. What types of material are poor conductors?

Fuels

We use a wide vareity of different fuels, including petrol, wood, oil and natural gas. When fuels are burnt, they release energy. All of these different fuels contain the elements carbon and hydrogen. When we burn hydrogen, it reacts with oxygen in the air to form water vapour.

hydrogen + oxygen → water vapour

When carbon is burnt in a good supply of air, the gas carbon dioxide is produced.

carbon + oxygen → carbon dioxide

Some fuels contain the element sulfur. When this is burnt, the gas sulfur dioxide is formed. If sulfur dioxide is released into the atmosphere, it can cause acid rain. This can damage plants and aquatic life.

7 What is the gas required for things to burn?

8 What gas causes acid rain?

Important chemicals made from crude oil

Crude oil is a mixture of compounds called hydrocarbons. These are compounds made up of hydrogen and carbon only. Crude oil can be separated into fractions using a process called fractional distillation. In this process, hydrocarbons which have different boiling points are separated. The fractions that are produced from crude oil are very useful. Petrol, diesel and liquid petroleum gas are three very important fractions that are obtained from crude oil.

9 Give the names of three fractions that can be separated from crude oil.

10 How does fractional distillation separate crude oil into fractions?

Oil from plants

Oils are not just found in the ground. Many oils are found naturally in plants and animals, and they can be very useful. Oil and water do not mix and so can be easily separated from each other. They could also be separated using distillation since they have different boiling points.

When oils are burnt, heat energy is released, so they can be used as fuels. When we eat oils in plants and animals, oils provide us with energy so that we can live and have healthy lives. However, it is important that we do not eat too much oil, since this may be bad for us.

11 What is seen when water and oil are shaken together and then left?

12 Why it is important that we eat oils in our food?

The Earth

The Earth is a planet and orbits the Sun. The Earth is made of rock of many different types. The rocks are called sedimentary, metamorphic and igneous rocks. Rock can change over many millions of years by means of the processes of weathering and erosion. Rocks are changing all the time. The three main rock types will change into other rock types. This process is called the rock cycle.

Pollution that is produced by humans can also change rocks. Acid rain, for example, will weather rocks. This type of rain is formed when some gases dissolve in rainwater to make acids.

13 What are the three types of rock classes?

14 How is acid rain made?

The atmosphere

The atmosphere is a layer made of air that surrounds the Earth. It contains many gases, some are really important for life, like oxygen. Other gases like nitrogen and argon are also found in the air but these gases are a lot less reactive than oxygen. Air is therefore a mixture of gases. Plants photosynthesise by taking in carbon dioxide gas and making oxygen gas. Photosynthesis is a very important chemical reaction that allows life to be found on our planet.

15 Give the names of three gases found in the air.

16 What is the name of the chemical process that plants use in order to grow?

Heat and heat flow

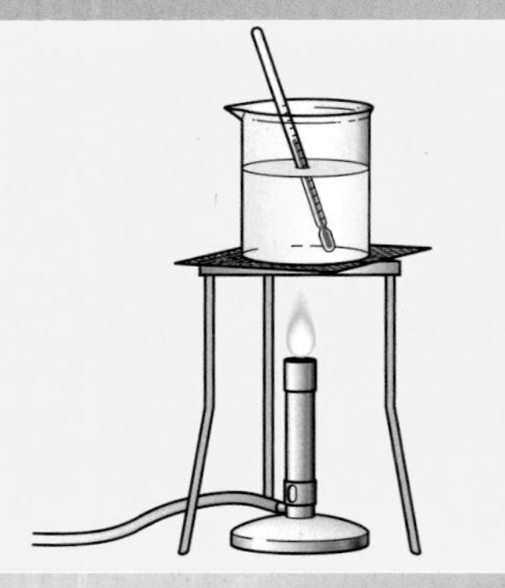

Heat is a type of energy. When objects gain heat energy, they get hotter. When they lose heat energy, they get cooler. We use a thermometer to measure the temperature of something, to tell us how hot it is. The unit of temperature is degrees Celsius (°C). There are three ways objects can gain or lose heat energy – by conduction, by convection or by thermal radiation.

1 What instrument is used to measure temperature? What is the unit?

2 What will happen to the temperature of something when it gains heat energy?

Energy and energy changes

Whenever we see any change happening, we know that energy is involved. We use different names to describe the energy that we see in different places or doing different things. For example, we could say that this motorbike has kinetic energy (movement energy), sound energy and heat energy. Lots of the things we use change (or transform) energy from one form to a different form. For example an electrical heater transforms electrical energy into heat energy.

3 How could you tell that the motorbike has heat energy?

4 What energy changes happen in you when you eat food, then run a race?

Saving energy

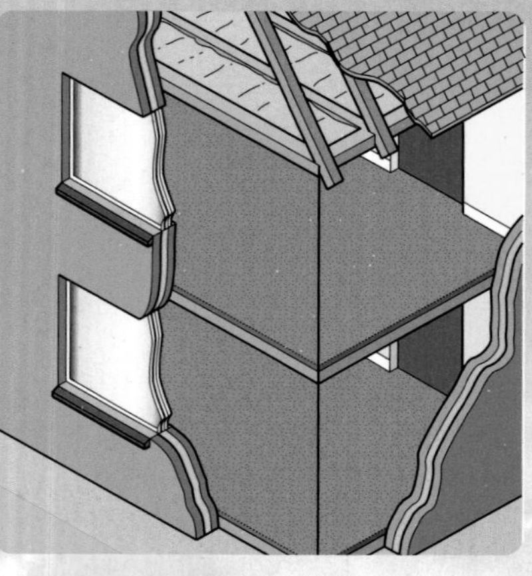

All the energy we use costs money, and affects the environment in some way. So it is good for us and for the environment if we can use less energy. There are lots of ways we can save energy, such as fitting our homes with insulation, turning our central heating down, walking or cycling to school, or turning off electrical appliances when we are not using them.

5 List three types of insulation we fit in our homes, to save energy.

6 List six things that you could do to help save energy.

Electrical energy

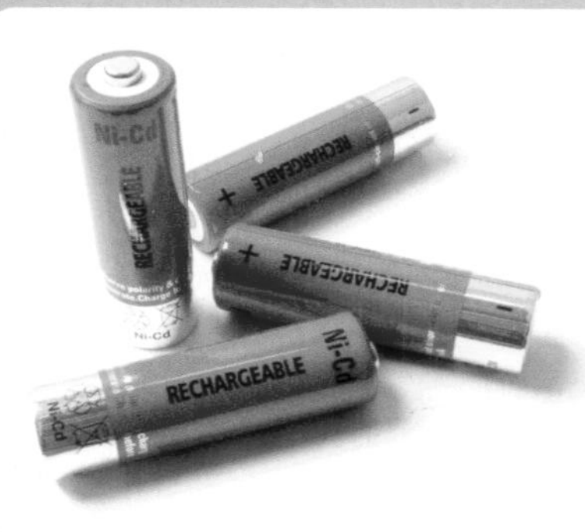

We use a lot of electrical energy, either from mains electricity or from batteries. The energy in batteries comes from the chemicals in the batteries. The energy in mains electricity comes from fuel at the power station. The voltage tells us how hard the current is pushed round the circuit, and tells us about the energy. Mains electricity has a much higher voltage than batteries and supplies a lot more energy.

7 What energy change happens when a battery is connected in a circuit?

8 Why is mains electricity much more dangerous than electricity from batteries?

Fossil fuels

Fossil fuels are fuels that have formed over millions of years from dead plant and animal material. Coal, oil and natural gas are all fossil fuels. When they are burned, their stored energy is released as heat energy. Burning fossil fuels also releases carbon dioxide, which causes climate change. Since they take millions of years to form, fossil fuels are non-renewable. Once they are used up they cannot be replaced.

9 What are fossil fuels formed from?

10 Explain why coal is a non-renewable fuel, but wood is not non-renewable.

Renewable energy resources

Renewable energy resources are energy resources that are always available, or that can be replaced as we use them. Solar power is renewable, because energy is always coming to us from the Sun. Wind and water power are renewable because the air and water are always moving. Biomass is renewable because as we use the wood or plant material we can grow more trees or plants to replace the ones we have used.

11 Describe what is meant by a 'renewable energy resource'.

12 List five different types of renewable energy resource.

Earth and beyond

The Earth spins on it axis once every 24 hours, giving us day and night. The Earth orbits the Sun once every 365 days. Due to the Earth's tilt, we experience four seasons.

The solar system consists of the Sun and nine planets; Mercury, Venus, Earth, Mars, Saturn, Jupiter, Uranus, Neptune and Pluto.

The Earth has one natural satellite, the Moon. Today there are many artificial satellites orbiting the Earth. Satellites are used for communications, weather forecasting, military purposes and surveying. Probes like Voyager have been launched to explore the solar system.

13 Describe the solar system and name the force that holds it together.

14 Why are there so many satellites orbiting the Earth? What other type of space craft have been launched from Earth?

Radiation and radioactivity

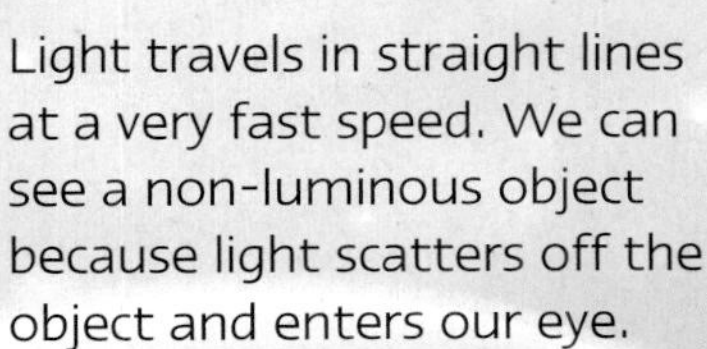

Light travels in straight lines at a very fast speed. We can see a non-luminous object because light scatters off the object and enters our eye. When light is completely absorbed by an object, the object will look black. Light is reflected from plane surfaces like mirrors. Light is refracted (bent) as it passes from one medium to another.

Light travels like a wave through space (a vacuum). Because it is a wave form, it has wavelength, amplitude and frequency.

Some substances are radioactive. They give out invisible radiation that can be quite dangerous to living things. Radioactivity can be detected using a Geiger counter.

15 Describe the three things that can happen to light.

16 What do you know about radioactive substances?

Biology 1a – Human biology

DISCOVER BLOOD!

Blood is the body's main transport system and one of its communication systems. Like a train on the underground, blood allows passengers to board in one place and get off at another.

The red blood cells pick up oxygen at the lungs and offload it at any tissue that is respiring. Smoking interferes with their ability to complete this task.

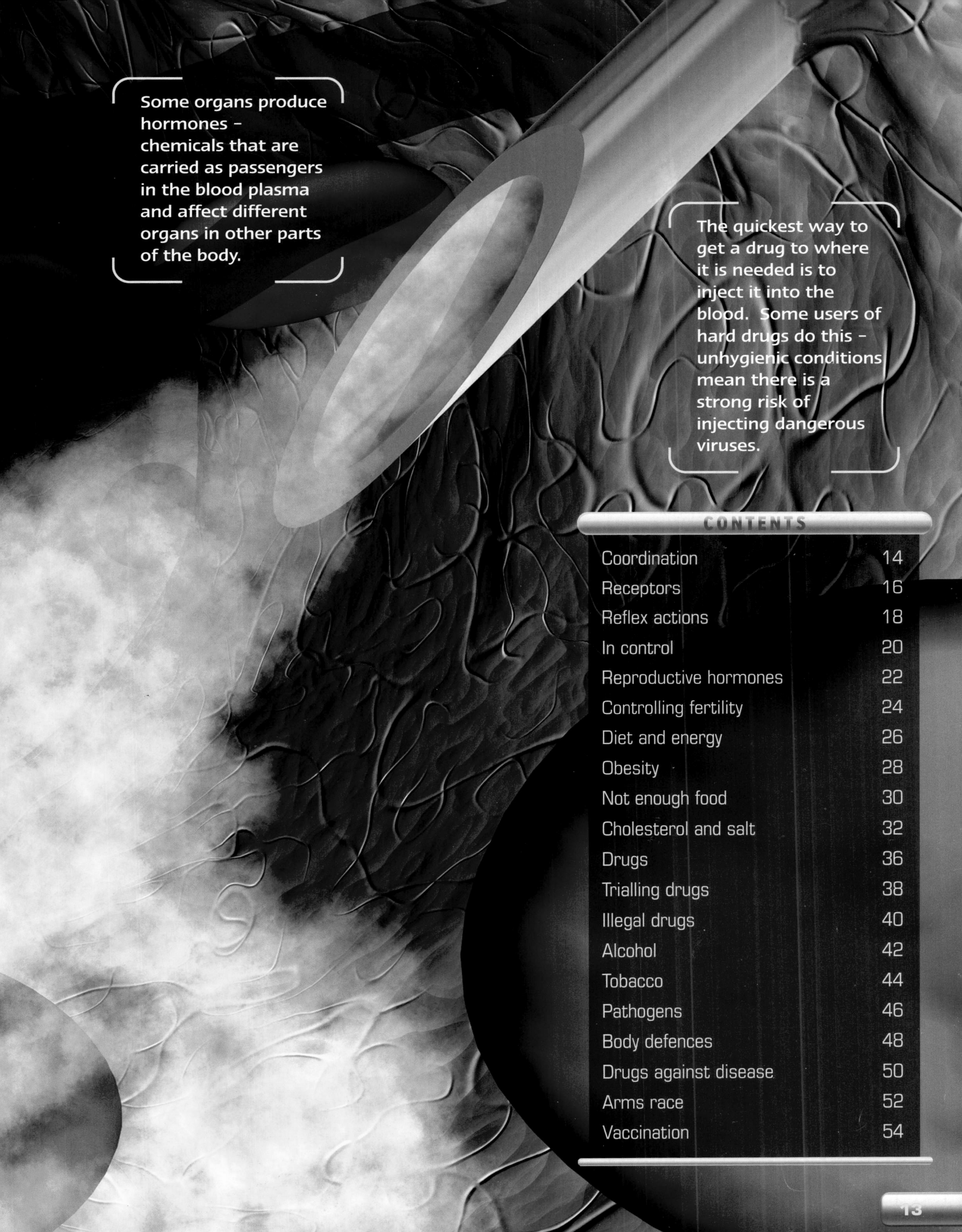
Some organs produce hormones – chemicals that are carried as passengers in the blood plasma and affect different organs in other parts of the body.
The quickest way to get a drug to where it is needed is to inject it into the blood. Some users of hard drugs do this – unhygienic conditions mean there is a strong risk of injecting dangerous viruses.

CONTENTS

Coordination

You will find out:

- That nerves and hormones coordinate body activities
- That glands secrete hormones into the blood
- That the central nervous system is brain plus spinal cord
- That nerves carry information

Keeping it together

A football player must be strong, fit and fast, and understand the game instinctively. But to excel at the game, he or she needs excellent eye–leg coordination.

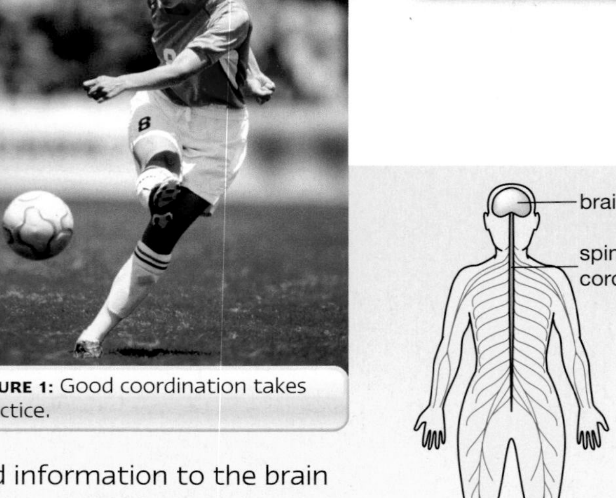

FIGURE 1: Good coordination takes practice.

Nerves and hormones

How good is your hand–eye **coordination**?

Think about putting the middle finger of your right hand onto the nose on this face.

FIGURE 2: Target the nose.

Now do it.

Your eyes see the nose and send information to the brain about where it is. The information travels from the eyes to the brain along **nerves**, as fast-moving electrical impulses (signals). Then the brain sends more impulses to the muscles in your arm and hand, telling them how and where to move.

Nerves carry information to and from the brain and spinal cord. The brain and spinal cord make up the **central nervous system**.

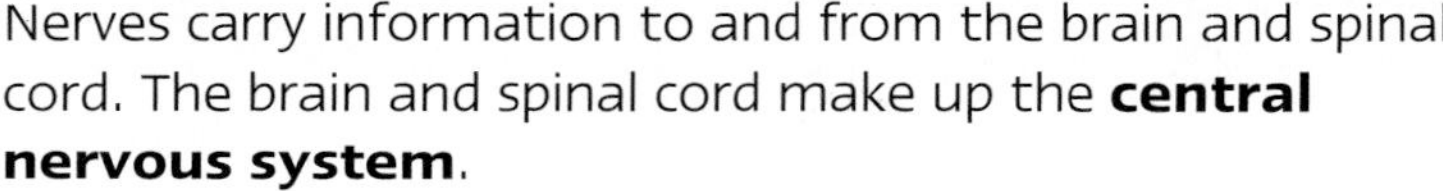

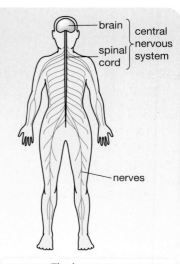

FIGURE 3: The human nervous system.

Nerves contain special cells called **nerve cells**. They carry information as electrical impulses.

The human body contains many different organs. These organs must work together so they must be able to communicate with one another. As well as nerves, **hormones** convey messages between organs.

Hormones are chemicals. They are made by **glands**. A gland is an organ that makes and releases a useful substance. The release process is called **secretion**.

The glands secrete the hormones into the blood. The hormones are carried all over the body in the bloodstream.

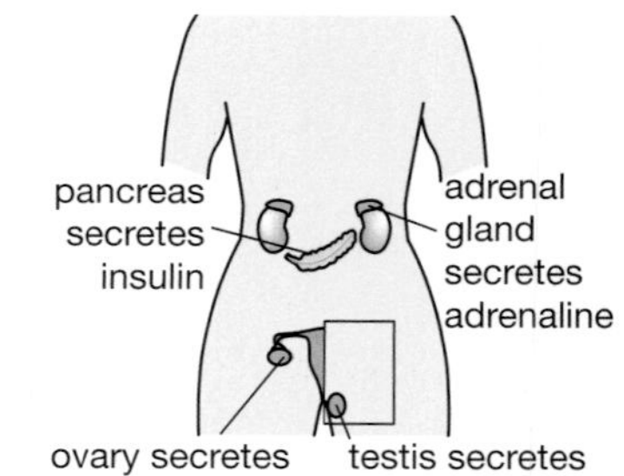

FIGURE 4: Four glands that secrete hormones.

QUESTIONS

1 List some of the organs that the footballer is using as she kicks the ball.

2 The excitement of a match causes a hormone called adrenaline to be secreted in the footballer's body. Name the gland that secretes adrenaline.

3 The adrenaline makes the footballer's heart beat faster. How do you think the adrenaline is carried to her heart?

Nerves and behaviour

Think about what happened when you touched the nose on the face with your finger.

As your arm and fingers move, the brain constantly monitors their positions in relation to the nose. It adjusts their movements so that your middle finger lands directly on the nose.

While you are making this simple movement, huge amounts of information are buzzing along nerves between your eyes, brain and muscles. Constant tiny adjustments are being made.

Try doing it slowly. You will be able to feel how tiny muscle movements make your arm and finger home in on the target.

In this simple action, your brain is using information from your surroundings, and also from inside you. It puts all this information together and then produces a perfectly coordinated piece of behaviour.

Hormones and target organs

In the nervous system, nerves carry information between one organ and another in the form of electrical impulses. Hormones move around the body in a different way. Hormones, made in glands, dissolve in the blood plasma, and are carried all around the body inside blood vessels.

Most hormones affect just a few different organs. These are called their **target organs**. The hormone **adrenaline** has more target organs than most hormones do. Adrenaline affects the heart, breathing muscles, eyes and digestive system.

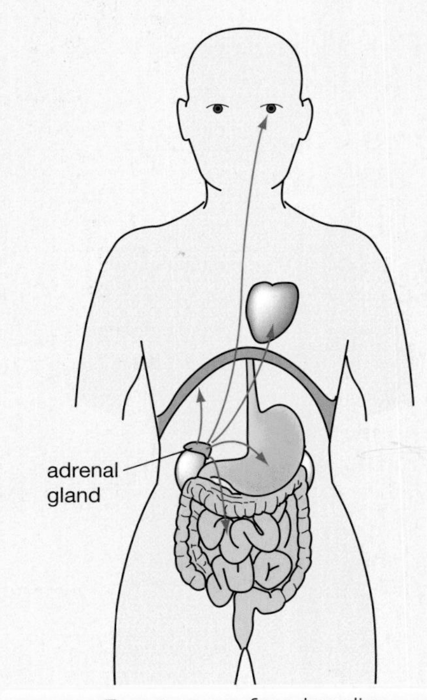

FIGURE 5: Target organs for adrenaline.

QUESTIONS

4 What information was your brain receiving about your surroundings as you thought about touching the nose?

5 What information was your brain receiving from inside your body?

6 Suggest why nerves, and not hormones, are used as the way of transferring information when you carry out an action like this.

7 In figure 5, identify the target organs of adrenaline by name.

8 Adrenaline is sometimes called the 'fight or flight' hormone. Think about how you feel when you are frightened or very excited. How is adrenaline affecting its target organs?

Response duration

A simple piece of behaviour such as the nose-touching exercise takes only a short period of time. Impulses travelling along nerves are an ideal way of achieving this. They are fast and short-lived.

Where a longer-term response is needed, hormones are often a more appropriate method of communication. For example, if you are frightened by a bull chasing you, it is probably a good idea to stay frightened until you have run across the field and leapt over the fence. Some hormones have even longer effects than this. You will read about some of them on pages 22 to 23.

However, you wouldn't want to go on feeling frightened for days. To avoid this, the liver gradually breaks down hormones. The products of this breakdown return to the blood and are excreted in urine.

ELECTRICITY IN PLANTS

Although plants don't have nerves, they do use electrical impulses for coordination. These impulses are like ours, but much slower.

FIGURE 6: This fly did not respond quickly enough to escape the Venus flytrap.

QUESTIONS

9 Draw a table with two columns, headed NERVES and HORMONES. Complete the table to compare these two methods of communication and coordination in the body.

Receptors

You will find out:

- That receptors have different positions in the human body
- That receptors detect stimuli – changes in the environment
- That muscles and glands are effectors

A painless life

The young boy with this hand was born with a rare condition called CIPA. He has no sense of pain. He bites his tongue so badly that the tip has gone. He burnt his hand like this by holding on to a very hot radiator. He didn't realise he was hurting himself.

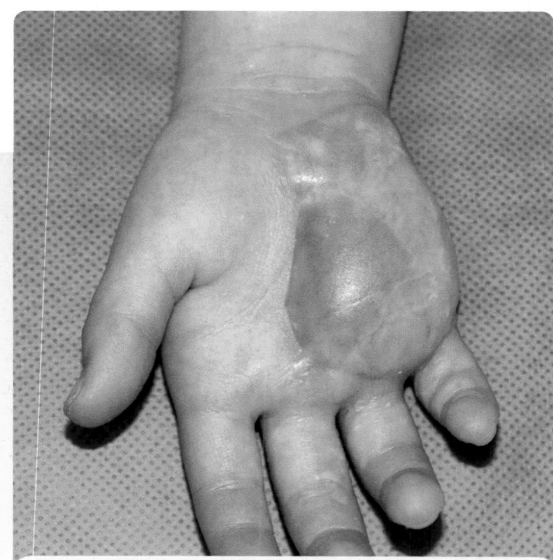

FIGURE 1: The hand of a boy who feels no pain.

Receptors and effectors

The boy did not feel his fingers burning because his brain did not get the right information from the **receptors** in his fingers.

Receptors are special cells that detect stimuli. A **stimulus** is a change in the environment. In this case, the stimulus was the very high temperature of the radiator.

If you touched a hot radiator, receptors in your fingers would send electrical impulses along nerves to your brain. This did not happen in the boy's body.

Your brain would then send impulses speeding along other nerves to the muscles in your arm and hand. The **muscles** would contract. They would pull your hand away from the radiator.

All your muscles are **effectors**. An effector is an organ that does something in response to a stimulus.

As well as muscles being effectors, our **glands** are also effectors. For example, our salivary glands respond to a stimulus by secreting saliva.

We have many different kinds of receptors. Figure 2 shows the positions of the other kinds of receptors that we have in our head.

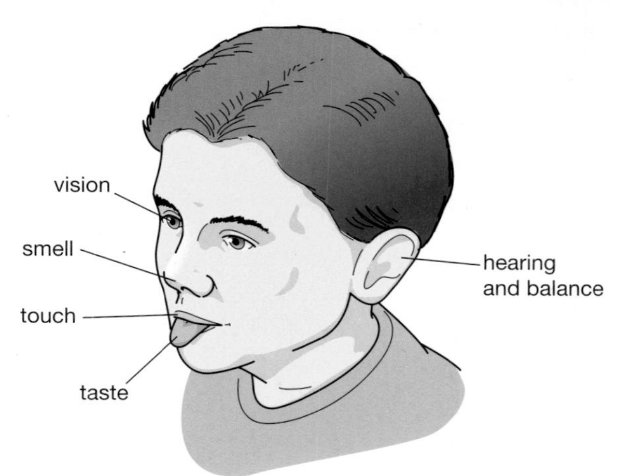

FIGURE 2: Some of the receptors in your head.

QUESTIONS

1 When you hear a sudden bang behind you, you jump. Where are the receptors that hear the bang? Where are the effectors that make you jump?

2 When you smell food cooking, saliva is produced in your mouth. Which receptors are involved in this action? What are the effectors?

WOW FACTOR!

Each off your fingers has about 3000 touch receptors. This is as many as the whole of your back and chest.

...*effector* ...*gland* ...*motor neurone* ...*muscle*

Neurones

You know that information is carried in the nervous system as electrical impulses. The cells that carry this information are called nerve cells. Another name for them is **neurones**.

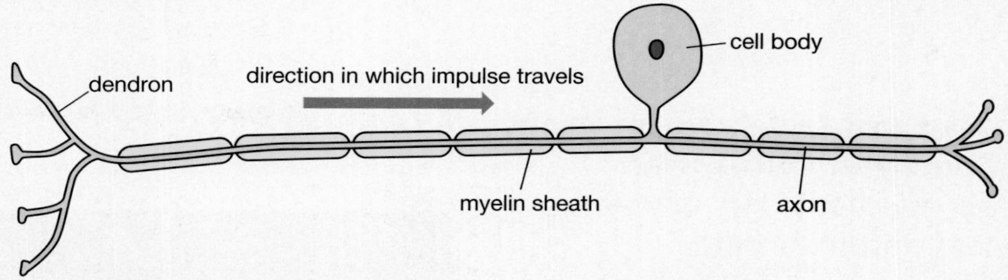

FIGURE 3: A sensory neurone.

The neurones that carry information from receptors to the central nervous system are called **sensory neurones**.

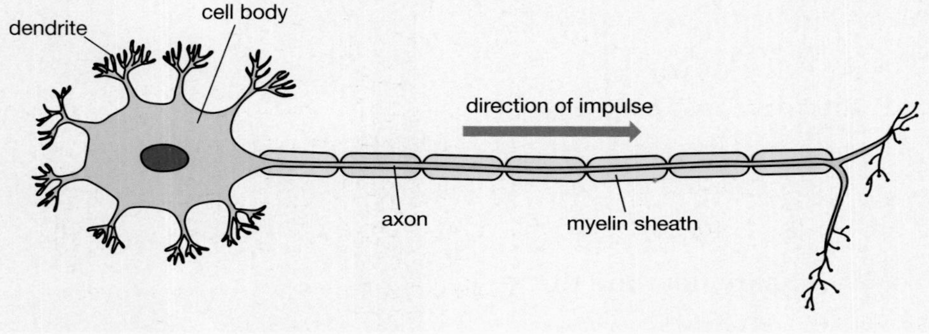

FIGURE 4: A motor neurone.

The neurones that carry information from the central nervous system to effectors are called **motor neurones**.

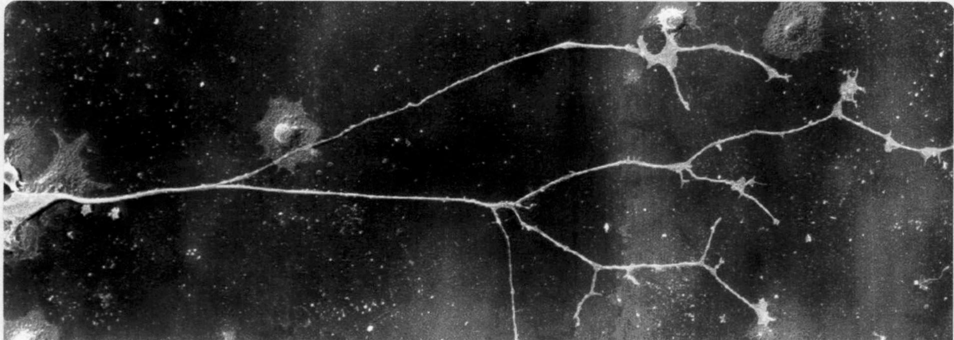

FIGURE 5: A scanning electron micrograph of a nerve cell with a branching axon.

QUESTIONS

3 Think back to what you know about the structure of animal cells. What features does a sensory neurone share with other animal cells? How is it different?

4 What features does a motor neurone share with a sensory neurone? How do they differ from one another?

ONE PHOTON

A single photon of light – the smallest quantity you can get – is enough to stimulate a rod cell.

Transducers

Receptors are transducers. A transducer is a device that converts one form of energy into another kind of energy, when one of them is electrical energy. Receptors transfer energy from a stimulus to electrical energy in neurones.

For example, in your eyes there are receptors called rod cells. When light energy hits a rod cell, the light causes changes to happen in the rod cell. This starts up an electrical impulse that travels in a neurone along the optic nerve to the brain. The rod cell is a transducer because it has transferred the light energy to electrical energy in a neurone.

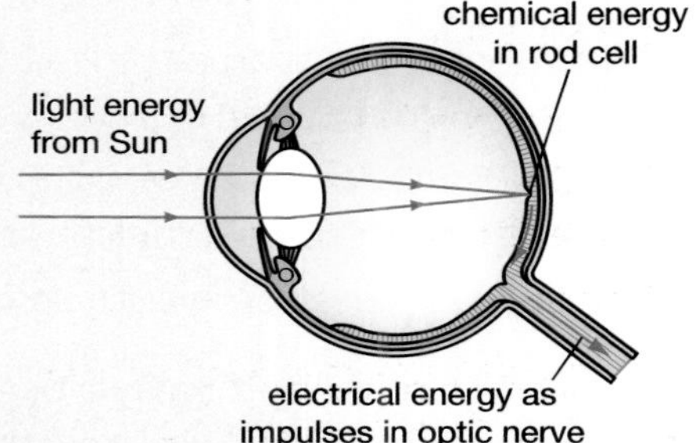

FIGURE 6: In the eye, energy in light is transferred to electrical energy.

QUESTIONS

5 Choose **two** other receptors, and describe how they act as transducers.

6 The energy that is picked up by a receptor is not enough to send an impulse all the way along a neurone to the brain. The neurone itself also has to provide some energy. How do you think it can do this? (Think back to what you know about how cells get energy.)

...neurone ...receptor ...sensory neurone ...stimulus

Reflex actions

You will find out:
- That a reflex action is fast and automatic
- That it involves sensory, relay and motor neurones in a reflex arc
- That synapses are present at neurone junctions and a chemical crosses them

Reflexes

If a doctor thinks you may have damaged your spinal cord, he might test your knee-jerk reflex. He will tap your knee with a small hammer. If you are OK, then your lower leg should kick upwards. You don't think about it – it just happens automatically.

Stimulus and response

The tap on the knee is a **stimulus**. It is detected by **receptors** in the thigh muscle connected to your knee. The receptors send nerve impulses to your spinal cord. The spinal cord then sends nerve impulses to your leg muscles. The leg muscles respond by contracting. This pulls your lower leg upwards.

This is a **reflex action**. A reflex action is a fast, automatic **response** to a stimulus.

In any reflex action, the sequence of events is as follows:
- A receptor detects a stimulus.
- The receptor sends an electrical impulse along a **sensory neurone** to the central nervous system (CNS).
- The CNS sends an electrical impulse along a **motor neurone** to an **effector**. The effector could be a muscle or a gland.
- The effector does something as a response to the stimulus.

The knee jerk reflex isn't really a useful one – except for testing if your spinal cord is working normally. But most reflexes are useful.

For example, if something moves really fast towards your face, you blink. This protects your eyes.

If you touch something burning hot, your hand pulls away from it. This stops you from getting burnt.

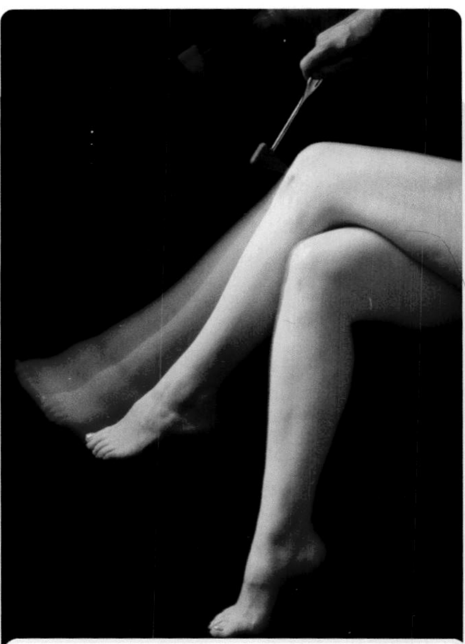

FIGURE 1: The knee-jerk reflex.

Your reflexes stop you getting hurt

QUESTIONS

1 In the 'blinking' reflex, what is the receptor? What is the effector?
2 In the 'hand pulling away from hot object' reflex, what is the receptor? What is the effector?
3 Think of **two** more reflex actions. Remember, each one must be something automatic, that happens without you thinking about it.
Describe each one. Say what the receptor is and what the effector is. Say why each reflex is useful.

GETTING OLD ALREADY!

You were born with 1000 trillion synapses. You have already lost at least half of these.

...effector ...motor neurone ...receptor ...reflex action ...reflex arc

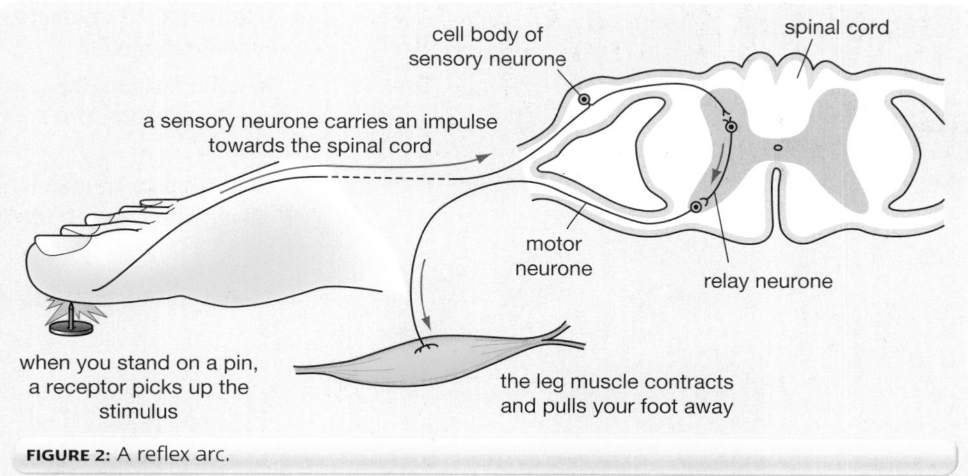

FIGURE 2: A reflex arc.

A reflex arc

A **reflex arc** is the pathway taken by a nerve impulse as it passes from a receptor, through the central nervous system, and finally to an effector.

The odd-shaped object at the right of figure 2 is what your spinal cord would look like if you viewed a slice across it end on.

In real life, your spinal cord is inside your spine. It runs inside a tunnel formed by holes in the bones that make up the spine and protect the spinal cord.

Put your finger on the receptor in figure 2. Run your finger along the sensory neurone, into the spinal cord, along the relay neurone, and then along the motor neurone until you arrive at the effector.

It takes a nerve impulse only a fraction of a second to go along this route. That is why reflex actions are so quick.

Synapses

If you look carefully at figure 3, you will see that there is a tiny gap between the end of one neurone and the start of the next. The gaps are called **synapses**.

Electrical impulses cannot jump across these gaps. Instead, when an impulse gets to the end of a neurone, it causes a chemical to be secreted. This diffuses across the gap, but at a slower rate than an electrical impulse travelling the same distance.

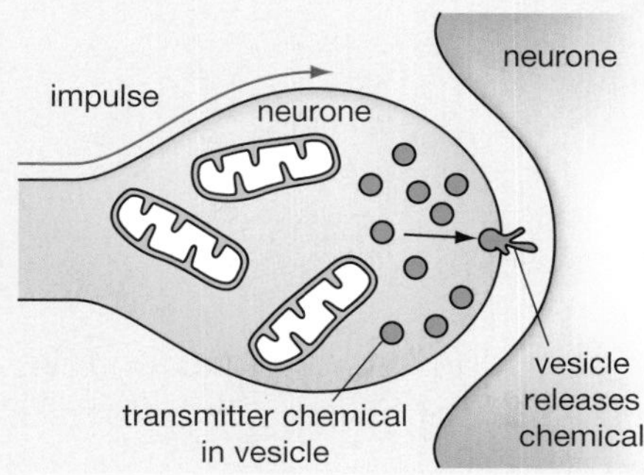

FIGURE 3: What happens at a synapse.

The chemical diffuses across the gap and arrives at the beginning of the next neurone. This starts off an electrical impulse that whizzes along that neurone.

QUESTIONS

4 How many neurones are there in the reflex arc? How many synapses are there?

5 Where is the cell body of the sensory neurone?

6 Where are the cell bodies of the relay neurone and the motor neurone?

7 Explain the difference between a reflex action and a reflex arc.

Why have synapses?

Synapses slow down the nerve impulse as it passes from a receptor to an effector. So why have them? Wouldn't it be better just to have the neurones all joined together to make a simple, fast-track pathway?

The advantage of synapses is that they make it possible for us to respond in more than one way. For example, the relay neurone in the spinal cord will have synapses to other neurones that can carry nerve impulses down from the brain. If the really hot thing that you grasp is the only thing to hold on to in order to stop you falling, your brain may send an impulse down towards the relay neurone that overrides the one coming along the sensory neurone. This stops it sending impulses on to the motor neurone. So you hang on to the hot rail, even though it may burn your hands – your brain has decided this is a better option than falling.

The billions of synapses between the millions of neurones in our brain are what allow humans to have such complex and infinitely variable behaviour.

QUESTIONS

8 Explain why synapses slow down the passage of a nerve impulse.

9 Think of another reflex action that can be overridden by your brain. Draw a flow diagram, using boxes and arrows, to show how the reflex action happens and how the brain can override it.

10 Discuss the advantages of **a)** reflex actions and **b)** behaviour that involves conscious thought. Use examples to illustrate your answer.

In control

You will find out:

- That conditions inside the body are controlled
- That this includes the body's water and ion content
- That temperature and blood sugar concentration must be controlled

Keeping the balance

Exercise hard on a hot day and in one hour you could lose up to 2500 cm^3 of water in your breath and sweat. A person running a marathon needs to replace this lost water during the race. Because **ions** are also lost in sweat, it is best to drink water that has ions in it. Isotonic drinks have the same balance of water and ions as the body has.

FIGURE 1: Isotonic drinks are great for replacing body fluid - but do they really do everything they say on the label?

Your body is about 60% water

What is controlled?

The cells in your body are always working. Chemical reactions take place inside them. These reactions must happen at the right time and at the right speed. For this, the conditions around each cell must be perfect – and constant.

These conditions include:

- the water content
- the ion (salt) content
- the temperature
- the concentration of sugar in the blood.

Controlling water and ions

Your blood has many different substances dissolved in it. Some are ions, such as sodium and chloride, both found in **salt**.

Too much salt and not enough water in the blood can lead to high blood pressure. People who eat too much salt can increase their risk of having a heart attack.

The kidneys help to keep the balance of water and ions just right. They do this by varying the amount of water and salt excreted from your body in urine.

from lungs in breath

from skin in sweat

from kidneys in urine

FIGURE 2: Ways the body loses water.

QUESTIONS

1. Make a list of the ways in which water is lost from the body. How is water gained by the body?
2. Why do you think a person running a marathon on a hot day loses much more water than usual?
3. All the chemical reactions in the body are controlled by **enzymes**. Enzymes work best at a particular temperature. Suggest what temperature a human's enzymes work best at.

TOO MUCH WATER

In the Boston marathon in 2003, a healthy woman athlete died because she drank too much water without replacing ions as she ran.

Sweating

Sweating keeps us cool. Sweat is made by glands in the skin. The glands take water and ions out of the blood, to make sweat. The sweat travels up through a sweat duct, and lies on the surface of the skin.

Sweat is a mixture of water, ions and a small amount of urea. So when you sweat, you lose all of these things from the body.

The water in the sweat evaporates. As it changes from liquid water to water vapour, it takes heat out of the skin. This cools your body.

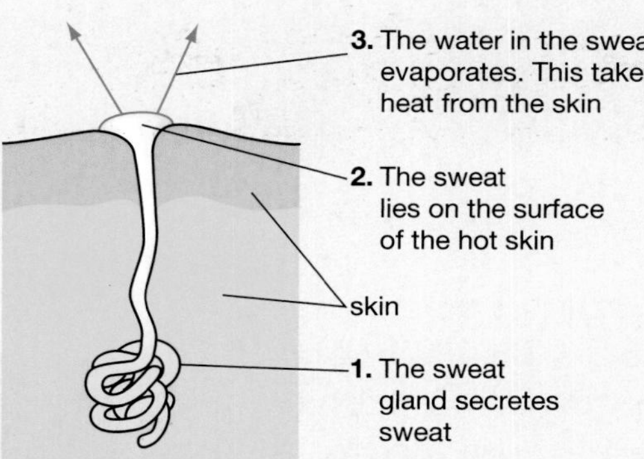
3. The water in the sweat evaporates. This takes heat from the skin
2. The sweat lies on the surface of the hot skin
skin
1. The sweat gland secretes sweat

FIGURE 3: How sweating cools you down.

Insulin

The sugar content of the blood is controlled by a **hormone** called **insulin**.

When you eat a meal with starch or sugar in it, a sugar called **glucose** is absorbed into the blood. The blood carries glucose all over the body. Cells need glucose to give them energy.

If your meal contained a lot of starch or sugar, then your blood glucose level might get too high. The **pancreas** detects this. It responds by secreting the hormone insulin.

Insulin is carried to the **liver** in the blood. Insulin makes the liver take glucose out of the blood. The liver stores it away.

Later, between meals, when your blood glucose level might go too low, the liver releases some of its glucose stores back into the blood.

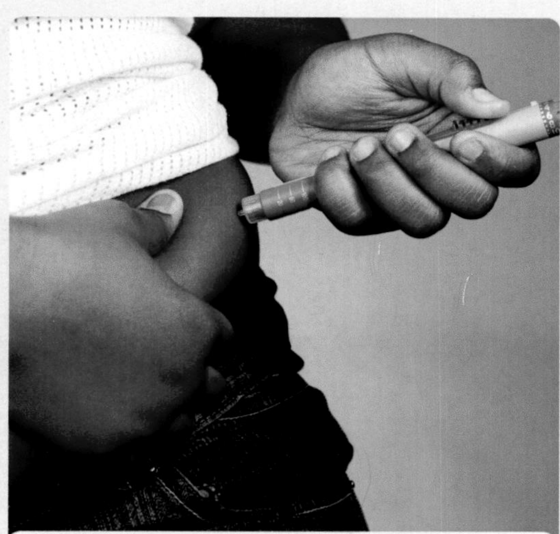

FIGURE 4: Some people with diabetes have to control it by injecting themselves with insulin.

WATER BEATS FOOD

You can survive for weeks without food, but only a few days without water.

QUESTIONS

4 Where is the **receptor** that detects an increase in blood glucose (sugar) level?

5 What is the **effector** that responds to this stimulus?

Survival in the desert

Your car has broken down in a desert. You don't know where you are, but you've been driving all day and haven't seen anyone else on the road. You don't have much water. You can't get a signal on your mobile phone. All you can do is wait and hope that someone comes along before you die of dehydration or heatstroke.

FIGURE 5: Lost in the desert.

How can you maximise your chance of survival?

An SAS manual for survival in a desert has the following advice:

- avoid exertion
- keep cool. Stay in the shade
- don't lie on the hot ground
- don't eat, because digestion uses up fluids
- talk as little as possible. Breathe through your nose rather than your mouth.

QUESTIONS

6 Explain how following each point in this advice could help you to survive. Use what you know about heat transfer, as well as what you have learnt in this lesson.

Reproductive hormones

You will find out:

- That hormones from the pituitary gland and ovaries control the menstrual cycle
- That FSH causes egg maturity and oestrogen secretion while LH causes egg release from the ovaries

The master gland

Figure 1 is a computer-enhanced MRI scan of a person's head. The little green C-shaped blob is the **pituitary gland**. This gland controls many of the other glands in the body. It also has overall control of sex cell production by the **testes** and **ovaries**.

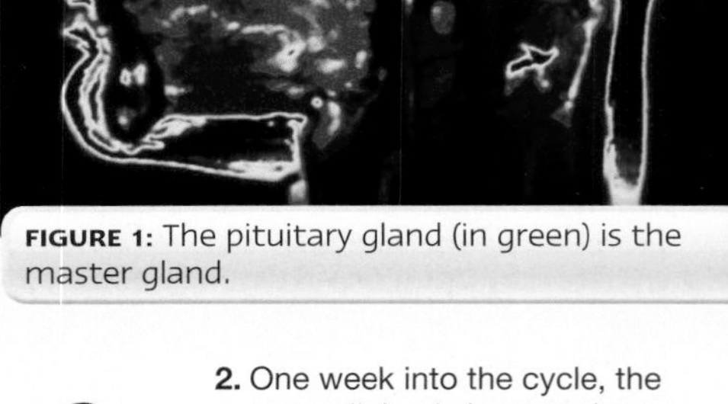

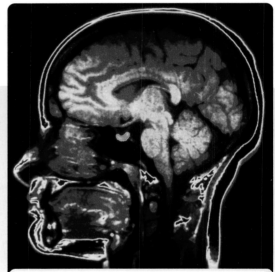

FIGURE 1: The pituitary gland (in green) is the master gland.

The menstrual cycle

In the **menstrual cycle**, one egg is released from a woman's ovaries every 28 days.

Before the egg is released, the lining of the womb (also called the **uterus**) thickens. So if the egg is fertilised, the womb is ready to receive the tiny embryo.

If the egg is not fertilised, the lining of the womb breaks down. It is lost through the vagina. This is called menstruation.

The menstrual cycle is controlled by **hormones**. These include:

- a hormone called **FSH**, secreted by the pituitary gland
- a hormone called **LH**, secreted by the pituitary gland
- a hormone called **oestrogen**, secreted by the ovaries.

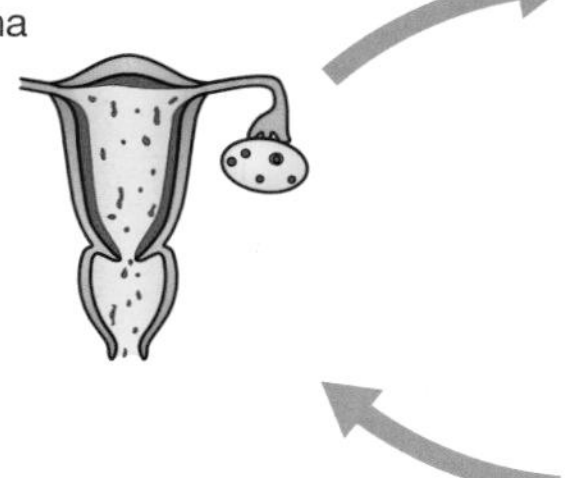

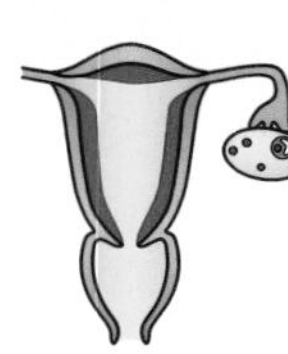

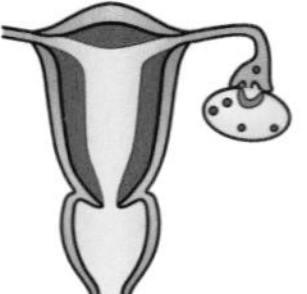

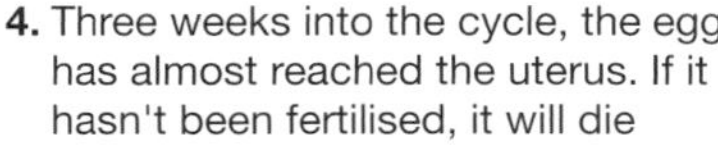

1. On the first day of the cycle, menstruation begins. The thick lining of the uterus breaks down and is lost through the vagina
2. One week into the cycle, the uterus lining is just starting to build up again. An egg is ripening in the ovary
3. Two weeks into the cycle, an egg is released from the ovary. The lining of the uterus is soft and thick, ready to receive the egg if it is fertilised
4. Three weeks into the cycle, the egg has almost reached the uterus. If it hasn't been fertilised, it will die

FIGURE 2: The menstrual cycle.

QUESTIONS

1. How many days does the menstrual cycle last?
2. A woman starts to menstruate on March 2nd. Predict the date when an egg will next be released from one of her ovaries.
3. Where are FSH and LH made?
4. How will FSH and LH be carried to the ovaries?

FSH AND LH SPELT OUT

FSH stands for follicle-stimulating hormone and LH stands for luteinising hormone.

...FSH ...hormones ...LH ...menstrual cycle ...oestrogen

Hormones and egg production

Figure 3 shows how FSH, LH and oestrogen are involved in the release of an egg from one of the ovaries.

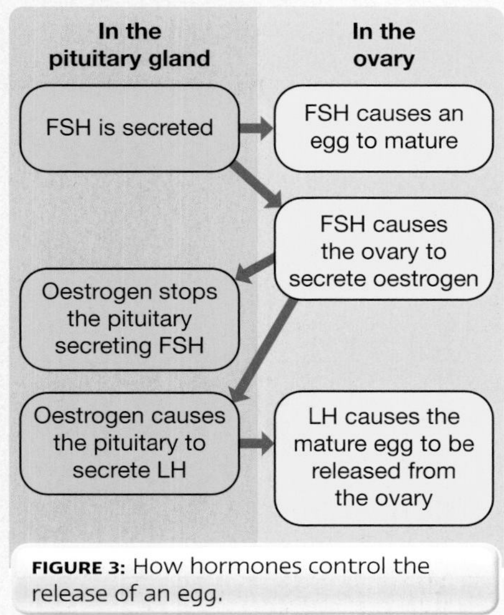

In the pituitary gland
In the ovary
FSH is secreted
FSH causes an egg to mature
FSH causes the ovary to secrete oestrogen
Oestrogen stops the pituitary secreting FSH
Oestrogen causes the pituitary to secrete LH
LH causes the mature egg to be released from the ovary

FIGURE 3: How hormones control the release of an egg.

PMT

During the menstrual cycle, the hormones circulating in a woman's blood change quite a lot.

These hormones can affect other parts of her body too. For example, many women feel tense in the last few days of the cycle when the hormones have dropped to quite low levels. This is called **pre-menstrual tension** or PMT.

This can work the other way round, too. Other things in the woman's life can affect her menstrual cycle. For example, travelling can delay a period, or make it happen earlier than it normally would.

QUESTIONS

5 What is the stimulus that causes the ovary to secrete oestrogen?

6 Name **one** target organ for oestrogen.

7 Suggest an advantage of this process being coordinated by hormones, rather than by the nervous system.

Hormones and the menstrual cycle

During the menstrual cycle, changes occur in the concentrations of FSH, LH and oestrogen in the blood. It is the change in concentration of oestrogen that causes the changes in thickness of the uterus lining. As oestrogen concentrations rise, this causes the uterus lining to thicken. When oestrogen concentration falls below a certain point, the uterus lining breaks down.

WOW FACTOR!

Women who live close together, such as female students living in the same house, often find that their menstrual cycles synchronise with one another.

Figure 4 shows how the concentrations of FSH, LH and oestrogen change during the menstrual cycle. It also shows how the thickness of the uterus lining changes.

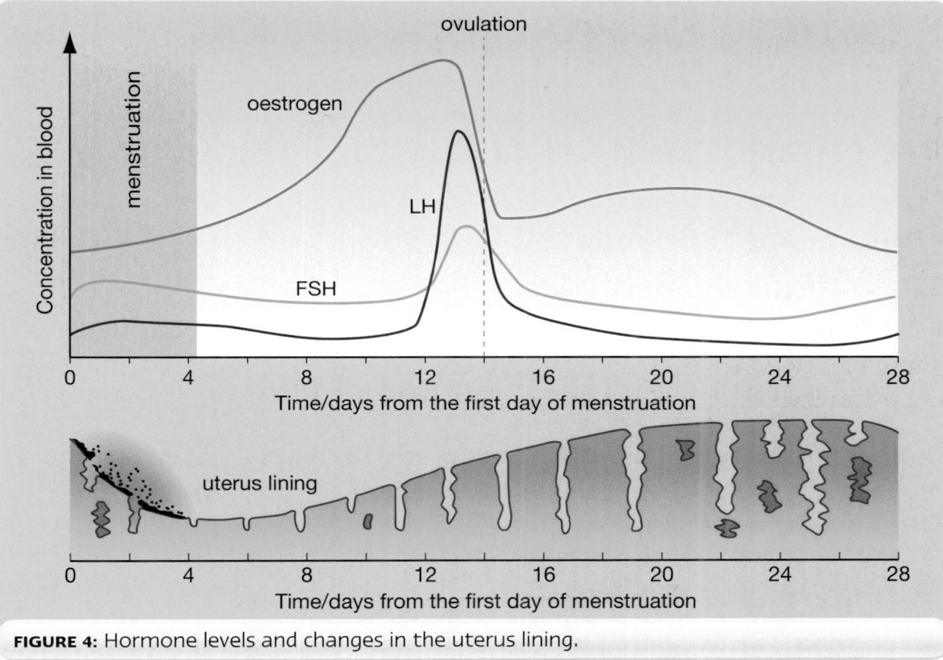

ovulation
Concentration in blood
menstruation
oestrogen
LH
FSH
0
4
8
12
16
20
24
28
Time/days from the first day of menstruation
uterus lining
0
4
8
12
16
20
24
28
Time/days from the first day of menstruation

FIGURE 4: Hormone levels and changes in the uterus lining.

QUESTIONS

8 Describe the pattern of oestrogen secretion throughout the 28 days of this cycle.

9 Use the information on the graph, and what you know about FSH, LH and oestrogen, to explain why the concentration of oestrogen rises between days 1 and 13.

10 What causes the egg to be released from the ovary on day 14?

11 Although the oestrogen level starts to drop on day 13, the lining of the uterus does not start to break down until day 28. Using the information on the graph, explain why it is important for there to be a delay between the beginning of the fall in oestrogen levels and the breakdown of the uterus lining.

Controlling fertility

You will find out:

- That FSH can help an infertile couple to have a baby
- That oral contraceptives work using hormones
- That using hormones to control fertility has both benefits and problems

Too much of a good thing?

This couple tried for a baby for nearly two years, with no success. They asked for help, and were given fertility treatment. Eventually it succeeded – even more than they had hoped. Instead of one baby, they now have three.

FIGURE 1: IVF enabled this couple to have a family.

Fertility treatment

Many couples trying for a baby are not successful. They may ask for help at their local fertility clinic.

Sometimes, the problem is that the woman is not producing eggs. To get egg production started, she may be given a course of hormone treatment. The hormones are sometimes called **fertility drugs**.

The hormone **FSH** can be used as a fertility drug. FSH stimulates the woman's eggs to mature in her ovaries. When an egg is released from her ovary into an oviduct, she can conceive in the normal way.

It is difficult to get the dose of the fertility drugs just right. If the dose is too low, the woman still won't be able to get pregnant. But if it is too high, she could make several ripe eggs at the same time, so she could get pregnant with twins, triplets or even quadruplets.

Another possibility is to use **IVF**. Some of the woman's eggs are put into a dish with some of her partner's sperm. One of the fertilised eggs is then placed in her uterus, where it grows into a baby in the normal way.

Oral contraceptives

Other women may have the opposite problem. They want to be able to have sexual intercourse without running the risk of getting pregnant.

A woman can be prescribed **oral contraceptives** – the contraceptive pill. The pills contain hormones such as oestrogen. The hormones stop FSH being produced, so her eggs do not mature. So there is never an egg in her oviducts and she cannot get pregnant.

QUESTIONS

1. What does 'fertility' mean?
2. Name a hormone that can be used as a fertility drug.
3. How does this hormone help a woman to get pregnant?
4. How does the contraceptive pill work?

ORAL CONTRACEPTION

Oral contraceptives were first developed in the 1960s. Before that, women could only avoid pregnancy by not having sex, or by their partner using a condom.

...fertility drugs ... FSH

IVF

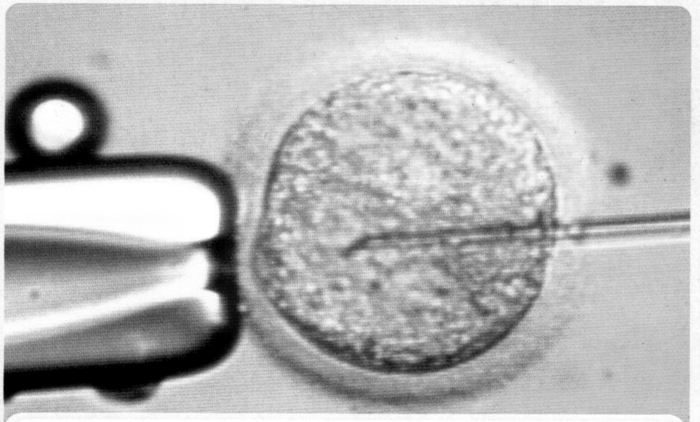
FIGURE 2: Sperm being injected into an egg cell.

IVF stands for '*in vitro* fertilisation'. '*In vitro*' is Latin for 'in glass'. The name comes from the fact that fertilisation happens inside a piece of laboratory equipment – which might or might not be made of glass.

The woman is given hormones to make her ovaries produce several eggs. Then the eggs are removed by a simple operation, done under anaesthetic. Some of them are put into a dish with a fluid at just the right temperature and nutrients to keep them healthy. Then some of her partner's sperm are added, and given time to fertilise the eggs.

When the eggs have been fertilised, they divide to make tiny balls of cells – embryos. One of the embryos is chosen and replaced in the woman's uterus. With luck, it will sink into the uterus lining and develop into a baby.

Benefits and problems of oral contraceptives

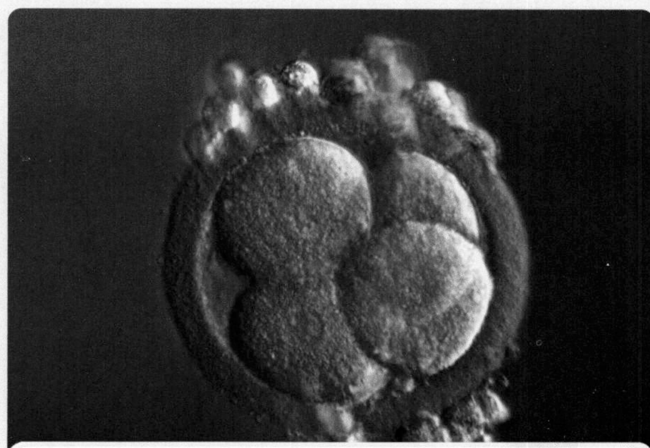
FIGURE 3: An embryo developed *in vitro*, just before being implanted in the mother's uterus.

The following are some of the benefits of using oral contraceptives:

- They can prevent unwanted pregnancies. This should mean that fewer women need abortions.
- They can help couples to plan their families so that every child is a wanted child.
- They could help to reduce the number of births in the world each year. This could help to slow down the growth of the world's population.

But some people argue that the widespread use of oral contraceptives may not be altogether a good thing. For example:

- With oral contraceptives easily available, a young woman may increase the number of times she has sex, and do so with more and different partners. This can increase the risk of herself and her partners catching sexually transmitted diseases such as chlamydia or HIV/AIDS.
- Some cultures and religions teach that any form of contraception, other than avoiding sex, is wrong.

QUESTIONS

5 Write a short paragraph outlining your own views on the use of oral contraceptives. Try to explain why you hold these views.

FERTILITY TREATMENT?

Of all the couples in the UK who want fertility treatment, the man is the only cause of infertility in 32% of cases and the woman is the only cause in 29%.

Multiple births

Most women would prefer to have one baby at a time, not twins or triplets. It is obviously much easier to care for one baby than several. Even one is demanding enough. Moreover, twins or triplets are more likely to have problems while developing in the uterus than a single baby. They are more likely to be underweight at birth.

In Britain, almost 98% of women who conceive naturally give birth to a single child. Only 2% of births are twins, 0.05% are triplets and only 0.001% are quads or more.

For women who have fertility treatment with FSH, the figures are very different. About 20% of births are twins, 8% are triplets and 3% are quads or more.

QUESTIONS

6 Display these results in a table.

7 Use your table to construct a block graph (bar chart).

8 Explain why multiple births are more common after fertility treatment with FSH than when a woman has conceived completely naturally.

9 Discuss the benefits and problems associated with the use of hormones to increase fertility.

Diet and energy

You will find out:

- That a balanced diet contains all the nutrients and energy you need
- That energy needs differ between people
- That brown fat keeps babies warm

Body heat

People are hot. This photo is taken using a camera that is sensitive to infra red light. The white, red and yellow areas are hottest, and the green and blue ones coldest.

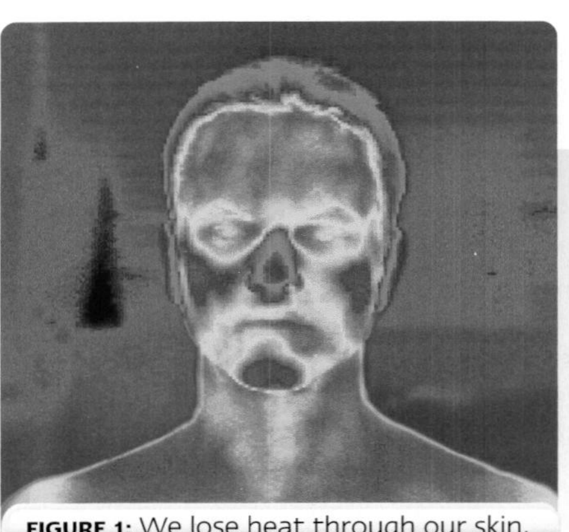

FIGURE 1: We lose heat through our skin.

Energy balance

Ten people dancing generate as much heat as a gas fire. All this heat **energy** comes from the food we eat.

Each day, you use up energy. Every cell in your body uses food to supply the energy it needs to stay alive and function properly. A person needs to eat food containing the right amount of energy to balance their needs.

If you take in more energy than you use, your body stores the extra energy as fat. If you take in less energy than you use, your body will raid its fat stores to provide your cells with the extra energy they need.

A balanced diet

The food that you eat each day is your diet. Most people eat a **balanced diet**. It should contain some of all these different kinds of nutrients:

- **carbohydrates** for energy
- **fats** for energy and making cell membranes
- **proteins** for growth, repair and energy
- vitamins and minerals for keeping healthy
- roughage (fibre) to keep the digestive system working well
- water.

ENERGY YOU TAKE IN
ENERGY YOU USE
If this end of the seesaw goes down, you put on weight
If this end of the seesaw goes down, you lose weight

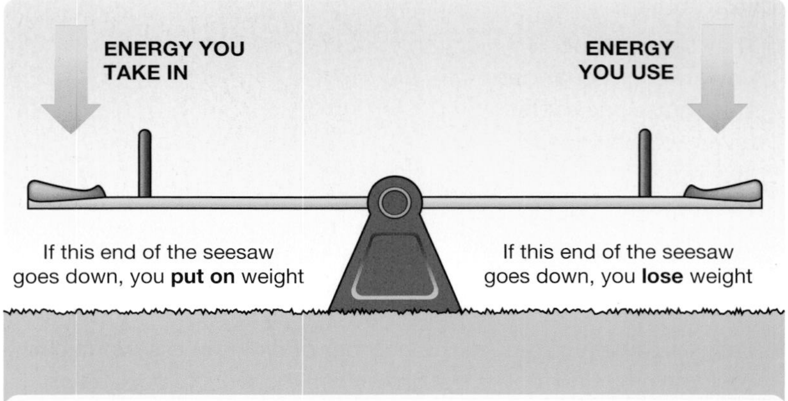

FIGURE 2: Energy balance.

If you eat plenty of different foods, you will probably get all the different nutrients that you need.

If your diet is not balanced, you are **malnourished**. This can lead to being too fat or too thin, or to deficiency diseases.

QUESTIONS

1. Which three types of nutrients provide energy?
2. What happens if you take in more energy than you use?
3. Explain what is meant by a balanced diet.

WOW FACTOR!

For the film *Super Size Me*, Morgan Spurlock ate nothing but fast food for a month. He gained 11 kg and his body fat went up from 11% to 18%.

...balanced diet ...brown fat ...carbohydrates ...energy

Energy needs

Different people have different energy needs. Taking exercise uses a lot of energy. So people who do manual work, or who do a lot of exercise like dancing, riding a bike or playing football, need to eat more energy-containing foods than people who don't exercise much.

Another reason we don't all need the same quantity of food is that our metabolic rates are different. Your metabolic rate is the rate at which chemical reactions take place in your cells. Even if two people are just sitting and resting, they may have different metabolic rates, and so use up different amounts of energy.

FIGURE 3: Exercise increases your metabolic rate.

On the whole, men have faster **metabolic rates** than women. Young people have faster metabolic rates than older people. Your metabolic rate rises when you exercise and stays high for some time after you finish. The greater the proportion of muscle to fat in your body, the higher your metabolic rate is likely to be. And it can be affected by your genes, too.

We need less food in the summer than in the winter. This is because respiration of glucose in our cells produces heat to keep us warm. If it is warm anyway, then we don't need to produce so much heat inside our bodies.

Fat

We all have some fat in our bodies. Most of it is white fat. It is found beneath the skin and around some organs, such as the kidneys. It is an energy store.

Babies have another kind of fat. It is called **brown fat** because it looks dark. Almost 5% of a baby's body weight is brown fat. But by the time you are an adult, you have practically none.

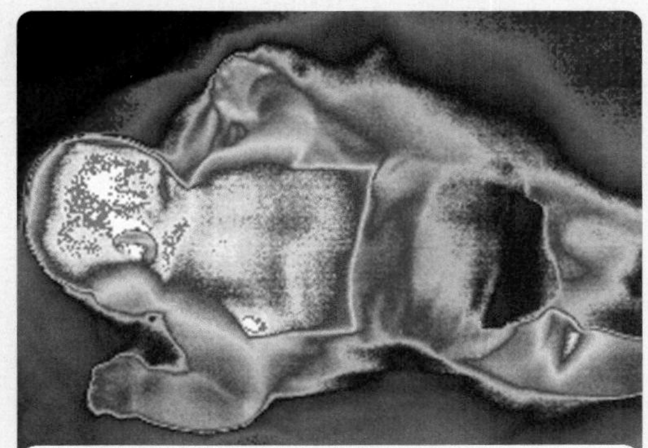

FIGURE 4: Thermogram of a sleeping baby.

Brown fat cells have a very high metabolic rate. They are used for generating heat. If a baby is cold, its brown fat cells switch on and generate heat fast. This is important in a tiny baby, because its small body can lose heat really quickly.

QUESTIONS

4 What is meant by your metabolic rate?

5 Explain how different people may have different metabolic rates.

6 Look at the thermogram of the baby. Where in its body do you think its brown fat is?

LESS FAT

A healthy man should have about 15% of his weight as body fat. A healthy woman should have about 25%.

Respiration

Cells release energy from food by **respiration**. Nutrients such as glucose are combined with oxygen. The glucose is broken down to carbon dioxide and water, and energy is released.

One gram of fat releases almost twice as much energy as one gram of carbohydrate (such as glucose). Proteins release about the same amount of energy as carbohydrates. Proteins are not usually a major source of energy for the body because they have other more important roles, such as repairing cells or making enzymes.

Calculating BMR

BMR is the shorthand for Basal Metabolic Rate. It is your metabolic rate when you are just sitting and resting quietly.

If you are between 10 and 17 years old, you can calculate your probable BMR like this:

Female

(body mass in kg × 0.056) + 2.898

Male

(body mass in kg × 0.074) + 2.754

This gives you your probable BMR in MJ (megajoules) per day.

QUESTIONS

7 Angie is 17. She has a body mass of 51 kg. Calculate her BMR.

8 Explain why a calculation like this cannot be sure to give you your actual BMR.

Obesity

You will find out:
- That regular exercise helps you to stay fit
- That being overweight increases your risk of getting several illnesses
- About the different types of diabetes

Keep it off

People who exercise regularly are fitter than people who don't. Any kind of exercise helps you to use up energy from the food that you eat. Cycling to school or to work can be a good way of keeping **fit**. It helps to stop you getting too fat.

FIGURE 1: Our bodies need exercise to stay fit.

FIGURE 2: Obese people are more likely to get heart disease.

Having a little fat is good

Eat more food than you need each day, and the excess will be stored in your body as fat. It's good to have some fat in your body, but you don't want too much.

People who are very overweight are said to be **obese**. Being overweight, and especially being obese, increases the risk of getting ill. Overweight people are more likely to get:

- arthritis
- diabetes
- high blood pressure
- heart disease.

Figure 3 shows the ideal weight for people of different heights. It has been worked out by looking at records of thousands of people's heights and weights and keeping track of their health throughout their lives.

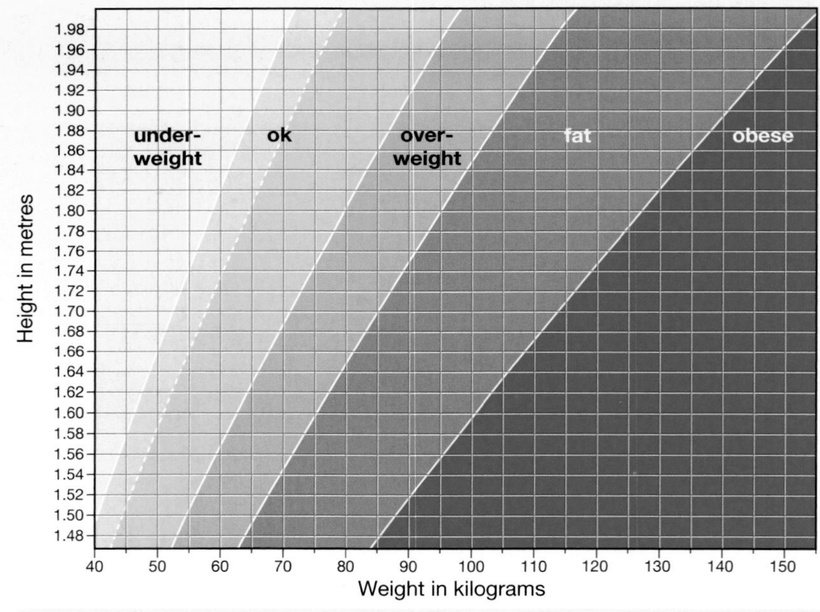

FIGURE 3: Chart of weight against height.

QUESTIONS

1. Jen is 1.64 metres tall. Her weight is 60 kg. Is she the right weight for her height?
2. Alan is 1.70 metres tall. What weight should he be for his height?
3. Peter is 1.90 metres tall. His weight is 145 kg. How much does he need to lose to end up with a weight that is OK for his height?
4. List **four** illnesses that Peter is more likely to get if he doesn't lose weight.

HEAVY STATISTIC

In the United Kingdom 20% of people are obese.

Arthritis

Arthritis means 'inflammation of the joints'. Anyone can get arthritis, but it is more common in people who are overweight.

Arthritis in the knee **joint** is the most common cause of disability in Britain. More than half a million people suffer from it. Drugs and exercise can help up to a point, but many need to have their knee joints replaced. This is a major and expensive operation.

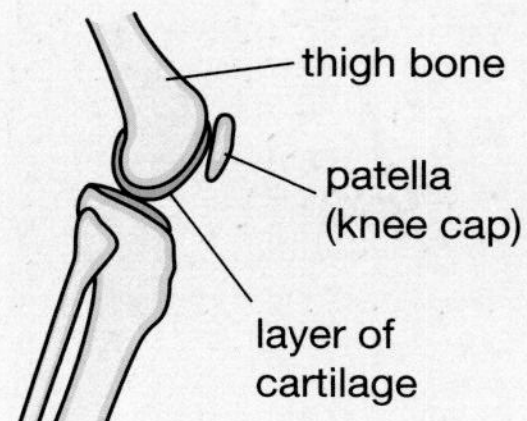

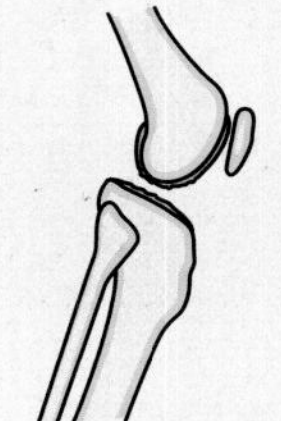

thigh bone

A normal knee joint has a thick cushion of smooth cartilage that allows the bones to slide easily over one another

An arthritic joint has thinner cartilage, and there are rough edges that grate against each other, causing pain and loss of mobility

FIGURE 4: A healthy knee joint and one with arthritis.

THREATENED KNEES

It is thought that up to half the cases of arthritis in the knee joint could be avoided if people were not obese.

Diabetes

Diabetes is an illness where a person can't control their **blood glucose** level. In Type 1 diabetes, the pancreas does not make enough insulin. In Type 2 diabetes, the body cells do not respond to insulin.

Type 2 diabetes is much more common in overweight people than in people who are the right weight for their height. Diabetes is dangerous because you can have too much glucose circulating in your blood. This can damage cells because it draws water out of them.

High blood pressure

Your **blood pressure** is the pressure of the blood in your arteries. The pressure is highest just after the heart beats. The pressure falls in between heartbeats.

For the blood pulsing through your arteries, a good blood pressure to have is about 130 over 85. The first figure is the highest pressure, and the second is the lowest pressure.

People who are overweight often have blood pressure that is too high. This is not good for your health. It puts a strain on your heart, and increases the risk of blood vessels getting damaged.

30% of the population have increased blood pressure as a result of eating too much salt.

QUESTIONS

5 Suggest why overweight people have an increased risk of getting arthritis in their knees.

6 Sally is told that her blood pressure is 150 over 100. What do these two numbers mean? Is Sally's blood pressure OK?

Who gets diabetes?

The number of people getting Type 2 diabetes is increasing. Mostly they are over 40, but in recent years it has become more common in younger people, even in children.

It still isn't known exactly why someone gets Type 2 diabetes. It certainly runs in families, which suggests that your genes have something to do with it. But your environment is also very important, especially your diet and your body weight. Smoking also increases the risk. All the same, even really fit people can get it. The rower Sir Steve Redgrave, who won five Olympic gold medals in five successive Olympic Games, has Type 2 diabetes.

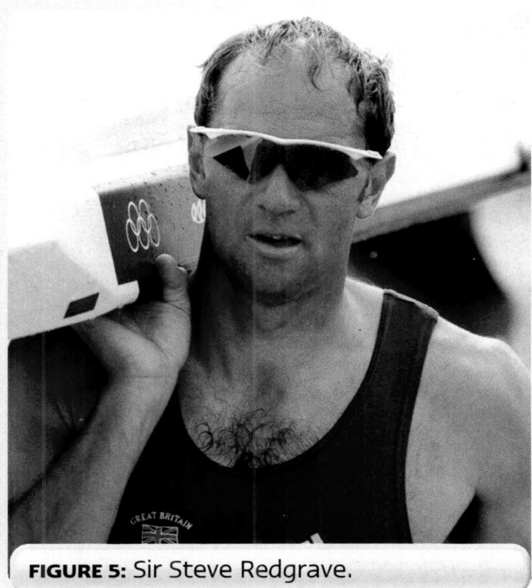

FIGURE 5: Sir Steve Redgrave.

Type 1 diabetes starts earlier in life, and has nothing to do with being overweight. In Type 1 diabetes, the cells in the pancreas that make insulin are destroyed. It is thought that this might be caused by the person's own immune system.

At the moment, there is no cure for either type of diabetes. In the future, though, it may be possible to cure Type 1 diabetes by transplanting healthy cells into the pancreas.

QUESTIONS

7 Explain the differences between Type 1 diabetes and Type 2 diabetes.

Not enough food

You will find out:

- That in poor countries, lack of food causes many health problems
- That these include reduced resistance to infection and irregular periods

Starvation

There is more than enough food in the world for everyone to have plenty to eat. But many people are starving or suffering from **malnutrition** because their diet is inadequate. Most of these people live in the developing world. Each year, we see reports on television of children in developing countries who are dying from lack of food.

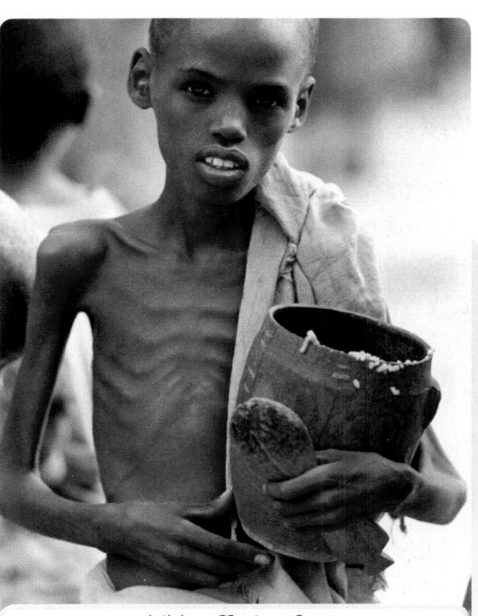

FIGURE 1: A child suffering from malnutrition.

Going hungry

In some countries, many people survive by growing their own crops. It is sometimes difficult for everyone to get enough food to eat. This may be because:

- there has been a drought or floods, so the crops have not grown well.
- there has been war, so the people have not been able to tend their fields or look after their children.
- people are too poor to buy food.

FIGURE 2: The rains came and this Somalian farmer is fortunate to have a crop of sorghum.

When someone does not have enough to eat, their resistance to infectious diseases is lowered. They are more likely to die from infections such as cholera or tuberculosis. Women may find that their periods stop or become irregular.

At the same time as people in the developing world are going hungry, some of us in developed countries eat too much. Many people want to be slimmer than they are. They may try **slimming programmes**. Many different programmes are advertised, all claiming to be a sure-fire way of losing weight. Most people who try them find that they don't really work, usually because they would have had to follow the programme for the rest of their lives, and they could not.

The best way to lose weight is to eat a bit less and do more exercise.

QUESTIONS

1. How can war lead to malnutrition?
2. Describe **one** health problem that can result from lack of food.
3. Suggest why people who want to lose weight often decide to spend money following a commercial slimming programme.

Every day, 40 000 children die from malnutrition

Health and malnutrition

When people are short of food, malnutrition usually affects small children first. This is because their bodies are still growing. They need protein so that their cells can grow and divide. If they do not get enough protein, they cannot grow. They stay very small for their age. They become very weak and some may die.

When a child does not get enough food, it cannot fight diseases. It has reduced resistance to infection because its white blood cells cannot destroy bacteria and viruses. (You can read more about this on pages 46 to 47.)

A child is at most danger of suffering from malnutrition when it stops feeding on its mother's milk and begins to eat normal food. The milk provided a **balanced diet**. But the only food a mother can then give her child may be low in protein. For example, the food may be made from maize flour or ground rice. This gives the child plenty of energy, but not enough protein for normal growth. And it may be lacking in important vitamins or minerals.

FIGURE 3: Breast milk is a healthier diet than food made from cereal flour.

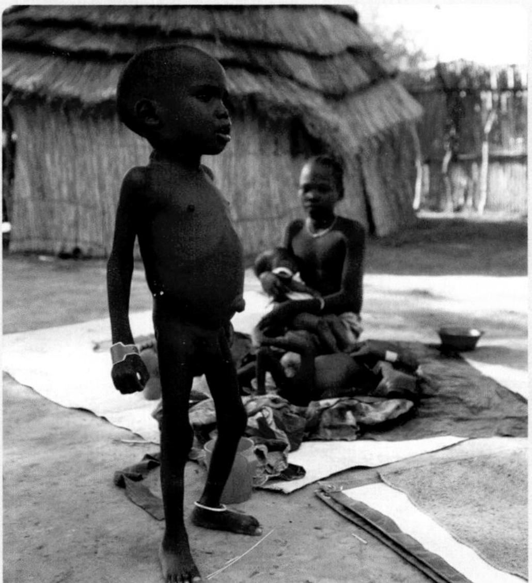

FIGURE 4: A child with kwashiorkor has a large abdomen but thin limbs.

A child on such a diet may suffer from **kwashiorkor**. This is an African word meaning 'disease suffered by a child removed from the breast'. A child with kwashiorkor is usually between one and three years old. Its arms and legs are thin, because its muscles have not developed. But it may have a swollen stomach because fluid accumulates in its tissues.

When given a good diet, a child with kwashiorkor will often recover fully.

QUESTIONS

4 Explain why children are often the first to suffer when there are serious food shortages.

5 What causes kwashiorkor?

6 Describe the symptoms of kwashiorkor.

Dieting

Doctors usually encourage patients who are overweight to try to lose some of their excess weight. This will improve their health.

The best way to lose weight is to change your diet so that you eat less overall but still have a balanced diet. Taking extra exercise also helps. The idea is simple: use up more energy than you take in. Then your body has to raid some of its energy stores.

Some companies make millions of pounds selling foods associated with their special slimming programmes. Some of these programmes have been well thought out and they work well. But many do not work for most people, so a person considering diets needs to choose with care.

FIGURE 5: A balanced diet.

For example, if a person follows the Atkins diet, they can eat as much protein and fat as they like but must cut down on carbohydrates. It is thought that this might increase the risk of developing heart disease.

QUESTIONS

7 Work in a group. You are a policy maker in the government. You have been given the task of developing a Health Promotion programme, to reduce illnesses caused both by obesity and by obsessive dieting.

Using information on the last four pages, discuss with your group the possible strategies you might use. Decide on a list of bullet points that summarises your message.

Work out how you could persuade the Chancellor of the Exchequer to give you funding for your programme.

Cholesterol and salt

You will find out:
- That eating saturated fats increases blood cholesterol level
- That too much salt can increase blood pressure
- That fast foods often contain lots of saturated fat and salt

Fast food or fat food?

Lots of people don't want to spend time cooking or shopping. Fast food is easy – it's cheap, it can taste good and it fills you up. But take care. Some fast foods contain more fat and salt in one serving than you should be eating in a whole day.

Cholesterol

Everyone knows **cholesterol** is bad for you. Too much cholesterol in your blood can form blockages in blood vessels, and that increases the risk of **heart disease**.

FIGURE 1: A meal packed with fat and salt.

What you eat can increase your cholesterol level. **Saturated fats** are especially to blame. These are the kind of fats that you find in animal products – foods like eggs, dairy products and meat.

Eating other kinds of fats isn't so bad. Some kinds actually seem to lower your blood cholesterol level. These are called **monounsaturated** and **polyunsaturated fats**. They are found in plant oils, like sunflower oil.

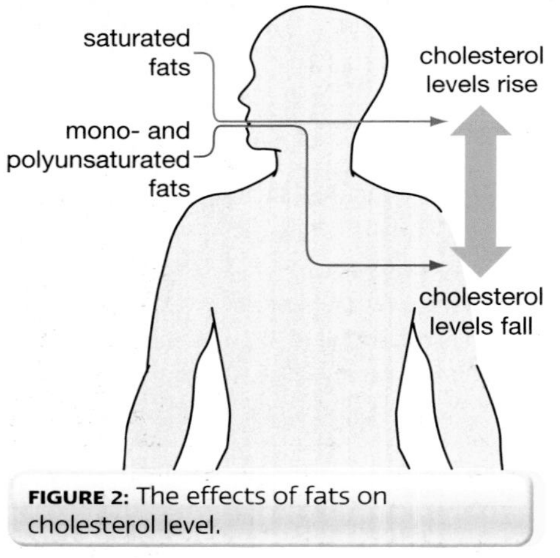

FIGURE 2: The effects of fats on cholesterol level.

But cholesterol isn't all bad. We need some cholesterol to make cell membranes. So your liver makes cholesterol. If you eat a diet that is low in saturated fats, the liver will make more cholesterol to ensure your cells have enough. If you eat a lot of saturated fats, the liver will make less. Different people make different amounts of cholesterol. It seems to depend on your genes and not just on how fat you are or what you eat.

Cholesterol is carried in your blood in two ways. **LDL** cholesterol is 'bad' and can cause heart disease. **HDL** cholesterol is 'good'. To stay healthy, it is best to have more HDL than LDL in your blood.

Salt

Like cholesterol, we need some salt, but not too much. Too much salt in the diet can lead to increased blood pressure.

Many processed foods contain a lot of salt. This includes snack foods like crisps and salted nuts. So people who eat a lot of these kinds of foods often eat too much salt.

QUESTIONS

1. Which are best to eat – saturated fats or mono- and polyunsaturated fats?
2. Give an example of a food containing saturated fat.
3. Give an example of a food containing polyunsaturated fat.
4. Which type of cholesterol is best to have in your blood – HDL or LDL?

...cholesterol ...heart disease ...high-density lipoprotein (HDL) ...low-density lipoprotein (LDL)

Cholesterol and heart disease

Cholesterol won't dissolve in water, so it cannot dissolve in your watery blood plasma. It is carried around in tiny balls mixed up with protein. These are called lipoproteins.

There are two kinds of these, **high-density lipoproteins** (HDLs) and **low-density lipoproteins** (LDLs).

A high level of LDLs in the blood increases the risk of developing **plaques** in the walls of the arteries. The diagrams show how this can happen.

A healthy artery has a stretchy wall and a space in the middle for blood to pass through

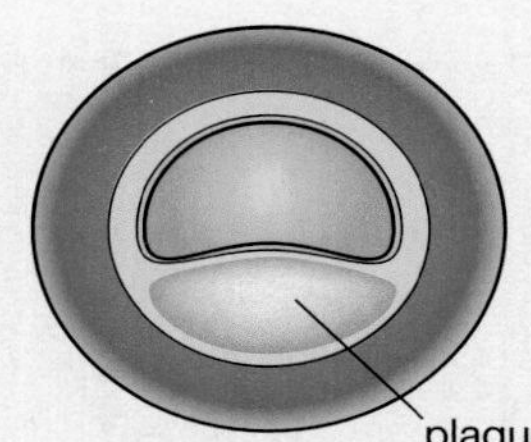

Sometimes, a substance called plaque builds up in the wall. This is more likely to happen if you have a lot of cholesterol in your blood

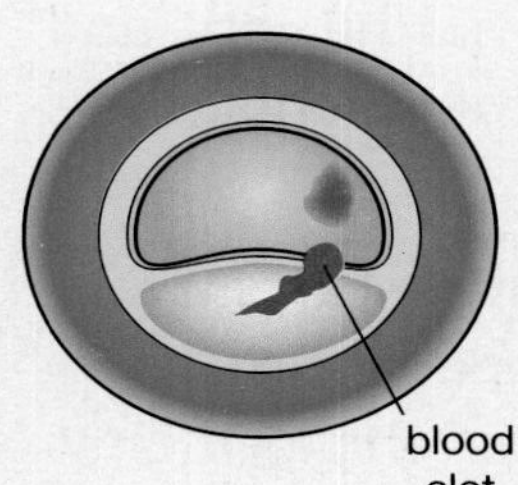

The plaque slows the blood down, and a clot may form. Or a part of the plaque may break away

FIGURE 3: How a plaque develops in an artery.

The plaque reduces the space that the blood can flow through. It can slow the blood down so that it clots. If a clot breaks away, it can get carried along in the blood and then get stuck in a smaller blood vessel, blocking blood flow.

Sometimes a clot blocks one of the arteries that take oxygenated blood to the heart muscle. The muscle can't work any more, so the heart can't beat properly. This is how someone has a heart attack.

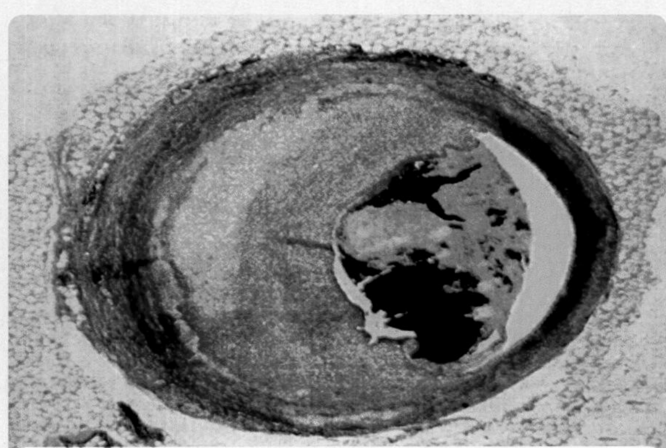

FIGURE 4: An artery almost blocked by plaque. Blood has to flow through the small space shown in blue.

HDLs can actually protect against heart disease. They help to remove cholesterol from the walls of your blood vessels.

QUESTIONS

5 Explain how cholesterol is involved in making a plaque in an artery.

6 Why is this dangerous?

Statins

The liver adjusts the amount of cholesterol that it makes according to how much you have in your blood. So it is difficult to have a really big effect on your blood cholesterol levels just by eating a good diet. If you eat less saturated fat, the liver compensates by making more cholesterol.

Some people's livers seem to have their cholesterol-making 'switch' set permanently at 'high'. It probably depends on your genes. It is particularly difficult for these people to keep their blood cholesterol down, no matter how careful they are with their diet.

For some people, drugs called statins can help. These affect the enzymes that control cholesterol synthesis in the liver. Taking statins inhibits cholesterol production.

Research has shown that statins can help everyone, not only people who have high blood cholesterol levels. Anyone who is at risk of having a heart attack, perhaps because they have high blood pressure, can reduce their risk by taking statins. The government is so sure that statins are useful that they have made them available to buy in a pharmacy, without the need for a prescription. Statins come as tablets, so they are easy to take.

FIGURE 5: A home cholesterol test.

QUESTIONS

7 Why do we need cholesterol?

8 Under what circumstances does the liver make cholesterol?

9 Explain why statins could have a bigger effect than diet alone in keeping blood cholesterol at a low level.

Bouncing off the walls

SELF-CHECK ACTIVITY

CONTEXT

Andy is a lively, enthusiastic eleven year old boy – full of confidence and keen to have a go at anything. His mother worries about his diet though, and she has good reason. He's fussy about what he eats, and the idea of healthy eating isn't one that troubles him.

He eats meat of various sorts, and chips. He also eats fish but won't eat vegetables (apart from cucumber). He'll eat pizza or pasta (as long as it only has butter or cheese on it) and ice cream or some kinds of yogurt. He'll eat chocolate in almost any form (his record is 25 Mars Bars in one day!) He'll drink milk occasionally, but much prefers fruit juice (as long as it doesn't have 'bits' in it) and loves cola. Breakfast is a chocolate flavoured cereal with no milk on it.

Andy is certainly not fat. He's one of the shortest in his class. He's active and alert. When he starts at secondary school he wants to join the school cross-country running team, though in a few of the practice sessions he seems to lack stamina. He goes to the local playing field with his friends sometimes and they kick a ball around. His mother's worried, though, that his poor eating habits may put him at a disadvantage when he's older. In the winter he spends a lot of time in front of the TV, though he does like reading and doing puzzles as well.

CHALLENGE

STEP 1

Read the information about Andy and discuss whether his mother is right to be concerned about his diet. List the strengths and weaknesses of his current diet.

STEP 2

Andy says he's doing fine and that his mother should 'lay off'. He points out that he's not fat, that he's active and gets energy from his food to do loads of energetic things. To what extent is he right?

STEP 3

His mother says he only eats what he fancies: sometimes he will eat a whole packet of biscuits and barely any tea. She knows he's slim and active at the moment, but thinks that sport may not be a big part of his life in the future and that his body shape may then change. Is she right to be concerned?

STEP 4

What might the future hold for Andy? Suggest two different outcomes. For each one refer to diet, activity levels and physical health.

Maximise your grade

These sentences show what you need to include in your work to achieve each grade. Use them to improve your work and be more successful.

Grade	Answer includes...
	Describe one way in which excess body mass can cause health problems.
F	Describe several ways in which excess body mass can cause health problems.
	Describe one way in which someone may try to control their body mass.
	Explain one way in which someone may try to control their body mass.
C	Explain how energy intake from food is balanced against energy requirements from physical activity.
	Explain how different people have different levels of energy requirement.
A	Explain how even if a younger person has a large intake of energy from foods but uses it up through an active lifestyle, problems may arise from poor eating habits linked to a more sedentary lifestyle later in life.
	As above, but with particular clarity and detail.

Drugs

You will find out:

- That drugs change the body's chemical processes
- That drugs have been used for thousands of years and can be used for health and recreation
- That drugs can be legal or illegal

What is a drug?

Almost everyone takes drugs sometimes. A **drug** is something that changes the chemical processes in the body. Lots of drugs are helpful. For example, antibiotics are drugs that help us to recover from infections. But some drugs are dangerous, especially if they are used wrongly.

FIGURE 1: These are what we think of as drugs.

Using drugs

People have been using drugs for thousands of years. Many come from plants and other natural substances. An example is aspirin which is found in willow bark. People used to chew the bark to relieve pain.

Drugs are very helpful to us. They can help to make us feel better when we are ill, and cure us of diseases.

Some people take drugs not because they need them, but because taking them makes them feel different. We describe this as a **recreational use** of drugs.

FIGURE 2: Coffee contains the drug caffeine which helps us stay alert.

Dangers of drugs

Many different kinds of drugs can be harmful. They include:

- alcohol
- cannabis
- cocaine and heroin
- tobacco

Alcohol and tobacco are **legal** drugs. Cannabis, cocaine and heroin are **illegal** drugs.

Some people become **addicted** to a drug. They are **dependent** on it, meaning that they feel they cannot manage without it.

A drug addiction can have dangerous long-term effects. Over time, the lungs, brain and **liver** can be seriously damaged. The liver is damaged because it has the job of destroying harmful chemicals in the body.

Although illegal drugs do a lot of harm, so do legal drugs if they are misused. Alcohol and tobacco are legal but claim thousands more lives each year than heroin or cocaine. This is because far more people use legal drugs than illegal ones.

QUESTIONS

1. What is a drug?
2. Name **two** useful drugs.
3. Name **three** drugs which are sometimes misused.
4. Why can the misuse of drugs cause liver damage?

...addicted ...dependent ...drug ...illegal

Addiction and dependency

Taking any drug changes the way that the body works. Sometimes, these changes mean that a person feels they can't manage without the drug.

If someone is dependent on a drug, they constantly crave it. Perhaps they started taking the drug to help them through a bad patch in their life. Perhaps they associate it with something they enjoyed. Whatever the reason, later they can't manage without it.

If someone is addicted to a drug, they feel really ill if they stop taking it. They may suffer from very unpleasant **withdrawal symptoms**. These can last for days or weeks.

There isn't any hard and fast dividing line between addiction and dependency. They are both really difficult to escape from. People often need a lot of help to get away from their drug habit and be able to live a better life.

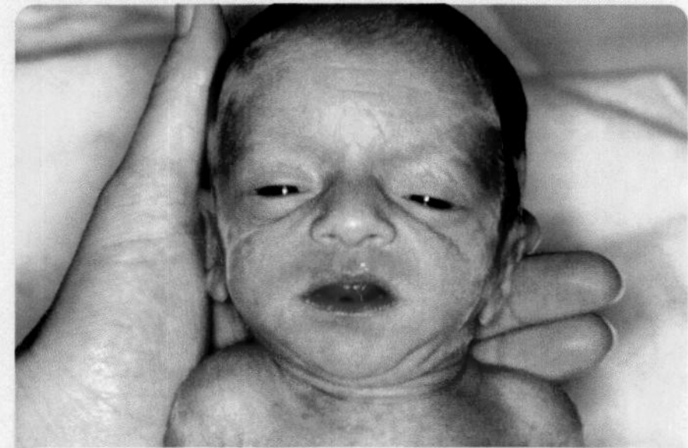

FIGURE 3: A mother may pass on a drug addiction to her baby.

QUESTIONS

5 Explain what is meant by 'dependency' on a drug.

6 Using your knowledge of how a baby grows in the uterus, suggest how a developing baby may become addicted to the same substance as its mother.

SOLVENTS KILL

Each year, about 70 people die from solvent abuse in Britain. People can die the very first time they sniff solvents.

Deaths from drug use

Each year, thousands of people in Britain die from misusing illegal drugs. Some of these deaths are from poisoning. Some of them happen because the drug affected someone's brain and made them behave in a dangerous way.

Most of the deaths happen in people between the ages of 20 and 39.

Figure 4 shows the number of deaths from misuse of illegal drugs in England and Wales between 1993 and 2003.

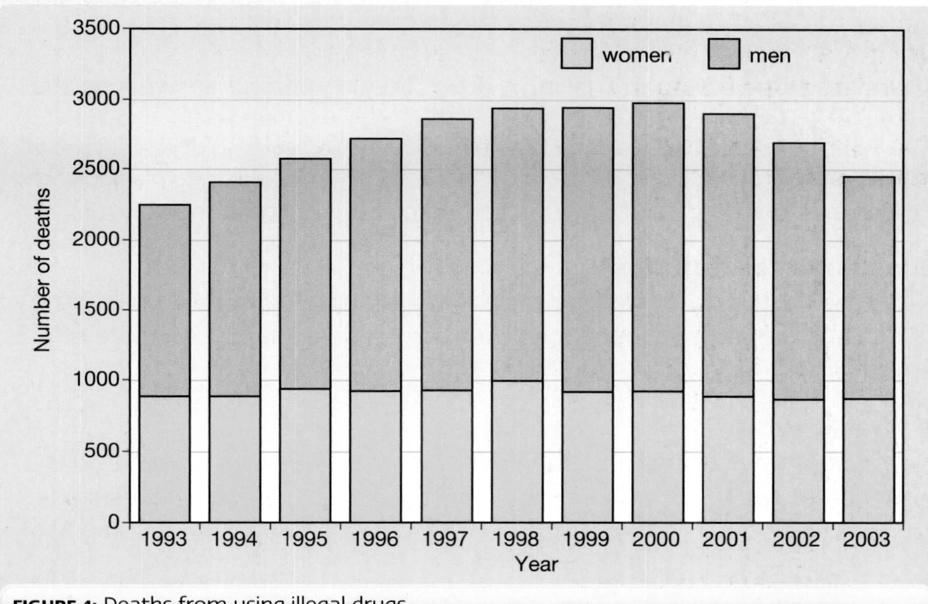

FIGURE 4: Deaths from using illegal drugs.

QUESTIONS

7 Are men or women more likely to die from drug poisoning?

8 How many women died from drug poisoning in 1998?

9 There were 2445 deaths from drug poisoning in 2003. How many of these deaths were of men?

10 Describe the trends in the number of deaths from drug poisoning between 1993 and 2003.

11 Over this time, in which group, men or women, have there been the greatest changes?

12 Many people become addicted to nicotine in cigarettes. Research some of the methods they use to try to give up. Which ones seem to work best?

Trialling drugs

You will find out:

- That new drugs are tested before being used
- That though trialled, thalidomide harmed fetuses
- That thalidomide is banned for pregnant women, but is used to treat leprosy

Thalidomide

In the early 1960s, many pregnant women were prescribed the **drug thalidomide** to treat morning sickness. Not until they gave birth did anyone have any idea that the drug was dangerous. Women who had taken thalidomide in early pregnancy often gave birth to babies with short arms or no arms. Immediately the connection was realised, thalidomide was banned worldwide, but not before more than 10 000 children had been affected.

FIGURE 1: A child affected by thalidomide.

Testing drugs

Whenever a new drug is discovered or made, it has to be thoroughly tested before doctors are allowed to prescribe it.

There are three stages in trialling a drug. They try to find answers to the following questions.

1 Is it safe?
The drug is tested in a laboratory, to find out if it is **toxic** (poisonous).

2 Is it safe for humans?
Next, the drug is given to volunteers. They are given different doses to try to find out what is the highest dose that can be taken safely. Any side effects are recorded.

3 Does it work?
Next, the drug is tested on people who have the illness that the drug is intended to treat. If it makes people better, then the drug may be sold commercially.

The trialling process can take years and may not result in a new drug. The media often report some major new breakthrough in the treatment of cancer, AIDS or other diseases. Then we never hear about it again. Probably, the planned drug failed at some stage of the trials. Even if it did get through the trials, it will be at least 5 years before it is available in chemists. And when it does, it quite often fails to be the miracle cure everyone was expecting.

FIGURE 2: A child in a trial of a drug to treat asthma.

Thalidomide had been thoroughly trialled for use as a sleeping pill. But no-one had thought to test it on pregnant women.

Now, thalidomide is being used to treat a disease called leprosy. But no woman who might be pregnant is allowed to take it.

QUESTIONS

1. What was thalidomide originally used for?
2. Why was thalidomide banned in the 1960s?
3. At which stage of a drug trial do we first discover whether or not the drug makes people better?
4. What is thalidomide used for today?

...double blind ...drug ...placebo

Testing an antiviral drug

GlaxoSmithKline have developed a drug called zanamivir. The drug looked as though it might help to lessen the symptoms of influenza – flu. Flu is hard to treat because it is caused by a virus.

Zanamivir passed all the early stages of the trials with flying colours. GlaxoSmithKline then tested it very thoroughly on several groups of volunteers. These included young soldiers, people over 65, members of families (to see if the drug helped stop everyone in the household catching flu), adolescents and adults, and – when they were sure it was safe – they tested it on children aged between 5 and 12.

They used a kind of test called a **double-blind** trial. The volunteers were divided into two groups. Half of them were given the drug, and the other half were given a **placebo**. This is a pill or other treatment that doesn't have the drug in it. The volunteers don't know which they are getting, and nor do the doctors and others involved in the trial.

HIGH FAILURE RATE

Of every 100 new drugs that are tested, about 20 will eventually be approved for marketing.

The table shows some of the results from a trial of the drug in young soldiers in the Finnish army. When one of them got flu, they were given either zanamivir or a placebo.

	Given zanamivir	Given a placebo
number of subjects	293	295
mean age in years	19	19
number of days until their temperature went down to normal	2.00	2.33
number of days until they lost all their symptoms and felt better	3.00	3.83
number of days until they felt just as well as before they had flu	4.5	6.3
average score the volunteers gave to their experience of the five major symptoms of flu	23.4	25.3

TABLE 1: Effect of zanamivir and a placebo on soldiers suffering from flu.

QUESTIONS

5 The trials with the other groups of people all gave similar results. If you had to decide whether or not zanamivir should be distributed, what would you say? How would you support your decision?

A question of cost

Zanamivir has been approved for use in Britain, as well as in the rest of Europe and in the USA. It is marketed as Relenza.

But just because a drug is approved doesn't mean you will be able to get it on the National Health. The NHS has only so much money to spend, and careful thought is given to the choice of drugs that should be freely available and which should not.

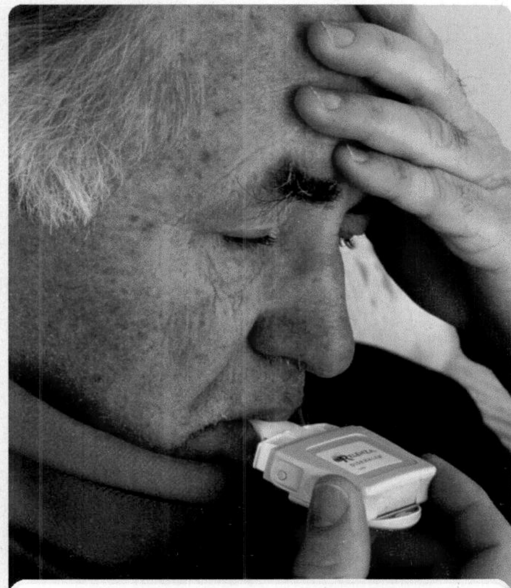

FIGURE 3: This man has been prescribed zanamivir because at his age flu can be dangerous.

It is the National Institute for Clinical Excellence – NICE – that decides this. They recommend that zanamivir should not be given to people with flu unless there is some reason to think they are at risk of developing other conditions which may be dangerous.

QUESTIONS

6 What evidence from the study shown in table 1 might help to explain NICE's decision?

7 What issues do you think NICE should take into account when making their decision?

8 What groups of people do you think should be part of the NICE committee? Explain your suggestion.

Illegal drugs

You will find out:

- That using cannabis can cause psychological problems and lead to using hard drugs
- That hard drugs, such as heroin, are very addictive
- That drugs can cause severe health problems

The danger of illegal drugs

Cannabis, **heroin** and **cocaine** are illegal drugs. They all come from plants. They all affect the brain and can do serious, permanent damage.

Cannabis

Cannabis is a **drug** made from the dried leaves of the cannabis plant. Some people smoke cannabis like smoking tobacco. Just like tobacco, cannabis can cause bronchitis and lung cancer.

Cannabis makes the user feel relaxed and happy. Some think that cannabis is safe to use. People with long-term illnesses such as multiple sclerosis claim that cannabis helps them feel better. But careful scientific research has not found any evidence that it really does help.

Doctors now think that young people who smoke cannabis are more likely to develop a serious mental illness called schizophrenia. This is very worrying. It looks as though cannabis is much less safe than many people thought in the past.

FIGURE 1: Cannabis plants.

Heroin and cocaine

Heroin and cocaine come from opium poppies. The poppies are grown by farmers in poor countries including Afghanistan and Colombia.

It is illegal to import heroin or cocaine into Britain. But drug dealers keep doing it. They can sell the drugs for large amounts of money.

People use heroin and cocaine because these drugs make them feel happy and relaxed. But heroin and cocaine are very dangerous. They are known as **hard drugs**. Cocaine is very addictive – someone can become a cocaine addict after using it only once. The drug dealers know this. Once someone is **addicted**, they will pay a lot of money to get their next fix of the drug.

Almost everyone who takes hard drugs has previously smoked cannabis. This suggests that using cannabis may lead a person to use hard drugs. However, there could also be other explanations for this link.

FIGURE 2: Opium poppies in Afghanistan.

QUESTIONS

1 List **three** ways in which cannabis can be harmful.
2 Why are cocaine and heroin said to be 'hard drugs'?
3 Suggest other explanations for the link between smoking cannabis and using hard drugs.

...addicted ...cannabis ...cocaine ...drug

Hard drugs

Opiates are drugs that are made from opium, which comes from opium poppies.

Diamorphine is an opiate that is used in hospitals to relieve pain. Used in this controlled way, it is a useful and safe drug. People will not become addicted to it.

But heroin and cocaine are much more dangerous. People can quickly become addicted to them. An addict may use a syringe to inject the drug directly into a vein, because it gets to their brain faster. This adds extra dangers. If several people use the same syringe, they can transmit infections such as HIV/AIDS or hepatitis.

People who are addicted to hard drugs will do anything to get the drug. It takes over their life.

If they stop taking it, they develop **withdrawal symptoms**. They cannot sleep, their eyes constantly water, they yawn, sweat and feel sick. They may feel pain all over their body.

Is cannabis safe?

This is what two young people have to say about cannabis.

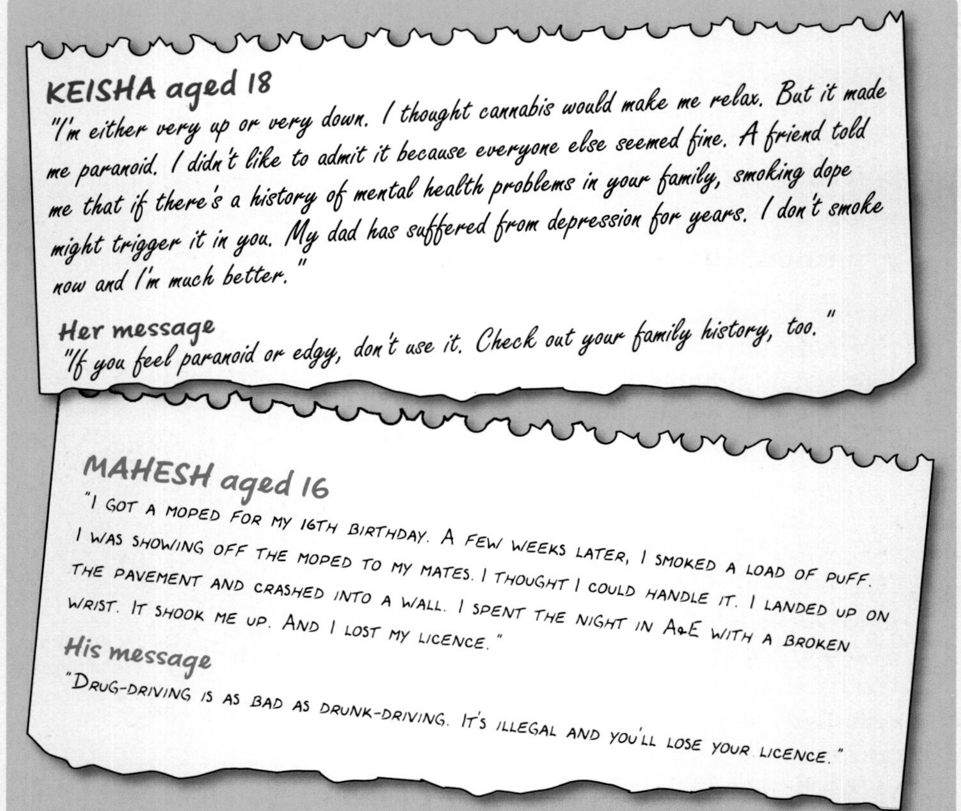

KEISHA aged 18
"I'm either very up or very down. I thought cannabis would make me relax. But it made me paranoid. I didn't like to admit it because everyone else seemed fine. A friend told me that if there's a history of mental health problems in your family, smoking dope might trigger it in you. My dad has suffered from depression for years. I don't smoke now and I'm much better."
Her message
"If you feel paranoid or edgy, don't use it. Check out your family history, too."
MAHESH aged 16
"I GOT A MOPED FOR MY 16TH BIRTHDAY. A FEW WEEKS LATER, I SMOKED A LOAD OF PUFF. I WAS SHOWING OFF THE MOPED TO MY MATES. I THOUGHT I COULD HANDLE IT. I LANDED UP ON THE PAVEMENT AND CRASHED INTO A WALL. I SPENT THE NIGHT IN A&E WITH A BROKEN WRIST. IT SHOOK ME UP. AND I LOST MY LICENCE."
His message
"DRUG-DRIVING IS AS BAD AS DRUNK-DRIVING. IT'S ILLEGAL AND YOU'LL LOSE YOUR LICENCE."

QUESTIONS

4 Explain how opiates can be useful drugs.

5 Explain why a person who starts taking cocaine may not be able to give it up.

6 Find out what 'paranoid' means. Explain why Keisha decided not to smoke cannabis.

Craving for drugs

Drugs such as heroin and cocaine affect synapses between our brain cells. The chemicals that carry nerve impulses across the synapses are altered. This is why the person develops an overwhelming craving for the drug. If they stop taking the drug, withdrawal symptoms can last for weeks, until the brain chemicals eventually get back to normal.

If someone really wants to break their heroin or cocaine habit, they can be given a different drug, methadone, on prescription. Then they can get back to a normal life, because they don't have to worry about where their next dose of the drug will come from.

But then they are addicted to methadone. The dose they take can be slowly reduced so that eventually they are no longer addicted.

FIGURE 3: An addict receives supplies of methadone.

QUESTIONS

7 Some people argue that it is wrong to give drug addicts free supplies of methadone on the NHS. Others say that this can help an addict to give up. Discuss these two points of view.

Alcohol

You will find out:

- That alcohol affects the nervous system, slows down reactions and can lead to loss of self-control
- That excess alcohol can cause unconsciousness or coma and damage the liver and brain

Alcohol is dangerous

Alcohol is a very commonly used **drug**. Most people who drink alcohol do so sensibly. But misuse can kill. Sometimes it is not the drinker who is harmed, but someone else. About 15% of road deaths are caused by a driver who has been drinking alcohol.

FIGURE 1: If you drink and drive, you increase the chance of killing and being killed.

An ancient drug

People have been drinking alcohol for thousands of years. The ancient Egyptians made beer. Beer is made from cereal grains, such as barley. Yeast uses the sugars produced by the grains as they germinate. Wine is made from the sugars in grapes.

FIGURE 2: Ancient Egyptians brewed alcohol on a large scale.

Alcohol is a poison

Alcohol affects the nervous system. It causes:

- reactions to slow down
- loss of self control
- **unconsciousness**, **coma** and even death, when a lot is drunk.

Alcohol damages the **brain** and the **liver**. Brain cells are quickly affected by alcohol. The cells shrink. A person who drinks a lot of alcohol for many years may have permanent brain damage.

The liver gets damaged because it has the job of breaking down alcohol. It changes the alcohol into harmless substances. But too much can kill the liver's own cells. Each year, 30 000 people are admitted to hospital in Britain with liver disease caused by drinking alcohol.

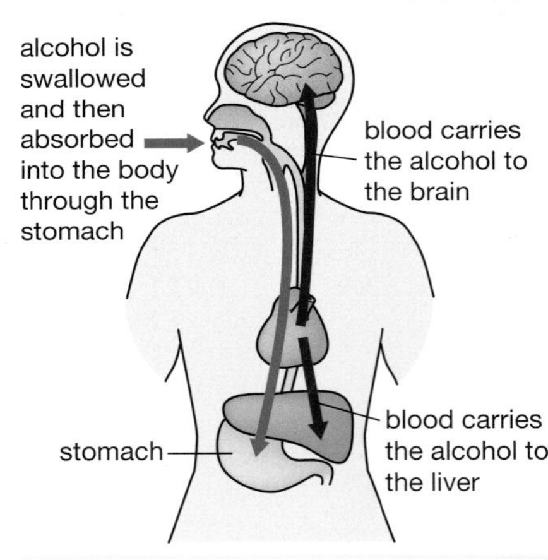
alcohol is swallowed and then absorbed into the body through the stomach
blood carries the alcohol to the brain
stomach
blood carries the alcohol to the liver

FIGURE 3: How alcohol reaches the brain and liver.

QUESTIONS

1 How does alcohol affect the nervous system?

2 Use your answer to question 1 to explain why no-one should drink and drive.

3 Name **one** body organ, other than the brain, that is damaged by alcohol.

4 Explain why this organ is damaged by alcohol.

THE GRIM FACTS

Almost one in 13 people in Britain are thought to be dependent on alcohol.

...alcohol ...brain ...coma ...dependent

An acceptable drug?

Because alcoholic drinks have been around for so long, many people don't think of alcohol as a dangerous drug. But if alcohol were to be discovered for the first time today, it would almost certainly be banned. Some cultures and religions actually do ban alcohol.

FIGURE 4: In many groups of people, alcohol is a socially acceptable drug.

Different people react differently to alcohol. Some just relax and enjoy themselves, since alcohol makes them feel relaxed. Others get aggressive and violent, even after just a few drinks. They can do things that harm themselves and others.

Here are some figures about alcohol abuse in Britain:

- around 150 000 people are admitted to hospital each year because of drinking alcohol
- one in every three people going to Accident and Emergency is there for reasons connected to drinking alcohol
- 40% of people arrested for criminal damage test positive for alcohol.

Alcohol dependency

Some people become **dependent** on alcohol. They cannot manage without it. This can ruin their lives. They spend so much money on alcohol that they cannot support themselves or their families. They may lose their jobs and friends.

QUESTIONS

This table shows the number of people who died in England and Wales because of drinking alcohol in 2000, 2001 and 2003.

Year	2000	2001	2003
number of women who died	3800	3815	4281
number of men who died	5970	6033	6580

5 Draw a bar graph to display these figures.

6 Describe what this data shows. Try to say something about:
- the trends over the three years
- the differences between the figures for men and women.

FAST EFFECTS

Alcohol gets from the stomach to the brain in just a few minutes.

Depressants

Alcohol is an example of a **depressant**. Depressants are drugs that slow down the brain's activity.

A part of the brain called the cortex allows a person to think clearly and make decisions. Alcohol greatly hinders this ability. It also inhibits the brain's cerebellum in its task of coordinating body movements.

If drunk in large enough amounts, alcohol can kill. It can inhibit the parts of the brain that control breathing. The person then becomes unconscious and may fall into a coma or die.

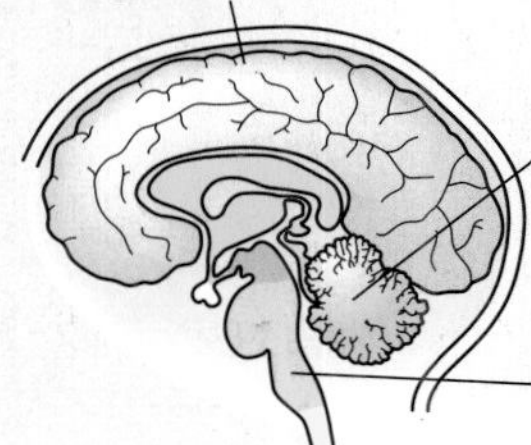
The cortex (the wrinkled surface layer of the brain), which is responsible for conscious thought and actions
The cerebellum, which controls movement and posture
The medulla, which controls breathing and heart rate

FIGURE 5: Parts of the brain that alcohol affects.

QUESTIONS

7 Using what you know about how alcohol affects the body, suggest reasons for the large number of hospital admissions connected with alcohol.

Tobacco

You will find out:

- That substances in tobacco smoke cause many diseases
- That carbon monoxide in smoke can harm a fetus
- That the link with lung cancer was made in the 1950s

Smoking kills

Smokers are 20 times more likely to die from **lung cancer** than non-smokers. Many types of cancer can now be cured, but lung cancer is not so easy to cure. In this man's treatment, X-rays are being targeted at the tumour in his lungs. The X-rays will kill the cancer cells. This is called radiotherapy.

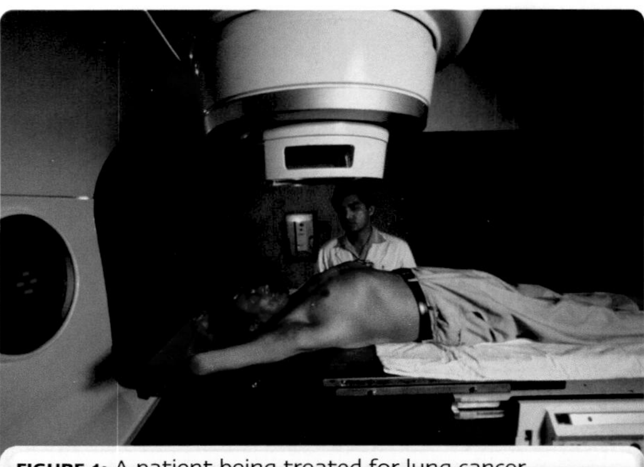

FIGURE 1: A patient being treated for lung cancer.

Cigarette poisons

Tobacco smoke contains many different substances including nicotine, tar and carbon monoxide. Some of them are poisons.

Nicotine affects the brain. It is **addictive**.

Tar is a poison that causes cancer. It is a **carcinogen**. Cancer is a disease where cells divide uncontrollably. The cancerous cells form lumps called tumours. Cigarette smoke often causes lung cancer, but it also increases the risk of developing many other kinds of cancer. About a quarter of regular smokers die of cancer.

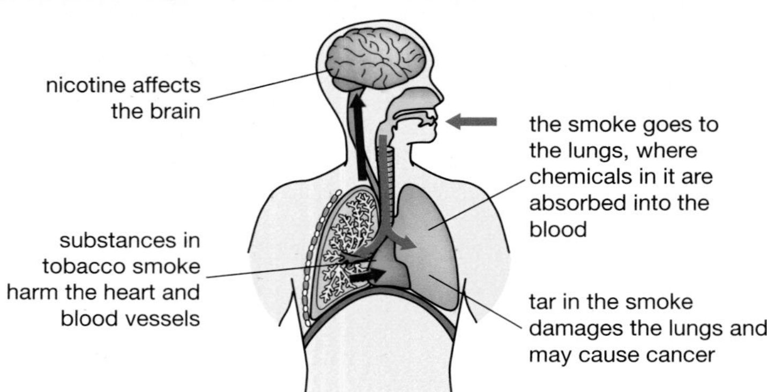
nicotine affects the brain
the smoke goes to the lungs, where chemicals in it are absorbed into the blood
substances in tobacco smoke harm the heart and blood vessels
tar in the smoke damages the lungs and may cause cancer

FIGURE 2: How tobacco smoke affects organs in the body.

Carbon monoxide takes the place of oxygen in the red blood cells so the blood cannot carry as much oxygen as it should. This can harm body cells. It is especially damaging for pregnant women. The developing baby does not get enough oxygen. It may not grow properly and is likely to have a low birth weight. A person who smokes is also more likely to have a disease of the heart and blood vessels.

Lung diseases

A regular smoker often gets infections in their lungs and airways. In **bronchitis**, the person's **bronchi** get inflamed and painful. A lot of **mucus** is produced. Some of the mucus trickles down into the lungs. The smoker coughs to try to remove the mucus.

The walls of the air sacs in a smoker's lungs lose their stretchiness. Some of them break. Instead of millions of tiny air sacs, a smoker may end up with far fewer of them. It is difficult to get oxygen into the blood. This condition is called **emphysema**. Someone with emphysema may have to breathe oxygen from a cylinder.

QUESTIONS

1. List **three** harmful substances in tobacco smoke.
2. What makes tobacco addictive?
3. What is cancer? Which kinds of cancer are you more likely to get if you smoke?
4. What is bronchitis?
5. What is emphysema? How is it caused?

...addictive ... bronchi ...bronchitis ...cancer ...carbon monoxide ...carcinogen

Making the link

Cigarettes first became popular during the First World War, round about 1915. At first, only men smoked. By the 1940s, women were smoking too. No-one had any idea that they were dangerous. By 1954, 80% of adults in Britain smoked.

But as early as the 1930s, doctors began to notice that more and more people were getting lung cancer. In the late 1940s, a doctor called Richard Doll tried to find out why. To start with, he thought it might be tar on the roads. He knew that substances in tar could cause cancer.

He and his research team interviewed 700 people with lung cancer. Soon, he realised that there was a **correlation** between smoking and lung cancer. In other words, people who smoked were much more likely to get lung cancer than people who did not smoke. Richard Doll stopped smoking.

But the correlation didn't prove that smoking actually caused lung cancer. There could have been something else going on. For example, more people were driving cars and there was more air pollution. Perhaps air pollution was causing the increase in lung cancer.

Richard Doll kept on with his work. He gradually found more and more evidence that lung cancer was linked with smoking. By the late 1950s, those in the medical world were convinced he was right. Today there is absolutely no doubt that smoking causes lung cancer. Scientists now understand how the chemicals in tar from tobacco smoke change cells so that they become cancerous.

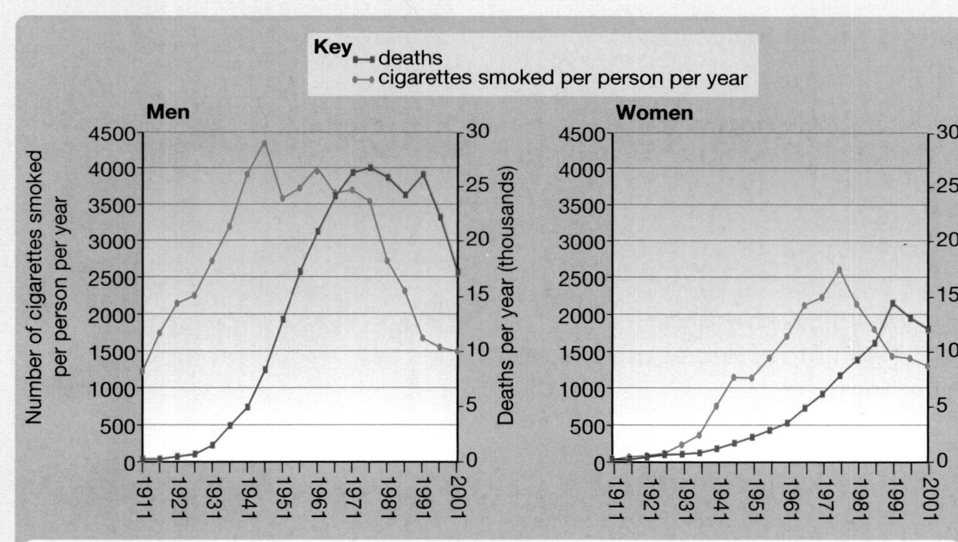

FIGURE 3: The link between smoking and deaths.

QUESTIONS

6 Describe the pattern of smoking by men shown in the graph.

7 How does the graph suggest that smoking could cause lung cancer?

8 Explain why the graph does not prove that smoking causes lung cancer.

9 Predict what will happen to the number of deaths from lung cancer in women after 2001, and explain why you think this will happen.

In 1954, 80% of adults in Britain smoked

Tar and cancer

Cells divide as a zygote (fertilised egg) grows into an embryo, a fetus and then into a child and finally an adult. But cells don't go on dividing forever. Once a brain or a heart or a lung has developed, most of the cells in it settle down and don't divide again.

The timing of a cell dividing is controlled by the genes in its nucleus. Some genes tell a cell to divide, while others stop it dividing. Usually, these are kept in balance.

Some chemicals cause mutations – changes – in these controlling genes. The chemicals are called carcinogens. Tar in tobacco smoke contains many different carcinogens.

The mutations can switch on the genes that stimulate cell division, while the genes that stop cell division switch off. This is why a cell becomes cancerous. It divides over and over again, out of control.

QUESTIONS

10 Smoking causes not only lung cancer, but also cancer in organs such as the pancreas. Explain how this could happen.

11 Although Richard Doll published a paper in 1951 showing a correlation between lung cancer and smoking, few people believed him when he said that smoking caused lung cancer. Suggest why the link was not accepted then.

Pathogens

You will find out:

- That microorganisms that cause disease are pathogens
- That bacteria and viruses reproduce rapidly and their toxins make us feel ill
- That Ignaz Semmelweis showed how to control infections

Food for thought

This is a piece of roast beef, magnified 2000 times. The green blobs are *Salmonella* bacteria. They probably got onto the beef on the feet of a visiting housefly. If the beef is left in a warm place, the bacteria will multiply. If you then ate the beef, the thousands of bacteria could make you very ill.

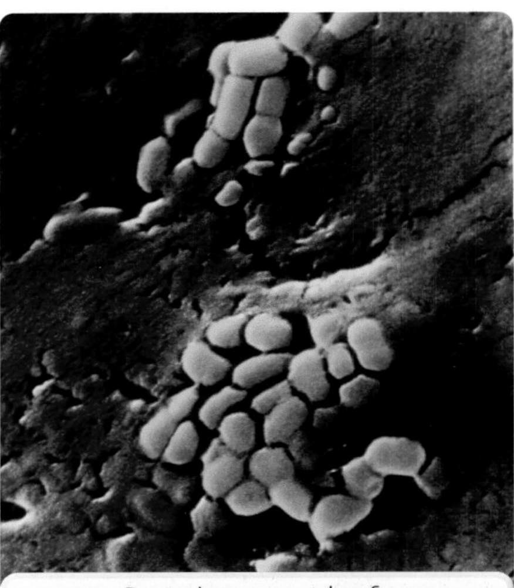

FIGURE 1: Bacteria on roast beef.

Microorganisms

Microorganisms are living things that are too small for us to see without a microscope. They include **bacteria** and **viruses**.

Visible organisms, such as humans, are made of many cells. But each bacterium is made of just one cell. And their cells are much smaller than ours. You can't see bacteria clearly with even the very best school microscope.

Look at the millimetre markings on a ruler. You could fit 1000 bacteria, lined up side by side, into one millimetre.

Viruses are even smaller. You could pack more than 1000 viruses inside a bacterium. And there are some viruses that actually do get inside bacteria. So even bacteria can get ill.

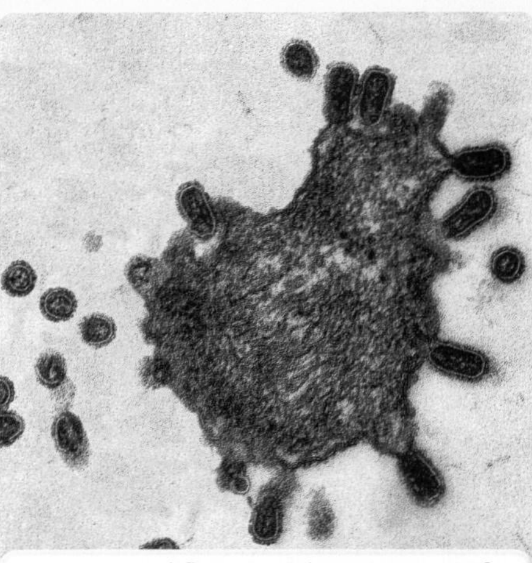

FIGURE 2: Bird flu viruses bursting out of a human cell and destroying it.

Microorganisms and disease

Some bacteria and viruses cause disease. The scientific name for a microorganism that causes disease is a **pathogen**. Lots of people use the word 'germs', but it's much better to use the proper term.

If bacteria get inside the body, they can reproduce rapidly. They may produce waste substances called **toxins** (poisons) that make you feel dreadful. The toxins get carried all round the body in the blood. So even if the bacteria are breeding only inside your intestines, you can feel ill all over.

A virus can actually get inside a cell of yours and reproduce there. When lots have been produced, they burst out of the cell, completely destroying it. The viruses then invade other cells. Next time you have a sore throat, imagine the viruses bursting out of the cells on the skin in your throat. No wonder it feels sore.

THREAT TO THE HEART

Current research suggests that bacteria might be responsible for some kinds of heart disease.

QUESTIONS

1. What does pathogen mean?
2. How do bacteria make you feel ill?
3. How do viruses damage the body?
4. Arrange these in order, smallest first: human cell, virus, bacterium.

Ignaz Semmelweis

Semmelweis was a Hungarian doctor who worked in a labour ward in Austria in the 1840s. There were actually two wards. One contained women due to give birth and was run by midwives. The other was used as a teaching hospital for medical students. The wards were cleaned no more than once a month. The doctors rarely washed their hands and often wore dirty coats.

Semmelweis was horrified by the number of women who died after births that were trouble free. The women developed a very high temperature and died within a few days from an illness called puerperal fever. No-one had any idea what caused this disease. No-one knew about bacteria or viruses then.

FIGURE 3: Ignaz Semmelweis.

Semmelweis realised that more than three times as many women died from puerperal fever in the teaching ward than in the midwives' ward. He was determined to try to reduce the number of deaths.

He looked at each factor that was different between the two wards, but nothing that he thought of seemed to make any difference to the deaths. Then a professor was accidentally cut with a knife that was being used to study the body of a woman who had died. The professor himself died, from a disease whose symptoms were very like puerperal fever.

Semmelweis thought that there must have been something on the knife that had caused the disease. So perhaps there was something on the doctors' hands that carried disease to the women in the wards. He made all the doctors wash their hands in chlorine water before examining the women. Within a very short time, the death rate had plummeted.

Today, we know about bacteria and how important it is to keep everything clean in hospitals. But there are still problems of people in hospital dying from infections. You can read more about this on page 52.

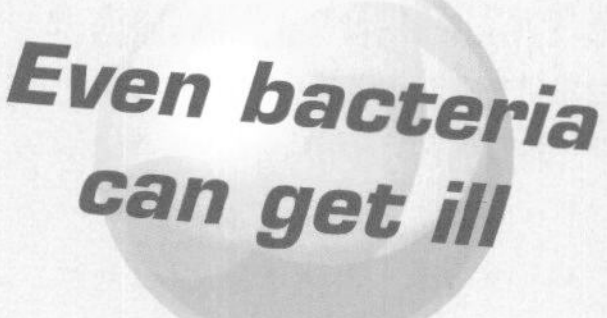
Even bacteria
can get ill

FIGURE 4: A hospital ward in the 19th century.

QUESTIONS

5 Explain how arrangements in Semmelweis's hospital helped him to find out which variable was causing the high death rate in the teaching ward.

6 Why was so little attention paid to hygiene in the labour wards?

Helicobacter

We are still learning a lot about pathogens today.

A stomach ulcer is a sore, raw patch in the stomach wall. For years, people thought it was caused by stress or an over-secretion of acid in the stomach.

But in 1982, two Australian researchers, Marshall and Warren, found bacteria in the stomachs of people with ulcers. The bacteria were spiral (helix) in shape, so they were given the name *Helicobacter pylori* ('spiral bacterium of the stomach'). Marshall and Warren put forward the startling hypothesis that these bacteria were actually causing the ulcers.

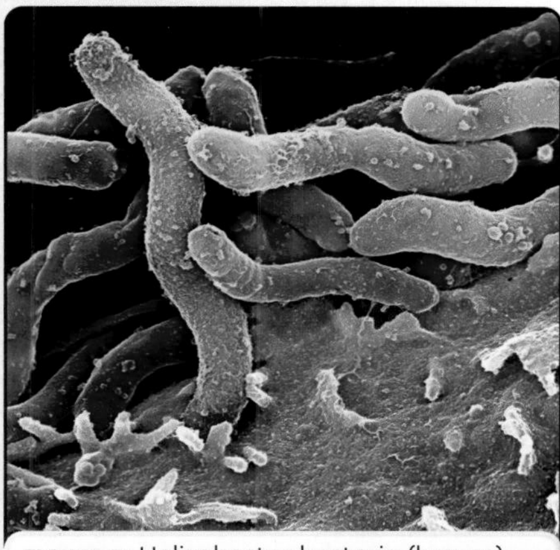

FIGURE 5: Helicobacter bacteria (brown) on a stomach wall (green).

But doctors weren't ready to believe them. To convince people they were right, Warren swallowed some of the bacteria, and, as he expected, developed a bad stomach ulcer.

Nowadays, stomach ulcers can be treated with antibiotics, which kill the *H. pylori* bacteria.

QUESTIONS

7 Suggest why people were so reluctant to accept Marshall and Warren's idea.

8 Suggest some less drastic methods that Marshall and Warren could have used to collect evidence to support their hypothesis.

Body defences

You will find out:

- That white blood cells fight against pathogens inside the body
- That some white blood cells ingest (take in) pathogens and kill them
- That some make antibodies and antitoxins

Infection

This 18-year-old's body piercing has become infected. Bacteria have got in through the wound. Now it is swollen, red and painful. This shows that her **white blood cells** are trying to destroy the bacteria causing the **infection**. The wound probably needs to be treated with something to kill the bacteria, or they may begin to spread through her body in her blood and make her very ill.

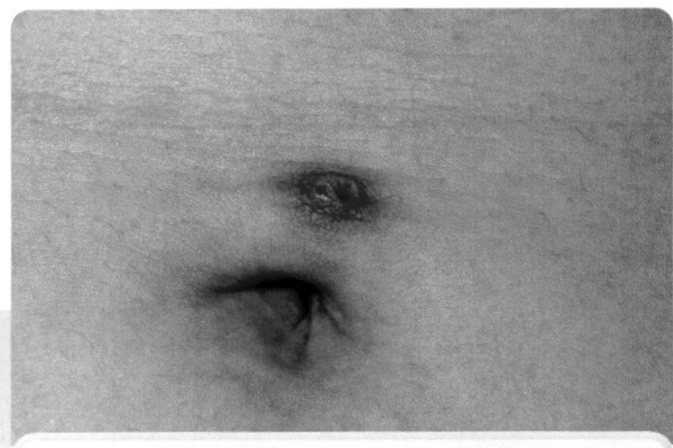

FIGURE 1: An infected navel piercing wound.

White blood cells

White blood cells are our defence forces. They attack and destroy pathogens that have found their way inside the body. White blood cells are part of your **immune system**.

Some white blood cells surround bacteria and take them into their cytoplasm. Then they kill them. Other white blood cells make chemicals called **antibodies**, which destroy the bacteria. Or they may make **antitoxins**, which neutralise the poisons that the bacteria are making.

The antibodies and antitoxins have to be exactly the right kind to match a particular bacterium. White blood cells can produce the right ones much more quickly if they have met that kind of bacterium before.

Epidemics and pandemics

During some winters, everyone seems to get flu. When lots of people have an infectious disease at the same time, we say there is an **epidemic** of the disease.

In 1918–1919, people all over the world were infected by flu. When an epidemic spreads worldwide, it is known as a **pandemic**. The 1918 flu was a new kind. The virus that causes flu had changed. It was called Spanish flu. The Spanish flu pandemic killed more than 50 million people worldwide.

Spanish flu spread so quickly because no-one's immune system had met this new form of the flu virus before. No-one had **immunity** to it. For a while, the virus was able to infect and breed in almost anyone without being destroyed by their white blood cells.

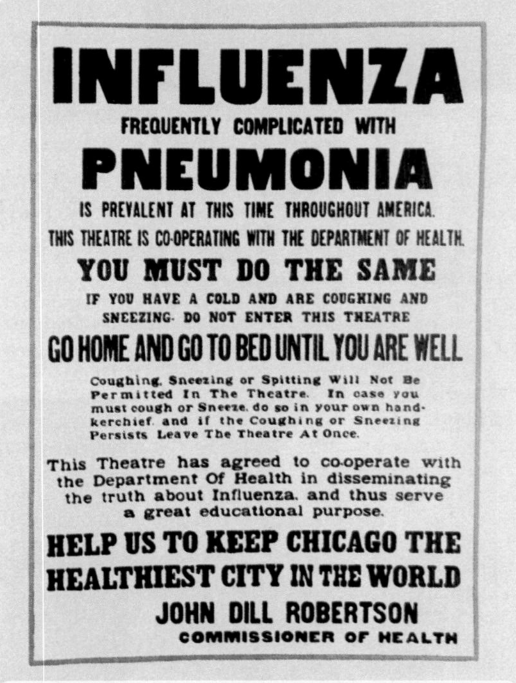

INFLUENZA
FREQUENTLY COMPLICATED WITH
PNEUMONIA
IS PREVALENT AT THIS TIME THROUGHOUT AMERICA.
THIS THEATRE IS CO-OPERATING WITH THE DEPARTMENT OF HEALTH.
YOU MUST DO THE SAME
IF YOU HAVE A COLD AND ARE COUGHING AND SNEEZING. DO NOT ENTER THIS THEATRE
GO HOME AND GO TO BED UNTIL YOU ARE WELL
Coughing, Sneezing or Spitting Will Not Be Permitted In The Theatre. In case you must cough or Sneeze, do so in your own handkerchief, and if the Coughing or Sneezing Persists Leave The Theatre At Once.
This Theatre has agreed to co-operate with the Department Of Health in disseminating the truth about Influenza, and thus serve a great educational purpose.
HELP US TO KEEP CHICAGO THE HEALTHIEST CITY IN THE WORLD
JOHN DILL ROBERTSON
COMMISSIONER OF HEALTH

FIGURE 2: A poster in Chicago about Spanish flu.

Spanish flu killed more than 30 million people

QUESTIONS

1. How do white blood cells protect you from bacteria?
2. Explain the difference between an epidemic and a pandemic.
3. Why did so many people get Spanish flu in 1918–1919?

Phagocytosis

Figure 3 shows how a type of white blood cell, called **phagocytes** (see figure 4), can surround and ingest bacteria. This activity is called **phagocytosis**.

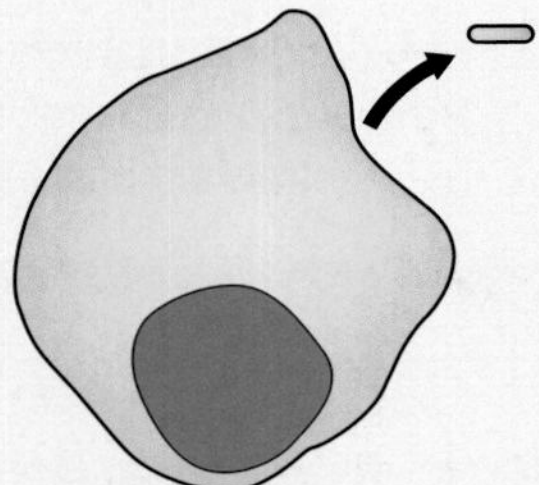

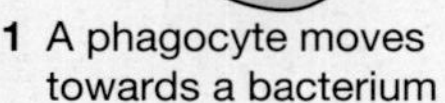

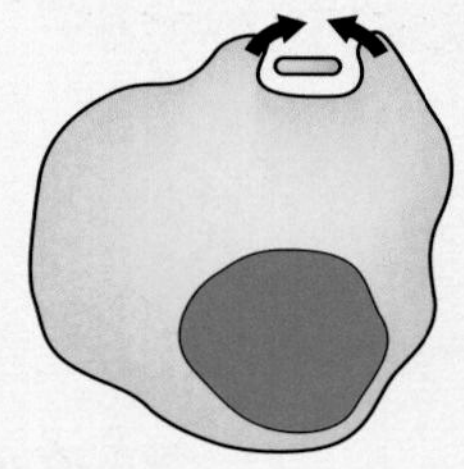

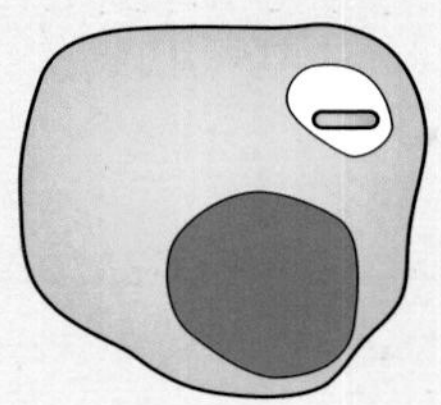

1 A phagocyte moves towards a bacterium

2 The phagocyte pushes a sleeve of cytoplasm outwards to surround the bacterium

3 The bacterium is now enclosed in a vacuole inside the cell. It is then killed and digested by enzymes

FIGURE 3: Phagocytosis.

This is what happens when you have an infected wound. Some of the cells around the wound produce chemicals that act as a signal to tell the phagocytes they are needed. Extra blood flows to the infected site, bringing more phagocytes with it. The wound becomes inflamed and red. But underneath the skin, phagocytes are doing their best to kill the invading pathogens before they do you too much harm.

Antibodies

Other white blood cells, called **lymphocytes**, attack pathogens in a completely different way. They produce chemicals called antibodies.

Figure 5 shows an antibody molecule. The bits on the end of the Y arms can come in millions of different shapes. Each lymphocyte can make just one kind.

The end bits fit onto molecules on the pathogen. Each shape only fits one kind of pathogen. So we have millions of different lymphocytes. Between them, there should be a few that can make antibodies to fit almost any pathogen that gets into us.

The antibodies group round and stick to the pathogen. Sometimes they kill it directly. Sometimes they stick the pathogens together into clumps, so that phagocytes can gather and destroy them more easily.

Some of the chemicals that the lymphocytes make can stick to the dangerous toxins made and given off by bacteria, and destroy them. These chemicals are called antitoxins.

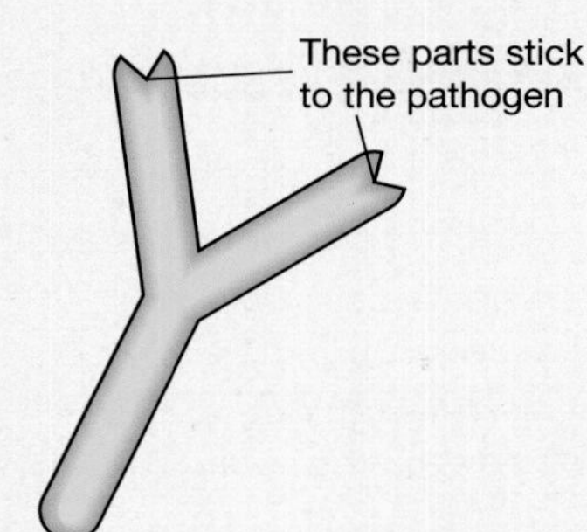
These parts stick to the pathogen

FIGURE 5: A simplified antibody molecule.

QUESTIONS

4 What do phagocytes do?

5 What do lymphocytes do?

6 Why do we need to be able to produce many different kinds of antibodies?

7 Which of these are *cells* and which are *molecules*?
lymphocyte, pathogen, antibody, toxin, antitoxin, phagocyte

FIGURE 4: A phagocyte (brown) ingesting bacteria (red).

SCID

The white cells that protect us from disease need to be able to make many different enzymes. Very rarely, a baby is born without one of the genes needed to make these enzymes.

FIGURE 6: An Apache baby with SCID.

The child will then have an illness called SCID – Severe Combined Immunodeficiency Disease. Any pathogen that gets into his body can run riot. Before long, he will die from one or other infection.

Children with SCID can be kept alive if they have no direct contact at all with anything that might have pathogens on it. They live inside a sterile plastic box or bubble.

Some of these children have been amongst the very first successes of gene therapy. They have been given the gene for the missing enzyme. As long as the gene keeps working, they can live normal lives.

QUESTIONS

8 What is meant by the term 'sterile'? Suggest how the environment of a child with SCID could be kept sterile.

Drugs against disease

You will find out:

- That painkillers reduce pain but don't cure disease
- That antibiotics kill bacteria inside the body but don't kill viruses
- How our understanding of antibiotics has changed the treatment of disease

Kill or cure?

Even in the late 19th century, doctors in Europe treated many illnesses by blood letting – which probably made many patients even more ill than they already were.

Until the 1940s, we really had no weapons at all against **bacteria**, and thousands of people died from infections of wounds and bacterial diseases. Then **antibiotics** were discovered, and within a few years doctors could cure illnesses that would previously have been fatal.

FIGURE 1: Bloodletting was once thought to be good for health.

Painkillers

You would have to be a bit unusual if you didn't occasionally get a headache. Thousands of people have pain that is with them almost all the time – for example pain in their joints because of arthritis, or pain in their back.

Most people take some kind of drug to try to get rid of pain. **Painkillers** you can buy 'off the shelf' include aspirin, paracetamol and ibuprofen. For really serious pain, you might be prescribed more powerful painkillers.

Painkillers can reduce the symptoms of whatever is wrong with you. But they can't actually cure the underlying problem.

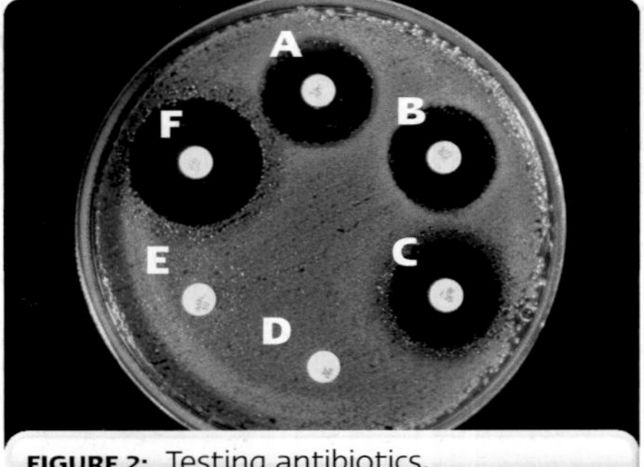

FIGURE 2: Testing antibiotics.

Antibiotics

Antibiotics are drugs that kill bacteria inside your body, without killing your own cells. Antibiotics don't kill viruses.

There are lots of different antibiotics. They include penicillin and streptomycin. We need different ones because they don't all work equally well against all kinds of bacteria.

Figure 2 shows a test being carried out to find the best antibiotic to kill a kind of bacterium called *E. coli*. The dish contains a clear jelly that was wiped over with a liquid containing the bacteria. Then little paper discs, each soaked in a different antibiotic, were placed on the jelly. The antibiotic seeped out of the discs and spread over the jelly. If the antibiotic kills the bacteria, they can't grow around the disc. The bigger the 'no-grow' area around the disc, the more effective the antibiotic.

QUESTIONS

1. Which kind of drug, painkillers or antibiotics, might be able to cure a disease?
2. Why won't antibiotics help you to get over a cold?
3. Which **two** antibiotics shown in the photograph aren't having any effect on the bacteria?
4. Which antibiotic would you choose to treat an illness caused by *E. coli*? Explain why.
5. How do you think the antibiotics spread out of the discs and through the jelly? Choose from: diffusion, radiation, secretion, infection.

Sources of antibiotics

You probably already know that one of the most well-known antibiotics, penicillin, comes from a fungus. The blue-green mould that sometimes grows on the skin of an orange or lemon that has been left around too long is often the penicillin mould.

The pharmaceutical (drug) companies are always on the look-out for new antibiotics. Quite a lot of antibiotics now don't work against bacteria that they killed in the past so we need to keep finding new ones.

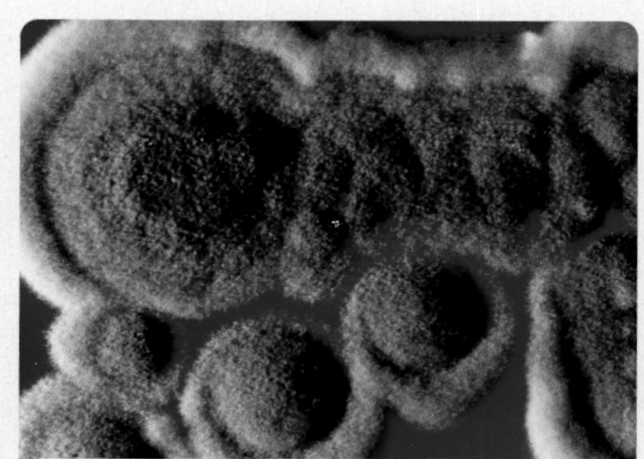

FIGURE 3: A growth of the fungus Penicillium that gives us penicillin.

Although most antibiotics have been discovered in fungi, people are now looking in many different places for them. They are finding them in some very odd places, such as on the skin of frogs.

Nowadays, most antibiotics are made chemically. This is better than extracting them from fungi or other organisms, because you know exactly what you are getting. If you extract an antibiotic from a fungus, you can't be sure what strength it will be. It's also difficult to get just the antibiotic – it may be contaminated with other substances as well. Making it chemically means you can get absolutely pure antibiotic every time.

Antivirals

Viruses are more difficult to kill than bacteria. Viruses get right inside our cells. It is practically impossible to kill the viruses without killing the cells as well.

Drugs to kill viruses are called **antivirals**. The big pharmaceutical companies would love to be able to make a really safe and really effective antiviral.

HIV/AIDS is caused by a virus. As yet, no cure has been developed. An antiviral drug called AZT does help to slow down the development of AIDS. Some people, though, experience severe side effects when they take AZT.

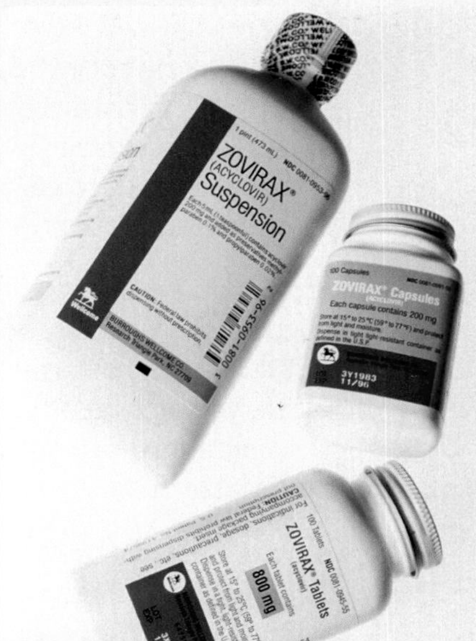

FIGURE 4: The antiviral drug acyclovir, with the trade name Zovirax, is used to treat herpes.

QUESTIONS

6 Explain why is it better for drugs to be made chemically rather than extracted from fungi or other organisms.

7 Why is it proving so difficult to make effective, safe antivirals?

Watch Out Don't get antibiotics mixed up with antibodies! You can get antibiotics from a chemist's shop. Antibodies are made inside people's bodies.

Prescribing antibiotics

We now know that we must not use antibiotics unnecessarily. Overuse makes it more likely that bacteria will become resistant to them (see page 50).

In Scotland, there was a big campaign to persuade doctors not to give out antibiotic prescriptions to everyone who wants them. This table shows the number of prescriptions for each 100 members of the population in six different years. The second column shows all the prescriptions for any antibiotic, and the third column shows just penicillin.

Drug	All antibiotics	Penicillin
1992	95.6	51.4
1995	105.6	59.8
1999	86.1	47.5
2002	82.0	44.9
2003	81.9	44.7
2004	79.2	41.7

QUESTIONS

8 Display the results in the table as a graph.

9 Describe the trend in total antibiotic prescription between 1992 and 2004.

10 Does prescription for penicillin follow a similar trend?

11 This data could be taken to mean that in 1992 only 4.4 people out of every 100 weren't prescribed an antibiotic. But this isn't a correct conclusion. Explain why.

Arms race

You will find out:

- That bacteria develop resistance to antibiotics
- That this happens because of natural selection
- That we need to avoid over-using antibiotics

War against infection

The man having the injection became infected with **bacteria** while he was in hospital. He is very ill. His white blood cells are losing the fight against the infection. He is being given a large dose of **antibiotics** to help his body defeat the bacteria.

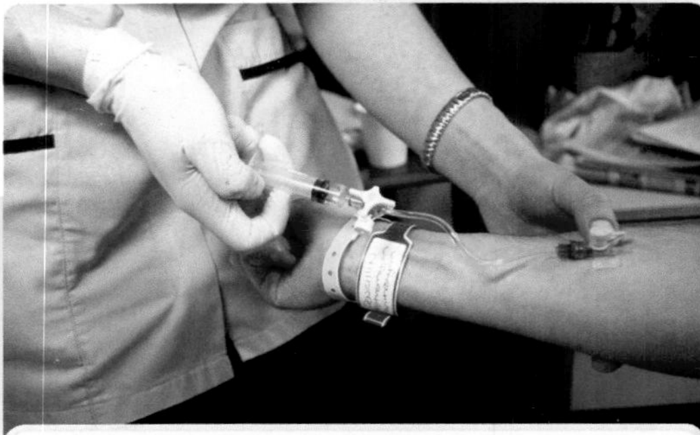

FIGURE 1: An antibiotic injection.

Resistance to antibiotics

When antibiotics were discovered in the 1940s, people thought that was the end of deaths from illnesses caused by bacteria. But the bacteria fought back. Many of them have become resistant to the antibiotics. This is how it happens.

This is a population of bacteria in someone's body. By chance, one of them happens to be a bit different from the others.

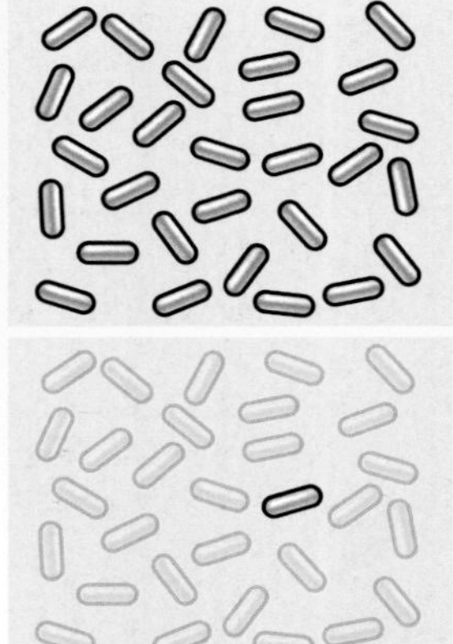

The person takes antibiotics to kill the bacteria. It works – except on the single odd one. This one is **resistant** to the antibiotic.

This bacterium now has no competitors. It divides and makes lots of identical copies of itself. Now there is a population of bacteria that the antibiotic cannot kill.

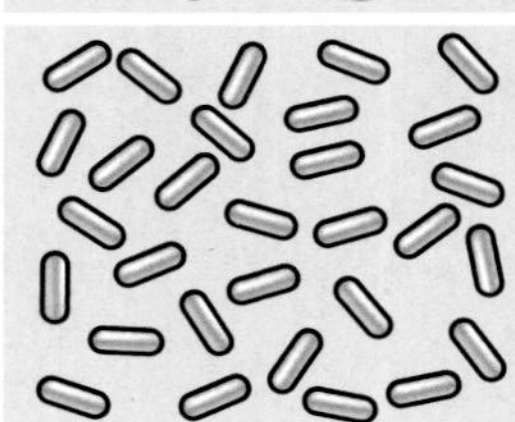

FIGURE 2: How a resistant strain of bacteria develops.

This process is an example of **natural selection**. You can read more about it on pages 76-77.

MRSA

The full name for **MRSA** is 'Methicillin Resistant *Staphylococcus aureus*'. This explains why the newspapers like to call it the 'super bug' instead of its proper name.

FIGURE 3: MRSA, the bacterium that is resistant to most antibiotics.

Staphylocccus aureus is a common bacterium. It usually does no harm. But it is a risk to someone who is weak, very young or very old. Then the bacterium can get inside them and make them very ill.

Most infections by MRSA happen in hospitals. MRSA can't be killed with all the usual antibiotics. It is really difficult to kill once it has infected someone. Each year, lots of people die of it.

QUESTIONS

1 What is wrong with the sentence below?
When you take an antibiotic, the bacteria try to become resistant to it.

2 Use what you know about how your body fights pathogens, and suggest why people who are weak, very young or very old are most likely to be made ill by a bacterial infection.

3 Use what you know about how bacteria become resistant to antibiotics, and suggest why MRSA is most often found in hospitals.

New diseases

In early 1993, people in China and other parts of south-east Asia began to die from a new disease. It was called **SARS** and was caused by a new kind of **virus**. There was panic, because people thought that SARS might be the next **pandemic**. Doctors couldn't treat it. If people got it, they often died.

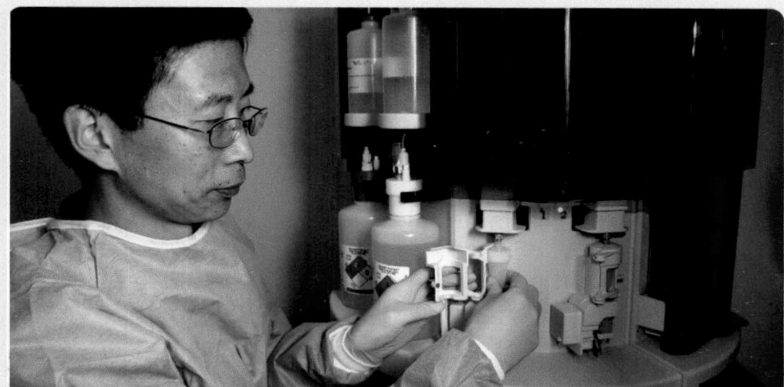

FIGURE 4: Removing DNA from SARS to develop a vaccine against it.

The SARS virus spread very quickly round the world, carried by people travelling on aeroplanes. Before long, there were cases of SARS in countries far from China, including Canada.

Scientists all over the world worked together to develop a vaccine against SARS. Every country set up rules to detect anyone with SARS and stop them passing it on to anyone else.

The world was lucky this time. The new disease was brought under control by 2003.

Bird flu

Could a similar disease appear again? Can we be sure we can always get a new disease under control before it spreads across the world and kills millions of people?

In 2004, there was an outbreak of a new kind of **bird flu** in Asia. Bird flu sometimes infects humans, and when it does, it is deadly. Students in Hong Kong sterilise their hands as they go into school, to try to reduce the chance of infection.

At the moment, bird flu does not seem to be able to spread from one person to another. You can only get it from birds. But scientists are worried that the bird flu virus might mutate into a type that can pass from person to person. Health agencies all over the world are very worried that there could be a worldwide pandemic of bird flu.

QUESTIONS

4 Why might we expect the next new virus to spread even more quickly than the Spanish flu, described on page 48?

FIGURE 5: Bird flu is very dangerous and has killed many people.

What next?

There are thousands of pathogens out there. There's a good chance that some kind of virus or bacterium will mutate and cause a new infectious disease that we can't control. Viral diseases are especially dangerous, because we have so few antiviral drugs.

The emergence of SARS underlined how vitally important it is for countries to work together. At first, China would not admit that a new disease had appeared. This gave the virus time to infect many people.

Figure 6 shows the number of people who died from *S. aureus* between 1993 and 2003. The yellow bars are deaths from 'ordinary' *S. aureus*, while the light green ones are deaths from MRSA.

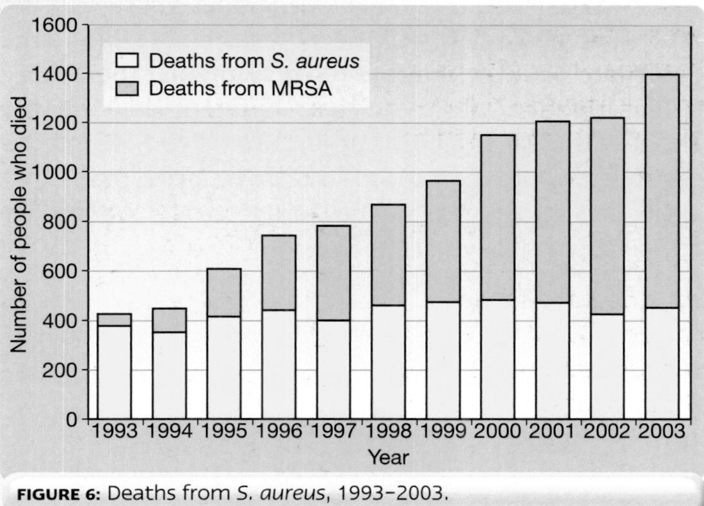

FIGURE 6: Deaths from *S. aureus*, 1993–2003.

QUESTIONS

5 Describe the trend in total deaths from all types of *S. aureus* between 1993 and 2003.

6 Which form of *S. aureus* has been responsible for this trend?

7 The government puts heavy pressure on hospital managers to do something to reduce these deaths. Suggest what the managers could do.

Vaccination

You will find out:

- That you can be immunised by an injection of an inactive form of a pathogen
- That vaccination is our best protection against viruses
- About the MMR vaccination

Smallpox is history

About 30 years ago, this Bangladeshi man had smallpox. It was a dreadful disease caused by a virus. In 1956, the World Health Organisation began a programme to wipe it out completely. They succeeded by vaccinating at least 80% of people in places where they were at risk from smallpox. This man was one of the last people to get smallpox. The WHO announced in 1980 that the world was free from smallpox.

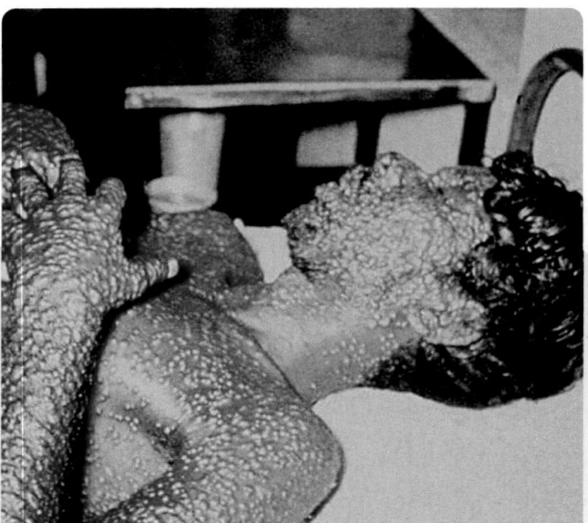

FIGURE 1: Smallpox was a deadly disease.

Immunisation

Immunisation means 'making immune'. You have probably been immunised against many different diseases. These could include **mumps**, **measles**, **rubella**, polio and diphtheria. When you have the jab, a small amount of dead or inactive viruses or bacteria are being pushed into your blood. Your white blood cells don't know they are harmless, and attack them just as they would attack living pathogens.

Some white blood cells make **antibodies**. These stick to bits on the surface of the bacteria or viruses. The surface bits are different on each kind of bacterium or virus. They are called **antigens**. The white blood cells make a different antibody to match each different kind of antigen. For a new antigen, this takes a bit of time. Later, if you are infected with the real, live pathogen, your white blood cells are ready to make the right sort of antibodies straight away. They will destroy the pathogens before they have a chance to make you ill.

The MMR jab

The **MMR** jab protects children against measles, mumps and rubella. It is sometimes called the 'triple vaccine'. These diseases are caused by viruses.

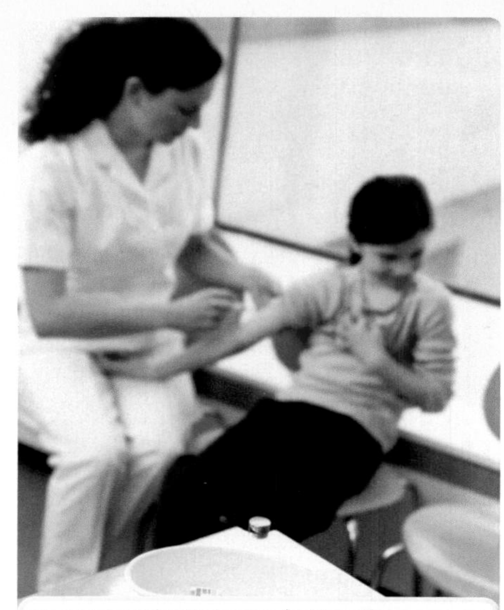

FIGURE 2: Injections are better than infections.

QUESTIONS

1 What is the difference between an antigen and an antibody?

2 A measles jab injects you with weakened measles viruses. How does this make you immune to measles?

3 What does MMR stand for?

Watch Out Don't get MRSA and MMR mixed up! Work out a way you can remember which is which.

...antibodies ...antigens ...autism ...immunisation

The MMR controversy

FIGURE 3: Parents' fears were echoed in the media.

In 1998, a group of scientists published an article about **autism**. It included a suggestion that the MMR jab might cause autism. An autistic person can't relate to other people in the way most people can.

The article made headlines. Parents were frightened for their children. Many of them decided not to let their child have the MMR **vaccination**. The government tried to reassure them that no link had been proved. But some parents did not trust the government.

Later, almost all the scientists who had published the original article published another one, saying that there wasn't a link. They said there had never been any scientific evidence for a link and that the first article should not have been published.

Many other studies have been carried out. None of them has found any link between the MMR jab and autism.

The table shows the number of children who were given the MMR jab each year from 1996 to 2003, and also the number of mumps cases from 1996 to 2004.

Year	Percentage of children having MMR jab	Number of mumps cases
1996	92	94
1997	92	180
1998	91	119
1999	88	372
2000	88	703
2001	87	777
2002	84	502
2003	82	1549
2004	(no figure available)	8104

QUESTIONS

4 Draw a graph to display these results.
5 Describe the trend for MMR jabs over these years.
6 Suggest reasons for this trend.
7 Describe the trend for the number of mumps cases.
8 Suggest reasons for this trend.

Mumps epidemic

In 2005, students starting at university were asked to make sure that they had had the MMR jab. Since it was only introduced in 1989, they were too young to have had it as babies.

The request was made because, in the first four months of 2005, there were 28 470 cases of mumps. What has caused this epidemic?

It is almost certainly because fewer babies are now being given the MMR jab. More babies get mumps, and so there are more mumps viruses around.

Mumps is usually not too unpleasant in young children, but it can be very nasty and dangerous in teenagers or adults.

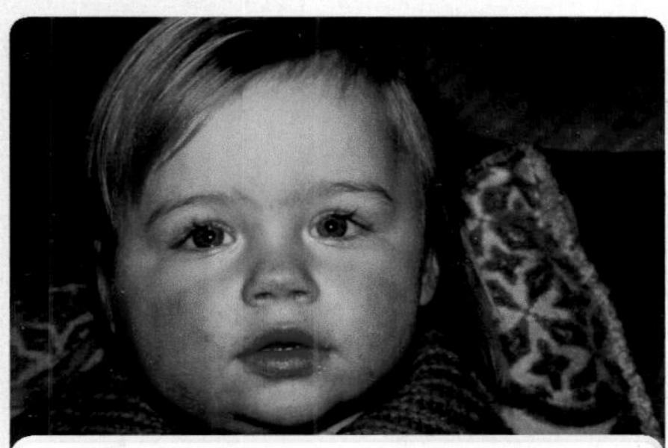

FIGURE 4: Mumps is uncomfortable.

QUESTIONS

9 In the first 4 months of 2004, there were 1811 mumps cases. How do the figures for the same period in 2005 compare with this?
10 Suggest why students starting at university are especially likely to get infectious diseases such as mumps.
11 The Health Protection Agency would like all babies to have the MMR vaccination, because this would protect the whole population against mumps. Do you think parents should take this into account when deciding whether to let their child have the MMR jab?

Unit summary

Concept map

Nerves and hormones

These coordinate body processes and help control water content, ion content, blood sugar concentration and temperature of the body.

Reflex actions are automatic and very fast. Nerve impulses pass along a reflex arc that contains: a sensory neurone; a relay neurone; a motor neurone, and synapses between them.

Receptors detect stimuli; information passes to the brain; effectors (muscles and glands) respond.

The menstrual cycle is controlled by FSH, LH and oestrogen.

Diet

A balanced diet is varied and contains some of each nutrient.

Energy needs vary due to differing metabolic rates and levels of activity. Taking in more energy than needed may lead to being overweight.

Obesity increases the risk of getting arthritis, diabetes, high blood pressure and heart disease.

Anorexia nervosa sufferers diet obsessively which causes health problems.

Too much cholesterol or salt increases the risk of heart disease.

Drugs

Solvents affect people's behaviour and can damage the brain.

Alcohol slows down reactions and can damage the liver and brain.

Hard drugs such as cocaine are very addictive and often cause severe health problems.

Tobacco smoke:
- contains nicotine, which is addictive
- causes cancer, bronchitis, emphysema and diseases of the heart and blood vessels
- contains carbon monoxide, which can harm unborn children.

Disease

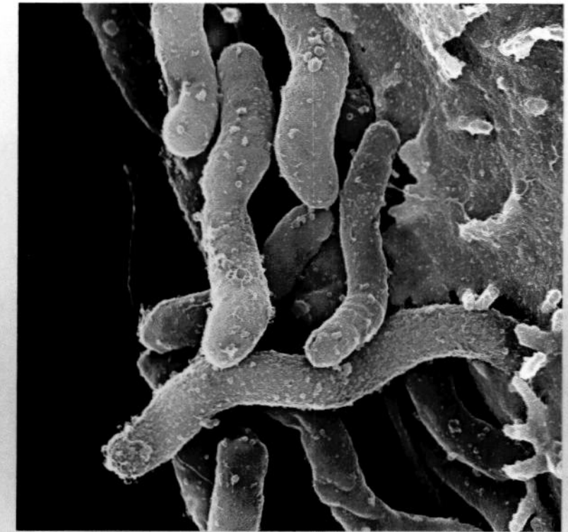

Bacteria and viruses produce toxins and damage cells, which makes people feel ill.

Outside help:
- painkillers relieve symptoms but don't cure diseases
- antibiotics can kill bacteria, but bacteria can develop a resistance to them
- immunisations and vaccinations offer protection from infectious diseases.

Pathogenic micro-organisms cause infectious diseases.

Self-help:
- skin, mucus and blood clots help stop pathogens getting into the body
- white blood cells ingest pathogens or produce antibodies and antitoxins.

Unit quiz

1 Which two organs make up the central nervous system?

2 What is the stimulus to which receptor cells in the eye are sensitive?

3 Put the following in the right order for a reflex arc.

effector **relay neurone** **sensory neurone** **receptor** **motor neurone**

4 What effect does insulin have on blood sugar level?

5 Name the gland where FSH and LH are made.

6 Name a reproductive hormone secreted by the ovaries.

7 Who has brown fat, and what does it do?

8 Which fats are healthiest: saturated, monounsaturated or polyunsaturated? Why?

9 Name **two** parts of the body that can be damaged by solvents.

10 Which component of tobacco smoke is addictive?

11 How does alcohol affect reaction times?

12 What kind of pathogen causes flu?

13 What do phagocytes do?

14 Is penicillin an antibody or an antibiotic?

15 What is the name for a drug trial where neither the patients nor doctors know who is getting the drug?

16 What does MMR stand for?

Numeracy activity

High blood pressure

The table below shows the percentage of men and women in England who had high blood pressure.

Percentage of people in England with high blood pressure, 1998–2003

Year	1998	2000	2001	2002	2003
Men	40.8	39.7	40.8	37.4	37.8
Women	32.9	33.2	34.7	33.8	31.7

QUESTIONS

1 Draw a bar chart to show these results.

2 Compare the percentage of men and women who had high blood pressure in 2003.

3 In which year did the highest percentage of people have high blood pressure?

4 Out of 200 men in 2001, how many would you expect to have high blood pressure?

5 The government is trying to reduce the number of people who have high blood pressure. Does the data suggest they are succeeding?

6 Explain why it is not good to have high blood pressure.

7 Describe **two** things a person can do to help reduce their blood pressure.

Exam practice

Exam practice questions

1 The diagram below shows a reflex arc. The arrows show the direction of the nerve impulse.

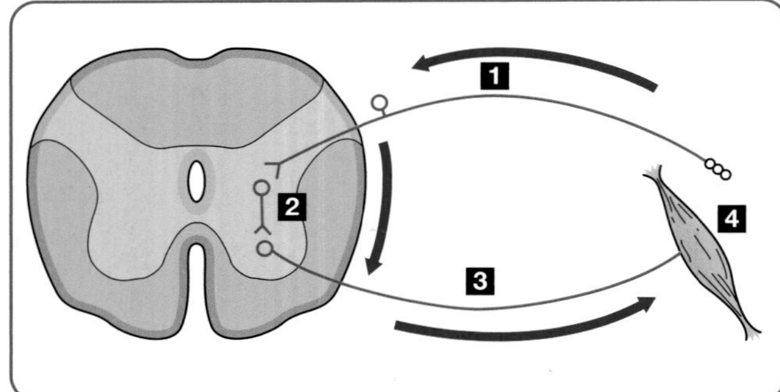

Match the words A, B, C and D to the missing information, 1–4, on the diagram.

A effector **B** relay neurone
C motor neurone **D** sensory neurone [4]

2 The human body's internal conditions are controlled in different ways. Match the words A, B, C and D to the spaces 1–4 in the sentences below.

A blood sugar levels **B** temperature
C water content **D** ion content

Shivering helps to control the (1) of the body. (2) is affected by adding salt to your food. Diabetics have difficulty in controlling their (3) . If the (4) of the body is too high, it can be controlled by producing more dilute urine. [4]

3 Humans take a wide range of drugs, usually to achieve changes in their bodies or minds. Match the words A, B, C and D to statements 1–4 in the table below.

A stimulants **B** sedatives
C pain killers **D** hallucinogens

1	Drugs, such as alcohol and barbiturates, which slow down the nervous system and calm the mind.
2	Drugs, such as LSD, which produce strange and intense effects in the mind.
3	Drugs, such as amphetamines and caffeine, which make people feel more awake.
4	Drugs, such as aspirin and heroine, which lower the activity of pain centres in the brain.

[4]

4 The kidneys control the body's water content by controlling the concentration of the urine. The diagram shows the body's response to low amounts of water in the blood, starting from 1 on the diagram.

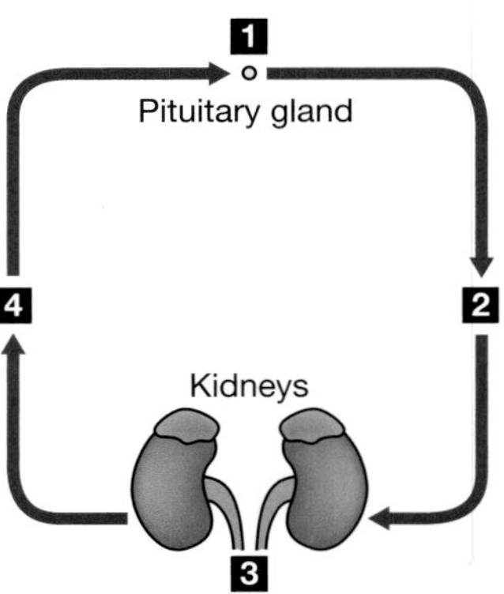

Match the statements A, B, C and D to the missing information, 1–4, on the diagram.

A More concentrated urine is produced.
B More ADH is carried in the blood.
C More water is contained in the blood.
D More ADH is produced. [4]

5 Using the information contained in the graph below, choose the most appropriate answer.

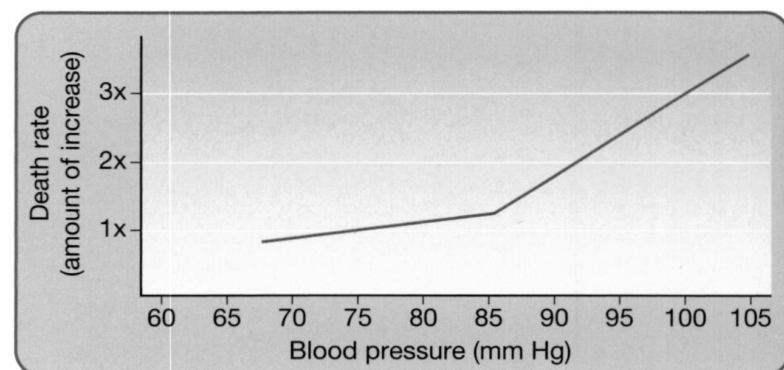

a During which range of blood pressure values does the death rate increase most rapidly?

A 80–85 mm Hg
B 68–83 mm Hg
C 95–100 mm Hg
D 80–90 mm Hg [1]

b What is the best description for the relationship between blood pressure and death rate?

A As blood pressure increases, death rate steadily increases.
B As blood pressure increases, death rate steadily decreases.
C As blood pressure increases, death rate increases then decreases.
D As blood pressure increases, death rate increases slowly, then rapidly. [1]

c The increase in death rate from 2 to 3 corresponds to a rise in blood pressure ...

A from 92 to 98 mm Hg.
B from 85 to 90 mm Hg.
C from 83 to 93 mm Hg.
D from 73 to 96 mm Hg. [1]

(Total 19 marks)

Worked example

Using the information contained in the graph choose the most appropriate answer.

a Which one of the following statements is correct?

A Hormone 1 is oestrogen; Hormone 2 is progesterone.
B Hormone 1 is progesterone; Hormone 2 is oestrogen.
C Hormone 1 is luteinising hormone; Hormone 2 is follicle-stimulating hormone.
D Hormone 1 is follicle-stimulating hormone; Hormone 2 is luteinising hormone. [1]

b What is the period during which the lining of the womb (uterus) is at its thickest?

A Days 11–12
B Days 7–28
C Days 15–22
D Days 11–26 [1]

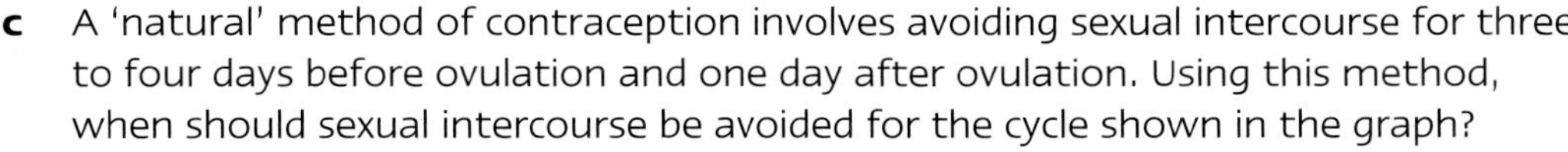

c A 'natural' method of contraception involves avoiding sexual intercourse for three to four days before ovulation and one day after ovulation. Using this method, when should sexual intercourse be avoided for the cycle shown in the graph?

A Days 9–13
B Days 10–12
C Days 10–15
D Days 13–16 [1]

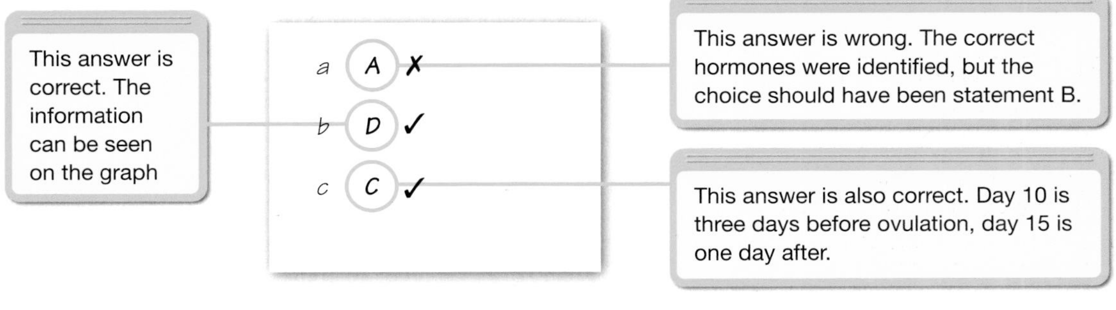

This answer is correct. The information can be seen on the graph
a A ✗
b D ✓
c C ✓
This answer is wrong. The correct hormones were identified, but the choice should have been statement B.
This answer is also correct. Day 10 is three days before ovulation, day 15 is one day after.

Overall Grade: B

How to get an A

Revise the menstrual cycle by drawing a graph like the one here without looking at the book, then check to see if yours is correct.

Biology 1b – Evolution and environment

DISCOVER NARWHALS!

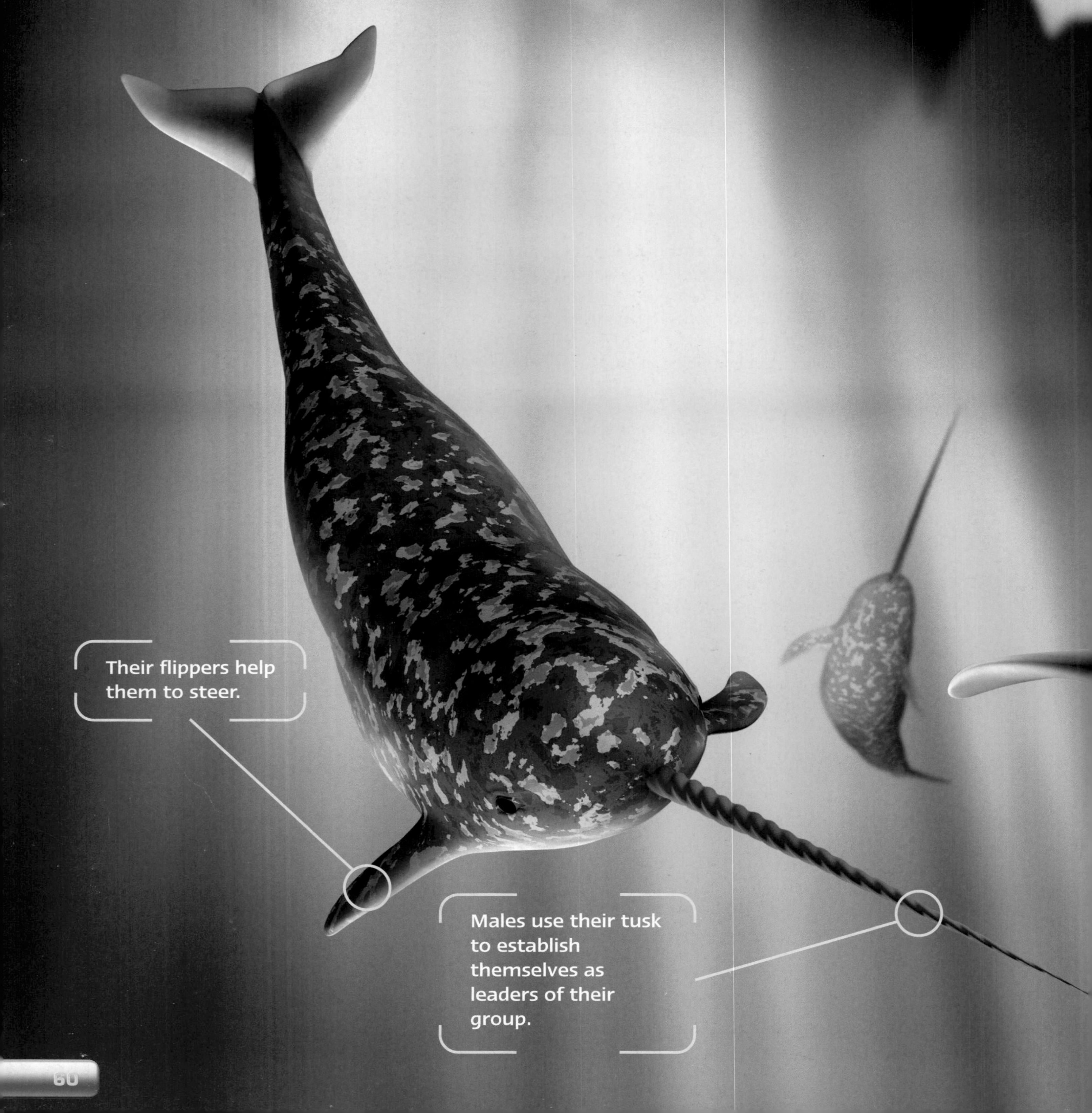

Their flippers help them to steer.

Males use their tusk to establish themselves as leaders of their group.

Living things are adapted to survive. Adaptations will help them to find a mate and reproduce, to get food and to defend their space from others. These Narwhals live in the cold seas of the Arctic.

Their strong tail helps Narwhals to swim.

Their streamlined shape allows them to swim quickly through the water.

CONTENTS

Hot and cold

You will find out:

- How plants are adapted to survive in extreme habitats
- How animals are adapted to survive in extreme habitats

Chilling out or heating up

Most plants and animals need similar things to live: food, water, space and a mate to reproduce with. So how can desert animals survive in hot, dry places where the temperature is often over 50 °C? Other animals live in the Arctic where the temperature can fall to below -50 °C. How do they cope? How are they **adapted**?

FIGURE 1: How is this polar bear adapted to life in extreme cold and this sun bear adapted to much warmer places?

How some animals adapt

Where it's hot Staying cool is very important when you live in a hot place. *You* can take your coat off but this is not an option for animals! Though elephants are mammals, they do not have fur. To lose heat to the air, warm blood flows through arteries and veins in their large thin ears.

Where it's cold Keeping warm when you live in a cold place is also important. Arctic foxes have thick fur and small ears. Their bodies are compact so they have a small **surface area** compared to their volume. All this helps to **insulate** them and helps them to **survive**. They are hunters and their white fur camouflages them.

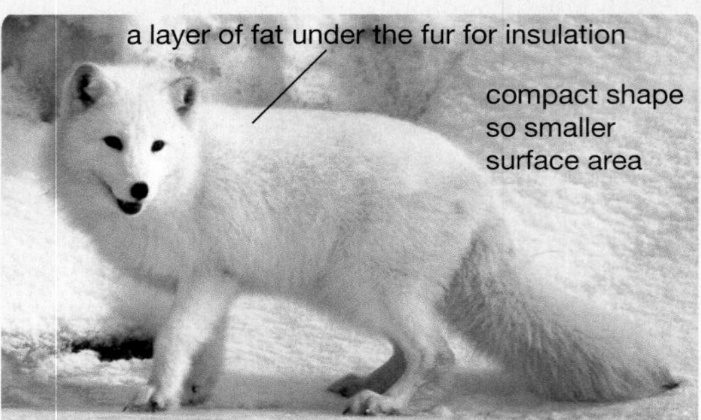

FIGURE 2: An Arctic fox insulated against the cold.

How some plants adapt

Plants need warmth, sunlight and water to grow.

Where it's hot In arid deserts, what little rain does fall drains away quickly. Plants need water for lots of reasons such as for photosynthesis to make their food; to transport various substances; and for support. Most of the water that plants absorb from the soil, evaporates to the air. Cacti are adapted to conserve and store water. They have a swollen stem to store water; a thick waxy cuticle (cover) to reduce water evaporation; spines instead of flat leaves to reduce water loss; and shallow roots to absorb lots of water when it rains.

Where it's cold Compared with the tropics, not many plants live in very cold places. The Arctic willow avoids the freezing winds by growing low over the ground – its trunk and branches are never more than a few centimetres off the ground. The dark Arctic soil is warmed by the sun. So the willow can absorb warmth from the ground.

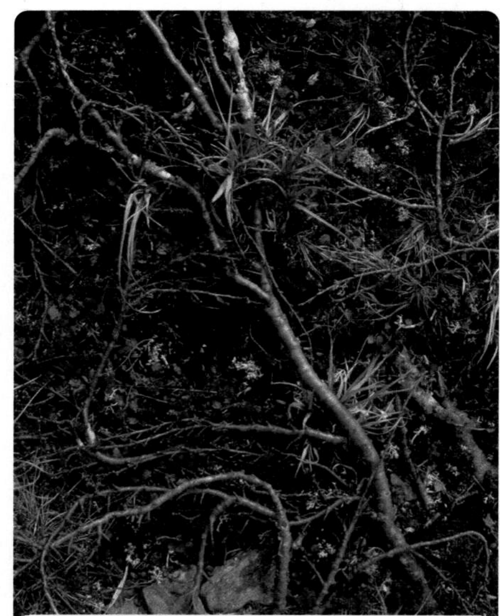

FIGURE 3: This Arctic willow grows in biting cold winds.

QUESTIONS

1. How are elephants adapted to living in hot places?
2. Describe how Arctic foxes are adapted to living and hunting in the cold.
3. Draw a picture of a cactus in outline, then label it to show how it is adapted to conserve water.

Cold enough to freeze your legs off?

In a caribou's **habitat**, winter temperatures can drop below −50 °C. Even summer temperatures often hover around 0 °C. Caribou spend time standing in deep snow, yet their legs do not freeze. This is because they have a 'heat exchange system' in their legs.

FIGURE 4: This caribou's legs are adapted to freezing temperatures.

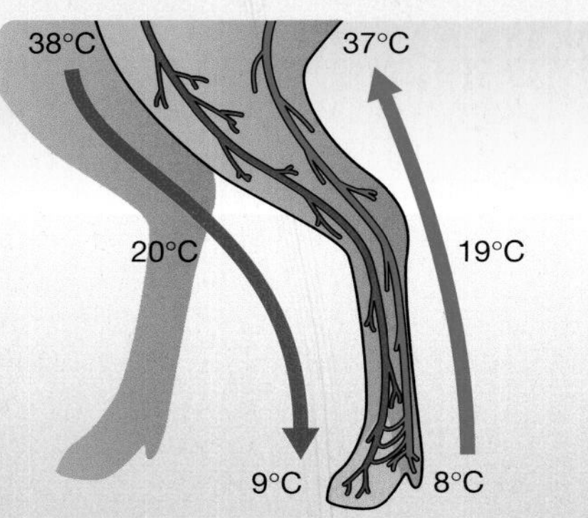

FIGURE 5: Heat exchange in a caribou leg.

The arteries and veins in their legs are close together. Warm blood flowing from their heart heats up the cold blood returning from their legs. This is a very good adaptation to life in such a cold place.

So dry it makes a camel thirsty?

Camels are adapted for life in deserts.

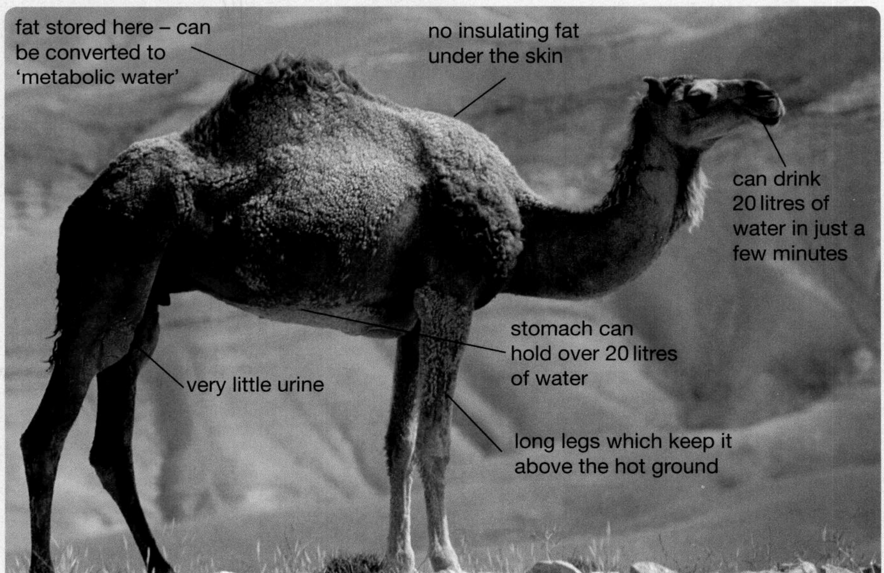

FIGURE 6: How a camel is adapted to desert life.

QUESTIONS

4 At what temperature does water freeze?

5 Describe how a caribou's 'heat exchange system' stops the blood in its legs from freezing.

6 How is a camel adapted for life in hot dry deserts?

7 Why would a camel not be expected to have a 'heat exchange system' in its legs?

Camels can drink 20 litres of water in a few minutes

Comparing climatic adaptations

The Fennec fox which lives in deserts and the Arctic fox are related, but they show different adaptations. These adaptations help them to survive in their own habitats. Look at Figure 2 and compare it to Figure 7.

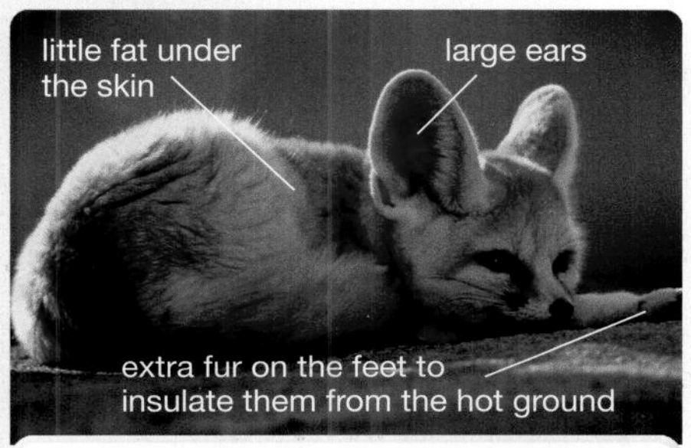

FIGURE 7: A Fennec fox surviving the heat.

QUESTIONS

8 Draw a table that compares the adaptations of the Arctic and the Fennec fox. Explain how each adaptation helps to keep the foxes alive.

9 Reindeer live in the Arctic Circle. Their fur is hollow. Each hair is a tube. How is this an adaptation to life in the cold?

10 Design an experiment which could test the idea that animals with a large surface area in relation to their volume (like a mouse) cool down faster than animals which have a small surface area in relation to their volume (like an elephant).

11 Why is it important for animals to keep a constant temperature?

Adapt or die

You will find out:
- What animals compete for in a habitat
- How plants and animals are adapted to compete for the things they need to survive

Colours aid survival

Animals are coloured for different reasons. Some, like the bittern bird, are camouflaged so well that they blend in perfectly with their surroundings. Some male animals are vividly coloured in an attempt to attract a mate. Others are very brightly coloured to warn off predators. So why are elephants grey?

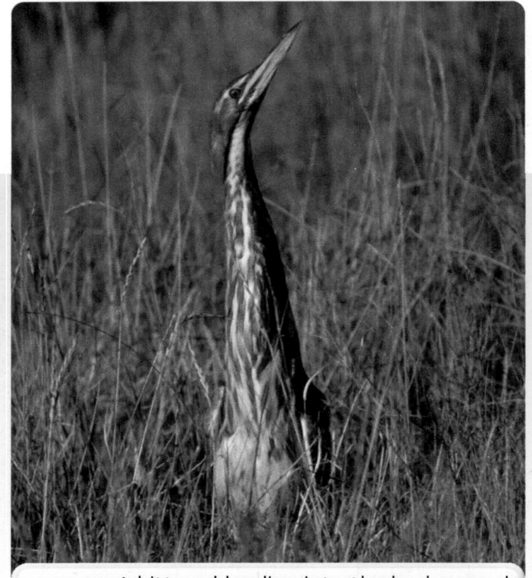

FIGURE 1: A bittern blending into the background.

Competing to survive

Plants and animals need to be **adapted**. This means that they will survive in the conditions in which they normally live. If they are adapted this means that they can **compete** with each other for the things they need. If they are not adapted for life in a particular habitat they will either die or they will move to another area. All living things compete for the following:

- food
- territory
- a mate

Some adaptations

Different living things are adapted in different ways. Adaptations help them survive. Moles, for example, feed by digging through the soil and catching worms. They have poor eyesight but an excellent sense of smell.

Butterflies feed by sucking up nectar from flowers. To do this, they have a coiled mouth tube – like a drinking straw.

When looking for a mate it is often the males that impress. The peacock, for example, is able to make a stunning display by spreading out its tail feathers.

Moles have poor eyesight but an excellent sense of smell

Plant adaptations

Plants compete for various resources including water and nutrients from the soil, and light from the Sun.

Plants which are better adapted will have:

- leaves that do not overlap each other
- a large root system.

FIGURE 2: The coiled mouth tube of a butterfly.

QUESTIONS

1. What makes a mole and a butterfly well adapted?
2. What makes a plant well adapted?
3. Suggest a way in which a plant is adapted to not being eaten.

...adapted ...compete ...mimic ...mimicry

Special adaptations

Plants that live in arid places often have sharp **thorns** instead of leaves. Thorns reduce the amount of water plants lose as well as stopping animals from eating them.

Some plants, as well as animals, protect themselves from being eaten by making **poisonous chemicals**. Often plants and animals that make poisons are also very brightly coloured. These colours act as a warning to predators – *eat me and it might kill you*.

Warning signs

In nature some colours say 'danger'. Black and yellow do it very effectively. We all know wasps can sting. They have a yellow and black abdomen. Hoverflies do not sting. They are harmless. But they, too, are black and yellow.

FIGURE 3: A wasp and a pretender (a hoverfly).

As hoverflies look like wasps, other animals will avoid them because they might get stung. There are advantages to looking like a wasp. It helps the hoverflies to survive. The hoverfly **mimics** the wasp.

Beware – poisonous

Another way of protecting yourself from being eaten is to be poisonous. Some tree frogs in Central and South America have very brightly coloured skin. This skin makes a poison. The frog's bright colours make it very conspicuous. Predators can easily see the frogs and know to avoid them. The poison is used by tribespeople. They put it on to the tips of their arrows (called darts) when they go hunting.

FIGURE 4: Why would a predator avoid this blue poison dart frog?

QUESTIONS

4 Why do harmless hoverflies look like dangerous wasps?

5 How does looking like a wasp help a hoverfly to survive?

6 Why are poison dart frogs brightly coloured?

Pretending to be another

The coral snake and the kingsnake look similar. One is venomous and the other is not. This is an example of **mimicry**. The kingsnake mimics the venomous coral snake. Some predators eat snakes.

FIGURE 5: The coral snake (bottom picture) is the venomous one; the kingsnake mimics it.

QUESTIONS

7 With a bit of paper, cover up one of the snakes above, and look at the other one for 2–3 seconds. Now do the same to the other snake. What, if any, are the differences between the two snakes?

8 What are the survival advantages to the kingsnake of looking like the coral snake?

9 Are there any advantages to the Coral snake of being mimicked by the Kingsnake?

Two ways to reproduce

You will find out:

- That there are two types of reproduction
- The differences between them
- The advantages of each type of reproduction

Keeping species alive

Sooner or later all living things die. To prevent a species from completely dying out, individuals need to reproduce. There are two ways to reproduce and different species normally use one or other of these. Most species reproduce **asexually** or **sexually**. Some are able to do both. So what are the differences between asexual and sexual **reproduction** and what are their advantages?

On to the next generation

Nothing lives for ever. Living things need to reproduce. Reproduction allows **genes** to be passed on from one generation to the next – from parents to offspring.

FIGURE 1: Dogs reproduce sexually – so all these puppies are different.

Sexual reproduction

Dogs reproduce sexually. The puppies in figure 1 are all different, despite having the same 'mum and dad'. In sexual reproduction the new individual gets genes from both parents. This means that it will inherit a mixture of features from both of its parents. When living things reproduce sexually, the two parents each give half of the genes to the offspring.

Asexual reproduction

The little strawberry plants (figure 2) are all genetically identical offspring of the main plant. They have been produced by asexual reproduction and are therefore naturally produced **clones**. The offspring produced by asexual reproduction get all their genes from just one parent. This means that they have exactly the same genes as their parent. All the offspring of a parent therefore have the same genetic make up as the parent. This makes them all clones.

FIGURE 2: Strawberry plants reproduce asexually – so all these offspring are identical.

QUESTIONS

1. What is the point of reproducing?
2. What are the two types of reproduction?
3. What is the difference between the two types of reproduction?
4. What is a clone?

...adult cell cloning ...asexual ...clone ...eggs ...fertilisation ...fuse

How sexual reproduction works

Females produce **sex cells** (**gametes**) called **eggs**, male gametes are called **sperms**. A sperm cell and an egg cell join, **fuse** together, to make the offspring. This is called **fertilisation**. The head of the sperm, shown in Figure 4, contains its genes (chromosomes) and the tail helps it to swim to the egg.

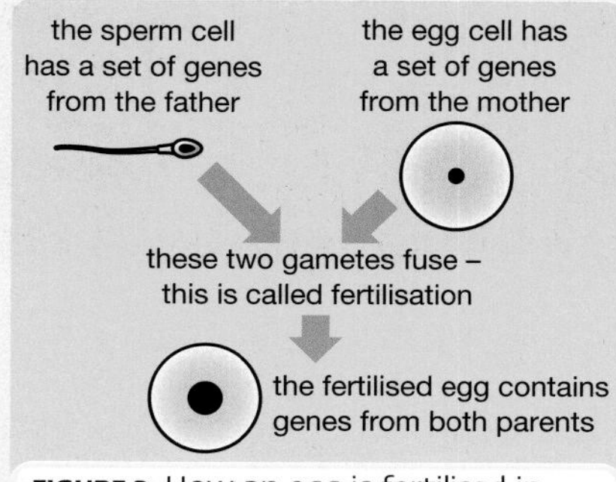

the sperm cell has a set of genes from the father
the egg cell has a set of genes from the mother
these two gametes fuse – this is called fertilisation
the fertilised egg contains genes from both parents

FIGURE 3: How an egg is fertilised in sexual reproduction.

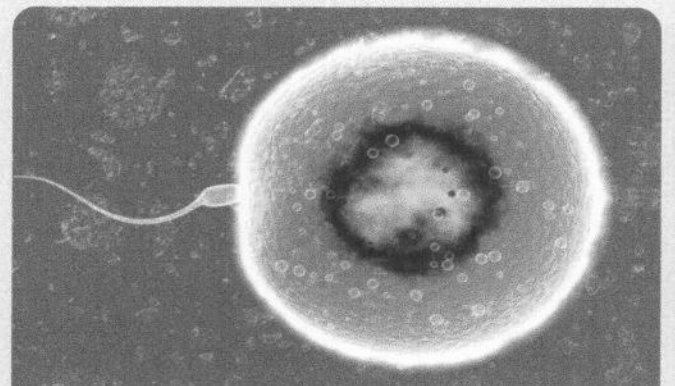

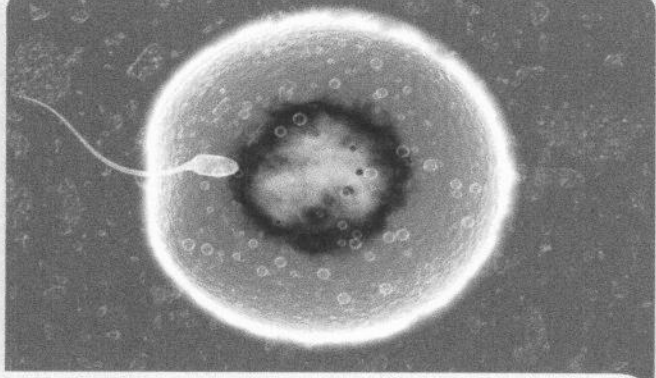

FIGURE 4: The sperm reaches the egg... and fertilises it.

How asexual reproduction works

Asexual reproduction does not need sex cells. An individual just splits in two (as in bacteria), or a part divides off, and this is the offspring. So, no male sperms, no female eggs and no fertilisation.

the parent cell copies all of its genes

a set of genes goes to the two new cells

each cell is a clone – they all have the same genes

FIGURE 5: Asexual reproduction – the first steps.

How they differ

There are advantages and disadvantages to both types of reproduction.

The advantages of asexual reproduction:

- only one parent is needed
- all offspring have the same genes – they are all clones.

There is really only one advantage to sexual reproduction:

- all the offspring will be different – they will have a mixture of genes from the two parents.

This means that the offspring will show more **variation** than offspring produced by asexual reproduction. But variation can also be a disadvantage. If the parents were adapted to live in a particular habitat, then identical offspring (as in asexual reproduction) will also be well adapted. But if variation leads to differences between individuals (as in sexual reproduction), what will happen to the offspring that are not so well adapted?

QUESTIONS

5 Look at the list of advantages of asexual reproduction. What do you think are the disadvantages?

6 Explain why variation is sometimes an advantage and sometimes a disadvantage.

7 Start off with one bacterium and assume it reproduces once every 20 minutes. How many bacteria would you have after three hours? Draw a graph of this reproductive rate.

Cloning sheep – then humans?

Dolly the Sheep was the first cloned mammal. She burst onto the scene in 1996 when the Roslin Institute near Edinburgh announced that it had created her. She was made by replacing the nucleus of an egg cell with the nucleus of a mature body cell. This procedure is called **adult cell cloning**.

Normally sheep live for anything between 10 and 16 years but Dolly was put down when she was six years old. She was suffering from arthritis and a lung disease. Both of these conditions develop in older sheep and some scientists suggest that Dolly was prematurely ageing. Was this early onset of ageing the result of her having been cloned?

Should we clone people? We have the ability to do it.

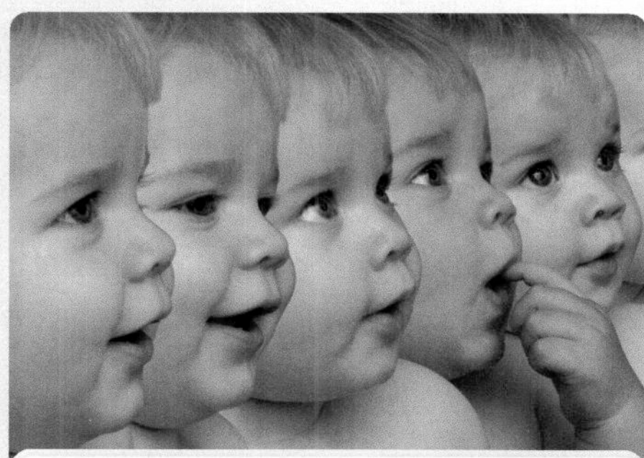

FIGURE 6: Human clones – or a multiple birth?

QUESTIONS

8 Was cloning Dolly the Sheep, a mammal like us, a good idea? Explain your answer.

9 Are there any circumstances in which producing a human clone could be acceptable?

10 Imagine that The Roslin Institute is threatened with closure. You have been asked to write an article for the local paper *The Roslin Courier* arguing why the Institute should be kept open.

11 Now write a second article supporting the opposite view.

Genes and what they do

You will find out:

- What genes and chromosomes are
- Where they are found
- Why young plants and animals resemble their parents
- How the resemblances are passed on

The ultimate information store

Chromosomes store the information living things need to survive. There is a species of fern that has 1260 chromosomes; and a species of ant is able to function on just one chromosome. Some people argue that humans are the most advanced living thing on Earth. Are we the most complex of all living things? We certainly do not have the most chromosomes!

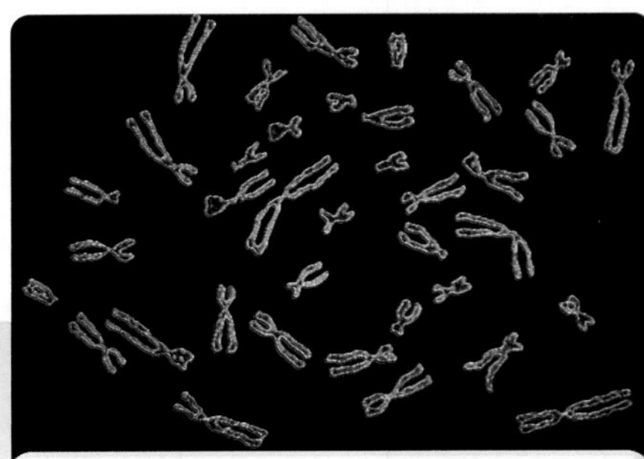

FIGURE 1: The full set of human chromosomes.

Just like your Mum or Dad?

Have you noticed that some children look just like their Mum or Dad? They might have the same coloured hair, or the same shape of nose as one of their parents.

Young animals, and plants, look like their parents because they **inherit** information from them. This information is passed on from parents to offspring by **genes**.

Genes are linked together in long chains called **chromosomes**. The **nucleus** of a cell normally has two sets of chromosomes in it. Genes and chromosomes are made from a chemical called **deoxyribonucleic acid** – **DNA** for short.

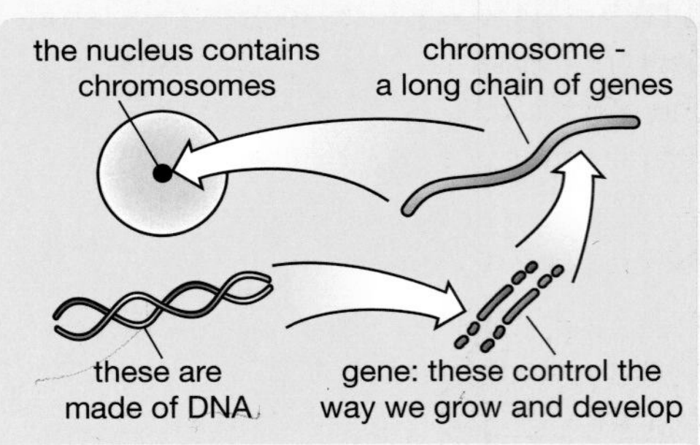

the nucleus contains chromosomes
chromosome - a long chain of genes
these are made of DNA
gene: these control the way we grow and develop

FIGURE 2: Looking at the detail – from DNA to nucleus.

Where do our genes come from?

We get one set of genes from our mother's egg cell. The second set comes from our father's sperm cell.

Eggs and sperms are special cells which contain half of the genes that normal cells have – that is, only one set. These two **sex cells** (**gametes**) join together during **fertilisation**. We develop from a fertilised **egg**. Fertilised eggs have two sets of genes. The genes we get control the development of characteristics we inherit.

But some of our features are not inherited. We get them during our life. Scars from cuts, tattoos and big muscles are just three of the features we do not inherit.

Many plants and animals develop from a fertilised egg.

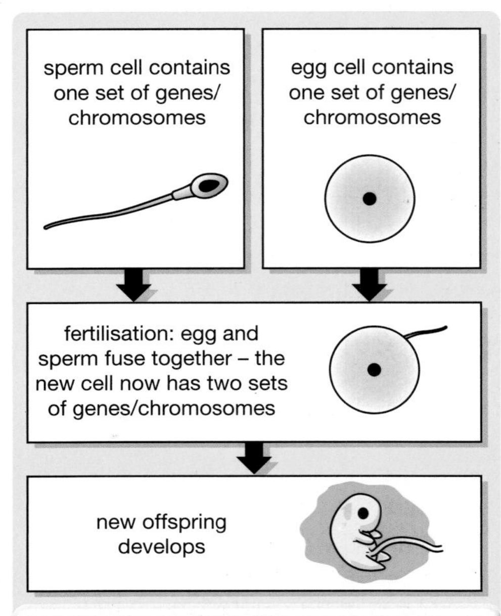

sperm cell contains one set of genes/ chromosomes
egg cell contains one set of genes/ chromosomes
fertilisation: egg and sperm fuse together – the new cell now has two sets of genes/chromosomes
new offspring develops

FIGURE 3: From egg to offspring.

QUESTIONS

1. Why do young plants and animals look like their parents?
2. What are genes and what do they do?
3. What are gametes?
4. Why are some features not inherited?

...*chromosomes* ...*deoxyribonucleic acid (DNA)* ...*egg* ...*fertilisation* ...*gametes*

What are your ears like?

Scientists have found some evidence that the type of ear lobe you have is inherited. Ear lobes can be either attached or unattached. Figures 4 and 5 show the different types.

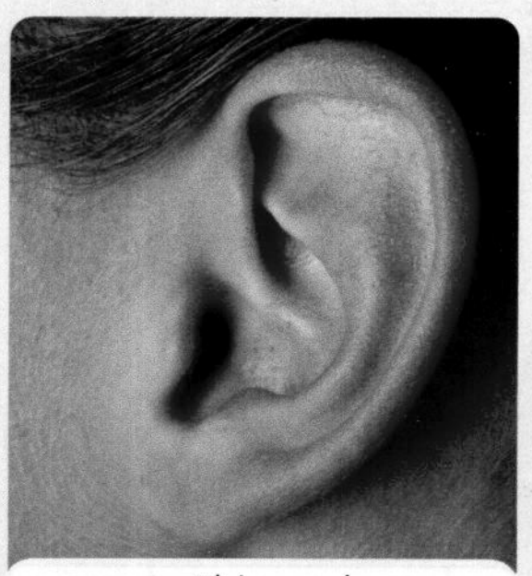

FIGURE 4: This ear has an attached lobe...

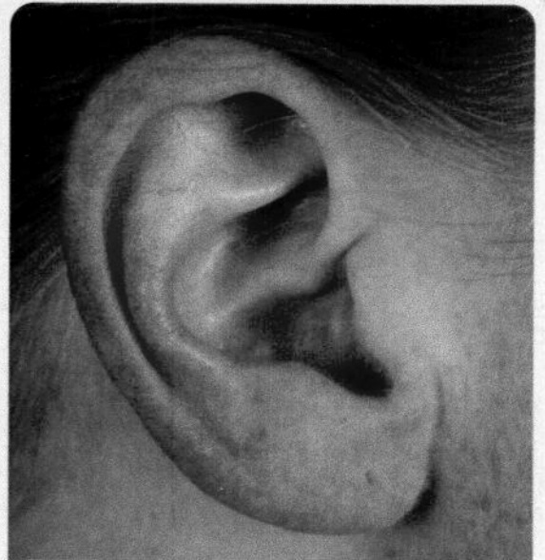

FIGURE 5: ...whereas this has an unattached lobe.

If you have attached ear lobes, you will have been given the *attached ear lobe* gene from both of your parents. This means you will have two genes for *attached ear lobes*. If your ear lobe is unattached, you only need to have received the *unattached ear lobe* gene from one parent. So you only need one of these genes to have unattached ear lobes.

A monk and his peas

In plant reproduction, the pollen grains contain the male gamete. The female gamete is in the ovary of the flower. Once pollination has happened, the seeds will develop. The seeds will contain genes from both the male and the female. The seeds will grow into plants.

Gregor Mendel lived about 150 years ago. In his spare time he busied himself in the monastery garden tending to his plants, especially his precious pea plants.

Though he wasn't the first person to notice that plants often looked like their parents he was probably the first to try to explain why. His observations eventually led to the discovery of how genes are passed on from parents to offspring and why offspring often resemble their parents.

Even though his scientific work is very important, it was never properly recognised during his own lifetime.

FIGURE 6: Gregor Mendel – it all started with his pea plants!

QUESTIONS

5 Why do gametes have only one set of genes and chromosomes?

6 How many *unattached ear lobe* genes do you need for you to have ears with unattached lobes?

7 Where can you get the *unattached ear lobe* genes from?

8 What did Gregor Mendel discover?

The Human Genome Project and life insurance

Many scientists think that if we know what all of our genes do we will be closer to understanding the secret of life.

The **Human Genome Project** was set up to help solve this mystery.

When you want to buy life insurance you will be asked lots of questions about your family's health history. If there is a history of particular illnesses then you may well be asked to pay more for the insurance. But your DNA could give insurance companies a much clearer picture about the diseases you may develop. So should you have a DNA test before getting life insurance?

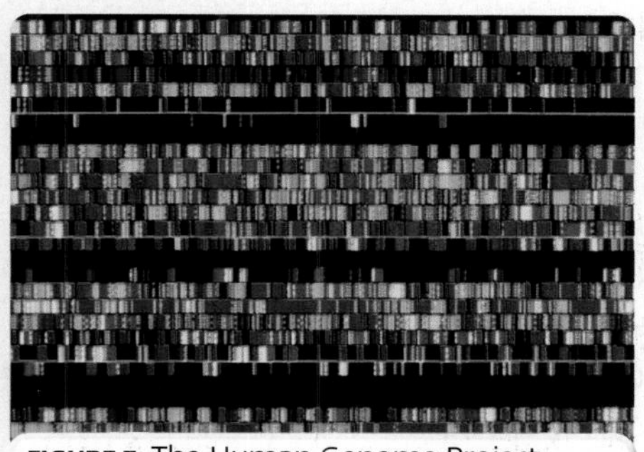

FIGURE 7: The Human Genome Project – are there any secrets left?

QUESTIONS

9 Do you think that information about your DNA should be made available to insurance companies?

10 In your group, discuss what the advantages and disadvantages would be of having a law allowing insurance companies to have your DNA information.

Cuttings

You will find out:

- What cuttings are
- How to make cuttings
- That all cuttings are genetically identical

Mutant oranges

We've probably all eaten them. Oranges are a great source of vitamin C. On average, one orange a day is all we need for our daily vitamin C requirements. Navel oranges have no seeds. All the navel orange trees in the world come from one mutant tree. About 200 years ago, this tree was found growing in a Brazilian orange plantation. Today, navel orange trees are grown all over the world.

FIGURE 1: All navel oranges come from 'cuttings' from the same tree!

Growing plants from cuttings

Planting seeds is the most obvious way of producing new plants. But seeds are produced by sexual reproduction. There is no way of telling that the new plants will be just what you want. Taking **cuttings** is another way of making new plants. They will be exactly the same as the original, parent, plant. They will be **genetically identical**. Figure 2 shows the stages involved in making cuttings.

The **hormone rooting powder** speeds up the growth of new roots.

Taking cuttings does not involve male and female gametes or fertilisation. The cuttings will therefore grow into new plants which are identical to the original parent plant. All the cuttings will be genetically the same as each other and the parent. They have the same genes as the parent plant and each other. This makes them all clones.

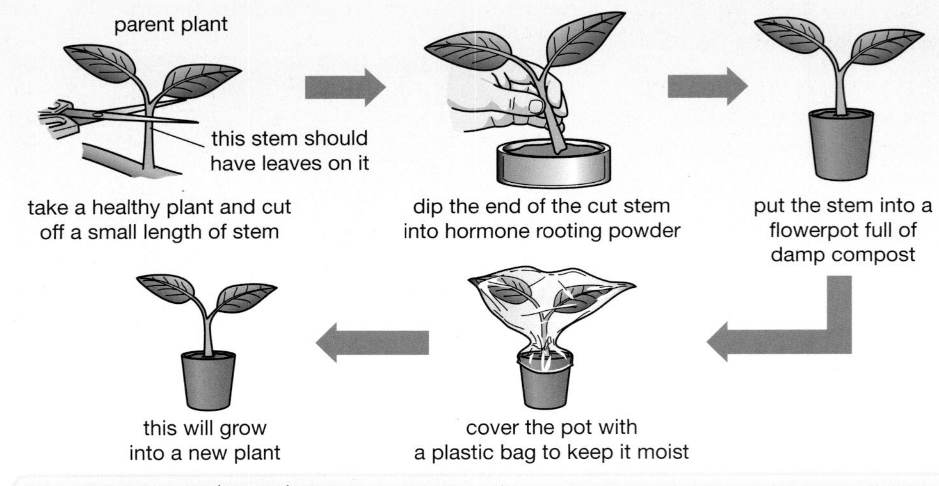
parent plant
this stem should have leaves on it
take a healthy plant and cut off a small length of stem
dip the end of the cut stem into hormone rooting powder
put the stem into a flowerpot full of damp compost
cover the pot with a plastic bag to keep it moist
this will grow into a new plant

FIGURE 2: How to take cuttings.

QUESTIONS

1. Why is it impossible to say what a plant from a seed will be like?
2. Why is it important to use a healthy plant to take cuttings from?
3. Write a paragraph to explain how you would take a cutting.
4. Why do all cuttings have the same genes?

Getting good cuttings

Most plants that reproduce sexually do so in the spring. When you take cuttings from a plant, you are actually making it reproduce asexually. There is no best time of the year to do this. It all depends on the plant and its age. Generally, when the plant is actively growing is a better time than when it's not, and younger plants are better to take cuttings from than older ones.

The best cuttings are not always taken from stems (**stem cuttings**). Some plants can be grown from **leaf cuttings** or **root cuttings**. Whether cuttings are made from stems, leaves or roots, the way you do it is the same. When you have made your cuttings and the new plants have grown, you then need to plant them out in the ground. There are advantages and disadvantages to making new plants by taking cuttings.

Here is a list of advantages:

- all the new plants will be identical to the original plant
- all the new plants will be identical to each other
- all the new plants will grow at the same rate
- making cuttings is easy
- making cuttings is cheap
- all the new plants will show the same adaptations.

Figure 3 shows cacao cuttings being prepared for planting. Cacao is used for the production of chocolate.

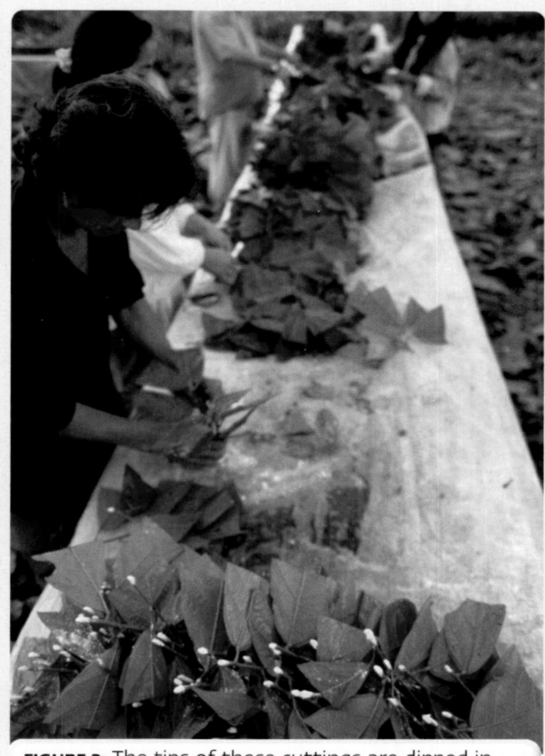

FIGURE 3: The tips of these cuttings are dipped in rooting powder.

EXAM HINTS AND TIPS

Make sure you understand the difference between sexual and asexual reproduction in terms of genes and chromosomes.

QUESTIONS

5 What parts of a plant can you take cuttings from?
6 What are the advantages of taking cuttings?
7 What disadvantages are there to growing cuttings?
8 Explain why taking a cutting is like making the plant reproduce asexually.

When you take cuttings, you are making a plant reproduce asexually

Planting a new tea crop

Tea is drunk world wide. To satisfy the huge demand, vast quantities are grown in India and Sri Lanka, as well as in many other places. A tea farmer who wants to plant a new crop must plan ahead as it can take between one and two years to prepare the ground for tea plants. A decision needs to be made whether to use seeds or cuttings. Farmers often use leaf cuttings rather than planting seeds.

FIGURE 4: Tea-plant leaf cuttings ready for planting out.

QUESTIONS

9 Why would tea farmers use cuttings in preference to seeds when setting up a new tea plantation?
10 A Sri Lankan tea farmer sent some leaf cuttings to a friend in northern India, over 2000 km to the north. Most of the cuttings failed to grow. Suggest why?
11 Write a short article for your school newspaper, or local newspaper, explaining why cuttings are clones.

Clones

You will find out:

- What tissue cultures are
- What tissue cultures are used for
- What embryo transplants are
- What embryo transplants are used for

When more is better

Dancer is an extraordinary horse. Her racing career is taking off. But she is special for another reason too. She is an embryo donor.

She is patiently standing in her vet's surgery. The vet, eyes glued to a microscope, holds her breath. 'Yes, we have an embryo.' Everyone breaths a sigh of relief! Dancer has donated an embryo which will be transplanted into another mare.

FIGURE 1: Dancer is so good – can they have another?

Tissue culture

What do you think would happen if you cut off the very top of a carrot and put it in water? After a few days it will have grown a stem and leaves. **Tissue culture** is a bit like this. It is a way of growing whole plants from small groups of cells. You place these cells on a special jelly that contains all that they need to grow, that is, all the nutrients they need. The cells divide and grow. Eventually you will have lots of plants that are exactly the same as each other. They have the same genes. They are clones.

FIGURE 2: These plants growing in tissue culture are all identical.

Embryo transplants

You can do something similar with animals. There are five steps.

1 Take a fertilised egg (called a **zygote**).

2 Let it divide a few times so that you have a ball of cells.

3 Split these cells up before they become **specialised**.

4 Let each cell divide into its own ball of new cells (**embryos**).

5 **Transplant** each ball of cells into a replacement (surrogate) mother.

The separated balls of cells will grow into individual animals. As in tissue culture, embryo transplants give you clones as they all have the same genes. If you started off with a fertilised egg from a cow, then the separated balls of cells would develop into cloned cows.

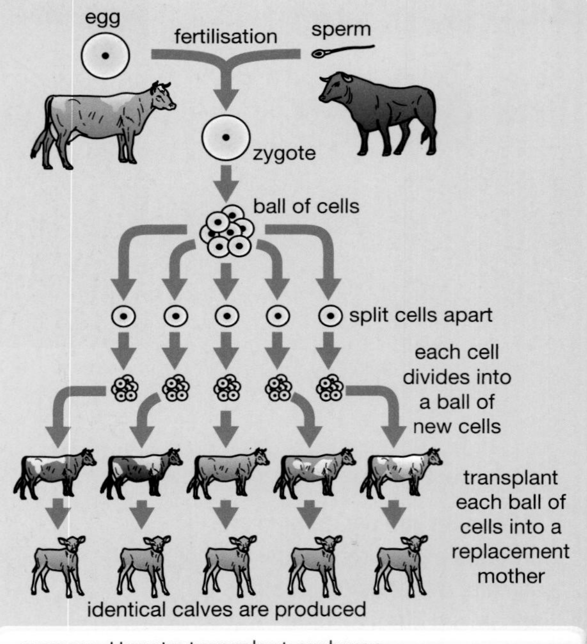

FIGURE 3: How to transplant embryos.

QUESTIONS

1 Explain what a tissue culture is.

2 Why are the plants produced by tissue culture called clones?

3 Why might a farmer want to transplant embryo calves?

4 Are the calves produced by embryo transplant clones? Explain your answer.

What is adult cell cloning?

This is when the nucleus from an egg cell is removed and replaced with the nucleus from a mature body cell. When this new cell eventually develops into an individual it will be a clone. It has the same genes as the mature body cell had. This procedure is called **adult cell cloning**. This is how Dolly the Sheep was cloned. You can read more about Dolly on page 67.

Replacing damaged skin

If someone has been badly burned, they will need new skin to replace the damaged skin. Skin transplants can be done. This involves 'harvesting' skin from a donor and transplanting it to the burns victim. Unfortunately, the body's immune system does not recognise the **skin graft** and so it is rejected.

Taking skin from another part of the victim's body is possible. Sometimes the burns are very extensive. In such cases there might not be enough undamaged skin, so another solution needs to be found.

Growing new skin

Tissue culture techniques can be used to grow new skin. Skin cells are put into a dish containing growth medium.

The cells are able to divide and grow because they are provided with the raw materials they need. An Australian company specialises in doing this. The manager says that all they need is about 4 cm^2 of a person's undamaged skin. In about three weeks they will then be able to culture up enough new skin to cover the victim's body. Growing skin must be done in sterile conditions. The process is very expensive.

Once enough skin has been made, plastic surgeons use it to cover the burns.

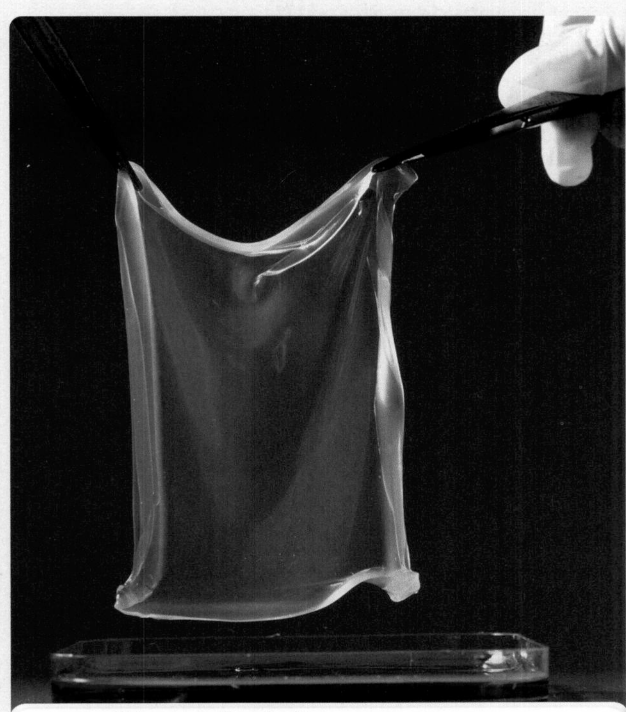

FIGURE 4: Skin ready for plastic surgery.

QUESTIONS

5 What might the growth medium for skin contain?

6 Why does the growing of skin grafts need sterile conditions?

7 Suggest an advantage of growing skin over using skin transplants.

Mothers of a different species

Scientists at the Zoological Society of London transplanted an embryo. It was 0.5 mm in diameter and consisted of about 100 cells. What made this so different was that the embryo was from a rare species of zebra and the surrogate mother was a horse.

Such 'cross-species' embryo transplants can be used to re-establish many types of endangered species. The zebra mother became pregnant again shortly after this, so the zoo had two young zebras in more or less the time it normally takes to produce one.

FIGURE 5: Could embryo transplants be used to breed endangered species?

QUESTIONS

8 Some people say that if a species is going to become extinct then so be it. Scientists should not interfere with the natural course of events. Write a letter to the Director of London Zoo supporting this view. Give as many reasons as you can think of in support of it.

9 Now write another letter expressing the opposite view.

Genetic engineering

You will find out:
- What genetic engineering is
- How genetic engineering is carried out
- Why genetic engineering is carried out

Engineering the tomato

How many cheese and tomato sandwiches could you make with one of these tomatoes? Is there no limit to **genetic engineering**? Big is beautiful, but this is ridiculous! Tomatoes like this are science fiction but genetic engineering isn't. Tomatoes which are resistant to moulds and other diseases are now commonly available. They have a longer shelf-life which means less wastage.

Genetic engineering could help to cure many diseases and help feed millions of people, but is it safe?

FIGURE 1: Real or imagined: have these been genetically modified?

GM Soya

Soya beans are a very important food. They contain lots of protein. The conditions in which they grow are also ideal for lots of weeds. Farmers spray their fields with herbicides to kill the weeds. The spray contains glyphosate. Because the beans have been **genetically engineered** they are not affected by the weedkiller. The weeds die but the bean plants continue to grow.

How to produce resistant soya beans

1 Find any plant that is able to withstand the weedkiller.
2 Search the plant's chromosomes and find the gene that made it resistant.
3 Transfer the gene into the cells of embryo bean plants and watch them grow.
4 Spray the plants with weedkiller to see if they are resistant (and keep your fingers crossed).
5 If they survive – great, they are resistant.
6 If they die – start again!

Moving genes from one living organism to another is called genetic engineering.

The plant which receives the gene is now **genetically modified** – it's a **GM** plant.

FIGURE 2: These GM soya bean plants will withstand the weedkiller.

QUESTIONS

1 Why are these bean plants not killed by the weedkiller?
2 What does 'genetic engineering' mean?
3 Describe how to make a weedkiller-resistant bean plant.
4 Why do you have to spray the new genetically engineered soya plants with weedkiller?

Genetic engineering could help to cure many diseases, but is it safe?

...diabetes ...enzyme ...genetic engineering

Insulin and diabetes

Lots of people suffer from **diabetes**. In some cases this happens because the pancreas does not produce the **insulin** needed to keep blood sugar at the right concentration. For some reason the gene that controls insulin production has stopped working. Blackouts and eventually death will result if the blood sugar levels are not controlled. Diabetes can be controlled by regular insulin injections and people with diabetes need a constant supply of this hormone.

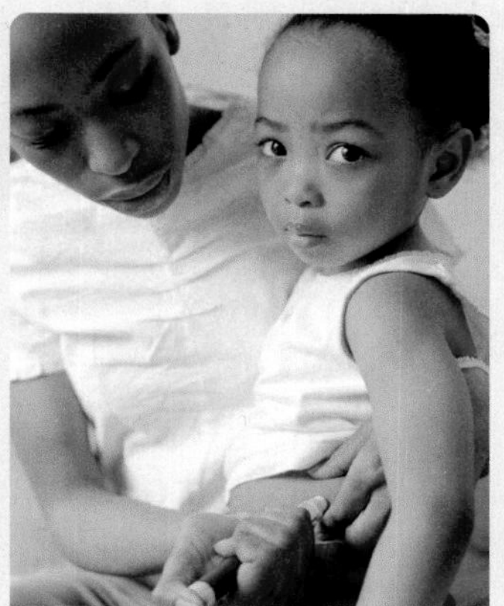

FIGURE 3: This four-year-old girl is having her insulin injection.

The manufacture of insulin

Genetic engineering has meant that enough insulin is produced for diabetics. Key to the process is a special **enzyme** (a complex protein). Figure 4 shows how this is done.

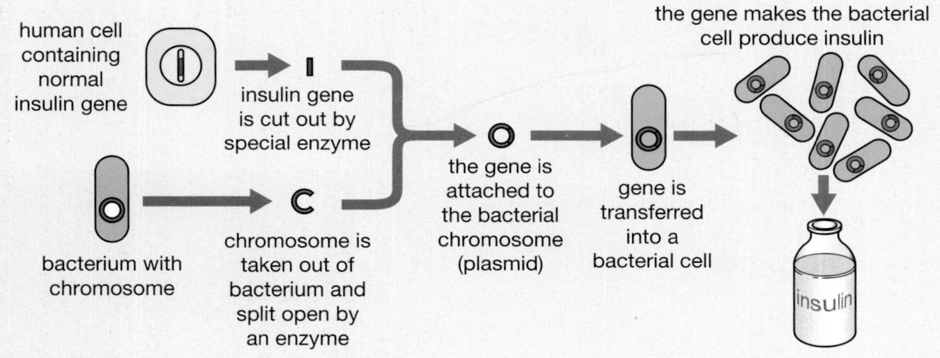
human cell containing normal insulin gene
insulin gene is cut out by special enzyme
bacterium with chromosome
chromosome is taken out of bacterium and split open by an enzyme
the gene is attached to the bacterial chromosome (plasmid)
gene is transferred into a bacterial cell
the gene makes the bacterial cell produce insulin
insulin

FIGURE 4: The genetic engineering of insulin.

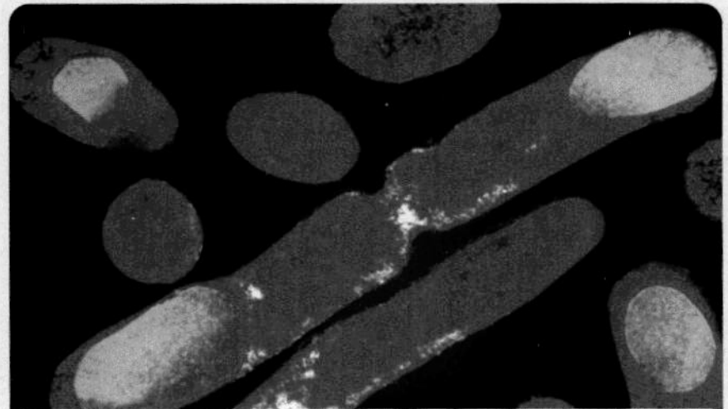

FIGURE 5: Genetically engineered bacteria producing insulin – the orange areas.

FIGURE 6: A fermenter producing insulin from GM bacteria in India.

QUESTIONS

5 What can cause someone to suffer from diabetes?

6 Describe the stages in the production of genetically engineered insulin.

7 Why are bacteria used for the production of genetically engineered insulin?

8 Human Growth Hormone is another hormone that some people do not produce. These people do not grow very tall. Its production is controlled by a gene. How would you go about getting bacteria to produce this hormone?

Genetic modification – good or bad?

Genetic modification is not unusual. Almost every aspect of our lives is touched by GM products. Many of the foods we eat and the medications we use are the product of GM technology.

Here are a few ways in which genetic engineering has been used:

- to make various plants resistant to microbes
- to speed up the growth of salmon which we eat
- to inject GM hormones into cattle, which we also eat
- to reduce the accumulation of toxic substances by some plants
- to reduce the rate at which some fruits and vegetables ripen, and so increase their shelf life.

Concerns about genetic engineering include:

- Are GM plants safe? Will they spread their genes to other plants?
- Are there long-term problems associated with eating GM foods?

QUESTIONS

9 Some people think that genetic engineering will bring enormous benefits. Write a letter to your Member of Parliament asking him or her to support the granting of further funding for genetic engineering.

10 Other people argue that GM is against the 'Natural Laws of Nature'. Draw up a table summarising the arguments against genetic engineering and explain each argument as fully as you can.

Theories of evolution

You will find out:
- About different theories of evolution
- About the different people who put these forward
- Darwin's theory of evolution
- Why scientific theories of evolution were unacceptable in the past

Earth's life came from...?

We cannot be sure when or where life began, but scientists estimate it was about 3500 million years ago. Some people say that there is no origin – life was always there. Others say that life came to the Earth from outer space.

What is evolution?

Evolution is how living things **change** (and have changed) from one generation to the next. Evolution is going on all of the time.

FIGURE 1: Lamarck's theory on the evolution of giraffes.

Old and new ideas

Originally people believed that living things were created by God. But not everyone thought this.

Aristotle (384–322 BC) was an ancient Greek philosopher. He thought that living things 'wanted' to change from being simple to being more complex. For example, from being single-celled to multi-celled.

In medieval times, about 800 years ago, people went back to believing in creation again.

Jean-Baptiste Lamarck (1744–1829) was a French scientist. He suggested that organisms could change as the result of their surroundings. This change can be passed on to their offspring. Lamarck said that, as a giraffe stretches up to eat leaves from a high tree, its neck will get longer. It gradually **acquires** a longer neck. This will then be passed on to the next generation. In this way, over the generations, giraffes have grown long necks.

Charles Darwin (1809–82) Charles Darwin's famous book *On the Origin of Species* was first published in 1859. He suggested that **species** gradually changed from one form to another by a process of natural selection. His ideas about evolution were based on observation and science. The book challenged all the established thinking of the day. It was a bestseller. In spite of this, Darwin's ideas were not accepted at first because they questioned religious belief.

FIGURE 2: Darwin in 1854, five years before his theory was published.

As so often happens in science when big ideas are being developed, more than one person had the same idea. Alfred Russel Wallace (1823–1913) was a naturalist. He was coming, independently, to exactly the same conclusions as Darwin. Both were extraordinary scientific thinkers.

QUESTIONS

1. What does evolution mean?
2. What was Aristotle's idea?
3. What was Lamarck's theory of evolution?
4. Why was Darwin's idea not accepted at first?

Watch Out Lamarck made his name with a theory of evolution – but got it wrong!

Charles Darwin and HMS Beagle

As a young man, Darwin sailed round the world on the ship *HMS Beagle*. He was the on-board biologist. The trip started in 1831 and lasted five years. Everywhere the ship landed, Darwin collected specimens to study. On his journey he visited the Galapagos Islands.

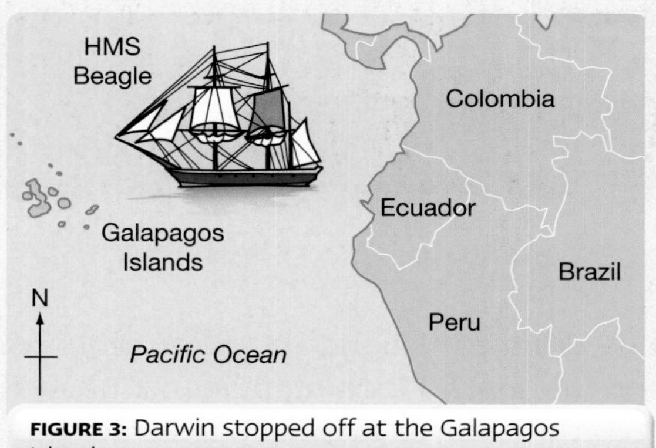

FIGURE 3: Darwin stopped off at the Galapagos Islands.

Darwin's famous Galapagos finches

Darwin collected small birds (all types of finches) from the different islands. Years later, back in England, he realised that they held the key to his theory of evolution. Darwin noticed that they all had different beaks and they all fed in different ways. There was one type of finch on the South American mainland. Perhaps the Galapagos finches evolved from this one type – gradually changing their feeding habits depending on the available food? The table shows how different species of finch found on the Galapagos Islands get their food from different places.

Type of finch	Food sources
Ground finch	eat seeds which they crush with their strong beaks
Cactus finch	long, slender beaks suck up nectar from cactus flowers
Vegetarian tree finch	curved beaks, like a parrot, eats buds and fruits
Insectivorous tree finch	stubby beaks to eat beetles and other insects
Warbler finch	small beaks to catch little insects and spiders from leaves and twigs
Woodpecker finch	use a cactus spine to prize small insects out from cracks in tree bark

QUESTIONS

5 Why was Darwin's *On the Origin of Species* such a sell out?

6 What is wrong with Lamarck's theory of evolution? (Hint: What do genes do?)

7 How did the finches help Darwin sort out his ideas about evolution?

The giant tortoises of the Galapagos Islands

It is thought that giant Galapagos tortoises live for a very long time. Scientists have identified 15 races of tortoise on the islands. They can be divided into two groups:

- dome-backed – the front edge of the shell arches high over the tortoise's neck; this lets them lift their heads up more
- saddle-backed – the shell forms a low line over the neck; this keeps their head relatively low.

Four races are already extinct. A fifth is down to just one male. Not surprisingly he is called Lonesome George. The remaining ten races remain in low numbers.

FIGURE 4: Giant tortoises – living long but facing extinction.

QUESTIONS

8 Suggest what sort of food the two types of tortoise can feed on.

9 How could the two different shell types, dome-backed and saddle-backed, have evolved?

10 In your group discuss what can be done to increase the numbers of these tortoises.

Natural selection

You will find out:

- What natural selection is
- Why natural selection is important
- What mutations are
- How mutations affect evolution

Darwin's big idea

Charles Darwin was interested in many different things, including pigeons. People have bred all sorts of weird and wonderful looking pigeons. Darwin believed that if people could choose which features to select, then so could Nature. When people choose a feature to breed then it's called '**artificial selection**'. When Nature does it, it's called '**natural selection**'.

FIGURE 1: The Victoria crowned pigeon – a wild relative of the Dodo.

Genes and survival

Having the right genes lets you survive. Surviving means you are well adapted to cope with your surroundings. It's a bit like having your radio tuned in well. This lets you hear the radio station properly. If it's even slightly 'untuned' then reception is poor. If your genes are 'untuned' then your chances of survival are low.

When your cells divide, changes to chromosomes and genes might happen. These changes are called **mutations**. Actually, mutations are quite common. As the result of mutations, new genes are made. The new genes could make an individual better able to survive. Individuals with characteristics most suited to their environment are more likely to survive. They will be able to breed and pass their new genes on to their offspring.

Genes formed as the result of mutations can lead to more rapid changes in a species. If a mutation is beneficial then we get survival. If a mutation is not beneficial then survival becomes less likely. Organisms compete to survive. The ones best suited to their environment make it and the others don't.

This is called natural selection. Charles Darwin put forward a theory of evolution based on natural selection (see figure 2).

Darwin's theory of natural selection works like this.

1 Organisms produce lots of offspring.
2 These offspring will not be identical, they will show **variation**.
3 Some will be better suited to survival than others.
4 This means there is a **struggle for survival**.
5 Many will die and only a few survive.
6 The survivors have the edge over those that die.
7 Their genes have helped them survive.
8 They then reproduce and pass on their genes to their offspring.

All the baby rabbits in this family are different.

This young rabbit has poor hearing.

The rabbit did not hear the fox creeping up.

FIGURE 2: How natural selection can be seen in the wild.

QUESTIONS

1 Why do organisms have to be adapted?
2 What is a mutation?
3 What is natural selection?

THE BIG QUESTION

Natural selection helps organisms survive. Of course the BIG QUESTION that scientists have not been able to fully answer is: How did life start?

Natural selection in action

The evolution of a black moth – the black peppered moth – is a case of natural selection in action.

The peppered moth is a light colour with speckles. A hundred and fifty years ago they lived in the countryside where there was no pollution. When they rested against lichen-covered tree trunks they were almost invisible. They were very well **camouflaged** and so were able to survive.

FIGURE 3: Can you see the light coloured moth in this photo?

However, during the Industrial Revolution, there began to be a lot of air pollution in cities like Manchester. The buildings and tree trunks were black with soot. If the moths landed on these they were easy to spot and birds ate them. Then, spontaneously, a mutation happened. Black moths appeared. Now there was variation in the peppered moth population. Some were black and others were light-coloured with speckles. The black ones were camouflaged when they rested against polluted buildings but hopelessly obvious against unpolluted tree trunks.

Because of natural selection, the light speckled ones survived in the country and the black ones survived in the cities.

A scientist set up an experiment to see if moths survived in the 'wrong' place. He released lots of black ones in the clean countryside and the same number of speckled ones in a city.

FIGURE 4: Which moth will survive in the city?

QUESTIONS

4 Explain why peppered moths are camouflaged.

5 Why do the speckled moths survive in the country but not in the town?

6 Why did the scientist release the same number of moths in the country and in the city?

7 What do you think the scientists' results were?

Sparrows that had medium-length legs survived

Tornado kills 'selected' sparrows – but only if their legs were the wrong length!

In 1890 a tornado struck Canada. As it swept over the land it killed lots of animals, including large numbers of sparrows. An ornithologist (someone who studies birds) measured the leg lengths of sparrows that survived and also those that were killed. She noticed that most of the birds that were killed either had very short legs or very long legs. Those sparrows that had medium-length legs survived.

FIGURE 5: Would this sparrow survive a tornado?

QUESTIONS

8 Is this an example of natural selection? Explain your answer.

9 What is the disadvantage to the sparrow of having either long legs or short legs?

10 Suggest a reason why the sparrows with medium length legs survived.

Fossils and evolution

You will find out:
- What fossils are
- That they give us evidence of how organisms have changed since life started
- What evolution is
- What evidence there is for evolution

When the Antartic was hot...

Scott of the Antarctic was not the first person to reach the South Pole. Amundsen, a Norwegian explorer got there first. In March 1912, having failed to get there first, Scott and his companions died on their way back. Their bodies were found the following year. Amongst their belongings was a piece of rock. This rock was a bit of fossilised tropical plant. This suggests that Antarctica was once a hot, humid land. Studying **fossils** helps us learn about the ancient history of the world.

What are fossils?

Fossils are the remains of plants and animals that lived millions of years ago. This is how fossils are made:

- dead plant or animal bodies get buried by **sediments** (sand and clay)
- layers of sediments press down on them
- the pressure of the sediments becomes very high
- over millions of years, this pressure gradually changes the remains into stone

We can compare fossil remains with present day plants and animals. This can tell us how much (or how little) things have changed since life began.

The origins of life

Scientists believe that all living things came from **life-forms** that lived billions of years ago. Life began about 3.5 billion years ago. Studying the similarities and differences between living species and extinct ones is useful because it helps you to understand how they lived. Did they, for example:

- live in the same sort of habitat?
- feed on the same sorts of things?
- move about in the same sort of way?
- look as if they could be related to each other?

Studying the similarities and differences also helps you to see if they are related to each other.

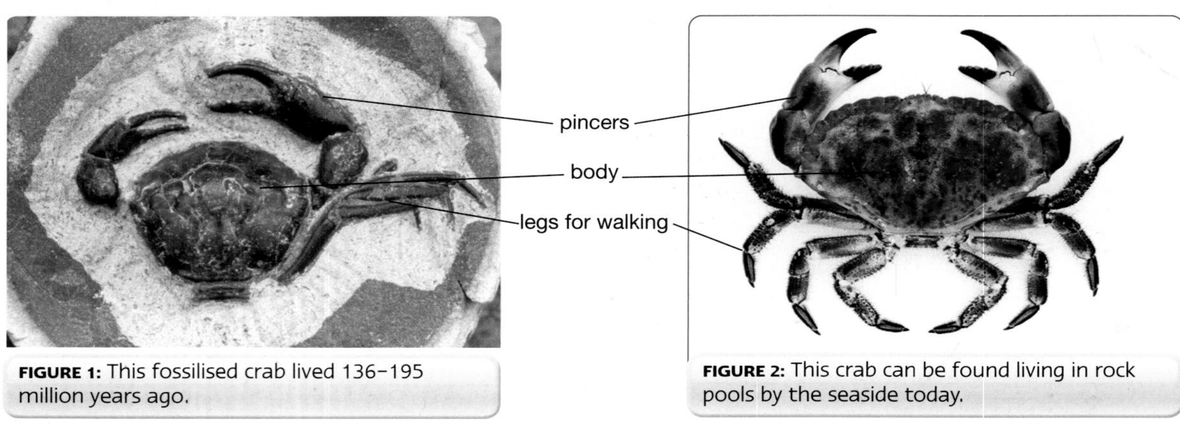

FIGURE 1: This fossilised crab lived 136–195 million years ago.

FIGURE 2: This crab can be found living in rock pools by the seaside today.

QUESTIONS

1 What is a fossil?
2 Write down **three** things that are the same in the two pictures of the crabs.
3 Did these two crabs feed in the same way? Explain your answer.

...fossils ...life-forms

What do fossils tell us?

Fossils give us evidence which suggests that all species of living things which exist today have evolved from simpler life forms.

The fossil record for most species is incomplete.

But the fossil record for the horse does show us how it has evolved over the last 50–60 million years. The table shows the key stages in the evolution of the horse.

Years ago	What it looked like and idea of size	Bones of its front leg	How it lived
1 million	**Modern horse** height: 1.6 m		lives on grassland; it is a fast runner
10 million	height: 1.0 m		lived in very dry places; it was a fast runner
30 million	height: 1.0 m		lived in dry conditions; it relied on speed to escape being eaten
40 million	height: 0.6 m		lived in dryer conditions; needed to be able to run away from predators
60 million	height: 0.4 m		lived on soft ground near water; its feet could support its weight without sinking into the mud

QUESTIONS

4 What can studying fossils tell us about living things from the past?
5 What has happened to the size of the horse as it has evolved?
6 How has the horse's leg and foot changed?
7 Why has it changed?

Fossils from Mars or just a meteorite?

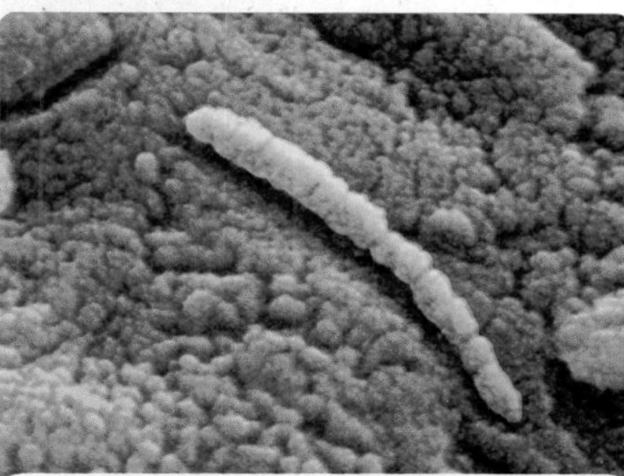

FIGURE 3: This is a Martian micro-fossil. Its name is 'Allan Hills 84001'.

Scientists estimate that this **meteorite** is over 4.5 billion years old. It shows what some scientists think is a fossilised life-form similar to bacteria. The big difference here is that this fossil comes from Mars. Many other scientists either disagree or are not sure. This fossil is seen as evidence that there once was life on Mars. In recent years none of the Martian landers have found any evidence that life now exists there.

"We are not talking about 'little green men' here" said a scientist "but it is evidence that life did exist on Mars."

We are not talking about little green men

QUESTIONS

8 What does this fossil suggest to you about the conditions on Mars in the past?
9 If there is no life there now, what must have happened?
10 Some people say that scientists should not be trusted because they cannot agree. Others say that discussion and debate help us all to get to the truth. Discuss this idea in your group.

She's got her Grandad's eyes!

SELF-CHECK ACTIVITY

CONTEXT

Will (14) has a brother, Andy (11), and a sister, Ellie (16). All three are blonde, though Ellie has brown eyes, unlike her brothers' blue eyes. All three are slim, though Will has a rather stockier build.

They all inherited characteristics from their parents, of course. The nuclei of the sperm and egg cells that formed them contained chromosomes, and each chromosome contains genes, which determine their characteristics.

Some of these characteristics are easy to see. Their mother has brown eyes and their father has blue eyes (not that sons inherit from fathers and daughters from mothers). However, brown eyes are dominant over blue, so why haven't all three children got brown eyes? This is because we all carry two sets of genetic data for each characteristic. We display the one that is dominant, but still carry the other. We pass one of these on to our children, and it's just as likely to be the recessive one as the dominant one. The mother was carrying a 'blue eye gene' (from her mother) as well as a 'brown eye gene' and it was the first of those that she happened to pass onto the boys.

With other features it's not quite so obvious. Brown hair is dominant over blonde, so it's perhaps rather surprising that all three children are blonde, since their mother has brown hair and their father is fair. However, a look in the family photo album reveals that the mother was fair until into her teens, and one of her grandfathers was fair, so she may be carrying a 'blonde hair gene'.

CHALLENGE

STEP 1

Read the information to see how the children compare with their parents. Why is it that certain features of the children are similar to those of their parents? How does the information travel from parent to child? Why is the mother mildly surprised to have three blonde children?

STEP 2

Was it inevitable that at least some of their children would have blonde hair? Explain the reasoning behind your answer.

STEP 3

Will is rather stockier in build than the other two. He's like both his grandfathers in this respect. The other two are slimmer and slightly taller. Suggest two reasons why Will should be different to his brother and sister in this way.

STEP 4

This rather complex system means that humans vary (as do all organisms that reproduce sexually). This variation rarely amounts to anything significant – blondes are no better (or worse) at surviving than people with any other hair colour. Why do living things vary?

Maximise your grade

These sentences show what you need to include in your work to achieve each grade. Use them to improve your work and be more successful.

Grade	Answer includes...
	Start to indicate how organisms formed as a result of sexual reproduction have a mix of the parents' characteristics.
F	Describe how organisms formed as a result of sexual reproduction have a mix of the parents' characteristics.
	Describe how different genes control different characteristics.
	Describe how genetic information is transferred from parent to child.
C	Explain how characteristics are passed on from parent to child.
	Start to explain how genetic information is passed on down through generations.
A	Explain how genetic information is passed on down through generations.
	As above, but with particular clarity and detail.

Extinction

You will find out:

- What extinction means
- What causes extinction
- If anything can be done to prevent extinction
- About the Tasmanian wolf

Mass extinction

Dinosaurs lived between 225 and 65 million years ago. They ruled the Earth. Some were herbivores. Others, like *Tyrannosaurus rex*, were fierce carnivores, killing their victims with their powerful jaws. Then, something happened to the world, and they all became extinct. So what could have happened that caused all the dinosaurs to die?

FIGURE 1: What caused their extinction – a giant meteorite or asteroid?

Extinction – what it means

Life on dry land started about 550 million years ago. The world was very different then. As it slowly changed, many different plants and animal species also changed, gradually died out, then were replaced by new types. When a species dies out and there are no more individuals left we say that it has become **extinct**.

There are thought to be more than 20 million different species of plants and animals alive today. Scientists think that since life began *billions* of different species have become extinct.

Living things become extinct for lots of different reasons. Here is a list of the main ones.

FIGURE 3: Now extinct – this Giant Club-moss lived about 300 million years ago.

- The **environment** in which they live changes.
- All the animals in a species might be eaten by a **predator**.
- A **disease** might kill them off.
- A new, more successful, **competitor** might move in to the **habitat**.

The Dodo lived on the island of Mauritius. The species became extinct about 300 years ago when sailors brought dogs, pigs and, accidentally, rats, to the island. Dodos did not taste nice – but their eggs did.

The Giant Club-moss lived up to its name – it grew 30 metres high. Why do you think it became extinct?

Dodos did not taste nice – but their eggs did

FIGURE 2: The Dodo – extinct since 300 years ago.

QUESTIONS

1. What happens to a plant or animal that becomes extinct?
2. Give an example of an animal which is extinct.
3. Explain what caused it to become extinct.
4. What could have been done to stop it becoming extinct?

...competitor ...disease ...environment ...evolution

Causes of extinction

There are lots of reasons why a species becomes extinct but they all involve individuals dying. It can be caused by changes in the environment, a new or altered predator, fatal diseases, or a more successful predator.

Environment change

This is when the place where a species lives changes, for example the temperature might increase. This means that the individuals living there are not adapted to the new conditions and so, unless they can adapt or move away, they will die out. Building cities and towns can also lead to species becoming extinct because the natural habitat has been changed. Actually the habitat has been destroyed.

A species will become extinct unless individuals can cope with the changes. This is the basis of **evolution**.

Predator

When a new predator is introduced into a habitat, it eats prey which is not adapted to get away. This can lead to the extinction of the prey species.

The Javan tiger is extinct because of human action – hunting. Does that make us the ultimate predator?

Fatal diseases

Plants and animals are naturally immune to lots of different diseases. However, if a new, fatal, disease is introduced to a habitat some species will not cope and so will die. Often a few individuals of the species are left. If there are not enough to keep the species going, then when the last few die of old age, that's it – extinction!

Figure 4 shows Mr Benjamin in his garden on the island of St Helena. The year is 2002. He is standing by the very last St Helena olive tree. The tree has since died from a fungal infection. The species is now extinct.

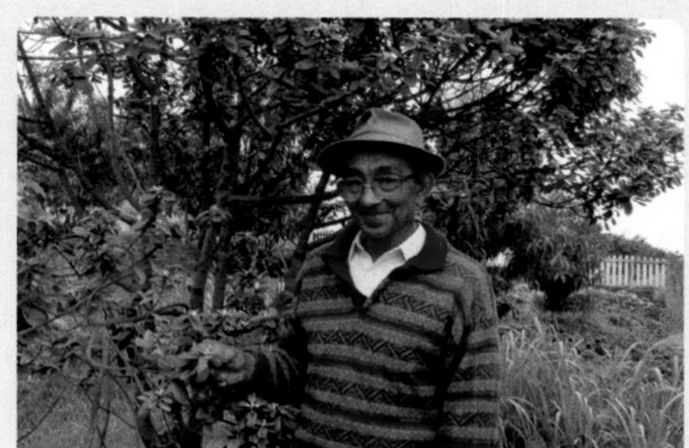

FIGURE 4: Last of its kind – now gone – the St Helena olive tree.

A more successful competitor

If there is a limited amount of food in a habitat and two different species are competing for it then the better adapted species will survive and the less well-adapted one will become extinct.

Humans endanger many species and hunting has caused lots of species to become extinct.

QUESTIONS

5 Explain how each of the main factors listed above has caused the extinction of a species.

6 What are humans doing that leads to other species becoming extinct?

7 A very rare butterfly is about to become extinct because a new road is to be built through its unique habitat. Write a letter to your local newspaper protesting against the road.

8 Now write another letter expressing your support for the road.

A kangaroo-like wolf

The Tasmanian wolf was hunted to extinction and by 1936 the last one died in captivity. Though it looks a bit like a tiger, has stripes and the shape of a wolf, it was actually closely related to kangaroos and wallabies and it had a pouch for its young. Since its extinction, many people believe that it still lives in remote parts of Tasmania but no proper sighting has been made since 1936.

FIGURE 5: A mystery disease and hunting made these Tasmanian wolves extinct.

QUESTIONS

9 How do we know if a species is truly extinct in the wild?

10 How long after the last verifiable sighting should a species be officially declared extinct?

11 The Tasmanian wolf was known to eat sheep. So does it matter that it is now extinct? Discuss.

12 What could have been done to prevent it from becoming extinct?

More people, more problems

You will find out:
- That the human population of the world is growing
- That this population is using up raw materials
- That more waste is being produced

Population rise, population fall

There are more and more people in the world, but this growth is not spread evenly. In the next 40 years the population of Niger, in north-western Africa, is expected to increase from 12 million to 53 million people. During the same time, in Europe, the Bulgarian population is expected to drop from 8 million to just 3 million.

Countries of the developing world have increasing populations; whereas the populations of most developed countries are stable or dropping.

FIGURE 1: People just keep on coming – can the world cope?

Standing room only!

The number of people in the world is increasing. More children are being born and we are all living longer. By the year 2035, the **population** of the world will have exceeded 10 000 000 000. A hundred years ago it was only about 2 000 000 000. This vast increase is having an enormous impact on the supply of **raw materials** and the **environment**.

What are raw materials?

We get raw materials from the Earth and we use them to make useful things.

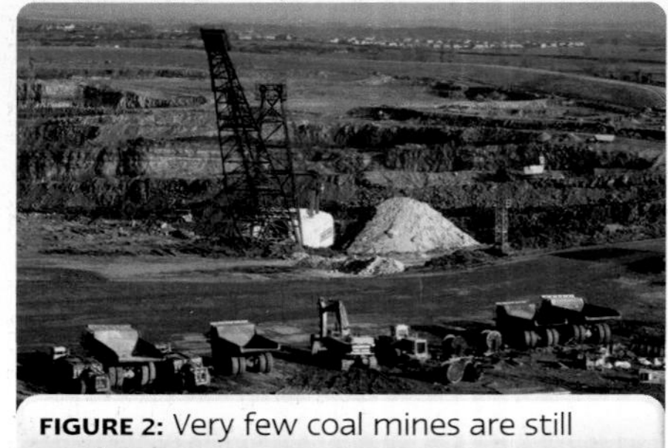

FIGURE 2: Very few coal mines are still working.

FIGURE 3: Crude oil is gradually running out – though this refinery is still operating.

Coal is used for burning in power stations. It is dug out of the ground or scraped up from opencast mines. Coal is made from the dead remains of plants which lived millions of years ago.

QUESTIONS

1. Why is the human population increasing?
2. By how many has the human population increased over the last 100 years?
3. Name **two** raw materials.
4. Why are raw materials running out?

Crude oil is extracted from the ground. When crude oil is refined we get lots of useful things including various types of fuel, lubricating oil and solvents.

Coal and crude oil, as well as natural gas, are **non-renewable energy resources**. Once these have been used up they cannot be replaced.

In the past, forests were much larger than today. They have been cut down to make furniture, build homes and to clear the land for farming.

We dig up various metal **ores** and **rocks** from **quarries**. All of these raw materials are gradually being used up as the world's population gets bigger.

As the world population continues to rise, the demand for raw materials also continues to soar. This results in more **waste** being produced. And, of course, more waste can lead to more **pollution**.

...coal ...crude oil ...environment ...non-renewable energy resources ...ores ...pollution

Population growth

At present there is a human population explosion. This means that the population is increasing very rapidly. This explosion tends to be in the developing countries. In many developed countries the size of the population is stable, or even falling. An increasing population puts great pressure on land and raw materials.

Land is needed for:

- building new towns and cities
- constructing roads.

All this contributes to the loss of natural habitats.

But it wasn't always like this. For thousands of years the human population was small. Diseases, poor shelters and inadequate food all meant that people did not live very long. As living conditions improved, so life expectancy increased.

In Britain, as the table shows, you can expect to live for much longer now than you did a hundred years ago.

	Life expectancy if born in 1901	Life expectancy if born in 2003
boys	45	76
girls	49	81

You now live much longer than your ancestors did because we have:

- better food
- improved hospitals and medical care
- better water supplies
- fewer people dying in childhood.

Figure 4 shows how the world's population is growing. In parts of the world the population is growing much more than in others.

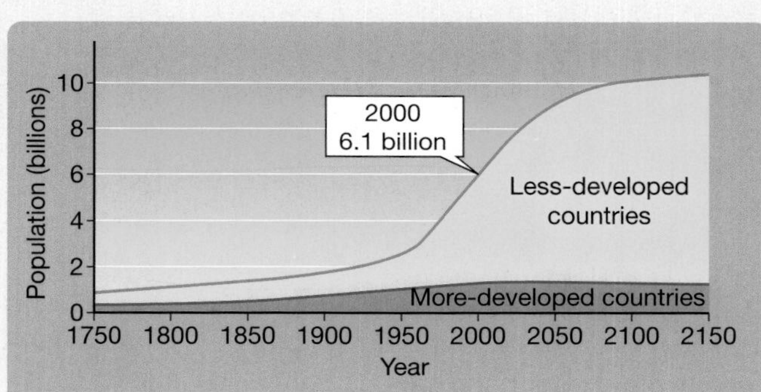

FIGURE 4: Human population growth – will it level off or continue to rise?

QUESTIONS

5 Why are people living longer now than a hundred years ago?

6 Explain the effect the increase in population is having on the demand for natural resources and the production of waste.

7 What effect does a large population have on pollution levels?

8 What is the difference between the population growth of more developed countries and the less developed countries?

More waste can lead to more pollution

Superquarries

Vast quantities of crushed rock (called aggregate) is needed for road building. Most new roads are built where the human population is high, such as in the Midlands and south-east England. These areas do not have their own quarries to meet the demand. '**Superquarries**', as they are called, are found on the west coast of Scotland where few people live. They are very big. Aggregate can be transported from them to areas where it is needed by road, rail or ships. Though superquarries provide employment for locals, many people object to them.

FIGURE 5: This large quarry gives us iron ore which is used to make steel.

QUESTIONS

9 Why would people object to superquarries?

10 Suggest **two** advantages of having superquarries.

Land use

You will find out:

- That an increased population uses up more land for building, farming and quarrying
- That this results in more dumping of waste
- That this contributes to the loss of natural habitats

Your rubbish says it all

Two thousand years ago the Romans invaded Britain. For the next 300 years they built forts, towns and roads. When they went back to Rome, they left these things behind. There are lots of Roman remains still to be seen today. Archaeologists dig up the remains of the past so as to learn something about Roman life in Britain. Roman rubbish dumps can tell us a lot – what will our rubbish dumps say about us?

Where have all the meadows gone?

As our population increases so our need for space and resources also grows. We need more homes and to build them we need more **building materials**, like rocks and stone. We get these from quarries. To feed everyone we need more food. A lot of our food comes from farms. When there are lots of people, there will be lots of rubbish and other waste. Waste can lead to **pollution** unless it is disposed of properly.

FIGURE 1: These homes were built on green fields.

Buildings

Houses, blocks of flats, shops and all the other **buildings** that we use take up space. When will the meadows, at the bottom of figure 1, be used up for more building?

Quarrying

Digging rocks out of the ground involves blasting it with explosives. We need the rocks to build homes and roads, but it's dangerous work. Few wild plants and animals can live in quarries.

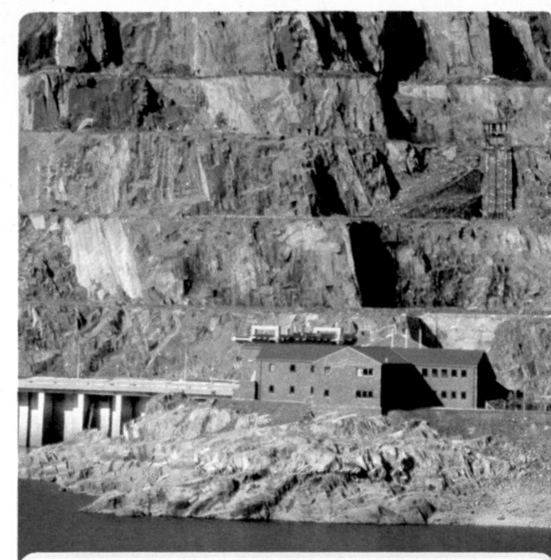

FIGURE 2: Do you think quarries scar the landscape?

Farming

People have changed **natural habitats** so that they can produce more food. So now there's less land available for wild species. Previously, the land would have supported whole communities of different plants and animals.

Dumping waste

Rubbish is a big problem. Its disposal costs a lot of money. Rubbish is either put in large holes in the ground (called landfill sites) or else it is incinerated (burned).

QUESTIONS

1 Why do we need more homes?
2 What do we get from quarries?
3 What has farming done to natural habitats?
4 What do we do with all the rubbish we produce?

What will our rubbish dumps say about us?

...building materials ...buildings ...dioxins ...fertilisers

Intensive farming

The demand for cheap food has resulted in greater mechanisation of farms. Over the last 50 years the number of farms in Britain has reduced but they have got bigger. Several small farms will have joined together into one big one. This can lead to **intensive farming** where lots of **fertilisers** and **pesticides** are used to increase production of crops and livestock. Thousands of chickens, hundreds of cows or vast fields of wheat mean that intensive farming methods give us cheaper food.

Battery hens, for example, are kept in very confined spaces in order to produce lots of cheap eggs.

Intensive farming of wheat means large fields of the same crop, so combine harvesters can be used and there is less wastage of land.

FIGURE 3: This farm has small fields with different crops.

FIGURE 4: Combine harvesters are suited to large fields of the same crop.

QUESTIONS

5 What is the difference between intensive farming and the more traditional ways of farming?

6 Why are there fewer farms today?

7 Look at Figure 4. Why do large fields mean less wastage of land?

8 What could you suggest to a farmer to get him to encourage wild plants and animals onto his land?

NIMBY (Not In My Back Yard)

Incinerating household rubbish can be a health hazard. **Dioxins** are chemicals which are produced when plastics are burned. After burning, these dioxins are released into the environment. Domestic rubbish has lots of plastic things in it. People who are exposed to dioxins can suffer because it can affect the working of many parts of their body, including the:

- liver
- immune system
- nervous system
- endocrine system
- reproductive system.

There is even some evidence from experiments that animals exposed to dioxins develop several forms of cancer. County Wicklow is on the east coast of Ireland. The local council want to build an incinerator near Redcross. Not surprisingly many locals are protesting against its construction.

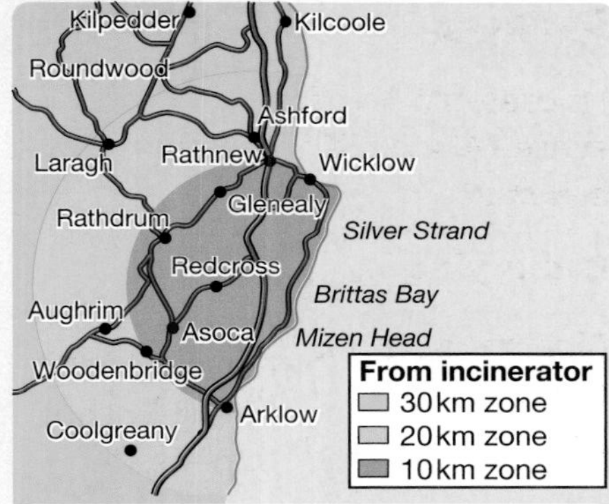

FIGURE 5: What do you think this map of the Redcross area shows?

QUESTIONS

9 What arguments could the council use to convince local people that the incinerator is a good idea?

10 You are a doctor. Write a letter to the *Wicklow Gazette*, the local newspaper, outlining the health dangers of the incinerator.

11 In your group, discuss what alternatives there are to building an incinerator.

Pollution

You will find out:

- What pollution is
- That more waste can lead to pollution
- That sewage and fertilizers can cause pollution
- That toxic chemicals cause pollution

Oil spill kills thousands

The following quote is from the *Tenby Observer*, 23rd February 1996. *'The whole of Pembrokeshire (west Wales) is bracing itself this weekend for a* ***pollution*** *nightmare that seems set to pose a threat to the county's economic and environmental future.'*

In February 1996 the supertanker *Sea Empress* spilt over 80 000 tonnes of crude oil into the sea. This was the biggest oil spillage, ever, in British waters. It's the equivalent of 3200 road tankers emptying their loads of crude oil into the sea. Over 4500 birds were killed by the oil's **toxic** effects.

FIGURE 1: Dead sea birds on a Welsh beach – when will this happen again?

How do we pollute

Pollution happens when things are added to our environment that damage it. Land and water pollution can be caused by **sewage**, **fertilisers** and **toxic chemicals**.

Sewage

Raw sewage contains:

- human waste
- industrial waste
- micro-organisms
- debris, such as sanitary towels, toilet paper, condoms and bits of plastic.

The table shows some of the diseases you can get if you come in contact with microbes from untreated sewage. Sewage treatment works can remove these things. If it has been dealt with properly, then treated sewage is quite safe to return to the environment.

Name of disease	Its symptoms
gastroenteritis	stomach cramps, diarrhoea and vomiting
Weil's disease	liver and kidney damage, it can be fatal
allergic alveolitis	fever, breathlessness, cough

Fertiliser

Farmers add fertilisers to help their crops grow. If these get washed into streams and rivers, they can cause the water plants to grow a lot. Eventually the plants die because there is not enough light for them all to photosynthesise. Bacteria feed on the dead plants. They **respire** and use up the oxygen. This kills other things like fish and snails.

Toxic chemicals

Toxic means poisonous. Toxic chemicals include **herbicides** and **pesticides** which are used to kill pest plants and animals. They are sprayed onto crops. But does spraying in this way only harm pests?

Lots of industrial processes produce wastes which are also toxic. They affect people as well as plants and animals.

QUESTIONS

1 What is pollution?
2 Name a disease that you can catch from sewage. How does it affect you?
3 Why do farmers put fertilisers onto their land?
4 Why would a farmer spray their fields with pesticides?

...fertilisers ...herbicides ...pesticides ...pollution ...respire

Health problems and water pollution

Lots of people are exposed to the dangers of sewage:

- builders and inspectors of sewers
- water treatment plant workers
- sludge tanker drivers
- plumbers
- workers who clean out toilets on trains and empty aircraft toilets.

These people have to take great care. They put on special clothing to protect themselves from contact with sewage.

Fertilisers and toxic chemicals

Artificial fertilisers contain chemical elements that plants need for healthy growth.

These include:

- nitrogen for growth
- phosphorus for healthy roots
- potassium for healthy stems and leaves.

Fertilisers can drain from the land into our drinking water reservoirs. This can cause a major health problem. High levels of nitrogen, as nitrates, causes blue baby syndrome – where babies are not able to transport oxygen around their body properly. The condition can be reversed quite easily. Just change the baby's water supply. Fortunately this is very rare as there are laws to limit the nitrate levels in our water supplies. Adults and older children are not affected.

Herbicides and pesticides are used by farmers and plant growers to kill weeds and insects so that their crops can grow properly. Unfortunately, some of these chemicals can have devastating **side-effects**. One such chemical is DDT.

DDT

Fifty years ago DDT was used as a pesticide. It was very effective and only small quantities were needed. The problem was that it did not break down in the environment, so it was there for a long time. It was passed along the food chain. It remained in the bodies of bigger animals where it would build up until it reached lethal concentrations. It is not used now.

All the problems that sewage, fertilisers and toxic chemicals cause can be solved. We have to deal with them in a safe and proper way.

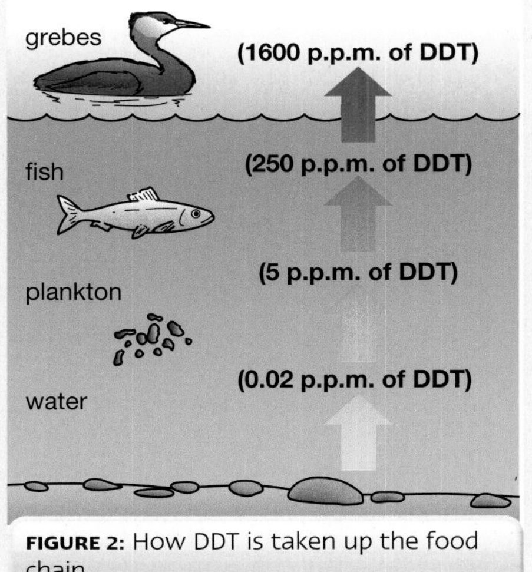

FIGURE 2: How DDT is taken up the food chain.

QUESTIONS

5 As well as wearing protective overalls, what else should sewage workers do to protect themselves from infection?

6 How could you cure a baby with *blue baby syndrome*?

7 What might happen to crops if farmers did not add fertilisers to their fields?

8 Why is DDT not used now?

Death in the Caspian Sea

The Caspian Sea is about 1 100 kilometres long.

FIGURE 3: The Caspian Sea, photographed from space in 2004.

There are 130 rivers flowing into the Caspian Sea. In the north, the river Volga, carrying farm run-off (containing fertilisers) flows in. The only way water can leave is by evaporation as there are no rivers flowing away. The light blue areas are shallow water and the black part is deep. The green zone at the top is where the water is rich in fertilisers. Plants are dying here. Bacteria are using up the available oxygen, breaking the dead plants down. As a result, fish and other aquatic organisms are also dying. The northern end of the Caspian Sea is virtually dead.

QUESTIONS

9 What effect does the fertiliser have on plant life in the northern Caspian Sea?

10 Why is there no oxygen here?

11 Some people say that what is happening in the Caspian Sea is an *ecological disaster*. Explain why they say this.

12 What could be done to stop the disaster continuing?

Air pollution

You will find out:

- What smoke is
- Why smoke is a pollution problem
- About the health problems caused by smoke
- About the effect of sulfur dioxide on living things

World history in a cup

The air is full of bits. Tiny particles float around, too small to be seen. An empty cup might look empty but inside there will be more than 30 000 particles. These are fragments of the whole world. From volcanic eruptions to atomic bombs, they all produce dust and smoke. Some of it is called pollution because people made it. But what about smoke from natural events? Volcanoes produce millions of tonnes of smoke. Is that pollution?

FIGURE 1: Mount St Helens erupting in 1980.

Smoke, smog and sulfur dioxide

When you burn a fuel you make smoke. Smoke is tiny particles which did not burn properly. Instead they float off into the air.

Smoke is a technical term. It refers to the size of these particles. They are incredibly small. If you lined them up, end to end, you would get about 5 000 in a millimetre!

Lots of industries produce smoke. This smoke causes air pollution. Power stations, for example, produce a lot of smoke.

When smoke mixes with fog we get **smog**. The particles of smog damage your lungs when you breathe them in. Though smog has not been a problem in London for a long time, there are cities in other parts of the world where it still is.

Cars, buses and lorries produce a lot of smoke. This smoke pollutes the air we all have to breathe.

Most **sulfur dioxide** pollution comes from burning **fossil fuels** (especially coal). Over 70% comes from power stations. When coal is burned, it releases sulfur dioxide into the air. This eventually falls as **acid rain**.

FIGURE 2: London, 1952, over 3 500 people died because of the smog.

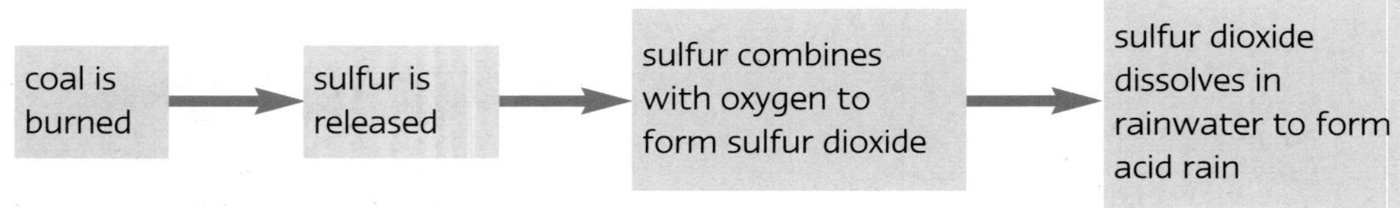
coal is burned
sulfur is released
sulfur combines with oxygen to form sulfur dioxide
sulfur dioxide dissolves in rainwater to form acid rain

FIGURE 3: How acid rain is formed.

QUESTIONS

1. What is smoke?
2. What can be done to reduce the air pollution in cities?
3. What is smog?
4. Describe how acid rain is made.

WOW FACTOR!

When Mount St Helens erupted, 3 cubic km of rock was pulverised into smoke, ash and dust and flung into the sky.

What air pollution does

Smoke and **soot** can damage living things as well as buildings and other man-made structures.

How to deal with air pollution

Many factories have filters to clean the smoke before it goes into the air. Power stations have gas scrubbers. Cars have catalytic converters. These remove the harmful chemicals.

The effects of sulfur dioxide and smoke

Sulfur dioxide causes:

- some elderly people, as well as the young, to get bronchitis
- asthma attacks
- plant leaves to turn yellow so that they cannot photosynthesise properly
- the limestone used in buildings to dissolve.

Smoke causes:

- breathing problems and coughing
- lung damage
- asthma attacks
- the blackening of buildings.

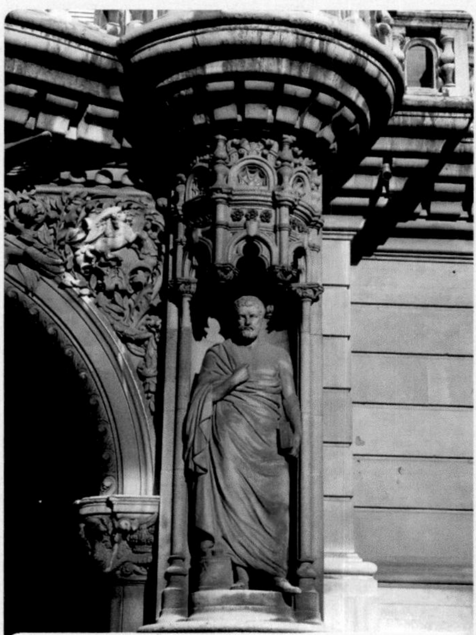

FIGURE 4: Smoke can turn buildings black.

QUESTIONS

5 Plants are able to get the carbon dioxide they need through their pores (shown in yellow in the greatly magnified undersides of holly leaves in figure 5). The pores are called stomata. Describe what is happening to the holly in the polluted area.

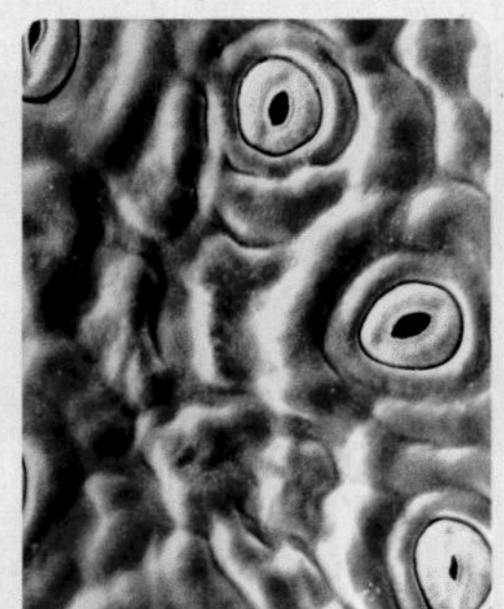

FIGURE 5: Which of these is from a polluted area?

6 What are the main effects of sulfur dioxide on people?

7 In your group, discuss what laws you would pass to reduce smog levels. Write these down.

Space waste

Since the 1950s, Soviet (Russian) and American space exploration programs have been sending rockets and satellites into space. Sometimes parts such as spent fuel canisters fall back to Earth. They often burn up on re-entering the atmosphere. Lots of bits are still up there, orbiting the Earth at speeds of between 30 000 and 45 000 km/h. At these speeds even the smallest bit of debris can cause serious damage to a spaceship or satellite.

The table gives some detail of this.

Size of object (cm)	Number of bits	% of total	% mass of total
0.1–1	35 million	99.67	00.035
1.1–10	110 000	0.31	00.035
over 10	8 500	0.02	99.930

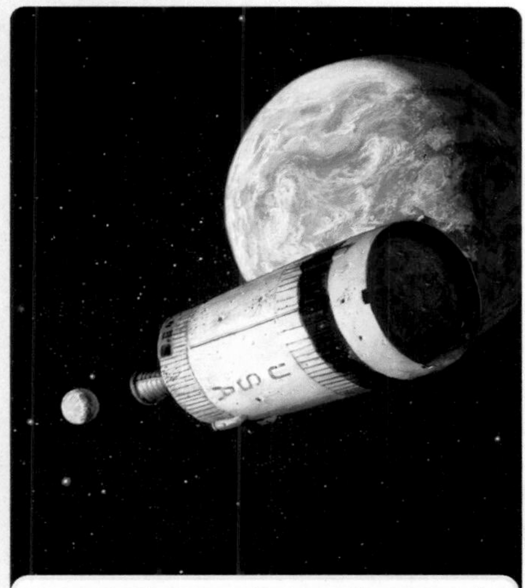

FIGURE 6: Space waste – another type of pollution?

QUESTIONS

8 Is space waste pollution? Explain your answer.

9 How should space waste be cleared away?

10 Some people would argue that a '*few nuts and bolts*' in space are not a problem. Discuss this in your group and try to get as many points opposing this view as possible.

What causes acid rain?

You will find out:

- What fossil fuels are
- What fossil fuels are used for
- What acid rain is
- What the effects of acid rain are

Modern cars are still a problem

The first car was built in 1769. It had a steam engine and its fuel was coal. This car was used to pull a cannon! Today there are over 500 million vehicles in the world. There are different types of cars, buses and lorries, but they all have one thing in common: they pollute. A modern car produces about 1/20th of the pollution that an old car did.

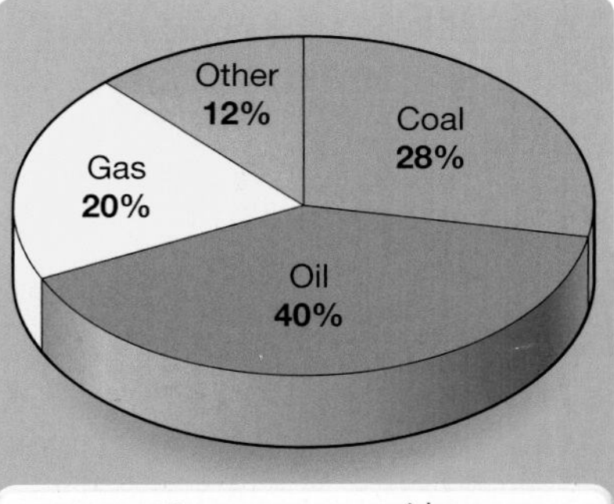

Other 12%
Coal 28%
Gas 20%
Oil 40%

FIGURE 1: Our energy providers.

Burning fossil fuels

Coal, oil and natural gas are made from the fossilised remains of plants and animals. They are called **fossil fuels**. Fossil fuels are very important as they satisfy most of our energy needs.

Many power stations also use fossil fuels to generate electricity.

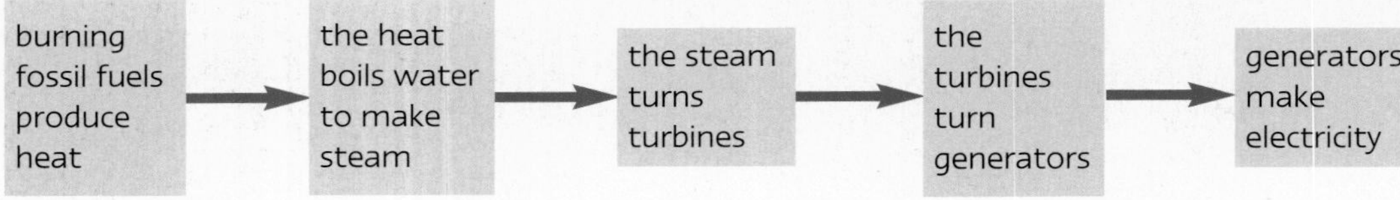

burning fossil fuels produce heat
the heat boils water to make steam
the steam turns turbines
the turbines turn generators
generators make electricity

FIGURE 2: How fossil fuels are used to generate electricity.

The chemical energy in fuels is converted into electrical energy for us to use.

Pollution from fossil fuels

Burning coal and other fossil fuels causes pollution. These fuels produce sulfur dioxide. When this polluting gas dissolves in rain it makes acid rain. Normal rain has a pH of 5.6. This is because there is some carbon dioxide dissolved in the rain.

carbon dioxide + water → carbonic acid

FIGURE 3: What has caused these trees to die?

Acid rain

Acid rain is pH 4. Acid rain kills trees, makes lakes too acid so that many plants and animals die; and **dissolves** rocks, buildings and statues.

Fossil fuels are **non-renewable energy resources**. This means that they cannot be replaced. Petrol and diesel are fossil fuels. Most vehicles use one of these.

QUESTIONS

1. What proportion of our energy needs do we get from fossil fuels?
2. What causes trees to die?
3. What could be done to reduce the amount of acid rain?
4. Why does burning fossil fuels make acid rain?

WANT TO KNOW MORE?

www.theaa.com has lots of information about exhaust emissions and 'green' cars.

...dissolve ...fossil fuels ...lime ...limestone

Why trees die

Acid rain washes important minerals out of the soil. Trees need these minerals for healthy growth. If they are missing, the trees eventually die. When acid rain falls on their leaves it strips off their waxy coating. This damages the leaves and stops them from photosynthesising. They turn yellow and fall off.

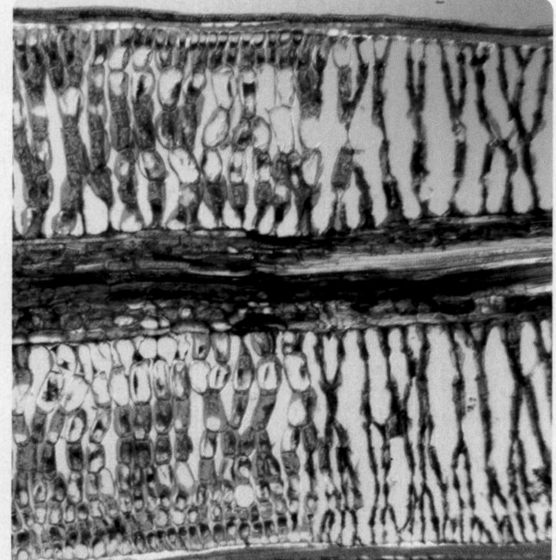

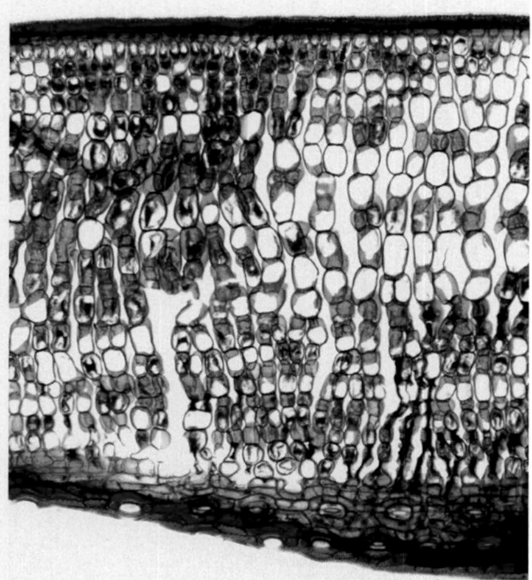

FIGURE 4: A cross section through a pine needle affected by acid rain (left) and a healthy one.

Why statues dissolve

Statues and buildings all suffer from the effect of acid rain. Water, wind, ice and snow all help to erode stone. As well as dissolving the rock, acid rain helps to make erosion happen more quickly. The worst affected things are made from **limestone** (see figure 5) and **sandstone**.

FIGURE 5: Why is this stone lion eroding away?

Acid lakes

Acid rain runs off the land and ends up in streams, rivers and lakes. It also falls directly into them. As the acidity increases, the fish, snails, shrimps and other water animals die. The eggs of the fish are also affected. The acidity can deform the young fish or prevent them from hatching properly.

People add **lime** to acid lakes to neutralise the effects of acid rain.

QUESTIONS

5 What effect does acid rain have on plants?

6 Why don't limestone statues last for ever?

7 Why do lakes become acidic?

8 What can be done to neutralise acid lakes?

Car exhaust emissions

If car engines were 100% efficient the only waste products would be carbon dioxide and water. Even though all new cars are fitted with catalytic converters and are much more efficient, they still produce polluting gases. Look at the table below, which shows the effects of the waste.

Exhaust content	Its effect
water	no harmful effect
carbon dioxide	greenhouse gas
carbon monoxide	prevents blood from carrying oxygen
nitrogen oxides	cause acid rain
sulfur dioxide	causes acid rain
benzene	can cause leukaemia
lead	affects nervous system – many cars now use unleaded petrol

Exhausts also give out oxygen and nitrogen which are normal constituents of the air.

QUESTIONS

9 Why do cars produce carbon dioxide and water?

10 Why do they produce the other gases?

11 Some cars are described as being 'ecologically friendly'. What does this mean?

12 Imagine a car manufacturer has designed a car engine that is 100% efficient. You have been asked to write a paragraph for a promotional leaflet explaining why people should buy this car.

Pollution indicators

You will find out:

- What pollution indicators are
- That lichens are air pollution indicators
- That invertebrates are water pollution indicators
- Why pollution indicators are useful

Anyone for a swim?

For hundreds of years the Thames was used as a dump for all sorts of waste. This cartoon is from 1855. It shows Michael Faraday, the famous British chemist, talking with 'Father Thames'. The smell of sewage and dead animals must have been overpowering, especially in the summer. London's sewage system was built from 1859–75. But is it good enough for today's needs?

FARADAY GIVING HIS CARD TO FATHER THAMES;
And we hope the Dirty Fellow will consult the learned Professor.

FIGURE 1: This cartoon says it all.

Pollution indicators

When a habitat is polluted, it changes. The organisms that normally live there will either die or move away. Sometimes other organisms move in. These have adaptations which let them live in polluted conditions.

Lichens are often used as indicators of sulfur dioxide **air pollution**. **Invertebrate animals** are often used as indicators of **water pollution**.

There are many different species of lichen. They tend to have one thing in common – they can't cope with sulfur dioxide.

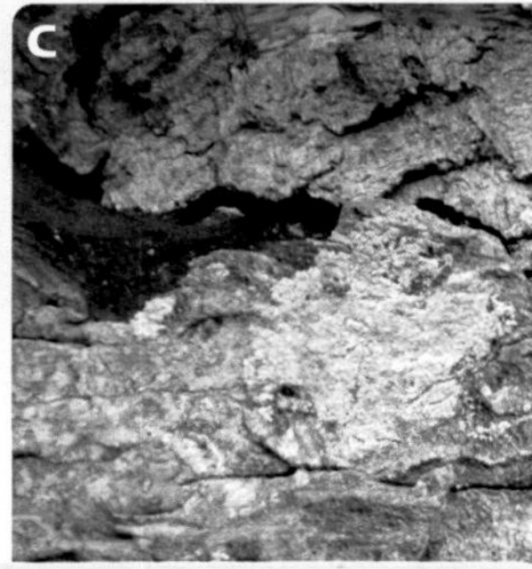

FIGURE 2: Lichens from an area with **A** clean air (no sulfur dioxide) **B** low levels of sulfur dioxide air pollution **C** high levels of sulfur dioxide air pollution.

Some invertebrates, like mayfly nymphs and rat-tailed maggots, are able to survive in polluted water. Others can't and die as the result of the pollution.

Here is what happens when a stream or river is polluted:

1. Pollutant is added, which kills some living things.
2. Microorganisms decompose them, they respire and use up the oxygen.
3. Lack of oxygen kills other organisms, but a few species stay alive.
4. As the water flows, oxygen levels gradually increase.
5. Other living things recover too.

The organisms in polluted water tell you that there is something wrong. These are the **pollution indicators**.

QUESTIONS

1. What are pollution indicators?
2. Look at figure 2 (**A**, **B** and **C**). What is the relationship between the lichen and the levels of sulfur dioxide pollution?
3. What happens to the invertebrates when water is polluted?
4. Describe what happens when a stream becomes polluted.

Sulfur dioxide, cities and lichens

A scientist surveyed the distribution of lichens. She counted the number of different species that grew on tree trunks at various distances from the centre of a polluted city. She also measured how much sulfur dioxide there was in the air. As she was collecting her results, she noticed that the lichen tended to grow on the dry parts of tree trunks only. Where the tree trunk was wet from rain, there were no lichens. Her results are shown in table 1.

Distance to the town centre (km)	0	1	2	3	4	5	6	7	8	9	10
Number of different species of lichen	0	1	2	6	8	10	30	44	51	56	56
SO_2 levels/ (arbitrary units)	180	160	145	119	93	71	49	35	11	5	0

TABLE 1: Sulfur dioxide levels and lichen growth as distance increases from polluted city centre.

Sewage pollution and invertebrates

Some invertebrates are able to live in sewage pollution and others are not.

Distance downstream from where sewage enters the river (m)	What the water is like	Invertebrates found (not drawn to scale)	Oxygen levels
Sewage enters here 0–10	dark and cloudy very smelly	Chironomous larva, rat-tailed maggot	falling quickly
10–100	cloudy bad smell	tubiflex worm (sludge worms), mosquito larva	very low
100–200	slight smell beginning to clear	flatworm, caddis fly larva	gradually rising
200+	clear	freshwater shrimp, mayfly larva, stonefly larva	back to normal

TABLE 2: The effects of untreated sewage in a river.

Scientists take samples of the animals living in a river to see if it is polluted. They use special nets with a fine mesh. If the holes in the mesh were too big some of the invertebrates would pass through and the scientists would not be able to judge how polluted the water really was.

QUESTIONS

5 Draw graphs of the data in table 1.

6 What is the relationship between the number of species of lichen and the distance from the centre of the city?

7 Name **one** invertebrate that can survive where there is little oxygen and another **one** that needs normal clear water to live in.

Pollution in the Thames

Over the last 30 years the water quality of the Thames has improved. Now over 120 species of fish inhabit the river. On the 4th August 2004, 100 000 fish were killed as raw sewage was accidentally washed into the River Thames. The sewage reduced the water's oxygen levels. In some parts of the river, where the water flows very slowly, oxygen levels fell to almost zero. This was the worst incident of this type of pollution since 1986. Fish, like invertebrates, are good pollution indicators. The authorities tried to **oxygenate** the river by using special boats that churn the water up. This helps some of the oxygen from the air dissolve in the water.

Over 120 species of fish now inhabit the Thames

QUESTIONS

8 Why did the oxygen levels fall?

9 What does the word oxygenate mean?

10 Why are fish considered to be good pollution indicators?

11 In your group, discuss what the authorities could do to prevent this sort of thing happening again.

Deforestation

You will find out:

- What deforestation is
- Why deforestation happens
- What the effects of deforestation are
- That many medicines originate from the world's rainforests

Once it's gone – it's gone!

We are losing rainforests at an alarming rate. Each year an area the size of Wales is cut down. Rainforest used to cover about 15% of the Earth. It's less than half that now. Scientists have estimated that the rest could be lost by 2050. Figure 3 shows the rainforests of the world.

What is deforestation?

Deforestation is the permanent clearing of forests. When people talk about deforestation they usually mean in relation to **tropical rainforests**. But it refers to the cutting down of forests anywhere. Britain experienced deforestation, but it was a very long time ago. Figures for England show that in 1086 there was about 15% woodland. Today it's about 8.5%.

FIGURE 1: Burning rainforest.

Why do it?

Tropical rainforests are cut down for two important reasons:

- to provide **timber** for building homes and furniture
- to clear the land for **agriculture** (farming).

Sometimes, when the forests are cleared for farmland, the trees are just **burned**.

Watch Out The greenhouse effect is not the same as global warming – it can lead to it.

Effects of deforestation

Green plants remove a lot of **carbon dioxide** from the air when they photosynthesise. When trees photosynthesise, they use some of the carbon dioxide to make wood.

Because of deforestation, less carbon dioxide is removed. This leads to an increase in the greenhouse effect which results in global warming. You can find out more about this on page 100. Of course burning trees also adds carbon dioxide to the air.

Wood contains a lot of carbon. As deforestation reduces the rate at which photosynthesis removes carbon dioxide form the air, it means that less carbon is 'locked up' as wood.

The loss of forests leads to a reduction in **biodiversity**. This means that:

- some species will die out – become **extinct**
- there will be less **variation** in the species that survive
- **habitats** will be lost.

Some of the species that become extinct like this could have been of use in the future.

QUESTIONS

1. What does deforestation mean?
2. Give **two** reasons why tropical rainforests are cut down.
3. What effect does deforestation have on carbon dioxide levels in the air?
4. Why is deforestation such bad news for the Earth?

EXAM HINTS AND TIPS

Be ready to explain how deforestation contributes to global warming.

Deforestation and the carbon cycle

Plants need carbon to make their food. They get it from the air. All living things produce carbon dioxide when they respire. The carbon cycle shows how carbon goes from one living thing to another. It also shows how this relationship can be disrupted by human activity.

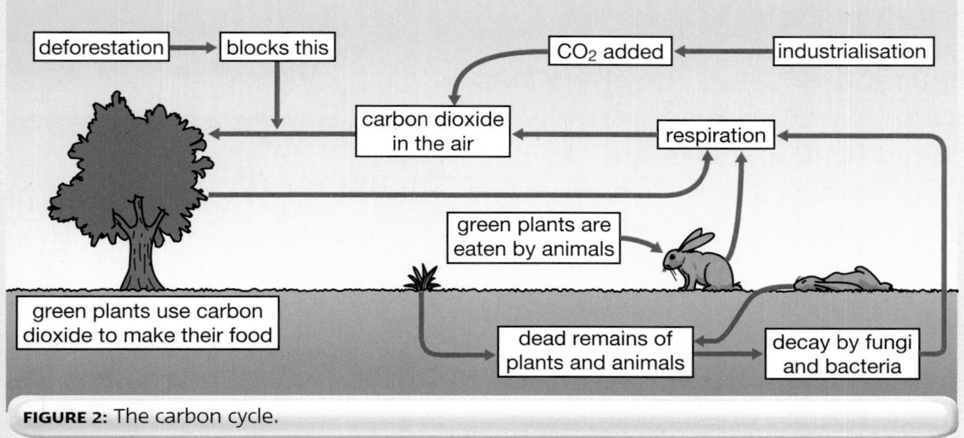

FIGURE 2: The carbon cycle.

Garden furniture, paper pulp and chopsticks

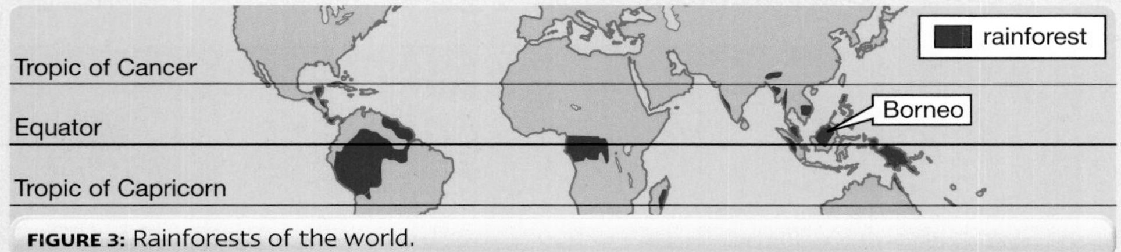

FIGURE 3: Rainforests of the world.

Borneo is the third biggest island in the world. Great Britain would easily fit into it three times! Originally 75% of Borneo was covered in dense tropical rainforest. But in the last 20 years it has undergone a massive change. So much rainforest has been either cut down or burned that now only half is left. The land has been cleared for palm oil plantations. Palm oil is used for cooking as well as in the manufacture of soap, cosmetics, chocolates and candles.

The rainforest that has not been burned has been cut into logs and exported to Japan and the United States. The timber is used to make:

- garden furniture
- paper pulp (for paper production)
- disposable chopsticks.

The global impact of this forest destruction is that carbon dioxide levels in the air will go up. The local impact is that natural habitat is lost. There are over 40 species of mammals that live only in Borneo. So, for example, the population of orang-utans is likely to die out.

QUESTIONS

5 What are the **two** processes that keep the carbon cycle balanced?

6 What can people do to disrupt the carbon cycle?

7 Why is the Borneo rainforest being cut down?

8 What could be done to protect the wild population of orang-utans?

Rainforest timber is used to make disposable chopsticks

The world's natural pharmacy

It has been estimated that about 25% of all medicines originate from the world's rainforests. Many of these medicines have anti-cancer properties. The Madagascar periwinkle contains chemicals which are used in chemotherapy for some forms of leukaemia. These chemicals are particularly useful in the treatment of children. Some scientists and doctors believe that we should look to the rainforests if we are to find a cure for HIV/AIDS.

FIGURE 4: The Madagascar periwinkle – used in cancer treatment.

QUESTIONS

9 Why have rainforests been called 'The Pharmacy of the World'?

10 Parliament is about to discuss its position on deforestation. Your MP is not convinced about the importance of rainforests. Write a letter to her which will persuade her of their value to medicine.

...extinct ...habitats ...timber ...tropical rainforest ...variation

The greenhouse effect – good or bad?

You will find out:

- What the greenhouse effect is
- What causes this effect
- That global warming is the consequence of the greenhouse effect

The greenhouse effect on Venus

The surface temperature of Venus is about 460 °C. It is the greenhouse effect that has made the temperature so high. The atmosphere is 96.5% **carbon dioxide**. This traps a lot of heat. The average temperature on Earth is about 21 °C and there is 0.04% carbon dioxide in our atmosphere. The level of carbon dioxide is slowly increasing.

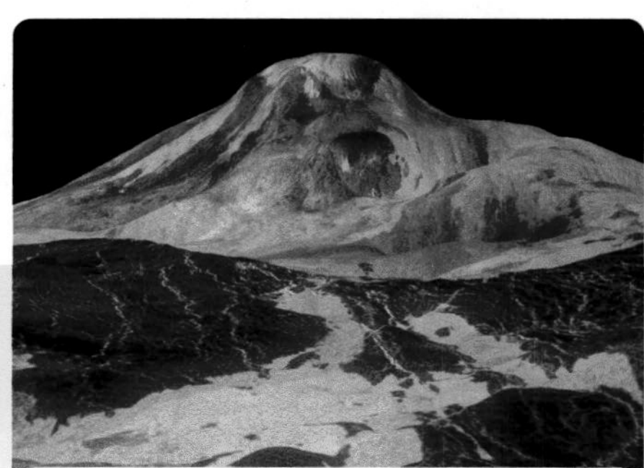

FIGURE 1: A mountain on Venus – clearly too hot for ice caps.

What is the greenhouse effect?

Some gases in the air trap heat from the Sun. This warms the **atmosphere** which heats up the Earth. The gases act like the glass in a greenhouse. Just as the glass traps the heat in a greenhouse so these gases trap the heat around the Earth. That's why it's called the **greenhouse effect**. As the greenhouse effect increases we get **global warming**.

Two important **greenhouse gases** are responsible for this:

- carbon dioxide
- methane.

If it wasn't for the greenhouse effect the temperature of the Earth would be about 35 °C colder than it is. It would be about -20 °C. So the greenhouse effect actually keeps the Earth warm enough for normal life to exist.

The problem is that we are adding more greenhouse gases to the air. Gradually this is making the temperature go up. The extra carbon dioxide comes from burning fossil fuels. The **methane** comes from increased numbers of cattle and rice fields.

Global warming will result in: flooding, storms, and droughts.

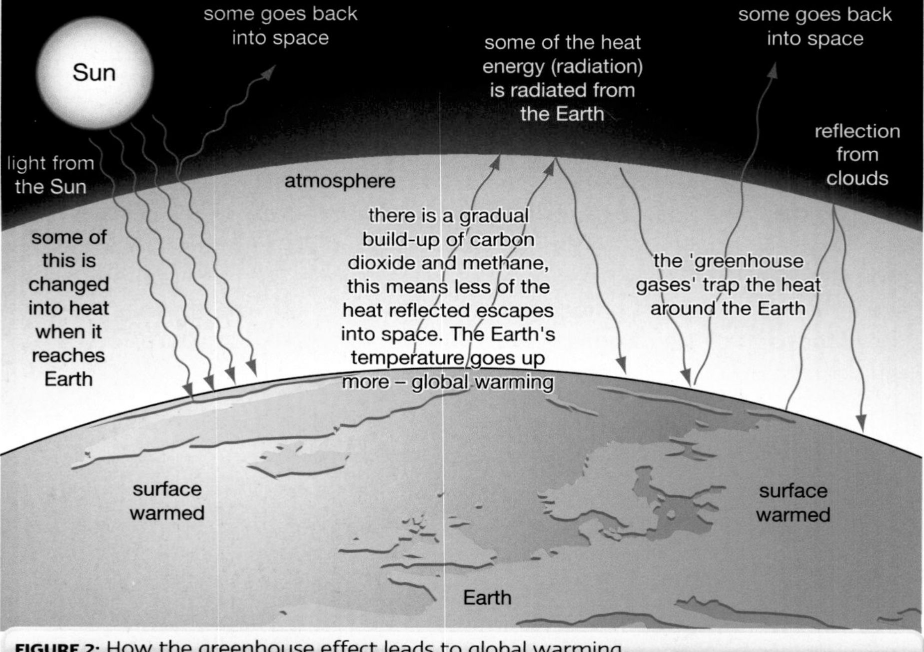
Sun
some goes back into space
some of the heat energy (radiation) is radiated from the Earth
some goes back into space
reflection from clouds
light from the Sun
atmosphere
some of this is changed into heat when it reaches Earth
there is a gradual build-up of carbon dioxide and methane, this means less of the heat reflected escapes into space. The Earth's temperature goes up more – global warming
the 'greenhouse gases' trap the heat around the Earth
surface warmed
surface warmed
Earth

FIGURE 2: How the greenhouse effect leads to global warming.

Cutting down forests is called deforestation. Trees photosynthesise, which removes carbon dioxide from the air. Deforestation adds to the problem of increased carbon dioxide levels in the air. You can find out more about deforestation on page 98.

QUESTIONS

1. What are the greenhouse gases and where do they come from?
2. What is the greenhouse effect?
3. Give **two** effects that global warming will have?
4. What should be done to reduce global warming?

...atmosphere ...carbon dioxide ...global warming

Carbon dioxide levels in the atmosphere

By looking at the air trapped in the Antarctic, ice scientists are able to measure carbon dioxide levels from the past. The deeper the ice comes from, the older it is. What the scientists have found was that in the last 250 years the carbon dioxide level has gradually increased. It was about 270 parts per million (that's 0.027%). Since then it has increased. Figure 3 shows carbon dioxide levels over the last 300 years.

Global warming

The Earth has been gradually getting warmer. Your summer holidays are warmer now than summer holidays were 100 years ago. Look at figure 4 to see how the temperature has increased over the last 300 years.

But global warming is a big problem. It melts the snow and ice from the polar ice-caps as well as from high mountain ranges. All the melted water eventually flows into the sea. Sea levels rise which means that coastal areas are flooded. This rise in sea level is also due to water expanding when it is heated. Engineers have built defences against rising sea levels.

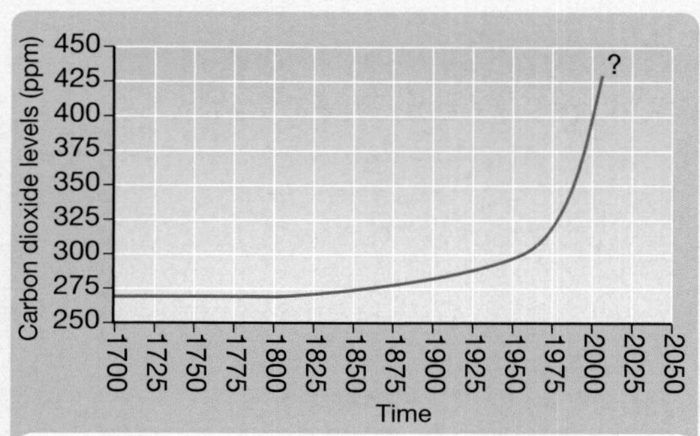

FIGURE 3: Carbon dioxide concentrations in the atmosphere.

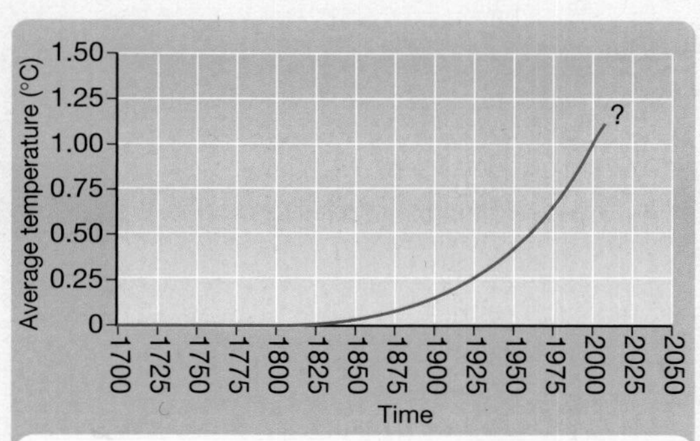

FIGURE 4: Increases in temperature over the last 300 years.

The rise in sea level is also due to water expanding when it is heated

FIGURE 5: The Thames Barrier – can it continue protecting London from flooding?

QUESTIONS

5 By how much have the carbon dioxide levels risen in the last 250 years?

6 What has caused these levels to rise?

7 Look at Figures 3 and 4. What is the relationship between the carbon dioxide levels and global warming?

8 Why will low-lying land flood?

Methane from rice paddies

FIGURE 6: Rice field or methane factory?

Between 50 and 100 million tonnes a year of methane are released into the atmosphere from rice paddy fields.

Methane is a very important greenhouse gas. It is about 21 times more potent than carbon dioxide. This methane is produced by bacteria (anaerobic bacteria as they don't need oxygen to survive). They live in the soil where rice grows.

It has been found that as a consequence of draining paddy fields for part of the rice growing season, two things happen:

- more rice is produced
- less methane is released into the air.

Rice is a staple food for hundreds of millions of people in the developing world. Draining paddy fields in the middle of the rice-growing season is not a traditional practice.

QUESTIONS

9 Imagine you are a rice farmer. Which of the **two** consequences of draining paddy fields is more important to you? Explain why.

10 Now imagine you are a government official working on the Reduce Global Warming Committee. Which of the two consequences is more important to you? Explain your answer.

Sustainability – the way forward?

You will find out:

- What sustainability is
- That improving the quality of life involves sustainability
- Sustainability involves recycling, more energy-efficient homes and changes to transport use

You look flushed

We all need clean water. In Britain each one of us uses about 125 litres each day, that's about 45 000 litres a year. About a third of this we flush down the toilet. Most of the rest we use for washing and cooking with.

Sustainable development

The world's population is increasing. This is resulting in the **natural resources** also being used up at an increasing rate. We all need to find ways of **conserving** these.

Improving the quality of everyone's life without damaging either the environment or the future chances of **survival**, is known as **sustainable development**.

Sustainable development has to be planned for at all levels of our society: locally; regionally; nationally; globally. There are lots of things that we can do.

Recycling

We need to see waste as a **resource** rather than a problem. Most towns and cities now have the facilities to **recycle** glass, paper, aluminium (cans) and rags (old clothes). It is possible to recycle other things too.

Energy efficient homes

Keeping your home warm is expensive, especially in winter. So what can be done to keep the heat in? **Insulation** is the answer (see figure 1).

Your home can be insulated using: double glazing; draught-proofing around the front door; curtains in the windows.

FIGURE 1: This thermogram shows heat loss as red and yellow, insulation as blue.

Walking and cycling

Most car journeys in Britain are very short, less than 3 km. That's a 30-minute walk. Often cars have only one or two people in them. Walking and cycling are better for your fitness levels and the environment.

Public transport

One bus can take 60 to 70 people. That's the equivalent of about 50 cars.

QUESTIONS

1. What does sustainable development mean?
2. Apart from what is listed above, name **three** more things that can be recycled.
3. Which natural resources will be conserved by insulating your home and using public transport?
4. Suggest why so many people go by car rather than by public transport.

...conserve ...insulation ...natural resource ...recycle

Carbon dioxide and you

Carbon dioxide is a greenhouse gas. It is produced when things are burned. Fossil fuels (coal, oil and gas) are often used as the fuel for power stations. Power stations provide the electricity we use every day. The table compares the amount of carbon dioxide produced by the different types of power station.

FIGURE 2: A power station – is it part of sustainable development?

Type of power station	Carbon dioxide produced (tonnes)
coal-fired	11 million
oil-fired	9 million
natural gas-fired	6 million
nuclear-powered	none
wind turbine	none
hydroelectric (from rivers)	none
wave power	none

Another very important source of carbon dioxide is the combustion of petrol in cars and other vehicles. So how much carbon dioxide are you responsible for? The table below summarises how much carbon dioxide a typical family is likely to produce each year.

Source of production	Carbon dioxide produced (tonnes)
electricity used	1.9
gas heating	2.7
petrol	5.0*
Total	9.6

(* this will depend on the type of vehicle – it could be as high as 10 tonnes)

QUESTIONS

5 Which type of fossil fuel power station produces the least carbon dioxide?

6 Give **one** advantage and **one** disadvantage of using nuclear power stations.

7 List **three** things that you could start doing today that would reduce the amount of carbon dioxide being produced.

8 What have car manufacturers been doing to reduce carbon dioxide emissions?

U-values

Architects and builders use 'U-values' and a formula to calculate heat loss from a house. The smaller the U-value, the better the insulator and the less energy is lost.

The formula is:

heat energy loss in watts (J/second) = U-value × area (m^2) × temperature difference

You have to know:

- U-values (see table below)
- the area through which heat energy is lost (m^2)
- the difference in temperature between inside the house and outside the house (°C).

The house that Jack built

The average temperature difference between the inside of the house and the outside is 17 °C.

Structure	U-values
tiled roof without insulation	2.0
tiled roof with insulation	0.3
cavity wall without insulation	1.4
cavity wall with foam insulation	0.4
single-glazed window	5.7
double-glazed window	2.9

QUESTIONS

9 A roof measures 12 m by 11 m. How much heat would be saved if it was insulated?

10 The single-glazed windows in a house have an area of 4 m^2. The double-glazed windows have an area of 5 m^2. How much energy is lost through the windows?

11 List as many other ways in which heat energy can be lost from Jack's house as you can.

Unit summary

Concept map

Animal and plant adaptations

- Colour is used as an adaptation for survival in number of ways: camouflage, mimicry, and danger colouring.
- Plants need to be able to conserve water.
- Animals, such as hoe camels, caribou and foxes, have had to adapt to a variety of extreme environments.

Reproduction and genes

- There are two types of reproduction: asexual and sexual reproduction.
- Genetic engineering produces a totally unique set of genes. Genetically modified organisms have medical applications.
- DNA is the genetic material that controls our inherited characteristics. In most cells, it is found in the form of chromosomes.
- Cloning takes place in nature but can also happen as a result of human intervention, through tissue cultures or embryo transplants for example.

Evolution

- Ideas about evolution have developed over time.
- Charles Darwin and Alfred Russel Wallace both proposed theories of evolution by Natural Selection.
- There are a number of factors that can contribute to the extinction of a species, including impact of man and climate change.
- Fossils can tell us about evolution and the similarities and differences between prehistoric and present day species.

Our impact on the environment

- Sustainable development is development that improves our quality of life without compromising future generations.
- Land has a number of different uses: farming, building, quarrying and waste disposal.
- Burning fossil fuels causes acid rain pollution. Deforestation increases carbon dioxide levels.
- The growth of the human population is affecting the environment.
- Lichens and invertebrates can be used as pollution indicators.
- The greenhouse effect can lead to global warming.

Unit quiz

1 List **three** ways in which plants are adapted to life in the desert.

2 Explain why living things need to be adapted.

3 Which type of reproduction makes clones?

4 How can genetic engineering help diabetics?

5 Why do children not look exactly like one of their parents?

6 Why are cuttings clones?

7 What does 'extinct' mean?

8 What is the difference between Darwin's and Lamarck's theories of evolution?

9 What is pollution?

10 What effect does acid rain have on living things?

11 What effect is deforestation having on the environment?

12 What is the relationship between the greenhouse effect and global warming?

13 What does 'sustainable development' mean?

Literacy activity

Rubbish

The key date was 16 July 2004. On this day the EU Landfill Directive brought radical change to the way hazardous waste was to be defined, treated and disposed of. Broadly speaking, 'hazardous' and 'special' waste is material liable to cause death, injury or illness to people who touch it, or that can damage the environment. Until the summer of 2004, England and Wales annually produced some 5 million tonnes of such waste, of which a little under half went into landfill. At midnight on 15 July, however, everything changed. It was no longer lawful for hazardous and non-hazardous waste to be mixed in the same landfill. As the clock struck twelve, the number of sites allowed to receive 'special' material fell from about 240 to fewer than ten.

(Taken from: 'Rubbish' by Richard Girling 2005)

QUESTIONS

1 What does the word 'radical' mean?

2 Why was the EU Landfill Directive made law?

3 What do you think were the consequences of this law?

Exam practice

Exam practice questions

1 Match the words, A, B, C and D, with the spaces 1–4 in the passage below.

A insulation **B** tolerate
C adaptations **D** conserve

Camels live in dry desert conditions. The camel's long eyelashes and closable nostrils are (1) to keep out wind-blown sand. Dry mucus within the nose helps to (2) water by trapping it before it is breathed out. The camel's fur is thick, providing (3) against both extreme hot and cold temperatures of the desert. The camel can (4) water loss of up to 25% of its body weight. [4]

2 There is a range of methods available to produce new, cloned offspring from organisms, using asexual reproduction.

Match the letters A, B, C and D with the descriptions 1–4 below.

A Adult cell cloning **B** Tissue culture
C Cuttings **D** Embryo transplants

1	Replacing the nucleus of an egg cell with a nucleus from a developed cell. The resulting cell is placed into a host mother, where it develops into a new individual.
2	Small groups of undeveloped cells are added to a nutrient medium, then treated with hormones to produce a new individual.
3	Splitting cells apart from an embryo, then placing the cells into a host mother, where it develops into a new individual.
4	A piece of stem is removed and treated with hormones to promote root growth. It develops into a new plant.

[4]

3 The diagram shows adaptations of a water lily plant to its habitat.

Match the letters A, B, C and D with the descriptions 1–4 below.

A Underwater leaf **B** Floating flower
C Stem buried in mud **D** Floating leaf

1	Stomata on upper surface allow gas exchange with air
2	Allows pollination by flying insects
3	Absorbs minerals from the surrounding water
4	Anchors the plant and also stores food

[4]

4 The graph shows the number of butterflies at different distances from the edge of a grassland habitat.

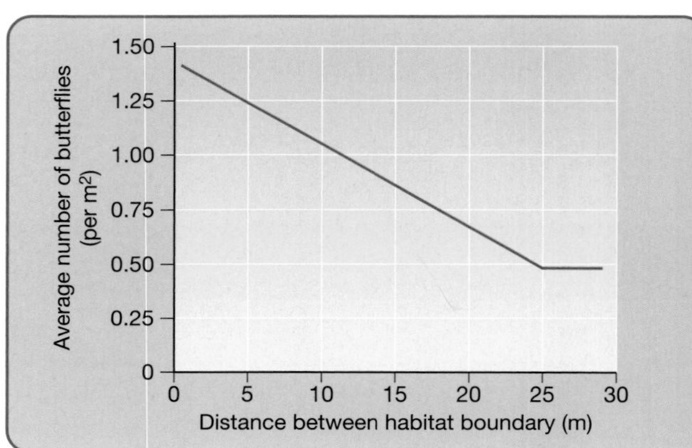

a What is the average number of butterflies found at 5 m from the edge of the grassland?

A 1.20 **B** 0.78 **C** 1.24 **D** 1.00 [1]

b The most suitable conclusion for the results shown in the graph is:

A As the distance from the edge of the grassland increases, the number of butterflies decreases at a constant rate

B As the distance from the edge of the grassland increases, the number of butterflies increases at a constant rate

C As the distance from the edge of the grassland increases, the number of butterflies increases, then stays constant

D As the distance from the edge of the grassland increases, the number of butterflies decreases, then stays constant [1]

(Total 14 marks)

Worked example

The graph shows the populations of two species of a micro-organism, called *Paramecium*, each grown in **separate** containers.

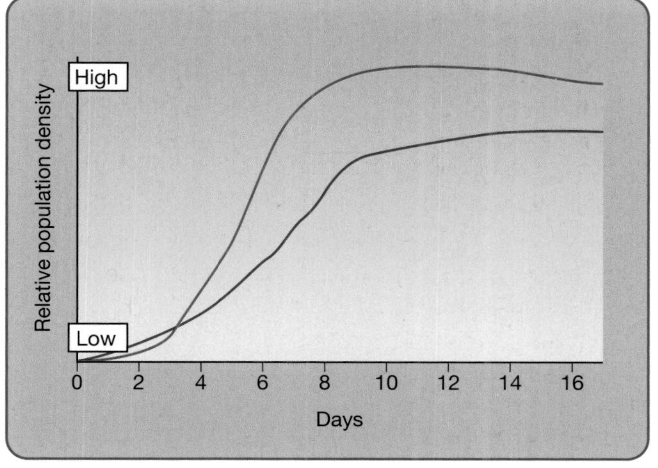

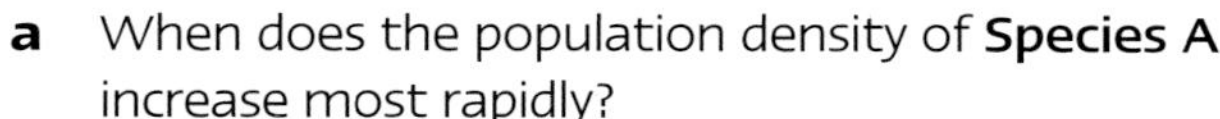

a When does the population density of **Species A** increase most rapidly?

A 2 – 10 days
B 5 – 8 days
C 8 – 10 days
D 3 – 5 days [1]

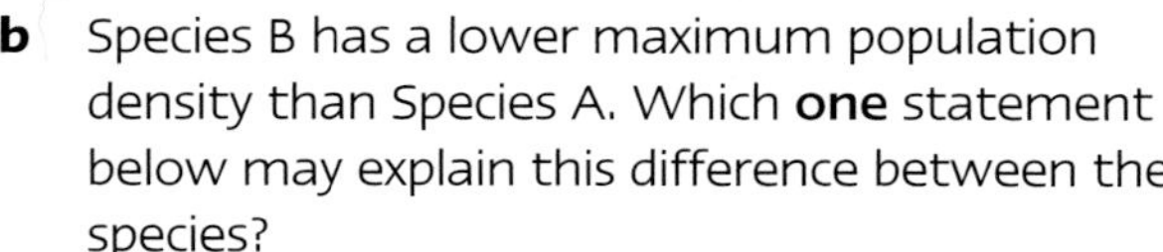

b Species B has a lower maximum population density than Species A. Which **one** statement below may explain this difference between the species?

A Species A tolerates higher population densities, compared with Species B
B Species B tolerates higher population densities, compared with Species A
C Species B has more space to live in, compared with Species A
D Species A has more space to live in, compared with Species B [1]

c For each species, growing in its own container, intra-species competition is occurring. What is the evidence for this?

A The graph for Species A goes higher than the graph for Species B
B The graph for Species B goes higher than the graph for Species A
C The size of both populations increases with time
D The size of both populations does not rise above a certain density [1]

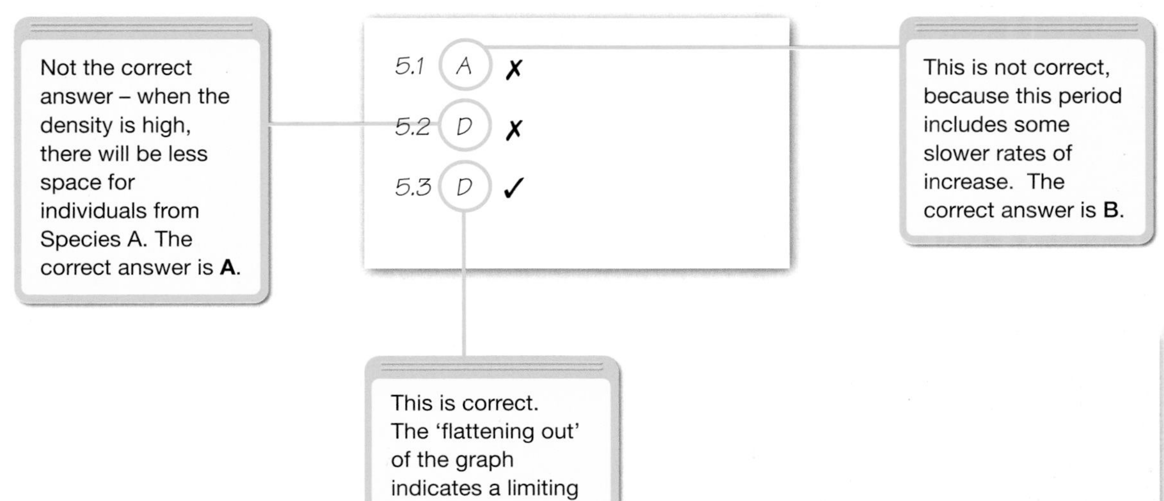

Not the correct answer – when the density is high, there will be less space for individuals from Species A. The correct answer is **A**.
5.1 A ✗
5.2 D ✗
5.3 D ✓
This is not correct, because this period includes some slower rates of increase. The correct answer is **B**.
This is correct. The 'flattening out' of the graph indicates a limiting factor, e.g. space.

Overall Grade: D

How to get an A

Make sure you get plenty of revision practice in analysing population graphs, and read all options carefully before answering.

Chemistry 1a – Products from rocks

DISCOVER DIAMONDS!

'Diamond' comes from the Greek word *adamas*, meaning 'unconquerable'. Its name reflects the fact that it is the hardest natural substance in the world.

Many tiny diamonds have been discovered in space. Scientists believe that they were formed when stars exploded.

Diamonds are just one of the useful products that we get from rocks. Diamonds consist of the element carbon. They form under intense pressure and extremely high temperatures deep underground. Diamonds only come to the Earth's surface via volcanoes.

A well-cut diamond appears to sparkle.

The carbon atoms in diamond are held together by strong covalent bonds.

CONTENTS

Elements and the periodic table

You will find out:
- That all substances are made of atoms
- What is meant by an element
- About the periodic table

Gold

The element gold has been known and prized since prehistoric times. It does not tarnish and is often used to make jewellery. Pure gold would be too soft for most jewellery and it is often mixed with other metals like silver or copper. The purity of the gold is then measured using the carat system. A rating of one carat means that the metal contains one part gold and 23 parts of other metals.

FIGURE 1: Unreactive metals like gold are found in the Earth.

What is an element?

All substances are made of tiny **particles** called **atoms**. An **element** contains just one type of atom. So all atoms of the element gold are alike, but they are different from the atoms of any other element. So far, we have discovered just over one hundred different elements.

Patterns in the elements

As new elements were discovered, scientists found that some groups of elements had similar properties to one another. They tried to find ways of showing the relationships between elements with similar properties. A huge breakthrough came when Dimitri Mendeleev, a Russian chemist, arranged the elements in something we now call the **periodic table**.

Look carefully at the periodic table in figure 3. Each vertical column is made up of elements with similar properties to one another. These vertical columns are called **groups**. The rows are called **periods**.

The first column is called Group 1. It's also known as the **Alkali Metals** and includes the elements lithium, sodium and potassium. These are metals that react quickly with water to form alkaline solutions and give off hydrogen gas.

FIGURE 2: All the metals in Group 1 react in a similar way.

The noble gases are in Group 0. They are all chemically unreactive, and are used in filament lamps and electric discharge tubes. Helium is much less dense than air and is used in balloons.

QUESTIONS

1 What is special about an element?
2 How many different types of element are there?
3 What is special about elements in the same vertical column?

WANT TO KNOW MORE?

For an interactive periodic table, visit www.chemsoc.org/viselements/

Why are the elements arranged in this order?

We arrange the elements in the modern periodic table in order of increasing **atomic number**. The atomic number tells you how many protons there are in the nucleus of an atom. We will look at this in the next lesson.

Hydrogen has an atomic number of one. All hydrogen atoms have one proton. The second element, helium, has an atomic number of two. All helium atoms have two protons. And so on.

The properties of an element depend on its atomic number. Elements with similar properties occur periodically and are found in the same vertical group.

Group I	Group II											Group III	Group IV	Group V	Group VI	Group VII	0
			$^{1}_{1}$H hydrogen														$^{4}_{2}$He helium
$^{7}_{3}$Li lithium	$^{9}_{4}$Be beryllium											$^{11}_{5}$B boron	$^{12}_{6}$C carbon	$^{14}_{7}$N nitrogen	$^{16}_{8}$O oxygen	$^{19}_{9}$F flourine	$^{20}_{10}$Ne neon
$^{23}_{11}$Na sodium	$^{24}_{12}$Mg magnesium											$^{27}_{13}$Al aluminium	$^{28}_{14}$Si silicon	$^{31}_{15}$P phosphorus	$^{32}_{16}$S sulfur	$^{35}_{17}$Cl chlorine	$^{40}_{18}$Ar argon
$^{39}_{19}$K potassium	$^{40}_{20}$Ca calcium	$^{45}_{21}$Sc scandium	$^{48}_{22}$Ti titanium	$^{51}_{23}$V vanadium	$^{52}_{24}$Cr chromium	$^{55}_{25}$Mn manganese	$^{56}_{26}$Fe iron	$^{59}_{27}$Co cobalt	$^{59}_{28}$Ni nickel	$^{64}_{29}$Cu copper	$^{65}_{30}$Zn zinc	$^{70}_{31}$Ga gallium	$^{73}_{32}$Ge germanium	$^{75}_{33}$As arsenic	$^{79}_{34}$Se selenium	$^{80}_{35}$Br bromine	$^{84}_{36}$Kr krypton
$^{85}_{37}$Rb rubidium	$^{88}_{38}$Sr strontium	$^{89}_{39}$Y yttrium	$^{91}_{40}$Zr zirconium	$^{93}_{41}$Nb niobium	$^{96}_{42}$Mo molybdenum	$^{99}_{43}$Tc technetium	$^{101}_{44}$Ru ruthenium	$^{103}_{45}$Rh rhodium	$^{106}_{46}$Pd palladium	$^{108}_{47}$Ag silver	$^{112}_{48}$Cd cadmium	$^{115}_{49}$In indium	$^{119}_{50}$Sn tin	$^{122}_{51}$Sb antimony	$^{128}_{52}$Te tellurium	$^{127}_{53}$I iodine	$^{131}_{54}$Xe xenon
$^{133}_{55}$Cs caesium	$^{137}_{56}$Ba barium	$^{139}_{57}$La lanthanum	$^{178}_{72}$Hf hafnium	$^{181}_{73}$Ta tantalum	$^{184}_{74}$W tungsten	$^{186}_{75}$Re rhenium	$^{190}_{76}$Os osmium	$^{192}_{77}$Ir iridium	$^{195}_{78}$Pt platinum	$^{197}_{79}$Au gold	$^{201}_{80}$Hg mercury	$^{204}_{81}$Tl thallium	$^{207}_{82}$Pb lead	$^{209}_{83}$Bi bismuth	$^{210}_{84}$Po polonium	$^{210}_{85}$At astatine	$^{222}_{86}$Rn radon
$^{223}_{87}$Fr francium	$^{226}_{88}$Ra radium	$^{227}_{89}$Ac actinium															

FIGURE 3: How are the elements arranged in the modern periodic table?

Typische Elemente							
			K = 39	Rb = 85	Cs = 133	—	—
			Ca = 40	Sr = 87	Ba = 137	—	—
			—	?Yt = 88?	?Di = 138?	Er = 178?	—
			Ti = 48?	Zr = 90	Ce = 140?	?La = 180?	Th = 231
			V = 51	Nb = 94	—	Ta = 182	—
			Cr = 52	Mo = 96	—	W = 184	U = 240
			Mn = 55	—	—	—	—
			Fe = 56	Ru = 104	—	Os = 195?	—
			Co = 59	Rh = 104	—	Ir = 197	—
			Ni = 59	Pd = 106	—	Pt = 198?	—
H = 1	Li = 7	Na = 23	Cu = 63	Ag = 108	—	Au = 199?	—
	Be = 9,4	Mg = 24	Zn = 65	Cd = 112	—	Hg = 200	—
	B = 11	Al = 27,3	—	In = 113	—	Tl = 204	—
	C = 12	Si = 28	—	Sn = 118	—	Pb = 207	—
	N = 14	P = 31	As = 75	Sb = 122	—	Bi = 208	—
	O = 16	S = 32	Se = 78	Te = 125?	—	—	—
	F = 19	Cl = 35,5	Br = 80	J = 127	—	—	—

FIGURE 4: How is the modern periodic table different from Mendeleev's original periodic table?

Why are there differences between the modern periodic table and Mendeleev's table?

Mendeleev's table contains fewer elements than a modern periodic table. This is because many elements had not yet been discovered. For example, Mendeleev's table doesn't include any elements from Group 0. These elements (also called the Noble Gases) were discovered later.

The brilliance of Mendeleev is shown by the gaps he left in his table – in anticipation of new elements being discovered. And he made detailed predictions about the properties of the elements that would fill these gaps. The later discovery of the 'missing' elements, with the properties Mendeleev predicted, showed that his ideas were correct.

QUESTIONS

4 How are the elements arranged in the modern periodic table?

5 Why are there gaps in Mendeleev's table?

6 Explain why scientists accepted that Mendeleev's ideas were correct.

Swapping the order

When Dimitri Mendeleev organised the elements into his periodic table he did not use the elements' atomic numbers, as we do today. Atomic numbers had not been discovered. Instead he placed the elements in order of increasing atomic mass. However, Mendeleev realised that sometimes he would have to be flexible about the exact order. Atoms of the element tellurium have a greater mass than atoms of the element iodine, so tellurium should be placed after iodine in Group 7 and iodine should be in Group 6. But when Mendeleev looked at the properties of the elements he realised that tellurium fitted much better into Group 6 and iodine fitted much better into Group 7. So he made the brave decision to swap the order of these two elements. By looking at their properties and not just their masses Mendeleev had actually placed the elements in order of increasing atomic number just as we do today.

QUESTIONS

7 Argon is heavier than potassium. When Mendeleev organised his table, why did he not include the element argon?

8 If he had included argon, how would he have been able to place it in the correct order?

Atomic structure

You will find out:

- That atoms of an element can be represented by a symbol
- That atoms have a central nucleus surrounded by shells of electrons

Mysterious mercury

Mercury is the only metallic element in the periodic table that is a liquid at room temperature. It has fascinated people since ancient times. Alchemists believed that mercury could be changed into gold! We now know that this is impossible, but alchemists tried to do it for hundreds of years. Mercury gets its symbol from its Latin name hydragyrum, or liquid silver.

FIGURE 1: Why is mercury such an interesting element?

How do elements get their symbols?

Each **element** can be represented by a symbol. This is a unique one or two letter code for the element.

Often the symbol is the first letter of the element's name, e.g.

- hydrogen is represented by the symbol H
- sulfur is represented by the symbol S.

Occasionally, an element takes its symbol from its Latin name, e.g.

- sodium is represented by the symbol Na, from its Latin name Natrium
- potassium is represented by the symbol K, from its Latin name Kalium.

Some elements start with the same letter. When this happens, we use the first letter plus another letter from the element's name, e.g.

- chlorine is represented by the symbol Cl
- chromium is represented by the symbol Cr.

Watch Out Protons and neutrons are so small that we do not measure their mass using grams, but instead use atomic mass units.

What is inside an atom?

Atoms are incredibly small. But scientists have discovered a lot about what's inside an atom. At the centre of each atom there is a **nucleus**. This contains **protons** and **neutrons**. The nucleus is surrounded by **electrons**. These move around the nucleus in energy levels called shells.

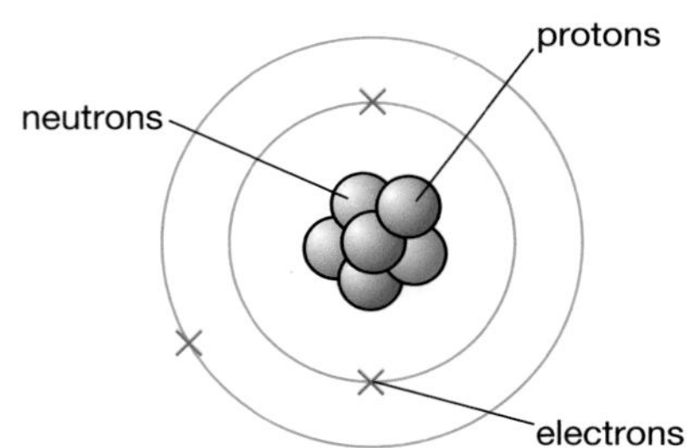

FIGURE 2: Which particles are found inside the nucleus?

QUESTIONS

1 Which element has the symbol O?
2 What is the centre of an atom called?
3 Which particles are found in the nucleus of an atom?

Properties of protons, neutrons and electrons

Protons, neutrons and electrons are unimaginably small. It's impossible to weigh them. However, we can measure their masses relative to one another. Sometimes we use **atomic mass units** to do this. Some particles also have a charge.

particle	relative mass	charge
proton	1	positive
neutron	1	neutral
electron	0.00055 (negligible)	negative

Any atom of any element always has the same number of protons as electrons. Furthermore, the number of protons and electrons is always the same for all atoms of a particular element. This number is called the element's atomic number. Each element has its own unique atomic number.

How are the electrons arranged?

Electrons are arranged around the nucleus in energy levels called shells.

- The first shell can hold up to two electrons.
- The second shell can hold up to eight electrons.
- The third shell can hold up to 18 electrons, but after eight electrons have been added, the next electron goes into the fourth shell.

The way the electrons are arranged in these shells is called the **electronic configuration**.

Sodium has 11 electrons. There are:

- two electrons in the first shell
- eight electrons in the second shell
- one electron in the third shell.

All atoms of a particular element have the same number of protons and electrons

QUESTIONS

4 Which particle found inside an atom has a positive charge?

5 If an element had seven electrons, what would its electronic configuration be?

6 If an element had 13 electrons, what would its electronic configuration be?

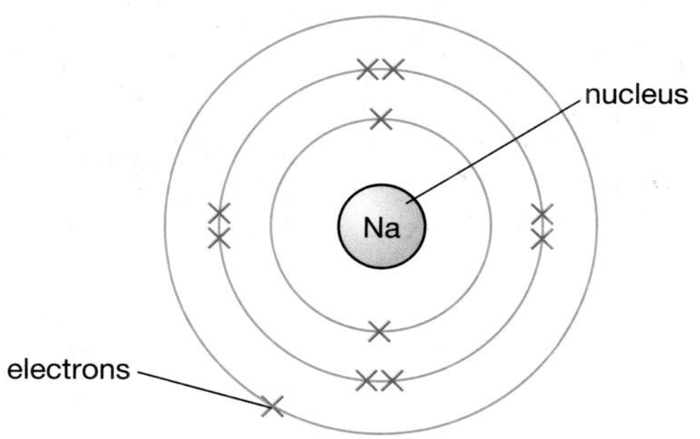

FIGURE 3: Sodium has two electrons in the first shell, eight in the second shell and one in the third shell. This gives it the electronic configuration 2,8,1.

Why is electronic configuration so important?

The elements lithium, sodium and potassium are in Group 1 of the periodic table. They react with water in a similar way to one another. Their other chemical properties are also similar. Why?

- The atomic number of lithium is 3. So each atom has three protons and three electrons. Its electronic configuration is 2,1.
- The atomic number of sodium is 11. Its electronic configuration is 2,8,1.
- The atomic number of potassium is 19. Its electronic configuration is 2,8,8,1.

All three elements have just one electron in their outer shell. They react in a similar way because they have the same number of electrons in their outer shell.

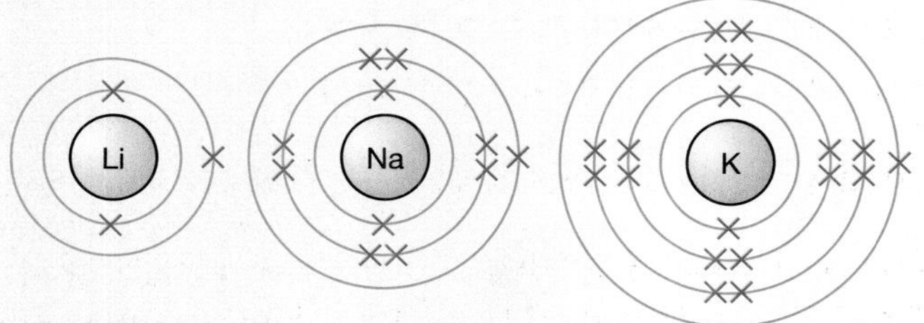

FIGURE 4: All these atoms have just one electron in their outer shell.

QUESTIONS

7 Work out the electron configuration of atoms of beryllium, magnesium and calcium. Would you expect them all to react in a similar way? Explain your answer.

Bonding

You will find out:

- That atoms of one element can join with atoms of another element to form a compound
- That atoms can join together by sharing electrons or by giving and taking electrons

Walking on water

This amazing Jesus Christ lizard appears to walk on water. But this is not really a miracle. It is made possible because there are forces of attraction not only between each of the atoms in a water molecule, but also between water molecules.

FIGURE 1: How can this lizard walk on water?

Molecules of an element

Many **elements** never exist as single **atoms**. Instead, two or more atoms join together to form **molecules**. We are surrounded by air, which is mainly a mixture of nitrogen molecules and oxygen molecules. Nitrogen molecules consist of two nitrogen atoms joined together, while oxygen molecules consist of two oxygen atoms joined together. The atoms are held together by shared pairs of **electrons**. This is called a **covalent bond**.

Molecules of a compound

Often atoms of two or more different elements join together to form **compounds** by sharing electrons. Water is a compound made when an oxygen atom shares two pairs of electrons, one pair with each of two hydrogen atoms.

FIGURE 2: What happens to the electrons when magnesium burns?

Ionic compounds

When we heat the metal magnesium, it reacts with oxygen in the air to form the compound magnesium oxide. However, magnesium and oxygen atoms do not share electrons to form covalent bonds. So magnesium oxide does not consist of molecules. When a metal reacts with a non-metal, electrons are transferred from the metal atom to the non-metal atom. This leaves both the metal atom and the non-metal atom with a charge. We call these **ions** instead of atoms. Metal ions always have a positive charge, and non-metal ions always have a negative charge. The **attraction** between these oppositely charged ions holds the compound together. This is an **ionic bond**.

QUESTIONS

1. What is a molecule?
2. What is a covalent bond?
3. If an atom loses electrons, what charge will it have?
4. If an atom gains electrons, what charge will it have?

How is the covalent compound water made?

Atoms with a full outer shell of electrons are **stable**. Covalent bonding occurs between two or more non-metal atoms. The atoms share pairs of electrons so that they can both have full outer shells. Water is an example of a covalent compound formed when an oxygen atom shares pairs of electrons with two hydrogen atoms.

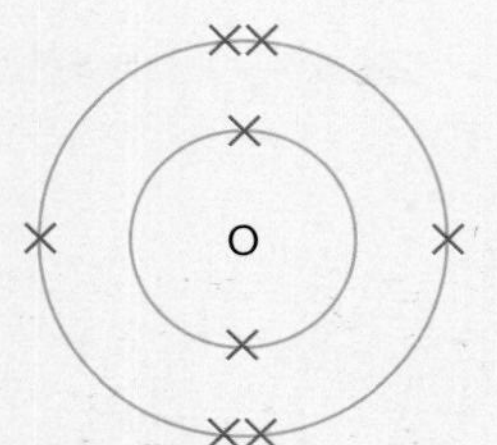

FIGURE 3: An atom of oxygen.

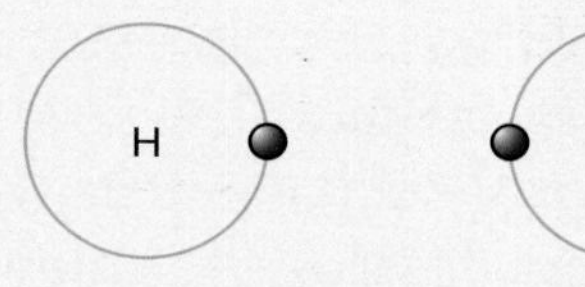

FIGURE 4: Hydrogen atoms.

Oxygen needs a share of two more electrons to get a full outer shell.

Both hydrogen atoms need a share of just one more electron to get a full, **stable** outer shell (remember there are only two electrons in the first shell).

In water, the oxygen and hydrogen atoms share pairs of electrons so that all the atoms have stable, full outer shells.

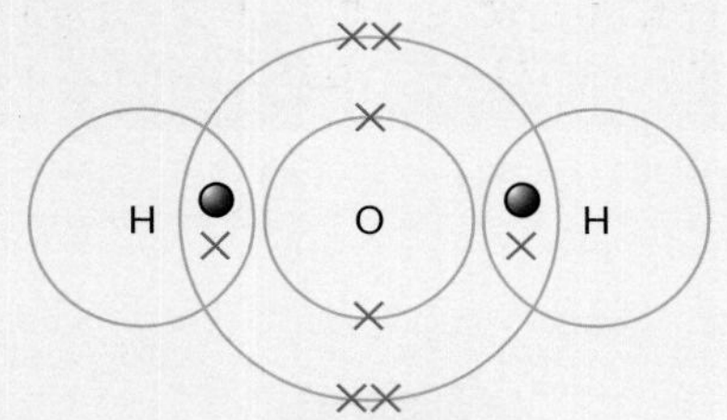

FIGURE 5: A water molecule.

Watch Out Although some electrons are drawn as dots and others as crosses, they are all identical.

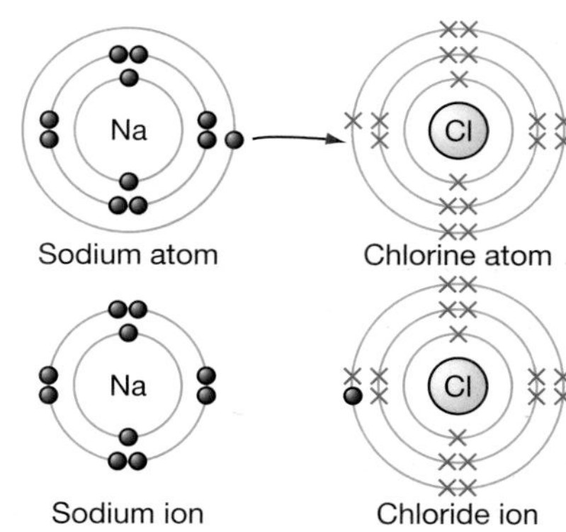

FIGURE 6: How do the sodium and chlorine atoms differ from the sodium and chloride ions?

How is the ionic compound sodium chloride made?

Ionic bonding occurs between metal and non-metal atoms. Again both atoms react to get a stable full outer shell of electrons. One electron is transferred from the outer shell of the sodium atom to the outer shell of the non-metal chlorine atom.

This means that the atoms have now got a charge so instead of being known as atoms, we now call them ions. The sodium ion has a positive charge (because it has lost an electron), while the chloride ion has a negative charge (because it has gained an electron). The strong force of attraction between these oppositely charged ions holds the substance together and is called an ionic bond.

QUESTIONS

5 Would the compound sulfur dioxide have covalent or ionic bonds? Why?
6 Why do atoms share pairs of electrons?
7 Would the compound calcium oxide have covalent or ionic bonds? Why?
8 During ionic bonding do metals gain or lose electrons? Why?

Representing covalent bonds

Scientists often use a short line drawn between atoms to represent the shared pair of electrons holding the atoms together in a covalent bond. Using this system, a chlorine, (Cl_2) molecule is shown as:

Cl - Cl

An oxygen, (O_2) molecule is shown as:

O = O

The double line between the two oxygen atoms represents a double covalent bond. This means that the atoms are held together by two pairs of shared electrons.

QUESTIONS

9 A molecule of the compound carbon dioxide (CO_2) can be represented as

O = C = O

Explain what this tells us about the bonding in carbon dioxide.

Extraction of limestone

You will find out:

- That limestone can be quarried and used as a building material
- The composition of limestone
- The consequences of extracting limestone

Building with limestone

St Paul's Cathedral is a well known London landmark. It has been the scene of many notable events. After Horatio Nelson died in 1805 at the Battle of Trafalgar, he was buried inside the cathedral. Nearly 140 years later during World War II, St Paul's famously survived the Blitz, even though much of the surrounding area was destroyed. Today it remains an important building, visited by people from all over the world. It is made from Portland Stone, which is a type of limestone.

FIGURE 1: How can you tell that St Paul's has been affected by London's pollution?

What is limestone used for?

Many public buildings, like town halls, are built from **limestone**. Can you think of any buildings made from limestone in your local town?

Limestone is mainly composed of **calcium carbonate**. Other materials made from calcium carbonate include:

- chalk
- egg shells
- marble
- stalactites and stalagmites.

All of these materials react with acids. In fact, buildings that are made from limestone can be badly damaged by acid rain.

FIGURE 2: These amazing structures are made of calcium carbonate. How did they form?

Are there different types of limestone?

Although all limestone rocks contain at least 50% of the compound calcium carbonate, the term 'limestone' covers a large range of rocks. Limestone sometimes has a yellow colour. This is due to the presence of the compound iron oxide in the rock. These rocks often become much darker upon weathering.

Limestone can also be made into useful new materials. Most of us live in homes, and use roads made with cement. Limestone is used to make cement, concrete and glass (see page 120) and is also used in the blast furnace during the **extraction** of iron (see page 122).

Limestone is extracted from the earth by removing the top layer of soil and then **blasting** the rock with explosives to dislodge pieces of limestone. This takes place in **quarries**.

FIGURE 3: Would you like to live near a quarry?

QUESTIONS

1 Give some uses of limestone.
2 How is limestone extracted?
3 Why is some limestone yellow?

What are the effects of a limestone quarry?

A limestone quarry can bring both advantages and disadvantages to an area.

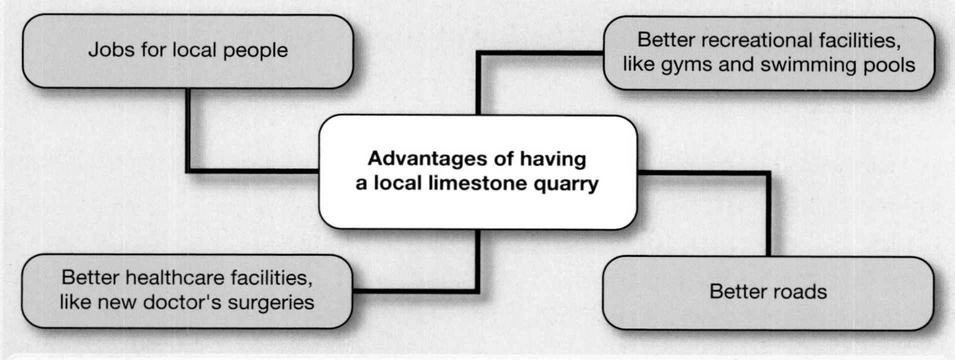
Jobs for local people
Better recreational facilities, like gyms and swimming pools
Advantages of having a local limestone quarry
Better healthcare facilities, like new doctor's surgeries
Better roads

FIGURE 4: The advantages of a limestone quarry.

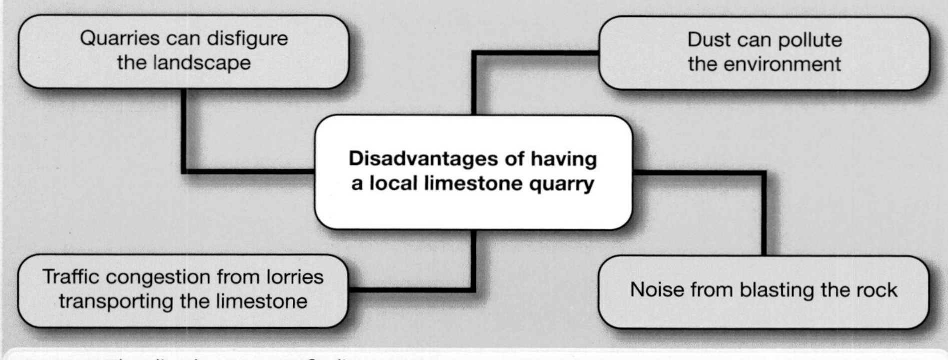
Quarries can disfigure the landscape
Dust can pollute the environment
Disadvantages of having a local limestone quarry
Traffic congestion from lorries transporting the limestone
Noise from blasting the rock

FIGURE 5: The disadvantages of a limestone quarry.

How can the unwelcome effects of limestone extraction be minimised?

Although there are some disadvantages to having a limestone quarry close to your home, with careful planning these problems can be minimised.

- Working limestone quarries can be seen as scars on the landscape, but once all the limestone has been extracted the area can be landscaped to provide nature reserves or new recreational areas.
- Railways can be used to transport limestone. This reduces the number of lorries causing congestion on local roads.
- Mines might only be allowed to work during the day and not at night or at the weekend.
- Have fewer, larger, well-managed quarries.

QUESTIONS

4 Look at figures 4 and 5 showing the advantages and disadvantages of a local limestone quarry. Which people are affected by each of the advantages and disadvantages shown? Choose from these categories:
a) Locals **b)** Visitors **c)** Everyone

5 Would you be in favour of a limestone quarry near your home? Explain your answer.

WOW FACTOR!

A large limestone quarry can produce up to 7 million tonnes of limestone per year.

Sites for new quarries

The Peak District National Park is an area of outstanding natural beauty. The National Park includes limestone areas. These limestone rocks were formed hundreds of millions of years ago in clear, warm seas so the limestone is very pure and has many uses. Mining is an important industry in the area, and limestone has been extracted from here since Roman times. Today all new quarries have to be approved by the local planning authority.

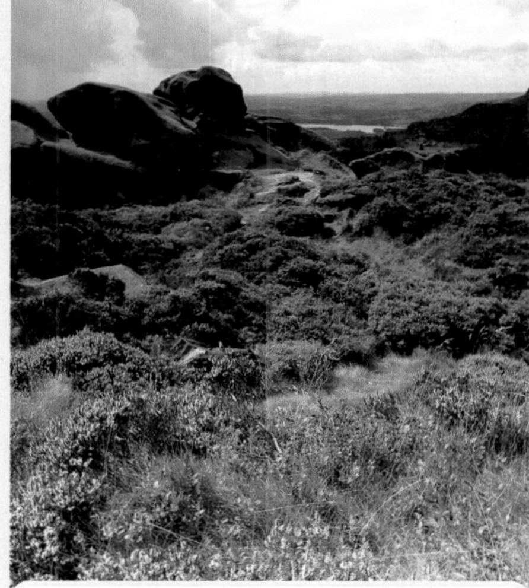

FIGURE 6: Why do so many people enjoy visiting the Peak District?

QUESTIONS

6 Imagine that you are a member of the local planning authority. What questions would you ask the owners of a new quarry before you would be prepared to grant them permission to open their quarry?

Thermal decomposition of limestone

You will find out:

- What happens when calcium carbonate is heated
- How limewater is used to test for carbon dioxide

Trilobites

This amazing fossil is the world's biggest trilobite. The fossilised bug is a staggering 70 cm long. It was found in limestone rock by a group of scientists working at Hudson Bay in Canada. The creature is thought to have lived 445 million years ago during the late Ordovician period. Limestone often contains fossils, though few are as large as this trilobite.

FIGURE 1: Limestone rocks often contain fossilised remains.

What is limestone?

Limestone is mainly **calcium carbonate**. Calcium carbonate is a compound. Its chemical **formula** is $CaCO_3$. This tells you the type and ratio of atoms that are joined together to make the compound.

In calcium carbonate, $CaCO_3$, the ratio of atoms is:

- 1 calcium atom
- 1 carbon atom
- 3 oxygen atoms.

What happens when limestone is heated?

If we heat limestone strongly it breaks down. Two simpler compounds, calcium oxide or **quicklime**, and carbon dioxide are formed.

The word equation for the reaction is:

calcium carbonate → calcium oxide + carbon dioxide

This type of chemical reaction is called **thermal decomposition**. It gets this name because heat breaks down the limestone into simpler substances.

Other metal carbonates react similarly, for example magnesium carbonate breaks down on heating to give magnesium oxide and carbon dioxide.

If water is added to quicklime we can make calcium hydroxide. This is also known as **slaked lime**.

We can represent this reaction by the word equation:

calcium oxide + water → calcium hydroxide

FIGURE 2: What is the main chemical compound in these limestone rocks?

QUESTIONS

1. What is the main compound in limestone?
2. Calcium carbonate has the formula $CaCO_3$. Explain what this formula means.
3. What happens when calcium carbonate is heated?
4. What does thermal decomposition mean?

Why does heating limestone make it react?

If we heat calcium carbonate strongly, it breaks down to form calcium oxide and carbon dioxide. However, no atoms are lost or made during the chemical reaction so the mass of the reactants equals the mass of the products.

We can write a symbol equation to show the reaction:

$$CaCO_3 \rightarrow CaO + CO_2$$

Why does a symbol equation have to balance?

Atoms are never made or destroyed during a chemical reaction, so there must be the same number of each type of atom on either side or the equation.

In this case, on each side of the equation there is:

- 1 calcium atom
- 1 carbon atom
- 3 oxygen atoms.

How can slaked lime be used?

Slaked lime is made by adding water to quicklime. Slaked lime is used by farmers. They spread it on soil that has become too acidic. The slaked lime raises the pH of the soil. This means that the farmer will be able to produce more crops from the same fields.

FIGURE 3: How could a soil become too acidic?

QUESTIONS

5 Write the word equation for the thermal decomposition of limestone.

6 What does 'slaked' mean?

7 Magnesium carbonate breaks down in a similar way to calcium carbonate when it is heated. Magnesium carbonate has the formula $MgCO_3$. State the type and ratio of atoms that are joined together to make the compound.

Limewater

If a little water is added to calcium oxide, solid calcium hydroxide or 'slaked lime' is formed. However, if more water is added, the solid calcium hydroxide dissolves to form a solution of calcium hydroxide called **limewater**. Limewater is used to test for the presence of the gas carbon dioxide. If carbon dioxide is bubbled through limewater, the limewater turns cloudy as a **suspension** of calcium carbonate is formed. This can be shown by the equation:

$$CO_2 + Ca(OH)_2 \rightarrow CaCO_3 + H_2O$$

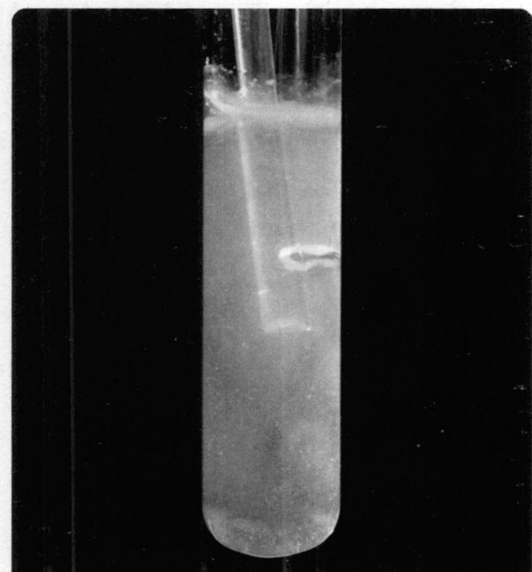

FIGURE 4: Why does this limewater change colour?

QUESTIONS

8 Write the word equation and the balanced symbol equation for the thermal decomposition of magnesium carbonate.

9 Draw a flow diagram to show how the calcium carbonate found in limestone is linked to the calcium carbonate made when carbon dioxide is bubbled through limewater.

Uses of limestone

You will find out:

- How limestone is used to make cement, concrete, mortar and glass
- That glass is a super-cooled liquid

Coloured glass

Stained glass windows like this one are often seen in churches and cathedrals. These wonderful colours aren't painted onto the glass, they are part of the glass itself! Glass of different colours can be made by adding metal salts to colourless glass. Cobalt salts produce blue glass, silver salts produce yellow glass, and copper salts can be used to make green glass.

FIGURE 1: Where else is coloured glass used?

Why is limestone important?

Think about your home. There is a very good chance that you live in a building that was made using **limestone** products. The importance of limestone lies in the useful materials that we can make from it.

- **How is cement made?**
  Cement is a very widely used building material. We can make cement by heating limestone and **clay** in a large oven called a **kiln**. If we add water to cement and allow it to set, it becomes as hard as stone.
- **How is concrete made?**
  If we mix cement, water, sand and rock chippings, we can make concrete. **Concrete** is used to make many buildings like multi-storey car parks.
- **How is mortar made?**
  Brick walls are held together by **mortar**. We can make mortar by mixing sand, water and cement. Originally, lime mortar was used. Slaked lime was used instead of cement. This is still used occasionally, usually with some cement added, for restoration work.
- **How is glass made?**
  Glass is used to make lots of things including windows and bottles. We can make glass by heating up a mixture of limestone, **sand** and **sodium carbonate**.

You probably live in a building that was made using limestone products

FIGURE 2: One of the many uses of glass.

QUESTIONS

1 How is cement made?
2 What is a kiln?
3 Give **one** use of concrete.
4 What raw materials are used to make glass?

...cement ...clay ...concrete ...glass ...kiln

What happens when mortar is made?

When we add water to a mixture of sand and cement, the cement absorbs the water. We say that the cement 'hydrates'. The wet mixture sets slowly and the hydrated cement holds the sand particles together. The result is called mortar.

The difference between mortar and concrete

Concrete is strong and very hard to squash or compress. It's an example of a composite material. Composites are mixtures of different substances that show properties that are different to those of their component parts.

Concrete is much stronger than mortar. The reason for this is that it contains rock chippings. The science is complicated, but the result is that a good mix of particle sizes in the concrete (small sand particles and various sized rock chippings) creates a strong material.

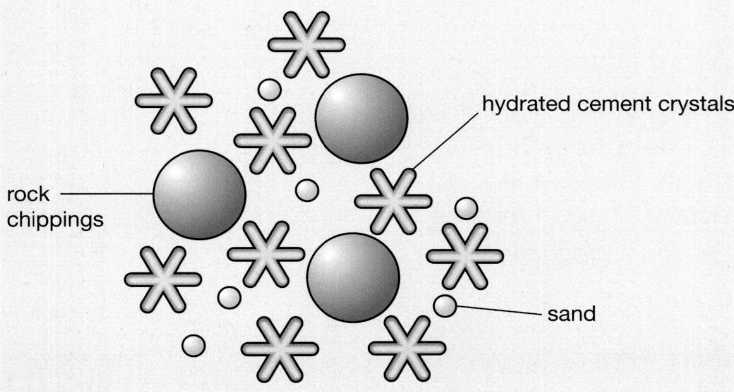

FIGURE 3: Which component holds concrete together?

What happens when glass is made?

Soda glass is the most common form of glass. It is made from a mixture of limestone, sand and sodium carbonate. The mixture is heated in a furnace to a temperature of around 1300°C. At this temperature, calcium carbonate and sodium carbonate break down. As the mixture cools, each silicon atom (from the sand) forms strong covalent bonds to four oxygen atoms. The silicon and oxygen atoms form a giant but irregular structure, trapping sodium ions and calcium ions within the structure.

QUESTIONS

5 People often think that cement and concrete are the same. Are they right?

6 Why is concrete stronger than mortar?

7 Describe how glass is linked to limestone.

WANT TO KNOW MORE?

www.bbc.co.ukschools/gcsebitesize/chemistry/usefulproductsrocks/index.shtm is a good site for revising and testing yourself on uses of limestone.

Why are old glass windows slightly thicker at the bottom than at the top?

Although glass appears to be a solid material, over a long period of time it does slowly flow. In fact, glass is an example of a super-cooled liquid. At room temperature, glass has been cooled down below its freezing point but it doesn't crystallise. This means it can still flow, but it does so very slowly.

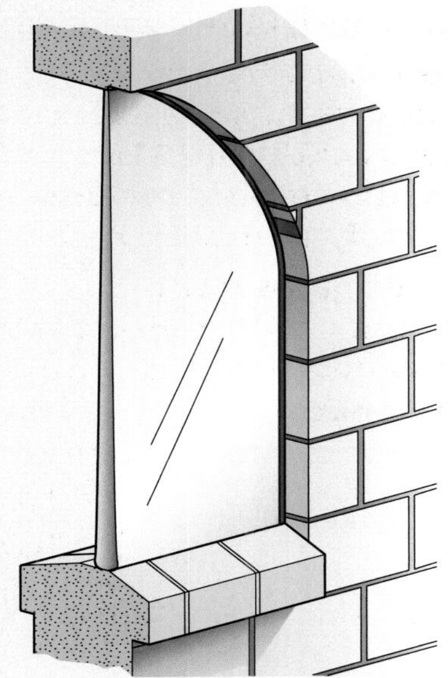

FIGURE 4: Why is this glass window thicker at the bottom than at the top?

QUESTIONS

8 Explain why glass can flow.

The blast furnace

You will find out:

- About some uses of iron
- How iron is extracted from haematite in the blast furnace
- About oxidation and reduction reactions

Tower of steel

The Burj Tower in Dubai will be the world's tallest building when it opens in 2008. It will be constructed from concrete and steel. Steel, an alloy of iron and carbon, is very strong. The Burj Tower will stand 800 m high. At this huge height, winds can be very strong – and damaging! Using steel, scientists were able to develop a special spiralling design that minimises damage by wind.

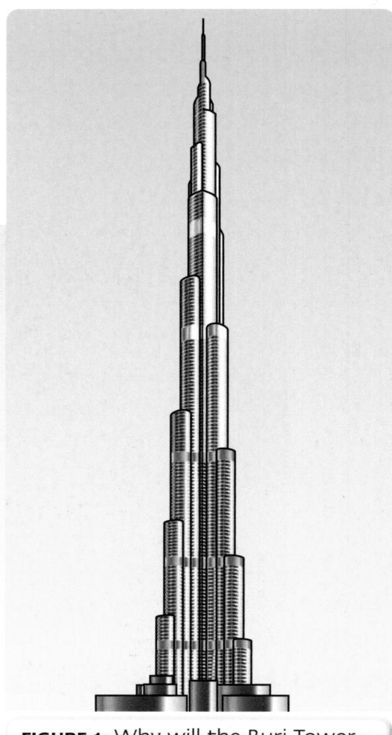

FIGURE 1: Why will the Burj Tower be made from steel?

Why is iron important?

Iron is abundant, cheap and strong. Like most metals, iron is found in compounds. Chemical reactions are used to extract it. This takes place in a **blast furnace**. Most of the iron made in the blast furnace is used to make **steel**. Steel is used in an enormous range of modern products including cars, trains and ships.

What are the raw materials needed in the Blast Furnace?

Iron is extracted in the blast furnace. Four raw materials are used:

- haematite
- limestone
- coke
- hot air

Haematite is an iron ore. It is mainly iron (III) oxide (Fe_2O_3), a compound of iron and oxygen.

Coke is made from coal, which has been heated but not allowed to burn. It is rich in the element carbon.

Limestone consists mainly of the compound calcium carbonate ($CaCO_3$). It reacts with impurities in the haematite.

Hot air is blasted into the furnace. This gives the 'blast furnace' its name.

FIGURE 2: Haematite contains the compound iron (III) oxide (Fe_2O_3).

QUESTIONS

1. What are the solid raw materials added to the blast furnace?
2. What is the chemical name of the main compound in the ore haematite?
3. What is the main element found in coke?
4. Why is limestone added to the blast furnace?
5. How does the blast furnace get its name?

...blast furnace ...carbon dioxide ...carbon monoxide ...coke ...exothermic

What happens in the blast furnace?

A series of chemical reactions takes place in the blast furnace to produce iron.

Initially the carbon-rich coke reacts with oxygen (from the hot air which is blasted into the furnace) to produce the gas **carbon dioxide**.

carbon + oxygen → carbon dioxide

$$C + O_2 \rightarrow CO_2$$

This reaction is very **exothermic** and releases a great deal of heat. Because it is so hot in the furnace, the carbon dioxide reacts with more carbon to form the gas **carbon monoxide**.

carbon dioxide + carbon → carbon monoxide

$$CO_2 + C \rightarrow 2CO$$

The carbon monoxide reacts with the iron (III) oxide from the haematite to produce carbon dioxide and iron.

carbon monoxide + iron oxide → carbon dioxide + iron

$$3CO + Fe_2O_3 \rightarrow 3CO_2 + 2Fe$$

The iron that is produced is so hot that it is **molten**. Its high density means that it sinks to the bottom of the furnace, where it is removed. This is an example of a metal that is less reactive than carbon being extracted by heating it with carbon.

Removing impurities

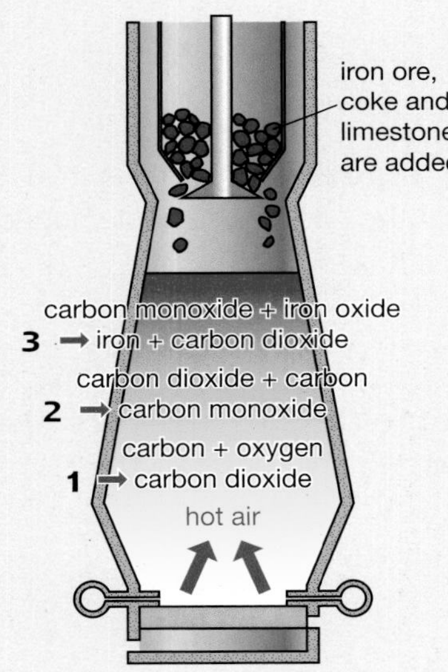

FIGURE 3: The chemical reactions that take place inside the Blast Furnace.

The ore haematite often contains silicon dioxide (sand) impurities. These are removed by adding limestone. At the high temperatures within the furnace, the limestone decomposes to form calcium oxide and releases carbon dioxide gas.

calcium carbonate → calcium oxide + carbon dioxide

$$CaCO_3 \rightarrow CaO + CO_2$$

The calcium oxide reacts with the silica impurities to form the compound calcium silicate which is known as **slag**.

calcium oxide + silicon dioxide → calcium silicate

$$CaO + SiO_2 \rightarrow CaSiO_3$$

The slag is less dense than the molten iron, so the slag floats on top of the iron. Once solidified, the slag can be used in making roads.

QUESTIONS

6 What does 'exothermic' mean?

7 Why is the iron made in the blast furnace molten?

8 Why does the molten iron sink?

9 Why does slag float on top of the molten iron?

EXAM HINTS AND TIPS

Remember the metal, iron, is reduced in the Blast Furnace. Always remember units – °C for temperature and J for heat

Oxidation and reduction

A series of **oxidation** and **reduction** reactions takes place within the Blast Furnace.

- Oxidation reactions occur when oxygen is added to a substance.
- Reduction reactions occur when oxygen is removed from a substance.
- Oxidation is the reverse of reduction.
- Oxidation and reduction must always occur together.

Most of the iron oxide is reduced by the gas carbon monoxide, which is made by a series of chemical reactions inside the Blast Furnace.

The carbon monoxide reacts with the iron (III) oxide, Fe_2O_3, to produce carbon dioxide and iron.

carbon monoxide + iron oxide → carbon dioxide + iron

$$3CO_{(g)} + Fe_2O_{3(s)} \rightarrow 3CO_{2(g)} + 2Fe_{(l)}$$

During this reaction, carbon monoxide is oxidised to carbon dioxide; and iron (III) oxide is reduced to iron.

QUESTIONS

10 When the carbon-rich coke reacts with oxygen to form carbon dioxide, is the carbon oxidised or reduced? Explain your answer.

11 When carbon dioxide reacts with more carbon to form carbon monoxide, which substance is oxidised and which substance is reduced? Explain your answer.

12 The metal aluminium is produced from its ore, aluminium oxide. Is the aluminium oxide oxidised or reduced? Explain your answer.

Using iron

You will find out:
- About the properties of cast iron and wrought iron
- About some uses of cast iron and wrought iron
- That steel is a useful alloy of iron

Iron engines

This engine block is made from cast iron. Cast iron is created when the iron made in the Blast Furnace is cooled down and allowed to solidify. In fact, most engine blocks in both petrol and diesel cars are made from this metal.

FIGURE 1: Engine blocks are made from cast iron.

FIGURE 2: This drain cover is made from cast iron. Why is cast iron used rather than pure iron?

Cast iron

Have you noticed the drain covers as you walk down the street? They are made from **cast iron**. Cast iron is made from the molten iron produced in the blast furnace, and it contains about 96% iron. The molten iron is poured into moulds called pigs. It cools and becomes solid, making cast iron. Cast iron is **hard** and **strong**. It doesn't **rust** as easily as pure iron. But it's also very **brittle** because it has impurities. In other words, it cracks easily. It is used when strength, rather than flexibility, is needed.

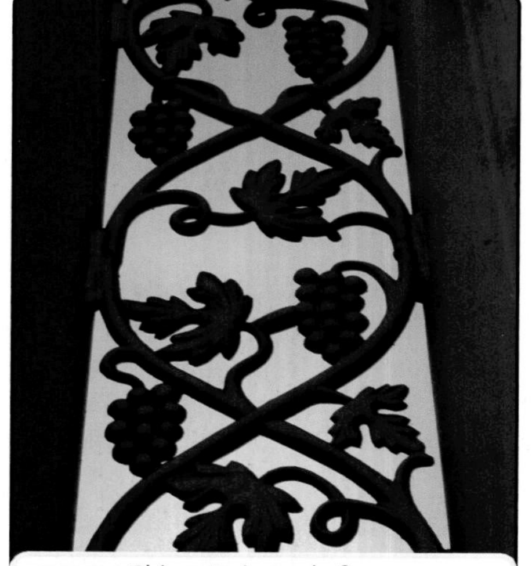

FIGURE 3: This gate is made from wrought iron.

Wrought iron

Wrought iron is pure iron. It is made by removing **impurities** from the iron that is made in the blast furnace. Wrought iron can be easily bent and shaped, but it is too soft for many uses.

Steel

Most of the iron produced in the blast furnace is converted into steel. First the impurities are removed. Then other metals and carbon are added to the molten pure iron. By varying the type and quantity of metals and carbon, 'designer' steels can be made with properties to suit their use.

QUESTIONS

1 Give **one** use of cast iron.
2 What are the properties of cast iron?
3 What are the differences between cast iron and wrought iron?
4 What are the properties of wrought iron?

EXAM HINTS AND TIPS

Pure metals are soft because the atoms form a regular arrangement. The layers of atoms can then pass easily over each other.

...brittle ...cast iron ...hard

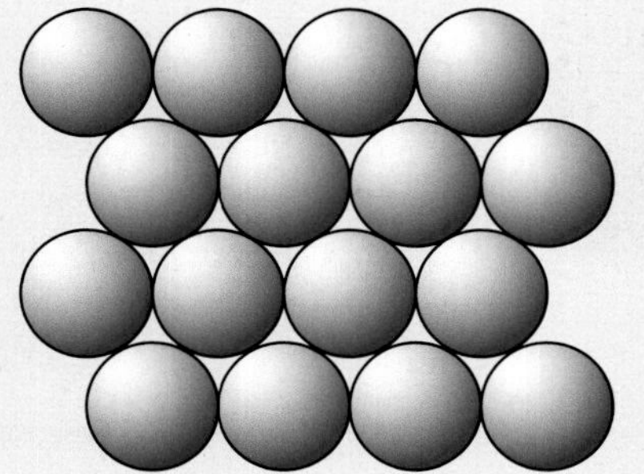

FIGURE 4: Why do the atoms in this wrought iron bar have a regular arrangement?

The structure of wrought iron

Wrought iron is made by removing the impurities from cast iron. Wrought iron therefore consists of the element iron. The atoms of iron form a very **regular** arrangement because they are all the same size. This regular structure gives wrought iron its special properties. The **layers** of iron atoms can pass over each other relatively easily, making wrought iron soft and easy to shape and bend. This means that wrought iron is very useful for making objects like gates and railings. However, it also means that it is too soft for most uses.

Most of the metal objects that we use every day are made from the metal steel. Steel is an alloy of iron. An alloy is usually a mixture of metals, but steel also contains some carbon, a non-metal element. Steel is much stronger than pure iron.

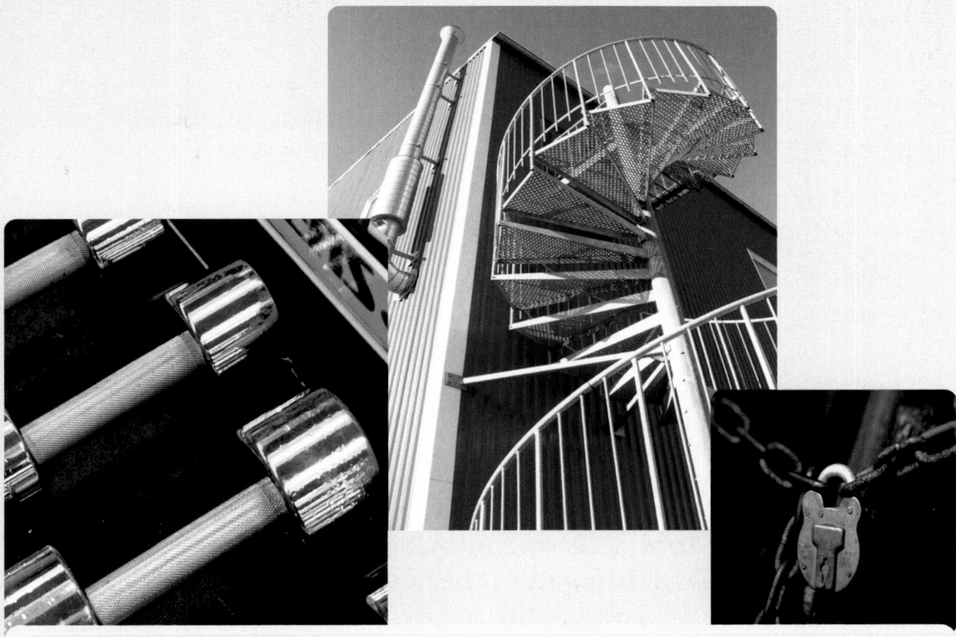

FIGURE 5: Steel is very widely used.

QUESTIONS

5 Describe the structure of the atoms in wrought iron.

6 Explain why wrought iron is soft.

7 Would you expect the atoms of pure copper to have a regular arrangement? Why?

Most iron is made into the alloy steel

The structure of steel

Pure iron is relatively soft, but the alloy steel is much harder. This difference in properties is caused by differences in how the atoms are arranged. In pure iron, all the iron atoms are the same size so they form a very regular structure. However, steel consists of iron atoms mixed with other metal atoms, plus atoms of the non-metal element carbon. These different types of atom are different sizes, and this distorts the regular structure of the metal. These distortions prevent the layers of atoms from passing easily over one another and make steel much harder than pure iron.

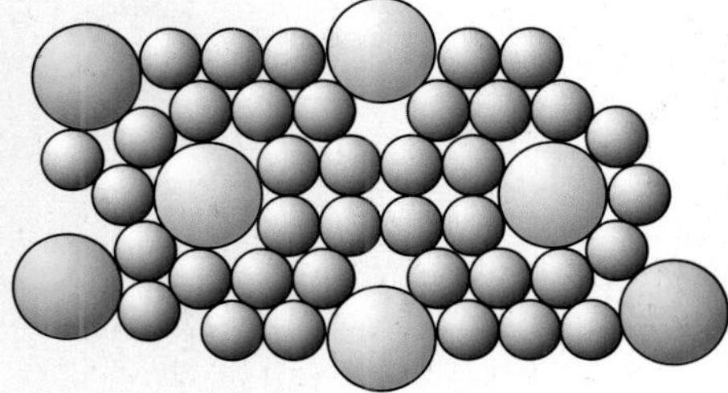

FIGURE 6: Why don't the atoms in this steel bar have a regular arrangement?

QUESTIONS

8 Explain why steel is harder than pure iron.

9 Would you expect pure copper to be hard or soft? Why?

...impurities ...layers ...regular ...rust ...strong

Using steel

You will find out:
- That different steels have different properties
- That the properties of different steels determine how they will be used
- That scientists can adjust the amounts of carbon and other metals in steel

Giant sculpture

The Angel of the North near the A1 in the North East of England is Britain's largest sculpture. It marks the southerly entrance to Tyneside. The Angel is made from an alloy called Cor-ten Steel. This alloy consists of iron with a small amount of copper. Around 90 000 motorists pass the Angel of the North every day. The sculpture stands over 20 m high and has a wingspan of 54 m, roughly the same as a jumbo jet.

FIGURE 1: The Angel of the North.

FIGURE 2: What properties of steel make it a suitable material to make this hammer?

FIGURE 3: What properties of steel make it a suitable material to make these scissors?

Designer steels

What **properties** do you think a hammer should have?

- Should it be hard?
- Should it be brittle?
- Should it rust?

What properties do you think a pair of scissors should have?

- Should they be hard?
- Should they be brittle?
- Should they rust?

Cast iron is too **brittle** for most purposes. Pure iron is too **soft** for most uses. However, scientists have found out how to add things to iron to give it just the properties they want.

Most iron is made into **steel**. Steel is an **alloy** of iron. It is a mixture of iron, other metals and small amounts of the non-metal element carbon.

The amount of carbon that is added to steel affects the **strength** and **hardness** of the steel that is made. It also affects how easily the metal can be bent and shaped.

WANT TO KNOW MORE?

For more information on iron and steel visit

www.howstuffworks.com/iron.htm

QUESTIONS

1. What is the main disadvantage of cast iron?
2. What is the main disadvantage of pure iron?
3. What is steel composed of?

...alloy ...brittle ...cast iron ...hardness ...properties

Low, medium and high carbon steels

Low carbon steels typically contain less than 0.4% carbon. These metals are soft and very easy to bend and shape. Low carbon steels are used in situations where an ability to be easily shaped is very important, e.g. car bodies are made from low carbon steel.

FIGURE 4: Low carbon steels are easy to shape but are also soft.

Medium carbon steels contain around 0.8% carbon. The addition of the extra carbon makes these steels harder and stronger, but they are also less easy to bend and shape. Objects such as the hammer in figure 2 are made from medium carbon steel.

High carbon steels typically contain between 1.0 and 1.5% carbon. These alloys are very hard and can be used to make objects such as knives or razor blades. The hardness of the metal allows them to remain sharp even after lots of use. However, high carbon steels are quite brittle and may snap if they are bent or misused.

Adding other metals to pure iron

Metals can also be added to iron to make different types of steel, called steel alloys. The chosen metal is dissolved in the molten iron. The exact metal chosen depends on how the steel will be used, and therefore the properties that it requires. One of the most widely used steel alloys is **stainless steel**. This is made from three different metals. It is about 70% iron, 20% chromium and 10% nickel. Stainless steel is enormously useful because it is very resistant to corrosion.

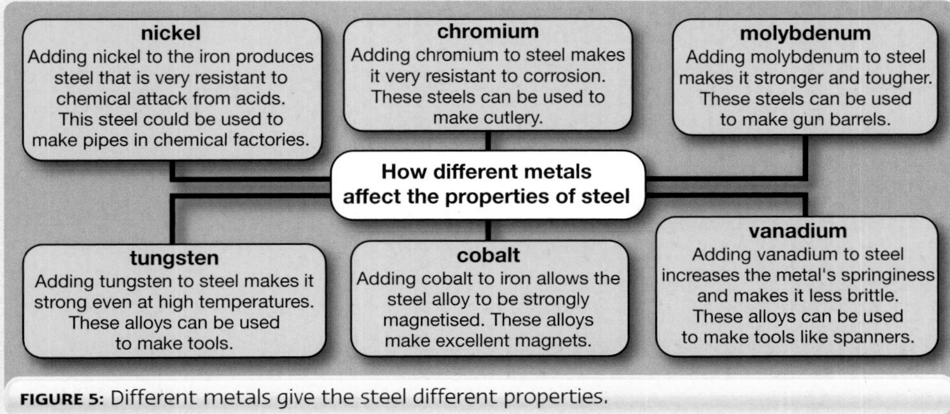

How different metals affect the properties of steel
nickel
Adding nickel to the iron produces steel that is very resistant to chemical attack from acids. This steel could be used to make pipes in chemical factories.
chromium
Adding chromium to steel makes it very resistant to corrosion. These steels can be used to make cutlery.
molybdenum
Adding molybdenum to steel makes it stronger and tougher. These steels can be used to make gun barrels.
tungsten
Adding tungsten to steel makes it strong even at high temperatures. These alloys can be used to make tools.
cobalt
Adding cobalt to iron allows the steel alloy to be strongly magnetised. These alloys make excellent magnets.
vanadium
Adding vanadium to steel increases the metal's springiness and makes it less brittle. These alloys can be used to make tools like spanners.

FIGURE 5: Different metals give the steel different properties.

QUESTIONS

4 Which metal should be added to iron to make the steel needed to make storage tanks for acids? Why?

5 Which metal should be added to iron to make the steel used to make drill tips? Why?

6 Which metal should be added to iron to make steel used to make the mechanism for a wind-up alarm clock? Why?

Removing impurities from iron

Iron is converted into steel by removing the carbon and other impurities, and then adding carefully controlled amounts of other metals and carbon. Molten iron straight from the blast furnace is poured into large furnaces. Jets of hot oxygen gas are then blown through the molten iron. The carbon impurities in the molten iron react with oxygen to form carbon monoxide and carbon dioxide. These are then removed with the other waste gases.

Iron from the blast furnace also contains small amounts of phosphorus and silicon impurities. The jets of oxygen blasted through the iron convert these two non-metal elements into their oxides. Non-metal elements form acidic oxides, so phosphorus oxide and silicon dioxide are both acidic. They react with calcium carbonate to form calcium phosphate and calcium silicate.

phosphorus oxide + calcium carbonate → calcium phosphate + carbon dioxide

$$P_4O_{10} + 6CaCO_3 \rightarrow 2Ca_3(PO_4)_2 + 6CO_2$$

silicon dioxide + calcium carbonate → calcium silicate + carbon dioxide

$$SiO_2 + CaCO_3 \rightarrow CaSiO_3 + CO_2$$

The calcium phosphate and calcium silicate form a slag, which floats on the top of the molten iron. The slag can be removed, and carefully controlled amounts of other metals and carbon then added to form different types of steel.

QUESTIONS

7 Name some everyday objects made from steel.

8 Why does the slag formed by calcium silicate and calcium phosphate float on top of the molten iron?

9 Why does the iron used to make steel come straight from the blast furnace?

Transition metals

You will find out:

- Where transition metals are found in the periodic table
- About the properties of transition metals
- About the uses of transition metals

Explosions of colour

Fireworks are often used in celebrations. One of the most stunning effects of any firework display is the amazing colours that they produce. These colours are caused by metal salts inside the fireworks. At the very high temperatures found inside exploding fireworks, the metal atoms emit coloured light. Different metals produce different colours.

FIGURE 1: A copper salt produces blue light.

Where are transition metals in the periodic table?

Look closely at the **periodic table** and you will see that **metal elements** are found on the left-hand side of the table, and **non-metal** elements are found on the right-hand side. The **transition metals** are found in the central block. They include elements such as copper, iron and titanium. Transition metals have many useful **properties**.

How are transition metals used?

Transition metals are strong, so they make excellent **structural** materials. Steel (which is made from the transition metal iron) is cheap and strong, and we use it extensively to make objects such as bridges, ships and cars.

Group I	Group II											Group III	IV	V	VI	VII	0
			$^{1}_{1}$H hydrogen														$^{4}_{2}$He helium
$^{7}_{3}$Li lithium	$^{9}_{4}$Be beryllium											$^{11}_{5}$B boron	$^{12}_{6}$C carbon	$^{14}_{7}$N nitrogen	$^{16}_{8}$O oxygen	$^{19}_{9}$F flourine	$^{20}_{10}$Ne neon
$^{23}_{11}$Na sodium	$^{24}_{12}$Mg magnesium											$^{27}_{13}$Al aluminium	$^{28}_{14}$Si silicon	$^{31}_{15}$P phosphorus	$^{32}_{16}$S sulfur	$^{35}_{17}$Cl chlorine	$^{40}_{18}$Ar argon
$^{39}_{19}$K potassium	$^{40}_{20}$Ca calcium	$^{45}_{21}$Sc scandium	$^{48}_{22}$Ti titanium	$^{51}_{23}$V vanadium	$^{52}_{24}$Cr chromium	$^{55}_{25}$Mn manganese	$^{56}_{26}$Fe iron	$^{59}_{27}$Co cobalt	$^{59}_{28}$Ni nickel	$^{64}_{29}$Cu copper	$^{65}_{30}$Zn zinc	$^{70}_{31}$Ga gallium	$^{73}_{32}$Ge germanium	$^{75}_{33}$As arsenic	$^{79}_{34}$Se selenium	$^{80}_{35}$Br bromine	$^{84}_{36}$Kr krypton
$^{85}_{37}$Rb rubidium	$^{88}_{38}$Sr strontium	$^{89}_{39}$Y yttrium	$^{91}_{40}$Zr zirconium	$^{93}_{41}$Nb niobium	$^{96}_{42}$Mo molybdenum	$^{99}_{43}$Tc technetium	$^{101}_{44}$Ru ruthenium	$^{103}_{45}$Rh rhodium	$^{106}_{46}$Pd palladium	$^{108}_{47}$Ag silver	$^{112}_{48}$Cd cadmium	$^{115}_{49}$In indium	$^{119}_{50}$Sn tin	$^{122}_{51}$Sb antimony	$^{128}_{52}$Te tellurium	$^{127}_{53}$I iodine	$^{131}_{54}$Xe xenon
$^{133}_{55}$Cs caesium	$^{137}_{56}$Ba barium	$^{139}_{57}$La lanthanum	$^{178}_{72}$Hf hafnium	$^{181}_{73}$Ta tantalum	$^{184}_{74}$W tungsten	$^{186}_{75}$Re rhenium	$^{190}_{76}$Os osmium	$^{192}_{77}$Ir iridium	$^{195}_{78}$Pt platinum	$^{197}_{79}$Au gold	$^{201}_{80}$Hg mercury	$^{204}_{81}$Tl thallium	$^{207}_{82}$Pb lead	$^{209}_{83}$Bi bismuth	$^{210}_{84}$Po polonium	$^{210}_{85}$At astatine	$^{222}_{86}$Rn radon
$^{223}_{87}$Fr francium	$^{226}_{88}$Ra radium	$^{227}_{89}$Ac actinium															

FIGURE 2: The transition metals are found in the shaded area of the periodic table.

The transition metal copper is an excellent **conductor** of electricity. We can also easily bend it into new shapes. Large quantities of copper are used for electrical wiring.

Copper is also a good conductor of heat. Some saucepans are made from copper.

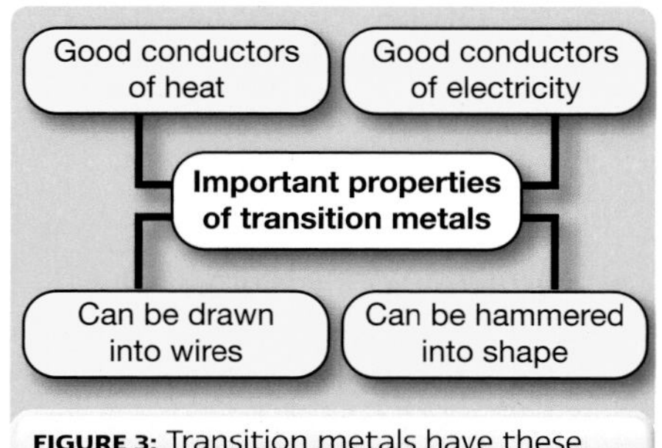

FIGURE 3: Transition metals have these properties because of the way that their atoms are arranged.

QUESTIONS

1 In which part of the periodic table are non-metals found?

2 Name **five** transition metals.

3 An element does not conduct electricity and is brittle. Is it a transition metal? Why?

4 Why is copper used in electrical wiring?

...atoms ...conductors ...delocalised ...electron ...elements ...layers

Why do metals have these properties?

The arrangement of **atoms** gives metals their special properties. Every atom has a small central nucleus, which has a positive charge. This nucleus is surrounded by negatively charged **electrons**. In metal atoms there are only ever a few electrons in the outer shell. These outer electrons are free to move through the structure. The electrons are **delocalised**, leaving the metal atoms with a positive charge. It's the attraction between these metal ions and the delocalised electrons that holds the structure together.

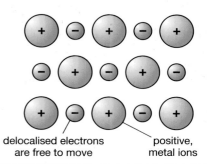

delocalised electrons are free to move

positive, metal ions

FIGURE 4: How does this structure give metals their properties?

Why can metals be drawn into wires and hammered into shape?

FIGURE 5: Why can metals be drawn into wires like this?

In metals, the force of attraction between the metal ions and the delocalised electrons is high. This means that metals are strong. However, **layers** of metal ions can slip over one another without the structure breaking. This allows metals to be drawn into wires and hammered into shape.

Why are metals good conductors of heat?

When we heat one end of a metal bar, the positive metal ions at this end start to vibrate more. The delocalised electrons collide with these vibrating metal ions and gain energy. As the delocalised electrons move through the metal, they conduct heat through the metal.

FIGURE 6: How does this metal conduct heat?

Why are metals good conductors of electricity?

Transition metals, for example copper, are good conductors of electricity because of their delocalised electrons. When an electrical voltage is applied across a metal, perhaps by connecting it to a battery, there is a flow of electric current. This is because the delocalised electrons are able to move through the whole structure.

QUESTIONS

5 What is a delocalised electron?

6 Why can metals be hammered into shape?

7 Why are non-metals poor conductors of electricity?

EXAM HINTS AND TIPS

Remember that metals are on the left-hand side of the periodic table, non-metals are on the right

Hot stuff

Have you noticed that when you touch some objects made from non-metals like plastics they feel warm, but that when you touch other objects made from metals they feel cold? In non-metals, the atoms are not packed together very tightly and there are no delocalised electrons. This makes non-metals poor conductors of heat. When you touch a non-metal it feels warm because it does not conduct heat away from your hand.

FIGURE 7: Why does this statue feel cold to the touch?

QUESTIONS

8 Explain why metal objects feel cold when you touch them.

Bridge the gap

SELF-CHECK ACTIVITY

CONTEXT

One of the greatest engineers of the 19th Century was Isambard Kingdom Brunel. He designed railways, bridges and ocean-going boats, often bigger or faster than anything built before. If you travel from London to Bristol by rail you will follow a route planned by Brunel, and as you leave the station at Bristol Temple Meads you will walk past the original station building designed by him. His ideas were exciting and challenging, and sometimes way ahead of their time.

When Brunel came to the river Tamar, between Plymouth in Devon and Saltash in Cornwall, he needed to build a bridge to carry the railway. He designed a suspension bridge that still stands today and is now the only mainline rail route into Cornwall. Brunel designed his bridge to be built partly of iron, a metal that he used a lot. Iron is strong and can be worked into a variety of shapes. Brunel used wrought iron plates to make tubes and then suspended the tubes between pillars.

Wrought iron has a very small amount of carbon in it, and other impurities called silicates. So, unlike pure iron, in which all the atoms are the same size, wrought iron has other atoms as well, which are different in size to iron atoms. Pure iron is rather soft: the layers of atoms slide over each other fairly easily. Wrought iron is stronger.

The bridge opened in 1859 (the year Brunel died). Just over 100 years later, in 1961, a new bridge opened next to it, this time to carry road traffic. This is also a suspension bridge, but with a significantly different shape. Much taller, the road bridge has a steel deck supported by steel cables from the concrete towers. Steel is basically iron with more carbon in it. The carbon atoms are a different size and alter the regular arrangement of iron atoms so they cannot slide over each other as easily.

CHALLENGE

STEP 1

Pure iron has a regular arrangement of atoms in layers. Draw what this might look like and explain why it is not a very strong metal.

STEP 2

Brunel used wrought iron to make the long curved tubes that form the top of his bridge (this was before the days of cheap steel). Look back to see what wrought iron consists of, then draw and label a diagram to show the arrangement of atoms in wrought iron.

STEP 3

When the bridge is loaded, forces are applied to the iron to try to make the layers move. Add labels to your diagram to show how easy you think it would be to make the layers slide over each other.

STEP 4

The road bridge engineers used steel – strong and cheap. The amount of carbon in steel is carefully controlled. Draw a diagram to show how you think the atoms might be arranged. Now add labels to say how this arrangement produces an extremely strong material.

STEP 5

The steel cables on the road bridge are stronger than they would be if made from iron. The steel contains more carbon than the iron does. What would happen to the strength of the material if the proportion of carbon was increased still further?

Maximise your grade

These sentences show what you need to include in your work to achieve each grade. Use them to improve your work and be more successful.

Grade	Answer includes...
	Start to describe how materials are selected for applications according to their properties.
F	Describe how materials are selected for applications according to their properties.
	Describe how particles are arranged in an element such as iron.
	Suggest how this arrangement can be disturbed by the introduction of other materials.
C	Explain how the properties of materials can be explained by referring to the arrangement of atoms.
	Start to use ideas about arrangements of atoms to suggest how disturbing the layers of iron atoms prevents slippage (thereby strengthening it) but too much disturbance weakens the iron.
A	Use ideas about arrangements of atoms to suggest how disturbing the layers of iron atoms prevents slippage (thereby strengthening it) but too much disturbance weakens the iron.
	As above, but with particular clarity and detail.

Aluminium

You will find out:
- Some properties of the metal aluminium
- Some uses of aluminium
- How aluminium is extracted from its ore

The multi-purpose metal

There is more aluminium in the Earth's crust than any other metal. Aluminium has many uses, from drinks cans to pylons and high voltage conductors. An alloy of aluminium and lithium was used to make the external fuel tank of the Space Shuttle. This alloy combined low density and high strength, both of which are properties of vital importance in the aerospace industry.

FIGURE 1: Why was the external fuel tank of the Space Shuttle made from an aluminium alloy?

Extracting aluminium

There is more aluminium than iron in the Earth's crust, but it is more **expensive** to extract.

Aluminium is extracted from its ore by **electrolysis**. The ore, called **bauxite**, is impure aluminium oxide. Bauxite is melted and an electric current passed through it.

aluminium oxide → aluminium + oxygen

The process uses a lot of electrical energy, which is why it's expensive.

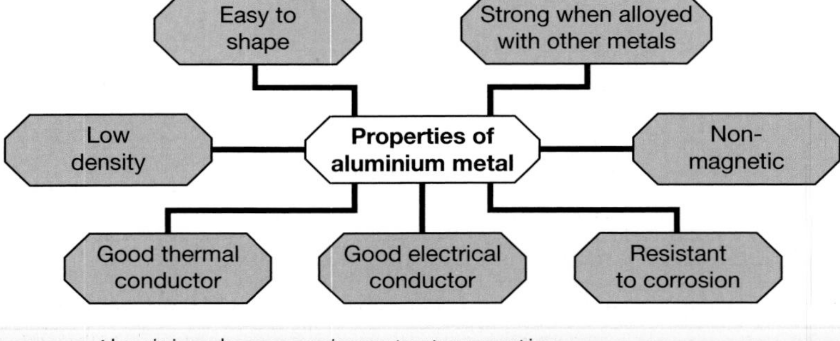

FIGURE 2: Aluminium has many important properties.

Uses of aluminium

You can buy aluminium foil in the supermarket. However, pure aluminium is not used very much.

Usually it is made into **alloys** with other metals. These alloys have many uses, for example:

- bicycle frames
- car bodies
- drinks and food cans
- pylons and high voltage conductors
- saucepans.

Can you think of other things that are made from aluminium?

FIGURE 3: Many bike frames are made from aluminium alloys.

QUESTIONS

1 Identify the properties that make aluminium a suitable metal from which to make aircraft wings.

2 Identify the properties that make aluminium a suitable metal from which to make greenhouse frames.

3 Identify the properties that make aluminium a suitable metal from which to make saucepans.

Electrolysis of aluminium oxide

Aluminium cannot be extracted from its ore by heating with carbon because it is more reactive than carbon. Therefore, the more expensive process of electrolysis must be used.

Bauxite has a very high melting point. Another ore of aluminium, called **cryolite**, is added to the bauxite. Cryolite melts at a much lower temperature and the bauxite dissolves in it. The aluminium **ions** and the oxide ions then become free to move.

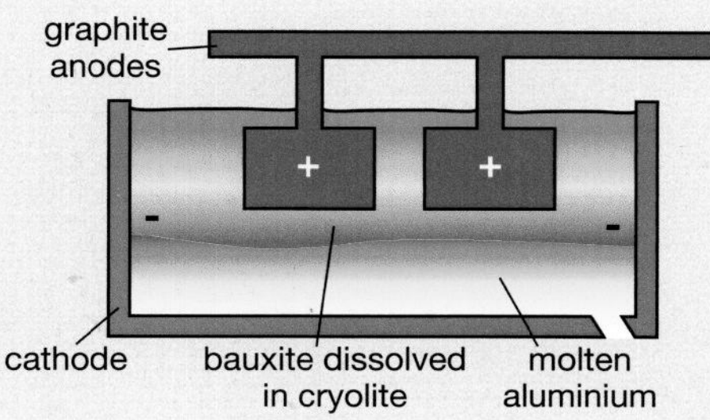

FIGURE 4: Aluminium is extracted by electrolysis. Aluminium forms at the cathode. Oxygen forms at the anode.

At the negative electrode (cathode):
aluminium ions gain electrons to form aluminium atoms. Molten aluminium metal is removed from the cell.

aluminium ions + electrons → aluminium atoms

At the positive electrode (anode):
oxide ions lose electrons and form oxygen molecules.

oxide ions − electrons → oxygen molecules

The oxygen formed reacts with the carbon-graphite electrodes and gradually eats them away. They have to be replaced regularly.

Explaining the properties of aluminium

- **Density** depends on how closely the particles are packed together. Aluminium atoms do not pack as closely as iron atoms. Aluminium is less dense than iron.
- Pure aluminium is quite soft. When alloyed (mixed with other metals), its strength increases dramatically. When an impurity is introduced, the layers of aluminium atoms do not slide over one another as easily. (See pages 126-127 to find out more about iron alloys.)
- Aluminium is a very reactive metal, but it doesn't **corrode**. The surface of pure aluminium reacts rapidly with oxygen to form a tough layer of **aluminium oxide**. This prevents the aluminium from reacting further, making the aluminium resistant to corrosion.

QUESTIONS

4 When aluminium metal is made, why is it molten?
5 When aluminium metal is made, why does it collect at the bottom of the cell?
6 Why must aluminium oxide be molten or dissolved but not solid?
7 What is unusual about graphite?

EXAM HINTS AND TIPS

Remember 'oil rig':
Oxidation Is Loss,
Reduction Is Gain
(of electrons)

Reduction and oxidation

The electrolysis of aluminium oxide is an example of a type of chemical reaction involving processes known as reduction and oxidation.

During reduction reactions a substance gains electrons. During oxidation reactions a substance loses electrons.

During electrolysis, each aluminium Al^{3+} ion gains three electrons to form a neutral aluminium atom. The aluminium ions gain electrons so they are reduced.

$$Al^{3+} + 3e^{-} \rightarrow Al$$

At the same time, pairs of oxide ions give up electrons to form oxygen molecules. The oxide ions lose electrons so they are oxidised.

$$2O^{2-} \rightarrow 4e^{-} + O_2$$

Because reduction and oxidation always occur together, these are often referred to as redox reactions.

QUESTIONS

8 Give the word and symbol equations for the reaction between the carbon cathode and the oxygen gas that is released there.
9 The melting point of pure aluminium oxide is over 2000 °C. Why is aluminium oxide not simply heated to this temperature?

Aluminium recycling

You will find out:

- The social, economic, and environmental impacts of extracting aluminium for its ore, and of recycling aluminium
- The importance of the rainforests

Billions of cans

The metal aluminium is used to make cans to hold fizzy drinks. Worldwide we use six billion aluminium cans every year. That is enough to reach to the Moon and back!

FIGURE 1: Worldwide we use an amazing six billion aluminium cans every year.

What can you recycle?

Do you **recycle** materials at home or at your school? Glass, paper, plastic and cans can all be recycled. But is it really worth recycling your old aluminium cans?

How do we get aluminium from its ore?

Aluminium is a useful metal that is extracted from its ore **bauxite**. In fact aluminium is quite a reactive metal, and a process called electrolysis is used for its extraction (see page 132).

What are the problems with extracting aluminium ore?

Extracting aluminium from bauxite by electrolysis is expensive because a lot of electricity is needed. Also, bauxite is often found in environmentally sensitive areas, such as the Amazon **Rainforest** in Brazil. These rainforests are very important ecosystems. Tomatoes, bananas and lemons were all discovered in rainforests.

FIGURE 2: All of these everyday foods were discovered in rainforests.

What are the advantages of recycling?

By recycling aluminium, we can stop rainforests being cut down to mine fresh bauxite. We can also help save **energy**. It takes the same amount of energy to make one new aluminium can as it does to make twenty recycled cans. By recycling our aluminium we also reduce the amount of **waste** that must be put into **landfill** sites.

By recycling aluminium we can stop rainforests being cut down

FIGURE 3: Do you recycle your used aluminium cans or do you just throw them away?

QUESTIONS

1. Which materials are often recycled?
2. What is the main ore of aluminium?
3. Give **two** reasons why recycling aluminium is a good idea.

WOW FACTOR!

Recycling one aluminium can saves enough energy to run your computer for three hours.

How does extracting bauxite affect local communities?

Bauxite is mined from big open-cast pits. Large numbers of trees have to be cleared every time a new mine is built. Trees also have to be cleared to build new roads for access to the mines. The trees are burnt and this produces carbon dioxide, a gas that contributes to global warming (see page 100). Global warming could affect weather patterns all over the world in unpredictable ways.

Mining for bauxite affects local people. In areas where bauxite is found, people traditionally live in a place for just a few years. They hunt and fish for food and farm the land. Then they move on, leaving the land to recover and restock. If more land is being mined, there is less land for these people to live on. Miners also bring diseases. Local people may never have been exposed to these diseases before so they have no natural **immunity**. This makes them very vulnerable, even to common diseases.

The mines can also pollute the local area in other ways, for example by **pollutants**, like litter and oil.

How is aluminium recycled?

Aluminium cans do not have labels so unlike many other containers they are 100% recyclable. Recycling aluminium is both straightforward and economically worthwhile. Cans are collected together, sometimes by local charities, and shredded and cleaned. The cans are then melted and the metal is reused. Aluminium can be recycled many times.

FIGURE 4: How could we make it easier to recycle aluminium?

QUESTIONS

4 For people living in the rainforest, what are the advantages of a bauxite mine being opened?

5 For people living in the rainforest, what are the disadvantages of a bauxite mine being opened?

6 Suggest **one** way to make people more likely to recycle aluminium.

Are there any other consequences of destroying the rainforest to extract bauxite?

It is estimated that half of the animal and plant species that are known to exist, are found in rainforests. Even today there are thousands of species living in rainforests that have not yet been discovered.

Perhaps the greatest loss to mankind will be the loss of plants that may have proved to be useful medicines. In this country, around a quarter of all prescription medicines are derived from plants that were found in rainforests. But we are now destroying these rainforests faster than we can test the plants that live there for their medicinal properties.

Half of the world's rainforests have already been lost. The more forest that is destroyed, the more plants will be lost to us forever.

FIGURE 5: What are the consequences of destroying the world's rainforests?

QUESTIONS

7 Write an article for your school newsletter explaining to students why they should recycle their aluminium drinks cans.

Titanium

You will find out:

- About some properties of titanium
- About some uses of titanium
- How titanium is extracted from its ore, rutile

Fighter aircraft

The F22 is considered to be the best fighter aircraft in the world. It is built from a **titanium** alloy. Titanium is an expensive metal but is ideal for applications where high strength, low density and an ability to withstand very high temperatures are essential.

FIGURE 1: Why is the F22 made from a titanium alloy?

Properties of titanium

Titanium is a useful metal because of its special **properties**.

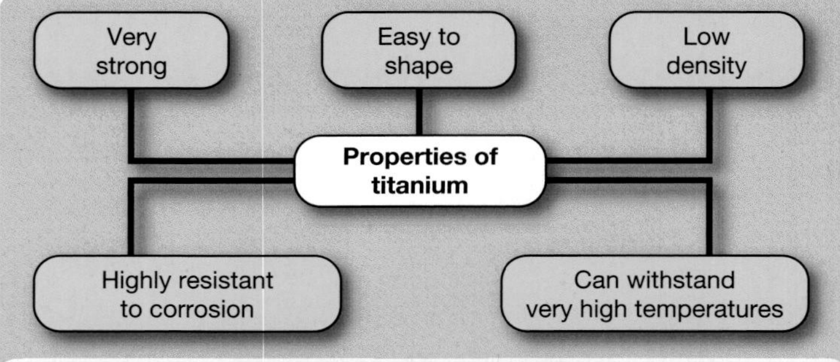

FIGURE 2: The properties of titanium.

Uses of titanium

Titanium has many uses including:

- replacement joints
- missiles
- rockets
- aircraft.

Do you know anyone who has had a hip replacement? The replacement joint is made from the metal titanium.

Extraction of titanium

Titanium is extracted from its **ore** called **rutile**. Rutile is a natural form of the compound titanium dioxide (TiO_2). It is converted into titanium chloride, which is then reacted with molten magnesium to produce pure titanium metal. This method of extracting titanium is very costly, which makes titanium an expensive metal.

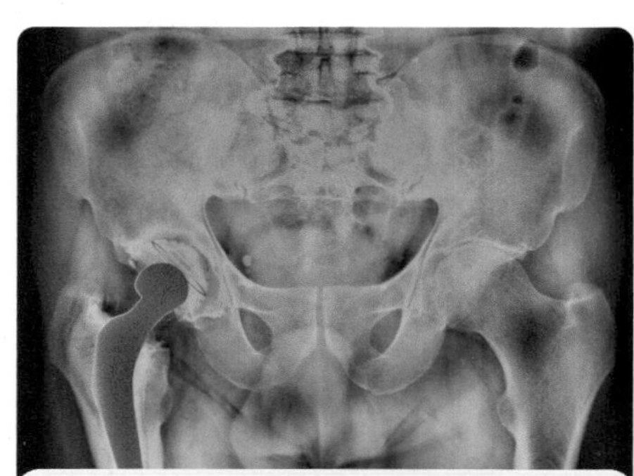

FIGURE 3: Why are replacement joints made from the metal titanium?

QUESTIONS

1 Identify the properties that make titanium a suitable metal from which to make artificial joints.

2 Identify the properties that make titanium a suitable metal from which to make missiles.

3 Identify the properties that make titanium a suitable metal from which to make the propellers of a ship.

4 Name the main ore of titanium.

...corrosion ...displaced ...ore ...properties

Why doesn't titanium corrode?

Titanium is a strong, light metal, and it is used to make replacement joints. So you might be surprised that a metal which can be safely placed inside the human body is actually very reactive.

In fact, it is such a reactive metal that the surface quickly reacts with oxygen to form a tough layer of **titanium dioxide**. Most of the time this is a good thing. The layer prevents the titanium from reacting further, and makes the object very resistant to **corrosion**.

The extraction of titanium

FIGURE 4: The main ore of titanium is called rutile and consists of titanium dioxide, TiO_2.

Titanium is the fourth most common metal in the Earth's crust, after aluminium, iron and magnesium. However, mining and extracting titanium from its ore is expensive. So despite its abundance and usefulness, its high cost has limited its use.

Rutile is very resistant to weathering, and it is deposited on certain beaches where it can be collected. The metal titanium is more **reactive** than carbon, so titanium cannot be extracted from rutile by simply heating it with carbon (the method used to extract iron from iron oxide). Nor can it be extracted by electrolysis (the method used to extract aluminium from its ore) because titanium chloride is covalently bonded so does not conduct electricity).

Instead, titanium dioxide is converted into titanium chloride, and then the titanium is **displaced** from this compound using a more reactive metal.

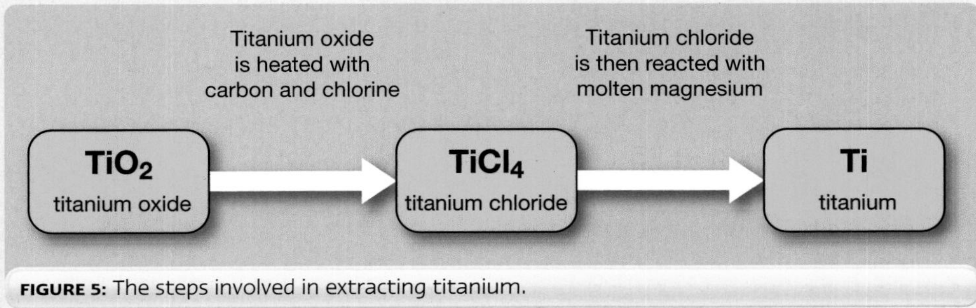

FIGURE 5: The steps involved in extracting titanium.

QUESTIONS

5 Why is titanium more resistant to corrosion than you might expect?

6 Explain why titanium cannot be extracted from its ore by heating with carbon.

7 Write a paragraph explaining how titanium is extracted from its ore. Ask someone else to read your explanation and ask them to write **one** good thing about your work and **one** way that it could be improved.

Extracting titanium

Titanium is extracted from its ore, rutile, by a series of chemical reactions.

First, titanium dioxide TiO_2 is converted to titanium chloride $TiCl_4$.

Then molten magnesium metal is reacted with the titanium chloride.

Magnesium is more reactive than titanium, and displaces the titanium from titanium chloride to form magnesium chloride and pure titanium.

titanium chloride + magnesium → magnesium chloride + titanium

$$TiCl_4 + 2Mg \rightarrow 2MgCl_2 + Ti$$

The hot titanium metal would quickly react with any oxygen that was present, so this reaction must be carried out under a vacuum or in an inert atmosphere.

Titanium extraction must be carried out in a vacuum or an inert atmosphere

QUESTIONS

8 Magnesium can be used to displace titanium from titanium chloride. Name another metal that could be used to displace titanium from titanium chloride. Explain why you chose this metal.

9 Would you expect titanium or magnesium to be more expensive? Why?

Copper

You will find out:

- About the properties of copper
- That copper-rich ores are limited, and how traditional methods of mining these ores cause problems

The Statue of Liberty

The Statue of Liberty in New York Harbour is famous all over the world. It is a symbol of freedom and democracy. The statue was given to the people of the United States of America by the people of France, in celebration of the friendship that the two countries established during the American Revolution. The outside of the statue is made from copper. Over time the colour of the statue has changed as the copper has weathered.

FIGURE 1: The outside of the Statue of Liberty is made from copper.

Properties of copper

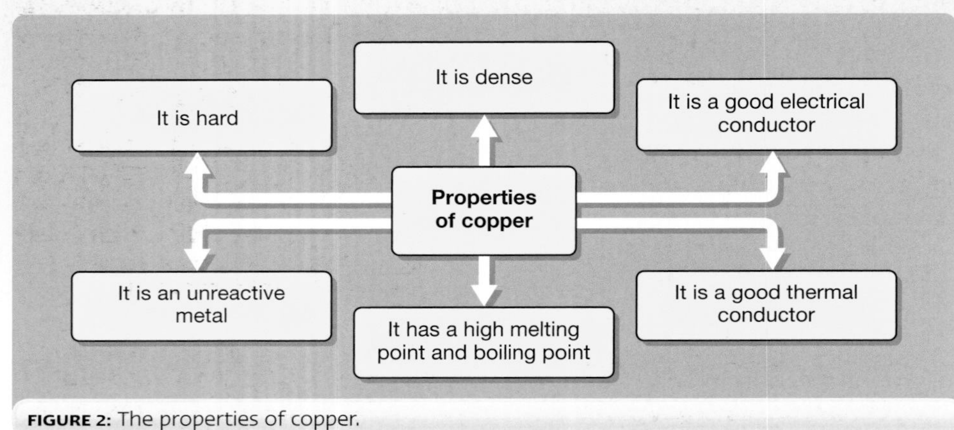

Properties of copper
It is hard
It is dense
It is a good electrical conductor
It is an unreactive metal
It has a high melting point and boiling point
It is a good thermal conductor

FIGURE 2: The properties of copper.

How is copper used?

Copper is a very **good conductor** of electricity. It is used for electrical wiring. Copper is also very **unreactive**. It is used in plumbing because the copper does not react with water.

How is copper extracted?

Copper ores are traditionally extracted from opencast pits. These pits often contain many copper-rich ores. The most important ores of copper are **chalcopyrite** and **chalcosine**.

Opencast mines cause significant problems to the environment.

FIGURE 3: Chalcopyrite is a copper-rich ore.

QUESTIONS

1. Why is copper used in electrical wiring?
2. Why is copper used in plumbing?
3. Name **two** ores of copper.

...chalcopyrite ...chalcosine ...concentrations ...good conductor

How is copper traditionally extracted?

Rocks containing copper ore are extracted from mines and then crushed into smaller pieces. A mixture of water and detergent is added to the rock pieces, and the copper-rich particles float to the top. These particles are collected and then dried. The copper ore is then heated in air to form copper oxide and sulfur dioxide. If we consider chalcosine, Cu_2S, the reaction is:

copper sulfide + oxygen → copper oxide + sulfur dioxide

$$2Cu_2S + 3O_2 \rightarrow 2Cu_2O + 2SO_2$$

The copper oxide then reacts with more of the copper ore, chalcosine, to form copper and sulfur dioxide:

copper oxide + copper sulfide → copper + sulfur dioxide

$$2Cu_2O + Cu_2S \rightarrow 6Cu + SO_2$$

Unfortunately, copper made by this method often contains small amounts of other metals and must be purified before it can be used.

What are the problems with extracting copper in this way?

Even in copper-rich rocks the copper is not present in very high **concentrations**. Typically these rocks only contain a few per cent of copper ore. This means that a lot of rock has to be extracted. This causes a lot of dust and noise pollution. The landscape is badly scarred and local wildlife destroyed. Finally, when copper sulfide is heated, the gas sulfur dioxide can be released and this can cause environmental problems. However, if this sulfur dioxide is collected it can be used to make sulfuric acid, which can then be sold on.

copper ore

rocks are crushed into smaller bits

copper-rich particles float to the top

rock, water and detergent

sulfur dioxide

flame

air

(Black) copper oxide forms

copper oxide is then reacted with more copper sulfide to form copper and more sulfur dioxide

FIGURE 4: This is one way of extracting copper from its ore.

How else can copper be extracted?

Recently scientists have been developing new ways of extracting copper from **low-grade ores**. These new methods are constantly being reviewed and refined. They involve **leaching** copper out of copper ore, to form a solution containing copper. The metal is then extracted from this solution using a process called electrolysis. This involves passing an electrical current though the solution. Very pure copper can be made in this way.

QUESTIONS

4 Explain how copper is extracted from chalcosine.

5 Give **two** problems with this method of producing copper.

6 Explain how copper can be extracted from low-grade ores.

Bronze and brass

Pure copper is quite soft and this makes it unsuitable for many uses. However, if copper is mixed with the metal tin, the alloy bronze is formed. Historically bronze has been used to make tools and weapons. Today it is often used to make statues.

FIGURE 5: This statue is made from bronze, an alloy of copper and tin.

Copper can also be mixed with zinc to make the alloy brass. Brass is stronger than either copper or zinc. It does not corrode easily and is a good electrical conductor. Brass is used to make musical instruments and electrical equipment.

FIGURE 6: Why is brass used to make these scales?

QUESTIONS

7 Draw a flow diagram showing the steps linking the copper ore chalcosine to the alloy brass.

Smart alloys

You will find out:
- That there are many different types of alloy
- That pure metals are too soft for many uses
- That smart alloys can return to their original shape after they are heated

Are silver coins really silver?

'Silver' coins have not contained any real silver since just after World War II. Instead we use a cupro-nickel alloy to make 5, 10, 20 and 50 pence pieces. This 50 pence piece contains 75% copper and 25% nickel. This copper and nickel alloy has a bright colour, good resistance to corrosion and is strong and hard wearing.

FIGURE 1: Why don't we make these coins from silver today?

What is an alloy?

Pure metals are too soft for many uses. To make metals harder we mix them together to make **alloys**. Useful alloys include:

- the copper alloys, bronze and brass
- steel, which is an alloy of iron, other metals and the non-metallic element carbon.

Why are smart alloys special?

Smart alloys are amazing new materials. Scientists have designed these alloys to have a **shape memory**. Like other metals, when smart alloys are stretched they change shape. However, unlike other metals, when smart alloys are heated they return to their **original** shape.

There are two main types of smart alloy:

- the cheaper copper-zinc-aluminium alloys
- the more expensive nickel-titanium alloys.

Scientists are using these new materials in many exciting ways.

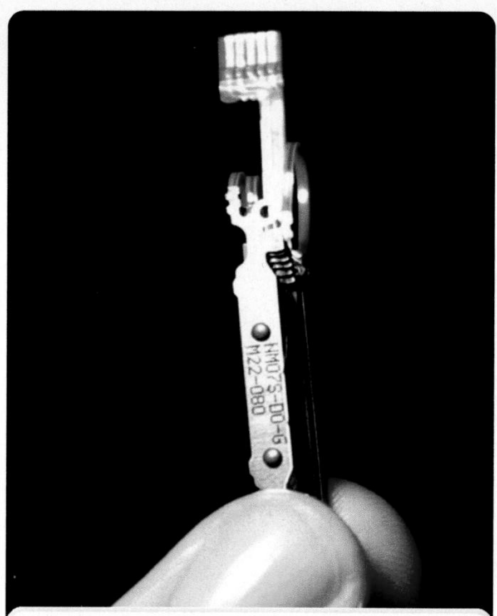
FIGURE 2: **Nitinol** is the trade name for the early nickel-titanium alloys.

Scientists have designed alloys with a shape memory

QUESTIONS

1. Name **two** alloys of copper.
2. How can you make a smart alloy return to its original shape?
3. Which metals are used to make the cheapest smart alloys?
4. Which **two** metals are used to make Nitinol?

...alloys ...deformed ...nitinol ...original

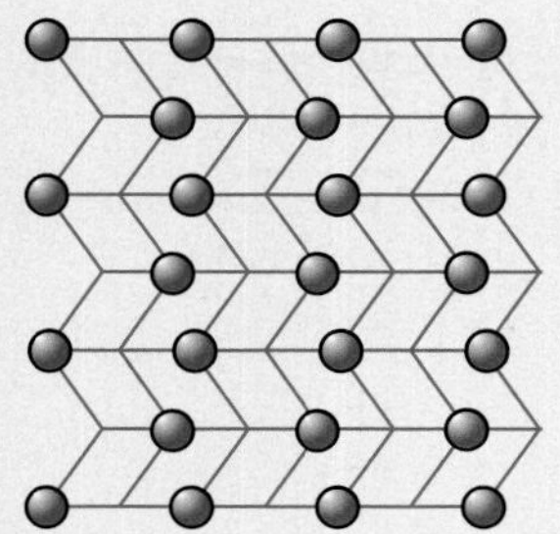

FIGURE 3: A smart alloy in its **undeformed** low-temperature form.

How do smart alloys work?

Smart alloys have amazing **properties** because they can exist in two different solid forms. A small temperature change of 10 °C to 15 °C is enough to trigger the change from one form to another.

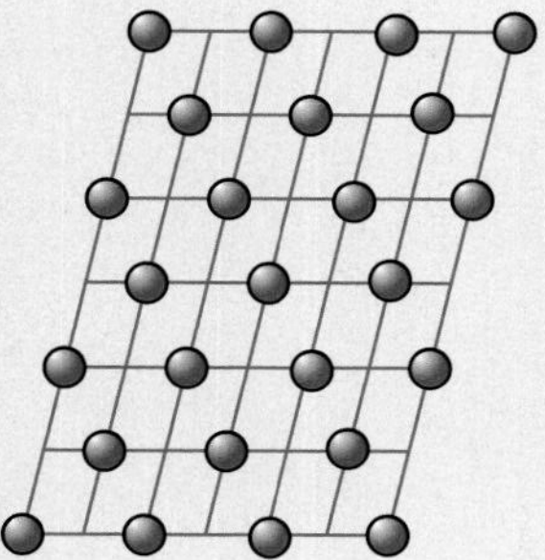

FIGURE 4: A smart alloy in its **deformed** low-temperature form.

If a force is applied to the smart alloy, it can be pulled into a new shape (see figure 4).

However, as soon as the smart alloy is heated it changes to a new form (figure 5). Smart alloys use the energy they absorb as they are heated to rearrange their atoms into this new form.

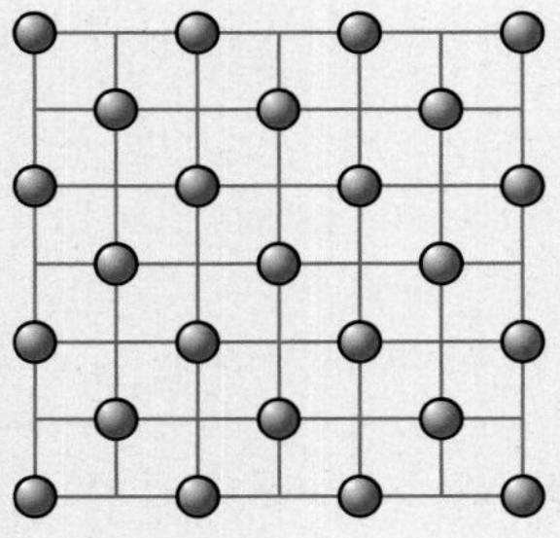

FIGURE 5: On heating, smart alloys change into a new high-temperature form.

The undeformed, low-temperature form of the smart alloy is exactly the same size and shape as the high-temperature form. So on heating, it appears that the smart alloy has returned to its original shape. In reality, at an atomic level the atoms are joined together in a different way but this cannot be easily seen. On cooling, the smart alloy returns to its low-temperature, undeformed form.

QUESTIONS

5 Describe how a low-temperature form of a smart alloy can be deformed.

6 What happens when a smart alloy is heated?

7 Why must a smart alloy be heated for the change to occur?

8 What happens to a smart alloy in its high-temperature form as it cools down?

How can smart alloys be used?

Smart alloys have been successfully used by doctors to help repair badly broken bones.

First, the bones are realigned. Often the damaged area can be held still in a cast to allow healing to occur. However, sometimes injury can occur to a part of the body where casts are not appropriate, for example the facial area. Traditionally, a titanium or stainless steel plate has been screwed onto the broken bones to hold them in place. The plate compresses the broken bones together. This increases the rate of healing.

With traditional plates, after just a few days as the bones start to grow, compression no longer occurs. Smart alloys can be used to keep the healing bones under sustained pressure. The smart alloy is cooled to below body temperature and then stretched as it is screwed onto the broken bone. Inside the body the smart alloy warms up. As it tries to return to its original size and shape it holds the bones together under tension which increases the rate of healing.

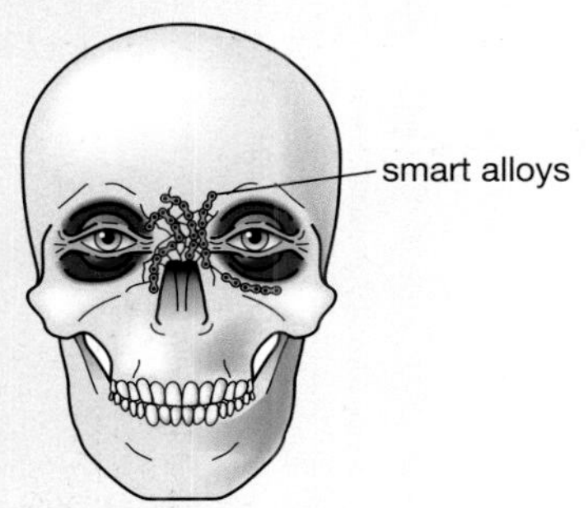

FIGURE 6: Smart alloys can be used to help bones heal faster.

QUESTIONS

9 Explain what happens, in terms of the arrangement of atoms, when smart alloys are used to help bones to heal faster.

Fuels of the future

You will find out:

- About the impact on the environment of burning hydrocarbon fuels
- About the environmental impacts of using different fuels

Lunar exploration

In 1971 the Apollo 15 astronauts David Scott and Jim Irwin explored the surface of the Moon using a lunar buggy. They used the vehicle to travel across the lunar surface and explore new areas. There is no air on the Moon so a fuel like petrol could not be used as it could not burn. Instead, the lunar buggy was powered by silver-zinc potassium hydroxide batteries.

FIGURE 1: Why was the lunar buggy battery powered?

Why are cars so important?

Today cars have become an indispensable part of many people's lives. However, more **pollution** is now caused by cars than by any other human activity. Although alternative public transport could be developed, many people would still not be prepared to give up their cars completely, so scientists need to develop ways of reducing the pollution that our cars produce.

FIGURE 2: Why are cars so useful?

What are the problems with the fuels that we use?

Today, **petrol** and **diesel** are the most popular fuels for cars. When we burn them they react with oxygen to release **carbon dioxide** and **water vapour**. However, combustion of these fuels is never complete and some **unburnt hydrocarbons** are released into the atmosphere. The gases **carbon monoxide** and **nitrogen oxides** are also released. These can all cause environmental problems.

In addition, while these fuels are quite cheap today, our reserves are **finite** and one day they will run out. So scientists are keen to look for alternative fuels for the future.

QUESTIONS

1 What human activity produces the most pollution?
2 What are the most popular fuels for cars?
3 Which gases are produced when petrol is burnt?
4 What is the longer term problem with using petrol as a fuel?

...carbon dioxide ...carbon monoxide ...diesel ...finite ...nitrogen oxides

What problems do petrol and diesel cause?

When petrol and diesel are burnt they release harmful pollutants into the atmosphere. The effects are particularly bad in big cities where there is lots of traffic and congestion. The exhaust gases can affect air quality and cause health problems. People with existing breathing problems, like asthma, may be particularly affected.

How can we reduce the problems with petrol?

All new petrol cars are now fitted with catalytic converters. These catalytic converters or 'cats' help reduce harmful emissions by converting:

- carbon monoxide to carbon dioxide
- unburnt hydrocarbons to carbon dioxide and water vapour
- nitrogen oxides to nitrogen.

Catalytic converters only work when they are hot, so for the first part of any journey harmful pollutants are still being released. Great care must be taken not to use leaded petrol in a car that has a 'cat' as it will be poisoned and no longer work.

What other fuels could we use?

Alcohol

Although fossil fuels like petrol are popular, they are not the only fuels we could use. We could use alcohol. Alcohol can be produced from sugar cane and is already popular in countries like Brazil where sugar cane is grown in large quantities. The alcohol is mixed with petrol. This mixture burns more cleanly than petrol so produces less harmful carbon monoxide. However, the alcohol methanol is a toxic chemical that can cause blindness and death. There are health concerns for people, such as petrol station attendants, that are exposed to it for long periods. Alcohols also release less energy than petrol when they are burnt.

Hydrogen

Another fuel which we already use is hydrogen. One way to produce hydrogen is by passing an electric current through water. When hydrogen is burnt it releases lots of energy. In addition, burning hydrogen produces water vapour which does not pollute the atmosphere. However, the production of hydrogen requires a lot of electricity and hydrogen is flammable so it has to be stored under special conditions.

QUESTIONS

5 Why is pollution worse in big cities like London?
6 How do catalytic converters reduce harmful emissions?
7 What are the disadvantages of using alcohol as a fuel?
8 Is hydrogen a good fuel? Why?

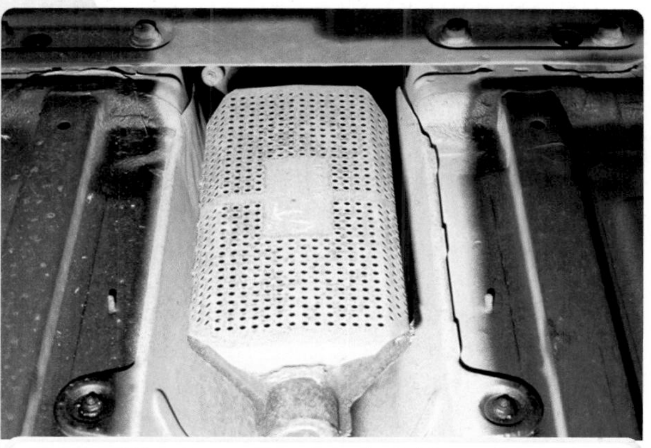

FIGURE 3: Why do new cars have 'cats'?

Electric vehicles

Electric vehicles which are powered by batteries do not emit any harmful pollution into the atmosphere. However, the batteries need to be recharged regularly and these vehicles have to carry around large, heavy batteries. Most of the electric vehicles in this country are milk floats, which are notorious for travelling quite slowly.

FIGURE 4: Why are most milk floats battery powered?

QUESTIONS

9 Electric vehicles do not emit pollutants themselves. How could an increase in the number of electric vehicles lead to an increase in the levels of carbon dioxide and sulphur dioxide in the atmosphere?

Crude oil

You will find out:

- That crude oil is a mixture of different compounds
- That most of the compounds in crude oil are hydrocarbons
- How crude oil can be separated by fractional distillation

New materials

These walkers are wearing fleece jackets. The jackets are lightweight, comfortable to wear and are quick to dry out if they get wet. They will keep these people warm even in very cold conditions. They are made from crude oil. Can you think of any other products that are made from crude oil?

FIGURE 1: You might have thought this fleece comes from a sheep, but it doesn't. This fleece started its life as crude oil.

Crude oil is a mixture

Most cars run on **petrol**. It is a colourless liquid that catches fire very easily. We say it's highly **flammable**. It must be stored very carefully. Petrol is one of the useful products that we get from **crude oil**.

Crude oil is a mixture of very many **compounds**, but the most useful compounds are called **hydrocarbons**. Petrol is a mixture of just a few of the compounds found in crude oil.

Hydrocarbons are compounds that only contain hydrogen atoms and carbon atoms. Crude oil is a mixture of lots of different hydrocarbons. Each compound is made up of molecules. The size of a molecule depends on the number of atoms it's made from. Some are short, made from just a few atoms. Others are longer, made from lots of atoms.

Name of fraction	Number of carbon atoms	Uses
petroleum gas	1 to 4	heating and cooking
naphtha	5 to 9	to make other chemicals
petrol	5 to 10	motor fuel
kerosene	10 to 16	jet fuel
diesel	14 to 20	diesel fuel and heating oil
oil	20 to 50	motor oil
bitumen	more than 50	in road making

Fractional distillation

Before we can use the different compounds in crude oil they have to be separated. They are separated into groups called fractions using a method called **fractional distillation**. Each fraction is a mixture of hydrocarbons with similar **boiling points**.

Separation by fractional distillation depends on the fact that different compounds boil at different temperatures.

How is crude oil used?

The table above shows the different fractions obtained from crude oil and how they are used.

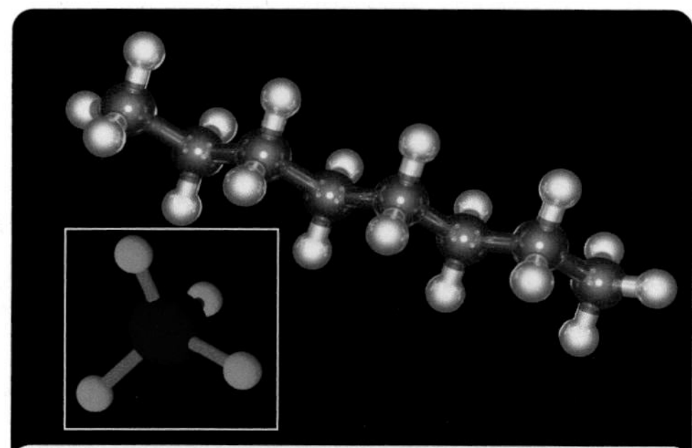

FIGURE 2: Methane has short molecules. It's a gas. Octane has longer molecules. It's the main hydrocarbon in petrol and it's a liquid.

QUESTIONS

1 Why do we have to store petrol carefully?

2 What is the name given to compounds that only contain hydrogen and carbon atoms?

3 What is the name used for groups of similar hydrocarbon molecules?

How is crude oil separated?

Because crude oil is a mixture, the compounds in crude oil are not chemically joined together.

- Within each hydrocarbon molecule there are strong **covalent** bonds (see page 114). However, the forces of attraction between molecules are much weaker. The boiling point of each hydrocarbon depends upon the strength of the forces between the molecules.
- Short hydrocarbon molecules have very weak forces of attraction between molecules. These molecules boil at low temperatures.
- Longer hydrocarbon molecules have stronger forces of attraction between molecules. These molecules boil at higher temperatures.

We can use the difference in boiling points to separate out the molecules in crude oil.

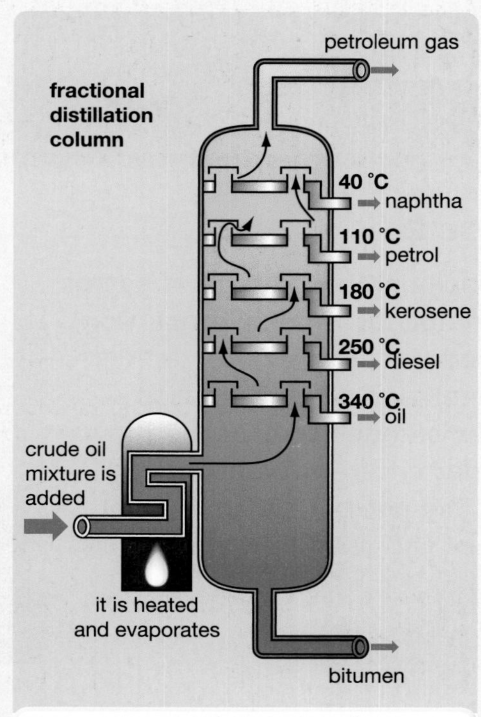

FIGURE 3: How are these hydrocarbons separated?

Fractional distillation takes place in a **fractionating column**. We heat the crude oil until it evaporates. The shorter hydrocarbon molecules evaporate first and reach the top of the fractionating column before they condense to form the petroleum gas fraction. The other hydrocarbon molecules in crude oil have longer carbon chains. When we heat crude oil these molecules will also eventually evaporate and move up the fractionating column. However, these longer chain hydrocarbons condense at higher temperatures so we collect these fractions lower down the column.

We use differences in boiling point to separate the molecules in crude oil

QUESTIONS

4 What are the shortest hydrocarbons used for?

5 You have two hydrocarbons. One is short and made of just a few atoms, the other is much longer and is made of more atoms. Which boils at the highest temperature? Why?

6 How high up a fractional distillation column would you expect to collect the shortest hydrocarbon molecules? Why?

Why can crude oil be separated by fractional distillation?

The difference in boiling point between different hydrocarbon molecules is caused by a difference in the forces of attraction between the molecules.

Short chain hydrocarbon molecules have weak forces of attraction between molecules. Less energy must be used to overcome these weak forces of attraction so short chain hydrocarbon molecules boil at low temperatures.

Longer chain hydrocarbon molecules align themselves in parallel. This increases the forces of attraction between the molecules. Because the forces of attraction between these molecules are greater, more energy must be used to overcome them so the longer chain hydrocarbons boil at higher temperatures.

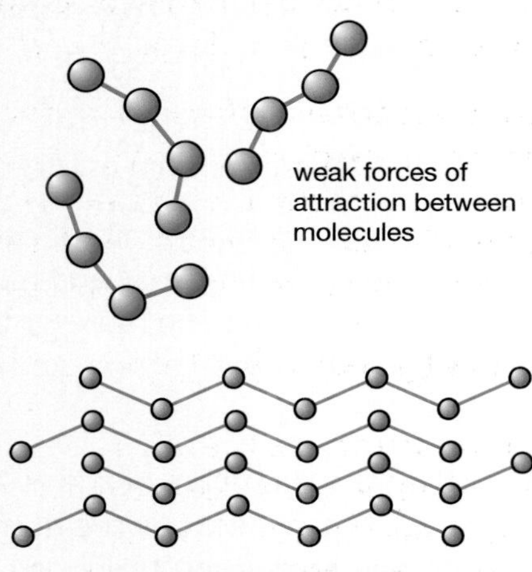

FIGURE 4: Which of these hydrocarbon molecules has the higher boiling point?

QUESTIONS

7 Which is stronger, the force between hydrocarbon molecules or the force within hydrocarbon molecules? How do you know?

Alkanes

You will find out:

- That crude oil is a mixture of compounds
- That most of the compounds in crude oil are hydrocarbons
- That most of these hydrocarbons are alkanes

Fuels for racing cars

This F1 racing car is fuelled by a specially prepared type of petrol. Petrol is a mixture, which consists mainly of small hydrocarbon molecules belonging to a family called the alkanes.
Each of these molecules has between 5 and 10 carbon atoms. The petrol used for F1 cars is specially blended to give the maximum possible performance under different weather conditions and on different circuits. The petrol used in normal cars is very similar and it is just one of the useful products obtained from crude oil.

FIGURE 1: Why is petrol such a popular fuel?

Methane

Have you ever used a Bunsen burner in your science lessons? The gas used in Bunsen burners is called **methane**. Methane is obtained from **crude oil** (see the previous section on crude oil to find out how crude oil can be separated).

Methane, like most of the compounds in crude oil is a **hydrocarbon** compound. These compounds contain only hydrogen and carbon atoms.

Methane belongs to a family of hydrocarbons called the **alkanes**. Methane is the first member of this family and has just one carbon atom and four hydrogen atoms. Methane can be represented by the formula CH_4. The next member of the family has two carbon atoms and six hydrogen atoms and can be represented by the formula C_2H_6.

In fact, all the members of the alkane family can be represented by the general formula C_nH_{2n+2} where n is the number of carbon atoms. To work out the number of hydrogen atoms you simply times the number of carbon atoms by two and then add two to your answer.

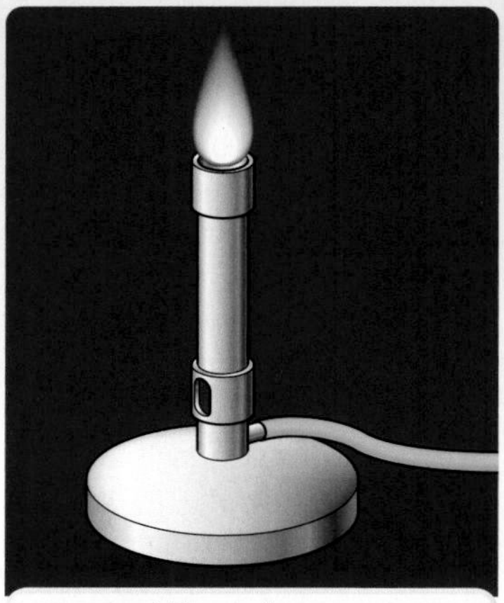

FIGURE 2: Where does methane come from?

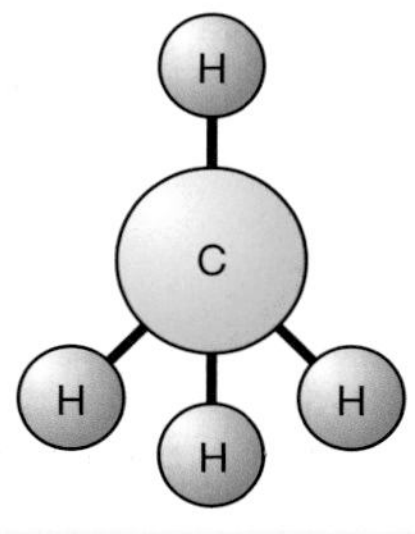

FIGURE 3: What atoms are present in a molecule of methane?

EXAM HINTS AND TIPS

Remember all members of the alkane family have the formula C_nH_{2n+2}.

QUESTIONS

1. What is a hydrocarbon?
2. What is the formula of methane?
3. An alkane has three carbon atoms. How many hydrogen atoms will it have?

The alkane family

All of the alkane compounds are made from the two elements, carbon and hydrogen. These atoms are held together by strong **covalent** bonds. (See page 114 to find out more about covalent bonds.) All alkanes share a similar structure. This means that all alkanes have similar properties. We can think of them as belonging to a family of similar compounds.

Naming hydrocarbons

All the members of the family have the general formula C_nH_{2n+2} and they all have names that end in 'ane', for example meth<u>ane</u> and eth<u>ane</u>.

Alkanes can be represented in many different ways as shown below.

name	formula	structure	atomic model
methane	CH_4	H H–C–H H	
ethane	C_2H_6	H H H–C–C–H H H	
propane	C_3H_8	H H H H–C–C–C–H H H H	
butane	C_4H_{10}	H H H H H–C–C–C–C–H H H H H	
pentane	C_5H_{12}	H H H H H H–C–C–C–C–C–H H H H H H	

QUESTIONS

4 Why do alkanes behave in a similar way?

5 Draw the structure of the alkane, hexane, C_6H_{14}.

6 An alkane has the formula C_7H_{16}. How many atoms of carbon and hydrogen are present in one molecule of this alkane?

7 A compound has the formula C_4H_8. Is this molecule a hydrocarbon? Is it an alkane?

How are the atoms arranged in alkanes?

Most of the compounds found in crude oil belong to the alkane family. Alkanes are hydrocarbon compounds. The carbon atoms are joined together by single covalent bonds. The carbon atoms also form single covalent bonds to hydrogen atoms. Notice how each carbon atom forms four single covalent bonds while each hydrogen atom forms just one single covalent bond. All alkanes have the general formula C_nH_{2n+2}. The carbon atoms in alkanes can be joined together in one straight chain as in this molecule called butane.

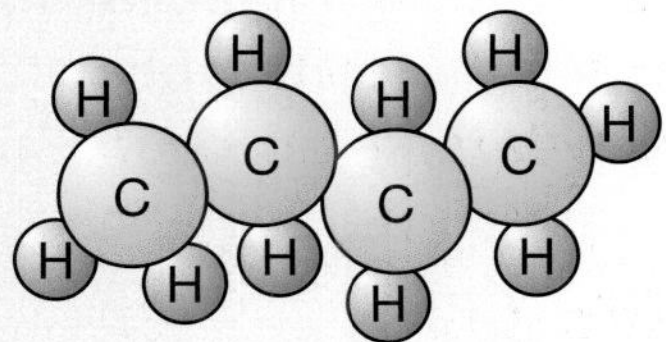

FIGURE 4: This alkane is called butane. What is its formula?

Or the carbon atoms can be joined together to form a branched chain as in methyl propane.

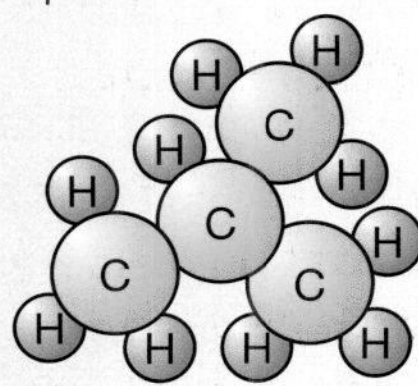

FIGURE 5: This alkane is called methyl propane. What is its formula?

- Both of these molecules have the same general formula C_4H_{10}
- Both molecules are members of the alkane family,

However, they are clearly different molecules. These two molecules are called **isomers**. They contain the same atoms but they have a different structure and different properties.

QUESTIONS

8 Draw the **three** possible isomers of C_5H_{12}.

9 Produce a leaflet that could be used by a Year 9 pupil to identify the names of the first five members of the alkane family.

Pollution problems

You will find out:

- That most fuels contain carbon and/or hydrogen and many contain some sulfur
- That when fuels are burnt carbon dioxide, water vapour and sulfur dioxide can be released

Krakatau

When the volcano Krakatau, part of a chain of Indonesian islands, erupted on August 26 1883, the explosion was heard more than 3000 km away in Australia. The volcano sent a massive cloud of dust high into the sky. This dust caused the area around the volcano to be shrouded in darkness for three days and three nights. The dust particles thrown out by the volcano spread around the globe and weather patterns were affected on a worldwide scale for many years. In addition, spectacular red sunsets were reported across America and Europe for several years.

FIGURE 1: The dust from the volcanic eruption at Krakatau caused dramatic red sunsets like this one.

What's in a fuel?

What happens when animals and plants die? Given a few million years they end up as **coal**, **oil** and **gas**. We call these three **fossil fuels** because they are formed from the fossilised remains of dead plants and animals. Fossil fuels release heat when they burn. Coal, oil and natural gas are made up from the elements carbon and hydrogen.

When carbon burns in oxygen, the gas **carbon dioxide** forms. This is the word equation:

carbon + oxygen → carbon dioxide

When hydrogen burns in oxygen, water vapour (steam) forms:

hydrogen + oxygen → water vapour

How does burning fossil fuels affect the environment?

Energy from burning fossil fuels heats our home, provides us with electricity and keeps our cars moving. It's impossible to imagine life without this source of energy.

However, there are problems:

- Carbon dioxide contributes to **global warming**.
- Some fuels release tiny particles into the atmosphere. We think these particles contribute to **global dimming**.
- Fossil fuels also contain small quantities of sulfur. When we burn sulfur we make **sulfur dioxide**

sulfur + oxygen → sulfur dioxide

Sulfur dioxide is poisonous. It pollutes the air and causes acid rain.

QUESTIONS

1. Name **three** fossil fuels.
2. Name the gas produced when carbon is burnt in a good supply of oxygen.
3. Which gas is thought to be linked to acid rain?

EXAM HINTS AND TIPS

Remember pH decreases as rain water becomes more acidic

How is acid rain caused?

Rainwater normally has a pH of around 5.5. It is slightly acidic because carbon dioxide, which is naturally present in the atmosphere, dissolves in the rainwater.

carbon dioxide + water → carbonic acid

However, in areas affected by sulfur dioxide pollution, the rainwater can become even more acidic. The sulfur dioxide can dissolve in rainwater and dramatically decrease its pH.

sulfur dioxide + water → sulfurous acid

Acid rain can attack and weather buildings. Luckily for us, limestone is a common rock in this country. When acid rain falls on limestone, the limestone reacts with and neutralises the acid rain. However, other areas are less fortunate and in these areas acid ran can cause serious damage to trees and aquatic life in affected lakes.

What is global warming?

Scientists believe carbon dioxide contributes to global warming. Although still small, the amount of carbon dioxide in the atmosphere has been rising since the Industrial Revolution. This was when we started to burn more fossil fuels.

The Earth gets energy from the Sun. It absorbs this energy and its surface becomes warmer. The Earth emits some energy back into space. Carbon dioxide absorbs some of this energy. As levels of carbon dioxide increase, more energy is absorbed. Less escapes back into space. Scientists think this process is gradually increasing the temperature of the Earth.

FIGURE 2: This increase in temperature could lead to changes in weather patterns and could produce floods and droughts which would have dramatic effects on agriculture and water supplies.

What is global dimming?

The smoke particles which are released into the atmosphere when we burn fuels may be leading to global dimming. Over the last 50 years, scientists estimate the amount of sunlight reaching the Earth has decreased by about 3% every 10 years. Some believe this dimming may lead to a lowering of the Earth's temperature. This, in turn, may affect weather patterns around the world.

QUESTIONS

4 Why is rainwater slightly acidic?

5 How is acid rain formed?

6 How do increased levels of carbon dioxide lead to global warming?

7 What are the effects of global dimming?

If the size of fish is increasing, why does that mean there is a problem?

One of the first pieces of evidence that acid rain was affecting lakes was that fishermen starting catching fewer fish. Those they did catch were often bigger, older fish than normal.

In the short term this may not seem to be a great problem but scientists wanted to know why it was happening. They discovered that fishermen were catching a greater proportion of big fish because there were far too few small, young fish in affected lakes. Acid rain was lowering the pH of the water in these lakes. This meant that fish born in these waters often had deformities. Many young fish died. With fewer young fish in the lakes, the older fish had little competition. They were able to grow to bigger sizes. But as these fish became older they eventually could no longer reproduce. In the long term this is disastrous for the fish population.

FIGURE 3: Why isn't it always good news for fisherman to be catching a lot of big fish?

QUESTIONS

8 Explain how burning fossil fuels in Britain could affect the size of the fish that are caught in lakes in Europe.

...global dimming ...global warming ...oil ...sulfur dioxide

Reducing sulfur problems

You will find out:

- That sulfur can be removed from fuels before they are burnt and how this is done
- That sulfur dioxide can be removed from waste gases and how this is done

Preserving food with sulfur dioxide

Fizzy drinks and fruit juices all contain the additive E220, or sulfur dioxide. There are concerns about high levels of this gas as it can cause asthma attacks in susceptible people but at low concentrations sulfur dioxide is an effective preservative. It works by killing bacteria, lowering the pH and by preventing the drinks from oxidising.

FIGURE 1: what effect could fizzy drinks have on this boy?

Sulfur problems

We know that:

- **Sulfur compounds** are found in **fossil fuels** (**coal**, **oil** and **natural gas**).
- When these fuels are burnt the gas **sulfur dioxide** is formed.
- That sulfur dioxide causes **acid rain**.

Removing sulfur

Sulfur compounds can be removed from oil and gas before they are burnt. This improves the fuels because when we burn them we will not produce sulfur dioxide. This means that we will not cause acid rain. There is another advantage to this process. The sulfur that we have removed is a valuable **resource** which we can sell.

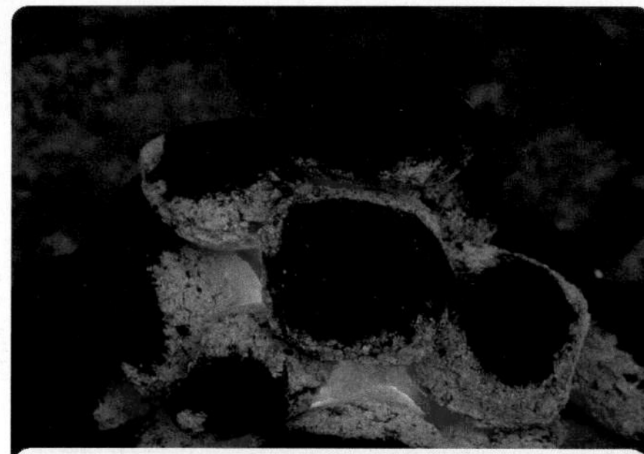

FIGURE 2: Why do we want to reduce the amount of sulfur dioxide produced when we burn fossil fuels such as coal?

Removing sulfur dioxide

Sulfur cannot be easily removed from the fossil fuel coal. Instead, we can burn the coal as normal and any sulfur will react to form sulfur dioxide.

sulfur + oxygen → sulfur dioxide

We can then remove any sulfur dioxide that has been formed from the waste gases before it can escape and cause problems in the **environment**.

QUESTIONS

1. Which gas causes acid rain?
2. Give **two** advantages of removing sulfur compounds from gas.
3. How are sulfur compounds removed from coal?

...acid rain ...coal ...environment ...fossil fuels ...hydrogen sulfide ...natural gas

How can sulfur be removed from fuels?

Natural gas and oil both contain a compound of sulfur called **hydrogen sulfide**. It is not desirable to leave this compound in the fuel because when it is burnt it will produce sulfur dioxide. To remove this compound, the hydrogen sulfide is dissolved in a solvent. The hydrogen sulphide can then be removed from the solution and the valuable sulfur can be extracted and then sold on. The fuel can be used as usual, but it will not produce sulfur dioxide when it is burnt.

How is sulfur dioxide removed from the waste gases at power stations?

Many power stations use coal to generate electricity. There is a lot more sulfur in coal than in oil or natural gas, so one easy way that we can reduce the amount of sulfur dioxide that we produce is to build new power stations which use a fuel that produces less sulfur dioxide. However, coal remains an important resource and scientists have found ways that allow us to continue using coal in existing power stations, but without producing lots of sulfur dioxide that can damage the environment.

Sulfur cannot be easily removed from coal but we can remove the sulfur dioxide (made when the sulfur is burnt) from the waste gases of the power station using **scrubbers**. The scrubbers remove around 95% of the sulfur dioxide that the power station produces. They work by injecting a mixture of limestone and water into the waste gases. Most of the sulfur dioxide that is present reacts to form calcium sulfate or 'gypsum'. The calcium sulfate can be sold to farmers to improve their soil.

FIGURE 3: How do we remove sulfur dioxide from the waste gases produced by this power station?

QUESTIONS

4 Name the compound found in gas and oil that can lead to the formation of sulfur dioxide.

5 Explain how the sulfur compound is removed from oil and gas.

6 How is sulfur dioxide removed from the waste gases of coal-fired power stations?

Pollution from ships

The problems of acid rain have been well known for the last thirty years. Since that time scientists have worked hard to reduce the amount of sulfur dioxide produced by power stations. In central and eastern England, where most of Britain's power stations are located, there has been a dramatic decrease in the level of acid rain and, as a consequence, aquatic life is beginning to recover in lakes and streams. However in most of Wales, aquatic life is still devastated. Scientists believe that this damage has been caused by acid rain made by sulfur dioxide pollution from ships operating in the North Sea and the north Atlantic.

FIGURE 4: Scientists believe that ships may be contributing to the acid rain problem.

QUESTIONS

7 Suggest how you could reduce the amount of sulfur dioxide produced by the ships operating in the North Sea and the north Atlantic.

Unit summary

Concept map

Atoms and rocks

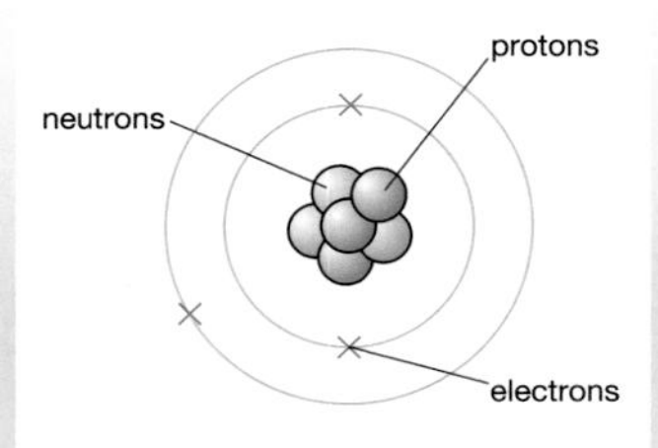

All substances are made from atoms, which have:
- protons and neutrons in a small nucleus
- electrons outside the nucleus.

An element consists of one type of atom; a compound consists of two or more types of atoms bonded together.

Bonds form between atoms when electrons are shared or transferred.

Limestone is mainly the compound calcium carbonate. It:
- breaks down when heated to give quicklime and carbon dioxide (adding water to quicklime makes slaked lime)
- can be used to make cement, concrete and glass.

Metals

Metals are elements that are extracted from their ores, often oxides, by chemical reactions (iron, titanium, copper), or by electrolysis (aluminium). They are sometimes mixed together to make alloys.

Iron is made in a blast furnace:
- impurities make cast iron from the furnace hard but brittle
- removing impurities makes wrought iron, which is easy to shape but soft
- adding metals and carbon to pure iron makes steel.

Shape memory alloys can be deformed, but return to their original shape when heated.

Aluminium:
- has low density and is soft
- forms strong, low density alloys when mixed with other metals.

Transition metals, such as titanium and copper, are:
- found in the central block of the periodic table
- hard and strong
- good conductors of heat and electricity.

Crude oil

Crude oil is a fossil fuel. It is a mixture of hydrocarbon compounds (made from carbon and hydrogen) that can be separated by fractional distillation.

Alkanes are an important type of hydrocarbon with the general formula C_nH_{2n+2}.

Scientists are working to reduce pollution and develop better fuels for the future.

Burning fossil fuels releases useful energy, but harmful substances are also made:
- carbon dioxide contributes to the greenhouse effect
- sulfur dioxide contributes to acid rain
- smoke particles contribute to global dimming.

Unit quiz

1 Which of these particles is not found inside an atom?

protons **electrons**
molecules **neutrons**

2 What is a covalent bond?

a shared pair of electrons
the gain of electrons
the loss of electrons
an attraction between molecules

3 What is the formula for quicklime?

$CaCO_3$ CO_2 $Ca(OH)_2$ CaO

4 Which of these materials is *not* a solid raw material added to the blast furnace?

haematite **coke**
air **limestone**

5 Which of these properties does cast iron *not* have?

hard **flexible** **strong** **brittle**

6 Which of these non-metal elements is added to iron to make steel?

oxygen **silicon**
carbon **nitrogen**

7 Which of these metals is not a transition metal?

gold **titanium**
chromium **aluminium**

8 What is the name of the main ore of titanium?

haematite **limestone**
chalcosine **rutile**

9 Which of these is a copper alloy?

brass **mild steel**
stainless steel **solder**

10 Which of these gases is not produced when petrol is burnt?

water vapour **carbon monoxide**
nitrogen oxides **hydrogen**

11 Which of these compounds belongs to the alkane family of hydrocarbons?

butane **butene**
methanol **ethene**

12 Which gas produces acid rain?

oxygen **sulfur dioxide**
carbon dioxide **nitrogen**

Literacy activity

Sustainable fuels

Wood pellets are a popular fuel for fires and stoves in North American homes. They are a good example of a sustainable fuel. Wood is a renewable resource; when old trees are cut down new trees are planted to take their place. The pellets are a by-product of the furniture making industry. They are made from the waste sawdust that would otherwise be dumped in landfill sites. The sawdust is compressed under high pressure to form pellets.

QUESTIONS

1 Explain why wood pellets are a sustainable fuel.

2 The pellets only contain trace amounts of sulfur so very little sulfur dioxide is produced when they are burnt. What is the problem with producing lots of sulfur dioxide?

Exam practice

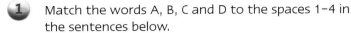

Exam practice questions

1 Match the words A, B, C and D to the spaces 1–4 in the sentences below.

A atom **B** neutrons
C electrons **D** nucleus

Atoms contain a central (1) surrounded by (2) . The central part of the atom contains protons and (3) . An element is a substance made of one type of (4) . [4]

2 Match the words A, B, C and D to the missing information, 1–4, on the diagram.

A calcium carbonate **B** heat
C add water **D** carbon dioxide [4]

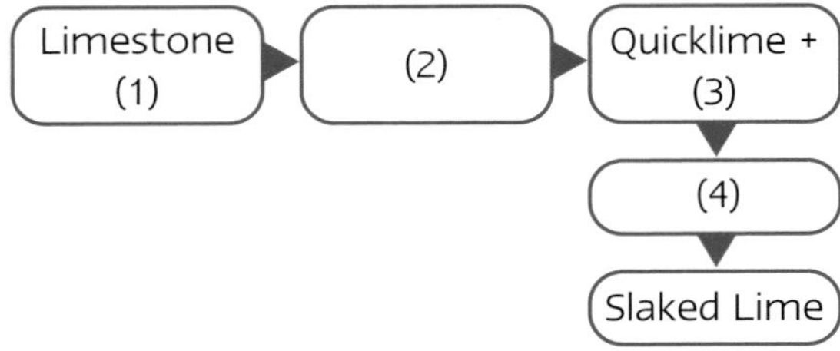

3 Match the words A, B, C and D to the spaces 1–4 in the sentences below.

A electrons **B** compounds
C mass **D** equations

When elements react their atoms combine to form (1) . This involves the taking and giving of (2) or the sharing of them. When elements react there is no loss of (3) which is why we can write balanced (4) for reactions. [4]

In questions 4 to 11, choose the best answer.

4 Copper is ...

A usually extracted by using electrolysis.
B useful for making bridges.
C in plentiful supply.
D not easily bent. [1]

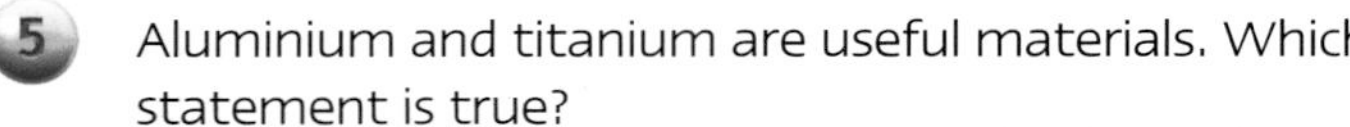

5 Aluminium and titanium are useful materials. Which statement is true?

A Aluminium is resistant to corrosion.
B They can both be extracted from their ores by heating with carbon.
C They are both cheap to extract.
D You cannot recycle aluminium or titanium. [1]

6 Iron ...

A is extracted using electrolysis.
B from a blast furnace is 90 per cent pure.
C when pure, is very hard.
D is made into stainless steel. [1]

7 Which one of these statements about alloys is false?

A Steel is an alloy.
B Smart metals return to their original shape when bent.
C In alloys the different sized atoms in the structure make the alloy softer.
D High carbon steels are good for tools as they are hard. [1]

8 Crude oil ...

A is a mixture of hydrocarbon atoms.
B is a mixture of hydrocarbon compounds.
C is a mixture and so it cannot easily be separated.
D is used as a fuel in power stations. [1]

9 Most of the compounds in crude oil ...

A are small molecules.
B are unsaturated hydrocarbons called alkanes.
C have no use.
D contain hydrogen and carbon only. [1]

10 Sulfur dioxide ...

A is found in crude oil.
B causes acid rain.
C is formed when pure hydrocarbons burn.
D cannot be removed from waste gases after fuels burn. [1]

11 Burning of fossil fuels ...

A leaves no environmental damage.
B produces gases linked with global warming.
C only produces sulfur dioxide as a pollutant.
D is our only option for road transport. [1]

12 Answer the following questions about metals.

a Give three properties of metals such as the transition metals. [3]

b Give two uses for copper and explain what property makes it useful for each purpose. [4]

c What makes titanium a particularly useful metal? [1]

d It is very expensive to extract titanium from its ores. Give two reasons why this is so. [2]

13 Limestone can be used directly for building or it can be used to make other substances.

a Give two other substances that can be made using limestone. [2]

b Limestone can be roasted in a kiln and broken down to make quicklime.

i What is the scientific term for breaking a substance down using heat? [1]

ii The reaction produces calcium oxide and carbon dioxide. Write a WORD equation for this reaction. [3]

14 A quarry owner in a National Park wants to expand her quarry to over ten times its current size. Give two good reasons for allowing this expansion and two reasons against. [4]

(Total 40 marks)

Worked example

Crude oil is a mixture of hydrocarbons, many of which are alkanes. Crude oil itself is not very useful and must be treated in order to obtain useful compounds from it. This produces different fractions which have different uses.

a Explain what you understand by the terms:

i fraction [1]

ii alkane [1]

b **i** Explain how crude oil is separated into fractions. [3]

ii What is the name of this process? [1]

c When a fuel burns it may release particles and three different gases into the air. Three of these four can cause environmental problems. Complete the following table. [6]

	Pollutant	Problem it causes
1		
2		
3		

(Total 12 marks)

a i A fraction contains molecules with the same number of carbon atoms in the molecule. ✗

ii An alkane is a hydrocarbon with the general formula C_nH_{2n+2}. ✓

b i Crude oil is heated and this evaporates the oil. ✓ *It is then condensed.* ✓

ii Fractional distillation. ✓

	Pollutant	Problem it causes
1	*particles* ✓	*global dimming* ✓
2	*carbon dioxide* ✓	*global warming* ✓
3	*??* ✗	*acid rain* ✓

In a) i the student has lost the mark. They should have written '**similar**' not '**same**'. Each fraction contains a range of molecules with similar numbers of carbons. The second explanation is a good answer.

Good answers but one mark has been lost in b) i where a third mark was available for saying, "It is condensed *at different temperatures*."

The student has forgotten that the gas sulfur dioxide is often formed when fuels burn but they did gain a mark by putting an answer down for the problem it causes.

Overall Grade: B

How to get an A

Always try to match the number of marks to the points you have made. If the question is open-ended, as in b) i, then you might write four points down just to make sure you score all of the marks.

Try not to leave blanks. A sensible guess might get a mark but a blank will not. This might be the mark that makes the difference.

Chemistry 1b – Oils, Earth and atmosphere

DISCOVER VOLCANOES!

Volcanoes can be dangerous to life on Earth. They show how powerful and destructive the Earth can be.

Lots of poisonous gases are formed when volcanoes erupt. However, many of these gases were important in creating the Earth's atmosphere.

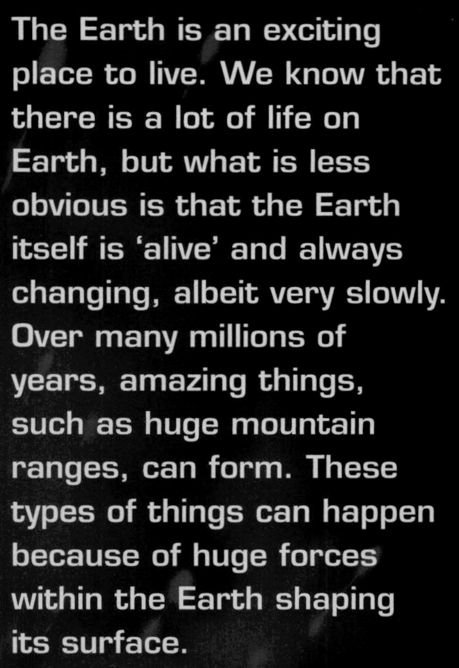

The Earth is an exciting place to live. We know that there is a lot of life on Earth, but what is less obvious is that the Earth itself is 'alive' and always changing, albeit very slowly. Over many millions of years, amazing things, such as huge mountain ranges, can form. These types of things can happen because of huge forces within the Earth shaping its surface.

We now know that the Earth's crust is like a broken eggshell. It is made up of many large pieces called plates, and these plates are always moving although only very slowly.

When the plates collide with each other, volcanoes may form or earthquakes may occur.

CONTENTS

Cracking

You will find out:

- That cracking produces useful substances from crude oil
- That cracking breaks down large molecules in crude oil to make them smaller
- That these include fuels and starting materials for plastics

Travelling in luxury

Figure 1 shows a powerful modern car that many people would like to own. The power it needs to run comes from petrol. In a car engine, petrol is the fuel. A fuel is a substance that burns to produce heat energy. The heat is then used to power the car.

FIGURE 1: Do you think this car is economical on petrol?

New molecules from crude oil

Crude oil is a valuable natural **resource**. It is a mixture of many substances. The substances can be separated out using a process called **fractional distillation**.

A lot of the separated substances become fuels, which are burnt to produce heat energy. Petrol is a mixture of some of them. Other fuels include diesel for lorries, fuel oil for ships and kerosene for aircraft.

Using a special process called **cracking**, new substances are made from crude oil.

What is cracking?

- The chemical compounds in crude oil are called **hydrocarbons**. These compounds are long chains of hydrogen and carbon atoms. They contain no other elements. They belong to a family called the **alkanes**.
- In cracking, the crude oil is heated to form a hydrocarbon **vapour**. This passes over a heated **catalyst**. This 'cracks' (splits) the molecules to form a mixture of new hydrocarbons. Using heat to split molecules and form smaller ones is called **thermal decomposition**.
- As a result of cracking, long alkane molecules in the crude oil are broken down to form shorter alkanes, plus a new family of hydrocarbons called **alkenes**.

long-chain alkanes → shorter-chain alkanes + alkenes

EXAM HINTS AND TIPS

Monkeys Eat Peanut Butter helps you count in carbon chemistry.

1 carbon in a molecule = meth-

2 carbons = eth-

3 carbons = prop-

4 carbons = but-

QUESTIONS

1 What is a hydrocarbon?

2 Give the names of **two** families (types) of hydrocarbons formed in cracking.

3 What needs to happen to a hydrocarbon for it to be cracked?

4 Give the names of **three** useful substances that come from crude oil and are used as fuels.

...alkanes ...alkenes ...catalyst ...chemical formula ...cracking ...fractional distillation

Why we need to crack hydrocarbons

Crude oil is a complicated mixture of alkanes. Some of the alkanes are very small, short-chain molecules and others are large, long-chain molecules.

Petrol is the main product made from crude oil. It is a mixture of alkane molecules that each contain between 5 and 12 carbon atoms. But crude oil only has a certain amount of hydrocarbons the right size to make petrol.

This is why larger hydrocarbon molecules that would not be useful are cracked to make smaller hydrocarbons. These are then used in petrol, mixed with the smaller molecules separated from crude oil in fractional distillation.

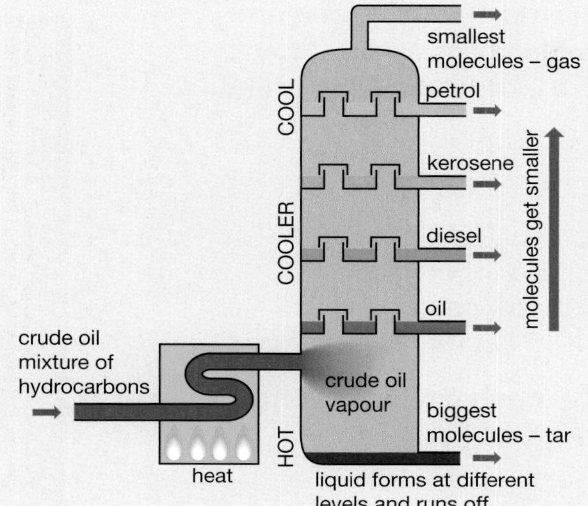

FIGURE 2: A fractional distillation plant separates the substances in crude oil.

When a long hydrocarbon molecule is cracked, an alkene is made as well as an alkane. Alkenes are more reactive than alkanes and can take part in many chemical reactions to make different compounds. This makes alkenes extremely useful.

One special reaction of alkenes produces **plastics**. Plastics are in the chemical group called **polymers**. Polymers are long-chain molecules formed when alkene molecules join together. Polymer molecules can contain millions of atoms joined together!

Plastics are everywhere in our lives. Many of the plastics we are familiar with are made from alkenes. Some names of polymers are polyethene and polypropene.

Polymer molecules can contain millions of atoms joined together!

QUESTIONS

5 Describe simply what is meant by 'polymer'.

6 What is the name of the new type of hydrocarbon made in a cracking process?

7 Give the names of **two** polymers.

How does cracking happen?

Alkane molecules can be represented by pictures. For each alkane, all the atoms are shown, and how they connect.

The molecule below is called decane, and is made up of 10 carbon atoms and 22 hydrogen atoms. It therefore has the **chemical formula** $C_{10}H_{22}$.

```
  H H H H H H H H H H
  | | | | | | | | | |
H-C-C-C-C-C-C-C-C-C-C-H
  | | | | | | | | | |
  H H H H H H H H H H
```

FIGURE 3: Decane – an alkane.

When decane vapour is passed over a heated catalyst, each large decane molecule breaks up to make smaller molecules. One of the smaller molecules is normally an alkene called ethene (C_2H_4).

```
  H H H H H H H H H H
  | | | | | | | | | |
H-C-C-C-C-C-C-C-C-C-C-H
  | | | | | | | | | |
  H H H H H H H H H H
         decane
           ↓
```

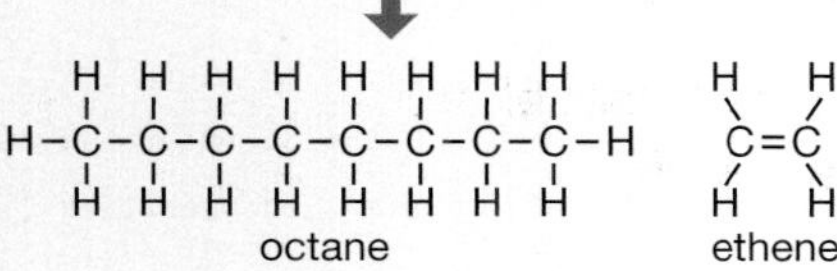

FIGURE 4: Cracking of decane. Which is the alkane formed?

The decane molecule can be broken in many different places when it is cracked. Think about how many different alkanes and alkenes can be made in this process.

QUESTIONS

8 What is the chemical formula for **a)** decane and **b)** ethene?

9 Suggest the name of the polymer formed when two ethane molecules join together.

10 Write a chemical equation to show decane being cracked to form ethene and octane.

11 Suggest the chemical formula for hexane.

Alkenes

You will find out:

- That alkenes are a family of hydrocarbons
- That all alkenes have a double bond
- That alkenes take part in useful reactions

Climbing mountains

Figure 1 shows a mountaineer climbing a high mountain. She carries a lot of equipment which she needs to make the climb as safe as possible. The rope the climber uses is very strong and is made from a polymer – a plastic – called polypropene. Many polymers, including polypropene, are made by reacting useful hydrocarbons called alkenes.

FIGURE 1: All the equipment must be strong, particularly the rope.

The alkenes

Alkenes are a family of **hydrocarbons**. This means that they are compounds made up of hydrogen atoms and carbon atoms only.

The smallest molecule in the alkene family is **ethene**. It has the formula C_2H_4. This is its molecular shape:

```
H     H
 \   /
  C=C
 /   \
H     H
```

Like all other alkenes, ethene has a **carbon double bond** in it. This bond is labelled red in the diagram.

The next member of the alkenes is called propene, it has the **chemical formula** C_3H_6:

```
    H   H   H
    |   |  /
H — C — C=C
    |      \
    H       H
```

All alkenes are called **unsaturated** hydrocarbons, because their molecules all have a carbon double bond in them.

Another family of hydrocarbons is called the alkanes.

Because of the carbon double bond, alkenes are a lot more **reactive** than alkanes. This means that alkenes can take part in more chemical reactions, which makes them a lot more useful than alkanes.

WOW FACTOR!

Propene is one of the most important industrial chemicals. Nearly 60 million tonnes are produced every year, much of it to make polypropene.

QUESTIONS

1 What is the chemical formula for **a)** ethene and **b)** propene?
2 What are the names of **two** families of hydrocarbons?
3 How many bonds does any carbon atom have in a molecule?

...carbon double bond ...chemical formula ...ethene

Why are alkenes more reactive than alkanes?

Let us compare the two hydrocarbons called eth**a**ne and eth**e**ne. Their names might sound similar, but their molecules are different. Ethane belongs to the alkane family, and ethene belongs to the alkene family.

```
ethene              ethane

H     H             H   H
 \   /              |   |
  C=C            H—C—C—H
 /   \              |   |
H     H             H   H
```

Alkanes and alkenes are two very different families of hydrocarbons. Ethene is a lot more reactive than ethane because of the carbon double bond it contains. The carbon double bond is the part of the molecule that makes all alkenes reactive.

EXAM HINTS AND TIPS

In all molecules, a carbon atom always forms four bonds. This is a good way to check if your structures are correct.

What is meant by a general formula?

Alkenes have the **general formula** of C_nH_{2n}. It shows that any molecule of an alkene always has *twice* as many hydrogen atoms as carbon atoms.

These are the chemical formulae of the first five alkenes:

ethene	C_2H_4
propene	C_3H_6
butene	C_4H_8
pentene	C_5H_{10}
hexene	C_6H_{12}

In alkenes, the number of carbons is '*n*', and the number of hydrogens is '2*n*'. This is why we write the general formula as C_nH_{2n}.

For alkanes also, we say the number of carbon atoms is 'n'. But the number of hydrogen atoms in alkanes is different. It is always '2*n* + 2', and therefore the general formula for alkanes is C_nH_{2n+2}.

If the number of carbon atoms in an alkane molecule was 100, the number of hydrogen atoms would be (2 × 100) + 2, making 202. So the formula for this alkane would be $C_{100}H_{202}$. Since it has 100 carbon atoms, we call this alkane centane (like 'century').

QUESTIONS

4 What is the name of the bond in an alkene molecule that makes it reactive?

5 What word describes all molecules which contain the bond you named in question 4?

6 Suggest a formula for the hydrocarbons called **a)** decene and **b)** decane.

7 A molecule of an alkane has 24 hydrogen atoms in it. How many carbon atoms must be present in the molecule?

Ripening fruit

Ethene gas can be used to increase the speed at which some types of fruit ripen. These fruit produce ethene themselves naturally as they ripen. The gas is 'sensed' in some way by nearby fruit, and this speeds up their ripening.

FIGURE 2: Explain how bananas use other bananas to ripen faster.

A clever way to make a bowl of green bananas go yellow is to place a yellow banana in with them, and then put all the bananas in a bag. The yellow banana makes the other bananas ripen a lot faster than they would on their own.

When bananas are grown in other countries, they are normally green when picked from the tree and transported to the UK. Here they are partly ripened before being sold in shops.

There may be occasions when you want to *slow down* the speed at which fruit ripens. This can be done by placing certain chemicals including potassium manganate near the fruit.

QUESTIONS

8 Which gas is used to ripen bananas?

9 Suggest how potassium manganate slows down the speed at which ripening takes place.

10 Describe an experiment that would show that mangoes ripen a lot more slowly when potassium manganate is present.

11 Suggest why ethane gas has little effect on the rate at which fruit ripens.

Making ethanol

You will find out:

- That ethanol (alcohol) is a compound that can be used as a fuel
- That ethanol is made from ethene derived from crude oil
- That it is also made by fermentation

Alcohol-powered cars

Worldwide, most cars use petrol as a fuel. Petrol comes from crude oil. However, one day crude oil will run out, and so we have had to start finding new fuels to power cars. **Alcohol** is a chemical compound which can be used as a fuel as well as a drink! It has been made for thousands of years from sugar. Now it is being made from sugar cane on a huge industrial scale.

FIGURE 1: Most cars in Brazil have run on alcohol since the time when the country could not afford crude oil.

Making ethanol

Ethanol is the chemical name that we use for alcohol. It is a colourless liquid, which looks just like water. However, unlike water, ethanol is highly **flammable**. This means that it can burn very easily.

This is the chemical structure of ethanol:

```
    H   H
    |   |
H — C — C — O — H
    |   |
    H   H
```

Notice that a molecule of ethanol has 2 carbon atoms, 6 hydrogen atoms and 1 oxygen atom. This gives it the chemical formula C_2H_6O. It is often written as C_2H_5OH because of the -OH at one end.

To make ethanol from crude oil takes two steps.

1 Crude oil contains large hydrocarbon molecules. In a process called cracking, these are broken up, and one of the smaller compounds formed is the gas **ethene**.

2 When a mixture of ethene and steam is passed over a **catalyst**, ethanol is made. The catalyst used is an acid called phosphoric acid. Catalysts speed up reactions, so in this reaction, ethanol is made faster.

Watch Out Ethanol is not a hydrocarbon because it contains oxygen as well as carbon and hydrogen.

QUESTIONS

1 What is the chemical name for alcohol?

2 What are the names of the **three** elements in the compound called ethanol?

3 What is a catalyst? Why is it useful to have a catalyst in a reaction?

EXAM HINTS AND TIPS

Ethanol is the chemical name for alcohol. It has the formula C_2H_5OH.

...alcohol ...biofuel ...catalyst ...ethanol ...ethene ...fermentation ...flammable

How ethanol is made from sugar

For at least 5000 years, people have made wine from grapes.

Sugars are found naturally in fruit, sugar beet and cane sugar. When sugar is dissolved in water and **yeast** is added, an important reaction called **fermentation** happens.

During fermentation, the sugar is changed chemically to ethanol.

When used as a fuel, ethanol burns very cleanly to produce heat energy. Since it is made from plants, such as sugar cane, it is called a **biofuel**. Ethanol can be added to petrol or it can replace petrol. Once the sugar cane is cut to make ethanol, it can then be grown again to make more ethanol.

Fuels that can be made over and over again are called **renewable** fuels. They can never run out. Ethanol is a renewable fuel since more sugar cane can be grown again to make more ethanol.

FIGURE 2: What do grapes contain that is used to produce ethanol?

FIGURE 3: Describe how sugar cane like this is used to make ethanol.

Renewable or non-renewable?

Ethanol can be made in more than one way. As we have seen, it can be made from sugar, which is renewable. It can also be made from crude oil, but crude oil will not last forever.

Since crude oil stocks will run out, it does make sense to find other ways of m… ethanol.

But is fermentation the answer? Think about the advantages and … making ethanol using either sugar or crude oil.

OIL IS RUNNING OUT

In 50 years, there will be very little crude oil left. We must find new fuels to replace those we use today.

How does fermentation work?

In a fermentation reaction, the sugars are changed chemically into ethanol and carbon dioxide gas.

We can show this reaction as a word and a symbol equation:

sugar in solution $\xrightarrow{\text{yeast}}$ **ethanol** + **…arbon dioxide gas**

$C_6H_{12}O_6 \longrightarrow 2C_2H$ … $OH + 2CO_2$

The alcohol forme… …ved in water is removed b… **…stillation** the mixtu… …ks beca… etha… …ent b…

QUESTION…

4 What is the name of the process used to ch… presence of yeast?

5 What is the chemical formula for ethanol?

6 What are the names of the **two** substances that rea… when crude oil is used?

...fractional distillation ...pharmaceuticals ...renewa…

Plastics from alkenes

You will find out:

- That alkenes react to make lots of new substances
- That alkenes are used to make plastics, which are polymers
- That polymers transform our lives

Plastics are everywhere!

Plastics are very important materials because they are used to make so many everyday items. For most objects we buy, plastics have replaced traditional materials like wood and metal. All the items in figure 1 are made from a plastic called PVC. PVC is very useful because it is flexible, **non-toxic** and is also easy to **recycle** when objects have come to the end of their useful life.

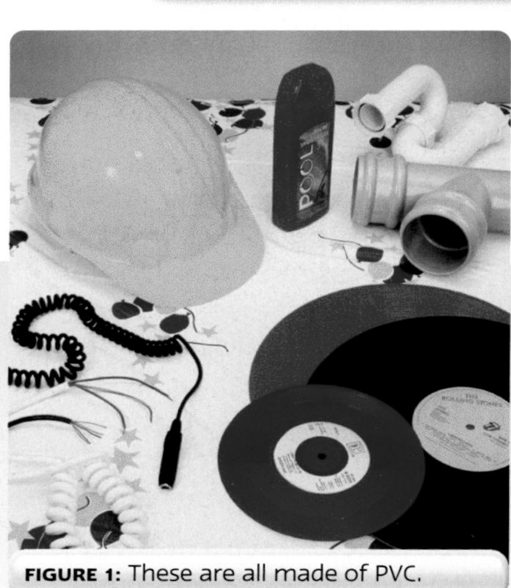

FIGURE 1: These are all made of PVC.

From crude oil to polymers

Plastics are known chemically as **polymers**. Polymers are very long molecules, or chains, containing up to millions of atoms all joined together like beads in a necklace.

To make long-chain molecules, small molecules are joined together chemically in a process called **polymerisation**.

The separate molecules are called **monomers**, and the long chain they make is the polymer.

[illegible] important monomer used to make a polymer, is the gas [illegible]ene. It is made from crude oil by the process of **cracking**.

[illegible]thene gas is squeezed at a very high pressure. At the [illegible]me, it is heated and a catalyst is added. In these [illegible]s, ethene molecules join together to make a new [illegible] called polyethene which we know as **polythene**.

[illegible] on the right shows how ethene monomers join [illegible]ke polyethene.

```
H   H  H   H  H   H       H  H  H  H  H  H
 \ /    \ /    \ /        |  |  |  |  |  |
 C=C    C=C    C=C   ➡ --C--C--C--C--C--C--
 / \    / \    / \        |  |  |  |  |  |
H   H  H   H  H   H       H  H  H  H  H  H
```

three ethene molecules → polyethene

Watch Out When a monomer forms a polymer, the double bond is [illegible]used up' – there is no double bond [illegible] the polymer.

WOW FACTOR!

Polymers can now be made that are stronger than steel!

QUESTIONS

[illegible] terms 'monomer' and 'polymer'.

[illegible]mer used to make polyethene?

[illegible]er used to make polystyrene.

How do alkenes join together to make polymers?

Alkenes are very reactive. This is because they contain a **carbon double bond**. Look at the ethene molecule on the right. The carbon double bond is present in all alkenes and it makes them react with many other chemical substances.

```
H     H
 \   /
  C=C
 /   \
H     H
```

The double bond can be imagined as 'sticky' because, when alkene molecules polymerise, it is the carbon double bonds that act as 'hooks' and help join the small molecules together to make a very long chain.

Polymerisation doesn't just work with ethene. The next member of the alkene family is called propene. It can polymerise too. It has three carbon atoms and 6 hydrogen atoms in each molecule. Its chemical formula is C_3H_6. This is the structure of a propene molecule:

```
      H   H
       \ /
H       C
 \     / \
  C = C   H
 /     \
H       H
```

When propene is compressed and heated with a catalyst, the propene molecules join together to make a polymer. This polymer is called **polypropene**:

```
    H  H        H  H        H  H             H CH3 H CH3 H CH3
H    \/     H    \/     H    \/              |  |  |  |  |  |
 \   C       \   C       \   C       ===>  ---C--C--C--C--C--C---
 C=C   H     C=C   H     C=C   H             |  |  |  |  |  |
 /  \        /  \        /  \                H  H  H  H  H  H
H    H      H    H      H    H
```

three propene monomers

a section of a strand of polypropene

This polymer is very useful because it is strong as well as being very light. It can be used to make mooring ropes like those that keep heavy ships from moving about while they are docked in a harbour.

FIGURE 2: Think of a chemical reason why these polymer ropes are so strong.

QUESTIONS

4 What type of chemical bond does a molecule need in order to make a polymer?

5 What is the chemical formula for propene?

6 Give a use for polypropene.

7 The monomer that is used to make PVC is called chloroethene. It has this structure:

```
H     H
 \   /
  C=C
 /   \
H     Cl
```

Draw the part of a polymer chain formed when three chloroethene molecules join together.

Polymers as smart materials

Chemists can design polymers that have particular properties. These are some of the very useful properties that they can build into new polymers:

- They have low densities.
- They can withstand corrosion by chemicals including acids and alkalis.
- They are flexible.
- They soften when heated – useful when polymers are recycled.

Polymers can now be made that conduct electricity, emit light or change shape when electricity passes through them. Polymers may also harden when a magnet is placed near to them. These amazing properties of polymers may prove very useful in future. Materials of this type that change rapidly when a condition, such as temperature, changes are called **smart materials**.

The flat screen monitor shown has a special polymer film for a screen. It is very thin and can be rolled up like a piece of paper!

FIGURE 3: Screens like this are made of light-emitting polymers.

QUESTIONS

8 What is meant by a 'smart material'?

9 Why is it environmentally useful for polymers to melt when heated?

10 Copper that is used as an electrical conductor in wires could be replaced by electrically conducting polymers in future. Give an advantage of polymers being used in this way.

Polymers are useful

You will find out:

- That polymers have very useful properties
- That many everyday objects made from polymers use these properties
- That some polymers cannot be recycled, and this causes environmental problems

Protection from plastic

Figure 1 shows someone in a bullet-proof vest. People wear these in war zones and wherever there is a risk of being shot. Bullet-proof vests are heavy and difficult to wear, but they do protect the wearer from being harmed by a bullet.

They are made of a special plastic called **Kevlar**®. This is a plastic (or polymer) made specially for the purpose of protecting people from bullets.

FIGURE 1: The plastic Kevlar can stop a bullet. What properties are needed to do this?

Slippery stuff

When people are older, their hips can sometimes start to wear out and it becomes difficult to walk. This is because the surfaces of bones that move against each other at the hip joint get worn away and become rough. When they grind together, it can be very painful.

Chemists have made a substance that helps with this problem.

Figure 2 shows an artificial hip joint. It is made of titanium and a special polymer called **Teflon**®. Teflon® is a slippery plastic that other substances just slide off!

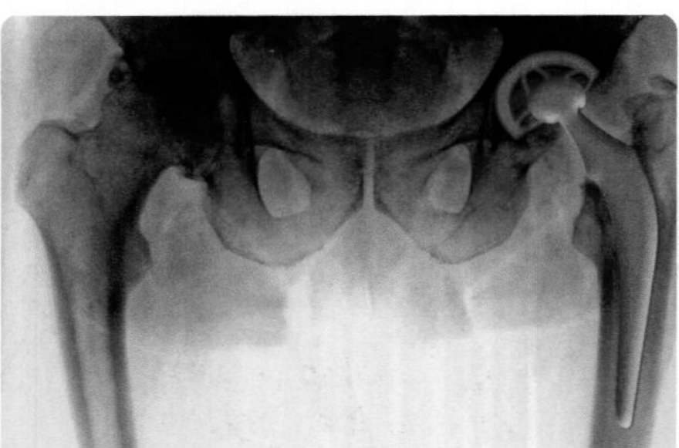

FIGURE 2: Teflon is used in artificial hip joints.

FIGURE 3: Surfers use the designer material polyurethane.

Tough stuff

The man in figure 3 is surfing. He uses a surfboard made of another special polymer called **polyurethane**. It is tough and light. It is not likely to break when he is surfing, even on the rough seas.

Polyurethane is one of many polymers we can manufacture and which make our lives more enjoyable.

QUESTIONS

1. What makes Teflon® special?
2. What is a surfboard made of?
3. Give an example of a very strong plastic used to make bullet-proof vests.

NEW PROPERTIES

Polymers can now do what only metals used to do: conduct electricity and light up when an electrical current passes through them.

...biodegradable ...cross-linkages ...Kevlar® ...polymer chains ...polyurethane

Slime!

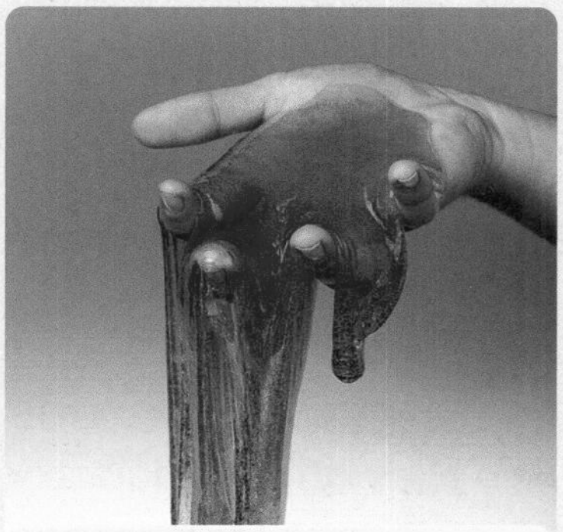

You can make a simple polymer by adding a solution of the chemical borax (which most chemists sell) to a glue called **PVA** (polyvinyl alcohol or polyethenol). The PVA consists of **polymer chains**, and the borax forms 'chemical bridges' or **cross-linkages** between these chains, linking them together. The substance formed is a soft, flexible polymer called 'slime'.

FIGURE 4: Slime! How is it made?

Slime can be formed into an elastic ball. If you then place the ball in your hand and tilt it slightly, the ball stretches out into a long column. It looks as if it is melting. If you tip further and the column is stretched quickly, it will break.

These properties of slime vary according to the conditions in which it is made. For example, how easily the slime will flow – its **viscosity** – will depend on the temperature and concentrations of the PVA solution and the borax solution.

More polymer uses

Polymers have many useful and new applications in our everyday world. A polymer can be tailor-made to have a specific list of properties. Polymers are known for being low density (they are lightweight), chemically resistant (they are not attacked by acids and alkalis), and some are also very strong. These are just some polymers and their uses:

- New packaging materials. They are strong, light and flexible.
- Waterproof coatings for fabrics. They repel water so that items made from them, such as tents and backpacks, are protected from water and last longer.
- Dental polymers. They are soft and flexible but become very hard when ultraviolet light is shone on them. They are used to make replacement teeth, including crowns, and also to make dentures.
- Wound dressings. These polymer fabrics allow wounds to 'breathe' so that they heal faster.
- Hydrogels. These polymers are squeezed from a tube onto wound dressings. They retain moisture, softening dead tissue so that it can be removed, and enabling wounds to heal more quickly.

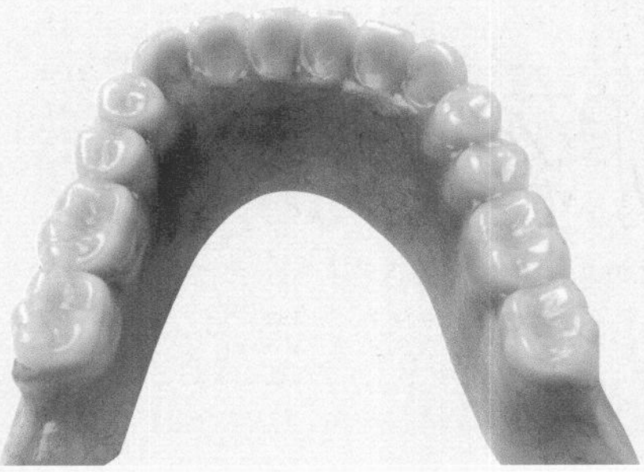

FIGURE 5: The polymer used for replacement teeth. What effect does ultraviolet light have on it?

WOW FACTOR!

Nylon is a polymer that, weight for weight, is stronger than steel.

QUESTIONS

4 Name **two** chemicals that are added together to make 'slime'.

5 Give **three** properties of normal polymers.

6 Polymers can be used to make car chassis (frames). List some properties that a polymer used for this purpose would need to have.

EXAM HINTS AND TIPS

Viscosity is a measure of the thickness or gooeyness of a liquid. The thicker it is, the higher its viscosity.

Polymers with a memory

Imagine if you could fix a dent in an object made from a polymer material just by heating it.

Polymers like this exist – they 'remember' the original shape of the object! They are called **shape memory polymers**. The impact that dented the object – deformed it – changes its form only temporarily. It changes back to the original form when heated.

Heat gives the polymer's 'memory' a boost. You can remove the dent merely by using a hairdryer. In effect, the plastic repairs itself.

In the world of surgery, it may be more convenient to put an implant into the patient's body with a smaller, temporary shape that, in the warmth of the body, reverts to its remembered larger shape. In other words, an implant in a compressed state takes up a small space until after the operation, and then it enlarges as it 'remembers' its original shape.

Such materials can also be completely **biodegradable**, eventually disappearing from the patient's body altogether.

QUESTIONS

7 What is a shape memory polymer?

8 When would it be useful to have a car body which had been made of a shape memory polymer?

Disposing of polymers

You will find out:

- About the problems caused by throwing rubbish away
- That recycling is the best option
- That there are other ways to deal with the rubbish that we produce

Bottles!

Most bottles used today are made of polymers. It takes a lot of energy to make polymers, and it causes a lot of pollution, too. We add to these disadvantages if we throw away bottles we have finished with, and put them into a landfill site like the one in figure 1.

Rubbish dumps don't look very nice, and they smell horrible. Also, most of the rubbish will still be there in 100 years. It doesn't break down naturally – it does not **biodegrade**.

FIGURE 1: A waste dump. Is this the best way to dispose of rubbish?

A waste time-bomb

When we have eaten food, we normally throw the packaging – wrappers, boxes, bottles – into a bin without thinking about it. We expect someone else to take it away. We then forget about it.

There are about 65 million people living in the UK. Everyone throws away rubbish, and most of it finishes up in a big hole in the ground.

The future – some important questions to think about

- Do you think it's right that we keep on filling up waste dumps with rubbish?
- If we can't see rubbish when it is in the ground, does it really matter anyway?
- If you think that we need to change our habits, what can we do about it?

FIGURE 2: Why is recycling a good thing?

Making rubbish useful

One thing that we can do is to turn rubbish into useful things. This is called **recycling**.

Instead of throwing objects made of polymers away, we can put them in special collection boxes like bottle banks.

Objects made of polymers can then be shredded and heated to melt them. The melted polymer is then made into pellets and sold to manufacturers who make them into new plastic objects.

WOW FACTOR!

Every two days, the UK throws away enough rubbish to fill the Royal Albert Hall in London.

QUESTIONS

1 Why are rubbish dumps thought to be a bad thing?
2 What does 'recycling' mean?
3 Name a substance that can be recycled.

...biodegrade ...environment ...microorganisms ...non-biodegradable

The case for recycling polymers

You may think that it would be too expensive to melt polymers to make new objects, melt glass to make new bottles, shred old paper to make new paper, and melt metal things to make new ones. However, costs of recycling in this way have been compared to the cost of starting with raw materials.

Raw materials have to be dug from the ground to produce metal and glass, and trees have to be grown and then cut down to make paper. Costs have shown that it is a lot cheaper to recycle.

Identifying different polymers

If you look at the base of objects made from **polymers**, you may find signs that look like the one in figure 3.

These signs tell us which polymer is used to make the object. For example, PP is polypropene, PS is polystyrene, HDPE is high density polyethene. This could be very helpful for recycling centres. They could sort out our everyday items according to the polymer they are made of. Then, for instance, all the objects made of polyethene could be shredded and melted together to make new polyethene items.

FIGURE 3: Look for signs on polymer containers and work out what they are made of.

However, in the UK, very few items made of polymers are recycled in this way. This is disappointing since, for example, all sorts of fleece garments such as jackets, jumpers and so on, can be made from recycled bottles.

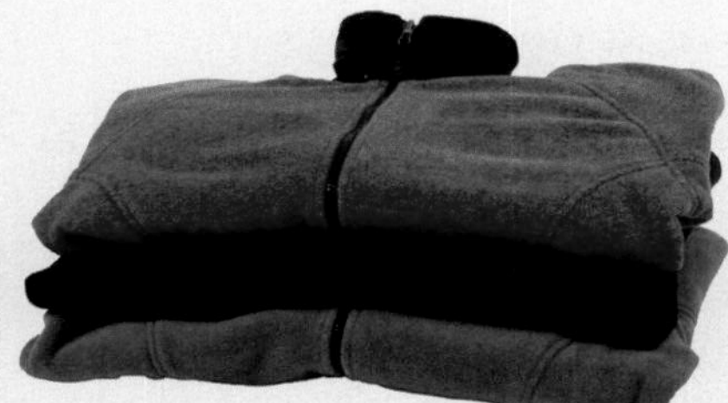

FIGURE 4: Clothes like this were once plastic bottles.

Other ways to dispose of polymers

We could burn waste polymers. This would produce heat energy that we could then use to make electricity. However, burning polymers produces a lot of air **pollution** and so causes a problem for the **environment**.

Few of today's polymers will rot down when buried in the earth. We say that they are **non-biodegradable**. This means that the buried material will never become useful as soil again in the future. Can we make polymers that we could bury without causing this problem?

In fact, we can make polymers that are broken down by **microorganisms**. If we are able to do this on a large scale, it will mean that we can dispose of rubbish in the ground knowing that it will not be there forever.

QUESTIONS

4 Why is it better for polymer objects to be recycled than to dispose of them in a landfill site?

5 What is the meaning of the term 'biodegradable'?

6 Why would it be thought good for the environment if polymers were made to be biodegradable? Explain your answer.

7 Give an advantage and a disadvantage of burning polymers as a method of disposal.

Plastic bones

Biodegradable polymers are seldom used for making food packaging – one reason why we produce such a lot of waste. But biodegradable polymers are being used for other purposes.

Scientists have worked out a new way of fixing broken bones using a biodegradable polymer.

They have developed a gel made up of several polymers. It glues the parts of a broken bone together and helps to support it as it heals.

Sometimes a metal pin has to be put into a broken bone to fix it together while it heals. This can be a complicated and painful operation.

Using metal pins, and the follow-up surgery needed to remove them, is not necessary when the polymer mixture is used. The bones are just glued together. Another advantage is that over time the polymer will biodegrade and disappear, and be replaced by new bone.

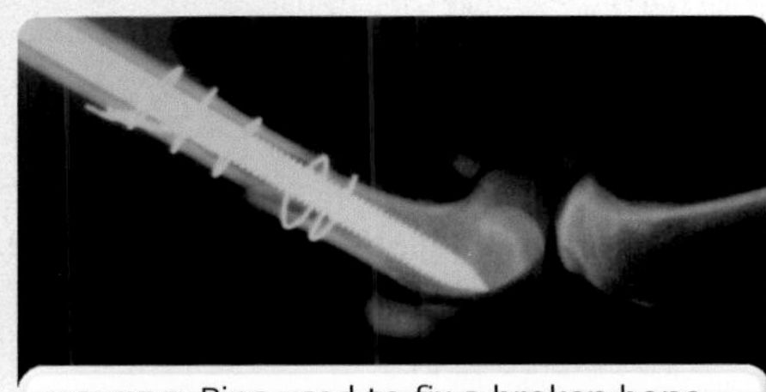

FIGURE 5: Pins used to fix a broken bone.

A stent is a coil that a surgeon inserts into a damaged blood vessel near the heart to support and repair it. In the past, stents have remained permanently inside the blood vessels, but now it is possible to make them biodegradable, so that they 'dissolve' and disappear as the blood vessel recovers.

QUESTIONS

8 What are the advantages of fixing a broken bone using a polymer glue rather than a metal pin?

9 Metal pins used for mending bones are made of titanium. Give **two** properties that titanium must have for this particular use.

Oil from plants

You will find out:

- About oils found in seeds, nuts and fruits
- That foods can be made from plant oils
- That oils are separated from plant material and then purified

Oil from sunflowers

The sunflower plant belongs to the daisy family. It probably came from North America or Mexico. It is known that North American Indians grew sunflowers as long as 2000 years ago.

When the seeds are removed from the sunflower, they can be crushed to make an oil. It is used in margarine, varnishes and soaps. The seeds can also be eaten whole, raw or cooked. Sunflower seeds are a good source of essential **minerals** in our diet, including potassium and phosphorus. They also contain **protein** and small amounts of iron and calcium, too.

FIGURE 1: Fields of sunflowers grown for their oil are increasingly common in the UK.

What useful substances come from plants?

Plants contain several very useful chemical substances, including **natural oils** that are found in the seeds or nuts of some plants.

For example, useful seeds come from cotton, rapeseed, mustard, sunflower and sesame plants. All these seeds are rich in natural oils that we can use.

Some nuts contain a lot of natural oils. Examples include coconut, groundnut and the shea nut. Even some fruits are rich in oils, like palm fruits, olives and avocados.

Watch Out Natural oils from plants are not the same as crude oil from the ground. They are very different chemicals.

How are oils removed from seeds and nuts?

Seeds and nuts normally have a hard coating which makes the inside difficult to reach. Therefore a press is used to crush the nuts and seeds and extract the oils.

As well as the natural oils, seeds and nuts also contain some water and other substances – **impurities** – that we need to remove before the oils are pure.

FIGURE 2: Olives like these are rich in natural oils.

QUESTIONS

1 Name **four** important chemical substances that are found in sunflower seeds.
2 What must happen to seeds or nuts before the oils can be removed?
3 Give **three** uses for the oil that is found in sunflower seeds.

How are plant oils purified?

Oils are large **molecules** made up of many carbon, hydrogen and oxygen atoms. Oils do not dissolve in water. They have a lower density than water, so they float on top of it forming an upper layer.

Although oils do not dissolve in water, they do dissolve in other **solvents**. So, to separate the oils, a solvent is added to the crushed seeds and nuts. The solvent dissolves only the natural oils but not the water and other impurities.

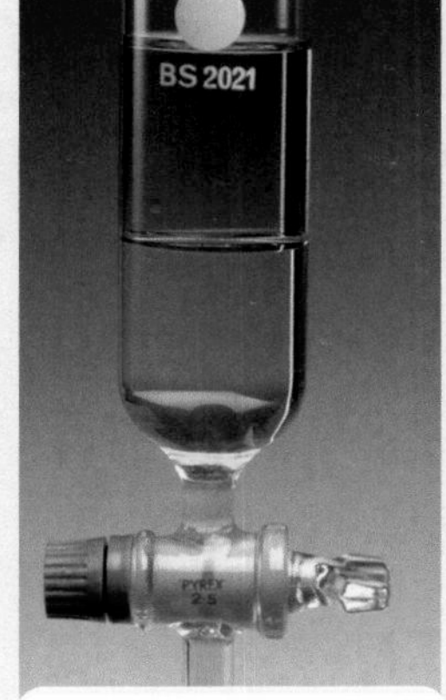

FIGURE 3: Which layer is the natural oil?

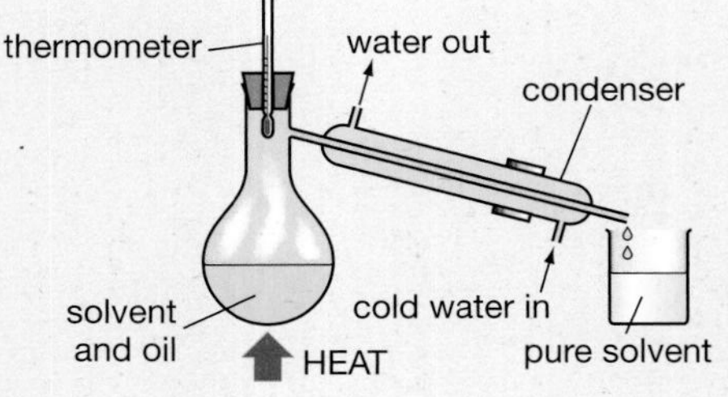

FIGURE 4: Why do water and oil leave the apparatus separately as the mixture is heated?

Oil and the solvent have different boiling points, so if we heat up a mixture of oil and solvent, the solvent will boil first, leaving the oils behind. This means that we could use a simple **distillation** apparatus to separate oil and the solvent, as shown in figure 4.

Why natural oils are important

Oils are very high in the chemical energy they contain. We call them high-energy foods. This means that natural oils in our diet provide us with a lot of energy, compared to other foods.

Nuts contain other nutrients that we need in a healthy diet. The nutrients include vitamins, which protect us from disease, and trace elements that are needed for health, but only in tiny amounts.

Almonds contain thiamine (vitamin B1), riboflavin (vitamin B2), niacin (vitamin B3), vitamin E, calcium, phosphorus, potassium, magnesium, manganese, copper and iron.

Brazil nuts contain thiamine (vitamin B1), calcium, magnesium, manganese, copper, phosphorus, potassium, selenium, zinc and iron. A single Brazil nut provides the daily allowance of selenium.

Pistachios contain beta-carotene, thiamine (vitamin B1), niacin (vitamin B3), folic acid, calcium, phosphorus, magnesium, manganese, copper, zinc and iron.

EXAM HINTS AND TIPS

A distillation works because liquids have different boiling points.

QUESTIONS

4 Name **three** elements present in a molecule of oil from a plant.

5 Name a nutrient that is present in Brazil nuts but is not found in almonds.

6 Name a vitamin that is common to almonds, Brazil nuts and pistachios.

7 Explain how natural oils are removed from seeds and nuts.

Are walnuts good for the heart?

Walnut trees with edible nuts include the black walnut in the USA, and the English variety, now grown worldwide because it is easier to harvest and shell.

FIGURE 5: Walnuts contain oils that are good for the heart.

English and black walnuts differ slightly in the nutrients they contain. Both are high in phosphorus, zinc, copper, iron, potassium and vitamin E, and low in saturated fat.

However, English walnuts have twice as much omega-3 fatty acids as black walnuts. Research suggests that omega-3 fatty acids may:

- lower blood triglyceride levels
- reduce the risk of blood clots
- lower blood pressure.

All these help to prevent heart disease.

The type of omega-3 fatty acids found in walnuts differs from the type found in fish oils, which are known to be healthy for the heart. More research is needed to compare the benefits of omega-3 fatty acids from plant sources, such as walnuts, and from fish.

QUESTIONS

8 What are the names of the **two** types of walnut?

9 What is the name of the fatty acids found in walnuts?

10 What does the passage suggest about the benefits for health of nut oils compared with fish oils?

11 Are scientists able to prove, beyond any doubt, that eating walnuts will prevent blood clots and reduce blood pressure? Explain your answer.

Green energy

You will find out:

- That rubbish is used as a fuel
- That fuels can be made from plant oils
- That plant oils could provide replacements for fuels such as petrol

Fuel from rubbish

When rubbish is buried in the ground, it breaks down and makes a gas called **methane**. This gas normally escapes into the atmosphere, but at some rubbish dumps it is being collected. It is taken to power stations and burnt to produce electricity. Your TV could be powered partly by the gas from rubbish.

FIGURE 1: Rubbish gives off methane that can be burned to produce electricity.

Tractor power

The tractor in figure 2 runs on rapeseed oil. Rapeseed is a common crop plant in the UK and in summer you see bright yellow fields of it in the countryside.

The crop is harvested and the seeds are separated. They are then crushed to extract the oil. After treatment, this oil can be burned as a **fuel**.

Fuels that are made from plants (like rapeseed oil, sunflower oil and wood) are called **biofuels**.

They can either be burned on their own, or can be mixed with other 'normal' fuels like petrol and diesel. Biofuels used on their own or in a mixture are called **green fuels**. These fuels are better for the environment than fossil fuels.

FIGURE 2: A tractor fuelled by rapeseed oil.

Why biofuels are better than fossil fuels

- Fossil fuels such as coal and crude oil will eventually run out. It took millions of years for fossil fuels to form. When we have used them all up, then we'll have to do without! This is why fossil fuels are called **non-renewable fuels**.
- Biofuels are burnt, but when we have used up one supply of them, we can grow more plants to make more fuel. These types of fuels are called **renewable fuels**.
- Plants' oils are called 'greenhouse neutral'. They do produce carbon dioxide when they burn, but when they were growing they absorbed the carbon dioxide from the air. So the carbon dioxide levels in the air stay the same.

QUESTIONS

1 What is the name of the gas produced from rotting rubbish?
2 What are biofuels?
3 Why are biofuels good for the environment?
4 What is a renewable fuel?

...biodegradable ...biodiesel ...biofuels ...carbon monoxide ...fuel ...green fuels

Why we need to look for new fuels

We use fuels in many of our everyday activities. Petrol and diesel are used to power cars and lorries, fuel oil powers ships, and kerosene is the fuel for aircraft. All of these fuels come from crude oil, but we know that within 50 years there will be very little crude oil left. We must therefore look around for alternative fuels.

Ordinary crude oil, known as 'black gold', has driven the economies of the world for more than a century. Over the next decades, 'green gold', or plant oils will become just as important to the world's economies and our lives.

FIGURE 3: An oil rig out at sea.

Are oils from plants the answer?

When plant oil is used as a fuel for a vehicle, it burns in the same way as petrol or diesel. The heat energy produced is used to power the engine. However, the plant oils in their pure form are usually too thick (viscous) to use as fuels. They are normally mixed with traditional fuels like diesel to make 'greener' fuels.

When a plant oil burns, it produces the gases carbon dioxide and water vapour. If there is not enough oxygen, **carbon monoxide** (chemical formula CO) is formed. This is a toxic gas. Also, some soot may form. This would happen if plant oil was burned in a traditional engine.

Therefore, if we want to power vehicles with pure plant oils, engines will have to be altered or replaced. This may prove expensive, but when fossil fuels run out or get too costly, we will be able to replace them with these new biofuels.

QUESTIONS

5 Give the names of **four** fuels made from crude oil.

6 Name a toxic gas that is produced when a fuel that contains carbon burns in air.

7 Give **one** disadvantage of using pure plant oil as a fuel.

Biodiesel – a fuel of the future?

Biodiesel is the name of a clean-burning fuel produced from renewable **resources**. Biodiesel is mixed with diesel to create a biodiesel 'blend'. It can be used in diesel engines that have had little or no modifications.

Biodiesel is simple to use, **biodegradable**, non-toxic, and free of sulfur.

FIGURE 4: Biodiesel is made from plant oils.

How is biodiesel made?

The plant oil reacts with methanol, an alcohol, to form a mixture of compounds called 'methyl esters'. This mixture is the biodiesel. The reaction also forms glycerol (glycerine). It separates from biodiesel because it is heavier, and is used to make soaps and cosmetics. The whole process is called 'transesterification'.

Why should we use biodiesel?

Biodiesel benefits the environment for several reasons.

- Burning it forms less greenhouse gases than burning diesel.
- It is completely non-toxic and biodegrades as fast as sugar.
- It is made from renewable resources, so using it means that we depend less on crude oil.

QUESTIONS

8 Describe what happens in the 'transesterification' of a plant oil.

9 Give an advantage of using biodiesel.

10 Give the name of the mixture in biodiesel.

Emulsions

You will find out:

- What an emulsion is
- How to make an emulsion
- About several everyday substances that are emulsions

The colourful world of paints

Emulsions are everywhere in our lives. They are in the processed foods and sauces we eat and the paints that decorate our walls.

What do we mean by an emulsion? It's a liquid, but what makes it different from other liquids?

FIGURE 1: These paints are emulsion based.

What is an emulsion?

We all know that oil and water don't mix. When oil is added to water, the oil floats on top. But when they are shaken together, the liquids form small droplets that mix together to make an emulsion.

French dressing is like this. You have to shake it hard to mix the oil and vinegar layers evenly and make an emulsion. Left on the table, it separates out into two layers. Some food manufacturers stop French dressing from separating out by adding an **emulsifier**.

Figure 2 shows an emulsion greatly magnified. It consists of tiny oil droplets suspended in water.

Milk is an emulsion. It has droplets of fat spread out in water. Butter is also an emulsion but it is the other way round. It is the water particles that are spread out in oil.

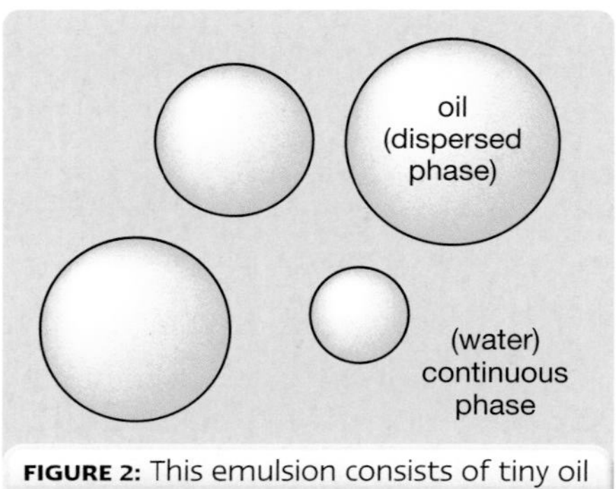

FIGURE 2: This emulsion consists of tiny oil droplets suspended in water.

FIGURE 3: French dressing. What does it contain? And when is it an emulsion?

QUESTIONS

1. Give **three** examples of emulsions you come across in everyday life.
2. What would happen if you left an emulsion of oil and water alone?
3. To stop what happens in question 2, you can add a substance to the emulsion. What do we call this type of substance?

...aqueous ...continuous phase ...disperse phase ...emulsifier ...emulsion

How do emulsions work?

Emulsions are made up of more than one **immiscible** liquid mixed together. An emulsion could contain droplets of oil suspended in a water-based (or **aqueous**) liquid (as in milk), or it could be an aqueous solution **suspended** in an oily liquid (as in butter). The different **phases** (liquids) in an emulsion have names. The supporting liquid is called the **continuous phase** and the liquid which forms the suspended droplets is the **disperse phase**.

FIGURE 4: Milk is an emulsion. But why is it white?

The harder you shake an emulsion, the smaller the droplets become. The droplets formed by shaking hard are very small. They are barely visible to the naked eye. Using a commercial emulsion mixer, it is possible to achieve a droplet size of 100 to 1000 **nanometres** (1000 000 nanometres = 1 mm). Droplets as small as this cannot be seen.

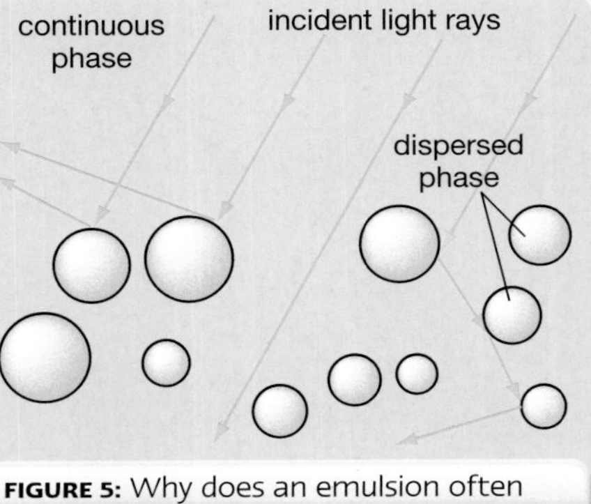

FIGURE 5: Why does an emulsion often appear opaque?

The tiny droplets in an emulsion scatter the light passing through it. The result is that the emulsion often appears to be either an opaque pale grey or white. This effect is similar to a bowl of salt – each individual grain is transparent (just like an emulsion droplet), but a collection of grains appears white since all the light is scattered.

EXAM HINTS AND TIPS

Remember that liquids that do not mix together are called immiscible liquids. Those that do mix together are called miscible liquids.

QUESTIONS

4 Is the continuous phase in butter the aqueous or fatty phase?

5 How large, in millimetres (mm), is 1000 nanometres?

6 Explain why milk appears as a white liquid.

What is mayonnaise?

Mayonnaise is a thick, creamy sauce made of oil, egg yolks, lemon juice or vinegar, and seasonings. It is an emulsion.

FIGURE 6: Mayonnaise is an example of an emulsion.

To emulsify the ingredients, you slowly add the oil to the water-based ingredients, mixing them vigorously. This disperses and suspends tiny droplets of one liquid through the other.

The oil and water are mixed permanently, so mayonnaise is a stable emulsion. Why don't the oil and water separate, as in French dressing?

This is because one of the ingredients is an emulsifier. Emulsifiers are substances added to a mixture of liquids to prevent them from separating – they stabilise the mixture. Egg yolk and gelatine contain emulsifying substances.

In mayonnaise, the emulsifier is egg yolk. It contains lecithin, which keeps fat emulsified by stopping its droplets from joining up again.

QUESTIONS

7 What is the name of the chemical substance in egg yolk that acts as an emulsifier in mayonnaise?

8 Gelatine is sometimes added to yoghurt. Suggest why.

Polyunsaturates

You will find out:

- That a polyunsaturated fat has several double bonds
- Evidence suggesting that polyunsaturated fats benefit health
- That there is a chemical test for an unsaturated fat

Fish oils

Many fish contain natural oils. Fish use these oils to provide them with energy. Mackerel, pilchards, salmon and sardines are fish that contain a special **polyunsaturated** oil which helps reduces the risk of death from heart disease.

FIGURE 1: Which fish oil is a benefit to health?

A closer look at oils and fats

Oils and fats occur naturally in animals and some plants. If we include these oils and fats in the foods we eat, we improve our chances of having good health. You may have heard about polyunsaturated fats and oils, and seen them listed on the packaging of some foods. What does 'polyunsaturated' mean?

Alkenes and alkanes – again

We have already learnt that we describe alkenes as **unsaturated** hydrocarbons, because they have a carbon double bond in them. Alkanes, on the other hand, are called **saturated** hydrocarbons since all their atoms are joined by carbon single bonds.

We can use words like 'saturated' and 'unsaturated' when talking about fats and oils, too. When a fat is described as being a saturated fat, it means that it is made up of molecules that contain only carbon single bonds.

Olives contain a **monounsaturated** oil. This means that each molecule of the oil in figure 2 has one carbon double bond in it.

Polyunsaturated oils, such as the oil in fish, has two or more carbon double bonds.

FIGURE 2: Olive oil contains monounsaturated oils.

QUESTIONS

1. What is meant by the term 'unsaturated'?
2. Name **three** fish that are considered healthy to eat.
3. What is the meaning of the term 'polyunsaturated'?

EXAM HINTS AND TIPS

Remember that oils tend to be liquids, and fats tend to be solids.

...bromine water ...monounsaturated ...polyunsaturated

How do we know whether fats are saturated or unsaturated?

We can test whether or not a fat or oil is saturated. This test distinguishes between an alkene and an alkane. It tells us if there is a double bond or not.

The bromine water test

When we add a few drops of orange **bromine water** (or iodine solution) to an alkene, the orange colour of the bromine decolourises. This happens only if a carbon double bond is present. If the solution remains orange, then there are only carbon single bonds present. (This matches what we know about alkanes: they are not as reactive as alkenes.)

The table shows the results expected when bromine water is added to a saturated fat and an unsaturated fat.

Compound	Observation on adding bromine solution	Conclusion
alkane	stays orange	saturated
alkene	goes from orange to colourless	unsaturated

What happens at the chemical level

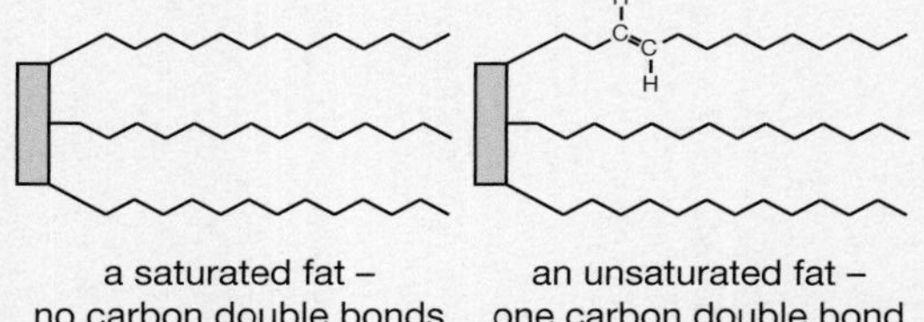

FIGURE 3: The general structures of saturated and unsaturated fats.

Figure 4 shows the general structures of a saturated and an unsaturated fat. Notice how a fat or oil molecule is made up of a small part (the rectangular bit) joined to three long chains of carbon atoms. These chains are the bits that have the double bonds in them, if any.

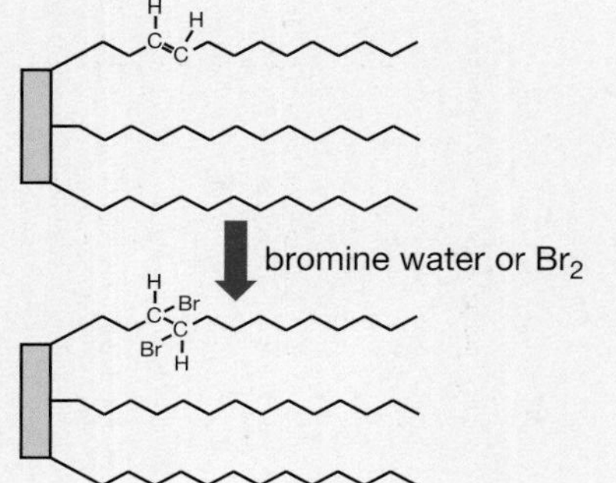

FIGURE 4: The effect of adding bromine water to an unsaturated fat.

When bromine water is added to the unsaturated fat, a bromine molecule 'attacks' the carbon double bond to form a saturated, colourless product.

QUESTIONS

4 What would you observe if you shake bromine water with **a)** ethane **b)** a polyunsaturated fat?

5 How does the molecular structure of a fat tell you that it is saturated?

6 Explain why the orange colour of bromine is decolourised when shaken with an unsaturated fat.

FIGURE 5: The saturated fat is on the left , the unsaturated fat on the right.

Polyunsaturated fats and monounsaturated fats

If the level of cholesterol in your blood is high, you are more likely to have a heart attack. Cholesterol can build up in arteries and block them. Tests show that polyunsaturates, and to a lesser extent monounsaturates, lower blood cholesterol levels.

The message is:

- eat foods rich in monounsaturates – olive oil and rapeseed oil – and in polyunsaturates – sunflower oil, soya oil and corn oil
- avoid foods rich in saturates, such as lard.

Some oils are labelled as vegetable oil or blended vegetable oils. All these are low in saturated fat. But remember, whichever unsaturated oil you use, try to use as little as possible.

FATS WE NEED TO EAT

Some polyunsaturated fats are essential in our diet because we do not make these fats in our own bodies.

QUESTIONS

7 Which types of fats are considered better for health, and which type of fat is considered to be unhealthy?

8 If you added a few drops of bromine water to sunflower oil, what would you expect to observe?

Spread it all around

SELF-CHECK ACTIVITY

CONTEXT

Will has just started doing a Food Technology course for GCSE and is really looking forward to the practical work. He's already cooked some pretty good meals at home, as well as one or two that hit the bin!

He's been told to bring in some ingredients for a practical lesson, which consists of planning and making a packed lunch for someone doing an Outdoor Education activity, such as sailing or climbing. The list of ingredients includes margarine, but he can't find any at home so takes butter instead. When he takes the butter from the fridge it feels as hard as a brick, but he's sure it will have softened by the time the lesson starts, even though it's the first period.

By the time the lesson starts, the butter is still brick hard. He tries to chip bits off to spread on the bread but it doesn't really work. His friend Pablo (who's better organised) has a small tub of margarine that spreads beautifully. The teacher is not impressed with Will, but uses the situation to explain how and why modern margarines have been developed.

Margarine manufacturers use vegetable oils. The molecules of these oils have a 'kink' in them, which means they don't pack together easily and therefore tend to be liquid at room temperature. A process called hydrogenation changes the molecules into new ones which are straighter. The molecules now pack together more easily and the melting point is raised to about $60^{0}C$, which means that they are solid at room temperature.

That evening, though, Will's mother tells him that she prefers butter and thinks she has read somewhere that hydrogenated oils are not good for you.

CHALLENGE

STEP 1

Will could have solved the problem of the hard butter by putting it in the microwave for a little while. However, this is a risky strategy as it is easy to end up with a large pool of liquid butter. Draw and label diagrams to show the difference in arrangement between the particles in Will's rock hard butter and liquid butter.

STEP 2

The molecules of vegetable oil have a kink in them, which means they don't fit together easily. Draw and label a diagram to show why oil is a liquid at room temperature.

STEP 3

Hydrogenated oil has molecules that don't have kinks in them. Draw and label diagrams to show how this means they will solidify more easily.

STEP 4

Why do you think that margarine and other spreads sell so well, with many people preferring them to butter?

Maximise your grade

These sentences show what you need to include in your work to achieve each grade. Use them to improve your work and be more successful.

Grade	Answer includes...
	Partially describe particle arrangements in solids and liquids.
F	Describe particle arrangements in solids and liquids using words or diagrams.
	Describe particle arrangements in solids and liquids using words and diagrams.
	Describe how some shapes of molecules will pack together more easily than others.
C	Explain how the ease with which molecules can pack together affects the melting point of a substance.
	Start to use molecular diagrams to explain a material's behaviour.
A	Use molecular diagrams to explain a material's behaviour.
	As above, but with particular clarity and detail.

Making margarine

You will find out:

- That margarine and butter are very different substances
- That margarine is made from natural oils and contains nutrients that make it a healthy alternative to butter

Spreadable butter

Many people today prefer margarine to butter. Margarine is considered to be a tasty and healthy alternative to butter. It certainly wasn't invented for these reasons.

Margarine was invented in France in the 1860s. It was Emperor Napoleon's idea to award a prize to the person who could make a butter substitute that very poor people could afford.

FIGURE 1: Margarine, the healthy alternative to butter?

What is margarine?

Margarine is a substitute for butter. Butter is formed from milk, an animal product, while margarine is formed from vegetable oils.

In the UK, the amount of each ingredient in margarine is controlled by law. Every 100 g of margarine must contain:

- between 80% and 90% fat
- between 800 mg and 1000 mg Vitamin A
- between 7.05 mg and 8.05 mg Vitamin D.

Making margarine

Margarine is made from natural vegetable oils including palm, sunflower, rapeseed and soya bean oils. To become margarine, the vegetable oil (liquid) has to be changed chemically into a fat (soft solid). The process is as follows:

- Hydrogen gas is passed through the oil, warmed to about 60 °C.
- Nickel is added as a catalyst to make the reaction go faster.
- In the process, the liquid vegetable oil is hardened. It hardens when the hydrogen reacts chemically with the carbon double bonds in the oil.
- The reaction between hydrogen and oil molecules is called **hydrogenation**. It only happens in the presence of a nickel catalyst.

GOOD OR BAD?

Bad: saturated fats, higher in butter than in margarine

Good: unsaturated fats, higher in margarine than in butter

Bad: trans fat, higher in margarine than in butter; raises 'bad' cholesterol levels in body

Bad: dietary cholesterol, in butter but not in margarine

QUESTIONS

1 Suggest why vitamins are added to margarine.
2 What is the chemical name for the process of hardening vegetable oils?
3 What do the carbon double bonds in oil react with?
4 Suggest why the temperature of the oil is raised and a catalyst is added.

...fatty acids ...hydrogenation ...partially hydrogenated

Hydrogenation of vegetable oils

Vegetable oils are liquids, so they are not suitable alternatives to butter. In hydrogenation, hydrogen gas combines chemically with the carbon double bonds in the vegetable oils. The oils become hardened to a soft solid – margarine.

Figure 2 shows two **fatty acids**, oleic acid and linoleic acid. They are commonly found in the vegetable oils used to make margarine. Notice that both these molecules contain carbon double bonds – oleic acid has one and linoleic acid has two. They are **unsaturated**.

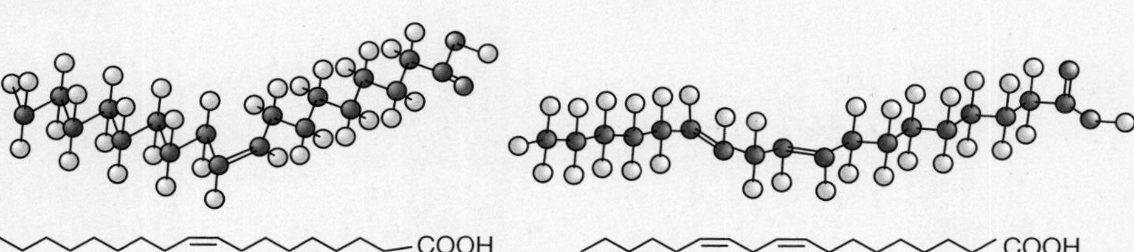

FIGURE 2: Molecules of two fatty acids in vegetable oils.

The carbon double bond gives the oil molecule its V shape. The V shape stops molecules from lining up close together. Having loosely packed molecules makes the oil less dense and so it is liquid at room temperature. Hydrogenation removes some carbon double bonds, the molecules straighten and pack more closely, and the vegetable oil becomes a solid – a fat.

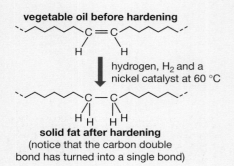

vegetable oil before hardening

C=C
H H

hydrogen, H_2 and a nickel catalyst at 60 °C

C–C
H H H H

solid fat after hardening
(notice that the carbon double bond has turned into a single bond)

FIGURE 3: Hydrogenation.

Saturated or unsaturated?

If all the carbon double bonds were removed from a vegetable oil it would be **saturated**. Saturated fats, of which there are more in butter than in margarine, are thought to be less healthy for the heart than unsaturated fats. So the oil is only **partially hydrogenated**, with some of the carbon double bonds left in. Manufacturers can then advertise their margarine as 'high in polyunsaturates'.

The trans fat issue

Trans fat is formed during hydrogenation. Its molecules have a double bond but are straight. Margarine has much more trans fat than butter. Research links diets high in trans fats with coronary heart disease. This makes people think that margarine is unhealthy. Now, new types of margarine are made that contain less or no trans fat.

QUESTIONS

5 Give the names of the **two** common fatty acids found in the vegetable oils used to make margarine.

6 Why aren't all carbon double bonds removed in the hydrogenation process?

Which is better for your health – butter or margarine?

People are concerned about the level of cholesterol in their blood. 'Bad' cholesterol is linked to heart disease. (We need 'good' cholesterol to make our body cells.)

Trans fat is formed when oils are hydrogenated to give margarine (and trans fat levels are therefore higher in margarine than in butter). There is evidence that trans fat raises 'bad' cholesterol levels and lowers 'good' cholesterol levels. For this reason, some people think that butter is better for health than margarine.

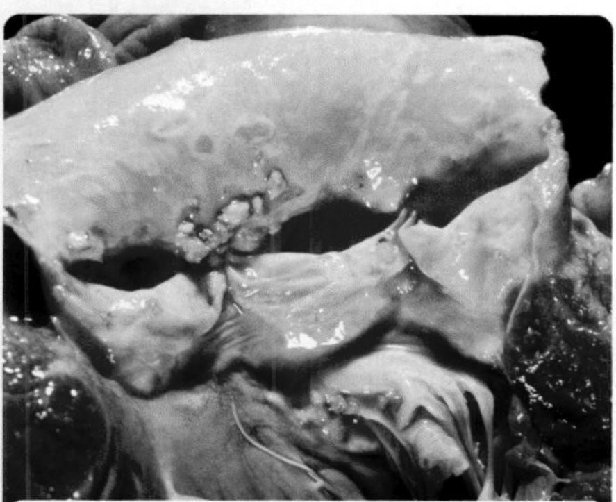

FIGURE 4: This is a diseased heart. The white deposit around the valve at the top is fat.

A simple way to judge the healthiness of a vegetable oil is to look at its viscosity – how runny the oil is. As a rule, saturated fats are solid and bad for your health, while liquids are better. The more liquid the substance is, the better.

QUESTIONS

7 Many people say that butter is healthier than margarine. What evidence in the text suggests that the situation is far more complicated?

8 Suggest the information you would need to show whether trans fats in margarine are harmful or not for health.

9 An undecided shopper wants to know whether to buy butter or margarine is totally safe or not. Why are scientists never able to say whether this is so?

Food additives

You will find out:

- That food additives are substances added to foods to improve their appearance, taste or to prolong their life
- About some important issues regarding some additives

Colour in sweets and foods

The appearance of food is very important to us when we shop. We think sweets and foods will be a lot tastier when they are brightly coloured or fresh looking. We are more likely to buy foods that are attractive, and often the foods look like this because they contain **additives**.

Colours in sweets

When we look at sweets and food in shops, we realise what a colourful world it is. Food looks a lot tastier when it is brightly coloured and looking fresh. We are more likely to buy it if it looks nice.

We are now more aware that some additives may have side effects that are not pleasant. At the same time, most people can eat additives without any risk to their health.

FIGURE 1: How are sweets made to look as colourful as this?

Additives – what are they?

Many chemicals in food could be harmful – **toxic** – but only if we eat too much of them. Some are naturally occurring, while others are man-made. Both types can be additives if they are added to the basic food. These chemicals are not necessarily harmful in small amounts, so the effects they have depend on the amounts that we consume.

Each additive has an **E-number**. For example, E330 is **citric acid**, naturally found in oranges and lemons but often added to other foods, and E102 is **tartrazine**, an orange dye made from coal tar.

FIGURE 2: The additives in this cream cake make eating it an even nicer experience.

An E-number shows that the additive has passed special safety tests and can be used throughout the European Union. If later evidence suggests an additive is unsafe to eat, it can be banned from use in foods.

Food packets must list practically all additives, whether natural or man-made. The list should either give the name or the E-number of each ingredient. The numbering system also tells you what job an additive does, such as adding colour or acting as a preservative.

Watch Out The term 'organic' is used to describe food that is grown without the use of chemicals, but it does not guarantee that the food is completely additive-free.

QUESTIONS

1 What is an additive?

2 'All additives that have E-numbers are man-made chemicals'. Is this statement true?

3 How do we know that food additives with E-numbers are safe?

...additives ...citric acid

Are additives safe?

Additives include chemicals that make food tastier, longer lasting and more colourful. The types of additive are:

- antioxidants
- colours
- emulsifiers, stabilisers, gelling agents and thickeners
- flavourings
- preservatives
- sweeteners.

Many additives occur naturally and others are made. Scientists test both types to make sure that they are safe.

Being man-made does not mean that a chemical is harmful. As well as food additives, we benefit from many man-made chemicals, such as medicines.

How safe is safe?

This is a really important question. Scientists can never say that any substance is 100% safe. Why it this?

To find out whether a chemical is safe or not, tests must be very thorough. A large group of people (or animals) is selected and the chemical is given to them. The health of the group is monitored.

If there are 1000 people in the group, how many people need to be affected by the chemical before we can say that the chemical is unsafe? What happens if one person in 1000 is affected? Is this safe? What if 1 million people are tested and one person is affected? Does this mean that the chemical is unsafe? It is certainly not 100% safe, but will it ever be?

In the end, we must accept that there will always be a risk, no matter how small. Measuring risk is difficult, and yet we do it every day. We cross the road, we drive cars, we use mobile phones. All these activities have a risk, but we decide whether the benefits of the activity outweigh the risks.

The important thing is to make sure that we are informed – that we have the correct information. We should try to find out the truth behind the risk. However, we must always realise that, in the end, there is no such thing as total safety.

QUESTIONS

4 'All chemicals are bad for us.' Is this statement true? Give an example of a piece of evidence which strengthens your answer.

5 A scientist may say that a chemical that is a food additive is safe when 1 person in 1000 000 has a bad reaction to it. Does this mean that the chemical is safe or not? Explain your answer.

6 In a scientific test, 3 people in 45 000 developed a minor skin rash when exposed to a certain chemical substance. How many people need to be in the group for us to be confident of 1 person developing a rash?

Sudan dyes

Sudan dyes are coloured substances. They are red dyes used for colouring solvents, oils, waxes, petrol, and shoe and floor polishes.

FIGURE 3: Additives that make food more colourful.

In the UK and the rest of the EU, it is not permitted for Sudan dyes to be added to food. But Sudan dyes were found in some chilli powder imported from India, and they were also found in a number of food products containing this chilli powder.

Tartrazine

Tartrazine (E102) is a food additive used to give food a bright orange colour. It is often used in crisps, custards, drinks, ice cream, sweets, jams and marmalades and in some cereals.

Tartrazine is known to make some children hyperactive. Scientists have suggested that it is also linked with various allergies, asthma, migraines and even types of cancer.

QUESTIONS

7 Give **two** uses of Sudan dyes.

8 How can food sold in shops still contain these dyes even though they are banned from food in the UK?

9 How would UK scientists know that Sudan dyes were unsafe to put in foods?

Analysing chemicals

You will find out:

- About chromatography – a technique used to separate chemicals
- That it can be used to look closely at substances in food
- How it is used to identify additives in food

Looking closely at food

'You are what you eat' is a well-known saying. But what is in our food? It may smell nice and be nice to look at, but that doesn't tell us what is in it.

A person may have an allergy. They will want to know if the foods they are buying contain additives that will trigger that allergy. Scientists need to know how to detect the additives in foods.

FIGURE 1: This looks nice, but what's in it?

Analysing food

A prepared salad in a supermarket cabinet may consist of tomatoes, lettuce, carrots and a dressing, but it could also contain some additives that keep the salad fresh for longer (increase its shelf-life), and others that make the salad tastier and nicer to look at. We need to know they are there, in order to decide whether the salad is safe for us to eat.

Scientists are able to analyse – look closely at – the chemicals in food. They use the methods of **chemical analysis**. One of the most important methods for analysing substances in food is called **chromatography**.

Chromatography is used to separate mixtures of substances. This is important because if we can separate the substances in a mixture, we can identify those substances and then use them for further study to check that they are safe.

Chromatography was developed about a hundred years ago by a Russian botanist named Michael Tswett, who used it to study plant pigments.

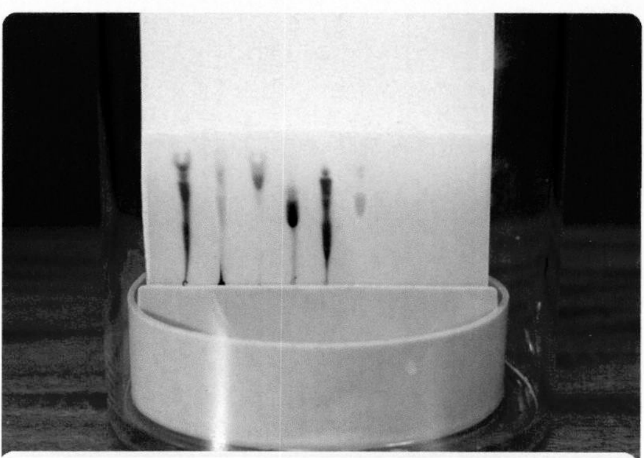

FIGURE 2: Carrying out paper chromatography.

QUESTIONS

1 Why it is important for scientists to be able to analyse food?

2 Give **two** reasons why additives are added to foods.

3 Some food dyes are mixtures of many different colours. What is meant by the term 'mixture'?

How is chromatography carried out?

Paper chromatography can be used to separate coloured substances in foods.

- A sample of the coloured dye from some food is spotted on a pencil line drawn near the bottom of a strip of chromatography paper.
- Known additives are then placed on the same pencil line and labelled.
- The bottom edge of the chromatography paper is placed in a **solvent**, for example water or ethanol. A solvent is chosen that dissolves the unknown substances easily so their spots move well up the chromatogram.
- The solvent then rises up the paper and, as it does so, the dyes separate out.
- When the solvent has moved a long way up the chromatography paper, the paper is removed and allowed to dry. It is now the completed chromatogram.

What does a chromatogram look like?

Look at figure 3. Look at how the spots have moved up the paper.

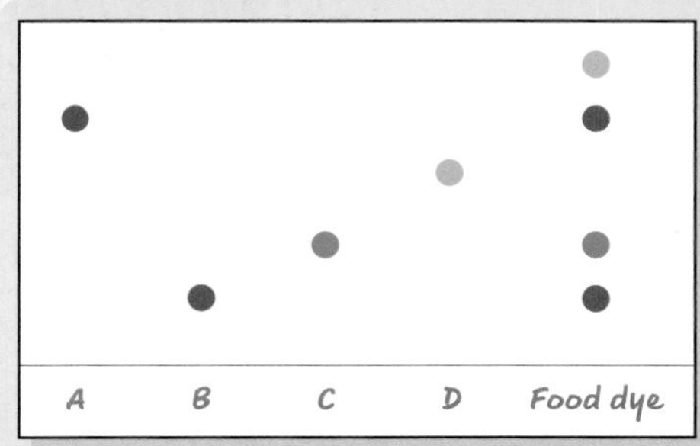

FIGURE 3: Chromatogram of a colour sample from food.

Points to notice in the chromatogram

- The colour from the food gives rise to four spots. This means that there are four different chemical substances in the original dye. Each spot is a separate chemical substance.
- The height of the spots is important. A particular chemical compound moves up the paper at a particular speed, whatever mixture it comes from. We can therefore say that dyes A, B and C are present in the food sample.

The orange spot at the very top of the chromatogram is not matched by any of the known additives A to D, so this is an unknown substance that will need to be analysed further.

QUESTIONS

4 In a chromatogram, six spots are produced from a dye sample taken from a cake dye. How many different substances are present in the dye?

5 Describe how you would use a chromatogram to identify the dyes in question 4.

6 Two spots are produced in a chromatogram. They are both brown spots but appear at different heights on the chromatography paper. Are the brown spots the same chemical substance?

Retention factors

A solvent rises up a chromatography paper faster than the spots of a substance. The **retention factor** compares the speed at which the substance rises up the paper, with the speed of the solvent.

The retention factor, R_f, is defined as:

$$\frac{\textbf{distance moved by the substance}}{\textbf{distance moved by the solvent}}$$

So, for example, if a solvent moves up the paper 10 cm and the coloured substance moves up 6 cm, then the R_f value is:

$$\frac{6\text{ cm}}{10\text{ cm}} = 0.6$$

The retention factor for a particular compound always has the same value. Scientists use this value to identify that particular compound in a dye. If there are more compounds in the dye, they will have other retention factor values. The R_f value for an unknown additive is calculated from the chromatogram. This value is then compared to a database of values to identify the additive.

QUESTIONS

7 Suggest why different substances have different R_f values.

8 A solvent moves up some chromatography paper 15 cm. Two different spots move up 5 cm and 3 cm respectively. What are the R_f values for these two spots?

9 If two spots have the same R_f value, and are the same colours, does this definitely prove that they are the same substance?

The Earth

You will find out:

- That the Earth is nearly a sphere and has a layered structure
- That the layers are: thin crust, mantle, core
- That the Earth's magnetic field protects life

Our planet

The Earth is a special place. It is the **planet** in which all the living things that we know about have evolved, including humans. It supplies everything we need: food, warmth and shelter. We think of it as huge, though it is small when compared to our Sun and the stars and other planets in space.

FIGURE 1: Planet Earth.

Earth facts

Our Earth is a planet. This means that it moves around a **star** – the Sun. So do the other planets in our Solar System.

The Earth is the largest rocky planet, but is small compared to others. Jupiter, which is mostly gas, has a diameter 11 times that of the Earth.

- The Earth is like a huge slightly squashed ball. Its diameter is about 13 000 km.
- The Earth is made of rock. About 70% of its surface is covered by water that forms the oceans, seas, lakes and rivers. It also has a very thin layer of air round it that we call the **atmosphere**.
- The Earth is ancient. It is about 4600 million years old.
- Life has been around on Earth for about three-quarters of this time. The first primitive forms of life appeared about 3400 million years ago.
- But the first humans appeared only 30 000 years ago. If we think of the story of the Earth spread over 1 year, with the Earth formed on 1st January, and 31 December being now, humans would have appeared at 11.58 p.m. on the final day (that is, two minutes before midnight).
- The Earth has a satellite, the Moon. Its diameter is only 3500 km, about 3 times smaller than the Earth's diameter.

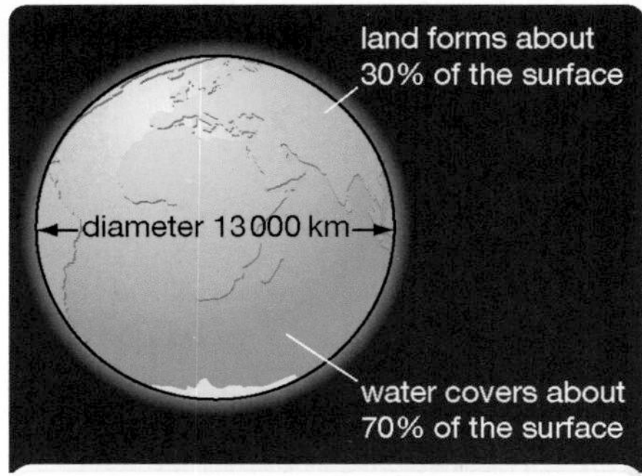

FIGURE 2: The size and features of the Earth.

EXAM HINTS AND TIPS

The Earth is a planet since it orbits a star (the Sun). A moon is an object that orbits a planet.

QUESTIONS

1 How old is the Earth?
2 What is the diameter and radius of the Earth?
3 Why is the Earth called a planet?

...atmosphere ...core ...crust ...magnetic field

What is the Earth like inside?

The Earth has a layered structure inside.

- There are three main layers. Each layer is different from the others.
- The layers are called the **crust**, the **mantle** and the **core**.

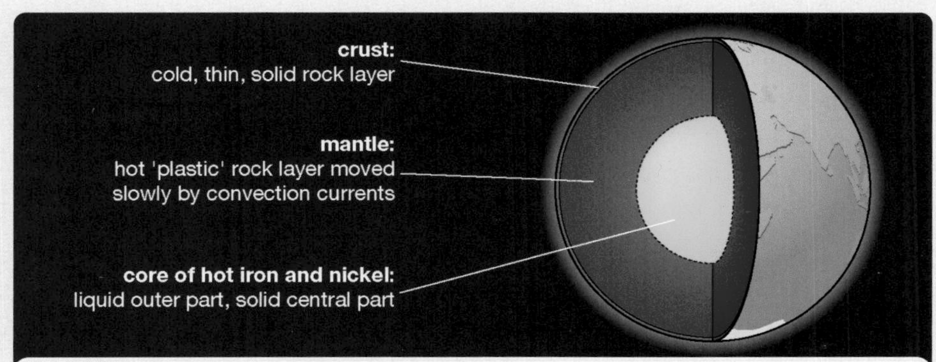

FIGURE 3: The layers of the Earth.

The crust

This is only thin and forms the outer layer around the Earth. It is solid rock.

The mantle

This is a very thick layer, about half of the Earth's diameter. It is made of rock, but a kind of 'plastic' rock that can move very slowly. The mantle is very hot and convection currents make it circulate below the crust. Radioactive materials inside the Earth produce the heat that drives the convection currents.

The core

As in an apple, the core is in the centre. This too is a large part of the Earth, about half of its diameter.

- The core is made up of a mixture of iron and nickel – these are both metals.
- The core is in two parts, the outer and inner core.
  - The outer core is a liquid mixture of the two metals iron and nickel.
  - The inner core is solid iron and nickel.
- We believe that the outer core is magnetic and gives the Earth its **magnetic poles**.

QUESTIONS

4 What are the names of the **three** main layers within the Earth?

5 What are the names of the **two** parts of the core of the Earth?

6 What are the names of the **two** largest layers within the Earth?

WOW FACTOR!

The deepest mine in the world is about 3.5 km in depth. It is two thousand times further to the centre of the Earth.

Earth loses its magnetism

The Earth is magnetic. This is why a metal compass needle lines itself up with the Earth's **magnetic field**. This field acts as a safety blanket, repelling dangerous electrically charged particles that stream from the Sun in what we call the 'solar wind'.

Scientists tell us that the Earth's magnetic field has lost about 10% of the strength it had 150 years ago and will disappear in 1500 to 2000 years' time. After a period of no magnetic field, it would gradually come back, but present-day compasses would then point south instead of north.

Over the life of the Earth, the magnetic field strength has steadily decreased, disappeared and switched over. While there is no magnetic field, the dangerous particles reach the Earth's surface and damage the cells of living things and many organisms become extinct.

It is hard to predict when the Earth's magnetic field will switch off, and how fast it will do this. The reversal pattern is not smooth and scientists find it difficult to predict when this process might happen in the future.

QUESTIONS

7 Which part of the Earth generates the magnetic field?

8 What is the 'solar wind', and how are we protected from it?

9 Why do scientists find it difficult to predict how the Earth's magnetic field will change in the future?

Earth's surface

You will find out:

- That the Earth's features were formed millions of years ago
- Alfred Wegener's explanation of how the Earth's structure changes
- That tectonic plates move against each other

The Grand Canyon

The Grand Canyon is one of Earth's most spectacular sights. It is huge – more than 300 km long and 1.5 km deep. Even the tallest skyscrapers would fit inside the inner gorge in the **canyon**.

The Grand Canyon is so vast that it is hard to work out what we are looking at. In fact, it was made by a wide Colorado River as it laid down silt layers that formed rocks. Then over millions of years the river slowly narrowed and wore the rocks away to form the steep-sided canyon.

FIGURE 1: The Grand Canyon.

The surface of our planet

When we look at the Earth, we realise what a beautiful place it is.

Over 70% of the planet is covered with water, forming the oceans, seas, rivers and lakes. The rest of the surface is land formed from rocks. We see mountain ranges, valleys, islands and wonderful countryside. Was it like this when the Earth first formed?

We now know that the Earth is not a static planet made of immobile rock. It is changing all the time, but so slowly that we don't notice.

People once thought that:

- features we now see on the surface were all formed when the Earth cooled down
- heat was left over from when the Earth first formed and this is why the centre of the Earth is very hot.

We now know that this is not what happened.

FIGURE 2: *Has this view always been the same?*

QUESTIONS

1 Briefly explain how the Grand Canyon was formed.

2 How was it first thought that the land features we see on Earth today were first formed?

3 What proportion of the Earth's surface is covered with land?

EARTH'S HEAT

The heat inside the Earth is produced when radioactive substances called isotopes decay. It is not heat left over from when the Earth first formed.

...canyon ...lithosphere ...mid-ocean ridge ...Pangaea

How do we know how surface features were formed?

In 1915, the German Alfred Wegener suggested that a **supercontinent** he called **Pangaea** existed in the past and broke up about 200 million years ago. He proposed that the pieces 'drifted' to their present positions. Most scientists at the time disagreed with these ideas, but Wegener was right.

Figure 3 shows Pangaea and outlines of the large continents and landmasses we know today. Notice how they fit together like a huge jigsaw puzzle.

We now know that the Earth's surface, called the **lithosphere** (the crust and the semi-solid upper part of the Earth's mantle), is broken into a number of large pieces called **tectonic plates**. Heat from radioactive processes within the Earth drives convection currents that circulate the material of the mantle. The tectonic plates 'ride' on the moving mantle, like slabs on a conveyor belt.

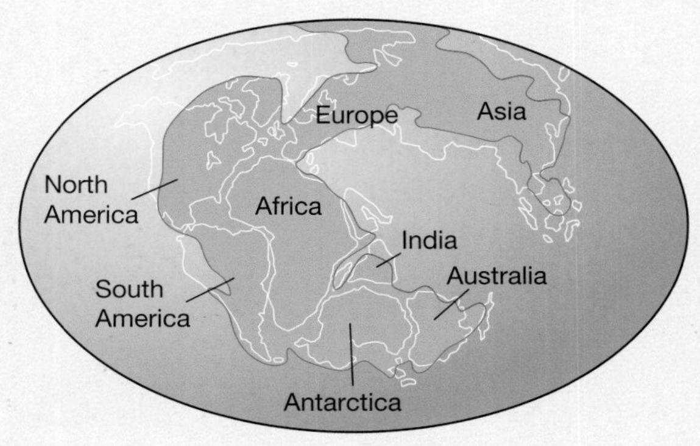

FIGURE 3: Pangaea, over 200 million years ago.

The tectonic plates move only very slowly, a few centimetres every year, at about the rate that human fingernails grow! We do not notice such small movements, but over millions of years they add up to a very large change.

The Himalayas form a giant mountain range that is still growing today. Two huge landmasses – India and part of Asia – are colliding and pushing each other upwards to form these amazing mountains. Before India collided with what is now Tibet, it was an island in the sea. The two crashed together, and the seabed was pushed upwards, carrying fossilised sea creatures with it. These are now found high in the mountains.

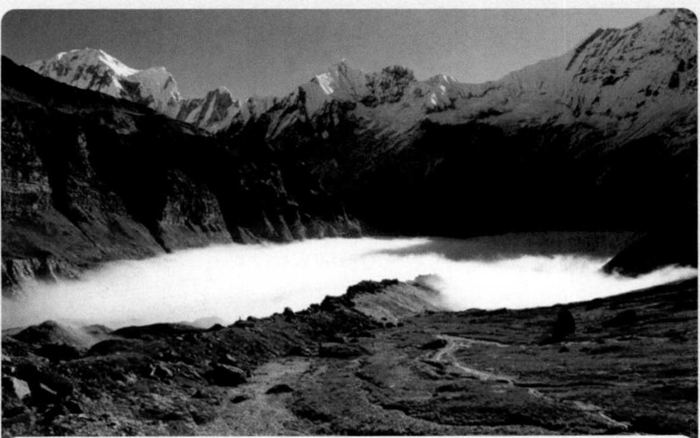

FIGURE 4: The Himalayas.

QUESTIONS

4 Name the island that existed millions of year ago and that moved apart to make the landmasses we see today.

5 What is the name given to the crust and upper part of the Earth's mantle?

6 Explain how fossils of sea creatures finished up at the top of the Himalayas, 8 km above sea level.

7 What is the name given to the broken pieces of Earth's crust?

Continents move apart

When tectonic plates move apart, magma (molten rock) pushes up from the mantle, forming new crust. Imagine two wide conveyor belts very slowly rolling away from each other. The gap between is filled by molten material that solidifies and moves away with the conveyor belts in both directions.

This is happening where plates meet at the Mid-Atlantic Ridge. It forms an underwater mountain range extending from the Arctic Ocean southwards to beyond the southern tip of Africa. It is just one part of the system of global **mid-ocean ridges** that circles the Earth.

The Mid-Atlantic Ridge spreads at about 2.5 cm per year, or 25 km in a million years. This **seafloor spreading** has changed the Atlantic Ocean from a tiny inlet of water between the continents of Europe, Africa and the Americas into the vast ocean it is today.

QUESTIONS

8 Explain how the plates are moving at the Mid-Atlantic Ridge.

9 How much has the ridge moved in 1000 years?

10 If new crust is being formed at the ridge, why doesn't the Earth become larger over millions of years?

Earthquakes & volcanoes

You will find out:

- That earthquakes are linked to the movement of tectonic plates
- That volcanoes form where magma bursts through the crust
- That some places are much more prone to earthquakes

Tsunami

On 26 December 2004, there was a huge **earthquake** on the floor of the Indian Ocean off the west coast of northern Sumatra in Indonesia.

The earthquake caused a great wave – a **tsunami** – to form. It spread outwards and crashed into the shores of Indonesia, Sri Lanka and southern India. It caused one of the deadliest disasters in modern history, killing well over 240 000 people.

FIGURE 1: Why do tsunamis happen?

Earthquakes

The Earth's surface is composed of large sheets of crust called tectonic plates. Some are **oceanic plates**, some are **continental plates**, and some are both. They are packed together and are always moving, though very slowly, driven by heat released by natural radioactive processes.

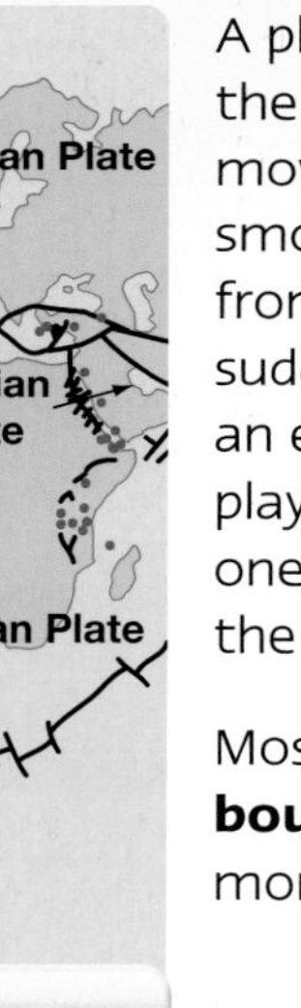

FIGURE 2: The main plate boundaries and active volcanoes.

A plate moves because of the pressure of currents in the mantle below – the plate 'rides' on top of the moving mantle. When a plate moves, it isn't a smooth movement. A neighbouring plate stops it from moving. The pressure gradually increases until suddenly one plate slips over the other, and there is an earthquake. It is like pushing the edges of two playing cards together. As you increase the pressure, one may buckle, then suddenly one slides on top of the other and all the energy is released.

Most of the world's earthquakes occur along **plate boundaries** where the rocks are usually weaker and more likely to give way to pressure.

MORE TO LEARN

We don't understand exactly how volcanoes and earthquakes work, and these events are not regular, so scientists cannot predict the next eruption or earthquake.

QUESTIONS

1 What is a tsunami and how does it form?
2 Explain briefly how an earthquake happens.
3 Why are earthquakes more likely to happen at plate boundaries?

...continental plate ...earthquake ...hot spot ...magma ...oceanic plate

How do volcanoes fit in?

Earthquakes are most likely to happen at plate boundaries, that is, at the join between one plate and another. The same is often true of **volcanoes**, as shown in figure 2.

A volcano forms when a bubble of **magma**, or hot molten rock, works its way up from the mantle and breaks through the Earth's crust to the surface. Imagine an apple pie being cooked and a bubble of hot apple mixture breaking through the pastry.

Between eruptions, the magma stays sealed in an underground chamber, often for hundreds of years, until the pressure builds enough for it to blast through a **vent** – a crack or weak spot in the crust. The blast creates a crater, and lava and gas pour out forming the familiar cone shape of volcanoes.

FIGURE 3: Mount Pinatubo in the Philippines erupted in 1991.

Hot spots and subduction zones

The dozen or so main plates of the Earth's crust move a few centimetres every year. Rising magma can push the Earth's plates apart at plate boundaries. When this happens, a **hot spot** occurs and at that point molten rock comes through to the Earth's surface. The Hawaiian Islands were created at a hot spot.

As shown in figure 4, an oceanic plate slides under a continental plate at a **subduction zone**. Magma rises to form a volcano, and the oceanic rock melts as it dives into the Earth. The Andes mountain range on the west coast of South America was formed in this way. Dotted up the coast is a series of extinct volcanoes that were formed when the oceanic plate moved under the continental plate.

QUESTIONS

4 Describe the plate movement at **a)** a hot spot and **b)** a subduction zone.

5 Give an example of islands created by a hot spot.

Very deep oceans

The deepest spot in all the oceans of the world is in the Pacific Ocean, just east of the Philippines. It is called the Mariana Trench. How did this trench form?

The oceanic crust is much heavier (denser) than the continental crust, so when they collide, the oceanic plate crashes downwards towards the molten mantle, while the lighter, continental plate rides up over the top. The forces driving the two plates together are enormously powerful, so the underlying oceanic plate creates a trench where it drags the edge of the continental crust down as it descends underneath.

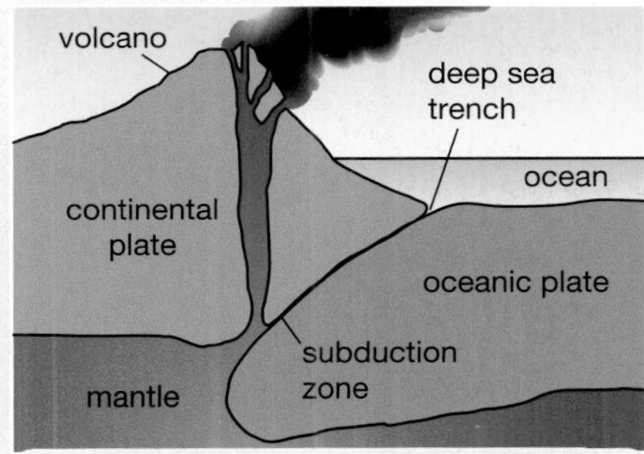

FIGURE 4: What happens at a subduction zone.

The really deep part of the ocean is at the bottom of the trench created by this subducting ocean crust. The Mariana Trench marks where the fast-moving Pacific Plate pushes against the slower moving Philippine Plate.

QUESTIONS

6 What is meant by the term 'subducting'?

7 Why does an oceanic plate move under a continental plate?

8 Why are volcanoes often found near to deep sea trenches?

The air

You will find out:
- That air is essential for life
- That air is a mixture of elements and compounds
- That the gases in air can be separated and put to use

Let there be life!

When a baby is born, it has to take its first breath of air to obtain **oxygen**. All animals need oxygen in order to live.

It may be an invisible, tasteless and odourless gas, but oxygen enables all life to exist. Without oxygen, there would be no living things on Earth.

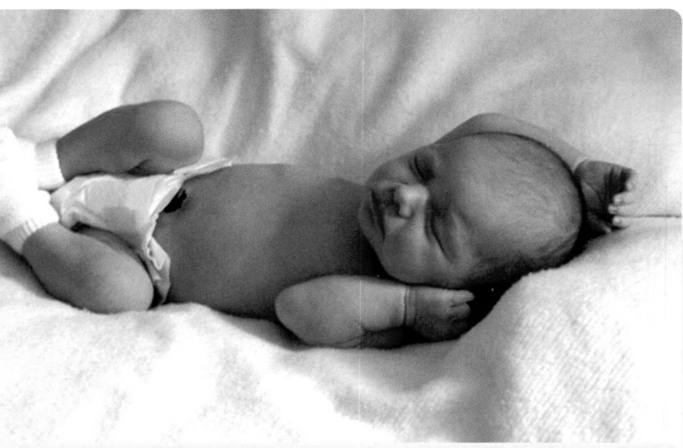

FIGURE 1: A newly born baby first fills its lungs with air.

The air we breathe

- **Air** is not a pure substance. It is a **mixture** of colourless gases.
- The main gases in air are oxygen and **nitrogen**. There are other gases in smaller amounts. One of them is **argon** which is a **noble gas**, meaning it does not react with other substances.
- Air also contains the gases carbon dioxide and water vapour in small amounts. The amount of water vapour tends to vary a lot.
- All of the gases that make up the air that we breathe are important – if one of them changed, even a little bit, life on Earth would be very different.

The man in figure 2 has been in a serious accident and is in hospital. The mask over his face is connected to a supply of pure oxygen gas. This helps him obtain enough oxygen if his breathing is shallow.

We have many uses for the different gases that make up the air, but we need to separate them out first.

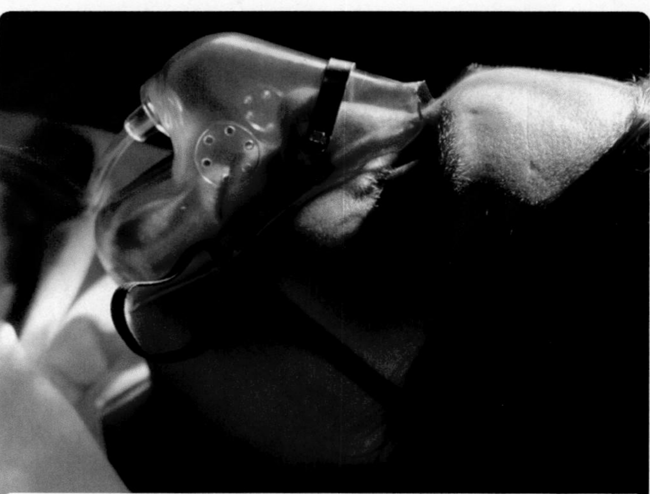

FIGURE 2: Seriously injured people are often given pure oxygen.

MAINTAINING OXYGEN

Oxygen was not in Earth's first atmosphere. It was the waste product of early organisms. It is still the waste product of plants today.

QUESTIONS

1 Which gas in the air do living things need in order to survive?
2 Name **three** gases found in the air.
3 Give a use for pure oxygen gas.

...air ...argon ...composition ...mixture

More about the air

The air that we breathe is a mixture of different elements and compounds.

Centuries ago, it was thought that 'air' was a single substance, not made up of anything else. Today we know that it contains many gases. Figure 3 shows the gases that make up the air.

About 80% of the air is nitrogen, and the rest is mainly oxygen. So the gas that supports life on Earth – oxygen – makes up only about 20%, or a fifth, of the air that we breathe. We have evolved so that 20% oxygen exactly matches our needs.

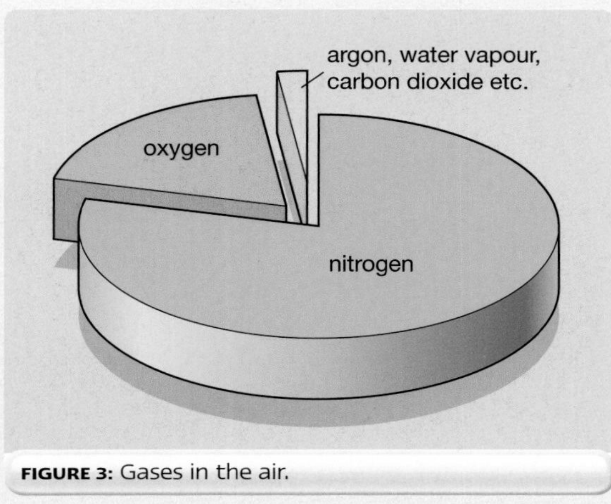

FIGURE 3: Gases in the air.

There are small percentages of other gases in the air, including carbon dioxide, water vapour and noble gases. The amounts of these gases can change.

It may be a surprise to learn that the mix of gases in the air, as well as their amounts, has not always been as it is today. The **composition** of today's air has been the same for only 200 million years. Since the Earth is 4600 million years old, for about 4400 million years the gases in the Earth's atmosphere were quite different.

A more precise breakdown of the composition of today's air is given on the next page.

QUESTIONS

4 Name **two** compounds present in air in very small amounts.

5 For what percentage of the Earth's age has air had today's composition?

6 Express 80% nitrogen and 20% oxygen as simple fractions.

How airbags work

Airbags have been used for many years. They were first used in fighter planes during the Second World War. Only since the 1980s have cars had airbags.

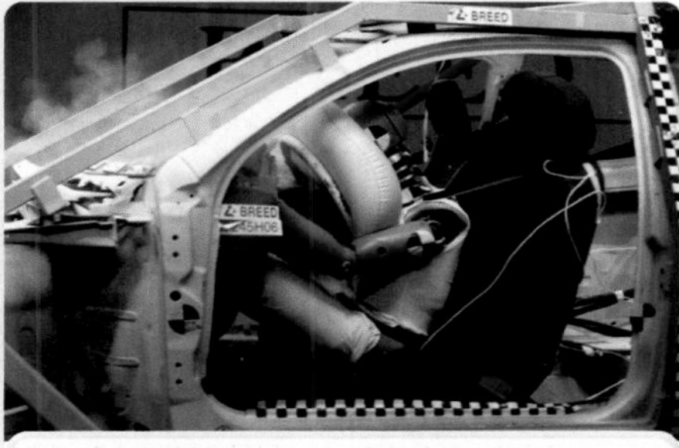

FIGURE 4: Airbags save lives.

All new cars must have dual airbags – for driver and front passenger. Airbags are known to reduce deaths in a head-on crash by about 30%. For safety, we may in the future have cars with six or even eight airbags.

Airbags work in a clever way. At a collision, a smart 'piezoelectric' material senses the change in force and immediately produces a small electrical charge that triggers a chemical reaction. In this reaction, a solid called sodium azide (NaN_3) decomposes very rapidly to form nitrogen gas which inflates the bag in a fraction of a second.

sodium azide → sodium metal + nitrogen gas

$$2NaN_3 \rightarrow 2Na + 3N_2$$

QUESTIONS

7 If 1000 people were killed during head-on collisions, how many would have survived if they had used airbags?

8 Name the gas that fills up the airbag.

Evolution of the air

You will find out:

- How volcanoes helped to produce Earth's early atmosphere
- How the composition of the atmosphere has changed over millions of years
- About Venus's atmosphere

Volcanoes

We think of **volcanoes** as dangerous because they have caused many human deaths.

However, volcanoes played a very important role in the formation of the Earth as we see it today. This is because the air was originally made up of gases that came from volcanoes.

FIGURE 1: Volcanoes formed Earth's first atmosphere.

'Modern' air

This is the composition of air that exists today.

Gas	Formula	% of air
nitrogen	N_2	78.084
oxygen	O_2	20.9476
argon	Ar	0.934
carbon dioxide	CO_2	0.0314
neon	Ne	0.001818
helium	He	0.000524
methane	CH_4	0.0002
krypton	Kr	0.000114
hydrogen	H_2	0.00005
xenon	Xe	0.0000087

The composition of air has not always been the same as in the table. It has changed greatly over millions of years.

How did the atmosphere begin?

We think the very first atmosphere was made of hydrogen and helium because these were the most common gases after the **Big Bang**. This was the explosion thought to have first formed the universe.

The two gases hydrogen and helium are light and could not have been held on Earth by **gravity**, so it would not have been long before they escaped into space.

QUESTIONS

1 What is the name and formula for the third most common gas in the air?

2 What are the names of the **two** gases that were believed to make up Earth's first atmosphere?

3 How many substances in the table above are compounds?

4 What is the meaning of the '2' in the formula for oxygen, O_2?

...Big Bang ...condense ...dissolve

How has the composition of air evolved?

Look at figure 2. It shows how the levels of the atmosphere's nitrogen (N_2), oxygen (O_2) and carbon dioxide (CO_2) have changed with time.

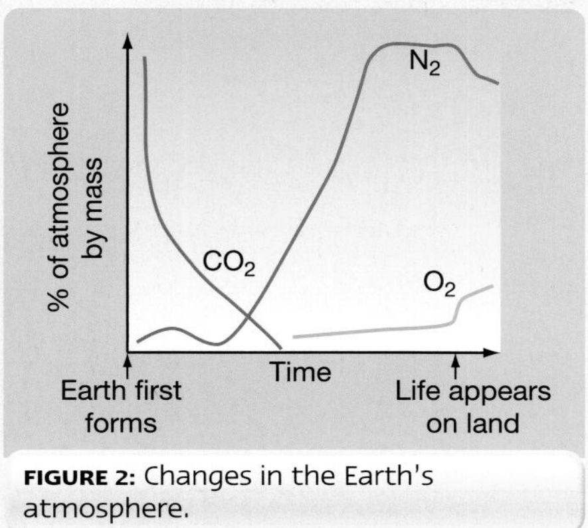

FIGURE 2: Changes in the Earth's atmosphere.

The following important stages in the Earth's history explain the graph.

- Levels of carbon dioxide were very high when the Earth first formed. We believe that this was because huge volumes of carbon dioxide gas were escaping from volcanoes.
- Volcanoes also produced water vapour. However, as the Earth started to cool, this **condensed** to form liquid water, which became the earliest seas and oceans.
- Carbon dioxide **dissolved** in these seas, so the carbon dioxide level of the atmosphere started to decrease.
- The first primitive life forms developed in warm shallow seas 3400 million years ago. The water protected them from the Sun's harmful rays. They produced oxygen as a waste product and this entered the atmosphere. Some of it was converted to ozone, O_3, which formed a layer in the atmosphere that protected the Earth's surface from the harmful rays. This allowed land plants to appear, about 400 million years ago. They photosynthesised, removing carbon dioxide and adding more oxygen.
- Ammonia (NH_3) from volcanoes reacted with oxygen gas and produced nitrogen, so nitrogen levels started to increase. Bacteria were also able to produce nitrogen gas from ammonia.
- Eventually the effects of life forms and volcanic processes began to balance each other and the composition of the atmosphere became steady.

QUESTIONS

5 Give **two** reasons why levels of carbon dioxide decreased over time.

6 Where did the nitrogen gas in today's air come from?

7 Why is photosynthesis important in maintaining the composition of the atmosphere?

Venus and the greenhouse effect

The swirling clouds around the planet Venus look peaceful, but they are definitely not.

FIGURE 3: Venus.

Venus is closer to the Sun than Earth. The Sun heats it and its thick cloud cover traps the heat. (On Earth, heat can escape back into space.) Venus's clouds have the same effect as a greenhouse on Earth. Temperatures can reach 600 °C. This makes Venus the hottest planet in the Solar System, even though Mercury is closer to the Sun.

Unlike Earth clouds, clouds on Venus contain deadly sulphuric acid droplets. Its atmosphere is mostly carbon dioxide, a poisonous, suffocating gas which would kill any living creature. It is thought that Earth's early atmosphere, with its high levels of carbon dioxide, may have been very similar to that on Venus.

QUESTIONS

8 Suggest how a gardener's greenhouse keeps flowers warmer than those outdoors.

9 Why would breathing in carbon dioxide be dangerous?

10 Why is there concern about the increasing levels of carbon dioxide gas on Earth?

Atmospheric change

You will find out:
- That changes in the atmosphere affect the Earth as a whole
- That gases that humans produce are making the atmosphere warmer
- That this is causing climates to change

Melting icebergs

Ice sheets cover massive areas of the world including the Arctic, Greenland and Antarctica. At the edges of these sheets, lumps of ice break off into the sea and form icebergs.

Icebergs can be enormous and contain huge volumes of frozen fresh water. They melt as they drift into warmer water. Ice is now being lost faster than snowfall can replace it, and this is seen as a worrying sign of **global warming**.

FIGURE 1: Spectacular icebergs in the Arctic Ocean.

The Earth is heating up

From records made over the last century, the average temperature of the Earth has risen by 1°C. Scientists say that the 1990s were the warmest 10 years in the last 1000 years. This **climate change** means our planet is becoming warmer. How much warmer will it be in another century, and what effects will that have?

The following things may happen if the Earth's temperature continues to increase.

- Ice sheets will melt. Water from ice on land will cause sea levels to rise. Small, low islands will be flooded forever.
- The world's weather will change. It may become stormier, hotter in summer and colder in winter: in general, the weather will become more extreme.

If the weather changes in this way, life will be very different in the future. Countries that are warm at the moment may become very hot. Other countries may become very cold.

FIGURE 2: Beautiful islands like the Maldives may disappear beneath rising oceans.

A GOOD IDEA?

One idea for disposing of carbon dioxide gas is to pump it to the bottom of the sea and store it there in large tanks.

QUESTIONS

1 What is the evidence that the Earth is becoming warmer?
2 What is the name given to the idea that the planet is getting warmer?
3 What may happen if sea levels rise?

Watch Out Saying, 'The evidence suggests that increased levels of carbon dioxide are contributing to global warming,' is not the same as saying 'The evidence proves that increased levels…'. We can only make definite conclusions when we have all the evidence.

What happens to carbon dioxide in the air?

Overall, the level of carbon dioxide in the atmosphere is increasing. At the same time, carbon dioxide constantly circulates between the atmosphere and living and non-living things on the ground.

- Carbon dioxide is quite soluble in water, and dissolves in rainwater as well as seawater. This decreases the level of carbon dioxide in the atmosphere.
- Once carbon dioxide is dissolved in water, it reacts to form **carbonic acid**. This acid can react with calcium-containing minerals dissolved in seawater. The reaction forms calcium carbonate, which is not soluble in water, and so sinks to the bottom of the sea. Over millions of years, a layer builds up and becomes rock.
- Chalk and limestone are calcium carbonate rocks. Carbon dioxide from the atmosphere is 'locked up' in them. We call these rocks **carbon sinks**.

FIGURE 3: Rocks like this act as a carbon sink.

- During **photosynthesis**, plants absorb carbon dioxide. If we grew more plants, especially more trees in **reforestation** schemes, more carbon dioxide could be absorbed. In the Earth's past, coal, which is a fossil fuel, was formed when trees were buried underground. Like calcium carbonate rocks, coal became a carbon sink.

Greenhouse gases

Carbon dioxide is known as a greenhouse gas. Water vapour is another greenhouse gas. They trap heat in the Earth's atmosphere. Without them, the Earth's temperature would be a lot lower than it is today.

QUESTIONS

4 Give **two** ways in which carbon dioxide is removed from the atmosphere.

5 The amount of carbon dioxide in the atmosphere is steadily increasing. What does this suggest about the rate at which carbon dioxide is being added to the air compared to the rate at which it is being removed?

A need for caution

Let us look at what we know about global warming.

- Scientists have measured the Earth's average temperature for over a century and have shown that it is increasing.

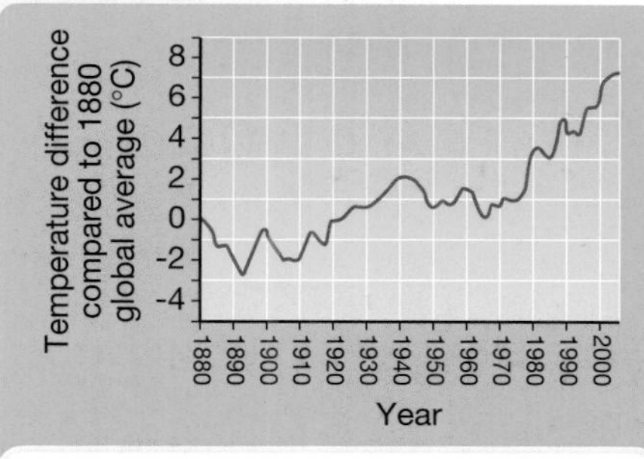

FIGURE 4: The changing temperature of the atmosphere.

- Scientists have measured the average levels of carbon dioxide gas in the air and have shown that it is increasing too.

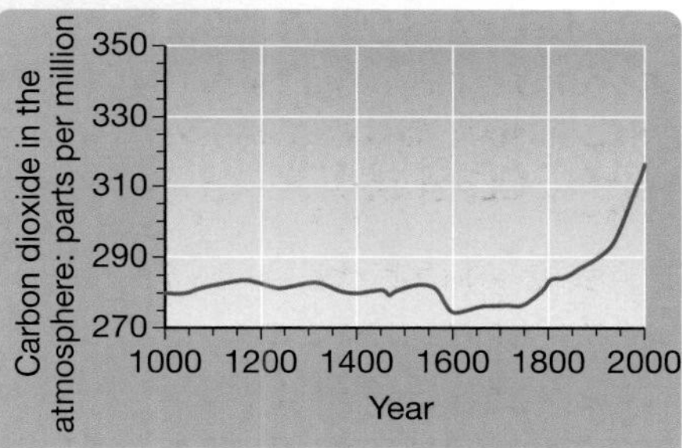

FIGURE 5: Changing carbon dioxide levels in the atmosphere.

- There is an increase in both the average temperature of the atmosphere and carbon dioxide levels. Are they linked? In other words, is the temperature increasing solely because levels of carbon dioxide are increasing? This is an important question, and the answer could be complicated.

QUESTIONS

6 Look carefully at the first graph. What evidence is there that the graph is not a measure of average global temperature?

7 In the second graph, suggest why the levels of carbon dioxide have rapidly increased since 1800.

Unit summary

Concept map

Making new substances from crude oil

Crude oil is made from hydrocarbons that can be cracked to form a new family called the alkenes.

Alkenes are unsaturated: they contain carbon double bonds.

Ethene gas is highly reactive and can form important chemicals such as ethanol.

Alkenes are useful as they can make polymers like polythene. Polymers are long chain molecules created when millions of carbon atoms join together.

Polymers are important as they are used to make many useful substances. But they represent an environmental problem when disposed of in landfill sites, as they do not biodegrade and so remain in the soil for a long time.

Plant oils

Many plants contain useful natural oils that can be extracted.

Some vegetable oils may be hardened by reacting them with hydrogen gas. This process (a hydrogenation) is important when making margarine.

Oils and water do not mix. When they are shaken together very hard, an emulsion is formed.

An emulsion will separate into two layers. Sometimes an emulsifier is added to stop this happening.

The Earth

The Earth has a layered structure. It consists of a crust, a mantle and an inner and outer core.

The Earth's crust is made of plates that are always moving slowly. When these plates collide with each other, volcanoes and earthquakes could form.

The Earth's atmosphere has changed over millions of years. Many of the gases that make up the atmosphere have come from volcanoes.

Unit quiz

1 What is the name of the process in which long chain alkanes are broken down to form smaller molecules?

2 Name the two elements found in hydrocarbons.

3 What is the general formula of an alkene?

4 What type of chemical bond is present in an alkene that makes it reactive and what substance is used to test for the presence of this bond?

5 What is the chemical formula for propene?

6 What is the name of the polymer formed using propene?

7 Why is the disposal of polymers an environmental problem?

8 Suggest **one** way of disposing of polymers that would benefit society.

9 Some plant oils are described as being 'polyunsaturated'. What does this mean?

10 Why is a diet high in saturated fats considered to be unhealthy?

11 What is the chemical formula for ethanol?

12 Name the process used to change sugars into ethanol in the presence of yeast.

13 Ethanol can sometimes be called a 'renewable' fuel. What does this term mean?

14 What is an emulsion?

15 Name the gas and the catalyst used to harden vegetable oils when making margarine.

16 What are the names of the four main layers within the Earth?

17 Explain why many earthquakes occur at the join between tectonic plates rather than within a plate.

18 What are the names and approximate percentages of the three main gases in the air?

19 Why is the burning of fossil fuels linked with global warming?

Literacy activity

Cancer scare

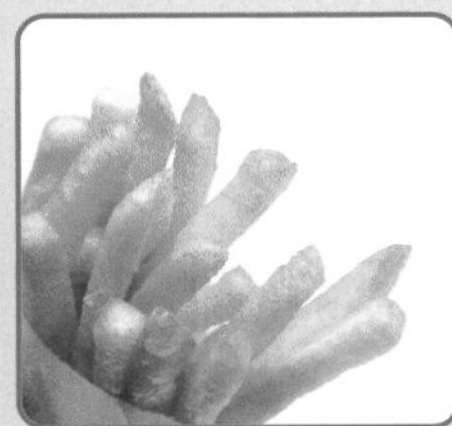

A study has suggested that staple foods, including bread, chips and crisps, may contain high levels of a substance believed to cause cancer. Tests have shown that they all contain high quantities of acrylamide, a chemical that is classified as a probable human carcinogen.

Researchers in Sweden found that acrylamide, a colourless, crystalline solid, was formed when carbohydrate-rich foods such as potatoes, rice or cereals are heated to a high temperature. Such foods could therefore pose a potential health risk to millions of people around the world.

The study found that an ordinary bag of crisps may contain up to 500 times more acrylamide than the highest level that the World Health Organisation (WHO) allows in drinking water. Similarly, French fries sold in some US fast-food chains were found to contain around 100 times more than the maximum permitted amount. The US Environmental Protection Agency classifies acrylamide as a medium hazard probable human carcinogen.

Animal tests have revealed that acrylamide induces gene mutations and can cause benign and malignant stomach tumours. It is also known to damage the central and peripheral nervous system.

QUESTIONS

1 What is the name of the substance that some people are concerned about?

2 How is this substance formed in foods?

3 What possible health problem may there be due to eating chips and crisps?

4 Is the passage a so-called 'scare story'? Explain your answer.

Exam practice

Exam practice questions

1 Match the words A, B, C and D to the spaces 1–4 in the sentences below.

A decomposition **B** vaporise
C cracked **D** catalyst

Hydrocarbons can be broken down, (1) , to make smaller more useful molecules. This involves heating them to (2) them, then passing the hot vapours over a (3) . The reaction that occurs is called thermal (4) . [4]

2 Match the words A, B, C and D to the missing information, 1–4, on the diagram.

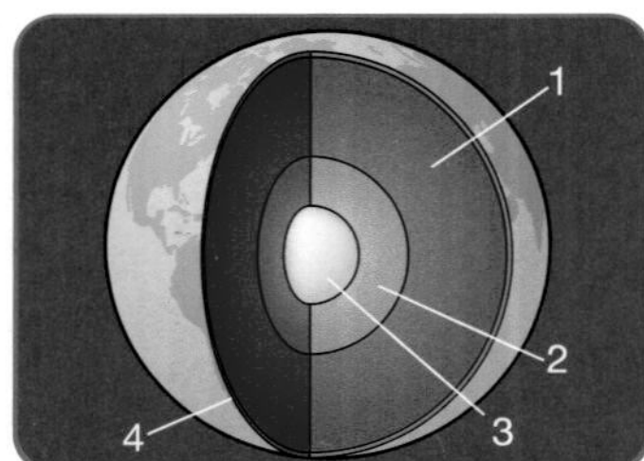

A inner core
B outer core
C mantle
D crust [4]

3 Match the words A, B, C and D to the spaces 1–4 in the sentences below.

A carbon dioxide **B** argon
C oxygen **D** nitrogen

For the last 400 million years, the Earth's atmosphere has been very like it is today. It contains about 80% (1) , 20% (2) and a small percentage of other gases including (3) , water vapour and noble gases, largely (4) . [4]

In questions 4 to 11, choose the best answer.

4 The molecule in Figure 1 ...

```
H       H   H
 \      |   |
  C  =  C - C - H
 /          |
H           H
```

Figure 1

A is saturated.
B contains only single covalent bonds.
C is an alkene.
D has the general formula C_nH_{2n+2}. [1]

5 The molecule in Figure 1 could be ...

A biodegraded.
B made by cracking a large hydrocarbon.
C a polymer.
D used to make polyethene. [1]

6 Which one of these statements about polymer applications is **false**?

A They pose few problems with their disposal.
B They can be used in dental treatments.
C Some can remember their shape.
D They can be used to waterproof fabrics. [1]

7 Which one of these statements about alloys is **false**?

A Steel is an alloy.
B Smart alloys return to their original shape when bent.
C In alloys the different sized atoms in the structure make the alloy softer.
D High carbon steels are good for tools as they are hard. [1]

8 The noble gases ...

A include nitrogen.
B have no uses.
C are chemically unreactive.
D are used in light switches. [1]

9 The early atmosphere ...

A was probably like that of Mercury and Mars.
B contained mainly water vapour and carbon dioxide.
C contained mainly water vapour, oxygen and carbon dioxide.
D formed as a result of many intense earthquakes. [1]

10 Carbon dioxide levels are increasing in the atmosphere because ...

A there has been much more volcanic activity lately.
B it is being locked up in sedimentary rocks as carbonates.
C it is being locked up in fossil fuels.
D there has been an increase in the amount of fossil fuels burnt. [1]

11 What will not occur at the boundary shown on the diagram?

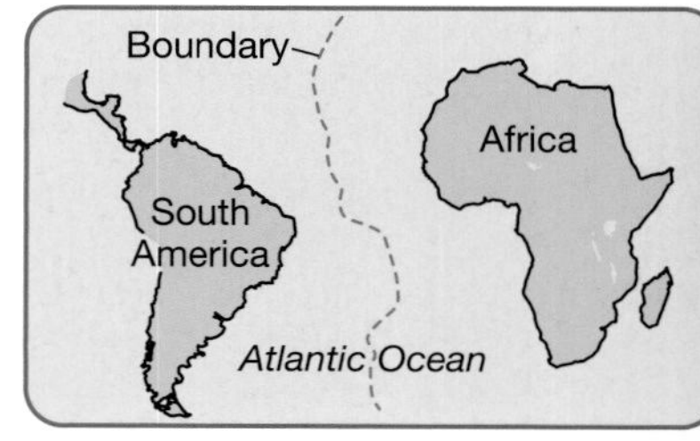

A Volcanic activity.
B Earthquakes.
C Oil formation.
D Further separation of South America and Africa. [1]

12 Ethene is a very useful molecule.

a Draw a diagram to show the structure of ethene. [1]

b Explain how it can be obtained from crude oil. [3]

c Describe how you would convert ethene into ethanol. [3]

13 The Earth's surface has many features, such as mountains.

a How did scientists in the past think these features had been created? [2]

b i The Earth's crust is cracked into a number of rigid plates. What are these plates called? [1]

ii These plates are moving at a rate of a few centimetres a year. What causes them to move and where is the energy derived from? [2]

iii The movement of these plates can cause two effects which can be disastrous. What are they? [2]

14 Chemical analysis can be used to identify the chemical substances present in food.

a How would you test whether a fat was saturated or unsaturated? [2]

b What is the name of the method you would use to identify artificial colourings in foods? [1]

(Total 37 marks)

Worked example

It is thought that several thousand people in Britain are running their cars on vegetable oil, having adapted their engines to run on oils bought from supermarkets. Indeed vegetable oils look set to make a more general comeback as a source of chemicals as well as food. Answer the following questions about vegetable oils.

a Why is there a move towards using vegetable oils? [1]

b Give two ways in which these oils can be extracted from seeds or nuts. [2]

c Why do vegetable oils make good fuels? [1]

d Oils do not dissolve in water but can be made into emulsions. Give three reasons why a salad dressing manufacturer might prefer to sell emulsified oils as salad dressing. [3]

e Vegetable oils can be turned into solids. Describe how and why this is done. [3]

a *Vegetable oils can replace chemicals from crude oil which is a non-sustainable resource.✓*

Good answer.

b *They can be pressed to squeeze the oil✓out or they can be distilled.✓*

Good answer again. If there had been more marks available then the student might have attempted to explain how the oil is distilled, but this is fine for two marks.

c *Vegetable oils contain lots of energy which can be obtained when they are burnt.✓In addition, they often burn more cleanly than some traditional fuels.*

Again the student has given more than is needed for the answer and has made sure of obtaining the one mark for the question.

d *Oils can be a bit runny and they can be made more viscous by emulsifying them. This can make the salad dressing stick to the food better✓and can make it look better✓and have a better texture when eating it.✓*

A complete answer.

e *They can be hardened and turned into solids like margarine by heating the oil at about 60 °C✓over a nickel catalyst.✓This makes them good for spreading and clean and easy for cooking.✓*

A good answer

Overall Grade: A

There is clearly no way of stopping this student! You can tell she has followed all the advice given. The work has been learnt thoroughly, probably with the specification for the course at her side. Careful attention has been made to the number of points needed and something written for each.

Physics 1a – Energy and electricity

DISCOVER LIGHTNING!

Energy cannot be created or destroyed. It can only be transformed from one type to another, or transferred from place to place. We find electricity an extremely useful type of energy, but the energy present in lightning, a form of natural electricity, can be very destructive.

The voltage of a bolt of lightning can be up to 300 million volts.

Lightning strikes somewhere on the Earth's surface about 100 times a second. A bolt of lightning can be three times as hot as the surface of the Sun, hot enough to turn desert sand into glass.

The energy in lightning is enough to crack bricks and stone in an unprotected building, and destroy electrical equipment inside. Each bolt of lightning contains about 1000 million joules of energy, enough to boil a kettle continuously for about two weeks.

CONTENTS

Heat energy

You will find out:

- The difference between heat energy and temperature
- About thermal radiation
- How an object's temperature is related to the internal energy of its particles

Got you!

This pit viper feeds mainly on small rodents, such as mice, which it can detect in total darkness, even when they are not moving. It has a pit on each side of its head, between its nostril and its eye, that detects the warmth of its prey's body. Scientists have shown that the snake can detect temperature differences as small as 0.02 °C, so small that it can even detect cold-blooded animals such as lizards.

FIGURE 1: A pit viper from the Amazon rainforest.

Heat and temperature

You already know that **heat** and **temperature** are not the same thing at all. Temperature is a way of measuring how hot something is. Things that are hot have a high temperature. We can measure temperature using a **thermometer**. The unit is degrees Celsius, written as °C. Heat is a type of energy, like light or sound energy. And **heat energy** can move around, just like light energy or sound energy can.

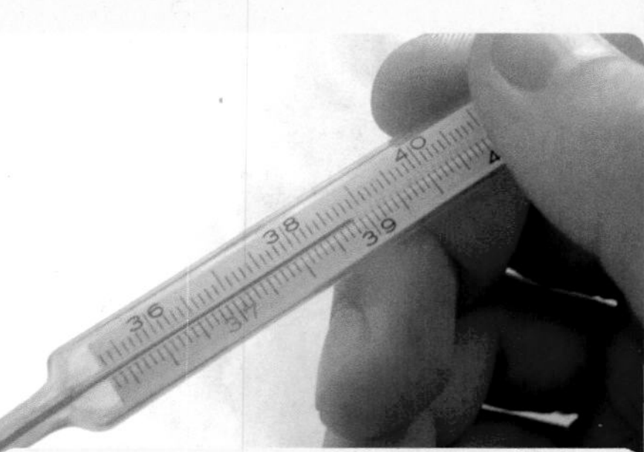

FIGURE 2: This clinical thermometer measures human body temperature. Can you read the temperature it shows?

Getting hotter, getting colder

When you make a hot cup of tea you know it will go cold if you don't drink it quickly. Heat energy flows from the hot cup of tea into the cooler room. The tea cools down and the room warms up a tiny bit, but not enough to notice.

When small children have ice lollies, the lollies nearly always melt! Heat energy flows from the warm surroundings into the cold ice lolly. This is because heat energy always flows from things that are hot to things that are cooler. The hot object loses heat energy and the cooler object gains heat energy.

FIGURE 3: Can you explain what the arrows on this diagram show?

QUESTIONS

1. What units are used to measure temperature?
2. Name **one** object with a high temperature and **one** object with a low temperature.
3. Name **three** different types of energy.
4. Describe how heat energy moves when an ice lolly is taken out of the freezer.

WOW FACTOR!

Just as solar cells generate electricity from light, thermophotovoltaic cells use waste thermal radiation from cookers or furnaces to generate electricity.

...absorb ...emit ...heat ...heat energy

What is thermal radiation?

Thermal radiation is heat energy being **transferred** by rays, similar to light rays. It is sometimes called infra red radiation. Thermal radiation is a type of electromagnetic radiation; other types of electromagnetic radiation include light, microwaves and X-rays.

Just like light, thermal radiation travels in straight lines and at the speed of light. We know that it can travel through a vacuum, because on a hot summers day we can feel the heat (thermal radiation) reaching us from the Sun.

Thermal radiation is a type of energy. When it hits an object, the particles in the object absorb some of the energy, giving them more energy and making them vibrate more. This makes the object hotter, since hot objects have particles that vibrate more than cold objects do.

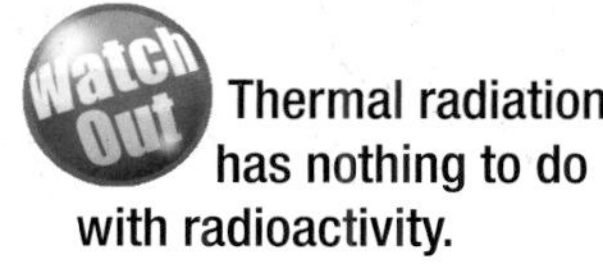

Thermal radiation has nothing to do with radioactivity.

Infra red cameras

All objects both **absorb** thermal radiation and give out, **emit**, thermal radiation. Hot objects give out more thermal radiation than cold objects do. That is why a hot object, such as a fire or an oven, feels hot when you hold your hand near to it. Your hand is detecting the thermal radiation being emitted.

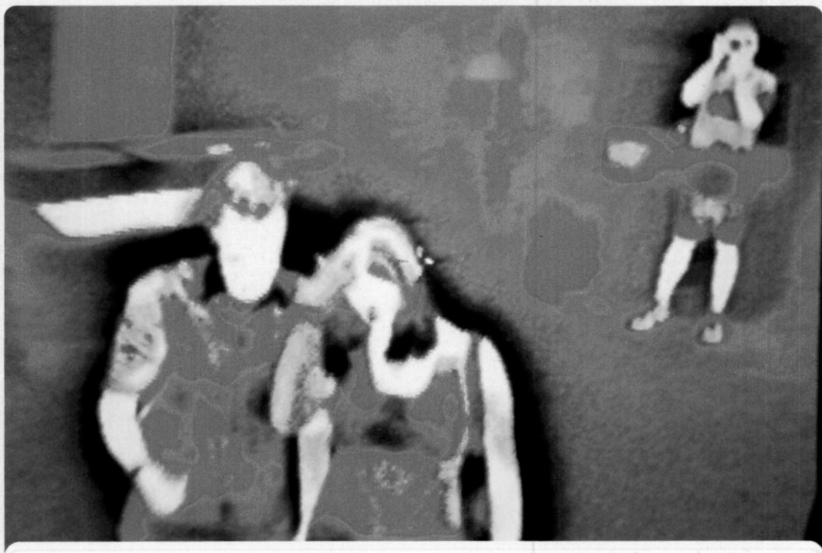

FIGURE 4: How does this image show you that the people are not wearing sleeves?

Infra red cameras, often called 'thermal-imaging cameras', detect the thermal radiation given out by objects so as to show a 'picture' of hot and cold objects. Hot objects usually show up as white or yellow; cooler objects show up as darker colours. Police and the military often use infra red cameras to find people hidden in woodland, or to detect enemy vehicles at night, because the warm bodies or warm engines show up clearly against their cooler surroundings.

QUESTIONS

5 Describe **three** properties of thermal radiation.

6 Describe how thermal radiation affects an object that it hits.

7 Suggest some clothing you could wear to make it harder for a thermal-imaging camera to detect you. Why would it work?

Internal energy

The amount of energy that the particles in an object have is called their internal energy. In any object, the particles have a range of different internal energies, and the temperature is a measure of the average internal energy of its particles. This is not the same as the total internal energy of the object. A very small piece of red hot metal has a very high temperature and a very high average internal energy, but the total heat energy in the metal is still very small, because it does not contain many particles.

FIGURE 5: The mug of water is hotter but contains less heat energy than the bath.

You could boil about 150 mugs of water with the heat energy needed to make a bath comfortably warm.

QUESTIONS

8 If you had two pieces of metal of different sizes and different temperatures, discuss how you could attempt to find out which contained most heat energy.

Thermal radiation

You will find out:

- That different surfaces give out different amounts of thermal radiation
- How to compare thermal emission and absorption in the laboratory
- The effects of thermal emission and absorption

Chilly satellites

It's cold in space. Satellites have to be made from materials that won't break when they get very cold. But satellites can also get very hot, when the Sun shines on them. So scientists have invented a paint that changes colour when the temperature changes. It absorbs heat when the satellite is cold and stops absorbing heat when the satellite is in danger of getting too hot.

FIGURE 1: It's very hot in the Sun and very cold in the Earth's shadow.

Giving out thermal radiation

Hot objects give out **heat energy** as electromagnetic waves. That's why they cool down. If you hold your hand next to, but not touching, a warm radiator you can feel the heat energy being given off. We say that the hot radiator is '**emitting** (giving off) **thermal radiation**'. That's how the radiator gets its name. Hot objects always give off more thermal radiation than cold objects and the bigger the difference between their temperature, and that of their surroundings, the faster the rate of heat transfer. The amount of thermal radiation given out also depends on the shape, dimensions and type of surface of the object.

Measuring thermal radiation

Scientists measure thermal radiation with a **thermopile**. The 'ear thermometer' that a doctor might use to measure your body temperature accurately is really a thermopile that measures the thermal radiation from your eardrum.

A Leslie's cube is a hollow cube with four different surfaces, shiny black, dull black, shiny white and dull white. The picture shows thermopiles being used to measure the thermal radiation from the surfaces of a Leslie's cube full of boiling water. The results show that:

- black surfaces give out more thermal radiation than the white surfaces
- dull surfaces give out more thermal radiation than shiny surfaces.

FIGURE 2: A hot bonfire might give off so much thermal radiation that you can't stand close to it.

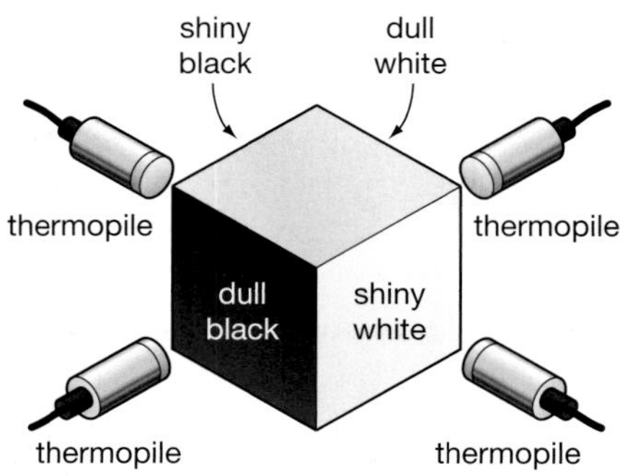

FIGURE 3: Scientists can use a Leslie's cube to compare the thermal radiation from different surfaces.

QUESTIONS

1. What does 'emitting thermal radiation' mean?
2. What type of thermometer do scientists use to measure thermal radiation?
3. List the **four** surfaces of the Leslie's cube in order of the amount of thermal radiation they give out, starting with the most.

...absorb ...emit ...global warming ...heat energy

Emission and absorption

Figure 4 shows how you can compare the thermal radiation emitted (given out) by different surfaces, in the laboratory. The thermometers show that the water in the dull black beaker cools down faster than the water in the shiny silver beaker. The dull black beaker is losing heat as thermal radiation faster than the silver beaker. The same equipment can be used to show that dull black surfaces also **absorb** more thermal radiation than shiny silver surfaces.

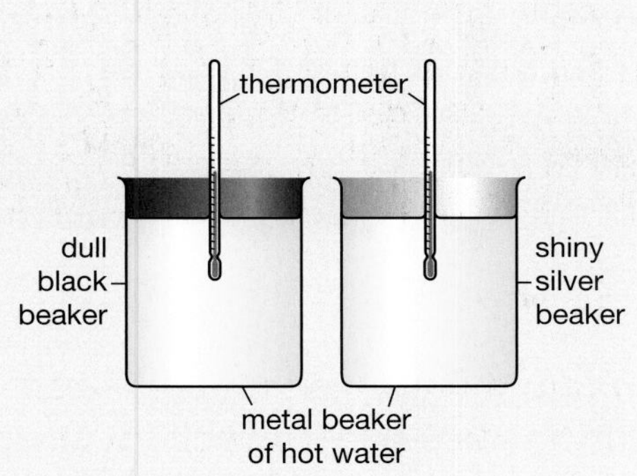

FIGURE 4: How could you use this equipment to compare the absorption of thermal radiation by different surfaces?

Using thermal radiation

There are examples all around us of where we use the colour of something to affect how much thermal radiation it emits or absorbs.

- The cooling fins on car radiators and the backs of refrigerators should be black, so they emit thermal radiation as quickly as possible.
- Newborn babies, and climbers or walkers suffering from hypothermia, are wrapped in shiny silver 'space blankets' to stop them losing heat so fast.
- Buildings and clothes in very hot countries are usually white or light-coloured, so they absorb less thermal radiation and the people inside them stay cooler.
- Fuel storage tanks are usually painted white or silver so that they don't overheat in hot weather.

You may be able to think of even more examples.

FIGURE 5: White buildings absorb much less thermal radiation than darker coloured buildings.

Thermal radiation and global warming

Some scientists fear that, as **global warming** makes ice at the North and South Poles melt, global warming will get even worse. The dark-coloured sea water absorbs more thermal radiation from the Sun than the light-coloured ice does. We don't know if they're right yet, because there are many other things that affect global warming too.

Watch Out **Remember, hot surfaces always give out more thermal radiation than cold surfaces, whatever their colour.**

QUESTIONS

4 What things would you have to do to make sure that the results from the thermal radiation experiments were fair and reliable?

5 What colour material would you make a firefighter's uniform from? Why?

6 Describe the colours the satellite should change to, in the introduction section.

Polar bears

Polar bears have white fur but they have black skin. The bear's fur scatters radiation from the Sun in all directions – that is why the fur looks white – but some of the Sun's radiation passes through to the skin, where it is absorbed. Black skin absorbs this radiation better than white skin would. It does not matter that black skin also emits radiation better because the polar bear's fur is a very good thermal insulator. When a scientist once tried to photograph a polar bear with a thermal imaging camera, the bear was completely invisible – the only bit that showed up was the puff of warm air the bear breathed out!

'If you hold your breath he won't spot us'

Black surfaces absorb and emit thermal radiation best

QUESTIONS

7 From the information above, what can you deduce about the absorption of heat and light by different surfaces? Explain how you reached your conclusion.

Conduction and convection

You will find out:

- How to compare conductors and demonstrate convection
- How to explain conduction and convection using the particle model
- About some familiar and unfamiliar examples of conduction and convection

Lava lamps

Decorative lava lamps like the one in figure 1 are very popular, but they could not work without **convection** currents. The solid wax at the bottom of the lamp melts when it is warmed by a light bulb. It becomes less dense than the liquid oil, and moves upwards. As it rises it cools, becomes more dense, and sinks back down again.

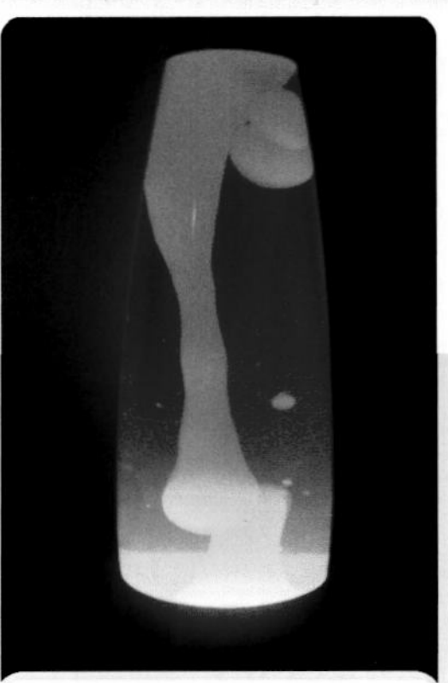

FIGURE 1: This lamp shows a popular use of a convection current.

Conductors and insulators

Thermal conductors, sometimes just called **conductors**, are materials that **heat energy** can flow through easily. Materials that heat energy cannot flow through easily are called **thermal insulators**, or just **insulators**. Metals are good conductors, glass and plastic are insulators. You can probably think of more insulators.

Figure 2 shows how we can compare materials to find out which is the best conductor. The better the conductor, the sooner the petroleum jelly melts and the sooner the drawing pin drops off.

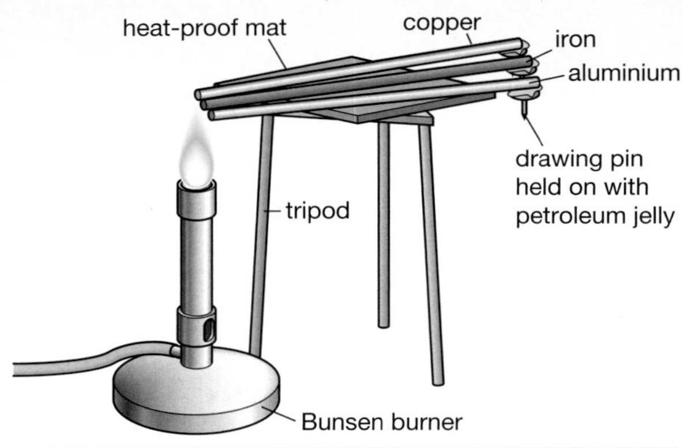

FIGURE 2: Do you know why the drawing-pin end of the best conductor feels hottest?

Convection

Have you ever heard people say 'Heat rises'? You know that is not true, but *warm liquids* and *warm gases* do rise upwards because they are less dense (lighter for their size) than cooler liquids or gases.

Figure 3 shows a convection current in a beaker of water. As the water gets warmer it rises up the side of the beaker, carrying the coloured dye with it. You can see the coloured dye falling down the other side of the beaker, as the water cools and gets more dense again.

FIGURE 3: It is important to use only a tiny amount of dye. Do you know why?

QUESTIONS

1. What is a thermal conductor?
2. Give **three** examples of thermal insulators.
3. What happens to liquids and gases when they are warmed?
4. Describe in your own words what a convection current is.

...conduction ...conductor ...convection ...expand ...heat energy ...insulator

The particle model

We can use the **particle model** to explain **conduction** and convection. You know that in all materials the particles **vibrate**, and in hotter materials they vibrate more. In a solid, the particles are in fixed positions. If one end of a solid is heated, particles at that end vibrate more and the vibrations are passed from particle to particle, **transmitting** the heat energy through the material.

In liquids and gases, the particles are free to move. When their particles vibrate more, they push on surrounding particles, making the particles move slightly further apart. The liquid or gas **expands**, becoming less dense, and causing convection currents.

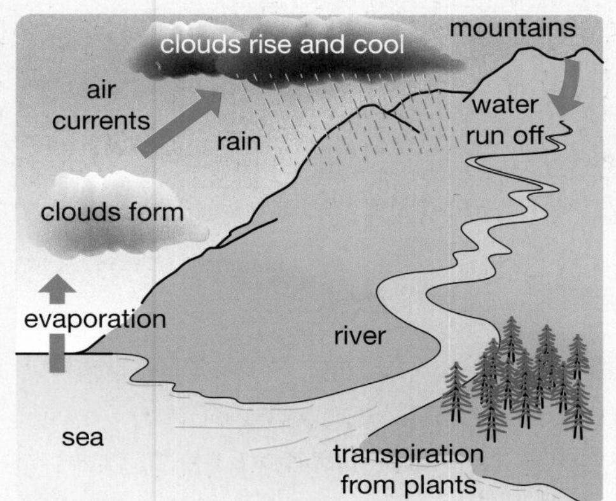

FIGURE 4: It is often wet in hilly areas near the sea, such as Wales or the Lake District. Can you use convection currents and the water cycle to explain why?

Watch Out Particles don't get bigger when you heat something – they just move further part.

Using conduction and convection

Choosing the right materials is very important.

- Most saucepans are made from metal, with plastic handles. The metal conducts heat easily from the cooker to the food; the plastic handles do not conduct the heat into your hand.
- Double-glazed windows have air or a partial vacuum between the panes of glass. Air is a very poor conductor; a partial vacuum is even poorer. The gap between the panes is narrow, so there is not enough room for a convection current to be set up.
- Computers, and other devices, use forced convection. A fan blows cool air across hot components. The air is heated and rises. This works just like an ordinary convection current but faster, because the components always have cool air next to them. Scientists think that the speed of the very newest computers being designed may be limited by how quickly they can be cooled.

Watch Out Don't confuse thermal conductors and electrical conductors. Sometimes they're both just called 'conductors'.

FIGURE 5: As modern computers get faster, stopping them overheating becomes very important.

QUESTIONS

5 Use conduction to suggest a reason why serving dishes are usually made from glass or china.

6 Explain why a partial vacuum is a poorer conductor than 'ordinary' air.

7 Describe another example, of your own, of using conduction or convection.

Water coolant

Engines, and other machines, often use water as a coolant, to transfer the heat energy away from the engine. Water is a good material for this as it takes a lot of heat energy to make water heat up a given amount.

Scientists say the water has a high specific heat capacity. The water is pressurised to keep it as a liquid even at temperatures above 100 °C, as steam takes up much more space than water and also heats up much more than water for a given amount of heat absorbed.

Thermal radiation is a type of energy

QUESTIONS

8 Land both warms up and cools down faster than the sea does. What does this tell you about their specific heat capacities?

Heat transfer

You will find out:

- How different materials transfer heat energy
- Why metals are so much better at transferring heat than most materials
- The connection between thermal conduction and other properties

Good enough to eat!

Baked Alaska pudding is amazing! The outside is meringue straight from a hot oven; the inside is frozen ice cream – so why doesn't the ice cream melt? The meringue is so poor at transferring heat that the ice cream in the centre stays cold, even when the meringue gets hot enough to cook.

FIGURE 1: How does the meringue on the outside of this pudding cook in a hot oven, without the ice cream in the middle melting?

Transferring heat

The **temperature** of the water in most swimming pools is about 25 °C to 30 °C. If you jumped into a pool where the water was at room temperature you'd soon feel very cold! The water can **transfer** (carry) heat away from your warm body better than air can. Liquids are poor **conductors** of heat, but gases are even poorer.

An ice cube at the bottom of a boiling tube (as in figure 2) takes a long time to melt, even when the water at the top of the boiling tube boils. **Heat energy** is only transferred very slowly through the water to the ice cube.

Figure 3 shows how a match has to be held very close to a Bunsen burner flame before it will catch alight. Air is very poor at transferring the heat from the flame to the match.

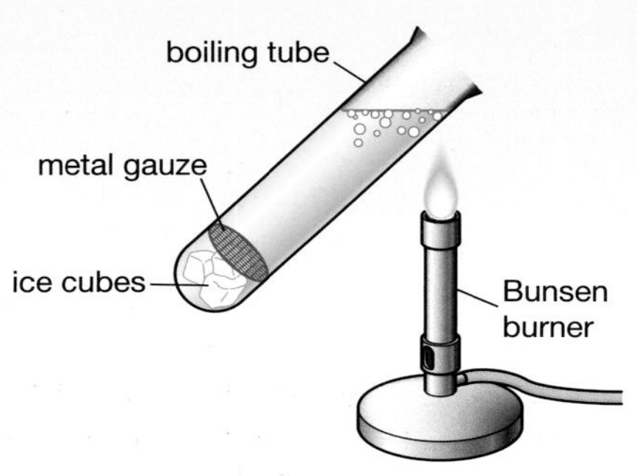

FIGURE 2: Heat energy is transferred very slowly through the water to the ice cube.

Keeping warm, keeping cool

When you put on a woollen jumper, it's the air trapped between the wool fibres that stops your body heat being transferred away from you. If you use a cool bag on a picnic, it is the trapped air in the padding that helps to stop heat from the warm surroundings being transferred to your cool picnic.

Animals that live where it is very cold tend to grow bigger, as large objects don't lose heat as quickly as small objects. Animals that live where it is very hot often have long legs or large ears, as a large surface area helps them lose heat to keep cool.

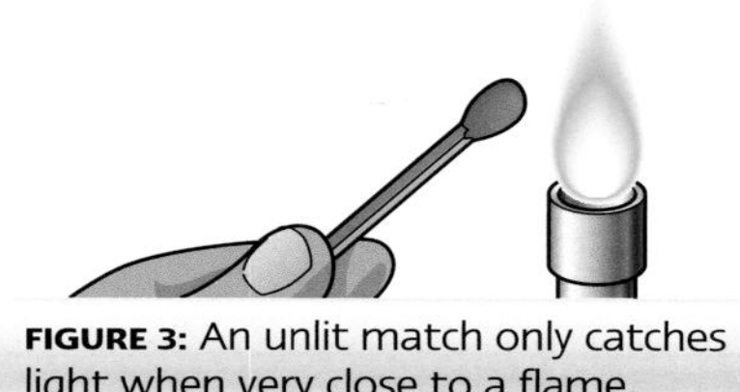

FIGURE 3: An unlit match only catches light when very close to a flame.

QUESTIONS

1. Which transfers heat energy best, water or air?
2. How does heat get to the ice cube at the bottom of the boiling tube, by conduction or by convection?
3. Would a woollen jumper make a snowman melt faster or slower? Why?

Watch Out Insulation doesn't make things warm, it just makes it harder for heat energy to flow.

The particle model again

In solids, the particles are held firmly together in fixed positions, often in a crystal lattice. This means that when one particle vibrates, its neighbours **vibrate** too, passing on the heat energy. Only the particles at the edge of the object can pass energy into the surroundings. That is why a large size or a small surface area slows down the rate at which objects lose heat.

In liquids, it is much harder for the vibrations to pass from particle to particle because the particles are not so firmly held together. In gases, the vibrations can only pass from particle to particle when one gas particle bumps into another, so gases are very poor conductors indeed. This description of the importance of particles in energy transfer is called the **particle model**.

Why are metals so good at transferring heat?

In metals, some heat is transferred by vibrations. But metals have another way of transferring heat too. Metals contain **free electrons**. These are electrons that are not firmly fixed to atoms, but are able to move through the metal transferring the heat energy faster than just vibrations can. Most of the heat energy transferred by metals is transferred by these free electrons moving. The electrons move in all directions, so they transfer the heat in all directions.

If a voltage is connected to the metal, it makes the electrons move in just one direction. The electrons carry electrical energy through the metal and we say there is an electric current. That is why metals are good conductors of both electricity and heat.

Thermal insulators do not have free electrons, which is why materials that do not conduct heat well, usually do not conduct electricity well either.

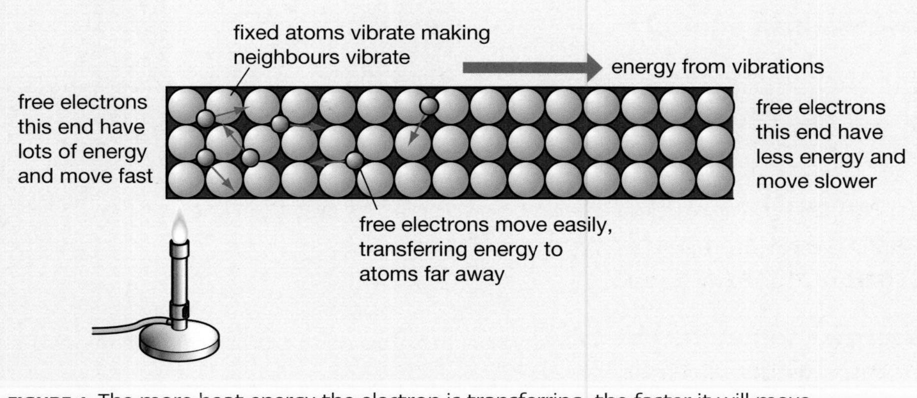

FIGURE 4: The more heat energy the electron is transferring, the faster it will move.

QUESTIONS

4 Use the particle model to explain in your own words why gases are very poor conductors of heat.

5 How is most heat energy transferred through metals?

6 Material X has no free electrons. Is it likely to be a good conductor of heat and electricity?

WOW FACTOR!

Water at 0 °C feels colder than ice at 0 °C, because water is better at transferring heat than ice is.

Real or fake?

Jewellers can tell if a diamond is a real diamond or a fake one made from glass, by holding it to their lips. A real diamond feels very cold, because diamond is very good at transferring heat – four or five times better than copper. However, diamond does not conduct electricity, because it has no free electrons. It is so good at conducting heat because its particles are very firmly bonded together; this is also what makes it extremely hard, and chemically unreactive.

FIGURE 5: How can you tell if this is a diamond or a piece of glass?

Diamond is very good at transferring heat

QUESTIONS

7 Graphite is made from layers of carbon atoms, with very firm bonds between the particles in each layer but weak bonds between the layers. What can you predict about the way graphite will conduct heat?

Types of energy

You will find out:

- The names of different types of energy, and where we find them
- The units of energy and how energy can be stored
- How much energy reaches us from the Sun and how it affects Earth

That's a lot of energy!

This spoonful of sugar contains about the same amount of energy as a modern power station supplies in a week! That's a lot of energy! Fortunately, when you eat the sugar it doesn't supply you with anything like as much energy as that. Most of the energy is being used to hold the atoms themselves together and cannot be released by any chemical changes.

FIGURE 1: There's a lot of energy in this sugar, but we can't use it all.

Energy everywhere

Whenever we see something happening, or we know that something could happen, we know that there is energy involved. We use lots of different names for energy to remind us where we find the energy or what it is used for.

- You already know a lot about **heat energy**, where we find it and how it moves around.
- You can probably describe places where we would find light or sound energy and how they move.
- Perhaps you remember that fuels contain **chemical energy** that is released as heat when we burn the fuels.
- Whenever you cook a microwave ready-meal you are using microwave energy to heat the food.
- Your television picture comes to you from the television studios as radio waves, travelling through the air. Radio waves are another type of energy.
- Everything that is moving has **kinetic energy** – sometimes we call it movement energy.
- Everything that is high up so that it could fall downwards, or is stretched so that it could spring back, has **potential energy**.

FIGURE 2: How many types of energy have you used today?

Whenever we see something happening, energy is involved

QUESTIONS

1 What type of energy is there in fuels?
2 What is the scientific name for movement energy?
3 Describe **two** things that could have potential energy.
4 Describe how we could tell if energy was involved somewhere.

...chemical energy ...heat energy ...joules ...kinetic energy

How much energy?

All energy is measured in **joules**. One joule of energy is about the same amount of energy as you would use to lift a small apple from the floor onto a table. Below are approximate values for the energy needed for different activities.

- 84 000 J – The energy needed to boil water for 1 mug of coffee.
- 216 000 J – The energy needed to use a 60 W light bulb for 1 hour.
- 280 000 J – The energy used to walk 1 km to school on level ground.
- 740 000 J – The extra energy you would need to climb Ben Nevis, compared with walking the same distance on level ground.
- 1 880 000 J – The energy used to play squash for 40 minutes.
- 3 600 000 J – The energy needed to run a one-bar electric fire for 1 hour.

We measure the energy we take in, in the food we eat, in kilocalories. One kilocalorie is about 4000 J, so a teenager may take in as much as 10 million joules of energy each day. Only a small amount of this is used for the activities we do; most of it is used for life processes such as keeping warm.

FIGURE 3: 'The walker will need to use more energy to get to the top of the mountain than the runner will.' Do you agree?

Storing energy

Fuels and batteries are stores of chemical energy. They are useful because we can release the **stored energy** when we need it, by burning the fuel or connecting a circuit to the battery. Energy can also be stored in stretched elastic bands, or in tightly wound springs, such as those used in old clocks and watches. Flywheels are rapidly spinning, heavy wheels that are used to store kinetic energy.

WOW FACTOR!

You use more energy eating a piece of celery than the celery provides!

QUESTIONS

5 Work out how much energy would be needed to use a 40 W light bulb for 2 hours.

6 Suggest how you could tell that coal is a more concentrated store of chemical energy than wood is.

Energy from the Sun

The Sun's radiation supplies virtually all the energy on Earth. About 1.7×10^{17} J of energy reaches Earth from the Sun every second. This means that in 45 minutes the Sun supplies as much energy as the total predicted global energy consumption for the year 2010. As well as providing energy for photosynthesis, this energy from the Sun causes the changes in temperature that drive the water cycle, weather patterns and ocean currents. The plant and animal growth made possible by the Sun's energy forms part of the carbon cycle that leads to the formation of fossil fuels such as coal and oil.

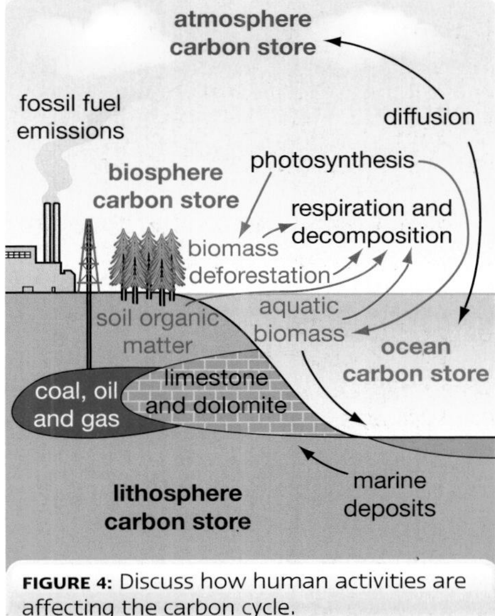

FIGURE 4: Discuss how human activities are affecting the carbon cycle.

Watch Out Energy is not 'stuff'. It's better to think about what energy can do, not what it might look like.

QUESTIONS

7 Explain why the natural release of carbon from decaying plant and animal material does not cause global warming, but the release of carbon dioxide from burning fossil fuels does.

Energy changes

You will find out:

- The difference between energy transfers and energy transformations
- About energy changes involving useful and wasted energy
- About the Law of Conservation of Energy

Bouncy balls

Each of the bouncy balls in figure 1 will only bounce a metre or so, dropped separately from shoulder height. The ball's potential energy changes to kinetic energy as it falls, then to potential energy again as it bounces. But dropped together, the small ball may bounce 10 metres! The small ball gains most of the potential energy of both balls. The more balls you use, the higher the top one will bounce.

FIGURE 1: What energy changes happen here when the balls are dropped?.

Transfer or transformation?

Scientists use two different names for energy changes.

- **Energy transfers** are energy changes where the energy just moves to a different place, such as an electric current carrying **electrical energy** from a cell to a component. You may like to think of it like a football transfer, where a player moves to a different team.
- **Energy transformations** are energy changes where the energy changes from one type (or form) to a different type (or form), such as when electrical energy changes to light energy in a light bulb.

Identifying energy transfers and transformations

You can probably think of lots of devices that were designed to make an energy change.

- A light bulb is designed to change electrical energy into light energy.
- A music system is designed to change electrical energy into sound energy.
- A battery is designed to change **chemical energy** into electrical energy.
- A bicycle is designed to change your **kinetic energy** into kinetic energy of the bicycle.
- A car is designed to change chemical energy into kinetic energy.

FIGURE 2: What energy changes happen in these devices?

QUESTIONS

1. What happens to the energy in an energy transformation?
2. Which of the energy changes listed above is an energy transfer? How do you know?
3. What energy change takes place in each of the pictures in figure 2? Is it an energy transfer or an energy transformation?
4. Name a device that is designed to change electrical energy into kinetic energy.

EXAM HINTS AND TIPS

Always remember to say if an energy change is an energy transfer or an energy transformation.

Wasted energy

If you have ever held your hand near a light bulb, you will know that light bulbs give out **heat energy** as well as light energy. Even though we design devices to change energy into useful forms that we want, some of the energy always changes into other forms as well. We call the energy that changes into forms we don't want '**wasted energy**'.

- A light bulb gives out useful light energy and wasted heat energy.
- A bicycle gives out useful kinetic energy and wasted heat energy, as friction between the moving parts.
- A jet engine or a rocket motor gives out useful kinetic energy and a lot of wasted heat and light energy.

Sometimes energy changes can be quite complicated. It isn't always easy to decide which energy changes are useful and which aren't. For example, is the useful energy from a barbecue the heat energy it gives out, or is it the chemical energy change that happens when raw meat becomes cooked meat? And is all the heat energy from a barbecue useful or is some of it wasted?

FIGURE 3: How many energy changes can you identify in this tumble drier?

Conservation of energy

Even though energy can move from place to place and can change from one form to a different form, it cannot just appear or disappear. The total amount of energy always stays the same. This is called the Law of **Conservation of Energy** and it is usually written as:

Energy cannot be created or destroyed.
The total energy always remains constant.

Energy cannot be created or destroyed

QUESTIONS

5 Identify the useful and wasted energy changes that happen in the tumble drier.

6 Identify **one** form of wasted energy from each of: a gas cooker, a television and a microphone.

7 A loudspeaker vibrates. Do you think this kinetic energy is wasted energy or not?

The Sun is shrinking!

The Sun's energy comes from nuclear reactions in the Sun. The main reactions change hydrogen atoms into helium atoms, giving off energy during this change. The mass of the helium atoms at the end of the reaction is slightly less than the mass of the hydrogen atoms at the start of the reaction. Einstein realised that mass is actually changing into energy! Fortunately, this only happens in nuclear reactions, so the Law of Conservation of Energy is true for all situations except stars and nuclear reactors. In stars and nuclear reactors, scientists say that mass-energy (the combination of mass and energy) is conserved.

FIGURE 4: This explosion is so powerful because some mass is being changed into energy.

Watch Out Some energy is always wasted. Try to spot the wasted forms of energy in any energy change.

QUESTIONS

8 Explain the energy changes that happen in the introductory paragraph. Discuss how the relative masses of the two balls might affect how high the small one bounces.

Energy diagrams

You will find out:

- How to draw and interpret energy transfer diagrams
- How to use energy transfer diagrams to compare devices

Is this car a good idea?

Many car manufacturers now make electric cars, which can be recharged from the mains. They seem like a good idea, because they produce less pollution than petrol cars, but how can we really tell? Energy diagrams are one of the tools that scientists use to compare different devices, to help them decide which one is more suitable.

FIGURE 1: How can we tell whether or not electric vehicles are a good idea?

Showing energy changes

You have probably seen diagrams like figure 2 showing the energy changes that happen in a device. The light bulb is changing **electrical energy** into useful light and wasted heat energy. The width of the arrows shows us that the light bulb gives out more energy as heat than it gives out as light.

Sometimes we need to know how much energy a device uses, or how much energy of different types it gives out. Then we draw a **Sankey diagram**, as in figure 3, to show the **energy input** and **energy output** each second. Adding up the energy input, and the useful and **wasted energy** outputs, shows us that the total amount of energy stays the same.

energy input for light bulb	=	100 J
energy output for light bulb	=	useful light energy + wasted heat energy
	=	10 J + 90 J = 100 J

This is because the Law of **Conservation of Energy** tells us that although energy can change from one form to another it can't be created or destroyed.

We can use the Law of Conservation of Energy to work out missing values. In the diagram for the car engine in figure 4, the total energy output must be 1000 J, because the input energy is 1000 J, so:

useful kinetic energy + wasted heat energy	=	1000 J
300 J + wasted heat energy	=	1000 J
wasted heat energy	=	1000 J − 300 J = 700 J

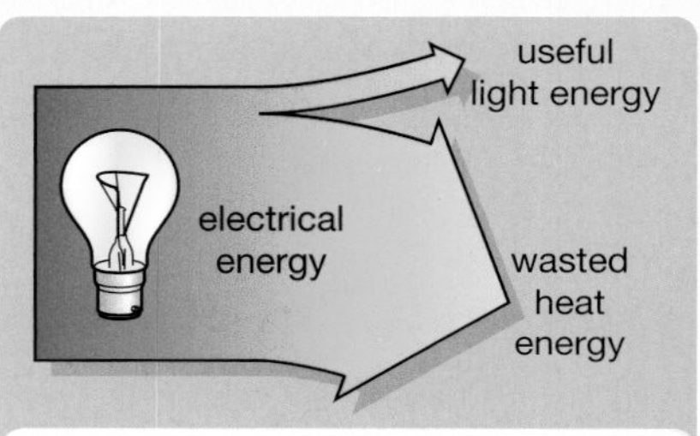

FIGURE 2: Energy changes in a light bulb.

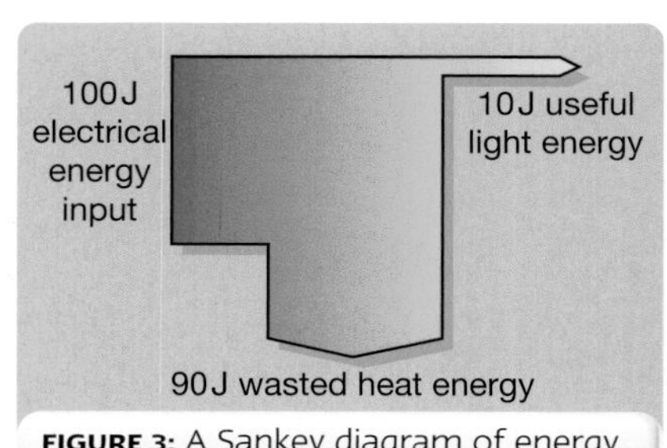

FIGURE 3: A Sankey diagram of energy input and outputs per second.

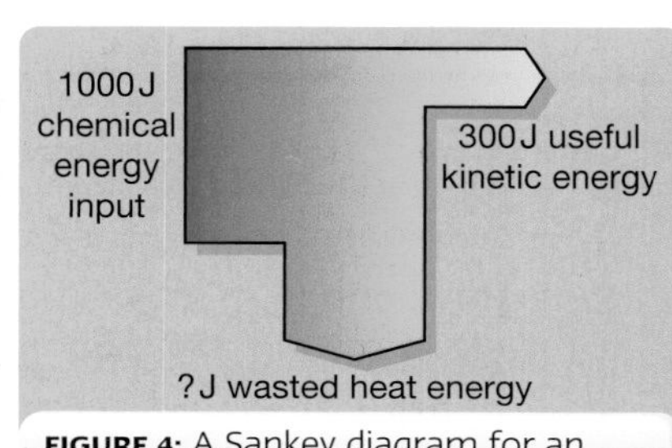

FIGURE 4: A Sankey diagram for an engine.

QUESTIONS

1. Draw an energy transfer diagram for a fan that transforms electrical energy into useful kinetic energy, wasted sound energy and wasted heat energy.
2. An electric bell transforms 100 J of electrical energy into 30 J of sound energy, 40 J of movement energy, and some wasted heat energy. Find out how much wasted heat energy is given out.

...conservation of energy ...electrical energy ...energy input ...energy output ...energy transfer

Comparing energy transfer diagrams

We can use **energy transfer diagrams** to compare different devices. Look at the energy transfer diagrams in figure 5 for an 'ordinary' incandescent light bulb, a fluorescent light bulb and a candle.

From figure 5 we can tell the following:

- The candle is very bad at transforming chemical energy into light energy. You would need 30 candles to provide as much light as one 'ordinary' light bulb.
- The 'ordinary' bulb will be much hotter than the fluorescent bulb. They are both giving out 6 J of light energy but the 'ordinary' bulb is giving out 54 J of wasted heat energy as well, while the fluorescent bulb is only giving out 6 J of wasted heat energy.
- The fluorescent bulb will cost much less money to run than the 'ordinary' bulb. To get 6 J of light energy from the fluorescent bulb you only have to pay for 12 J of input electrical energy. To get the same amount of light energy from the 'ordinary' bulb you have to pay for 60 J of input electrical energy.

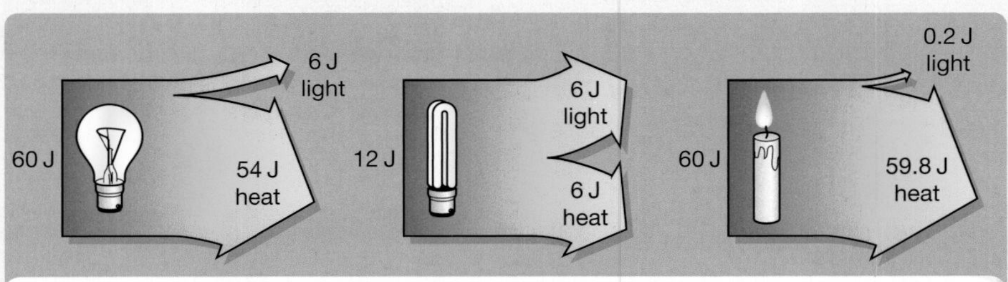

FIGURE 5: Energy transfer diagrams comparing different light sources.

More wasted energy

Even when a device has several energy changes, we can still use a Sankey diagram to show the wasted and useful energy changes. There will be some wasted energy given out every time there is an **energy transfer** or **transformation**. The most common type of wasted energy is heat energy. We can show all the wasted energy on one Sankey diagram.

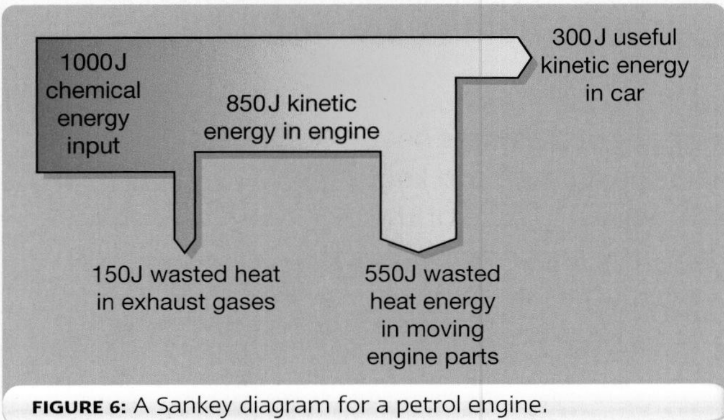

FIGURE 6: A Sankey diagram for a petrol engine.

QUESTIONS

3 How much light energy would the fluorescent bulb give out if its input energy was 60 J?

4 Petrol engines have oil in them to keep the moving parts sliding smoothly past each other. Describe or discuss how the Sankey diagram would change if this oil wasn't there.

Watch Out The output energy on any energy transfer diagram must add up to the input energy.

Electric vehicles

Most milk floats, and some cars and vans, are electric vehicles. Instead of a petrol or diesel engine they have an electric motor, driven by a large rechargeable battery. In 2000 the car company, Ford, introduced its 'e-Ka', an electric powered version of its 'Ka' car, which can travel for 200 km at 80 kph before its battery needs recharging. A completely flat battery takes 6 hours to recharge fully.

FIGURE 7: What disadvantages would electric cars have compared to petrol or diesel cars?

QUESTIONS

5 Draw an energy transfer diagram to show all the energy transfers and transformations for the Ford e-Ka. Start with the electrical energy at the power station.

6 Discuss what you would need to know to help you decide whether or not the e-Ka was better for you, or better for the environment, than a petrol version of the Ka.

Energy and heat

You will find out:

- How wasted and useful energy is transferred to the surroundings
- How the particle model explains why energy causes objects to heat up
- What happens to the usefulness of energy as it spreads out

Lasers

This robot is using a laser to cut metal. The laser is a beam of light that is so bright that it contains enough energy to melt metal, and so narrow that it can cut very accurately. Lasers are also used in surgery – they are much more accurate than scalpels – and in the detection and treatment of cancer.

FIGURE 1: Why is it helpful to have this laser held by a robot?

Wasted heat energy

Did you notice how many of the energy changes you looked at had wasted **heat energy**? Whenever there is an **energy transfer** or **transformation**, some of the energy always changes into heat energy. Most of the time this is wasted heat energy.

Have you ever wondered why you get hot when you exercise a lot? Respiration in your muscle cells transforms **chemical energy** stored in glucose into **kinetic energy** as your muscles contract. And in every energy transformation, some energy changes into heat energy. The harder your muscles work, the more chemical energy transforms into kinetic energy, but the more chemical energy transforms into heat energy as well, so the hotter you get.

FIGURE 2: Our cells transform chemical energy into kinetic energy. Can you remember what gas they need?

Where does the energy go?

The wasted heat energy 'disappears' into the surroundings by conduction, convection or thermal radiation – except that you know energy can't 'disappear'. It is absorbed by the surroundings and makes them just a tiny bit warmer than they were.

Even the useful energy in energy transfers and transformations becomes heat energy in the surroundings eventually. When you shine a torch beam you know the light doesn't go on for ever. When the beam hits something, some of the light is absorbed and transformed into heat energy. The same happens to sound energy, kinetic energy and all the other sorts of useful energy. Eventually they spread out and are absorbed by the surroundings.

QUESTIONS

1. What type of energy will you find in every energy transfer or transformation?
2. What energy transformation happens in your muscles?
3. Draw an energy transfer diagram for the energy transformation in question 2.
4. Use energy transformations to describe what happens when an object absorbs light energy.

Watch Out Energy can never 'disappear' – look for where it has gone to.

...chemical energy ...concentrated ...energy transfer ...heat energy

Why does energy make things warm up?

We can use the **particle model** to explain why the energy from energy transfers and transformations always ends up as heat energy in the surroundings. Inside all materials, the particles are **vibrating**. You know that as an object gets hotter, its particles vibrate more. When any sort of energy is absorbed by an object, the particles end up with a little bit more energy. This makes them vibrate a little bit more, and so the object is a little bit hotter.

Energy spreading out

As energy transfers and transformations make energy spread out, it becomes less and less useful. Fuels and batteries are useful because they are a **concentrated store of energy** that we can use to make other energy changes happen. A beaker or a saucepan of hot water contains much more energy than the same beaker or saucepan of cold water. The hot water is a more concentrated store of energy than the cold water – it contains more energy in the same mass of water. We can use it to make chemical reactions happen or to cook food (another chemical reaction).

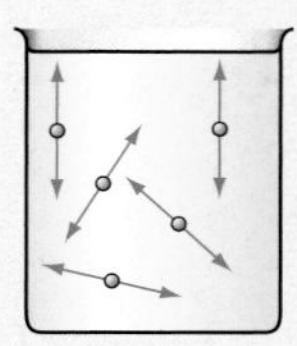

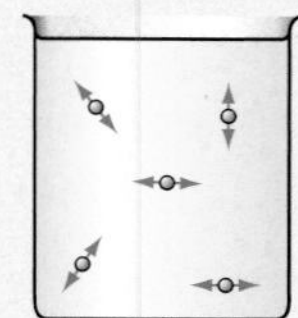

FIGURE 3: The hot water is a more concentrated store of energy.

FIGURE 4: How could you decide which is the more concentrated store of energy – the coal or the wood?

If we were to tip the saucepan or beaker of hot water into a bath full of cold water, so that the energy was spread out much more, it would be much less useful. A bath full of warm water contains much more energy than a saucepan of boiling water but you still can't cook your dinner in the bath full of warm water!

EXAM HINTS AND TIPS

The more spread out energy gets, the less useful it is.

QUESTIONS

5 Describe what happens to the kinetic energy of its particles when an object is heated.

6 Describe how the energy stored in a battery is transferred to the environment.

7 Suggest how you could show that coal is a more concentrated store of energy than wood.

Refrigerators

A refrigerator is a device that is designed to concentrate energy. The heat energy that was originally spread throughout the contents of the refrigerator becomes concentrated in the cooling fins at the back of the refrigerator, keeping the food cooler than normal and the cooling fins hotter than normal. This heat energy is moving in the opposite direction to the direction energy normally moves in – energy naturally tends to spread out, not concentrate. That is why the refrigerator needs a power supply – energy is needed to make heat energy from the contents of the refrigerator move in the opposite direction to normal.

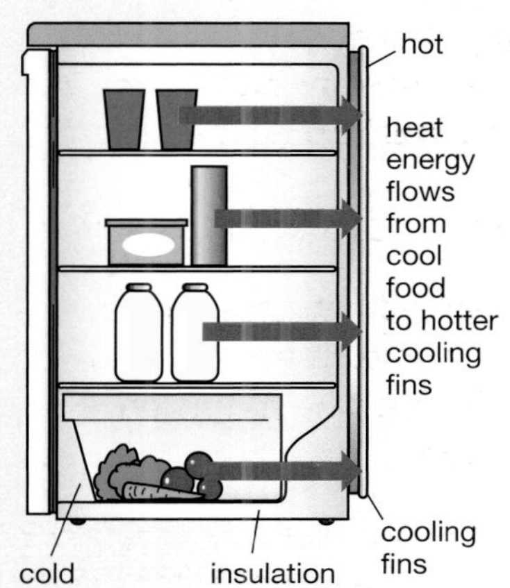

FIGURE 5: When will your fridge cost most to run, winter or summer? Do you know why?

QUESTIONS

8 Can you think of any natural systems which cause energy to be concentrated in one place? Do these systems obey the Law of Conservation of Energy?

Energy, work and power

You will find out:

- The scientific meaning of work and power
- How work, power and energy are related to each other
- How to calculate the work done, the energy used, and the power for a device

Mighty muscles

This bodybuilder needs to eat much more than most people to stay fit and healthy. Can you explain what happens to the energy in the food he eats? We might use words like '**work**', '**energy**', 'strong', '**powerful**' when describing this person or what he can do, but do you know what all these words mean, in scientific terms?

FIGURE 1: Can you describe the energy changes that happen as this bodybuilder lifts the weights?

Working hard

When you do work you use up energy. If you spent all day lifting bricks onto the back of a lorry you would feel tired and hungry. Tired because you had done a lot of work, and used up a lot of energy. Hungry because eating food is your body's way of replacing the energy you have used. The chemical energy in the food is transformed into kinetic energy and heat energy in your muscles. The kinetic energy in your muscles is transferred to kinetic energy in the bricks as they move, and finally it is transformed into potential energy as the bricks are on the back of the lorry, high above the ground.

Power

Most brick lorries have a crane to move the bricks. In one or two minutes, the crane can move as many bricks as you move in a whole day. The crane is a powerful machine, much more powerful than you are. We say that a machine is powerful if it can do a lot of work in a short time. Powerful machines use up energy very quickly.

We measure how powerful something is by measuring how many **joules** of work it can do in one second, or how many joules of energy it uses up in one second. The unit of power is the '**watt**' (symbol, W), named after the engineer James Watt. As 1 watt is the same as 1 joule per second (symbol, J/s), a machine with a power of 1 W uses up 1 J of energy each second.

FIGURE 2: Can you explain why this crane needs a powerful motor?

Energy and work are measured in joules. Power is measured in watts.

QUESTIONS

1. What do we mean when we say a machine is 'powerful'?
2. What is the unit of power?
3. If the crane moves the same number of bricks as you, in less time, does it do more work, less work or the same work as you do?

WOW FACTOR!

In 1985, Lamar Gant from the USA became the first man to deadlift five times his own body weight.

...energy ...joules ...power ...powerful

Finding the energy used

The amount of work done to lift bricks onto the back of a lorry is the same as the energy the bricks gain. This is often written as:

energy gained = work done

The work done by a force is calculated from the equation:

work done = force x distance moved

So if a force of 15 N moves an object 3 m, the work done on the object is:

work done = 15 x 3 = 45 J

and the object gains 45 J of energy.

FIGURE 3: Could you calculate the work you do to climb upstairs in your house?

We can use this to find out how much potential energy something gains when we lift it up.

Imagine we lift a person with a mass of 50 kg onto a table 1 m above the ground. The force we use to lift the person is the force used to overcome their **weight**. The weight of a person (in newtons) is their mass (in kilograms) x 10 (the force of gravity on a 1 kg mass). So:

potential energy gained = work done = force x distance moved

= weight x distance moved

= 50 x 10 x 1 = 500 J

Finding the power

The **power** of a machine tells us how much work the machine can do each second. We can calculate the power from the equation:

power (in W) = work done (in J) ÷ time taken (in s)

Suppose a crane can lift 2000 kg of bricks to a height of 2 m in 2 minutes. We can find the power of the crane, by first calculating how much work it does.

work done = force x distance moved

= weight x distance moved

= 2000 x 10 x 2 = 40 000 J

Then by calculating:

power = work done ÷ time taken

= 40 000 ÷ 120 = 333 W

(Did you spot that the time would have to be changed from 2 minutes to 120 seconds?)

FIGURE 4: Estimate your maximum power going upstairs. SAFETY: Don't try to measure it – it could be dangerous!

QUESTIONS

4 A crane lifts a mass of 60 kg to a height of 5 m. How much work does it do?

5 The crane takes 1 minute to do this. Calculate the power of the crane.

6 A crane has a power of 100 W. How far can it lift a 10 kg mass in 10 s?

The same work, but easier!

When the ancient Egyptians built the pyramids, they needed to get large blocks of stone to the top. They dragged the blocks up ramps because it was easier than lifting them. To lift the block, they would have to pull against the weight of the block, so they would need to use a very large force. To pull the block up a slope they only had to pull against the component of the weight that was acting down the slope. The shallower the slope, the smaller this component was. The work done was the same whether they lifted or dragged because the smaller force used to drag the block had to move it a much larger distance.

FIGURE 5: What forces are at work here?

The power is the work done each second

QUESTIONS

7 How many men, each pulling with a force of 80 N, would it need to drag a 1000 kg block to the top of a pyramid 40 m high, using a slope 500 m long?

Efficiency

You will find out:

- What is meant by 'efficiency'
- How to calculate the efficiency of machines or devices
- How to relate efficiency to energy transfer diagrams

Dying for efficiency?

The Arctic and the Antarctic are lonely and dangerous places. Explorers who walk to the North Pole or the South Pole have to pull all their food with them on sledges. If they get their calculations wrong they will starve, as Sir Ranulph Fiennes nearly did in 1992 to 1993. It is very important to know how efficiently they can use the energy in the food they take.

FIGURE 1: What forms of waste energy will this explorer have to consider?

What is efficiency?

Have you ever heard anyone say 'She's efficient'? An efficient person is someone who gets the work done without lots of fuss, and without using up lots of unnecessary energy. An efficient machine is just the same. It is a machine that uses as little energy as possible to get the work done. Scientists use an equation to describe **efficiency**:

$$\text{efficiency} = \frac{\textbf{useful energy output}}{\textbf{total energy input}}$$

The 'useful **energy output**' is the work that you wanted the machine to do, or the energy that the device transforms into useful forms. The 'total **energy input**' is all the energy that goes into the device.

Comparing efficiency

We can use the efficiency of machines or devices to help us decide which is the best one to buy. People like to buy efficient machines because they cost less to run. They use less energy to do the same amount of work. Suppose:

Crane X uses 2000 J of energy to do 800 J of useful work.

Crane Y uses 3000 J of energy to do 900 J of useful work.

It would be better to buy Crane X, because Crane X does 400 J of useful work for every 1000 J of energy it uses up. Crane Y only does 300 J of useful work for every 1000 J of energy it uses up. So Crane X is more efficient than Crane Y.

QUESTIONS

1. Write down the equation we can use to work out efficiency.
2. Describe what we mean by an 'efficient machine'.
3. Why does an efficient machine cost less to run than an inefficient machine?
4. How much energy would Crane X use to do 600 J of useful work?

WOW FACTOR!

Muscles are only about 10% efficient, much less efficient than most of the machines we use.

Efficiency and wasted energy

An efficient machine is one that does not waste much energy. As much of the energy that you put in as possible is transformed into useful forms or useful work.

We can use **energy transfer diagrams** to calculate the efficiency of devices and to compare the efficiency of different devices. Figure 2 shows a Sankey energy transfer diagram for the petrol engine.

We can calculate the efficiency from:

$$\text{efficiency} = \frac{\text{useful energy output}}{\text{total energy input}} = \frac{300}{1000} = 0.3 = 30\%$$

We can use either fractions or decimals to describe efficiency.

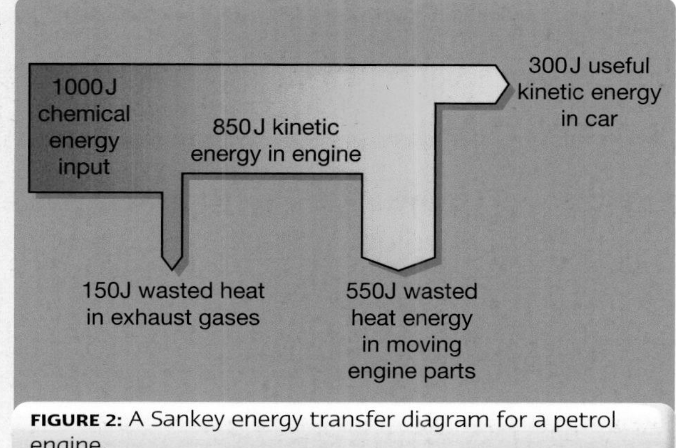

FIGURE 2: A Sankey energy transfer diagram for a petrol engine.

More energy transfer diagrams

We can also use energy transfer diagrams to compare different machines or devices.

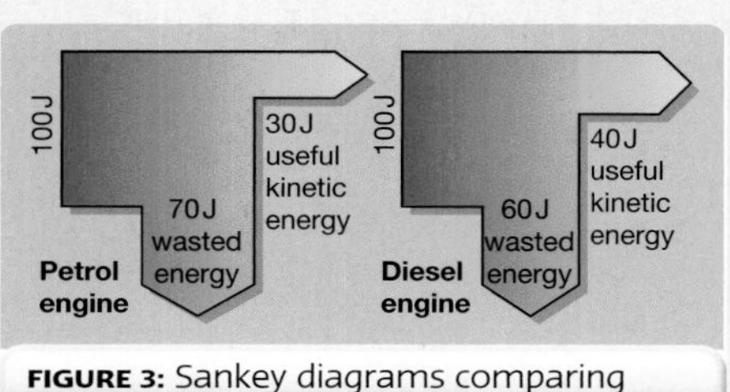

FIGURE 3: Sankey diagrams comparing different machines

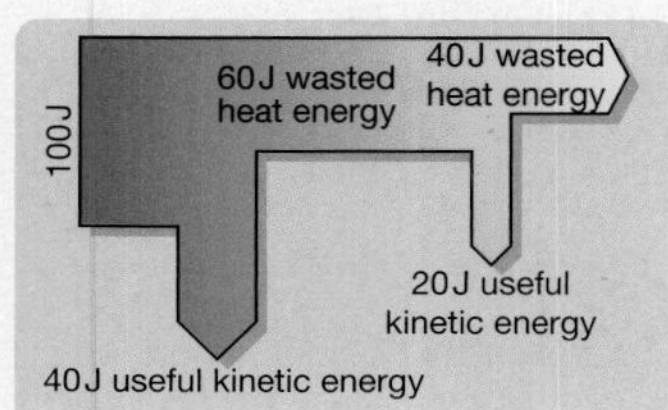

FIGURE 4: A steam-diesel hybrid engine

You can see that the diesel engine is more efficient than the petrol engine. In a steam-diesel hybrid car, **wasted heat energy** is used to heat water, to produce steam, to drive a turbine, to produce electricity, to drive the car at low speeds. One third of the wasted heat energy is transformed into useful **kinetic energy** in this way.

From figure 4, we can see that the efficiency of the steam-diesel hybrid is:

$$\text{efficiency} = \frac{(40 + 20)}{100} = 0.6 = 60\%$$

Efficiency and potential energy

We can calculate the efficiency of a crane used to lift masses. Suppose a crane using 5000 W of power can lift a 500 kg mass to a height of 6 m in 10 seconds. First we calculate:

useful work done by crane = force x distance = weight x height
= mass x 10 x height
= 500 x 10 x 6 = 30 000 J

Then we calculate:

useful work done each second = 30 000 ÷ 10 = 3000 J

total energy used each second by the crane = 5000 J

So: $$\text{efficiency} = \frac{\text{useful work done each second}}{\text{total energy used each second}} = \frac{3000}{5000} = 0.6 = 60\%$$

QUESTIONS

5 Draw an energy transfer diagram for a machine that is 25% efficient.

6 A 60 W light bulb emits 54 J of heat energy each second. Calculate its efficiency.

7 Describe why using lubricants in engines improves their efficiency.

Perpetual motion machines

The pendulum in this executive toy (Figure 5) appears to keep swinging continually, without 'running down'. Sometimes the toy is called a 'perpetual motion machine'. It has a battery and an electromagnet in its base.

Perpetual motion machines are machines that transform all the energy that is put into them into kinetic energy. Early scientists spent many years trying to design perpetual motion machines; occasionally inventors still try to make them today.

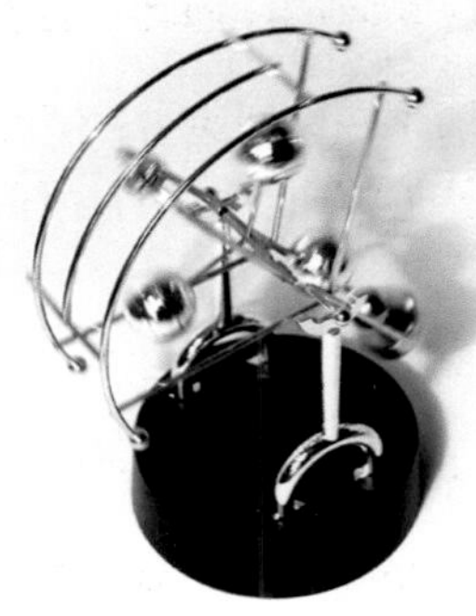

FIGURE 5: Is this toy a perpetual motion machine?

QUESTIONS

8 What is the efficiency of a perpetual motion machine?

9 Why is a true perpetual motion machine impossible?

10 Discuss how you think the 'perpetual motion machine' executive toy works.

Getting up steam

SELF-CHECK ACTIVITY

CONTEXT

In the 18th Century, Britain was on the verge of an Industrial Revolution that would bring about huge changes. People in their thousands would move from living in the country and working on the land to working in factories or mines, often in rapidly expanding towns and cities. New technologies would enable the large scale production of textiles, building materials and iron. Although flowing water was used as a source of energy, it was the development of the steam engine that made large factories and deep mines possible on a scale never previously seen.

Two of the people behind the development of steam power were Matthew Boulton and James Watt. Engines of their design powered machines, pumped water and lifted people and materials from the bottom of mineshafts.

A Boulton & Watt engine needs a supply of steam from a boiler. The boiler burns a fuel such as coal to heat water and turn it into steam. The steam goes into the engine and pushes a piston along a cylinder (imagine blowing into a syringe and making the plunger move). The piston is linked to a wheel which then turns (rather like when your leg pushing down on a bicycle pedal makes the wheels turn). This rotating movement could be linked to, for example, a water pump, or a cable down a mineshaft. These engines didn't move very quickly (they turned far slower than a car engine, for example) but they were large and powerful.

These engines were much more efficient than the crude atmospheric engines in use before, but not very efficient by today's standards. Compared with the energy content of the fuel, only about 5 per cent reached the machines being driven by the engine. In comparison, a gas turbine in a modern power station will run at about 60 per cent efficiency.

CHALLENGE

STEP 1

What do you think it would be like to be near a Boulton & Watt engine? Describe the sight, sounds and smells.

STEP 2

Tell the story of the transfer of energy, starting with the fuel in the boiler and finishing with the machine being driven by the steam engine.

STEP 3

Most of the energy ends up being transferred to the environment. How does this happen?

STEP 4

Why did factory and mine owners use Boulton & Watt engines if they were so inefficient?

Maximise your grade

These sentences show what you need to include in your work to achieve each grade. Use them to improve your work and be more successful.

Grade	Answer includes...
	Give an example of energy being wasted.
F	Explain that when energy is transferred some will be wasted.
	Describe one of the ways in which energy is wasted in a Boulton & Watt engine.
	Describe several of the ways in which energy is wasted in a Boulton & Watt engine.
C	Explain that a more efficient machine transfers more energy in a useful form.
	Explain what happens to the energy supplied to a Boulton & Watt engine.
A	Explain how both useful output energy and wasted energy end up raising the temperature of the surroundings.
	As above, but with particular clarity and detail.

Using energy effectively

You will find out:

- How using less energy helps us and the environment
- Some ways in which we can save energy
- How to work out how cost effective different methods of home insulation are

Better buildings?

Years ago, before people thought about using energy efficiently, no-one worried about the energy they used to heat their homes. Now most people are concerned about using energy carefully and scientists are designing new buildings that waste as little energy as possible. We can't all live in houses like this one, but we can improve the houses we do live in.

FIGURE 1: A modern, energy-efficient house, using solar energy.

Energy, money and the environment

It is worth us trying to use less **energy**, because using less energy saves us money. We have to pay for all the energy we use. Using less energy is good for the **environment** too. Most of the energy we use harms the environment in some way. You probably know lots of ways to save energy, such as turning off lights when you're not using them, or turning down the temperature of your central heating. Replacing old, inefficient devices with newer, more efficient ones helps too. More efficient devices waste less energy.

Energy-saver light bulbs

Have you ever seen **energy-saver light bulbs**? Do you have any in your home? Energy-saver light bulbs transform much more of the electrical energy into light and much less into **wasted heat energy**. An energy-saver light bulb that uses 11 J of electrical energy each second gives the same amount of light as an 'ordinary' incandescent bulb that uses 60 J of electrical energy each second.

Energy-saver light bulbs cost more to buy than ordinary bulbs, but because they last much longer, they actually cost less in the long run. And they save energy too. One energy company has suggested that if every household in Britain replaced just one ordinary light bulb with an energy-saver light bulb, it would save enough energy to close down two power stations.

FIGURE 2: How many ways do you know to save energy?

QUESTIONS

1. State **two** reasons why it is a good idea to use less energy.
2. Describe how energy-saver light bulbs save energy.
3. If an average house has six rooms, estimate how much energy we could save if every house in Britain replaced their ordinary light bulbs with energy-saver bulbs.

FIGURE 3: How would the energy transfer diagrams for this bulb and an 'ordinary' bulb differ?

...energy ...energy-saver light bulb ...environment

How much can we save?

In the average British home, the central heating costs could be reduced by tens of pounds a year by installing **insulation** to reduce the heat energy lost through ceilings, walls, doors and windows. But installing ways to save energy and money actually cost us money! So how do we decide if insulation is worth while?

FIGURE 4: Can you explain how different types of insulation reduce the heat energy lost from a house?

Table 1 shows approximately how much different methods of insulation cost, and how much they can save you each year.

Type of insulation	Installation cost, in £	Annual saving, in £	Payback time
Loft insulation	240	60	4 years
Cavity wall insulation	360	60	6 years
Draught-proofing doors and windows	45	15	3 years
Double glazing	2500	25	100 years

TABLE 1: Savings as a result of different types of insultation.

The **payback time** is the length of time the insulation takes to 'pay for itself', that is the time it takes to save as much money as the insulation cost to install. You can see that draught-proofing the doors and windows would pay for itself most quickly, and double glazing would not pay for itself in your lifetime.

Even though double glazing is the least cost-effective type of insulation, it is still Britain's most commonly installed type of home insulation. This is because people often install double glazing to cut out the sound of noisy roads or towns, or to save the time and money spent on repainting wooden window frames, rather than to save money on fuel bills.

QUESTIONS

4 Which type of insulation is cheapest to install?

5 Describe what is meant by 'payback time'.

6 If draught-proofing lasts 5 years before it needs replacing, and loft insulation lasts 10 years, discuss which you would install, and why.

Saving energy is good for us and the environment

The wider picture

The table only shows how much money each type of insulation would cost a homeowner. But this is only part of the picture. If governments and local authorities give grants to help people to pay for the cost of insulation, they also have to consider the energy used in manufacturing the insulation. For example, cavity wall insulation saves energy being used in homes, but factories need to use energy to make the foam originally.

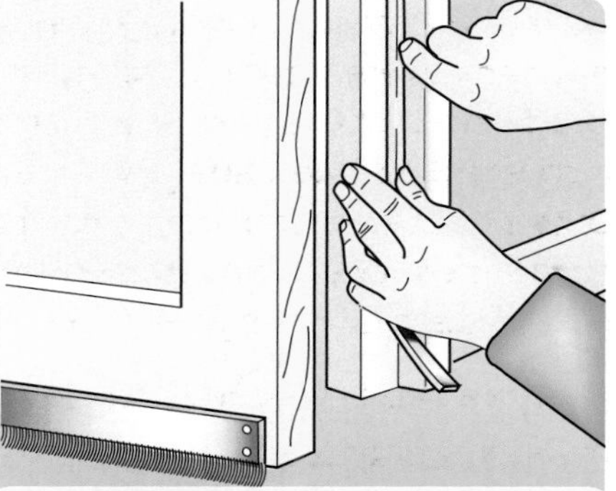

FIGURE 5: If you have gas fires or a central heating boiler, it is dangerous to eliminate all draughts. Do you know why?

QUESTIONS

7 Imagine you are on a local council deciding whether or not to give grants for installing home insulation. Discuss all the factors you would consider in making your decision, and what other information, if any, you would need to help you.

Why use electricity?

You will find out:

- Examples of devices that use energy transformations involving electrical energy
- Some of the alternatives to mains electricity and some of their limitations
- Alternatives to electrical energy for energy outputs

People power

The radio in figure 1 does not need mains electricity or batteries. Winding a handle turns a small electricity generator that makes electricity to charge up a built-in rechargeable battery. The 'clockwork radio' was invented in the 1990s by Trevor Baylis. Since then he has also invented clockwork torches, clockwork mobile phones, clockwork laptop computers and even a clockwork laser for eye surgery.

FIGURE 1: What advantages might 'clockwork' electricity bring a remote community?

Using electricity

We use a lot of electricity in our homes. Just think for a moment what your life would be like without electricity. What things would change? We use **mains electricity** because it is convenient, clean, safe and reliable. You just flick a switch, and there is the energy when you need it.

We don't usually want energy in the form of **electrical energy**, so we use a wide range of devices designed to transform the electrical energy into other forms. For example, a hairdryer transforms electrical energy into heat and kinetic energy, a television transforms electrical energy into light and sound.

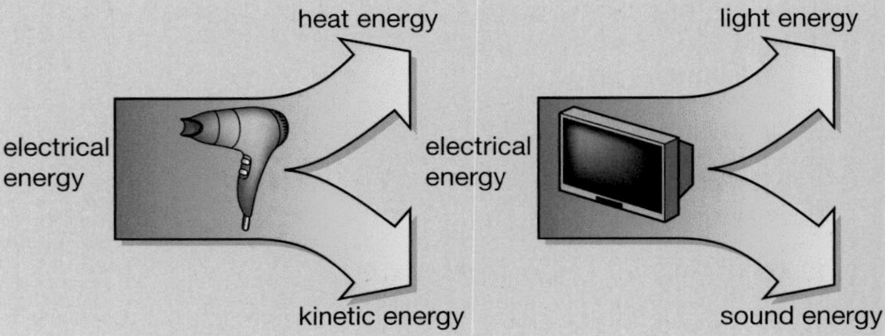

FIGURE 2: Devices transforming electrical energy. What type of wasted energy would you get from a television?

Batteries

Batteries allow us to use electrical energy in places where there is no mains electricity. Batteries do not contain electrical energy. They are stores of **chemical energy**, which they transform into electrical energy when it is needed, when a circuit is connected to the battery. Have you noticed how heaters hardly ever use batteries? That is because heaters need to use a lot of electrical energy, and batteries can only store a small amount of energy compared to the mains. A heater that ran on batteries wouldn't be very hot, and the batteries would go flat very quickly!

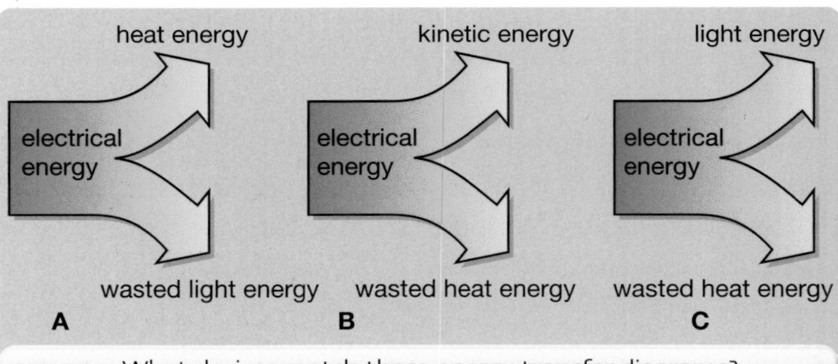

FIGURE 3: What devices match these energy transfer diagrams?

QUESTIONS

1. Draw an energy transfer diagram to show the energy transformations in an electric toaster.
2. Match these devices to the correct energy transfer diagrams A to C in figure 3: electric light bulb, electric fire, electric motor.
3. Mains electricity can be dangerous if we are not careful. Discuss what safety precautions you know for using mains electricity.

Remember to look for wasted energy in energy transfers.

...batteries ...biomass ...chemical energy ...electrical energy

Alternatives to electricity

Many of the things that we use electricity for can be done using some other form of energy. We can cook using the chemical energy stored in gas or various types of **biomass**. Before mains electricity, people used candles or gas or oil lamps to provide light; in many parts of the world they still do. Human, animal or steam power can be used to provide kinetic energy; all of these transform the chemical energy stored in either food or fuel. People even used to use wind-up gramophones to provide sound.

The reason we don't usually use these methods is that, compared with electricity, they are often smelly, dirty or hard to use. Using mains electricity often produces pollution too, but at the power station, not in our homes.

FIGURE 4: What disadvantages does this have compared to an electric locomotive?

Where there is no alternative

Sometimes it seems as though there is no alternative to electricity. It's very hard to imagine using interactive television, computer games or the Internet without electricity. These all have to use electrical energy to operate, but scientists are gradually developing other ways of supplying the electrical energy, other than the mains. **Solar energy** and the **potential energy** in clockwork springs are being developed to charge rechargeable batteries to allow people in the developing world, without mains electricity, to use telephones, computers and many of the other devices we take for granted.

WOW FACTOR!

About one-third of the world's population, that's about 2 billion people, don't have any electricity.

QUESTIONS

4 Give **three** examples of devices that transform electrical energy into some other form of energy. For each example, give an alternative way of obtaining the same type of output energy.

5 Draw a diagram to show the energy transformations when clockwork springs are used to provide the energy for a computer.

LEDs

Light emitting diodes (LEDs) look like tiny, coloured light bulbs, but actually they are quite different. LEDs don't have a filament inside them, like most light bulbs do. All atoms have electrons orbiting around the nucleus in different shells, or energy levels. The electrons that are further from the nucleus have more energy.

When a voltage is connected across an LED, it makes some electrons jump up to a higher level. They then fall back down again and give out a little bit of light. The light is always the same colour because the electrons always give out the same amount of energy as they fall from the high level to the lower one. Different materials give different colours because they have different electron energy levels.

FIGURE 5: Can you explain how these LEDs (balanced on a hand) differ from tiny light bulbs?

QUESTIONS

6 What does the passage above tell you about the colour of light and its energy?

7 LEDs last longer than ordinary light bulbs. Suggest a reason why.

Electricity and heat

You will find out:

- The link between electric currents and heating
- Examples of how we use the heating effect of an electric current
- Factors that affect the heating effect of an electric current

Electrical fires

Firefighters try to discover the cause of all house fires. Sometimes the fire is started by an electrical fault. Damaged wires, or fuses that have been replaced with ordinary wire or nails, are some of the most common causes of electrical fires. The electric current flows through materials it was not intended to flow through, and makes them so hot they catch alight.

FIGURE 1: What clues might help fire-fighters decide what caused this fire?

Getting warmer

FIGURE 2: Do you know what the holes in this monitor case are for?

If you put your hand on the back of your television when it has been on for a while, it probably feels warm. Lots of other **electrical appliances**, such as mobile phone chargers, or the power supplies for laptop computers, feel warm too. DVD players and video players often have warnings on them telling you not to stand anything on top of the player. This is to make sure there is always a good air flow around the player to keep it cool and stop it overheating. The **electrical currents** that flow through the appliances transfer **electrical energy**, and whenever there is an energy transfer or transformation some of the energy is transformed into **heat energy**.

Using the heat

There are lots of places where we use the heating effect of an electric current. Most light bulbs have a very thin wire, or **filament**, inside them. When a current flows, the filament glows white hot and gives out light. Electric heaters have very thin wires that glow red hot when a current flows. **Fuses** are safety devices that switch off the current if it gets too large. The fuse is a thin piece of wire that gets hot and melts if too much current flows through it, breaking the circuit so the current doesn't damage other **components**.

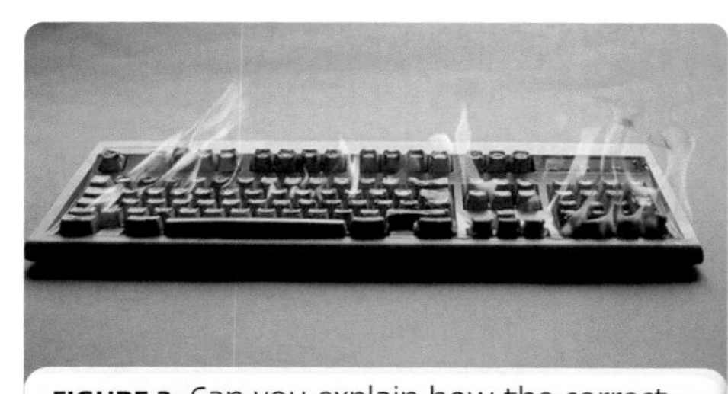

FIGURE 3: Can you explain how the correct fuse might stop this happening?

QUESTIONS

1 When air flows round a DVD player, does the player lose heat by conduction or by convection?

2 What type of energy does an electrical current transfer?

3 Describe the energy transformation that happens in the filament of a light bulb.

4 How does a fuse protect components in an electrical circuit?

WOW FACTOR!

Other safety devices include circuit breakers and trip switches. Do you have these in your labs?

...component ...electrical appliance ...electrical current ...electrical energy

Heat and resistance

Did you notice that all the wires that are designed to get hot, such as light bulb filaments or electric fire filaments, are very thin? Thin wires have a greater **resistance** than thicker wires, and wires with a greater resistance heat up more when an electric current flows through them. It is harder for the current to flow through the wire, and more of the energy carried by the current is transformed into heat energy.

Different metals have different resistances. That is one reason why most wires that carry electricity are made from copper, even though copper is more expensive than steel, for example. The copper wire has a lower resistance than a steel wire of the same thickness, so current can flow through it more easily. Less of the electrical energy carried by the current is transformed into heat, so more of it is available for the components in the circuit.

FIGURE 4: Why is the filament of this bulb so thin?

Heat and current

Larger currents carry more energy than smaller currents. This means that a large current causes more heating in any particular wire than a small current would. An appliance has to have the right thickness of wire for the current it uses, so that the current does not make the wire heat up. Telephones, which only use a very small current, have thin wires going to them; hairdryers or televisions, which use more current, have thicker wires; and if you have an electric cooker, which uses a very large current, you will see that the wire to the cooker is very thick indeed.

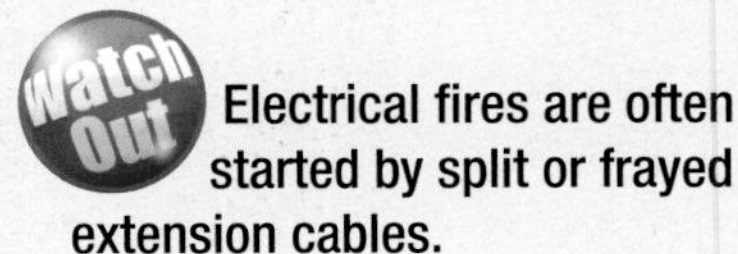

Electrical fires are often started by split or frayed extension cables.

QUESTIONS

5 What is the connection between the thickness of a wire and its resistance?

6 Give **one** advantage and **one** disadvantage of copper wires, compared with steel.

7 Suggest a reason why a cooker needs a large current.

Superconducting wire can carry currents for several years without any measurable loss of energy

Superconductivity

Scientists have discovered materials that are 'superconductors' at very low temperatures. These materials have such a low resistance that virtually all the electrical energy carried by the current is transferred to the components. Hardly any is lost as wasted heat energy in the wires.

Loops of superconducting wire have been shown to carry currents for several years without any measurable loss of energy! Many scientists are now working to discover or develop materials that are superconductors at room temperature, but at present the 'high temperature superconductors' are only superconductors at temperatures of below about −150 °C.

QUESTIONS

8 Superconducting wires can be made much thinner than normal wires for the same current. Can you explain why?

...filament ...fuse ...heat energy ...resistance

The cost of electricity

You will find out:

- What the 'power rating' of an appliance means
- How to calculate the energy an appliance transfers from the mains
- How to calculate the cost of the electricity we use
- What we are paying for when we pay for electricity

The football World Cup

Football World Cup matches need electricity for floodlighting, for public address systems, and for many other things. In 2006, the Hamburg Arena in Germany will need about 5 million watts of electricity, that's the same as a town of 5000 people use. And that's a huge electricity bill! After reading this page, try to estimate the bill for a match that lasts 90 minutes.

FIGURE 1: Can you work out the electricity bill for this match?

Paying for electricity

Electric current does not get used up. The same size current flows all the way round a **series circuit**. The same size current flows out of our house as flowed into it. When we pay an electricity bill we are paying for the electrical energy we have used. This electrical energy was transferred to our **electrical appliances** by the current, and was then transformed into lots of other types of useful energy.

You already know that some appliances transform much more energy than others. Electric cookers transform thousands of joules of electrical energy into heat energy every second. A radio may only transform 4 joules of electrical energy into sound energy each second. Appliances that give out heat transform the most energy.

Power rating

All electrical appliances have a **power rating**, given in **watts** (symbol, W) or **kilowatts** (symbol, kW). An appliance with a power rating of 1 W transforms 1 **joule** of electrical energy each second. So a 60 W light bulb transforms 60 J of electrical energy each second into light energy and heat energy. 1 kW is equal to 1000 W, so a 2 kW electric fire transforms 2000 J of electrical energy each second into heat energy.

Baum
Type 5468
220-240V ~ /50Hz/1600W
CE
made in EU
S/N D23891

FIGURE 2: An appliance's power rating value.

Appliance	Power rating	Appliance	Power rating
laptop computer	100 W	television	50 W
electric kettle	2.4 kW	microwave oven	1.2 kW
hairdryer	1.5 kW	electric fire	2.0 kW
radio	4 W	lawn mower	1.3 kW

TABLE 1: Power ratings of household appliances.

Appliances that give out heat transform most energy

QUESTIONS

1. What are we paying for when we pay an electricity bill?
2. What does the power rating of an appliance tell us?
3. Which appliance, from the table, transforms energy fastest?
4. A television transformed 1000 J of energy. For how many seconds was it switched on?

...electrical appliance ...electric current ...joule ...kilowatt

Calculating the energy transferred from the mains

To find out the total energy an appliance transfers from the mains, we need to know the number of joules transferred each second and the number of seconds the appliance is on for. The joules transferred each second is the power rating, so we can calculate the energy transferred using this equation:

total energy transferred (in J) = power rating (in W) x time (in s)

To find out the total energy used by a 1.2 kW microwave oven for five minutes to heat a ready-meal we use:

total energy transferred = 1200 x 300 = 360000J
(1.2kW = 1200W, 5 mins = 5 x 60 = 300 s)

FIGURE 3: How could you adjust the amount of microwave energy this microwave oven emits?

How much does it cost?

Electricity bills charge for the number of **kilowatt hours** (kWh) of electrical energy that we use. An electrical appliance with a power rating of 1 kW, left on for 1 h, uses 1 kWh of electricity. So to find the number of kilowatt hours used by an appliance, we can use the equation:

number of kilowatt hours used = power rating (in kW) x time (in hours)

So the 1.2 kW microwave oven, on for 5 minutes, uses:

1.2 x 5/60 = 0.1 kWh of electrical energy

To find the cost of using the appliance we have to use the equation:

total cost = number of kilowatt hours used x cost per kilowatt hour

So if each kilowatt hour of electrical energy used costs 2p, the cost of heating the microwave ready-meal will be:

total cost = 0.1 x 2 = 0.2p

Remember

- To work out the energy transferred, the time must be in seconds and the power in watts.
- To work out the cost, the power must be in kilowatts and the time must be in hours.

SEE Energy

Name **Ms F Eastwood**
Billing period **30 March to 30 May 2005**
Readings

Present	*Previous*	*Units*	*Per unit (p)*	*VAT (%)*	*Total (£)*
45698	44096	1602	6.03	zero	96.60
		Standing charge			8.50
		Total			105.10

FIGURE 4: Which two figures must we multiply together to find the total cost excluding standing charge?

QUESTIONS

5 Calculate the energy transferred by a laptop computer, used for 15 minutes.

6 If electricity costs 2p per kilowatt hour, how much would it cost to cut a large lawn that takes 3 hours to mow?

7 Calculate the energy transferred by 1 kilowatt hour of electricity.

WOW FACTOR!

Playing a computer game for nearly an hour uses the same amount of energy as boiling the water for one cup of coffee.

Switching to standby

The Energy Saving Trust is concerned that as people switch to digital television there will be a large increase in the emission of greenhouse gases from power stations.

The problem is that people tend to leave the set-top boxes used to receive the digital TV on standby when they are not using them. The set-top boxes use about 9 W of power but this only drops to about 7 W of power when they are on standby, compared with an analogue video recorder which uses about 3 W of power on standby. The problem is that so many manufacturers are competing to sell set-top boxes that some are using cheap, inefficient components to keep the prices low.

FIGURE 5: How much money would you save each year by switching this set-top box off for 10 hours each night instead of leaving it on standby?

QUESTIONS

8 Assume an analogue video recorder and a digital set-top box are both left on standby for 24 hours. How much extra energy does the digital set-top box use?

The National Grid

You will find out:

- What the National Grid is
- How the voltage changes throughout the National Grid
- The advantages of using very high voltages to transmit electricity

Are power lines safe?

In 2005 a study by the University of Oxford and the owners of the National Grid showed that children born within 200 m of overhead power lines had a 70% increased risk of developing childhood leukaemia. Those born between 200 m and 600 m away had a 20% increased risk. One month earlier, a UK Childhood Cancer Study showed there was no increased risk. Now scientists have to decide which report is correct.

FIGURE 1: Are these safe? Would you want to live near them?

What is the National Grid?

You know that the **mains electricity** we use is generated in **power stations**. The network of wires or cables that carries the electricity from the power station to our homes is called the **National Grid**. Sometimes the cables are underground, but in most places you can see pylons carrying the wires across the countryside.

The electricity coming from the power station has a very high energy. It needs to be high energy, because one power station may supply the energy for hundreds of thousands of homes and businesses. This high energy makes the wires extremely dangerous. You may have seen warning signs near canals or lakes saying 'Danger Overhead Cables'. This is to stop people accidentally touching the cables with fishing rods. If they did, an **electric current** would flow down the fishing rod and through them, killing them. You mustn't fly kites near overhead cables either, for the same reason.

FIGURE 2: Do you know what this sign means?

Changing voltage

The high energy electricity from the power station has a very high **voltage**. Most of it is transferred around the country at 400 000 V, but the mains supply in our homes is only at 230 V. **Step-down transformers** in large **substations** in cities change the voltage from the power station down to 132 000 V. Then more step-down transformers in several smaller substations change it down to the 230 V we need in our homes. You may have seen substations near your home or school. There is usually a small substation for every few streets.

FIGURE 3: Why is high voltage electricity dangerous?

QUESTIONS

1. What is the National Grid?
2. Why does the electricity coming from the power station have a high energy?
3. Explain in your own words why you mustn't fly kites near overhead power cables.
4. Describe what a substation does.

...electric current ...mains electricity ...National Grid ...parallel

Why use such high voltages?

To find the power of an electric current we have to multiply the current by the voltage.

power = current x voltage, or P = I V

The power tells us the energy that the current transfers each second.

You can see from the equation, that if we use a high voltage, we only need a small current to transfer the same amount of energy each second. By using such a high voltage, the power station can transfer huge amounts of energy using a relatively small current. And you already know that if the current is smaller, the wires can be thinner. Thinner wires contain less copper and so are cheaper. And that makes our electricity prices lower.

We don't end up with a huge current coming into our house when the voltage is changed down to the 230 V used in our homes, because the single current coming from the power station splits into lots of smaller, **parallel** currents all taking electricity to different groups of houses.

FIGURE 4: What advantages are there in using high voltages in these cables?

Heat losses

You know some of the energy transferred by an electric current is always wasted as heat energy, making the wires warm. This amount increases as the current increases, so keeping the current from the power station low helps reduce the amount of energy wasted as heat. About 10% of the energy supplied by power stations is wasted as heat in the National Grid. Sometimes if it is frosty you can tell where underground cables are because the wasted heat energy from them melts the frost.

QUESTIONS

5 If the voltage from a power station doubled, how would the current change?

6 Thinner wires are cheaper. Give one other advantage of thinner wires.

7 If 10% of the energy is wasted, what is the efficiency of the National Grid?

8 Explain why the current to our homes is not huge.

EXAM HINTS AND TIPS

Remember: very high voltages transmit very large amounts of energy with relatively small energy losses.

a.c. and d.c.

The current from a battery is direct current (d.c.). It flows in one direction only, from the positive terminal to the negative terminal. The current from the mains is different. It is alternating current (a.c.). It flows first in one direction then decreases to zero, before flowing in the opposite direction, in a continual cycle.

The frequency of the mains electricity is 50 Hz, which means there are 50 complete cycles of current flow every second. The reason mains is a.c. is because the substations that change the voltage of the National Grid only work with a.c., not with d.c.

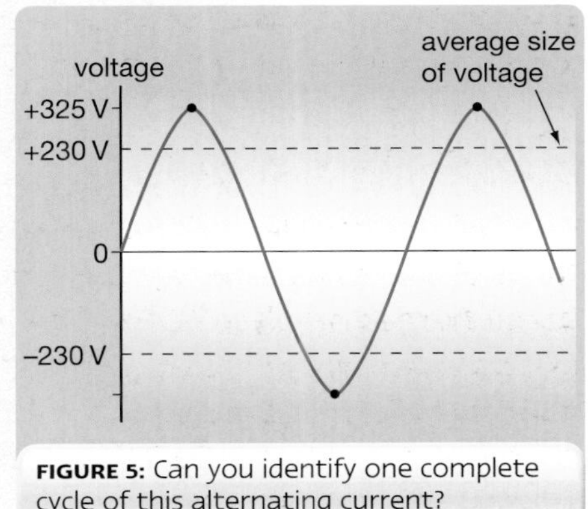

FIGURE 5: Can you identify one complete cycle of this alternating current?

QUESTIONS

9 The size of the mains voltage changes too, from +325 V to -325 V. The average size is 230 V. Why is it more useful to give the average size of the voltage than the maximum?

Generating electricity

You will find out:

- The energy changes that happen in electric motors and dynamos
- The connection between magnets, currents and movement
- How an electricity generator works

Where does electricity come from?

Have you ever felt a slight electric shock as you get out of a car? Sometimes you gain static electricity as your clothes rub on the car seat. Then you feel a shock as a tiny spark of electricity jumps from you to the car's metal bodywork. Lightning is the same thing, but on a much, much larger scale! Chemicals can generate electricity too. That's how batteries work. How else can we generate electricity?

FIGURE 1: How many ways do you know to generate electricity?

Electric motors

An **electric motor** transforms **electrical energy** into **kinetic energy**. You may have used a small electric motor at school to drive around the blades of a model windmill, or to drive a small, battery-powered fan. You may even have made a small electric motor from a motor kit.

If you change the electric motor circuit slightly, replacing the battery with a sensitive **ammeter**, you can use the electric motor 'in reverse' to generate electricity. Blowing hard on the windmill blades, or spinning them round by hand, makes the motor turn round. You can see this makes an electric current because the needle on the ammeter moves. If you are able to turn the blades fast enough you may even get enough current to make a small bulb light up dimly. The 'motor in reverse' is transforming kinetic energy into electrical energy.

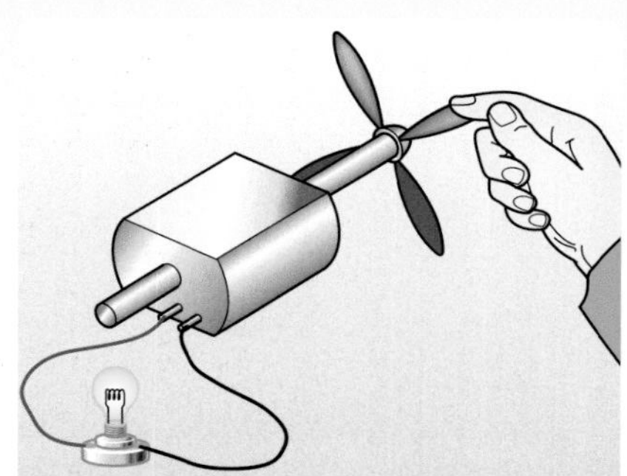

FIGURE 2: Where does the energy come from to make the bulb light up?

Dynamos

Years ago, when batteries didn't last as long as they do now, most cyclists used a **dynamo** to generate the electricity for their bicycle lights. The dynamo was just a 'motor in reverse' that was fixed to the back wheel, so it generated electricity as the wheel turned round. The problem was that if a cyclist went really slowly, uphill for example, their lights would go out!

You can often try generating electricity like this, by pedalling a bicycle, at Science Discovery Centres. The faster you pedal, the more current you generate and the brighter the bulb gets. Imagine how fast you would have to pedal to generate enough electricity for your home!

FIGURE 3: Do you think it is possible to play computer games and get fit at the same time?

QUESTIONS

1. When you use a model windmill and a 'motor in reverse', where does the energy to light the bulb come from originally?
2. Describe the energy transformations that happen in the windmill and 'motor in reverse'.
3. Discuss why a cyclist's lights may go out when they pedal uphill.

...ammeter ...dynamo ...electrical energy ...electric current ...electricity generator

Magnets, current and movement

Magnets, **electric current** and **movement** always go together. Wherever you find two of them, you will find the third as well. You may already have seen this with a coil of wire and a magnet.

When an electric current flows through the coil of wire, it becomes an **electromagnet**, attracting or repelling the magnet and making it move. An electric current and a magnet together always cause movement.

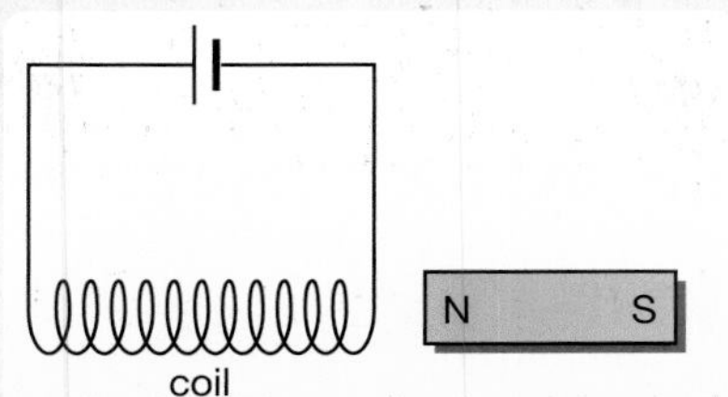

FIGURE 4: What will happen to the magnet?

If you replace the cell with a sensitive ammeter, you will see that an electric current flows (the needle moves) whenever you move the magnet. A magnet and movement together always cause an electric current. The faster you move the magnet, the bigger the current will be. If you move the magnet in the opposite direction, the current flows in the opposite direction too.

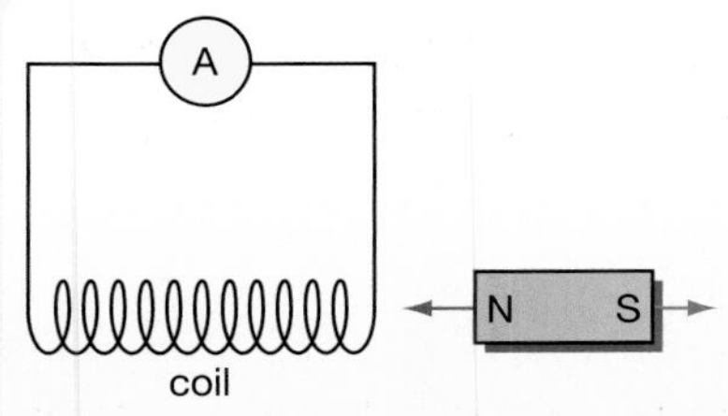

FIGURE 5: What affects which way the needle on the ammeter moves?

An electric motor works in the same way.

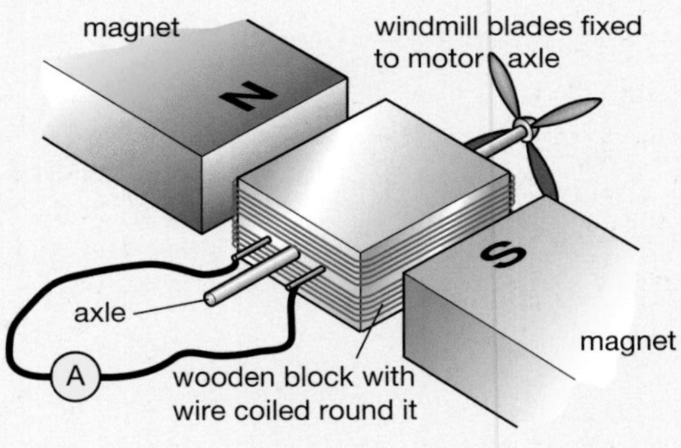

FIGURE 6: What effect would swapping over the poles of the magnet have?

The magnet and the electric current in the wires of the motor, together, make the motor move. The current flows down one side of coil and back up the other side (that is, in the opposite direction). So one side of the coil moves up, and the other side of the coil moves down (in the opposite direction). This makes the motor spin. The 'motor in reverse' works like this too. The magnet and spinning the motor coil, together, cause an electric current in the coil of wire, so the 'motor in reverse' is an **electricity generator**.

QUESTIONS

4 Describe the energy changes happening when a current flowing in a coil of wire repels a nearby magnet.

5 Use ideas of energy to suggest why a 'motor in reverse' gives a bigger current when the motor coil is spun round faster.

Larger motors

If you look at the motor from a washing machine or a lawn mower, you will see that it is not a rectangular coil of wire like the small motors used in school. It is cylindrical because it has many rectangular coils all wound at an angle to each other, and all surrounded by curved magnets.

A small rectangular motor moves fastest when the plane of the coil is parallel to the magnetic field lines (lines from the North pole to the South pole of the magnet). In a large motor, the curved magnets mean the coils are always parallel to a magnetic field, and more coils increase the force and make the motor move faster.

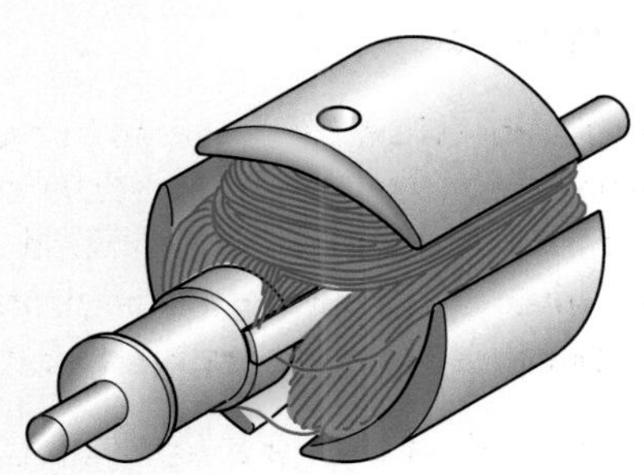
FIGURE 7: What are the advantages of having more than one coil of wire in a motor?

QUESTIONS

6 Suggest a reason why a small rectangular electric motor, such as is used in schools, will not work with an alternating current.

Power stations

You will find out:

- The main stages in a power station that burns fossil fuels
- The energy changes taking place inside a power station
- How the efficiency of power stations can be improved

Going with a bang!

Lake Kivu, in north-west Rwanda, is in an area with a lot of volcanic activity. Highly flammable gases from the volcanic activity, and from bacteria, are building up at the bottom of Lake Kivu. Scientists fear there may be a massive explosion, destroying local villages. In 2003, engineers started plans to pump the gas out and burn it in a power station to generate electricity for most of Rwanda.

FIGURE 1: Lake Kivu – could a power station be the answer to this area's problems?

How does a power station work?

Most of the **power stations** in Britain burn **fossil fuels**, such as coal, natural gas or oil. Figure 2 shows the main stages in one of these power stations. Look at the diagram and work out where each of these stages happens.

- Fuel is burned to heat water.
- The hot water changes to steam.
- The steam drives round a **turbine**.
- Steam condenses back into water and is returned to the boiler.
- The turbine turning round makes the **generator** turn round.
- The generator generates electricity.
- The **step-up transformer** increases the **voltage** of the electricity to the very high voltages needed for the **National Grid**.
- The National Grid transmits the electricity to homes and businesses.

EXAM HINTS AND TIPS

Remember, the *efficiency* of a power station tells us how much of the energy in the fuel changes to electrical energy.

A large power station may supply electricity for hundreds of thousands of homes and businesses. It takes a lot of fuel to supply that much energy. A large power station may burn a trainload of coal every half-hour. Coal, natural gas and oil are all **non-renewable** fuels and one day they will run out. How long they last will depend on how fast we use them and on whether or not we find any new supplies of them.

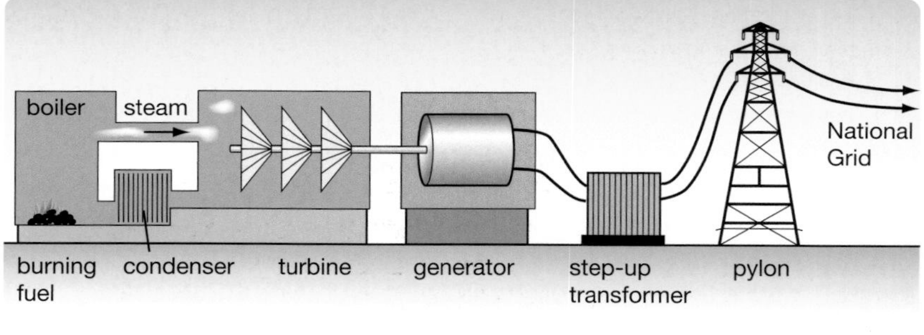

boiler, steam, National Grid, burning fuel, condenser, turbine, generator, step-up transformer, pylon

FIGURE 2: Can you describe what happens at each stage in the power station?

QUESTIONS

1. Which part of the power station generates electricity?
2. What happens in the boiler of a power station?
3. Describe what 'non-renewable' fuels are. Give **three** examples of non-renewable fuels.
4. Write down **two** things that will affect how long supplies of fossil fuels last.

Energy changes

You already know that whenever there is an energy transfer or transformation, some of the energy is transformed into '**wasted energy**', often heat. Power stations are no different.

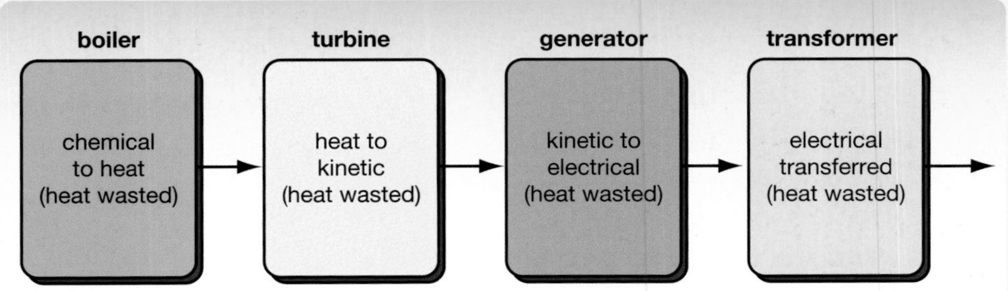

FIGURE 3: What would you need to know to work out the efficiency of this power station?

Figure 3 shows the main energy transfers and transformations happening in the power station described earlier. You can see that heat energy is wasted at every stage. In a typical coal-burning power station, only about 35% of the chemical energy in the coal is transformed into useful electrical energy, most of the rest is 'lost' as wasted heat energy. Perhaps it would be more accurate to call it a 'heat station'!

Most of the new fossil fuel power stations being built are 'combined cycle gas turbine power stations'. The first stage uses burning natural gas to drive round one turbine, connected to a generator. Waste heat from this 'gas turbine' is used to heat water to make steam to drive round a steam turbine. This type of power station is usually just over 50% efficient. The most efficient fossil fuel power stations are combined heat and power stations, where the waste heat is used to heat local houses and businesses. These are usually 70% to 80% efficient.

Nuclear power stations

Nuclear power stations work in the same way as standard fossil fuel power stations except that they use a nuclear reaction (the radioactive decay of uranium-235) to produce the heat needed to change water to steam. About 11% of the world's electricity is generated in nuclear power stations. Most nuclear power stations are only about 30% efficient.

EXAM HINTS AND TIPS

Make sure you know the stages in a power station, and the energy changes at each stage.

QUESTIONS

5 Explain why it might be more accurate to describe a coal burning power station as a 'heat station'.

6 Explain why a combined cycle gas turbine power station is more efficient.

7 Discuss where a combined heat and power station could, or couldn't, be used.

What should we burn?

FIGURE 4: How should we decide what to burn in power stations?

Large amounts of coal are present in deep underground seams that are inaccessible to mining. In 2002, some engineers suggested that it would be possible to burn this coal and trap the resulting gases at the surface, using them to fuel gas turbine power stations. Critics say the resulting fires in the coal seams would probably be impossible to put out and that the burning coal would release massive amounts of carbon, possibly causing unstoppable global warming, affecting the whole planet.

QUESTIONS

8 Discuss what extra information you would need to help you decide whether or not the plan to burn coal in deep underground seams is a good one.

...power station ...step-up transformer ...turbine ...voltage ...wasted energy

Renewable energy

You will find out:

- What renewable energy resources are
- How different renewable energy resources can be used to generate electricity

Energy everywhere?

Fossil fuels are non-renewable. One day they will run out. Fortunately, we can use many **renewable** energy resources to generate electricity. Renewable energy resources are ones that are always available, or that can be replaced as we use them. They include water power, wind power and solar power. Scientists are gradually getting better and better at finding ways to use the energy from these sources.

FIGURE 1: This power station generates electricity from the energy in moving water. What other renewable energy resources can we can use to generate electricity?

What else burns?

In 2003, there were 16 'energy-from-waste' power stations in the UK. These burn household rubbish or waste from industries to heat water. Each supplies electricity for about 50 000 homes. Many only burn waste that can't be recycled, and the ash from them can be used as fertiliser. Other power stations burn **biomass**, such as fast growing willow saplings. In 2005, building work began on the UK's first power station to burn grass.

Wind turbines

Have you ever seen a **wind farm** like this one on the right? Small wind farms may only have two or three **wind turbines**. The world's largest wind farms, in California, have thousands. Each wind turbine works a bit like the model windmill you may have used with a 'motor in reverse'. The wind makes the blades turn round, which turns a turbine connected to an electricity **generator**. The wind turbine transforms the kinetic energy of moving air into electrical energy.

FIGURE 2: Do you know the difference between a 'wind farm' and a 'wind turbine'?

Hydroelectric power

Hydroelectric power stations use falling water to turn round turbines, a bit like using a running tap to make a model water wheel turn round. A dam built across a river holds the water in a reservoir. Engineers open gates to allow water to flow through turbines, then back into the river lower down. As the turbines turn, they turn generators to generate electricity. Engineers can increase or decrease the amount of water flowing through the turbines. This makes them spin faster or slower, so the generators generate more or less electricity.

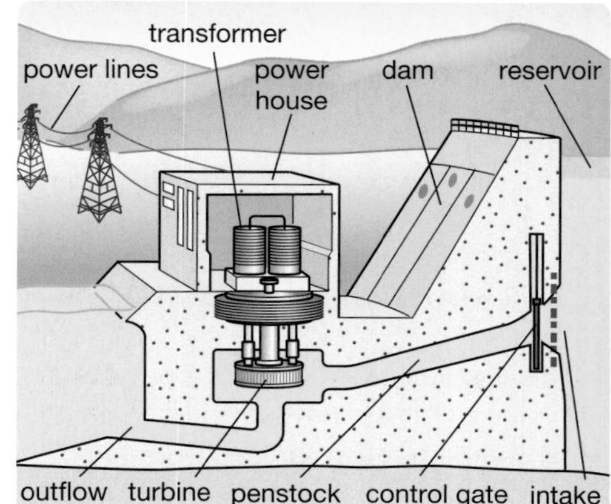

FIGURE 3: What energy changes happen in this hydroelectric power station?

QUESTIONS

1. Describe what an 'energy-from-waste' power station is.
2. What is the difference between a 'wind turbine' and a 'wind farm'?
3. How can engineers change the amount of electricity generated in a hydroelectric power station?
4. What is the main energy change that happens in a hydroelectric power station?

...biomass ...generator ...geothermal ...hydroelectric ...renewable

Tidal power

Tidal power stations use the movement of water as tides rise and fall. They are often built across estuaries, but can be built on some beaches as well. A wall is built across the estuary. As the tide comes in, it flows through turbines in the wall, making them spin to turn a generator to generate electricity. A gate behind the wall prevents water flowing back out again. As the tide falls, the gate is opened and water again flows through the turbines, in the opposite direction, generating more electricity. Tidal power stations only work well in areas where the difference between high tide and low tide is 15 metres or more.

WOW FACTOR!

In 2005, 24%, that's almost a quarter, of the world's electricity was generated using wind turbines.

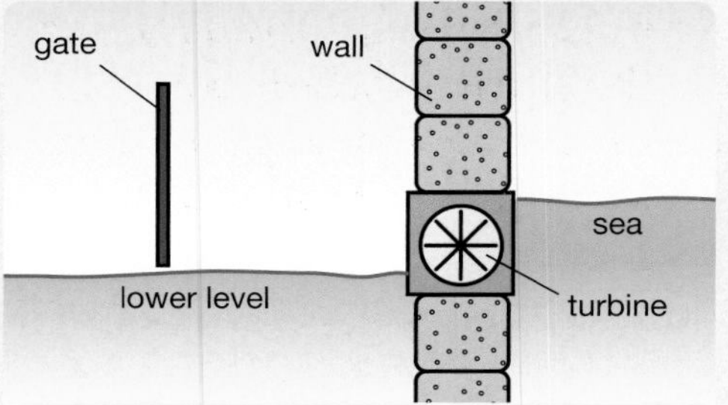

FIGURE 4: Where does the energy to generate the electricity come from originally?

Wave power

Wave power generators are tubes of air (like a chimney), dipping into the sea and open to the sea at the bottom, with a turbine at the top. They are anchored to the seabed, so have to be in fairly shallow water. When a wave hits the wave generator, the water inside the tube rises, forcing the air through the turbine, so the turbine spins. The turbine is connected to a generator. As the water level falls, air is sucked back down through the turbine again, so the turbine continues to spin. Scientists are still working to improve wave generators, as they are easily damaged by large waves.

Renewable energy resources can be replaced as we use them

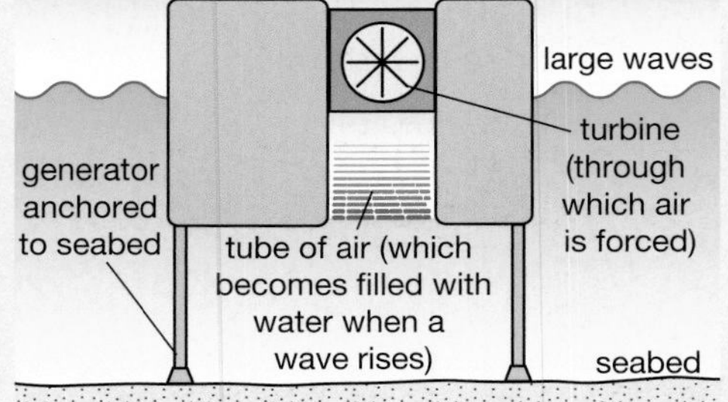

FIGURE 5: Can you draw an energy transfer diagram to show the energy changes happening here?

Geothermal power stations

The rocks deep underground are hot. In volcanic areas, steam sometimes rises to the surface. In **geothermal** power stations, this steam is used to drive a turbine connected to a generator. In other areas, holes are drilled down to the hot rock, and water pumped down. The steam that comes back up is used to drive a turbine.

QUESTIONS

5 Describe the energy changes that happen in a geothermal power station.

6 Compare tidal power stations and wave power generators, describing the similarities and differences between them.

Watch Out Nuclear power is not renewable, though supplies of nuclear fuel will last a lot longer than fossil fuels.

Solar power stations

In 2004, scientists in Spain announced that they had successfully built a prototype solar power station, capable of generating 1 megawatt of power. The solar power station has 300 heliostats (computer-guided reflective mirrors), each made from 70 square metres of glass, that reflect sunlight onto a central tower with a ceramic heat absorber.

The heat absorber reaches a temperature of 1000 °C. Air blown through the heat absorber, reaches a temperature of 680 °C. The hot air is used to heat steam, which drives a conventional steam turbine, driving a generator. In 5 to 10 years, Spain expects to have 15 to 20 commercial solar power stations.

FIGURE 6: The mirrors, or heliostats, at this experimental solar power station are all computer controlled to track the Sun. Why is this necessary?

QUESTIONS

7 Imagine you were the scientists working on the prototype solar power station. What things would you look at in order to try to improve its efficiency?

Electricity and the environment

You will find out:

- About the harmful effects of different methods of electricity generation
- The benefits of different ways of electricity generation
- The limitations on where different types of power station can be used

Britain's energy vision

Britain has a green energy strategy, intended to ensure that at least 20% of Britain's electricity is generated from renewable energy resources by 2020. Dutch scientists have calculated that wind power alone could supply six times as much energy each year as the whole world used in 2001. Their study did not include offshore wind farms, and assumed wind farms would not be put in any urban areas, nature reserves, lakes or mountains.

FIGURE 1: This is Britain's first offshore wind farm. What advantages or disadvantages does it have compared with wind farms on land?

Harmful effects

All the power stations that we use harm people or the environment in some way.

- Burning **fossil fuels** give off harmful gases that cause **global warming**.
- Toxic gases given off by burning waste may cause cancer or birth defects.
- Many people complain that **wind turbines** are noisy and ugly and kill birds.
- When they are set up, hydroelectric power station dams flood valleys, often destroying farmland, homes or wildlife habitats.
- Both tidal power and wave power can change water flow patterns, disrupting harbours or shipping and often destroying wildlife habitats such as mudflats.
- **Geothermal** power stations can release dangerous gases and minerals from deep underground, which can be difficult to dispose of safely.

FIGURE 2: What harmful effects might this geothermal power station have?

Benefits

All the different types of power stations we use to generate electricity have different benefits too.

- Burning fossil fuels is relatively cheap, and can generate large amounts of electricity.
- Wind turbines can generate electricity in very remote, rural areas. The alternative, of putting in National Grid wires to these places, is very expensive.
- Hydroelectric power stations across large rivers can supply very large amounts of electricity.
- Tidal power stations and **wave power generators** have very low running costs.
- Geothermal power stations are small and do not need fuel or other deliveries, so their impact on the environment is small.

FIGURE 3: Why do you think it is expensive to bring the National Grid to a place like this?

QUESTIONS

1. How can burning fossil fuels harm the environment?
2. State **two** types of power station that can damage wildlife habitats.
3. Give **one** advantage and **one** disadvantage of wind turbines.
4. How can geothermal power stations affect the environment?

Air pollution and climate change

People often think of **air pollution** as smoke that you can see. Scientists call this type of air pollution **particulate matter**, and it can be very harmful to health, making asthma and other breathing problems worse.

Some air pollution is invisible. All the fuels we use contain **hydrocarbons**. These release **carbon dioxide** gas into the atmosphere as they burn. More carbon dioxide in the atmosphere makes it harder for heat to radiate out from the Earth, so the Earth gradually warms up. This is global warming, or **climate change**. Burning fossil fuels increases the amount of carbon dioxide in the atmosphere because it releases carbon that has been trapped for millions of years. Burning renewable fuels, such as agricultural waste or grass, does not increase the amount of carbon dioxide in the atmosphere because it only releases carbon dioxide absorbed by plants in the last year or so.

Location matters

It is expensive to transfer electricity around the country in the National Grid. Wires and pylons cost money, as does installing them. And the longer the wires, the more wasted heat energy they give out. So power companies try to generate electricity near to where it is needed. This is not always possible.

- Fossil fuel power stations need to be near a river for water, and near railways or roads.
- Wind turbines work best where it is windy.
- Hydroelectric power stations only work where it is hilly.
- Geothermal power stations need to be on rock that is easy to drill through.

All power stations harm people or the environment in some way

FIGURE 4: What type of power station would you choose for the people who live here?

EXAM HINTS AND TIPS

Try to remember at least one advantage and one disadvantage for each type of power station.

QUESTIONS

5 Describe what 'global warming' is.

6 Explain why burning renewable fuels does not cause global warming.

7 Discuss what type of power station would be suitable for a small, hilly, windy, Scottish island, with only a few hundred inhabitants.

WOW FACTOR!

The Scottish island of Islay has a bus powered by electricity generated in a wave power generator.

Not so green hydroelectric power

Hydroelectric dams cause global warming by releasing methane gas into the atmosphere. This is because seasonal changes in water levels mean plants grow on the banks of the reservoir, then are flooded and rot. The dissolved methane is released as water passes through the turbines. In effect, the hydroelectric dam converts carbon dioxide absorbed by plants into methane, and methane gas causes far more global warming than the same amount of carbon dioxide.

One study estimated that, in 1990, one hydroelectric dam in Brazil caused more than three times as much global warming as generating the same amount of electricity using fossil fuels would have.

FIGURE 5: This looks harmless enough, but when reservoir water levels fall it can contribute to global warming.

QUESTIONS

8 Discuss what, if anything, could be done to decrease the amount of global warming caused by hydroelectric dams.

Making comparisons

You will find out:

- The factors we need to consider when deciding the best type of power station
- How the flexibility, cost and reliability of different types of power station vary

Nuclear power

Nuclear power stations produce about 11% of the world's electricity. Supporters say it is cheap, reliable, and does not produce the pollution that fossil fuels produce. Critics say that although it only produces a tiny amount of waste, that waste is very dangerous. A lot of money has to be spent on safety, as an accident could be a major disaster.

FIGURE 1: This is Sellafield nuclear power station. What do you think about nuclear power, and other types of electricity generation?

Which power station should we choose?

One day we will have to replace our old **power stations** that burn fossil fuels, because fossil fuels will run out and burning fossil fuels causes **climate change**. Some scientists work on improving the design of fossil fuel power stations, so they are more **efficient**. Then they burn less fuel to generate the same amount of electricity. Modern fossil fuel power stations that use the waste heat to generate more electricity are about 50% efficient, compared with about 35% for older power stations.

Some **renewable energy** power stations are much less efficient than fossil fuel power stations. Some are much more efficient. When the energy resource is renewable, efficiency is not as important as it is for fossil fuel power stations. It may matter more how much it will cost to build the power station, or to keep it running, or whether the energy source is **reliable**, or whether it can generate different amounts of electricity when the demand changes.

FIGURE 2: At half-time in a World Cup final, the demand for electricity suddenly goes up. Do you know why?

Electricity without power stations

About a third of the world's population does not have mains electricity. Usually they don't have batteries either. **Solar cells** are panels that transform light energy from the Sun into electricity. People in developing countries can use solar cells to generate electricity for lamps, telephones, computers, water-purifying machinery, fridges to keep vaccines cold, and other appliances to improve their quality of life.

FIGURE 3: How can solar power improve the quality of life of people in the developing world?

QUESTIONS

1. Give **two** reasons why fossil fuel power stations have to be replaced.
2. What do you think a 'renewable energy power station' is? Give an example.
3. Explain what a more efficient power station is.
4. List **three** things that may matter more than efficiency for a renewable energy power station.

...capital cost ...climate change ...efficient ...operating cost

Changing demand

Power stations cannot store the electrical energy they generate. Instead, they change the amount of electricity they generate when the amount that people use changes. For example, in Britain demand for electricity goes up in a cold spell in winter, when everyone turns their heating on for longer; and in the morning and evening, when people are making breakfast or evening meals. Fossil fuel and hydroelectric power stations can adjust the amount of electricity they generate more easily than wind, tidal or wave power generators can.

How much does it cost?

There are two costs that we have to consider for all types of electricity generation. The first is the **capital cost** – how much it costs to build the power station. The second is the **operating cost** – how much it costs to run the power station once it is built. At present, most types of renewable energy power stations – especially tidal and geothermal – have very high capital costs compared with a fossil fuel power station, but they have low operating costs. As the technology used in renewable power stations becomes more familiar, and as fossil fuel prices increase, the electricity from fossil fuel power stations is getting more expensive, and electricity from renewable power stations is getting cheaper.

Reliability

All power stations need an energy source, and some energy sources are more **reliable** than others. For example, wind turbines do not operate at all at low wind speeds and work best at wind speeds of over 50 kph. They are only a good choice in areas with steady, high winds. Hydroelectric power stations need a reliable rain supply, to maintain the water level in the reservoir.

FIGURE 4: This tidal barrage is on the Rance river in France. Do you think tidal power is a reliable source of energy or not?

QUESTIONS

5 What do power stations do when the demand for electricity changes? Why?

6 How reliable do you think geothermal energy is? Explain why.

7 Imagine the area you live in needs a new power station. Discuss what type of power station you would invest in, and why.

EXAM HINTS AND TIPS

When choosing a power station, we have to consider efficiency, cost, reliability and flexibility.

Electricity from sewage

In 2004, a group of American scientists announced that they had developed an electricity generator fuelled by sewage. Bacteria in the generator oxidise liquid organic waste, which releases electrons and protons. The electrons are attracted to a positive anode, and flow round a circuit connected to the generator. The protons move through the liquid to a negatively charged, central cathode where they combine with oxygen from the air and electrons from the cathode, to produce water.

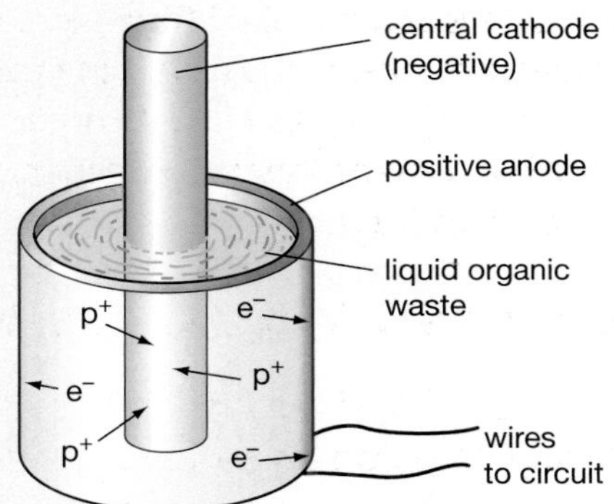

FIGURE 5: What factors might affect the amount of electricity produced by this generator?

QUESTIONS

8 The sewage electricity generator is still at the experimental stage. Discuss whether or not you think it could ever become a full-size power station and, if so, what its advantages and limitations would be.

Unit summary

Concept map

Energy

useful light energy
electrical energy
wasted heat energy

Metals conduct heat well because the heat is transferred by free electrons as well as vibrations.

The particle model explains conduction and convection.

All bodies emit and absorb thermal radiation – dull, dark surfaces do so more than shiny, light surfaces.

Important equations to remember:

Power = work done ÷ time taken
Units are: energy – the joule (J)
power – the watt (W)

Efficiency = useful energy output ÷ total energy input.

Moving energy from one place to another is transfer. Heat energy can be transferred by: thermal radiation (electromagnetic waves), conduction and convection.

Changing energy from one type to another is transformation.

Types of energy include: kinetic, potential, chemical, electrical, light, heat and sound.

Energy cannot be created or destroyed, but some is wasted during transfer or transformation. Energy transfer diagrams summarise transfer or transformation.

Electricity

We get electricity from the mains or batteries.

Mains electricity arrives via the National Grid:

- burning fossil fuels or nuclear reactions produce heat energy (the choice depends upon efficiency, capital and operating costs, reliability and flexibility)
- heat energy produces steam and this turns turbines
- turbines turn generators to produce electricity
- High voltages are used through distribution cables to reduce transformation into heat.

Some energy is transformed into heat when electrical energy is transferred – the larger the current and resistance, the more heat is produced.

Renewable energy resources include: wind, wave and tidal power, hydroelectric and geothermal.

All types of electricity generation have some harmful effects on people or the environment. There are also limitations on where they can be used.

The power rating of an appliance is the rate at which it transforms electrical energy:

Total energy transferred = power × rating time

Cost of electricity = number of kilowatt hours used × cost per kilowatt hour.

Unit quiz

1 What is thermal radiation?

2 Explain why fuel tanks are often painted white or silver.

3 Convection currents occur in liquids and gases because, when they get hotter, the particles get:

larger **denser** **further apart**

4 Which type of energy is contained in fuels?

5 Describe the difference between an energy transfer and an energy transformation.

6 To calculate the efficiency of a device, we divide the useful energy output by which of the following?

wasted energy **total energy input** **work done**

7 What type of energy is always given out when an electric current transfers electrical energy?

8 The amount of energy an electrical appliance transforms each second is called which of the following?

power rating **efficiency** **cost**

9 List the following in order of their voltage, starting with the smallest.

the National Grid **a battery** **mains electricity**

10 Which of the following is the odd one out? Explain why.

electricity generator **electric motor** **dynamo**

11 Name **five** different energy resources that could be used to drive the turbine in a power station.

12 List **three** factors that you would need to consider when deciding what type of power station to use in a particular location.

Numeracy activity

Electricity generation

The pie chart shows the proportion of the UK's electricity that is generated in different ways.

The bar chart shows the estimated maximum cost of electricity generation by various methods. This is not the price customers pay for electricity because it takes into account 'hidden' costs, such as the cost of pollution and health problems created by each type of electricity generation. These costs are usually paid for by the government. It is only an estimate because it is difficult to tell exactly how much of the health or climate change problems are caused by electricity generation, rather than by other causes.

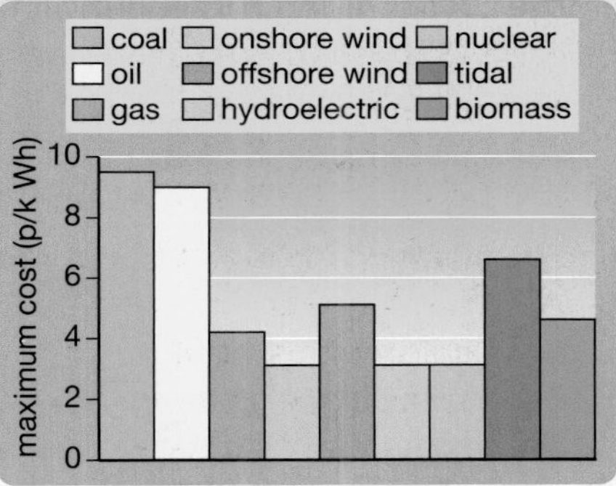

QUESTIONS

1 What is the most common energy source for electricity generation?

2 What percentage of electricity is generated using fossil fuels?

3 What percentage of electricity is generated using renewable energy resources?

4 Which type of electricity generation costs most?

5 Which type of renewable electricity generation costs most?

6 The government wants at least 20 per cent of electricity to be generated using renewable energy, by the year 2020. Using the information from the bar chart, discuss which type, or types, of power station you would replace with renewable electricity generation, and which types of renewable energy you would choose.

Exam practice

Exam practice questions

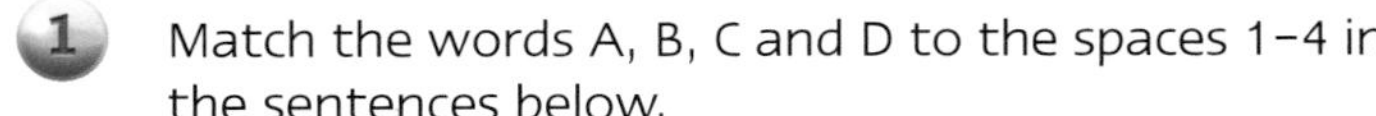

1 Match the words A, B, C and D to the spaces 1–4 in the sentences below.

A coal **B** hydroelectricity
C solar cells **D** uranium

An example of a fossil fuel is (1) . An example of a nuclear fuel is (2) . To produce electricity directly from the Sun, (3) can be used. A different renewable source of energy is (4) . [4]

2 Match the words A, B, C and D to the spaces 1–4 in the sentences below.

A boiler **B** generator
C jet of steam **D** turbine

Water is heated in the (1) which produces a (2) . This is used to spin the (3) , which in turn spins the (4) , changing kinetic energy into electrical energy. [4]

3 Match the words A, B, C and D to the spaces 1–4 in the sentences below.

A 1 **B** 10 **C** 100 **D** 1000

The efficiency of any appliance is never more than (1) %. The amount of energy transferred by a 4 kW appliance switched on for 15 minutes is (2) kWh. If the cost of using this energy is 10p, then one kWh costs (3) p. To convert watts into kilowatts, you must divide by (4) . [4]

In questions 4 to 7, choose the best answer.

4 The best absorber of infrared radiation is ...
A a matt white surface.
B a shiny white surface.
C a shiny black surface.
D a matt black surface. [1]

5 The National Grid ...
A uses step-up and step-down transformers to transfer electricity at high voltage.
B uses step-up transformers only to transfer electricity at high voltage.
C uses step-up and step down-transformers to transfer electricity at low voltage.
D uses step-down transformers only to transfer electricity at low voltage. [1]

6 Heat-transfer methods that involve particles are ...
A conduction and radiation.
B conduction and convection.
C convection and radiation.
D conduction, convection and radiation. [1]

7 The energy transfer that the battery in a torch is designed to do is ...
A electrical → light.
B chemical → light.
C chemical → electrical.
D electrical → light + heat. [1]

In questions 8 to 11, identify the answer that is **not correct**.

8 Nuclear fission ...
A takes place in solar cells.
B takes place in nuclear power stations.
C creates heat.
D is used to generate electricity. [1]

9 When a lamp is used ...
A some energy is transferred to its surroundings.
B electrical energy is transformed into heat and light.
C all of the electrical energy is usefully transformed.
D some of the electrical energy is usefully transformed [1]

10 A cup of tea cools down quicker if ...
A the tea is much hotter than its surroundings.
B the tea is cooler to start with.
C the cup is left in a draught.
D the cup is wide and shallow. [1]

11 Wind turbines ...
A cannot produce electricity if the wind speed is very low.
B do not produce gases linked with global warming.
C cannot produce electricity if the wind speed is very high.
D are a reliable way to generate electricity. [1]

12 The following table provides information about two types of light bulb.

	Filament bulb	Energy efficient bulb
Efficiency	4%	25%
Power	100 W	16 W
Cost when new	30p	£5.00
Lifetime	1 year	5 years

a Explain what is meant by 'efficiency'. [1]

b Each bulb is used for 1500 hours per year. Use this information to calculate the energy used by the filament bulb in a year in kilowatt-hours. [3]

c If each kilowatt-hour costs 8 p, calculate the total cost of using the filament bulb over five years. [2]

d The equivalent cost if energy efficient bulbs are used is less than £7. Give two reasons, apart from cost, why the use of energy efficient bulbs is being encouraged. [2]

13 Paramedics may wrap an injured person in an aluminium-coated survival blanket as they travel to hospital. This is designed to reduce several types of heat transfer.

a State the type of heat transfer reduced by choosing a silver colour. Explain how the choice of colour helps to reduce heat loss. [2]

b The blanket also reduces other forms of heat transfer. Complete the following table stating the type of heat transfer and how the blanket helps.

Method of heat transfer	How the blanket reduces this

[4]

14 There are plans to build a new power station near a large city. The choice is between an oil-fired power station or wind turbines set on nearby hills in a local beauty spot.

a Give one advantage and one disadvantage for each of these schemes.

Type of station	Advantage of the scheme	Disadvantage of the scheme
Oil-fired		
Wind turbines		

[4]

b Which scheme would you recommend and why? [2]

(Total 40 marks)

Worked example

Mayo leaves her radio on for 12 hours each night; Jim uses a microwave for 20 minutes to heat his meals. The power of the radio is 50 W, and the power of the microwave is 0.9 kW.

a Calculate the energy used in kWh:
i by Mayo
ii by Jim. [6]

b Explain why electricity is transferred from power stations at high voltages. [2]

a i 50 × 12 = 600 kWh ✓
ii 0.9 × 20 = 18 kWh ✓
b It reduces heat losses. ✓

In a) i the student has lost two marks. They should have converted watts to kilowatts (divide by 1000) so the answer is 0.6 kWh.

In a) ii the student has lost a further two marks. They should have converted time from minutes into hours (divide by 60) so the answer is 0.3 kWh. However, as the student showed working each time, they didn't lose all of the available marks.

The student gets one mark, but needs to write more for both marks. A better answer would have been: 'Increasing the voltage reduces the current. This means the wires heat up less. Less energy is lost as heat'.

Overall Grade: D

How to get an A

Always answer the question that is being asked, and be especially careful about units. If you show working, then the examiner will understand what you were trying to do and you will gain a few marks.

Physics 1b – Radiation and the universe

DISCOVER SOLAR ENERGY!

Huge solar panels can be placed in orbit around the Earth to capture the electromagnetic waves of visible light radiating from the Sun. The solar panels convert the energy carried by the electromagnetic waves into electricity.

The electrical energy from the solar panels can also be converted into laser light, which can be used to power vehicles working in orbit around the Earth. This can also provide the energy needs for the International Space Station.

The nuclear fusion of hydrogen in the Sun's core is virtually an endless source of energy. NASA scientists are developing methods of capturing some of this energy.

In space there is no atmosphere to block or absorb the Sun's electromagnetic radiation.

Electrical energy can be converted to microwaves and transmitted directly down to Earth. Microwave energy is then converted back to more useful forms of electrical and heat energy.

CONTENTS

Uses of electromagnetic radiation

You will find out:

- That electromagnetic radiation is a way of carrying energy
- That electromagnetic radiation is useful in many different ways

How energy travels through air

To get a good TV picture, you have to be in line with a transmission mast that sends the signal. In a deep valley with hills all round, you may not get a good TV picture. That tells us two things. The **wave** that carries the signal travels in a straight line. Also, the signal can move through the air, but if it reaches a hill, its energy is absorbed and goes no further.

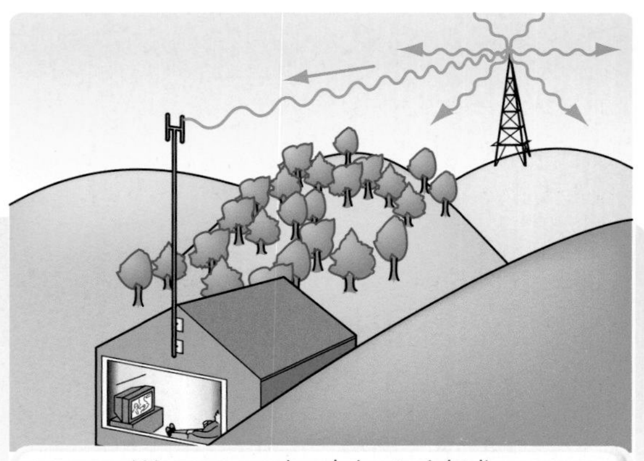

FIGURE 1: Waves carry signals in straight lines.

Invisible waves

TV and radio signals are carried by **electromagnetic radiation**. It is invisible, travels in waves at the speed of light and carries energy from one place to another. Electromagnetic radiation has a range – a **spectrum** – of energies. **Rays** with the greatest energy could cause us harm. But, handled carefully, we can make good use of the whole range.

Useful radiations

We use the energy of electromagnetic radiation for fun and to make living easier and more convenient. Some radiations save lives.

- **Radio waves** are low energy and are used for radio and TV.
- **Microwaves** are used in microwave ovens, and also for communications. A phone call to Australia uses a microwave signal bounced off satellites in space.
- **Infra red rays**. You feel these as radiant heat. The red glow of an electric bar heater is infra red.
- **Visible light** are the rays that enable us to see.
- **Ultraviolet rays** come from the Sun and give us a tan. Sun-beds use UV light to tan us artificially.
- **X-rays** have high energy. They are used to produce images of bones and teeth.
- **Gamma rays** have very high energy. They can kill cancer cells.

All electromagnetic waves can travel through air and through a vacuum (space) where there is no matter.

FIGURE 2: A thermogram reveals infra red radiation we cannot see.

ENERGY CAN'T BE SEEN

Like all energy, you can't see the energy of electromagnetic radiation. You know it's there only because it makes something happen.

QUESTIONS

1 List the different types of radiation. Give an example of how each is used in a helpful way.

2 Work in pairs to find other examples of good uses. Add them to your list.

3 Which are your top **three** most useful applications? What does your partner think?

...electromagnetic radiation ...gamma rays ...infra red rays ...microwaves

More about radiation and its uses

There is a range of radio waves with different energies. The lowest waves broadcast, national radio medium waves, carry local radio and police and ambulance messages, and the highest waves are for TV.

As well as in cooking, microwaves are used for telecommunications. Signals are transmitted between the ground and satellites in space. Police radar speed traps also use microwaves.

Anything warm gives off infra red rays, including humans, so infra red is used to make thermogram images. A person can be 'seen' when trapped in a collapsed or smoke-filled building, or if on the run at night, or breaking into a house. In medicine, a thermogram detects arthritis and cancer, because these parts of the body are warmer.

Visible light comes from the Sun, fluorescent lamps and lasers. We call it 'visible' because we can see its source and everything that absorbs it when it reaches them.

Ultraviolet (UV) rays come from very hot objects including welding equipment and the Sun.

X-rays and gamma rays are dangerous to body cells and so must be used carefully. X-ray images show when bones are broken, teeth decaying and lungs diseased. Radioactive substances, including uranium, produce gamma rays. They are used to sterilise food by killing bacteria. They are also used to kill cancer cells and in industry to check for faults and cracks in pipelines.

FIGURE 3: Using microwaves to detect speeding motorists.

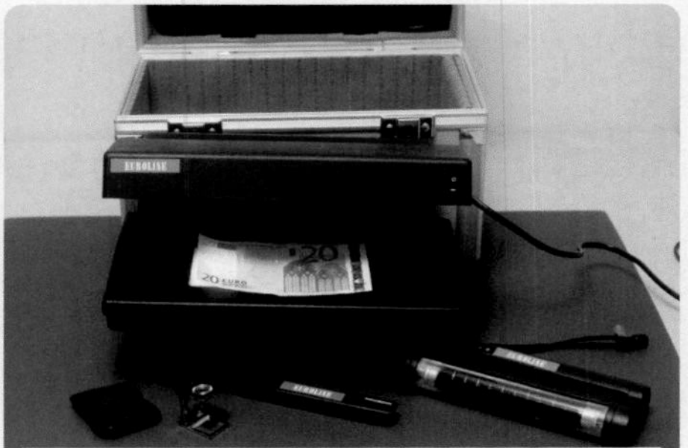

FIGURE 4: UV light is useful for checking bank notes for forgeries.

QUESTIONS

4 How can infrared rays be used to find people trapped in collapsed buildings?

5 As a group, discuss the safety measures we must take when using gamma rays.

6 What property of gamma rays makes them suitable for sterilising food?

WHITER THAN WHITE

Some fluorescent chemicals absorb UV light and re-emit it as white light. Clothes with special dyes that emit UV light make our clothes look 'brighter than bright' in the sunlight.

Security

Airport security makes sure that millions of passengers fly in safety. You may have passed through an airport security area. You put your baggage on a conveyor belt where it is X-rayed. Airport staff can see an image of the object on a screen. Also, passport control staff will check for illegal passports by exposing them to UV rays.

FIGURE 5: Airport security detects a gun in a suitcase.

An infra red burglar alarm picks up on an intruder by sensing their body heat. A laser beam acts as an invisible light 'trip wire': if the beam is broken it sets off the alarm.

Art galleries X-ray paintings to make sure that they are not forgeries. Banks use UV light to check for forged banknotes.

QUESTIONS

7 Describe ways that airport security ensures passenger safety.

8 How might you protect a valuable diamond necklace on display at an exhibition?

9 What can you do to check for forgeries?

Electromagnetic spectrum: 1

You will find out:

- That electromagnetic radiation travels in waves
- That wavelength, frequency and energy are connected

Building up the radiation picture

In 1666, Isaac Newton shone white light through a prism and revealed the seven colours of the **visible spectrum**.

In the 19th century, Herschel discovered infra red rays and then Ritter discovered ultraviolet rays. Maxwell calculated the speed of the rays. It was the same as the speed of light.

Hertz invented equipment that made low-energy **electromagnetic** waves. He found they travelled through air and could be picked up by a detector some way away. He called them 'radio waves'. His discovery made him the pioneer of radio communication.

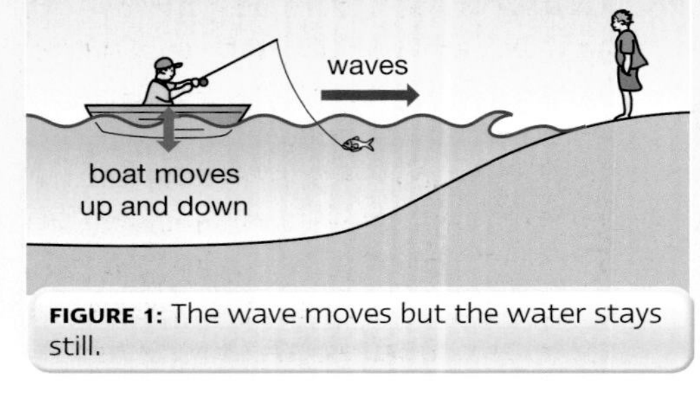

FIGURE 1: The wave moves but the water stays still.

Electromagnetic radiation

Electromagnetic radiation travels as waves that carry energy from place to place. The waves move in straight lines and all travel at the same speed in a vacuum (in space). The material they travel through does not move with them.

Imagine waves on the sea. Standing on the beach, you can see the waves rolling towards you and finally breaking on the shore. Oddly, the surface of the water is not moving towards you. You see a boat just offshore bob up and down, but it does not move forwards with the wave. In the same way, the electromagnetic wave carries energy forwards, but what it moves through stays still.

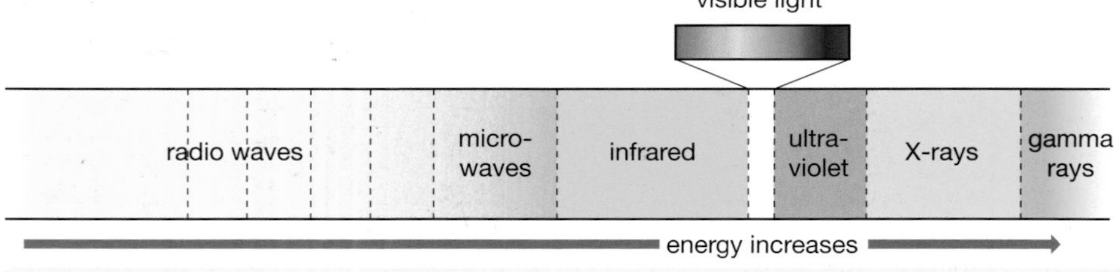

FIGURE 2: The electromagnetic spectrum.

We have seen that different radiations carry different amounts of energy. The electromagnetic spectrum gives the full range of radiations.

EXAM HINTS AND TIPS

Remember:

The shorter the wavelength, the higher the frequency.

The longer the wavelength, the lower the frequency.

The higher the frequency, the higher the energy.

QUESTIONS

1. In what form does electromagnetic radiation travel? How fast does it go and what does it carry?
2. Describe what the electromagnetic spectrum shows.
3. Make up a simple rhyme to remember the order of wave types in the electromagnetic spectrum

...alternating current ...amplified ...current ...electric charges ...electromagnetic

All about waves

As the electromagnetic spectrum in figure 4 shows, waves have different energies. Scientists can measure the length of a wave. This is its **wavelength**. It is measured in metres (m). The shorter the wavelength, the higher the energy it has.

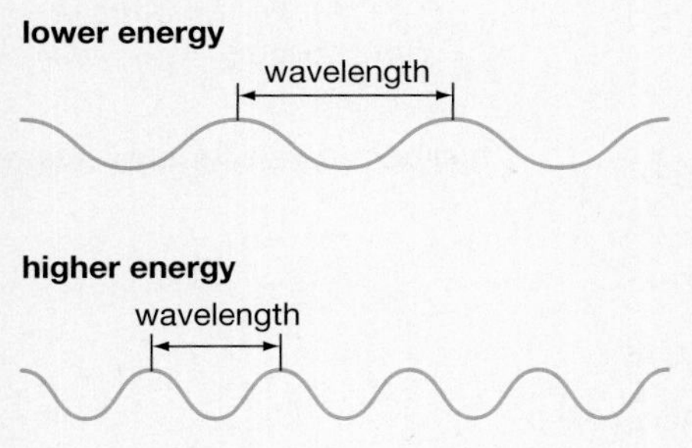

FIGURE 3: Wavelength, frequency and energy are linked.

If we could see a wave moving, we could count the number of waves passing a particular point in a second. That number is its **frequency**. It is measured in hertz (Hz). The greater the frequency of a wave, the higher the energy it has.

We can now adapt the electromagnetic spectrum to include wavelength and frequency.

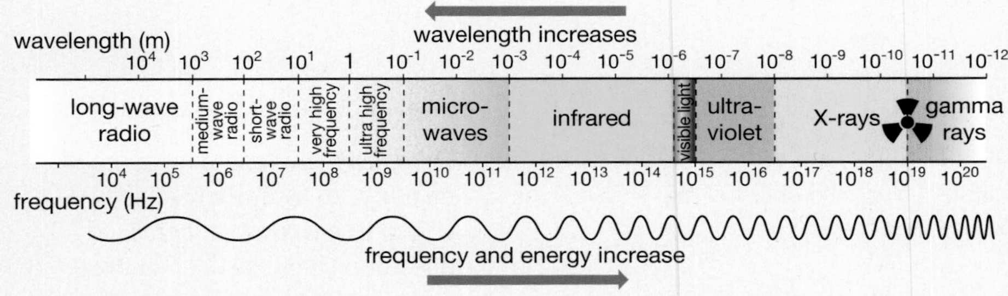

FIGURE 4: The electromagnetic spectrum with wavelengths and frequencies.

Comparing electronic waves with sound waves

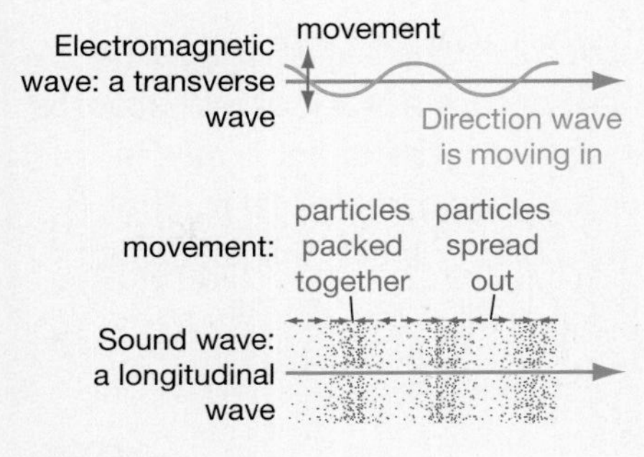

FIGURE 5: Transverse and longitudinal waves.

Electromagnetic waves move either side of the direction they travel in and are, therefore, **transverse waves**.

Like electromagnetic waves, sound waves carry energy. (When it reaches our ears, the energy in a sound wave is converted to an electrical signal that reaches our brain.) Unlike an electromagnetic wave, a sound wave travels because air particles are first packed together and then spread out along the direction of travel. They are therefore called **longitudinal waves**.

QUESTIONS

4 What is the relationship between energy and frequency?

5 What is electromagnetic radiation? Describe its features and characteristics.

6 List the different types of electromagnetic radiation in descending order of frequency.

7 What is the link between wavelength, frequency and energy?

Transmitting and receiving electromagnetic radiation

Imagine a wire with an electrical **current** in it. Electricity can go in one direction – direct current. But it can also go backwards and forwards – oscillate – as in the **alternating current** of our domestic electricity supply. At the sub-atomic level, **electric charges** (electrons) oscillate in the wire.

This oscillation produces electromagnetic radiation that is transmitted away from the wire. The speed at which the electric charges oscillate becomes the frequency of the electromagnetic radiation transmitted.

This process works in reverse. A wire antenna can receive radiation transmitted by an oscillating electric charge. The radiation travels through air or space, enters the metal of the antenna, and small electric alternating currents are formed. These are collected, **amplified** (the signal is strengthened) and converted to the TV pictures we see on our screens.

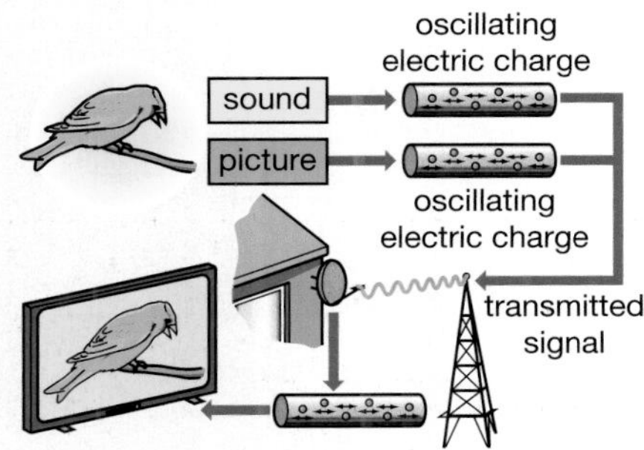

FIGURE 6: Transmitting and receiving a TV signal.

QUESTIONS

8 Describe how electromagnetic radiation is generated.

9 Discuss how TV images are transmitted from a studio to your home.

Electromagnetic spectrum: 2

You will find out:

- That visible light is one type of electromagnetic radiation
- That the colour of an object depends on the wavelengths it reflects and absorbs

Light, a wave or a particle?

The Ancient Greeks had two opposing theories about how we see things. Empedocles said that light rays from our eyes touch any object we look at. Plato thought that every object radiated light rays that entered our eyes.

Francesco Grimaldi, in 1665, first spoke of light as a form of wave. In 1704, Isaac Newton said that light behaved as if it were a particle. Einstein showed that light could 'knock' electrons off a metal surface - a particle property. He called light 'particles' photons. Louis de Broglie brought the two ideas together: light has the properties of both **particles** and **waves**. This idea became known as **wave-particle duality**.

Looking at colour

Electromagnetic radiation is not all the same. Think of it as a group of different types of radiation, with a different set of wavelengths in each type. Together, they make up the **electromagnetic spectrum**.

Radiation from the Sun, or a bulb or fluorescent lamp, includes a set of rays whose wavelengths are in the range we can see - the **visible range**. This means that when these rays reach an object, the object **reflects** them, and our eyes see the reflected rays. We say we 'see the object'.

If an object reflects all the rays in the visible range, we see it as white. If the object **absorbs** all but the red rays, we see only the reflected red rays, and the object looks red. If no rays are reflected, we see a black object. It has absorbed all the rays.

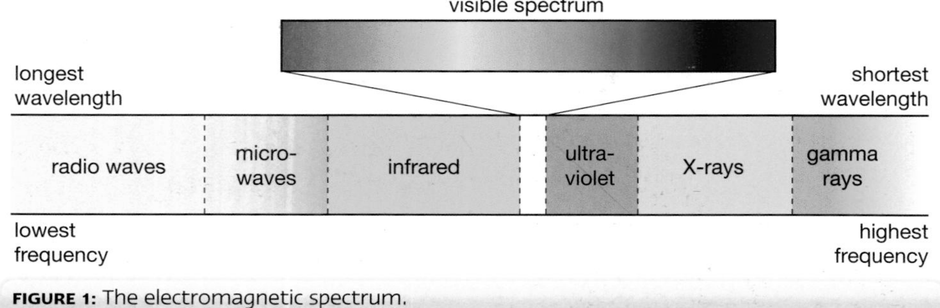

FIGURE 1: The electromagnetic spectrum.

QUESTIONS

1. Recall the rhyme you made to remember the order of wave types.
2. Which type of radiation allows us to see?
3. Which type has the longest wavelength? The highest frequency?
4. Decide whether this statement is true: Ultraviolet rays have more energy than infra red rays.

SPEED OF LIGHT

Galileo was the first to measure the speed of light. He flashed a lantern to an assistant across a measured distance. Galileo was intrigued. No matter how far the distance, the speed was always the same.

Remember that light rays carry energy. Since a black object absorbs all wavelengths of light, all the energy is transferred to it. That is why a black object in the Sun gets hotter than a white one.

FIGURE 2: Raindrops reflect the spectrum of colours in visible light.

...absorbs ...electromagnetic spectrum ...formula ...particles

Radiation types merge into each other

Visible light is only a small part of the electromagnetic spectrum. Our eyes just happen to be sensitive to this narrow range of energies.

We describe white light as being made up of the seven rainbow colours. But where does one colour finish and the next begin? There is no exact point: the colours merge into each other. The visible spectrum gradually appears in the infra red region and fades out through the ultraviolet.

The same applies for the whole of the electromagnetic spectrum. As wavelengths and frequencies gradually change, so do their properties. It is each range with similar properties that we group together and identify as a type of radiation.

The electromagnetic spectrum is, therefore, continuous, but we identify various types by banding together similar wavelengths, each with its own characteristic properties and uses. The table shows the characteristics of each band within the electromagnetic spectrum,

Wave type	Wavelength	Sources	Detectors
Gamma rays	10^{-12} m	Radioactive nuclei	Geiger-Müller tube
X-rays	10^{-10} m	X-ray tubes	Geiger-Müller tube
Ultraviolet	10^{-7} m	Sun, very hot objects	Photographic film; Fluorescent chemical
Visible light	0.0005 mm	Hot objects, Sun, lasers, LEDs	Eyes; Photographic film
Infra red	0.1 mm	Warm or hot objects	Skin; Thermometer
Microwaves	1-10 cm	Radar, microwave ovens	Aerial; Mobile phone
Radio waves	10-1000+ m	Radio transmitters	Aerial; TV; Radio

QUESTIONS

5 Suggest how each type of radiation is identified.

6 Make a list of the types and note key information (including wave length) about each wave type.

LONG WAVES

Long-wave radio waves can be more than a kilometre long.

Properties of all electromagnetic waves

We have seen that:

- the frequency of a wave = the number of waves travelling past a point in a second
- the wavelength is the distance from peak to peak.

We also know that:

- all electromagnetic waves travel at the same speed.

Therefore we can write a **formula** which enables us to find the frequency or wavelength of any wave:

wave speed = **frequency** × **wavelength**

(metre per second, m/s) **(hertz, Hz)** **(metre, m)**

Summary

- Electromagnetic waves transfer energy from one place to another.
- They can travel through a vacuum.
- They all travel at the same speed: 300 000 000 m/s in a vacuum.
- Wave speed = frequency × wavelength
- The higher the frequency (the shorter the wavelength), the more energy they carry and the more dangerous they are.
- Electromagnetic waves are transverse waves.

QUESTIONS

7 Working in groups, make a poster that highlights the key properties of electromagnetic waves.

Waves and matter

You will find out:

- That electromagnetic radiation can be reflected, absorbed or transmitted by matter
- That whether radiation is absorbed depends on its wavelength and the type of matter

Bounce, be absorbed or go right through?

When an electromagnetic wave reaches an object, it can bounce off, be absorbed or pass right through. It depends on how much energy the wave has.

We see the world because visible light rays bounce off objects and reach our eyes, where the retina in each eye absorbs the energy.

Glass and Perspex let light pass through. They are **transparent**. Black objects absorb the light waves completely. They are **opaque**. 'Black' is when no light energy reaches our eyes. So is black a colour?

How electromagnetic waves behave

Electromagnetic radiation travels as waves. They bounce off – are **reflected** – from particular kinds of surfaces including shiny ones, like waves in the bath bouncing off either end.

Try this experiment with the infra red remote TV control. Can you switch channels by pointing the control away from the TV? Now use a mirror to reflect the infra red waves back at the TV.

Materials **absorb** energy in different ways.

- Standing by a radiator or electric fire, you absorb infra red radiation (radiant heat) and begin to feel warm.
- Food in a microwave oven absorbs the energy of the microwaves and heats up.
- Dark surfaces tend to absorb a large range of waves, including light waves.

Radiation with very short wavelengths, like X-rays and gamma rays, can also pass right through objects because short waves tend not to transfer their energy to the particles of the objects.

FIGURE 1: The mirror reflects the infra red wave and the TV absorbs it.

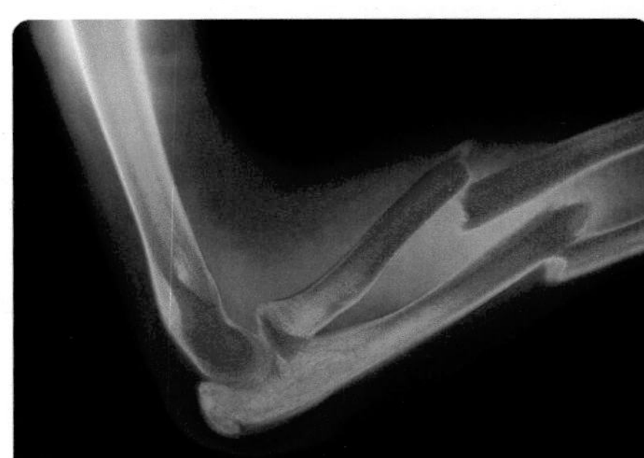

FIGURE 2: Most X-rays are transmitted through soft tissue, but bone absorbs them.

QUESTIONS

1. Give an example of when electromagnetic radiation is **a)** reflected and **b)** absorbed.
2. When would you need to take care if a surface begins to absorb electromagnetic radiation?
3. Which types of radiation can pass right through solid objects?
4. In the experiment with the remote control and the mirror, what do you think would happen if you covered the mirror with a black cloth? Explain your answer.

DEEP HEAT

Infra red radiation can penetrate body tissues and is used to heal deep muscle damage in injured athletes and footballers.

...absorb ...frequency ...gamma rays ...infra red ...microwaves ...opaque ...radio waves ...reflected

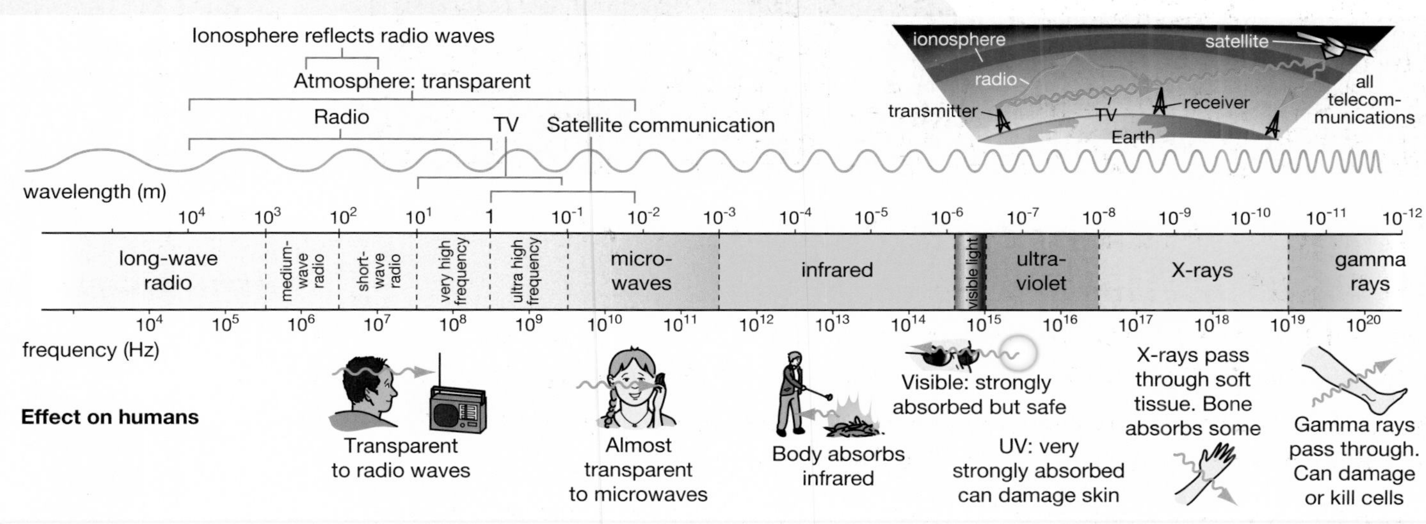

FIGURE 3: How waves across the spectrum behave.

How waves and materials interact

Whether radiation is reflected, absorbed or transmitted by an object depends both on the energy that the wave carries and on the type of material.

For a material to absorb a wave, and not to reflect or transmit it, the wave's energy has to match the range of energies which that material can absorb.

Figure 3 shows examples of how different waves interact with the atmosphere and with our bodies.

- **Radio waves** transmit through the atmosphere, but the ionosphere reflects some. All can be bounced by a series of transmitters and receivers round the world. Buildings and people are largely transparent to radio waves.
- **Microwaves** can transmit through the atmosphere and are used for telecommunications. They are absorbed only very slightly by humans. The water molecules in food absorb them: they vibrate more vigorously and heat up.
- **Infra red** is absorbed by human tissues to a limited depth.
- **Visible light** is strongly absorbed at the body surface but heats it only slightly.
- **Ultraviolet rays** are absorbed by our bodies. The shortest wavelength rays can do damage by ionising atoms in skin tissues.
- **X-rays**: soft tissues of our bodies are transparent to them, but bones absorb some radiation. X-rays can ionise tissue atoms.
- **Gamma rays** transmit through our bodies, and nearly everything else except lead. Gamma rays with very high energies can ionise atoms in human tissue.

QUESTIONS

5 Give examples of how different electromagnetic waves are reflected, absorbed and transmitted.

6 Why should you be careful with medium wavelength radiation?

7 Why do we have to be very careful with high frequency radiations?

Using the wave equation

We looked at the wave equation in the last spread, and now let's use it.

	Symbol	Unit
Speed	v (upsilon)	m/s
Wavelength	λ (lambda)	m
Frequency	f	Hz

The equation for the speed of a wave is:

wave speed = frequency × **wavelength**

$$v = f \times \lambda$$

Worked example: What is the speed of a sound wave with a frequency of 500 Hz and a wavelength of 0.75 m?

f = 500 Hz, λ = 0.75 m

QUESTIONS

8 What is the speed of a sound wave with a wavelength of 0.8 m and a frequency of 415 Hz?

9 A radio station transmits radio waves of frequency 150 000 Hz and a wavelength of 2000 m. What is the speed of radio waves?

10 BBC Radio 1 transmits on a wavelength of 285 m. What is the transmission frequency? (Check out the answer from Q9.)

Dangers of radiation

You will find out:

- That different types of electromagnetic radiation carry different hazards
- That there are ways to protect ourselves from these hazards

Danger or benefit?

Is **high-energy radiation** bad or good? Well, it's both. It depends on how we use it.

Strong **microwaves** can boil water, and we are about 2/3 (66%) water. **Infra red** can severely burn us. **Ultraviolet** can damage cells and cause skin cancer. X-rays and **gamma rays** penetrate deeply, damage and destroy cells, and even cause mutations that grow into tumours.

To balance that, all telecommunications depend on microwaves to carry information around the world. And doctors use infra red, **X-rays** and gamma rays to treat disorders and save lives.

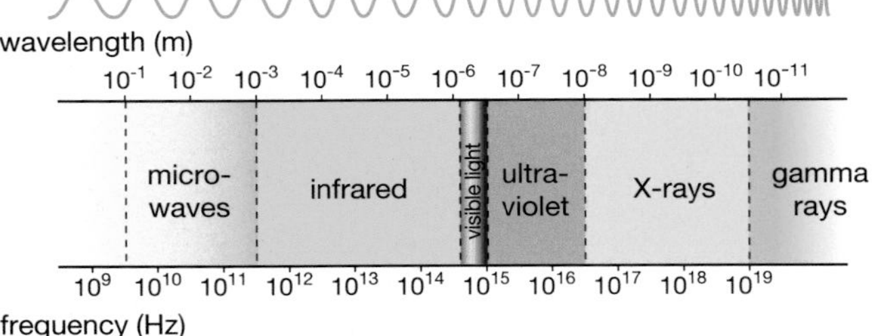

FIGURE 1: The high-energy end of the spectrum.

Protection from the danger

Microwave ovens cook by heating the water molecules in food. We are mostly water, so microwave ovens are designed to trap the waves inside and to start only when the door is closed.

The infra red radiation from a bonfire keeps us warm, but the soft tissue of our skin could be severely burnt if we stay close too long.

We need the Sun's ultraviolet rays to produce Vitamin D in our skin to form healthy bones that do not bend as they grow. But if the radiation is too strong and for too long, the same ultraviolet rays can damage the skin cells. Very high **doses** even cause skin cancer. This is why it is wise to use lots of sun-block in strong sun.

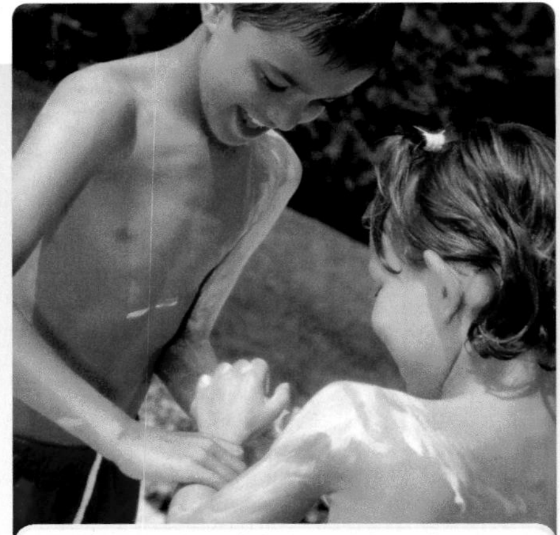

FIGURE 2: You can't have too much sun-block in strong sunshine.

Radiographers (operators of hospital X-ray equipment) wear a lead apron and stand behind a lead-glass screen. Only thick lead and concrete will stop gamma rays. Both types of radiation damage cells by ionising cell molecules. They are finely focused on the patient so as to kill cancer cells only. Radiation doses are very carefully controlled, for the safety of both patients and hospital staff.

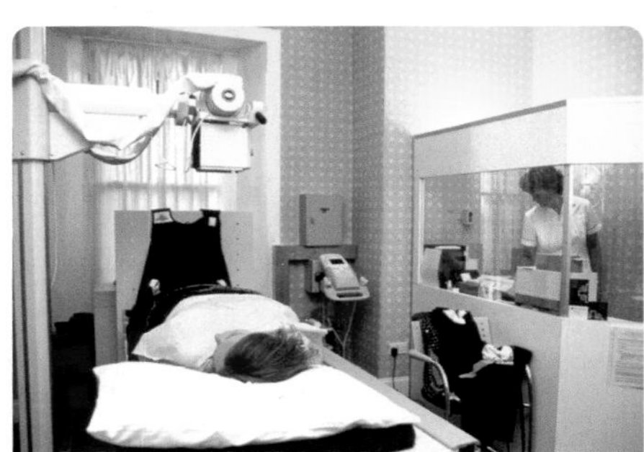

FIGURE 3: The radiographer stands behind a lead glass screen to protect herself.

QUESTIONS

1 Why can high frequency radiations be dangerous?

2 Why is staying out in the Sun for too long not good for you? How should you protect yourself?

3 How do radiographers protect themselves from dangerous gamma and X-rays?

4 Mobile phones work by using microwaves. Some people claim that using mobile phones could be dangerous. Can you suggest why?

...dose ...gamma rays ...high energy ...high-energy radiation ...infra red ...ionising

More about the dangers

Some microwaves pass through soft tissues, while some are absorbed by water molecules which heat up. Effects depend on the wavelength and the strength of the radiation.

Infra red radiation is absorbed by the skin and we detect it as heat. Too much can cause serious skins burns.

Visible light is the only part of the electromagnetic spectrum we can see. Though visible light does no harm to our bodies, very strong, bright light can damage the retina of our eyes, which is why we don't look directly at the Sun.

The dividing cells below the skin surface absorb the energy of ultraviolet radiation. If these cells die, skin is not replaced and becomes old and wrinkled. Too much exposure to ultraviolet can also cause skin cancer. (The pigment in darker skin gives some protection.) The ozone layer absorbs much of the Sun's ultraviolet radiation, but this layer is thinning.

FIGURE 4: Protective glasses are the only safe way to view a solar eclipse.

X-rays can easily penetrate soft body tissue, but are partially absorbed by denser substances like bone. An X-ray image is formed when sensitive film collects the rays that go through the patient.

When the nuclei of radioactive atoms break up, they give off extremely **high energy** as gamma rays. They are very penetrating. Nuclear power stations use very thick lead and concrete shields to absorb gamma radiation.

Unless carefully controlled, X-rays and gamma rays can kill or severely damage body cells.

OZONE LAYER

Fuel exhaust from air travel is the major reason why the ozone layer is thinning and allowing more of the Sun's ultraviolet rays to reach the Earth.

QUESTIONS

5 Make a table. List each type of high frequency radiation. Add a second column for their hazards, and a third to say how to protect yourself from exposure to each type.

6 Why is it dangerous to stay out in the hot summer sun for too long? How should we protect ourselves?

7 Which part of the electromagnetic spectrum is the only part visible to us? Can it be dangerous?

8 Microwaves are very useful, but why should we treat them with care?

RADIATION DOSE

The dose depends on the intensity of the radiation and the length of time of exposure.

The unit of radiation = rad

Mutations

Ultraviolet, X-rays and gamma rays are called **ionising** radiations. They have enough energy to penetrate our cells and kill or damage them.

If radiation hits the DNA molecules in the nucleus of a cell, it can damage the DNA structure. The cell may be killed outright. But, if the DNA is only slightly damaged, the cell will continue to divide, but with an altered genetic code. The new cells are a **mutation**, meaning they are changed. These mutated cells can divide out of control and form a cancerous **tumour**. If this spreads, it is known as **malignant**.

The chance of this happening depends on the type of radiation and the size of the dose. This depends on the strength (intensity) of the radiation and the exposure time. The bigger the radiation dose, the more likely it is that mutated cells will develop into a cancer.

QUESTIONS

9 Mutations occur regularly in nature and some help species to develop and survive. Are mutations caused by ionising radiation equally beneficial? What are the key points of this issue? In a small group, prepare a list of points. Discuss them, and protective measures that can be taken to avoid the dangers.

Telecommunications

You will find out:

- That radio waves, microwaves, infra red and visible light are used for communication
- That satellites in space give us instant communication across the world

Communications

'**Telecommunications**' means making connections over long distances – something we do all the time. Mobile phones have all but replaced telephone boxes which were joined by thousands of kilometres of wires. We talk instantly to friends and relations all over the world as if they were just next door. The signal is of a far better quality than from the old copper wire landlines. From all over the world, TV gives us high-quality pictures and we find information on the Internet. Many banks send their daily details to India. It is processed overnight, and is on the banks' computers the next day.

FIGURE 1: Satellites receive and transmit messages worldwide, and with space exploration probes.

Entertainment and information

Long ago, word messages were sent in Morse code in the form of a light beam turned on and off. Today, the energy of electromagnetic waves can be made into a **digital signal** carrying far more information, very clearly and at the speed of light.

All modern telecommunications use some form of electromagnetic radiation. Radio waves carry local radio, police bands and TV. Microwaves are used for mobile phones, radar and transmission to satellites in space. Infra red and visible (laser) rays are used to pulse digital information along **fibre optic** cables.

Fibre optic cables supply cable TV programmes. New technology gives us interactive TV, so you can choose the programme, pause live TV, record shows, and even order a pizza on line.

Most people have access to the Internet. E-mail transmits and receives our messages almost instantaneously. With broadband we can download information in seconds. A web-cam enables you to hear and see the person you are speaking to.

A mobile phone sends text messages and takes and transmits images. The new 3G technology will make videophones commonplace.

FIGURE 2: Radio waves help keep emergency and security services in touch.

QUESTIONS

1. Describe the wavelengths of radiations that are used in telecommunications, locally and worldwide.
2. Name the different types in this range of radiations, and describe the different types of communication each is used for.
3. What type of signal carries information through an optical fibre?
4. Describe how cable TV programmes reach homes.

ATLANTIC CROSSING

TAT-8 was the first fibre optic transatlantic cable. It went into service in 1988.

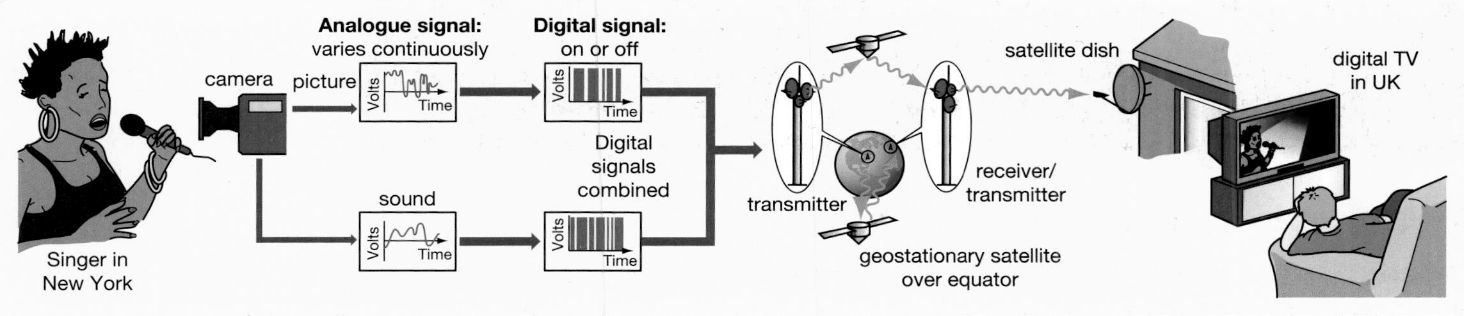

FIGURE 3: How a satellite TV programme travels.

Space technology

Microwave, digital and optical fibre technologies have all been combined to give us today's telecommunications systems. Microwaves travel in straight lines through the atmosphere and give a very sharp signal. We can connect to the other side of the world in milliseconds. **Communications satellites** including Intelsat and Satcom1 are **geostationary satellites** that stay over the same ground position and receive and transmit digital signals across the world.

Tall radio towers carry 'line-of-sight' microwave communications across cities, and transmit international calls via satellite. Today if you have a customer query, you might end up speaking to a call centre in the Far East, all for the cost of a local call.

Most large cities no longer use land lines for their telephone networks: it is just too expensive to keep digging up roads and laying cables.

E-commerce is the way to do business on the web. For example, Amazon.com has been selling books, music and video successfully for years. As time goes on, supermarkets and trading companies will sell more of their goods on line.

On TV, you see news as it happens. Correspondents give live reports from war zones and disaster areas via direct satellite hook-ups. The government doesn't want young people to miss out. All schools have internet access to 'National Grid for Learning'. NGfL provides websites that offer high quality content and information.

Modern radar and computer technology is so hi-tec that it can guide an Airbus jet through the roughest weather and land it automatically, even in thick fog when the pilot cannot see the runway.

FIGURE 4: Toronto's CN Tower, at 553 m, one of the tallest communications towers.

QUESTIONS

5 Why are microwaves used for telecommunications?

6 Describe how you receive satellite TV into your home.

7 Why are digital signals used in telecommunications?

Communications satellites

Geostationary satellites are used for all kinds of telecommunications. (They are also called geosynchronous satellites.) They stay above the same point on the ground, usually over the Equator, and appear to hang in space. In reality, they are orbiting at the same rate as the Earth – one orbit every 24 hours. The satellites are positioned far from the Earth, at a height of 36 000 km, about three times the diameter of the Earth away.

QUESTIONS

8 Why do telecommunications satellites appear to be stationary in space?

9 Can you suggest reasons why telecommunications satellites need to be in geostationary orbit?

10 Research other types of artificial satellites and their purpose. Are they all geostationary? Explain.

...geostationary satellite ...telecommunications

Fibre optics: digital signals

You will find out:

- That optical fibres are ideal information carriers
- That digital signals have advantages over analogue signals

Perfect partners

When you use a digital camera, light rays from the scene reach millions of tiny areas on a memory card in the camera. Each area develops a different electrical charge. The camera instantly scans the charges, producing a sequence of **digital signals**. You can then press 'view' to convert the signals to the image.

Telecommunications cables contain **optical fibres** – fine flexible glass threads. Each fibre can carry thousands of messages together at the speed of light. If you send your photo to a friend's computer, it will be crisp and clear. The new technologies of 'digital' and fibre optics work together perfectly.

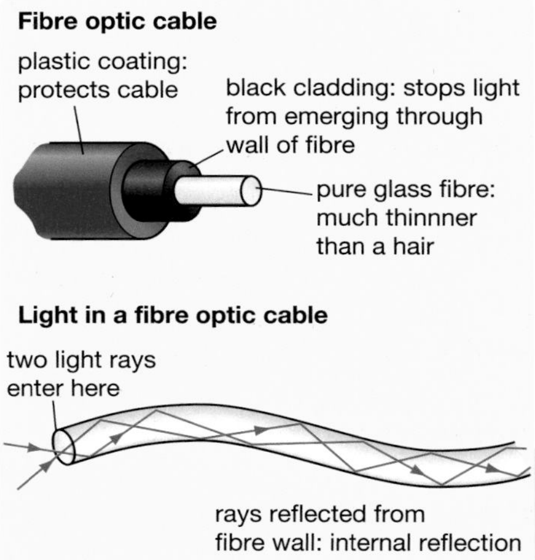

Fibre optic cable

plastic coating: protects cable

black cladding: stops light from emerging through wall of fibre

pure glass fibre: much thinnner than a hair

Light in a fibre optic cable

two light rays enter here

rays reflected from fibre wall: internal reflection

FIGURE 1: Fibre optic cables carry information for phones, cable TV and computers.

Optical fibres

Optical fibres are very fine, long, flexible threads of pure glass. A **pulse** of light shone at one end of a glass thread travels inside, through to the other end.

All telecommunications systems use laser light (infra red and visible light) to pulse digital signals over long and short distances. Landline telephone conversations and cable TV broadcasts reach your home through an underground optical fibre. When you access the Internet using broadband, the information comes to you by laser pulses through optical fibres.

Digital signals

TV and telephone signals once travelled as analogue signals. Electrical signals in copper wires would interfere with each other and give poor quality sound and vision. Today, everything is going digital. The big advantage of digital is quality. There is no interference or loss of strength in a digital signal travelling in an optical fibre.

CD players provide quality music sound using laser light and digital technology. This has also revolutionised the games industry. The Nintendo DS provides touch screen technology and wireless connection, and 3D virtual reality games put the player right in the middle of the action.

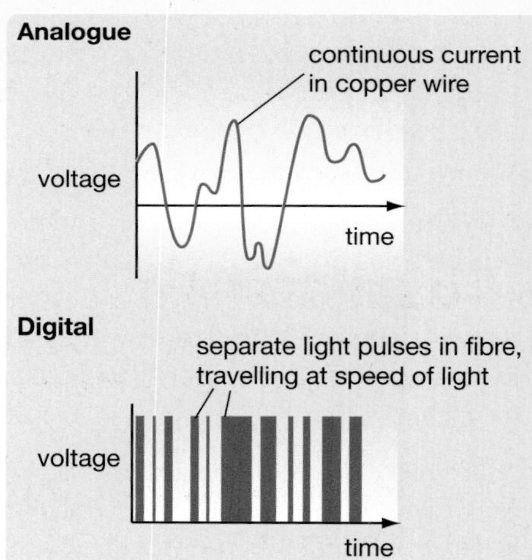

FIGURE 2: Analogue and digital signals shown as voltages.

QUESTIONS

1. What are optical fibres made from? How do they work?
2. Give **two** examples of how optical fibres are used in industry.
3. What shape are digital signals? Suggest why digital is replacing analogue.
4. Give an example of digital technology being used in the home.

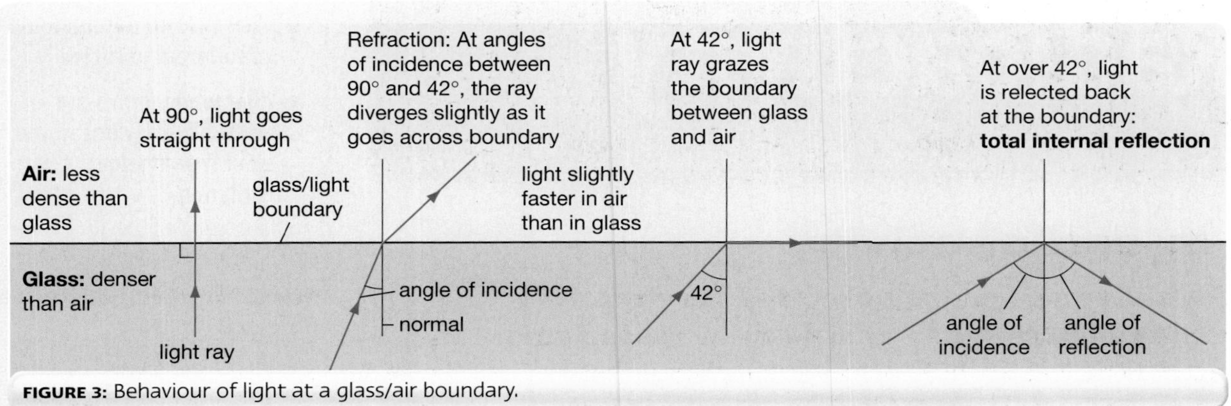
Refraction: At angles of incidence between 90° and 42°, the ray diverges slightly as it goes across boundary
At 42°, light ray grazes the boundary between glass and air
At over 42°, light is relected back at the boundary: **total internal reflection**
At 90°, light goes straight through
Air: less dense than glass
glass/light boundary
light slightly faster in air than in glass
Glass: denser than air
angle of incidence
normal
42°
light ray
angle of incidence
angle of reflection

FIGURE 3: Behaviour of light at a glass/air boundary.

Total internal reflection

Figure 3 shows how a beam of light inside an optical fibre behaves at the boundary with air. Follow it carefully. When the **angle of incidence** reaches the **critical angle** of 42°, the beam grazes the boundary. At greater angles there is **total internal reflection** of the light ray.

FIGURE 4: The base of the stomach, leading to the duodenum, seen through an endoscope.

Fibre optics

Optical fibres are very fine strands of pure silica glass. Light can travel along them, even if they are bent. Black cladding prevents the light from escaping. The light reflects internally until it emerges from the other end.

In commercial fibre optics, infra red and visual laser light rays transmit digital signals close to the speed of light. The signal remains pure, and over long distances the signal is boosted every kilometre or so to maintain its signal strength. Fibre optics are also used in medicine. Doctors use an endoscope to look inside your body and to perform keyhole surgery.

Analogue or digital?

The old telephone, radio and TV signals used to be analogue – a continuously variable electrical signal seen in figure 2 as a wave. Digital signals are simpler – rectangular pulses which are either on or off. Optical signals do not have the interference that electrical signals in adjacent cables had, so quality is far better – ideal for transmitting the accurate signals that computers require. Thousands of signals can go simultaneously down the same fibre.

Other advantages are: optical fibre cables are far cheaper than the old copper wire cables used for electrical signals; the cables do not heat up, so there is no fire hazard; being thinner, you can pack far more optical fibres into the same diameter of cable; the cable is lighter than copper cabling.

QUESTIONS

5 Explain the optical properties that make optical fibres so good for transmitting signals.

6 What is the main difference between an analogue and a digital signal?

7 What are the key advantages of digital over analogue signals?

'IT'S GOOD TO TALK'

One strand of optical fibre can handle up to 10 000 telephone conversations all at the same time.

Digital technology

Digital technology has crept into every part of our lives. Digital TV gives excellent quality pictures and allows you to be interactive.

Digital cameras are fast replacing traditional film equipment. You can download an image into a PC and crop, enhance, airbrush and edit the picture.

Smart ID cards are being developed. They can be a passport, national insurance card and driving licence all in one. The card could also hold biometric data like an eye retina scan and voice scan for unique identification and security. All of this data would be held digitally in the tiny chip.

QUESTIONS

8 Choose a topic connected with this spread that you want to know more about, and use the Internet to prepare a two-minute talk on it.

...optical fibre ...pulse ...total internal reflection

Radioactivity

You will find out:

- That the atom is made up of different particles
- That when atoms are unstable, they decay and emit high energy radiation

Pioneers in radioactivity

With her husband, Marie Curie won the Nobel Prize for Physics in 1903 for her work on **radioactivity**. In 1906, Marie was appointed the first woman lecturer at the Sorbonne in Paris, famous for its teaching and research. This was a great honour for a woman at the time.

There she continued to investigate ways to use radium for curing cancer. In 1911 she received a second Nobel Prize. Sadly, she died in 1934 from leukaemia, a cancer of the blood, due to overexposure to radiation.

FIGURE 1: Marie Curie and her husband, Pierre.

Structure of an atom

Scientists used to think of atoms as the most basic building blocks of matter that could not be broken down into anything smaller. Now we know atoms contain smaller particles. An atom has a small central nucleus made up of **protons** and **neutrons**, surrounded by **electrons**.

Isotopes

Atoms of an element always have the same number of protons and electrons. But some atoms have a different number of neutrons. When this varies, the different atoms of that element are called isotopes.

Some isotopes are stable, while others are **unstable** and can break down or decay. A very tiny amount of matter is converted to energy, which leaves the nucleus as particles and rays. This is called **radiation**.

As an example, the nucleus of a normal carbon atom, carbon-12, has 6 protons and 6 neutrons. An isotope called carbon-14 has 6 protons and 8 neutrons in the nucleus. It is unstable because it has too many neutrons. So when it decays, a neutron becomes a proton plus a beta particle (a high speed electron). The stable form of nitrogen is formed.

carbon-14 → nitrogen-15 + beta particle

This reaction happens naturally and the energy from it is not dangerous.

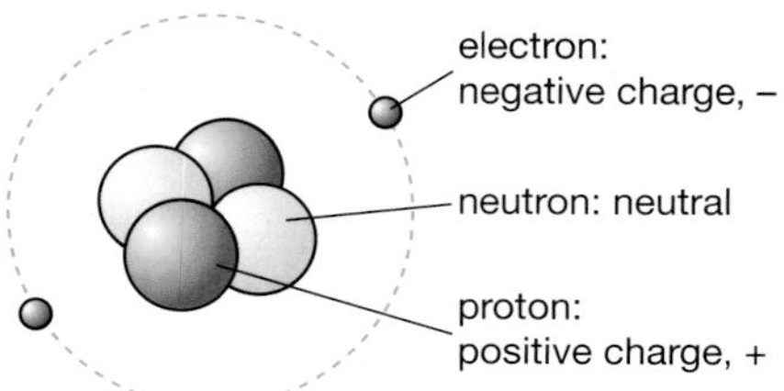

FIGURE 2: Structure of a helium atom.

QUESTIONS

1. What are the names of the **three** types of particles in an atom?
2. What do you understand by an isotope?
3. Sketch a picture of a stable atom of carbon-12.
4. Why is carbon-14 unstable?

...atomic number ...electrons ...mass number ...neutrons ...nuclear energy ...plutonium

More about atoms

The number of protons in an atom is called the **atomic number**. The number of protons added to the number of neutrons is called the **mass number**. A lithium atom has 3 protons and 4 neutrons. This is its full symbol:

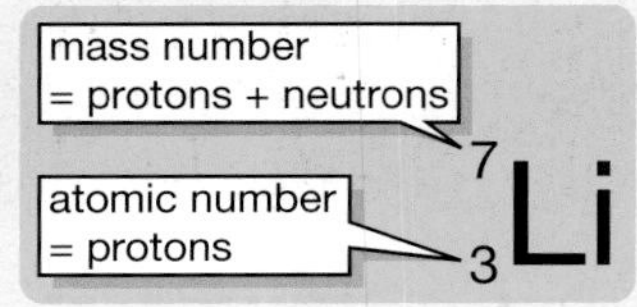

The table shows the first six elements in the Periodic Table.

Element	Atomic number	Full symbol
hydrogen	1	$^{1}_{1}H$
helium	2	$^{4}_{2}He$
lithium	3	$^{7}_{3}Li$
beryllium	4	$^{9}_{4}Be$
boron	5	$^{11}_{5}B$
carbon	6	$^{12}_{6}C$

Isotopes

Isotopes are atoms that have the same number of protons but a different number of neutrons. All isotopes of the same element have the same atomic number. Only the mass number is different because of the additional neutrons. All these are isotopes of iodine, and you can check the periodic table to find which is the stable isotope: $^{123}_{53}I$ $^{124}_{53}I$ $^{127}_{53}I$ $^{129}_{53}I$ $^{131}_{53}I$

Much heavier elements emit huge amounts of energy when they decay. One is **uranium**. Its isotope $^{238}_{92}U$ is used as the fuel for nuclear power stations. The plutonium isotope $^{233}_{94}Pu$ was used by the Apollo lunar missions to power their equipment on the lunar surface.

Radiation

Having many extra neutrons makes an atom unstable. It wants to reach a more balanced state. It breaks down in a process called decay, which happens independent of what is done to the atom.

When the nucleus of a heavy element decays, sub-atomic particles leave the nucleus as a huge amount of radiation, which we call **nuclear energy**.

Most elements have one or more isotopes that are unstable. As a nucleus breaks down, it can emit alpha particles, beta particles or gamma rays or a mixture of these. We call this **radioactive decay**, and we talk about nuclear radiation because it comes from within the nucleus itself.

QUESTIONS

5 Explain the meaning of 'atomic number' and 'mass number'.

6 Check out the Periodic Table: What is the full symbol for oxygen and sodium?

7 In what way is an isotope different from the stable isotope of the same element?

8 Describe what you understand by radiation and radioactive decay.

Nuclear fuel

Uranium is the fuel for nuclear reactors. Uranium-238 is the most common radioactive element found in the Earth's crust, but it has to be enriched before it can be used as a nuclear fuel. The enriched uranium, U-235 and also U-238, is pressed into pellets and placed into stainless steel tubes to become the fuel rods for the reactor. As the uranium fuel is used up, it changes into **plutonium**, which has to be disposed of safely.

The spent fuel can be reprocessed to recover useable uranium. This is then re-enriched and re-cycled back into the reactor. Sellafield in Cumbria is a reprocessing plant. The spent fuel can also be set into solid glass and stored deep underground.

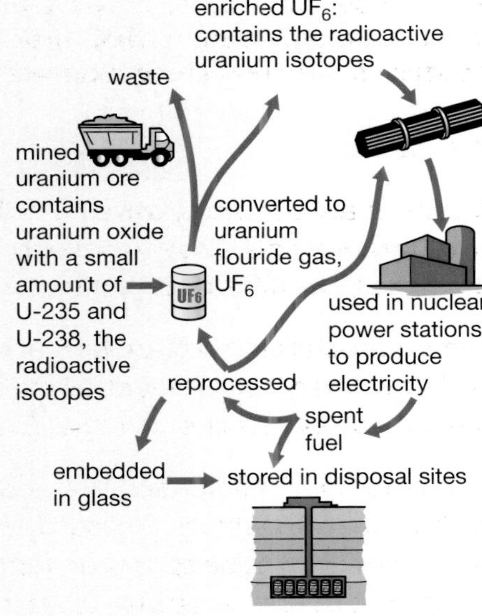

FIGURE 3: The nuclear fuel cycle.

QUESTIONS

9 Look at each step of the nuclear fuel cycle. Discuss it in small groups. What are your impressions?

10 Would you like to live close to the Sellafield reprocessing plant in Cumbria? Explain your answer.

Alpha, beta and gamma rays

You will find out:

- That there are three main types of nuclear radiation
- That they each have different properties and behaviour

Good guys or bad guys?

Radiation is often part of the doomsday scenario in fiction films where the bad guys hijack a nuclear bomb and the hero saves the world.

But the nuclear power station disasters at Three Mile Island in the USA in 1979 and at Chernobyl in the Ukraine in 1986 were not fiction. They really happened. Both nuclear reactors overheated and gave off radiation. The nuclear fallout from Chernobyl even reached the UK. Welsh farmers couldn't sell lamb for years because the hillsides were contaminated.

Nuclear radiation can be both dangerous and also beneficial. It just depends on how we use it.

FIGURE 1: Chernobyl after the disaster: nuclear reactors need the highest maintenance to be safe.

The three types of radiation

The isotopes of some elements are radioactive. They are unstable and give out radiation as their nuclei break up. There are three different types of nuclear radiation.

Alpha particles are helium nuclei – helium atoms without the electrons. They move relatively slowly. Although large, they have little penetrating power. They travel only a short distance in air and are stopped by a single sheet of paper.

Beta particles are electrons – beta radiation is a stream of electrons. They are small, light and move very fast. Beta particles have good penetrating power, though about 3 mm of aluminium sheet will stop them.

Gamma rays are not composed of particles, so they have no mass. They are waves (like electromagnetic radiation). The waves travel at the speed of light and carry a lot of energy. Gamma rays can penetrate almost everything. A block of lead about 10 cm thick will only stop half of them.

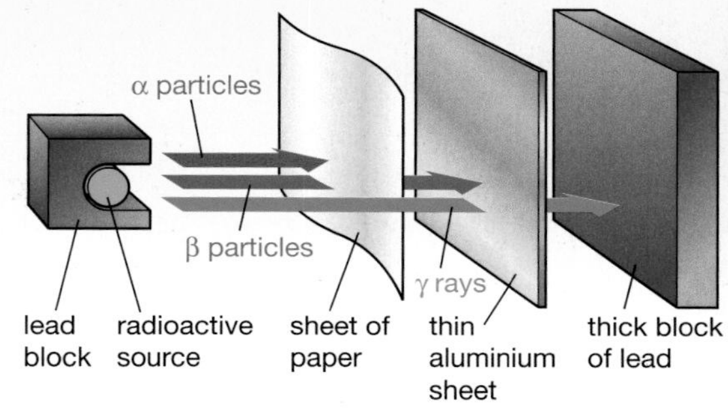

FIGURE 2: The three radiations and their penetrating properties.

QUESTIONS

1. What are the **three** types of nuclear radiation that can come from the nucleus of an unstable isotope when it decays?
2. Which radiation is big and heavy? How would you describe it to someone?
3. Which radiation is almost unstoppable? Write down its characteristics.
4. Which radiation needs about 3 mm of aluminium to stop it? Describe its properties.

AVERAGING THE COUNT

Atoms decay at irregular intervals. The Geiger counter measures radiation, counts the pulses and gives an average count per second.

...alpha (α) particle ...beta (β) particle ...gamma (γ) ray

Alpha, beta and gamma

All the radiations can **ionise** atoms. If one of them hits an atom hard enough, it can knock off an electron, which is negatively charged, and the rest of the atom becomes a positively charged ion.

An **alpha (α) particle** is a helium nucleus, ^4_2He, with a positive (+) charge. It moves at about a tenth of the speed of light. Because of its mass, it doesn't travel far before colliding with atoms in its path, knocking off electrons. It is a good ioniser but has poor penetrating power, stopped by a few centimetres of air or a sheet of paper. Alpha particles are harmful if they enter the body, but they seldom get that far.

Americium-241 is the alpha particle emitter used in smoke detectors. As the diagram shows, ions from air keep an electrical current flowing in the circuit. When smoke particles intercept the alpha particles, the current stops, and then the alarm goes off.

alarm battery

3. Current detector: when smoke prevents alpha particles from ionising air, the current stops and the detector triggers the alarm

1. Radioactive souce, americium-241, emits alpha particles. They collide with air and ionise its particles

2. Electrons move to positive electrode. Positive ions move to negative electrode

air enters

FIGURE 3: How a smoke detector works.

Beta (β) particles are electrons, so have a negative (-) charge. They are 1/7000th of the size of the alpha particle and move at half the speed of light. About 3 mm of aluminium stops them. Because of their small size, they frequently fail to hit atoms. But occasionally they collide and ionise an atom.

FIGURE 4: The gamma radiation from cobalt-60 kills cancer cells.

They are weak ionisers, but not safe: workers using them wear protective clothing. Strontium-90 is a source of β (or beta) particles that was present in the atmosphere when world powers were testing nuclear bombs. Eventually, atmospheric tests were banned.

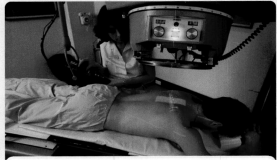

Gamma (γ) rays are electromagnetic waves and have no charge. They travel at the speed of light, carry a lot of energy and penetrate most materials easily.

Without mass or charge, they are poor ionisers. The dangers and uses of gamma rays are based on their high energy, which can disrupt living cells. This is why, carefully targeted, gamma rays from cobalt-60 are used to kill cancer cells.

QUESTIONS

5 What happens when a particle is ionised?

6 What makes alpha particles particularly strong ionisers?

7 Beta particles carry a lot of energy, but they are not strong ionisers. Can you explain why?

8 Why are gamma rays so different from the other two types of nuclear radiation?

Radiations in electric and magnetic fields

Alpha particles have a positive charge, beta particles a negative charge and gamma rays have no charge. These charges affect the way the radiations move in an electric field. Remember: like charges repel. The diagram shows how they move in the electric field between a positive and a negative plate.

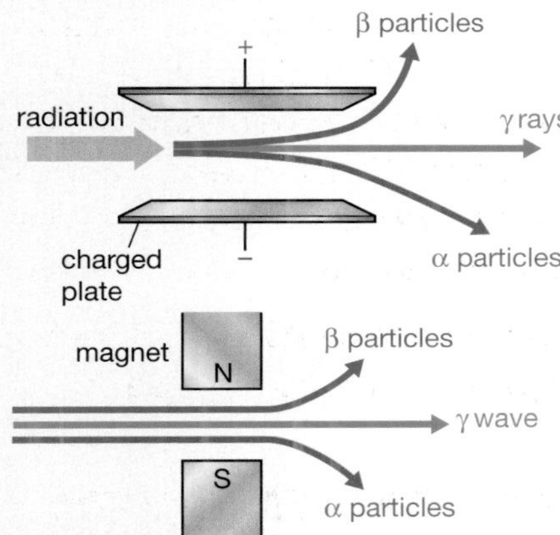

FIGURE 5: The effect of charged plates or a magnet on different types of radiation.

Similarly, a magnetic field affects how radiation moves: The positive alpha particle is attracted to the south pole of a magnet and the negative electron to the north pole.

Which is which?

During a laboratory experiment, three radioactive sources are accidentally mixed up. The technician knows that one is cobalt-60, one is strontium-90 and the third is americium-241, but cannot tell which is which just by looking. Now read question 10.

QUESTIONS

9 What effect would the north pole and south pole of a magnet have on a gamma ray?

10 Using the information from the text and figures 2 and 5, explain how you would identify each of the three sources. What piece of equipment would you need?

Background radiation

You will find out:

- That there is background radiation all around us
- That there are many sources of background radiation
- How living things have adapted to cope with background radiation

When life could start on land

When first formed, Earth had no atmosphere. There was no protection from harmful solar and **cosmic rays**. Levels were so high that no living thing could survive in the open. Gradually, over millions of years, the atmosphere formed and became a shield against the deadly radiation. Only then could living things that had evolved deep in the oceans emerge onto the land.

The atmosphere doesn't offer 100% protection; some radiation still gets through, but at very low levels. We need to look after our atmosphere; it's the only natural protection we have!

FIGURE 1: The whole Earth could be like this, but for our protective atmosphere.

Background radiation

We have seen that a radioactive isotope emits radiation as particles or rays and that we use a Geiger counter to detect and count them.

Switch on a Geiger counter in the laboratory with all radioactive sources safely put away. You will hear a low level of clicks from the counter. Go into the street or into the countryside with the counter. You will still hear the low level of clicks.

The Geiger counter tells you that there is a small amount of radiation all around us all the time. It's called **background radiation**, and it comes from various sources. Some comes from the soil and rocks of the Earth, some from space. Some of it is man-made. Fortunately, the amount of radiation is quite small and does not harm our bodies.

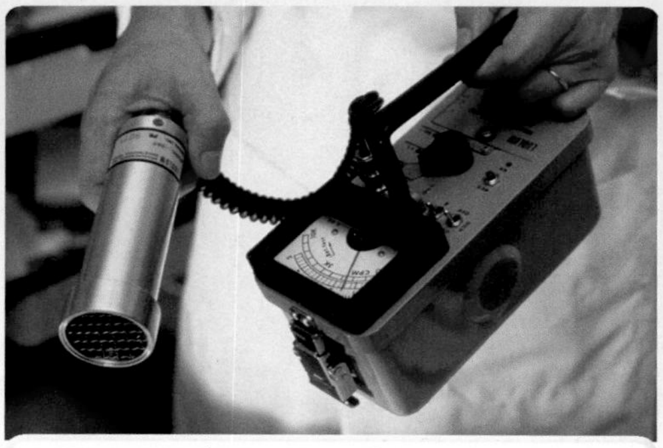

FIGURE 2: A Geiger counter in use.

Where does it come from?

Look at figure 3 for a detailed breakdown of where background radiation comes from.

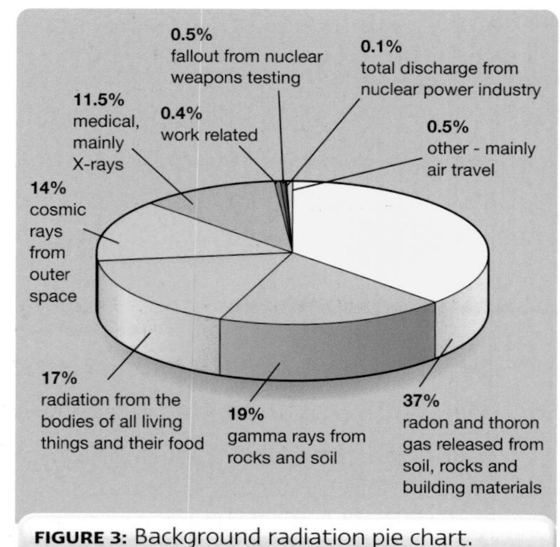

FIGURE 3: Background radiation pie chart.

QUESTIONS

1. What is background radiation?
2. Why does this radiation not harm us?
3. Which of the sources in the pie chart surprised you most? Why?
4. Give a reason why you might get an extra 0.5% radiation from air travel.

Sources of background radiation

Here on Earth, we experience a low level of radiation around us all the time. All living things, including humans, have adapted to this background radiation. Our cells have evolved ways to repair any damage that it might cause.

The amount of background radiation varies from place to place. In the UK, areas of granite rock, such as parts of Cornwall and Scotland, have much higher radiation than London or East Anglia.

Granite is also used for buildings and roads. Atoms decaying in it emit **gamma rays** and are converted to atoms of **radon** gas, which is itself radioactive. Radon can leak into people's houses and cause mysterious illnesses. Now that we understand this, ventilators are installed in buildings on granite or made of it, to clear the gas and restore the background radiation to safer levels.

Cosmic rays from outer space constantly bombard the Earth. Fortunately, the atmosphere can absorb much of this radiation. Pilots and aircrew who fly long-haul routes are exposed to more than ground-level doses of cosmic radiation. At altitude, about 12 km high, the atmosphere is very thin and offers little protection.

You may have been to hospital or the dentist for an X-ray. Radiographers are careful to use small doses to make sure we are not harmed.

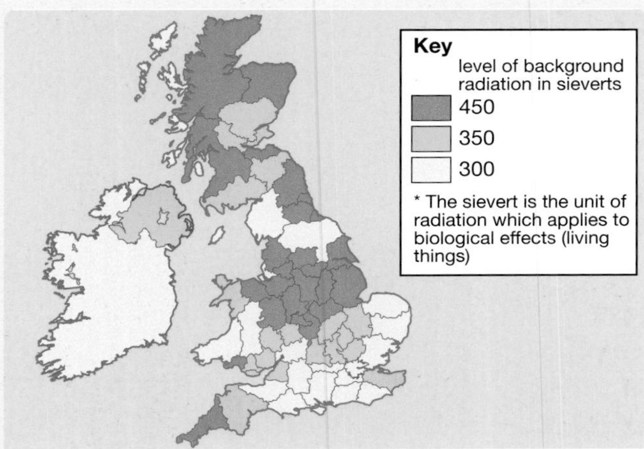

FIGURE 4: Background radiation in the UK.

Nuclear power stations and nuclear weapons testing are today's hot issues. Are we contaminating the environment? Check out the pie chart – what do you think?

All living things contain tiny amounts of radioactive material. So does the food we eat, since it once lived. Later on we'll learn how scientists use this phenomenon to work out the age of fossil remains.

SEVEN MILES HIGH

Pilots and air-crew wear radiation badges. If they get too much exposure to cosmic radiation, they are grounded until their levels return to normal.

QUESTIONS

5 What do you understand by the term background radiation?

6 Is background radiation harmful to us humans? Explain your answer.

7 State **two** sources of background radiation and give some information about each.

8 What is your opinion on the use of nuclear energy and nuclear weapons testing, and their effect on our environment?

FIGURE 5: Anyone working with or near to radioactive materials wears a radiation film badge to monitor how much radiation they are exposed to.

Taking into account?

Background radiation is always there. So if you do an experiment with a radioactive source, the Geiger counter will read its activity plus the background radiation.

The correct experimental technique is always to measure background radiation before you begin your experiment. Then once you have recorded your experimental results, remember to subtract the average background reading from each reading.

Averaging out

Radioactive decay is random and does not emit radiation in a regular stream. You might get three or four pulses almost together and then one on its own.

The right technique to measure the rate of radioactive decay is to use a stopclock, count the number of pulses for 10 seconds and then work out the average per second. Repeat several times. Eventually, you get a consistent average for the rate of decay.

QUESTIONS

9 During experimental work, why should you take background radiation into account? How would you do this?

10 Why is it important to use the word 'average' when measuring or discussing rates of radioactive decay?

The risk from radon

SELF-CHECK ACTIVITY

CONTEXT

Ellie lives in a house in Cornwall, down in the South West of England, with her parents and brothers. The house is quite new, but is built in an area where there is a lot of granite. In the science lessons at school, Ellie's teacher told the class about a gas called radon.

Radon is a gas that forms naturally due to the decay of uranium in the ground. It forms in greater quantities in areas such as Devon and Cornwall, where there is a large amount of granite in the ground. Radon decays to form radioactive particles, which remain suspended in the air. Normally this is not a problem, but inside a building, the levels can rise rather higher.

People inhaling air that contains these radioactive particles are exposed to alpha radiation and are at a greater risk of developing lung cancer. This is a particular problem in houses with well fitting doors and windows, as the air doesn't circulate as easily.

Ellie told her parents about this. Her mother said, "I've been meaning to get something done about this. Our neighbour Diane got a detector device to put in the house to see if Radon was a problem. We should do the same."

Her dad said that he'd find out where they could get a detector. "I don't know if we have to pay for it," he said, "but we should get one anyway. I just don't like the idea of there being any radiation in our house."

Ellie laughed. "Don't be daft," she said, "there's radiation around wherever you are. It's the amount that matters."

CHALLENGE

STEP 1

Think about Ellie's reaction to her dad when he said that he didn't want any radiation in their house. What might she have said to him to explain her ideas?

STEP 2

If Ellie's family lived far away from granite rocks and radon, where might the radiation around them have come from?

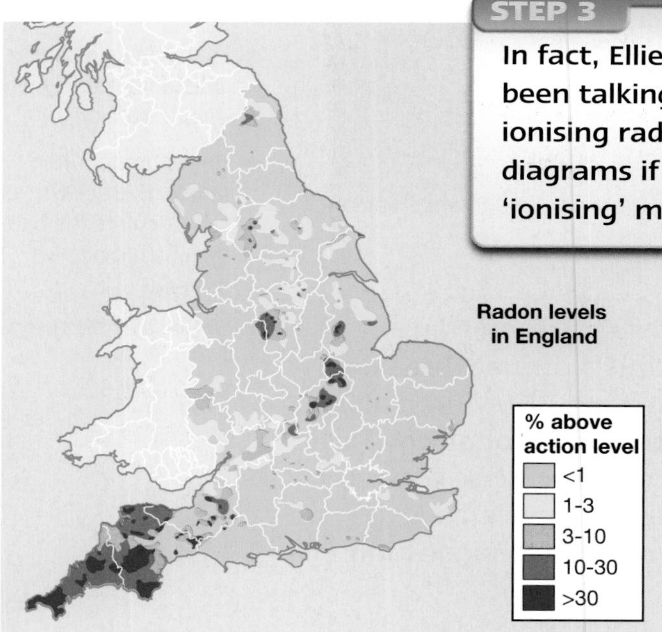

Note: Action level is the level at which the Health Protection Agency advise taking action to reduce radon levels.

STEP 3

In fact, Ellie's science teacher had been talking to the class about ionising radiation. Explain, using diagrams if it helps, what the word 'ionising' means.

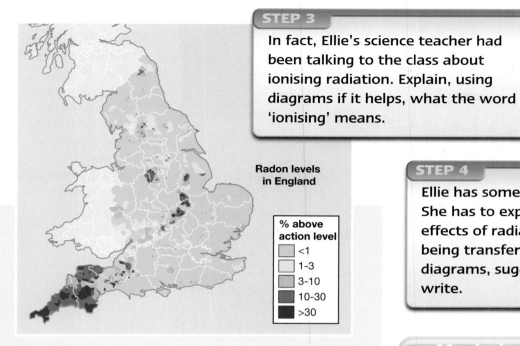

STEP 4

Ellie has some Science homework. She has to explain how the ionisation effects of radiation involve electrons being transferred. Using words or diagrams, suggest what she might write.

Maximise your grade

These sentences show what you need to include in your work to achieve each grade. Use them to improve your work and be more successful.

Grade	Answer includes...
	Suggest a source of background radiation.
F	State and recognise that there is background radiation in the environment that is always present.
	Describe background radiation.
	Describe background radiation and state one thing it is caused by.
C	Explain the meaning of ionisation. Describe background radiation and state that it is caused by radioactive substances, rocks, soil, living things and cosmic rays.
	Explain ionisation in terms of electron transfer.
A	Explain ionisation in terms of: • Removal of electrons from particles • Gain of electrons by particles.
	As above, but with particular clarity and detail.

Half-life

You will find out:

- That every radioactive substance has its own unique half-life
- How, from counting radioactive decays, you can calculate the half-life of a radioactive material

The mighty atom

In 1909 Ernest Rutherford, working at Manchester University with Hans Geiger (of counter fame) and Ernest Marsden, carried out a ground-breaking experiment which began to reveal the structure of the atom. They fired alpha particles at very thin gold foil. Most particles passed straight through the foil. This showed that a gold atom was mostly empty space. Some were scattered. This indicated that the nucleus was positively charged, and repelled a positively charged alpha particle. A very few bounced right back suggesting that the nucleus was very small but very dense.

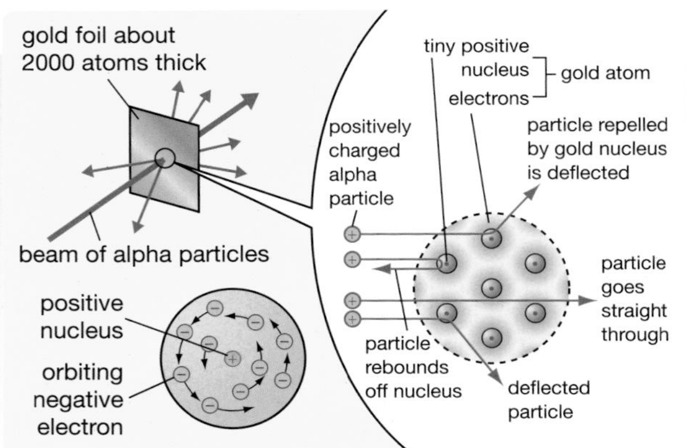

FIGURE 1: Rutherford's scattering experiment and his model of an atom.

Half-life

The **isotope** of an element that has an unstable nucleus is called a **radioisotope**. The nucleus can break down and emit particles or rays. This process is **radioactive decay**. Decays do not happen at regular intervals. You have to average the number of clicks of a geiger counter in a given time to get the **activity rate** or **count rate**. As time passes, the number of atoms of the original isotope decreases, so the activity rate slows down. Scientists have worked out a way to describe the rate at which the activity of an isotope changes. It is called **half-life**.

The half-life of a radioisotope is the average time it takes for half of the unstable atoms to decay.

No matter how much isotope you start off with, the half-life will always be the same. The first square in figure 2 represents the original amount of radioactive material. After one half-life, half the atoms have decayed, leaving the other half. In the next half-life, half of the atoms in the remaining part decay, leaving a quarter of the original number. After the next half-life, half the quarter of the atoms decay, leaving an eighth.

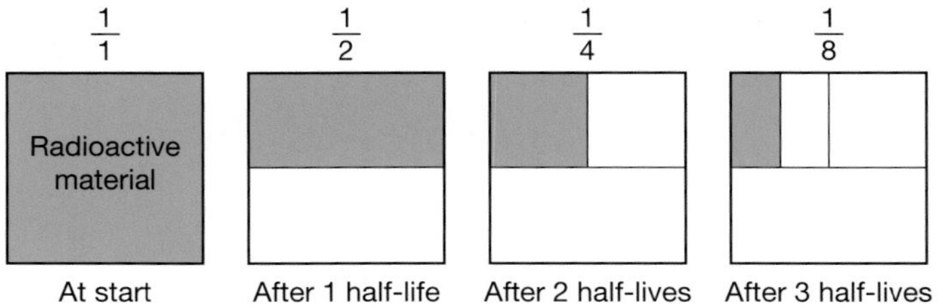

FIGURE 2: Amount of radioactive isotope left after each half-life.

Let's try an example using numbers:

A radioactive sample has 1000 atoms and a half-life of 1 hour. How many atoms will be left after three half-lives (3 hours)?

hours	No. of atoms left	Half-lives
0	1000	(start)
1	500	one
2	250	two
3	125	three

QUESTIONS

1. Write down the definition of half-life.
2. A sample of radioactive material has 800 atoms. How many atoms are left after two half-lives?
3. For the same material, how many half-lives does it take to reduce it to 50 atoms?
4. If the material has a half-life of 30 minutes, how long does it take for the number of atoms to reduce to 100?

...activity rate ...count rate ...half-life

Half-life of a radioisotope

- Radioactive decay is the emission of alpha, beta and gamma radiation from an unstable nucleus which is decaying.
- The activity rate or count rate is the average number of emissions in a given time.
- As the decay of nuclei continues, the activity rate decreases since there are fewer atoms left of the original isotope.

Scientists discovered that each radioactive material has its own unique, constant rate of decay. In a particular time period, called the half-life, half of the atoms in a sample will have decayed.

The half-life of a radioactive sample is the average time taken for half the radioactive nuclei to decay.

You can express this in terms of how it is measured as 'activity' or 'count rate'.

The half-life is the average time taken for the activity (or count rate) of a sample to decrease to half of its starting rate."

The table below shows the half-life of some radioisotopes.

Isotope	Radiation	Half-life
Uranium-238	alpha	5000 million years
Plutonium-239	alpha & beta	24 000 years
Carbon-14	beta	5700 years
Cobalt-60	gamma	5 years
Americium-241	alpha	460 years
Iodine-131	beta	8 days
Sodium-24	beta	15 hours
Strontium-93	beta & gamma	8 minutes
Barium-143	beta	12 seconds
Polonium-213	alpha	0.000 004 second

Half-life values vary enormously, from millions of years to milliseconds. The half-life is also unique to each individual type of isotope. For example, barium-143 has a half-life of 12 seconds. Any sample of barium-143 anywhere in the world will have the same half-life. Scientists use this characteristic to identify radioisotopes.

QUESTIONS

5 What is so special about the half-life of a radioactive isotope?

6 Iodine-131 has a half-life of 8 days. A sample has a count rate of 128 counts/min. What will the count rate be after three half-lives?

7 For the same isotope, what length of time will it take for the activity rate to drop to 4 counts/min?

ALWAYS THE SAME

The half-life is independent of the physical state (solid, liquid, gas), temperature, pressure, chemistry or any other outside influence.

How to determine half-life

The half-life of a radioactive material is a very useful characteristic. With data like that in the table opposite, you can work out the identity of an unknown radioactive isotope. You record its activity rate or count rate and then check your results against the table.

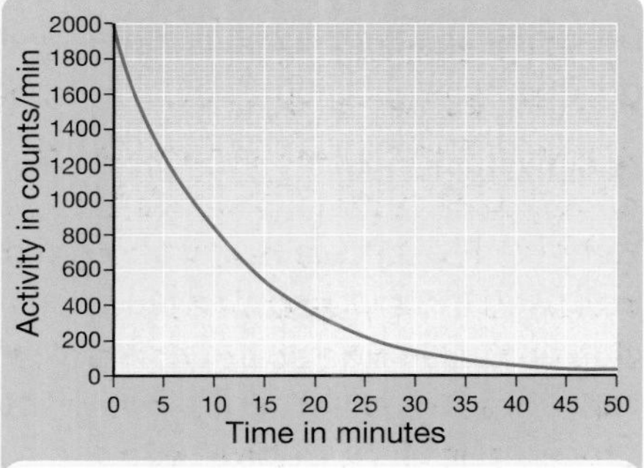

FIGURE 3: Radioactive decay graph for strontium-93.

QUESTIONS

8 Figure 3 shows the decay curve for strontium-93. Starting from the original reading of 2000 counts/ min, determine the half-life of Sr-93.

9 Using the graph and a new starting point on the y-axis, repeat the process to obtain a second value for the half-life. How does it compare with your first answer?

10 Use the graph to find the count rate after three half-lives.

11 How long would it take for the count rate to drop to 100 counts/min?

Uses of nuclear radiation

You will find out:

- That the three types of radiation have different uses
- How to recognise the benefits of using various radioisotope techniques

Releasing the energy

A uranium-235 atom is unstable because its nucleus has many more neutrons (143) than protons (92). It just takes a neutron fired into the nucleus for it to split in two. This is **nuclear fission**. It releases huge amounts of energy and a few extra neutrons. These neutrons move on and split more uranium-235 nuclei, releasing even more energy and more neutrons. This is called a **chain reaction**. The amount of energy released is immense. One gram of uranium can produce the same energy as exploding 22 000 tonnes of TNT (an explosive).

Radiation in medicine and industry

Handled safely, radiation can be a great benefit to us all. In medicine it saves lives. In industry it ensures the quality of products.

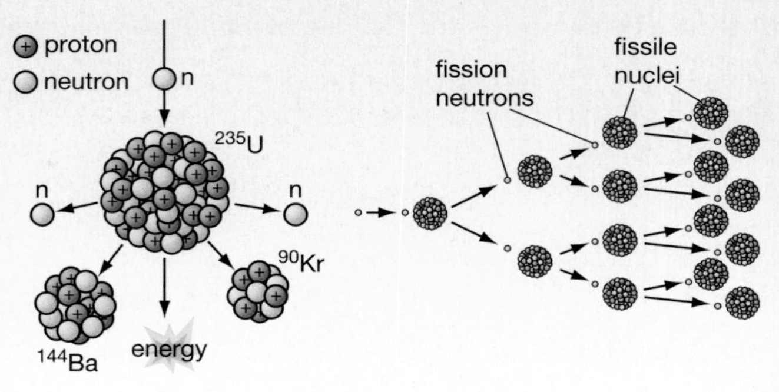

FIGURE 1: Nuclear fission and a chain reaction.

Radiotherapy

Here's a real conundrum: too much radiation can cause cancer, but used in small, controlled doses it can also help to cure cancer. A fine beam of gamma rays is aimed accurately at a tumour inside a patient's body. The gamma rays kill the cancerous cells without harming too many healthy cells (see page 269).

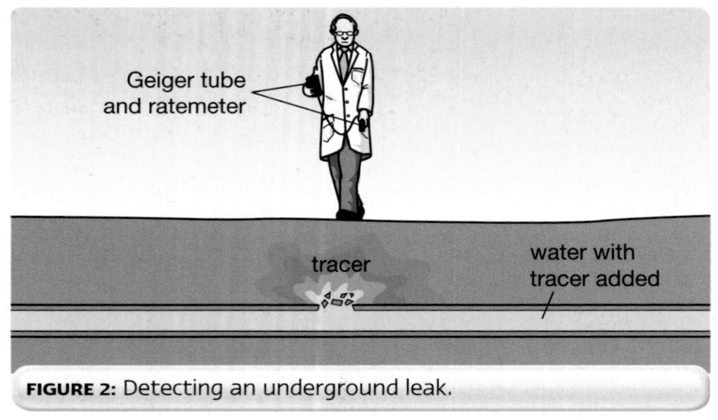

FIGURE 2: Detecting an underground leak.

Sterilising surgical instruments

The old way to sterilise surgical instruments was to 'cook' them with high-pressure steam. Today, instruments are washed and cleaned, sealed in cellophane packaging and **irradiated** with gamma rays. They kill all bacteria and the sealed package keeps the instruments clean and sterile.

Tracing leaks in pipes

We have thousands of miles of underground pipelines for water, gas and oil. How would you find a leak? You put a substance called a **tracer** – a radioisotope – into the pipeline and wait until it spreads through the pipes. Then you follow the pipeline overground with a Geiger counter. How will you know when you are above the leak?

QUESTIONS

1. How can gamma rays cause cancer and also help to kill the cancer?
2. How can gamma rays be used to help keep a surgeon's instruments clean and sterile?
3. Explain how radioactive materials can be used to find leaks in underground pipes.
4. Think of any other way in which radiation can be used for our benefit.

...chain reaction ...irradiated

More about uses of radiation

Medical tracers

When a patient has a problem with an organ in their body, a doctor injects a small quantity of solution containing radioactive material. It moves through the bloodstream and a radiation detector shows a picture of the organ, so the doctor can diagnose the disorder. Iodine-123 is used as a tracer for thyroid and kidney problems. Barium-143 is used for problems of the stomach and intestines.

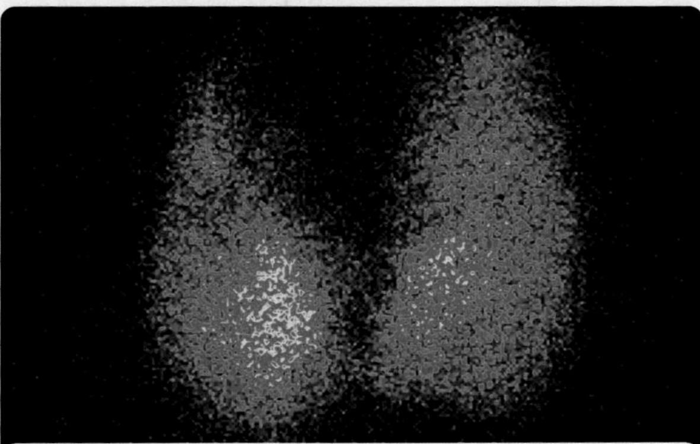

FIGURE 3: The thyroid glands of a patient where radioactive iodine-123 has been injected to allow a doctor to identify a goitre (or growth).

Sterilising food

The shelf life of many fresh foods can be extended if they are irradiated with gamma rays. All food contains bacteria and fungal spores which make it go mouldy and rotten. Gamma radiation (cobalt-60) kills the bacteria but does not damage the food itself (see figure 4).

Smoke detectors

Smoke alarms contain small amounts of americium-241 which emits alpha particles. The alpha particles ionise the air, releasing free electrons which maintain a tiny current in the detector circuit. Smoke particles absorb the alpha particles, ionisation stops, and the current ceases which sets off the alarm (see page 269).

Thickness control

In paper mills, the thickness of paper is controlled by measuring the amount of radiation that passes through it. If the paper is too thin, the Geiger counter will read high and send a signal to the rollers to open a little. If the paper is too thick, the counter will read low and send a signal to close the rollers.

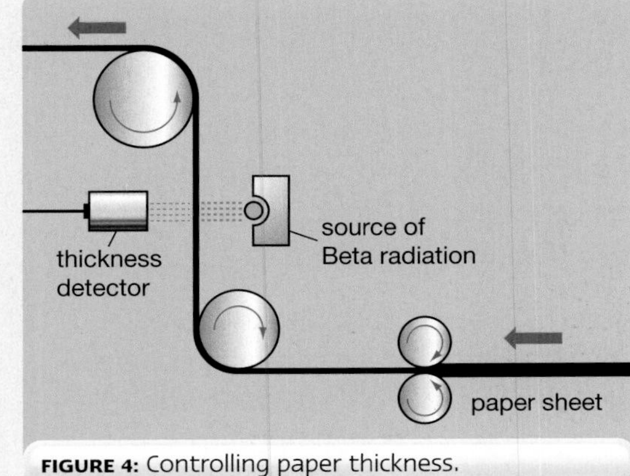

FIGURE 4: Controlling paper thickness.

QUESTIONS

5 What is a tracer? Explain how it is used in medicine.

6 Why is radiation used in the food industry? How do you feel about its use?

7 Explain how a smoke detector works.

8 Draw a diagram of how the thickness of paper is controlled. Describe how the control mechanism works.

FIGURE 5: Same-age strawberries: those on the left have been irradiated.

The three radiations: a review

- **Alpha** is a helium nucleus with a positive charge. It has very low penetration and can be stopped by a sheet of paper or a few centimetres of air; but it is a strong ioniser.
- **Beta** is a high-speed electron, so it has a negative charge. It has good penetration but can be stopped by 3 cm of aluminium. Beta is a weak ioniser.
- **Gamma** is a ray, not a particle, and has no charge. It penetrates everything. Even thick lead only slows it down. Gamma is a poor ioniser but carries a lot of energy.

All sources of these radiations have a unique half-life; it can be 50 000 years, or days, hours or seconds.

QUESTIONS

9 Study figure 3 on page 269. Then explain why a smoke detector needs an alpha source and would not work with a beta source.

10 Sr-90 and Cs-137 are both beta emitters and are used in industry to control the thickness of paper, aluminium foil and plastic sheeting. Suggest why beta particle sources are used and not alpha or gamma.

11 Strontium-90 is a beta emitter with a half-life of 59 years. Iodine-124 is also a beta emitter but with a half-life of 8 days. Which do you think is more suitable for use as a medical tracer? Why?

...nuclear fission ...tracer

Safety first

You will find out:

- That radioactivity has various dangers
- That to avoid the dangers, great care is taken to handle and dispose of radioactive waste safely

The answer to all our energy problems?

Nuclear energy seems to answer the world's energy problems. It is relatively cheap, clean (no burning of fossil fuels) and ecologically sound (no carbon dioxide emission, no greenhouse effect).

But what happens if things go wrong? The explosion at the Chernobyl nuclear power station deposited nuclear fallout across half of Europe. In the UK, families living near the Sellafield nuclear power station blame it for unusual illnesses. Hundreds of tonnes of nuclear waste are taken across the country for reprocessing or storage deep underground. What if a transporter were involved in an accident? What if terrorists hijacked it?

Is nuclear power a risk we must not take, or is it a risk we cannot afford not to take?

FIGURE 1: Sellafield nuclear power station.

Better safe than sorry

The three radiations, alpha, beta and gamma, carry energy in different ways. It is the high energy in them that makes radioactivity potentially dangerous.

Alpha particles are big and slow and can be stopped by a sheet of paper. No real danger? Well, yes, if they get inside our bodies. Once inside a person's body, alpha particles can damage cells and organ tissues.

Beta particles are small and fast and can penetrate our bodies. Gamma rays carry the most energy and can penetrate anything. Both beta and gamma are also dangerous to living cells. Sometimes cells are killed outright. Sometimes the nucleus is damaged so that the cell reproduces as a cancer.

All radioactive materials must be handled according to strict health and safety guidelines. Every care should be taken to prevent any radiation reaching people's bodies. Those working with radioactive materials keep them in special lead-lined containers and wear protective gloves and clothing when handling them.

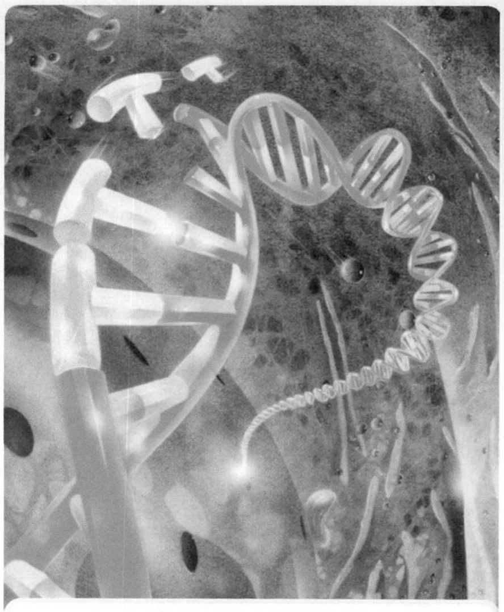

FIGURE 2: Radiation can ionise and damage the DNA in cells. Then, they divide uncontrollably and produce a cancerous growth.

QUESTIONS

1. What makes the various radiations so dangerous to living things?
2. Since alpha particles can be stopped by a sheet of paper, why are they dangerous?
3. What makes beta and gamma radiation dangerous?
4. How are radiation sources stored, and what care should people take when handling them?

The worst scenario

The nuclei of unstable elements **decay** and release large amounts of energy. This energy is carried away by the various particles and rays – alpha, beta and gamma. With enough energy, these radiations can knock electrons from atoms they collide with – they **ionise** the atom. If this happens inside our bodies, the consequences can be serious. Ionisation can alter the structure of our DNA, and when a damaged cell reproduces it **mutates**. This is how a cancerous growth often begins.

Up to a point, the body can repair damaged cells and replace cells that have been killed. Long, intense exposure leads to **radiation sickness**: there is so much damage that remaining cells cannot replace them quickly enough. Then, vital organs can fail and death follows. Some 70 000 people died in this way after an atomic bomb was dropped on Hiroshima during the Second World War.

Handle with care

The government has very strict health and safety regulations on radioactive materials. All radioactive sources and materials must be stored and handled safely to avoid any risk of radiation penetrating the body. In the nuclear industry, safety is of prime concern. Nuclear reactors are encased in steel and thick concrete. People who work in this environment wear protective clothing, overalls, gloves and headgear and use remote-controlled robot arms.

FIGURE 3: The most dangerous radioisotopes can only be safely handled by robots.

Nuclear waste

The nuclear industry produces large quantities of hazardous materials. Some of it is **spent nuclear fuel** (uranium-235 and plutonium-239) which cannot be further reprocessed. There is also contaminated equipment and discarded clothing and packaging materials. This has to be safely contained and disposed of.

Category of waste	Typical waste materials	Method of disposal
low-level	protective clothing and used packaging materials	buried on land or at sea
intermediate	irradiated equipment from reactors, cladding materials and reprocessing fluids	storage in concrete warehouses, or deep burial underground
high-level	spent nuclear fuel and other radioactive sources from the reactor	vitrification (sealing in glass blocks), deep burial

QUESTIONS

5 Explain fully why radiation is very dangerous to living organisms.

6 Why can alpha radiation be safe and yet also be very dangerous?

7 Why do you think there are many strict rules and regulations in the nuclear industry?

8 Nuclear waste has to be disposed of safely. Imagine the government plan to dig a deep mine in your area to store radioactive waste underground. What would your view be?

Radiocarbon dating

Neutrons in cosmic rays constantly bombard nitrogen (^{14}N) in the atmosphere, forming radioactive carbon-14. This stays at a steady percentage in the air. It combines with oxygen to form carbon dioxide, which is taken up by plants, so it enters the food chain and is present in all living things. When they die, the carbon-14 present gradually decays.

To determine the age of bones, wood, paper or anything that once lived, scientists compare the percentage of carbon-14 in the object with the percentage in air. Knowing the half-life of carbon-14, 5700 years, they can work out how much has decayed, hence how long it took. This is the age of the object, and the process is called **radiocarbon dating**.

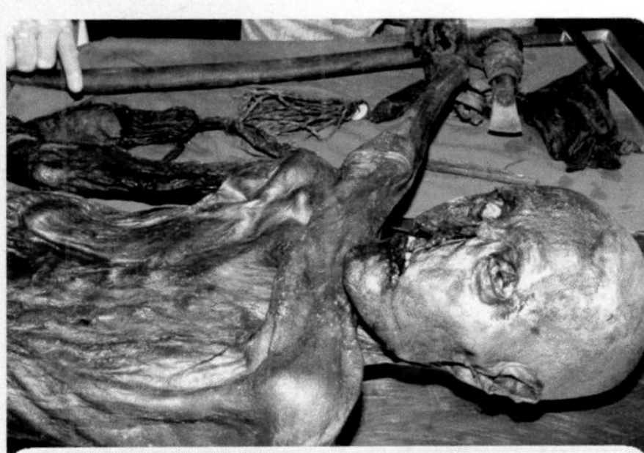

FIGURE 4: The body of the Iceman, found in Italy, is 5300 years old.

It takes only 6.6 half-lives – 38 000 years – for carbon-14 to fall to just 1% of the amount present when an organism was living. To age the Earth's rocks, scientists need a radioisotope with a much longer half-life. This is uranium-238, with a half-life of 4500 million years, by coincidence about the age of the Earth.

QUESTIONS

9 What are the properties of radioactive materials that make radioactive dating possible?

10 Do some research on the Iceman at: www.bbc.co.uk/science/horizon/2001/iceman.shtml. What extraordinary information were scientists able to find out about him?

Searching space

You will find out:

- How different types of telescopes are used to make discoveries about the Universe
- That they collect radiation right across the electromagnetic spectrum

Galileo Galilei (1564–1642)

Galileo invented the first optical telescope in 1609. It could only magnify eight times, but with it, Galileo was able to observe Jupiter and discovered that it had moons orbiting around it. From that observation he suggested that our own moon also orbited around the Earth.

He could study the phases of Venus and was the first person to see sunspots. These discoveries were early scientific evidence that the Sun was at the centre of the Solar System, and not the Earth as people believed then.

FIGURE 1: Galileo making discoveries using his optical telescope.

Telescopes

In its simplest form, an **optical telescope** is a long tube with a glass lens at each end. It is called optical because you see images with your eye. Today's optical telescopes for viewing planets and stars are bigger, more powerful versions of the model Galileo used. They are housed in large observatories where astronomers observe the night sky.

There is a problem. The Earth's atmosphere varies in density and this distorts the light from the stars and planets. An extreme effect is the mirage you see over a hot tarmac road in summer. Together with air pollution, this effect blurs and distorts images seen with ground-based optical telescopes. To minimise the distortion, most observatories are built high on the tops of mountains. The thinner, cleaner atmosphere means images are much clearer and sharper.

FIGURE 2: The Keck Observatory is built high up at Mauna Kea, Hawaii.

In 1990, the **Hubble telescope** was launched into orbit around the Earth, beyond its atmosphere. For the first time, astronomers could get very sharp images, and could see deeper into space than ever before. They discovered new galaxies, thousand of light-years away.

Scientists discovered that some objects in space emit radio waves. These are invisible to our eyes, so **radio telescopes** were built. A radio telescope has no glass lenses. Its large dish gathers the radio waves and focuses them to a receiving antenna. A computer then interprets them.

FIGURE 3: The Arecibo radio observatory in Puerto Rico can 'see' pulsars, which emit a pulse of radio waves about every second.

QUESTIONS

1. What is the name for a telescope that you look through with your eyes?
2. Why are many telescopes built high up on top of mountains?
3. Why is the Hubble telescope so important?
4. In what way does a radio telescope differ from an optical telescope?

Earth-based telescopes

The left-hand picture in figure 4 shows the classical optical telescope. Not enough light passed through the small-diameter glass lens, so the **reflecting optical telescope** was developed. Its large concave mirror gathers much more light. The larger the diameter of the mirror, the more light captured, and the clearer and sharper the image.

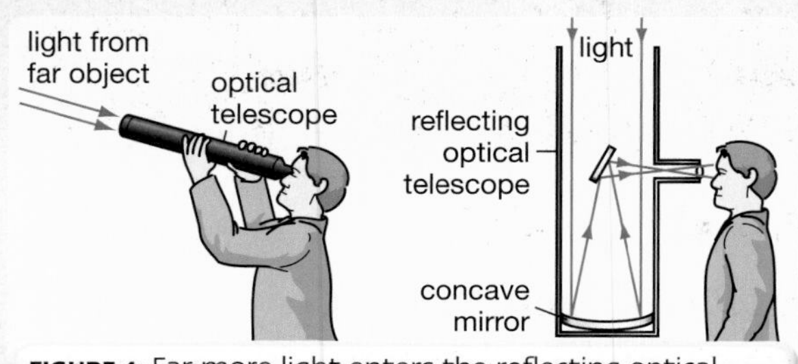

FIGURE 4: Far more light enters the reflecting optical telescope.

The problem with all Earth-based telescopes is the atmosphere. Its particles and its effect of distorting the light from space limit the sharpness and clarity of images. To minimise these effects, many observatories have been built high on the tops of mountains where the atmosphere is thin and clean.

Space telescopes

The best way to overcome the problem of image quality is to get out beyond the atmosphere, into space. The Hubble telescope is stationed in Earth orbit and looks through empty space and transmits images to Earth. Not only is the quality of these images superb, but Hubble has been able to look farther and deeper into the Universe than ever before. We have even been able to see the formation of new stars.

FIGURE 5: Gas clouds in the Eagle nebula, taken by the Hubble telescope.

FIGURE 6: The Hubble telescope in space has transformed optical images.

QUESTIONS

5 The original optical telescope was a wonderful invention. Why was it limited as a means to observe the night sky?

6 How did scientists overcome this problem? What was the name of the new type of telescope?

7 What is the problem that all Earth-based telescopes have? What was the solution to this problem?

8 How has this problem been solved today? Explain.

TWINKLE, TWINKLE

The reason stars seem to twinkle is because the atmosphere distorts the light reaching our eyes. Out in space, stars give a steady, clear light.

Seeing the invisible

Objects in space emit rays right across the electromagnetic spectrum, but only visible and radio frequencies can penetrate the atmosphere. To 'see' the other, invisible waves, scientists invented new types of telescope. For each kind of radiation, a large dish gathers the rays, brings them to a focal point, and a sensitive receiver captures and sends them to a computer for processing. Astronomers see a computer-enhanced image.

Wavelength	Objects 'seen' in space
gamma ray	neutron stars
x-rays	neutron stars
ultraviolet	hot stars, quasars
visible	stars
infra red	red giants
far infra red	protostars, planets
radio	pulsars

Today's space technology enables scientists to place new telescopes on orbiting satellites above the Earth's atmosphere. A whole new field of astronomy has developed which observes wavelengths other than visible light.

QUESTIONS

9 The title of this section is 'Seeing the invisible'. Why 'invisible'?

10 In what way are these telescopes different from the traditional optical telescopes?

11 Where do you find these telescopes?

Gravity

You will find out:

- That gravity is one of the fundamental forces in the Universe
- That gravity helps space rockets reach Neptune
- That the force of gravity keeps the planets in orbit around the sun

All objects have gravity

Gravity is a 'pull' force that acts between all objects. It pulls a ball you throw in the air back down to Earth. At the same time, the ball is pulling the Earth towards itself as well. However, it only does this to a tiny extent because it has a small mass.

Gravity also depends on distance. The further away something is, the smaller is its gravitational effect. A bus passing you in the street 'pulls' you about as much as the Moon does. Gravity holds the Universe together and determines the shape and size of stars and solar systems.

FIGURE 1: It would be easy to break the world high-jump record on the Moon.

The force of gravity

Every object (body) with **mass** has gravity and exerts a force on all other bodies. No matter where you are in the Universe, the force of gravity will pull you towards other objects.

The larger the mass, the larger is its force of gravity.
For an object in space, the Moon is small, so its force of gravity is small. Astronauts on the Moon can do effortless high jumps that they couldn't do on Earth where the force of gravity is stronger.

The Earth keeps the Moon in orbit. Gravity is like an invisible elastic band holding the Moon in place. But the Moon's gravity also affects the Earth. It pulls the water in the oceans and seas towards itself as a bulge that follows the Moon and gives us high and low tides.

*The further the **distance** between two objects, the weaker the force of gravity.*
As a Moon-bound spacecraft moves away from the Earth, the force of gravity gradually weakens until the astronauts become weightless. Then slowly, as they get closer to the Moon, its gravity begins to take hold. The astronauts feel its pull, but not as strongly as on Earth.

The force of gravity keeps all the planets moving in **orbit** around the Sun.

FIGURE 2: Gravity gets less, the further you are from large bodies.

Gravity keeps our Solar System the shape it is. If the planets were not on the move, orbiting the Sun, the Sun's gravity would pull them all into its fiery furnace. If the Sun's gravity suddenly stopped working, each planet, including our Earth, would shoot off into deep space.

QUESTIONS

1. What property of an object does gravity depend on?
2. What is the relationship between this property and the gravity of an object?
3. How does the distance between two objects affect gravity?
4. Give **two** examples of the force of gravity at work.

FIGURE 3: The planets of the Solar System don't fall into the Sun because they are moving in orbits.

Voyager's gravity-assisted flight to Neptune

Voyager was launched in 1977 to fly past the four largest of the outer planets, Jupiter, Saturn, Uranus and Neptune. No rocket could carry enough fuel to power it across the Solar System. The plan was to use the powerful pull of each planet's gravity to push Voyager, like a sling, on towards the next planet.

In 1979, Voyager reached Jupiter. Jupiter is huge, and its enormous force of gravity tended to pull Voyager towards it. But Voyager accelerated faster and was catapulted with great speed towards Saturn. As it shot past, Voyager was able to collect scientific data and fabulous images of Jupiter.

Voyager reached Saturn in 1981. Again, the planet gave Voyager the gravitational boost to accelerate it on to Uranus and Neptune.

Io is one of the moons of Jupiter. Both the Voyager fly-by and later images from the Hubble telescope confirmed that Io has enormous volcanic activity, with volcanic plumes jetting 100 km into space. Scientists suggest that gravity plays its part here, too. Jupiter's force of gravity is so great that Io is being continually pulled and stretched. This causes so much friction and heat that rocks melt, creating mighty volcanoes.

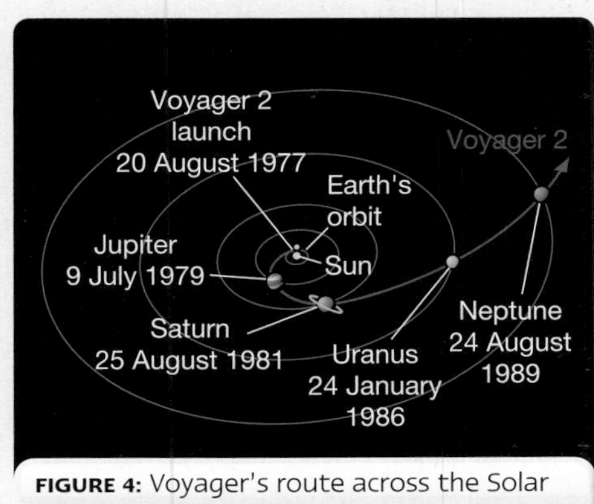

FIGURE 4: Voyager's route across the Solar System.

QUESTIONS

5 What is the problem with sending a rocket across the Solar System?

6 How did Voyager overcome this problem?

7 How do scientists explain the presence of active volcanoes on Io?

Weightless in space

For some of the time, astronauts on their way to the Moon are weightless. Thousands of miles away from the Earth, gravity is so slight that everyone and everything floats. So how can astronauts orbiting Earth in the Shuttle also be weightless when only two hundred or so kilometres above the Earth?

In fact it is not true weightlessness. The astronauts only *feel* weightless.

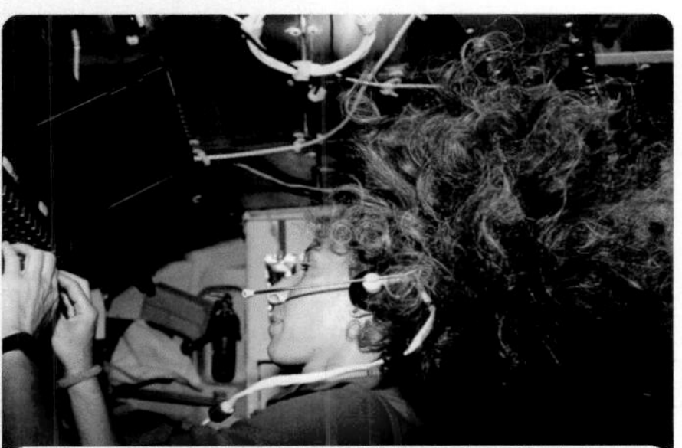

FIGURE 5: Astronauts feel weightless either far from large bodies or when moving at orbital velocity.

While in orbit, the astronauts and the Shuttle are falling towards the Earth at the same rate together: they cannot escape the pull of gravity. But, the velocity of the orbit is so great that it balances the pull of gravity. At 250 km above the Earth the **orbital velocity** needed to stay at the same height is about 28 000 kph.

Escape velocity is the velocity that a spacecraft needs to escape from Earth's gravity before travelling into space. This is 40 000 kph.

QUESTIONS

8 What is true weightlessness?

9 How can an astronaut be weightless if he is 200 km above the Earth?

10 What is escape velocity?

Birth of a star

You will find out:

- That a star is formed when gas and dust come together in space
- That the core of a star is a nuclear reactor

Risky business

The Solar System is littered with rocks, asteroids and comets journeying through space amongst the planets. Some of them collide with planets. Look at the surface of the Moon and Mars: they are pock-marked with craters. This is evidence that the danger of impact is very real.

Some 65 million years ago an asteroid 10 kilometres in diameter collided with an area in the Gulf of Mexico. This impact is thought to have made the dinosaurs extinct. We can expect an asteroid impact on Earth about every 100 million years.

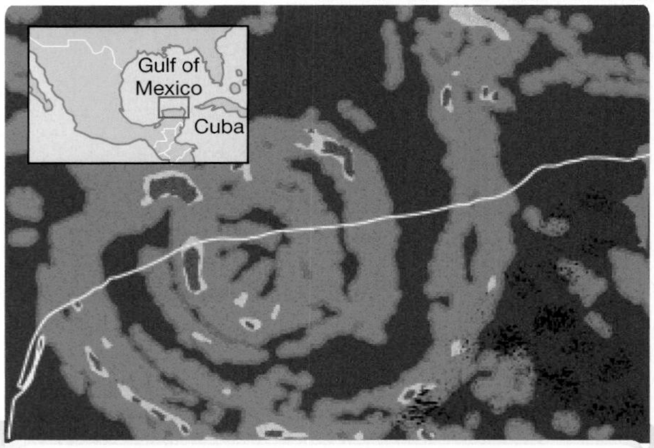

FIGURE 1: Geological surveys reveal the site of an asteroid impact thought to have wiped out the dinosaurs.

From gas and dust

It is usual to think of space as an empty void. But it contains gas and dust particles, much of it in huge clouds called **nebulae** (see figure 5 on page 281 for gas clouds in the Eagle nebula).

It is in these clouds that the universal force, **gravity**, comes into play. Gravity gradually pulls the gas molecules and dust particles together. They meet and stick, and slowly grow in size as they join up with other particles. Over millions of years they form a core which grows to the size of a planet. Gradually it becomes larger until it is about as big as our Sun.

As more material joins on, the pressure at the centre increases. Particles are squeezed together and gradually heat up. The core gets increasingly hot, and over millions of years it eventually reaches 15 million Kelvin.

At this incredible temperature, and with the immense pressures in the core, atoms behave in a way that only occurs on Earth in huge nuclear research equipment: the nuclei of atoms fuse together in a **nuclear fusion reaction**. This produces its own additional heat, and nuclear fusion becomes a **chain reaction**. Intense brightness spreads out to the surface, lighting up the sky. A star is born.

FIGURE 2: The Pleiades, young stars about 50 million years old, in the constellation of Taurus, surrounded by the gas cloud left over after their formation.

HOW OLD IS OUR SUN?

Our Sun is a middle-aged star. It's about 4600 million years old. it burns about 4 million tonnes of hydrogen every second.

QUESTIONS

1 What is a star formed from?
2 Which universal force is responsible for creating a star?
3 Describe the steps that make a star.

The birth of a star

Space isn't an empty void. It contains gas, mostly hydrogen, with dust and particles, in huge clouds called nebulae. Even the tiniest particle has mass, so each one has a gravitational attraction to its neighbours. The force of gravity gradually draws the gas and dust particles together to form a denser ball of gas in the cloud.

As particles round the ball are pulled into the mass, their potential energy changes to kinetic energy and they gain speed. Collisions between particles increase, and the mass heats up. As the ball enlarges, the pressure in the core increases and it becomes denser. Molecules begin to vibrate more vigorously and the core temperature rises until it becomes white hot. Most of the energy remains trapped inside, but some emerges as infra red radiation. The ball begins to look like a huge dull red glow hanging in space. At this stage it is called a **protostar**. These are the beginnings of a star coming to life.

It takes about a million years for a mass of gas to become a protostar. Then, the very hot core produces a stream of particles outwards in all directions, blowing away the gas and dust in the surrounding cloud. Slowly, the core starts to contract and, about 50 million years later, it reaches 15 million Kelvin – hot and dense enough for hydrogen atoms to undergo a nuclear fusion reaction. This releases vast amounts of energy, the temperature rises even further and the mass is seen as white-hot. It has become a real **star**.

FIGURE 3: The protostars in this cloud mass of the Orion and Monoceros constellations are strong infra red emitters.

The word equation for this nuclear fusion is:

hydrogen $\xrightarrow{\text{nuclear fusion}}$ **helium** + **Energy**

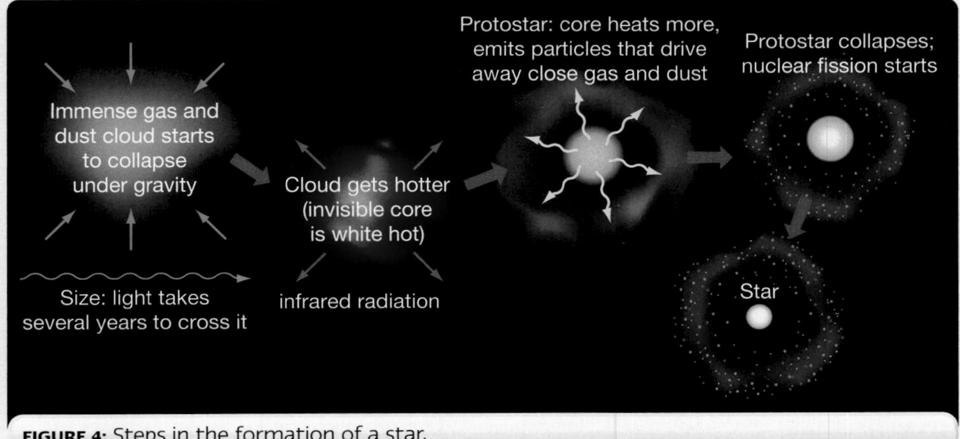

Immense gas and dust cloud starts to collapse under gravity
Size: light takes several years to cross it
Cloud gets hotter (invisible core is white hot)
infrared radiation
Protostar: core heats more, emits particles that drive away close gas and dust
Protostar collapses; nuclear fission starts
Star

FIGURE 4: Steps in the formation of a star.

QUESTIONS

4 Explain why the core of a protostar becomes hot.

5 15 million Kelvin is an important temperature. Why?

6 Suggest why an infra red telescope is used to find protostars.

KELVIN

Kelvin is a measure of temperature based on absolute zero. 1 kelvin (K) is -273 °C.

Getting the right balance

A star is not a burning object like a fire which uses oxygen. It is a huge, continuous and uncontrolled hydrogen bomb nuclear explosion. So how is it that the star does not just explode out into space? The answer lies in our old friend gravity again.

The nuclear explosion pushes outwards, but the force of gravity is so great that it pulls everything back in. It's a constant battle between the outward **radiation pressure** and inward gravity. As long as these two forces are in balance, the star is stable.

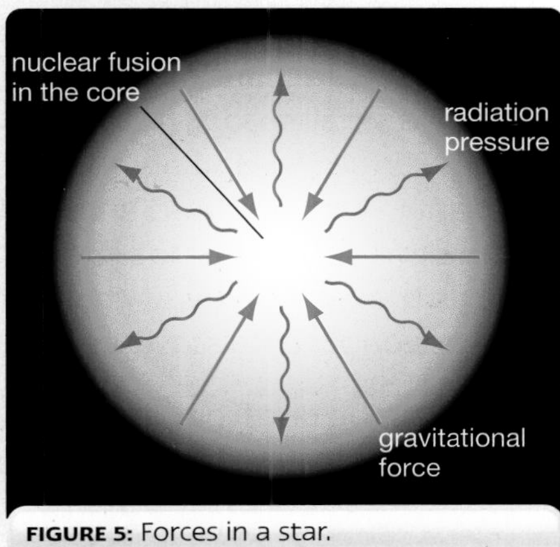

nuclear fusion in the core
radiation pressure
gravitational force

FIGURE 5: Forces in a star.

QUESTIONS

7 What is radiation pressure?

8 What role does gravity play in a star?

9 What does it mean to say that a star is stable?

Formation of the Solar System

You will find out:

- That the Solar System was formed from a huge cloud of gas
- That there are rock planets and gas giants
- Where comets and asteriods come from

Beyond our world

Humans are fearless explorers. Curiosity drives us to find out what is out there. From earliest times, people have looked up into the night skies and wondered what was up in the heavens. As technology has improved, we have been able to take the first few steps to find out.

The Solar System

Our Sun was originally formed from a cloud of gas and dust. Gravity pulled it all together into a huge ball; it heated up to immensely high temperatures and exploded like a hydrogen bomb in space. When the new Sun became stable, the surrounding gases, particles and rocks were still orbiting it. Gradually the particles and rocks joined together to become the nine (or ten, see below) planets of our Solar System.

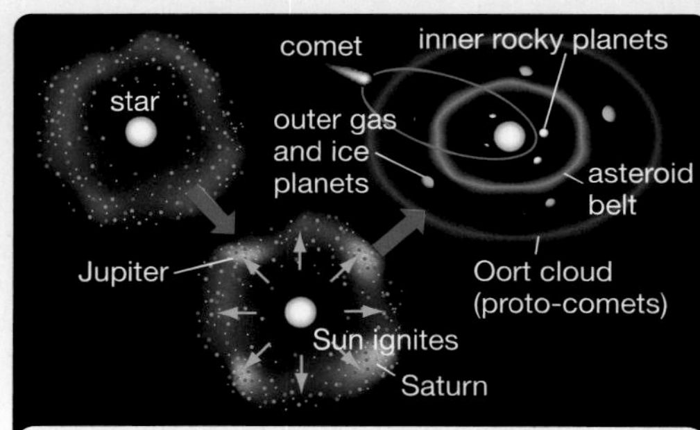

FIGURE 1: How the Solar System was formed.

Yet again, gravity played a part. It helped to make the Sun, then the planets, and now it keeps the planets in orbit around the Sun.

The four inner planets, Mercury, Venus, Earth and Mars, are known as the **rocky planets**: they contain iron and nickel and have a hard rock crust. The outer four planets are known as the **gas giants**: Jupiter, Saturn, Uranus and Neptune are huge, made of liquid gas with a small solid core. They have no hard surface to land on. Pluto is an odd planet. It is very small and made of rock and ice. Its orbit is not in the same plane as the others. It was thought to be furthest from the Sun until 2003 when astronomers discovered a tenth planet they named Sedna.

FIGURE 2: The Solar System showing the orbits of the planets round the Sun.

Looking at the disc from above the North Pole, all the planets orbit the Sun in an anti-clockwise direction, more or less in the same plane.

MOON ROCKS

The Moon contains a lot of basalt rock, which indicates early volcanic activity. But because it has no atmosphere and no water, there are no sedimentary rocks like sandstone and limestone.

QUESTIONS

1 Explain how the planets were formed.
2 What is special about the first four planets?
3 Name the next four outer planets. In what way are they different from the four inner planets?
4 What is special about Pluto?

...asteroid belt ...aurora borealis ...gas giants ...magnetic storm

How the Solar System became disc-shaped

The Solar System was formed from a huge mass of gas and dust particles. As it contracted under gravity, this mass started to spin and it flattened into a disc, like clay on a potter's wheel. Rocks started to form as dust particles came together.

When nuclear fusion began in the Sun, intense radiation blew the gases outwards, leaving only the hard rocks near the centre of the disc. They continued to collide and fuse with each other, eventually forming four large bodies. That is why the first four planets are rocky planets (see figure 1).

Beyond Mars, the fourth rocky planet, is the **asteroid belt**, composed of rocks and asteroids. These are the left-overs from the formation of the planets. Beyond the asteroid belt it is cold enough for gases from the original cloud to condense, and this is where the gas giants, made mostly of liquid hydrogen, were formed.

Way beyond Pluto, reaching into deep space, is a vast cloud of particles and ice called the Oort cloud. It is thought that all our comets and **meteorites** come from this outer zone at the furthest edges of our Solar System. By studying meteorites, scientists have worked out that the Solar System is 4600 million years old.

How was Earth's Moon formed? The current theory is that a 'planetoid' about the size of Mars collided with the Earth. The material dislodged from the Earth in this collision remained held in Earth's orbit by gravity and eventually formed the Moon.

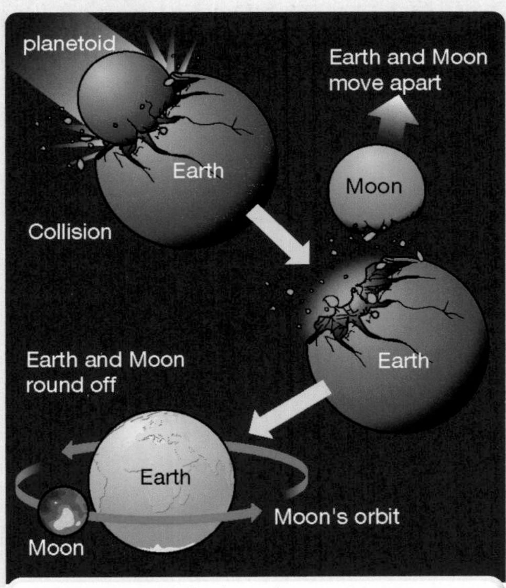

FIGURE 3: How it is thought our Moon was formed.

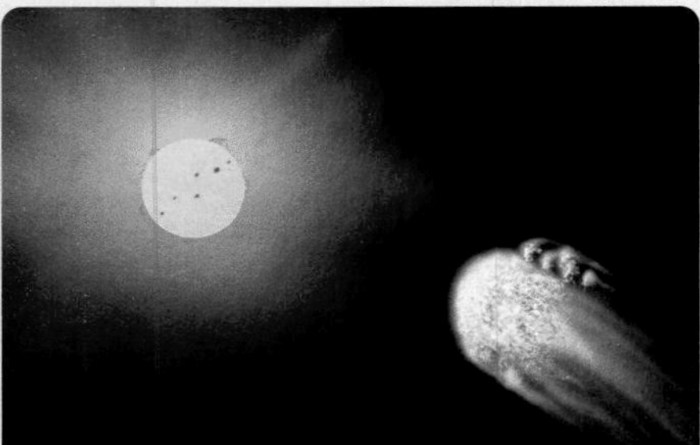

FIGURE 4: The tail of a comet reveals the direction of the solar wind, always streaming away from it.

COMETS

Comets come from deep space. As they get closer to the Sun they develop a tail of dust and ionised gas. The tail always points away from the Sun, even when it moves away back into deep space.

QUESTIONS

5 Suggest why some planets were formed of rock and others were formed from gas.

6 What is the asteroid belt?

7 What is the Oort cloud and what makes it interesting?

8 What is the current theory on how the Moon was formed?

Solar wind

The Sun throws 1 million tonnes of electrically charged particles out into space in all directions every second! This stream of material is called **solar wind**. Once away from the Sun, the particles speed up to travel at a supersonic 200 to 800 kilometres per second, reaching the Earth after two days, then continuing all the way past Pluto and on into deep space.

The solar wind is not steady. It has massive bursts called **magnetic storms**. During these, the electric charge and mass of the particles give rise to the following unusual events.

- The **aurora borealis** are the amazing northern lights that can be seen near the Arctic Circle. Charged particles in the solar wind interact with particles in the upper atmosphere, causing them to glow.
- Magnetic storms can affect telecommunications and satellites. In 1989 there was such a fierce magnetic storm that all radio and computer communications were knocked out across the whole of northern Canada.

FIGURE 5: The spectacular aurora borealis.

QUESTIONS

9 What is the solar wind?

10 Describe ways in which we experience the effects of the solar wind here on Earth.

11 Describe in your own words how the aurora borealis are formed.

...meteorite ...rocky planet ...solar wind

Life and death of a star

You will find out:

- That a star has a sequence of events in its life and then it dies
- That the events in a star's life depend on its size

The Sun is middle aged

At 4.6 billion years old, our Sun is an average-sized star halfway through its life. This gives us plenty of time to work out what to do when it dies, in about 4 billion years' time. By then, it will have used up its fuel and begun to change into a red giant. It will expand enormously and the surface will reach Earth's orbit. Before that, our atmosphere will have been blown away and the oceans will evaporate. Finally, the Earth itself will be vaporised.

Life history of stars

Nothing lasts forever, not even a star. Eventually the hydrogen fuel inside a star begins to run out. Meanwhile, the star is constantly losing mass in the form of energy and solar wind. The gravitational pull on its remaining material lessens. It begins to expand outwards and becomes a **red giant**. What happens next depends on the size of the star.

When the fuel finally runs out in a medium-sized star like our own Sun, its temperature drops. The red giant collapses under the force of gravity and becomes a **white dwarf**. Eventually it cools down even more to become a **black dwarf**.

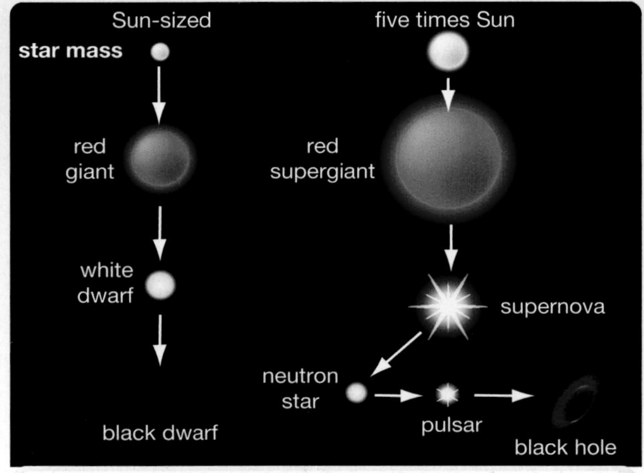

FIGURE 1: The life and death of stars.

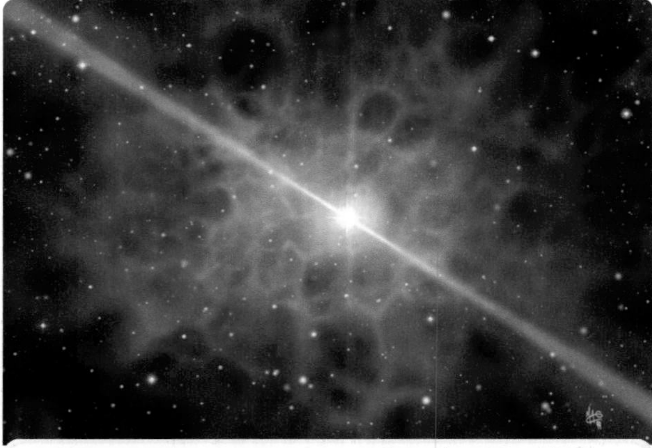

FIGURE 2: A pulsar rotates on an axis and emits radio waves from opposite points near its equator.

If it is a large star, it expands to become a **red supergiant**. Hydrogen burns to form helium and helium forms carbon. Then carbon starts to burn and, in one of the Universe's biggest explosions, the outer layers are blasted off and the whole thing becomes a **supernova**. The small core collapses inwards and becomes a **neutron star** that may develop into a **pulsar**. If it is large enough, gravity collapses the pulsar until it becomes a **black hole**. Its gravity is so immense that no light escapes from it.

QUESTIONS

1. What happens to a star when its fuel begins to run out?
2. What happens next to a medium-sized star like our own Sun?
3. What happens if it is a larger star?
4. Explain how a pulsar becomes a black hole.

BETELGEUSE

Betelgeuse is a red supergiant. It is located in the Orion constellation and is one of the largest stars visible.

...black dwarf ...black hole ...force of gravity ...neutron star ...pulsar

Two options for a star

You will recall that a star is in a stable state when the force of **radiation pressure** pushing outwards is balanced by the **force of gravity** pulling inwards.

With time, the hydrogen in the core is gradually used up. As the mass of the star decreases so does the force of gravity. Radiation pressure now has the upper hand and the star expands to become a red giant (see figure 1). What happens next depends on the initial mass of the star.

If it is a medium-sized star like our own Sun, it stays a red giant until most of the hydrogen in the core is used up. Hydrogen fusion moves to the outer shell of the star. it is here that the lighter elements like carbon, iron and nickel are formed. The core cools and begins to contract. Radiation pressure reduces and gravity begins to take over again. It pulls the red giant back into itself, which eventually collapses into a dense and very hot white dwarf. Eventually it cools even further, like a dying ember, to become a black dwarf.

Larger stars have a more spectacular ending. As hydrogen fuel is used up and mass is reduced, the radiation pressure expands the star into a huge red supergiant. As it is such a large star it uses up its fuel very quickly and becomes unstable. Cooling and collapse follow and the core becomes super-dense. This rapid contraction under the huge force of gravity raises the core temperature to millions of Kelvin. The star explodes as a most spectacular supernova, emitting the energy of ten billion stars. It is at this point that many of the heavier elements are formed.

The explosion blows off the outer layers of the star leaving a very dense neutron star. Some neutron stars rotate and emit short, regular pulses of radiation. These are called pulsars.

If the pulsar still has enough mass, the force of its own gravity will collapse it even further to become a black hole. The force of gravity in a black hole is so great that no radiation can escape from it.

FIGURE 3: A supernova and source of heavier elements.

QUESTIONS

5 What triggers a star to begin to move from its stable state?

6 Describe the phases that a star the size of our own Sun will go through.

7 If the star is very much larger than our Sun, what will it eventually become? Explain how this happens.

DAY-TIME STARS

Supernovae release enormous amounts of energy. In 1054, Chinese astronomers observed a supernova which was bright enough to be seen by day. It was visible for several months.

Children of the stars

Hydrogen fuels the nuclear reaction inside the core of a star that produces energy and helium. When the hydrogen runs out, the star begins to use helium as a fuel. The higher fusion temperature of helium allows new elements like carbon, oxygen, iron and nickel to be made.

During the last few moments as a supernova explodes, super-high temperatures create the heavy metals like gold, silver, copper and lead. The explosion scatters all these elements across space. These become the dust clouds (nebulae) from which the next generation of stars will be formed.

Our Earth and all the living things on it are formed from the elements made in earlier stars. We are truly children of the stars.

QUESTIONS

8 How are elements like carbon and iron made?

9 How are the heavier elements made?

10 The first gas clouds in space consisted of hydrogen. Can you explain why second generation clouds consist of hydrogen plus dust and particles of many elements?

11 What does 'we are truly children of the stars' mean?

In the beginning

You will find out:

- That the Universe began with a Big Bang
- How atomic particles and hydrogen were formed in the first seconds

Is this the answer?

'Where do we come from? What are we? Where are we going?' So said the artist Paul Gauguin.

Scientists have come up with answers about the material world. Stephen Hawking proposes that time and space began at the moment of the **Big Bang**: all the matter and energy of the Universe, compressed into the size of a pinhead, exploded. Before that there was nothing.

The M-theory adds to the picture: before the Big Bang, several hidden universes existed in parallel. Two of these collided and the resulting release of energy was the Big Bang.

The Big Bang

The physicist Edwin Hubble observed the galaxies and proposed that the Universe is expanding. The stars and galaxies are all moving outwards, away from each other at tremendous speeds. Where did they start from?

By observing the direction the galaxies are moving, then working backwards, it seems that a long time ago the whole universe began at one spot in space. Scientists believe that to start with, there was just a gigantic amount of energy. They don't explain where it came from or how it got there.

Suddenly the energy exploded, and at that moment, time and space came into being. The temperature of the explosion was enormous – billions of degrees. As the temperature cooled, energy began to change into matter. Within seconds, **protons**, **neutrons** and **electrons** were formed. They came together to make the first atoms of the first element, hydrogen. The hydrogen gathered as clouds in space, and over millions of years it became stars, planets and galaxies and all the stuff that makes up our Universe.

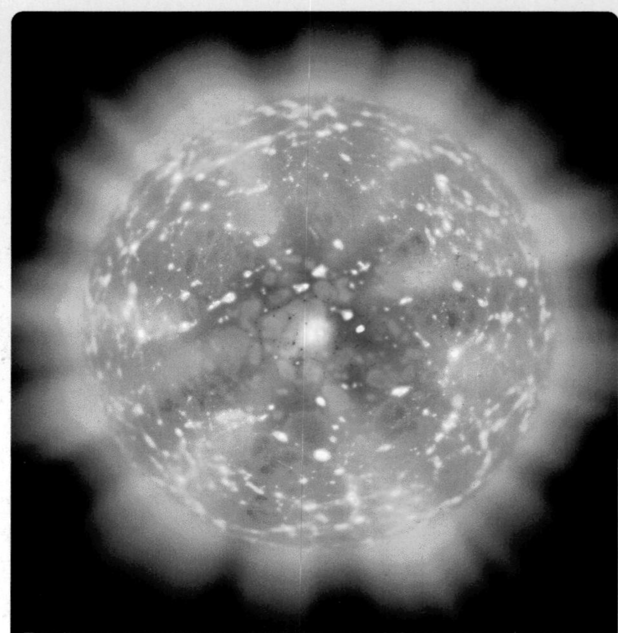

FIGURE 1: The Big Bang theory suggests that before any matter existed, the Energy of the Universe was concentrated in a space the size of a pinhead.

QUESTIONS

1. What did Hubble conclude from his observations of galaxies?
2. By looking backwards, what idea was formed about the beginning of the Universe?
3. What was the Big Bang?
4. What happened immediately after the Big Bang as the temperature cooled?

RECYCLING

Our Sun and Solar System are only 4.6 billion years old. That means that our part of the Universe has probably gone through the birth, life and death cycle at least three times already.

The birth of our Universe

About 15 billion years ago a tremendous explosion, the Big Bang, released vast amounts of energy. At that point all energy and matter were contained in a single point. At the instant of its release, time, space, matter and our Universe came into existence. What existed before this event is completely unknown and is anybody's guess.

You may know Einstein's famous equation $E = mc^2$. E is energy, m is mass and c is the speed of light – a huge value. The equation means that energy can be converted to mass and vice versa: (mass of matter) × (speed of light)^2 is the amount of energy you can get from that mass. In other words, energy and mass are interchangeable.

Instantaneously, as the temperature of the Big Bang explosion began to cool, energy began to change into matter. The expanding space began to fill up with the fundamental building blocks which make up our Universe: matter, anti-matter, quarks, photons, electrons and neutrinos. As the temperature cooled further, protons and neutrons formed, and eventually the first atoms of the first element hydrogen came into existence. This hydrogen made up the first gas clouds, which became the birthplace for the first stars.

The temperature at the moment of the Big Bang was unimaginably high: 10^{32} Kelvin (that's 10 with 32 zeros after it). As the Universe expanded the temperature dropped dramatically. Today, 15 billion years later, the average temperature of the Universe is just 3 Kelvin.

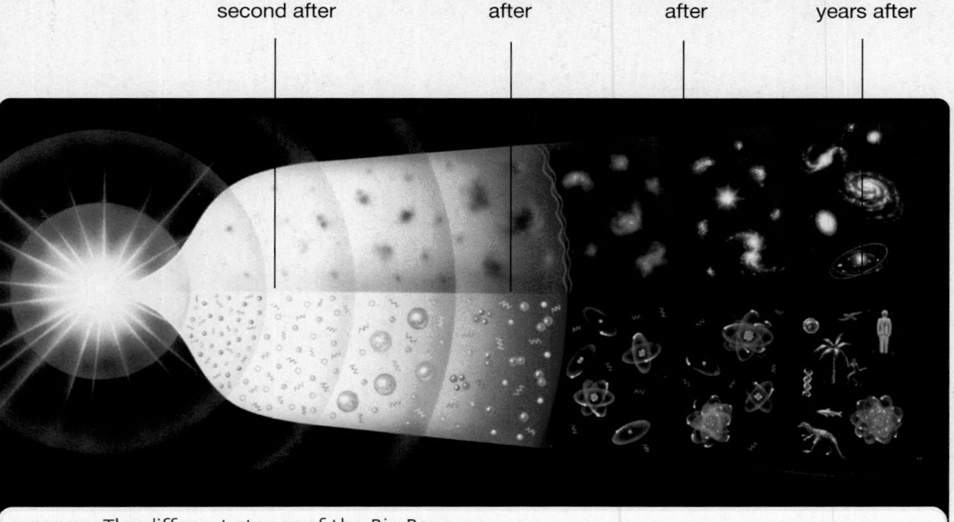

FIGURE 2: The different stages of the Big Bang.

QUESTIONS

5 What existed before and at the moment of the Big Bang? What happened to it?
6 How does Einstein's famous equation relate to the Big Bang?
7 What happened to the temperature, immediately after the Big Bang? What was formed?
8 Compare the temperatures at the time of the Big Bang and today.

Far away is long ago

Light takes time to travel: we see the Sun as it was when the light left it 8 minutes ago. The more distant the stars and galaxies that astronomers can observe, the further back in time they are looking. Light from the most distant galaxies observable has taken billions of years to travel to us.

The Hubble telescope has shown us images of some of the first galaxies formed after the Big Bang. This gives astronomers clues as to how the Universe developed in those early times.

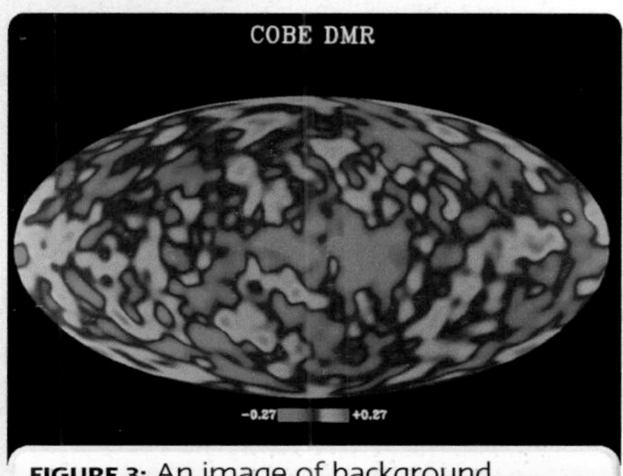

FIGURE 3: An image of background radiation, the afterglow of the Big Bang.

NASA's COBE satellite has a microwave detector. It was able to detect cosmic **background radiation** which is the afterglow of the Big Bang. This is key evidence of the huge temperatures which must have existed in those first few seconds.

QUESTIONS

9 Explain what is meant by 'far away is long ago'.
10 What information do we gain from observing the most distant galaxies?
11 The COBE satellite has an infra red detector. What was it able to detect, and why is this important?

The expanding universe

You will find out:

- That the red shift is proof that the Universe is expanding
- That galaxies are moving away from each other
- That our universe has three possible futures

Edwin Hubble again!

Edwin Hubble was one of the first astronomers to scan the night sky thoroughly. He invented a way to classify objects in space based on what they were made of, their distance and their shape and brightness.

He noticed that distant galaxies glowed redder than closer ones of the same kind. This meant that the galaxies had to be moving away from each other and that the Universe was expanding.

The red shift

Edwin Hubble discovered that, whichever way he looked in the night sky, all the galaxies were moving away from each other. Their light was shifted towards the red part of the spectrum. This happens when an object is travelling away from the observer – the wavelength appears to get longer. Hubble called this the **red shift**.

FIGURE 1: The redder the galaxy, the faster it is travelling away from Earth.

This is like the effect you hear when an ambulance drives past. As it comes towards you the siren seems to increase in pitch, but as it passes and moves away, the sound drops in pitch. This is because the wavelength reaching you is longer.

Hubble also discovered that the further away the galaxy, the bigger its red shift. This means that as the distance of a galaxy increases, so does the speed at which it is moving away. The closer the galaxy, the slower it is moving away from us.

George Gamow, a Russian scientist, had the idea that if all the galaxies are moving away from each other, then perhaps they are all travelling from the same original starting point. Perhaps there was one place where they all came from. He thought of the term Big Bang to describe this starting point of the Universe.

QUESTIONS

1. What did Edwin Hubble notice when he observed distant galaxies?
2. What did he call this effect?
3. Do all galaxies move at the same speed? Explain.
4. Explain how the Russian scientist George Gamow worked out the idea that the Universe started at one point.

DARK MATTER

Dark matter does not emit any electromagnetic radiation and therefore it cannot be seen by any of our telescopes. It is thought that 85% of the Universe could be dark matter.

Evidence for an expanding Universe

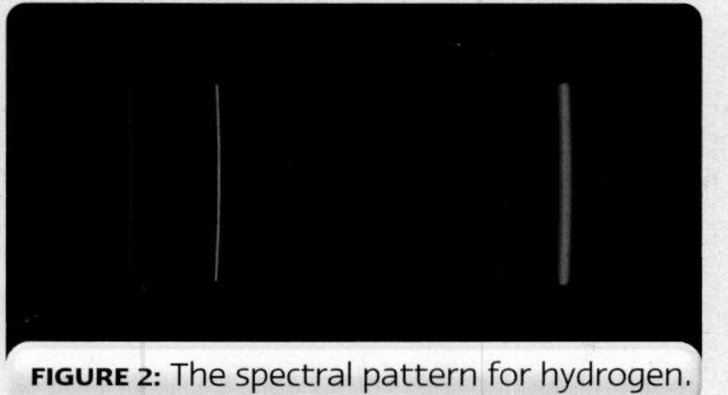
FIGURE 2: The spectral pattern for hydrogen.

When heated enough, every element emits visible light with a particular range of colours of the spectrum – its spectral pattern. A spectroscope shows these colours as bands at different wavelengths. So if you look at hydrogen through a spectroscope you always see the same **spectral pattern**. It uniquely identifies hydrogen.

All stars burn hydrogen to fuel their internal nuclear reactions. Edwin Hubble looked at the hydrogen pattern of different stars and galaxies. He noticed that it varied: the whole pattern moved towards the red end of the spectrum. He also observed that the further away the galaxies, the greater the shift into the red. He called this the red shift.

When a light source is moving away from the observer, the wavelength appears to stretch and get longer. This lengthening of the wave can be seen as light becoming redder. The reverse also holds: if light is moving towards an observer, the wavelength appears to shorten and moves into the blue. This is called blue shift. Both these are examples of the **Doppler effect**.

Hubble also observed that the further away the galaxy, the greater the spectral shift to the red. This meant that the further the galaxy is from Earth, the faster it is moving. Hubble concluded that all galaxies were moving away from the Earth, and the further away they were, the faster they were travelling.

George Gamow, a Russian physicist, came up with the idea that if all the galaxies were moving away from each other, it should be possible to look backwards and work out where they all originally came from. It seems that they all started from the same point and at the same time as a great big explosion! He called this the Big Bang.

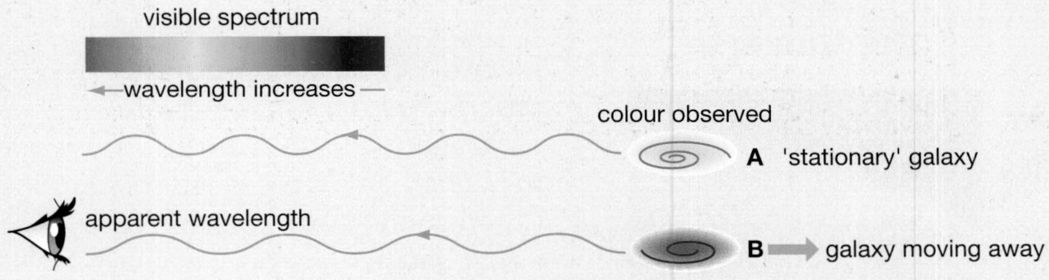

Light leaves galaxy B at exactly the same speed as from galaxy A. But B is moving away from the observer. So, from her viewpoint, it reaches her at the speed of light minus the speed of galaxy B. Therefore the wavelength she observes is longer than for A.

FIGURE 3: A galaxy shows a red shift because it is moving away from Earth.

QUESTIONS

5 What idea did Hubble use to interpret the observations he made?

6 Explain in your own words what causes the red shift.

7 What was the second observation that Hubble made about the speed of galaxies?

8 What piece of evidence did George Gamow use to work out the way the Universe began?

Three possible outcomes

What future do the discoveries suggest for our Universe? That depends on the total amount of matter in the Universe.

- The force of gravity may be strong enough to slow down the expansion, stop it and put it into reverse. The Universe will contract into a **Big Crunch**.
- If the force of gravity is not strong enough, the Universe will continue to expand and keep cooling.
- A third option is that the mass and gravity are in balance, and that the Universe will eventually stop expanding and remain in a stable state.

What is still missing is a value for the mass of the Universe. Current calculations suggest that there is a huge amount of mass unaccounted for. This is called **dark matter**.

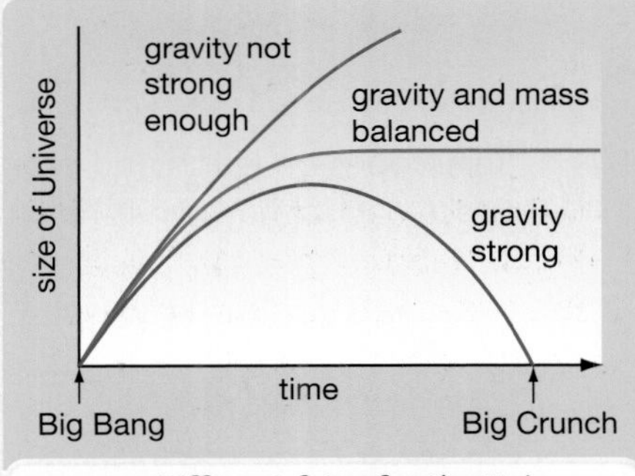

FIGURE 4: Different fates for the Universe.

QUESTIONS

9 What are the **three** possible outcomes for our Universe?

10 What is the key factor which determines each possible outcome?

11 What problem do astrophysicists face in trying to determine which way it will go?

Unit summary

Concept map

Electromagnetic radiation:

- travels as waves of defined wavelength and frequency that obey the wave formula: wave speed = frequency × wavelength
- transfers energy from one place to another
- can be reflected, absorbed or transmitted by substances.

Radiation can damage living cells.

The electromagnetic spectrum is continuous, but is divided into regions.

Each region has a specified wavelength range. From shortest to longest they are:

- gamma rays
- X-rays
- ultraviolet
- visible light
- infrared
- microwaves
- radio waves.

When a substance absorbs radiation it gets hotter and may create an alternating current.

Radiation has many uses in communication systems including: satellites, optical fibres, and mobile phone networks.

Communication signals may be analogue or digital.

Radioactivity

REACTOR AREA

CAUTION
RADIOACTIVE
AREA

The half-life of a radioactive substance is the time it takes for the number of radioactive atoms to halve.

Radioactive substances have unstable atoms that emit radiation. There are three forms (alpha particles, beta particles and gamma rays), each with uses and hazards.

The Universe

Telescopes on Earth and orbiting in space gather data that help us find out about the Solar System and the galaxies in the Universe.

Different types of telescope can detect visible light or other electromagnetic radiations, such as radio waves or X-rays.

A wave moving away from an observer will appear to increase in wavelength and decrease in frequency. This is called red shift. Observations show:

- that galaxies are moving away from each other at very high speed
- the further away a galaxy is, the faster it is moving away from us.

Current evidence suggests that:

- the universe is expanding
- matter and space expanded violently from a small initial point (the 'big bang').

Unit quiz

1 State the three characteristics of electromagnetic waves.

2 What is the electromagnetic spectrum? List the different groups in sequence starting with gamma rays.

3 What happens to an object when it absorbs radiation?

4 Which type of radiation kills living cells?

5 Which three types of radiation are used in communications technology? Suggest examples of each type of communication.

6 Which type of signal is better suited to modern technology such as optical fibres and computers: analogue or digital? Explain why.

7 What are the three types of nuclear radiation?

8 Which type of radiation is slow moving and can be stopped by paper? Which type travels at the speed of light and can penetrate anything?

9 Define the half-life of a radioactive substance.

10 What evidence is there to support the idea that the Universe is expanding?

11 What do you understand by the phrase 'big bang'?

12 Which type of telescope gives the best quality images when observing the night sky: Earth based or space platform? Explain why.

Citizenship activity

Mobile phones and transmission masts

The UK has the highest number of mobile phone users in Europe. Mobile phones are convenient, easy to use and very much the accepted technology. Many people need them for work, while for others they are a 'must have' fashion accessory.

In order to get an acceptable level of coverage for their networks, mobile phone companies have put up transmission masts on schools, churches and hospitals. This is because these buildings are located at good vantage points around the country.

Mobile phone masts receive and transmit radiation. The phone companies say that because the masts are tall, there is no danger to anyone walking or playing in the area around a mast, although some people have expressed concerns.

There is also some concern that people who use mobile phones for long periods might suffer damage to the brain. This is because there is some evidence that prolonged exposure to radiation increases the chance of developing brain tumours.

QUESTIONS

1 What are the attractions of owning a mobile phone?

2 What are the perceived dangers of using mobile phones?

3 Do you think the benefits outweigh the dangers? Explain your answer.

4 Would you agree to have a mobile telephone mast erected at your school? Why?

Exam practice

Exam practice questions

1 Match the words A, B, C and D to the spaces 1–4 in the sentences below.

A electrons **B** neutrons
C nucleus **D** protons

Atoms contain a central (1) surrounded by (2) . All atoms of a particular element have the same number of (3) . Atoms of one isotope of an element have a different number of (4) compared to atoms of a different isotope of the same element. [4]

2 The table shows typical wavelengths for different parts of the electromagnetic spectrum. Complete the table using the words A, B, C and D. (One part of the spectrum has already been done for you.)

A gamma rays **B** microwaves
C radio waves **D** ultraviolet radiation

Part of the electromagnetic spectrum	Typical wavelength
	1×10^{3} m
	1×10^{-2} m
	1×10^{-8} m
X-rays	1×10^{-10} m
	1×10^{-12} m

[4]

3 Match the words A, B, C and D to the spaces 1–4 in the sentences below.

A alpha particle **B** beta particle
C gamma ray **D** nuclei

Some substances give out radiation from the (1) of their atoms. The radiation may be an (2) which is the nucleus of a helium atom, or electromagnetic radiation in the form of a (3) , or a (4) which is an electron. [4]

In questions 4 to 7, choose the best answer.

4 Alpha particles are ...

A very ionising so they can penetrate long distances in air.
B charged so they cannot be deflected by magnetic fields.
C very ionising so they cannot penetrate more than a few centimetres in air.
D very ionising so they can penetrate through thin cardboard. [1]

5 The half-life of an isotope is three days. This means that ...

A the size of the sample halves in three days.
B the isotope is not radioactive after six days.
C the sample does not decay after six days.
D the count rate of the sample halves in three days. [1]

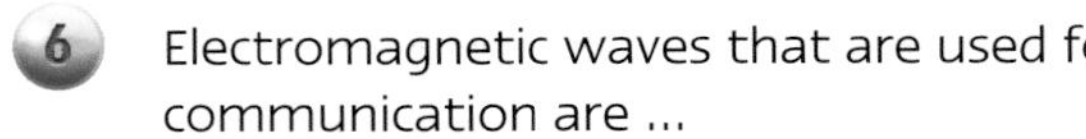

6 Electromagnetic waves that are used for communication are ...

A radio waves, sound waves and visible light.
B radio waves, microwaves and infrared.
C sound waves, seismic waves and visible light.
D radio waves, microwaves and ultraviolet. [1]

7 One advantage of using a satellite-based telescope is that ...

A pictures of fainter, more distant objects are possible.
B the satellite-based telescope is bigger than ground-based telescopes.
C pictures can be taken at night.
D the satellite-based telescope can get close to distant stars. [1]

In questions 8 to 11, identify the answer that is **not correct**.

8 Observations of the Universe are made using telescopes that detect ...

A visible radiation. **B** X-rays.
C radio waves. **D** seismic waves. [1]

9 Digital signals ...

A can be processed by computers.
B can be sent down optical fibres using infrared radiation.
C are less prone to interference than analogue signals.
D are signals that are continuously varying. [1]

10 A radioactive tracer ...

A can be used in hospitals.
B is safe to use in people if it emits alpha particles.
C will become less radioactive in time.
D can be used to trace leaks in a pipeline. [1]

11 Electromagnetic waves ...

A travel through a vacuum.
B can be reflected and transmitted by different materials.
C do not affect living cells.
D may be absorbed by some substances, heating them up. [1]

12 **a** Explain what is meant by the 'Big Bang' theory. [2]

b Explain what the red shift tells us about the movement of galaxies. [2]

c How can the red shift provide evidence for the Big Bang? [2]

13 Different types of electromagnetic radiation may affect cells differently.

a For each of the following, state its effect, if any, on living cells.

Type of electromagnetic radiation	Effect, if any, on living cells
Infrared	
Ultraviolet	
Gamma rays	
Radio waves	

[4]

b Complete the following table to show which type of electromagnetic waves is used for the different applications.

Type of electromagnetic radiation	Use
	to produce shadow pictures of bones
	to cook food
	to sterilise surgical instruments
	to transmit broadcasts

[4]

(Total 34 marks)

Worked example

A radioactive sample has a half-life of four minutes.

a How long will it take for the count rate of the sample to fall to a quarter of its original value? [3]

b The count-rate from the detector does not fall to zero even when there is no radioactive source nearby. Explain the cause of this reading. [2]

c The sample emits alpha particles and gamma rays only. Explain why the sample should be stored in a lead-lined box. [2]

d State three more safety measures that should be taken when the sample is out of its box. [3]

a *The count rate falls by half after one half-life.✓ It falls to a quarter after two half-lives.✓ The answer is 2 x 4 = 8 minutes.✓*

The correct answer – laid out so the examiner could follow the logic.

b *Background radiation✓ from nearby rocks, cosmic rays.✓*

A sensible answer; other sources of background radiation that could be included are radon gas, buildings and food

c *Gamma rays are very penetrating✓ and only lead will absorb them.✓*

This answer is correct and to the point.

d *Use tongs to handle the sample;✓ do not look at the sample;✓ do not leave it out of its box for a long time.✓*

Good answers – you could also ask anyone else in the room to stand away from the sample, or use a lead shield.

Overall Grade: A

The student explained their answers fully which helped to gain full marks. Always show working so you can get some credit even if you do make a mistake with calculations. Definitions and explanations are best written out as full sentences to avoid room for doubt.

Explaining the world we live in

Introduction

Science affects all our lives. We all need to know about how. Science tries to answer big questions such as:

- How did the world get to be the way it is?
- How can we make life safer for its inhabitants?
- How can we look after it for future generations?

Most **scientists** specialise in narrow areas of science. But together they build up evidence that allows us the tackle the big questions.

So what do scientists do? They gather **data**. Data is information. Scientists observe, count and measure things. Observing gives qualitative data. Counting and measuring give quantitative data.

Evidence

Scientists use data for **evidence**. It's like police work. Fingerprints, marks at the scene of the crime and DNA samples are examples of data gathered. They are evidence used in a court to get a conviction.

But is the evidence **reliable**? How confident are we about it and do we trust it? If it is reliable, can we be sure the data are interpreted correctly? Reliable evidence correctly interpreted is said to be **valid**. Whenever you read or hear about scientific work, or do it yourself, you should think about these questions. It's the basis of good science. It's the **thinking behind the doing**.

Sections A – H introduce the key ideas further.

A Fundamental ideas

A1 A difference of opinion

Fashion is a matter of opinion. What you like someone else might dislike. In life we all have preferences and favourites. We have feelings and prejudices. We all say things without the facts to back up what we say.

There's no place for prejudice, whim or hearsay in science. An opinion must be supported by valid and reliable evidence.

EXAMPLE

A friend says to you, "She's the best singer around today." You might not agree. What would your friend need to say to convince you?

You won't be persuaded by, "Because I think her voice is great." That's a matter of opinion. However, "Because she has a great vocal range", is different. It's something that can be measured. Even easier to measure is chart success, but you may not agree that this is the mark of the 'best singer'.

Questions

1. Look at the picture. Who is the best sprinter? Before you answer, remember this is just one race!
2. Do you think it is easier to say who is the best gymnast or the fastest runner in the world?

A2 Arranging data

Scientists arrange data in ways that help them to spot patterns and trends. How they do this depends on the type of data:

Arranging qualitative data into groups or categories is called **labelling**.

Counting gives quantitative data. The data can be arranged in order, either going up or going down. This is **ranking**.

Measurements can also be ranked. But we can do more with them. If we make measurements, we can say what the differences between them are. We call this **measuring a continuous variable**. Length, mass, time, temperature and electric current are examples of continuous variables.

EXAMPLE

How could you decide how effective a kettle is?

You might simply say the kettle boiled the water. This is labelling. Either it worked or it didn't. You might say it boiled the water faster than another kettle. This is ranking. You might say that it boiled the water in three minutes. This is measuring time. Time is an example of a continuous variable. We don't simply rank the kettle. By measuring other kettles we can say how much faster or slower the water boils.

Questions

1. If you are buying a kettle, which data would be most useful in helping you to choose?
2. A number of people are asked which type of shampoo they use. If you listed the shampoos in order of popularity, would you be labelling, ranking or measuring a continuous variable?

A3 One thing leads to another – or does it?

Things change, and this interests scientists. They like to explain changes. Often the hope is that changes can be predicted and managed.

Can we help ships by forecasting violent weather and seas?

Things that can change are called **variables**. Scientists look for links between variables and try to explain them.

Sometimes there's no explanation. We say it's a **chance occurrence**. While you are brushing your teeth in the morning, a new baby is born somewhere in the world. And this happens every day! But it's extremely unlikely the two events are linked.

Sometimes the link can be explained. Exercise actively for a period of time and your heart rate increases. One variable (how active you are) changes another variable (your heart rate). This is a **causal** link. Usually several variables are involved and linked. These variables are in **association**.

What variables influence how well this wheat grows? What can we do to increase the yields? We need to understand the relationships between the variables in association.

EXAMPLE

If you use a kettle to boil water, the kettle may fur up. How much it furs depends on the hardness of the water and how much water is boiled. The furring insulates the kettle's element, making it less efficient. It takes longer for a kettle of water to boil and uses more electricity.

Question

What are the variables in association?

B Observation

B1 Interpreting observations

Scientists spend a lot of time making **observations**. Your brain processes the information. It compares it with knowledge that you already have stored. This affects how you describe what you see.

EXAMPLE

When you look at a plant with some of its green leaves turning yellow, you might say, "Some leaves are yellow", "The plant looks ill" or "The leaves aren't getting enough light for chlorophyll formation." Your response depends on what you already know.

Questions

1. How would you describe what happens when sugar is added to a mug of tea or coffee and stirred?
2. How do you think a five-year-old child might describe the same thing?
3. Does observation give qualitative or quantitative data?

B2 Observe and group

We can use our knowledge to group things with similar properties. For example:

- organisms as animals, plants or micro-organisms
- substances as elements, compounds or mixtures
- materials as metals, polymers, ceramics or composites.

We can do this because we know about the properties of each group. Observing these properties lets you put things into the right groups.

Scientists use several terms for the same idea. They put things into:

- groups (grouping)
- classes (classifying)
- categories (categorising).

It all amounts to the same thing!

There are many ways to group things. Just imagine the different ways you might group the people you know or the types of music you listen to. The way we group things depends on how we want to use the groupings. For example, we might want to make a lightweight container to keep food cool. So we would look at materials with low density and good thermal insulation.

EXAMPLE

In the picture you can see different pieces of laboratory equipment. There are various ways in which they might be grouped. For example, some are used for making measurements, some are used for mixing substances and some are used for safety.

Questions

1. Look at the picture of the laboratory. List the equipment that might fall into the category 'measuring equipment'.
2. Imagine you are a technician and have to arrange the storage of the equipment. People need to be able to find the equipment they want easily and quickly. How does putting equipment into categories help?

B3 What matters and what doesn't

Careful observation helps you to narrow down what matters and what doesn't. It can tell you which variables are important to control and which are not.

EXAMPLE

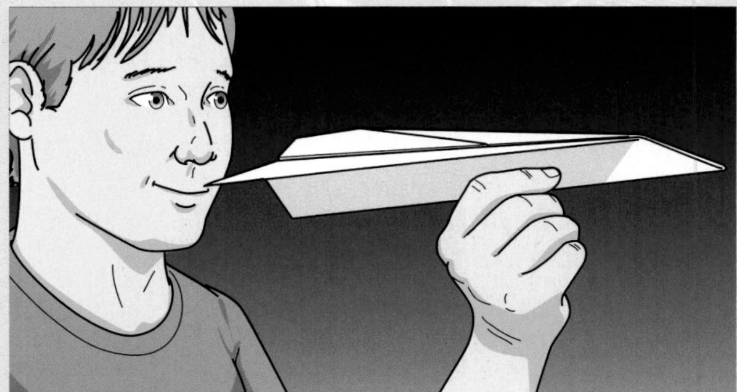

Suppose you were designing a paper glider. You know that the colour of the paper isn't important and so can be safely ignored. Its thickness may be important. But you might think design and wingspan are most likely to affect how far it can fly.

Question

Explain the relationship between chance occurrences and causal links when thinking about designing the paper glider.

Observations raise questions. These may lead to an investigation. For example, you might notice that some kinds of plants grow better in some parts of a garden than others. Why? You might map out the garden and investigate how factors such as soil type and shade vary in different parts of the garden.

Careful observation of rocks in Dorset led to oil being obtained commercially from Wych Farm near Wareham.

C Designing an investigation

C1 What is an 'investigation'?

A scientific investigation usually begins with a question. Data are collected, analysed and interpreted as we home in on an answer to the question. The number of questions is limited only by our curiosity!

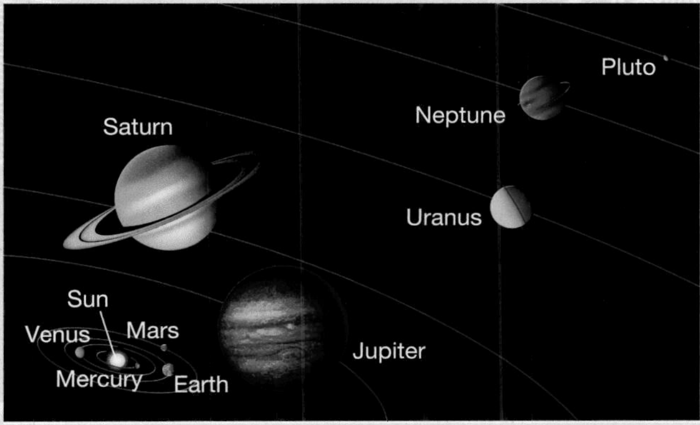

How do we know about our Solar System? How did the whole thing begin? Will it ever end? The questions are only limited by our curiosity!

Many investigations are 'application-led'. For example:

- searching for new drugs to combat cancer or heart disease
- trying to make mobile phones that work on the Underground
- finding alternative energy resources.

C2 Setting up an investigation

You think about the 'big' question. It gives rise to others. Investigation design starts with deciding which you are going to try to answer and seeing how, together, they might give you the answer to the 'big' question.

Tests used must be **fair tests**. It's usually better to do them in a laboratory where it's easier to control variables. Of course, it's not always possible and some tests must be carried out 'in the field'.

[C2 continued]

Typically in a fair test you choose one variable to study. This is the **independent variable**. You change this variable in a controlled way and see what happens to the **dependent variable**. Often some trial runs are necessary to find out what approximate values you are going to try to measure, how many measurements you should make and when to make them.

EXAMPLE

Enzymes are used to make, for example, yoghurt from milk and wine from grapes. The activity of an enzyme depends on the temperature and pH. To investigate the effect of temperature you need to:

- choose a method for measuring activity
- keep the pH the same
- use enough enzyme for its activity to be measured
- use a sensible range of temperatures
- take readings at smaller time intervals when the activity changes.

Questions

1. What do you think 'a sensible range of temperatures' means?
2. Why should you 'take readings at smaller time intervals when the activity changes'?
3. What variable must you keep constant if you want to investigate the effect of pH on enzyme activity?

Control groups are often used to check the effect of changing a variable. An example is testing the effectiveness of a new medicine. The control group might be split into two. One half is given the medicine. The other half is given a placebo (a substance that we know has no effect). Nobody is told which they have been taking.

An investigation must be designed to give data with sufficient accuracy and precision, and measurements that are reliable. Your conclusions must relate to the question asked. You should evaluate the reliability and validity of measurements made and their interpretation. You should justify your confidence in the outcome of the investigation, whether it's high or not so high!

D Making measurements

D1 Measuring instruments

Scientists measure things. They use a wide variety of instruments and apparatus. There are three important terms you should understand when using measuring instruments and apparatus.

- **Accuracy**: how close a measurement is to the true value. You are more likely to get accuracy with quality instruments (usually more expensive) than cheaper ones. They are better made and better calibrated. So you are more likely to be confident in a measurement if it is made with a quality instrument

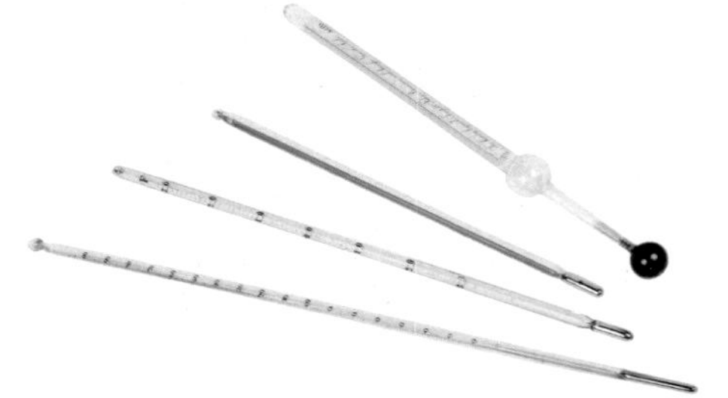

The quality of thermometers varies. On the whole the more expensive ones are more accurate. As well as 'liquid in glass' thermometers, scientists often use electronic thermometers.

- **Sensitivity**: the smallest differences that can be measured with an instrument or piece of apparatus.
- **Precision**: the reliability of an instrument. Measuring the same thing several times gives results that are close together.

EXAMPLE

Imagine measuring the mass of a sample of soil. You use two different balances and repeat the measurement six times with each. These are your results:

Balance A: 103, 104, 102, 103, 104, 104 grams
Balance B: 101, 109, 92, 106, 112, 103 grams

Question

Which balance has the greater precision?

D2 Measurement confidence

How confident can you be that your measurements are reliable?

If it was your job to analyse water and check its fitness for drinking, what would affect your confidence in your results?

Imagine you are testing tennis balls. Does a ball bounce to the correct height? When you measure the height of the bounce it might vary because the temperature is different. The hotter the weather, the more the balls bounce. Do you know why?

- Use **standard procedures**. They describe exactly how to make a measurement. Always follow the manufacturer's instructions when using an instrument.
- Look for **anomalous data**. These are data that don't seem to fit the pattern of the others. They 'look wrong'. Try to find out why. If the anomaly is due to poor measurement, ignore these data.
- Repeat the measurement. Getting the same value means the measurement is **reproducible**. It's probably reliable. A further check on reproducibility is that different people working in different laboratories, but using the same procedure, get the same result.
- Don't just repeat the measurement once. Often it is useful to repeat it several times. The difference between the minimum and maximum values is the **range**. The **mean** (or **average**) is the sum of the measurements divided by the number of measurements taken.
- If the measurement is not reproducible it might be that the **conditions** have changed.
- We all make mistakes. Practice can help to reduce **human error**. You can usually tell if there is a problem. Several measurements of the same thing vary randomly, in other words there is no pattern.
- On the other hand repeated measurements that are close to one another but not close to the true value suggest a different problem. It's likely that the instructions have been followed incorrectly or the instrument is poorly calibrated.

EXAMPLE

An ammeter is used in an electrical circuit to measure the current. In an investigation three ammeters were tried. Each was used to make repeat measurements. Here are the results (all measurements in amperes):

Ammeter A / amperes
1.35 1.45 1.29 1.22 1.38 1.30
Ammeter B / amperes
1.32 1.34 1.32 1.35 1.33 1.33
Ammeter C / amperes
1.45 1.44 1.44 1.45 1.45 1.44

The true value was 1.34 amperes.

Questions

1. Which set of readings suggests the greatest human error?
2. Which set of readings is accurate and precise?
3. Which set of readings is inaccurate but precise?
4. Which set of readings shows the greatest precision?
5. For each ammeter, say what the range of measurements was and calculate the average measurement.

E Presenting data

E1 Displaying data

Some data are:

- observed. They can be sorted into groups or categories. Each can be labelled. They are sometimes called **categorical data**.
- measured. They are **continuous data** and have no limits. When measurements are made it is essential to say what the units are.

It is useful to display data to help you to spot patterns, relationships and anomalous data. You could do this using:

- **tables** to set out data clearly (you must include the correct units)
- **bar charts** to show the relationship between categorical data and continuous data (you must label both axes and include units for the continuous data)
- **line graphs** to display data in which both sets of data are continuous (you must label both axes and include correct units).

One picture shows a beaker of water being heated and its temperature being measured. The other shows a field of coloured flowers. Which would you display as a bar chart and which as a line graph?

EXAMPLE

Six different types of tomato are grown from seed. After a period of time their heights are measured. You could record the results in a **table**:

Type of tomato	1	2	3	4	5	6
Height/cm	3.2	4.9	4.1	5.8	3.7	5.3

To look for patterns and relationships, you might display the data as a **bar chart**.

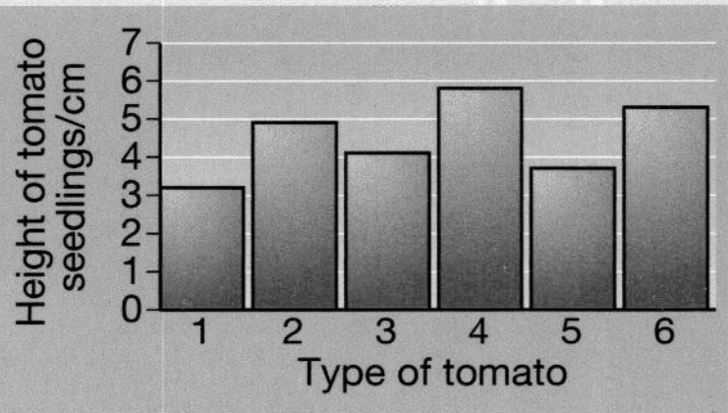

Questions

1. Which data are categorical and which are continuous?
2. It might seem that types 2, 4 and 6 are the strongest growers. How could you test this idea?
3. How would you display data showing how the height of a tomato plant changes according to the time it's been growing?

EXAMPLE

A candle was lit and its height after different periods of time was measured. You could record the results in a **table**:

Time/minutes	0	1	2	3	4	5	6
Height/cm	10	9.2	8.4	7.6	6.8	6.0	5.2

To look for patterns and relationships, you might display the data as a **line graph**:

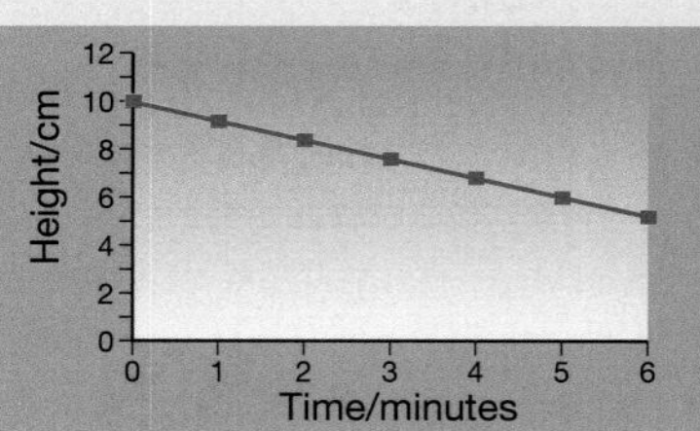

Questions

1. Describe in words what the line graph shows.
2. Why is it acceptable to use a line graph here but not for the tomatoes investigation above?
3. How could you compare the speed at which candles of differing diameters burn?

E2 Line graphs are really useful

When you plot a line graph, it can take many forms. Perhaps the most useful is the straight line graph. You get a straight line graph when one variable is directly proportional to the other. Let's look at a couple of examples.

EXAMPLE

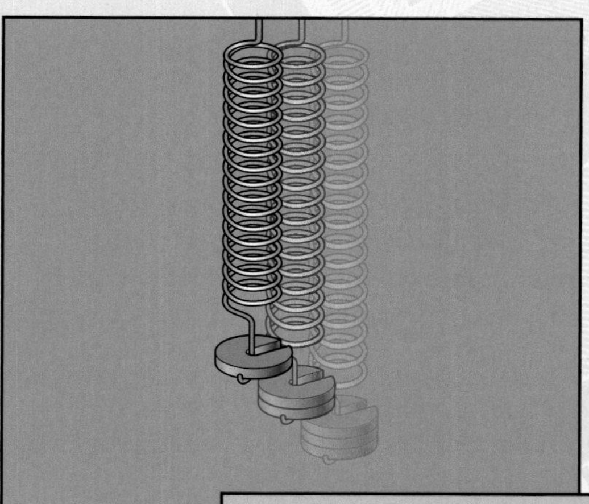

When masses are hung on this spring it stretches by the same amount each time. The graph shows this.

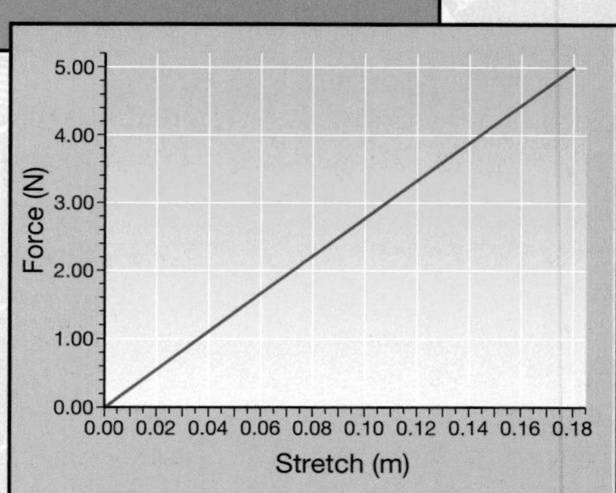

Questions

1. What are the two variables?
2. Which variable is being controlled?

EXAMPLE

Look at the graph showing how the height of a candle changes as it burns. It is a straight line graph. It shows that the height of the candle decreases by the same amount each minute that it burns.

Questions

1. What type of data is plotted?
2. What are the units for the height of the candle?
3. Do you think there are any anomalous data?

F Identifying patterns and relationships in data

Patterns and relationships in data can show the behaviour of the variables in an investigation. However, we need to remember that the data is often limited, and that this may affect our conclusions.

How do we identify patterns and relationships? We can use tables and graphs. On a graph with scattered data, we often use a line of best fit to reveal what the underlying pattern is. Tables and graphs will also often help show 'odd' or anomalous data that needs more examination.

When examining data we look for relationships that are either linear or directly proportional. An example of a linear relationship might be pumping water out of a barrel – the volume of water left depends on the time spent pumping. An example of a directly proportional relationship could be stretching a rubber band – the stretching relates to the amount of force used.

It is important to remember the limitations of your data. An investigation conducted on members of your own school may not mean that your conclusions are correct for the whole world! Consider also how reliable the data actually is, and what we might do to improve it.

EXAMPLE

Suppose you want to investigate how physical activity affects heart rate and breathing rate. You should:

- choose a suitable method for measuring heart rate and breathing rate
- keep the physical activity the same for each of these two measurements.

Questions

1. In this investigation there are two dependent variables. What are they?
2. Why is it important to 'keep the physical activity the same for each of these two measurements.'?
3. Why might it be useful to group the data into categories such as 'Age range', 'Occupation' or 'Diet'?
4. Construct a graph of the heart rate versus breathing rate results. What does this tell you about the relationship between the variables?
5. What can we conclude from this investigation? Can we say that all people with a lower heart rate are 'physically fit'?

G Societal aspects of scientific evidence

G1 There's no place for prejudice

There's no place for prejudice, whim or hearsay in science. An opinion must be supported by valid and reliable evidence. However, history shows that the acceptance of new scientific ideas may not depend on the reliability of the evidence alone.

G2 Does it fit with or go against current ideas?

Evidence that supports what we already think and know tends to be accepted more readily. Evidence that seems to go against our present understanding often takes more time to be accepted.

EXAMPLE

Giordano Bruno

Giordano Bruno was an Italian philosopher and astronomer born in 1548. He became interested in the ideas of Nicolaus Copernicus, but these went against Church thinking. He fled Naples, his home, to avoid the Inquisition and develop his idea in safety.

Bruno believed the Earth moved, an idea now universally accepted. He thought the Earth wasn't special, just another heavenly body in the Universe. This didn't find favour with the Church. In fact, the pattern throughout his life was to fall foul of the Church having gained favour from lay authorities.

He was denounced to the Inquisition on 22 May 1592. In 1600 Bruno was burned at the stake for his beliefs. Four hundred years later Pope John Paul II expressed 'profound sorrow' and acknowledged an error had been made.

G3 Is it balanced and not biased?

Evidence is scrutinised to check that it doesn't show bias by omitting or playing down the significance of some data. Potentially researchers might present biased evidence for various reasons.

They may have preconceived ideas about why something works the way it does. They set out to provide evidence for their hypothesis.

They may feel pressure from other people or organisations. For example:

- Somebody has to fund their research. Might this influence the data presented?
- The researchers' findings might cause concern amongst the public or government. Might this influence the data presented?

G4 Purpose of scientific evidence

Scientific evidence is gathered for many purposes. The nature of the evidence and how it is presented depends on these purposes. In other words, the evidence must be fit for its purpose. A couple of examples will show you what we mean.

A new drug is discovered that can be used to treat an illness or disease. It is highly effective. However, before doctors prescribe it we must be sure that it is safe to use. We need highly reliable and valid evidence.

Sometimes a lesser degree of reliability and validity in evidence is acceptable. For example, gardeners use soil testing kits to decide how to treat the soil. For example, soil may be acidic. The measurement allows gardeners to work out how much lime should be added. But the exact quantity is not critical.

However, whatever the investigation, it's essential that the conclusions are based only on the evidence. For example, it might be shown that a new drug works well on young women. It would be wrong to say it works on everybody. Of course, it may work on everybody but there is no evidence for this.

G5 Does status matter?

A scientist with academic or professional status, experience and authority will be listened to with more confidence that those with less experience. To act as an expert witness in a court of law, a scientist must have appropriate academic and/or professional qualifications.

EXAMPLE

Marie Curie

With her husband Pierre, Marie Curie discovered radium. They were awarded a Nobel Prize in 1904. Pierre Curie died in 1906, but Marie devoted her life to finishing their work. In 1911 she received a second Nobel Prize. Their research on high energy radiation led to the development of X-rays in surgery.

Marie Curie was an outstanding scientist yet she initially faced great opposition from male scientists in France. She died in 1934 from leukaemia, due to exposure to high-energy radiation used in her research.

H Limitations of scientific evidence

Science does not have all the answers. Our scientific knowledge and understanding is still limited. Every day we make new discoveries, but there are always questions to which we do not have the answers. Consider global warming, for example. Is it caused by mankind's excessive use of fossil fuels? We believe so, but there are many who argue that we simply do not have enough evidence to prove it.

Sometimes science simply cannot answer the question at all. Should we eat meat? Should we clone human organs? Should we introduce life to other planets? We cannot rely on science to tell us.

There are some questions that only society can provide the answers for.

How Science Works – in your practical and investigational work

Throughout your GCSE Science course, you will be encouraged to carry out practical and investigational work. Remembering the key points of How Science Works will help you to do your very best work.

At certain points, your teacher will set **Investigative Skills Assignments**, to test the quality of your work. You can find examples to practise on at www.collinseducation.com/gcsescience and at www.aqa.org.uk

Your teacher will **Assess your Practical Skills** during the course of your normal practical work. They will be judging your ability to...

- use equipment and materials in an appropriate and careful way
- carry out work in an organised way
- work safely and with consideration for the well-being of living organisms and the environment.

This table provides an indication of how performance is judged. Compare your work to this table, and think of ways to improve.

Performance level	Skills
2 marks	Practical work is done safely, but sometimes in a disorganised way. The student uses the equipment and materials with some assistance.
4 marks	Practical work is done safely and in a fairly organised way. The student uses the equipment and materials well, without needing assistance.
6 marks	Practical work is done safely, and in a well organised way. The student uses the equipment and materials well in a demanding context.

Alkane molecules can be represented in the following forms:

C_2H_6

```
      H     H
      |     |
H --- C --- C --- H
      |     |
      H     H
```

Unsaturated hydrocarbon molecules can be represented in the following forms:

C_3H_6

```
      H     H     H
      |     |     |
H --- C --- C === C
      |           |
      H           H
```

$$\text{efficiency} = \frac{\text{useful energy transferred by the device}}{\text{total energy supplied to the device}}$$

energy transferred (kilowatt-hour, kWh) = power (kilowatt, kW) x time (hour, h)

wave speed (metre/second, m/s) = frequency (hertz, Hz) x wavelength (metre, m)

The Periodic Table

Key: relative atomic mass / **atomic symbol** / name / atomic (proton) number

1	2											3	4	5	6	7	0
							1 **H** hydrogen 1										4 **He** helium 2
7 **Li** lithium 3	9 **Be** beryllium 4											11 **B** boron 5	12 **C** carbon 6	14 **N** nitrogen 7	16 **O** oxygen 8	19 **F** fluorine 9	20 **Ne** neon 10
23 **Na** sodium 11	24 **Mg** magnesium 12											27 **Al** aluminium 13	28 **Si** silicon 14	31 **P** phosphorus 15	32 **S** sulfur 16	35.5 **Cl** chlorine 17	40 **Ar** argon 18
39 **K** potassium 19	40 **Ca** calcium 20	45 **Sc** scandium 21	48 **Ti** titanium 22	51 **V** vanadium 23	52 **Cr** chromium 24	55 **Mn** manganese 25	56 **Fe** iron 26	59 **Co** cobalt 27	59 **Ni** nickel 28	63.5 **Cu** copper 29	65 **Zn** zinc 30	70 **Ga** gallium 31	73 **Ge** germanium 32	75 **As** arsenic 33	79 **Se** selenium 34	80 **Br** bromine 35	84 **Kr** krypton 36
85 **Rb** rubidium 37	88 **Sr** strontium 38	89 **Y** yttrium 39	91 **Zr** zirconium 40	93 **Nb** niobium 41	96 **Mo** molybdenum 42	98 **Tc** technetium 43	101 **Ru** ruthenium 44	103 **Rh** rhodium 45	106 **Pd** palladium 46	108 **Ag** silver 47	112 **Cd** cadmium 48	115 **In** indium 49	119 **Sn** tin 50	122 **Sb** antimony 51	128 **Te** tellurium 52	127 **I** iodine 53	131 **Xe** xenon 54
133 **Cs** caesium 55	137 **Ba** barium 56	139 **La*** lanthanum 57	178 **Hf** hafnium 72	181 **Ta** tantalum 73	184 **W** tungsten 74	186 **Re** rhenium 75	190 **Os** osmium 76	192 **Ir** iridium 77	195 **Pt** platinum 78	197 **Au** gold 79	201 **Hg** mercury 80	204 **Tl** thallium 81	207 **Pb** lead 82	209 **Bi** bismuth 83	[209] **Po** polonium 84	[210] **At** astatine 85	[222] **Rn** radon 86
[223] **Fr** francium 87	[226] **Ra** radium 88	[227] **Ac*** actinium 89	[261] **Rf** rutherfordium 104	[262] **Db** dubnium 105	[266] **Sg** seaborgium 106	[264] **Bh** bohrium 107	[277] **Hs** hassium 108	[268] **Mt** meitnerium 109	[271] **Ds** darmstadtium 110	[272] **Rg** roentgenium 111	Elements with atomic numbers 112-116 have been reported but not fully authenticated						

* The Lanthanides (atomic numbers 58–71) and the Actinides (atomic numbers 90–103) have been omitted.
Cu and **Cl** have not been rounded to the nearest whole number.

acid rain	all rain is slightly acidic due to carbon dioxide naturally present in the atmosphere. Acid rain also contains stronger acids, made when sulfur dioxide and nitrogen oxides from pollution or volcanoes dissolve in falling rain.	92–95
adaptation	a feature of an organism that fits it to its environment: for example, the zebra's stripes are an adaptation that helps to camouflage it in the savannah of Africa.	62–65
addicted	people are addicted to something if they would suffer if it was removed. In psychological addiction, the suffering is mental – e.g. people can be very bad tempered or fidgety if they give up cigarettes. Physical addiction occurs with drugs like heroin. In this case the addict suffers from serious physical symptoms (sweating, headaches, diarrhoea, possibly even fits) when the drug is removed.	36–37, 40–41
additives, food	chemicals added to foods to improve the flavour or appearance or shelf life.	182–183
adrenaline	a hormone produced by the adrenal gland which prepares the body for vigorous activity.	14–15
air	the mixture of gases in the atmosphere.	92–97, 192–197, 242–243
alkanes	chemicals containing only hydrogen and carbon with the general formula C_nH_{2n+2}, for example methane.	146–147, 156–157
alkenes	chemicals containing only hydrogen and carbon with the general formula C_nH_{2n}, for example ethene.	158–161, 164–165
alloy	a mixture of two or more metals.	132, 140–141
aluminium	a shiny metal which is very light in weight.	132–135
antibiotic	a substance produced by a microbe which kills other microbes. Some antibiotics can be purified and used to treat infections.	50–52
antibodies	chemicals produced by cells called B lymphocytes which attack invading microorganisms.	54
antigens	chemicals found in cell membranes and cell walls which trigger a reaction by the immune system.	54
antivirals	drugs that act against viruses.	50–51
atoms	the building blocks of an element. Atoms consist of negatively-charged electrons flying around a positively-charged nucleus.	110, 112–113, 128–129, 266–267, 274–275
battery	a device that changes chemical energy into electrical energy.	228
Big Bang	the event believed by many scientists to have led to the start of the universe.	290–291
biofuel	a fuel that is produced from a living system, for example wood, or ethanol produced from maize starch.	172–173
biomass	the mass of living material in an area. Ecologists might talk of the biomass of lions in a safari park or the biomass of grass in a grassland area.	229, 240
blast furnace	a furnace that extracts iron from iron ore.	122–123
brown fat	a type of fat that seems to be able to burn glucose by respiration to produce heat rather than energy for the body. People with high levels of brown fat seem to be able to eat more food without getting so fat.	26–27
carcinogen	a carcinogen is a chemical known to cause cancer.	44
cast iron	iron produced from a blast furnace. It is just over 90% iron and is quite brittle.	124–127
central nervous system	the brain and spinal cord.	14
chromatography	the science of producing chromatograms. Chromatography can use paper or jelly-like films for the soluble substances to move along.	194–195
clones	two living things are clones if they have exactly the same genes.	72–73
conduction	movement of energy as heat (or electricity) through a substance without the substance itself moving.	208–209
convection	movement of a heated substance which carries energy with it as heat.	208–209
copper	a yellowy-orange metal.	138–139
correlation	a correlation is a link between two variables. You can decide that there is a correlation between two things, even if you do not understand how the link works.	45
covalent bond	a covalent bond is a link between two atoms where electrons move around both atoms in the pair. Covalent bonds tend to be strong bonds and form between non-metals.	114–115
cracking	the breaking of large organic molecules into smaller ones using heat, pressure and sometimes catalysts.	158–159
crude oil	oil extracted from the ground before it has been refined.	144–145
current	the flow of electrical charge through an electrical circuit.	255
cuttings, plant	parts of a plant that can, under certain circumstances, grow into a new plant.	70–71
deforestation	the loss of the tree cover in an area, usually through logging, but can also occur after a fire.	98–99
density	the mass of an object divided by its volume. Solids tend to be denser than liquids and much denser than gases.	133
dependent	if a person is dependent on a drug or alcohol, they constantly crave it and cannot manage without it.	36, 42–43

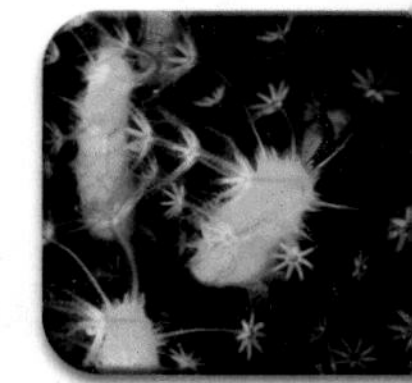

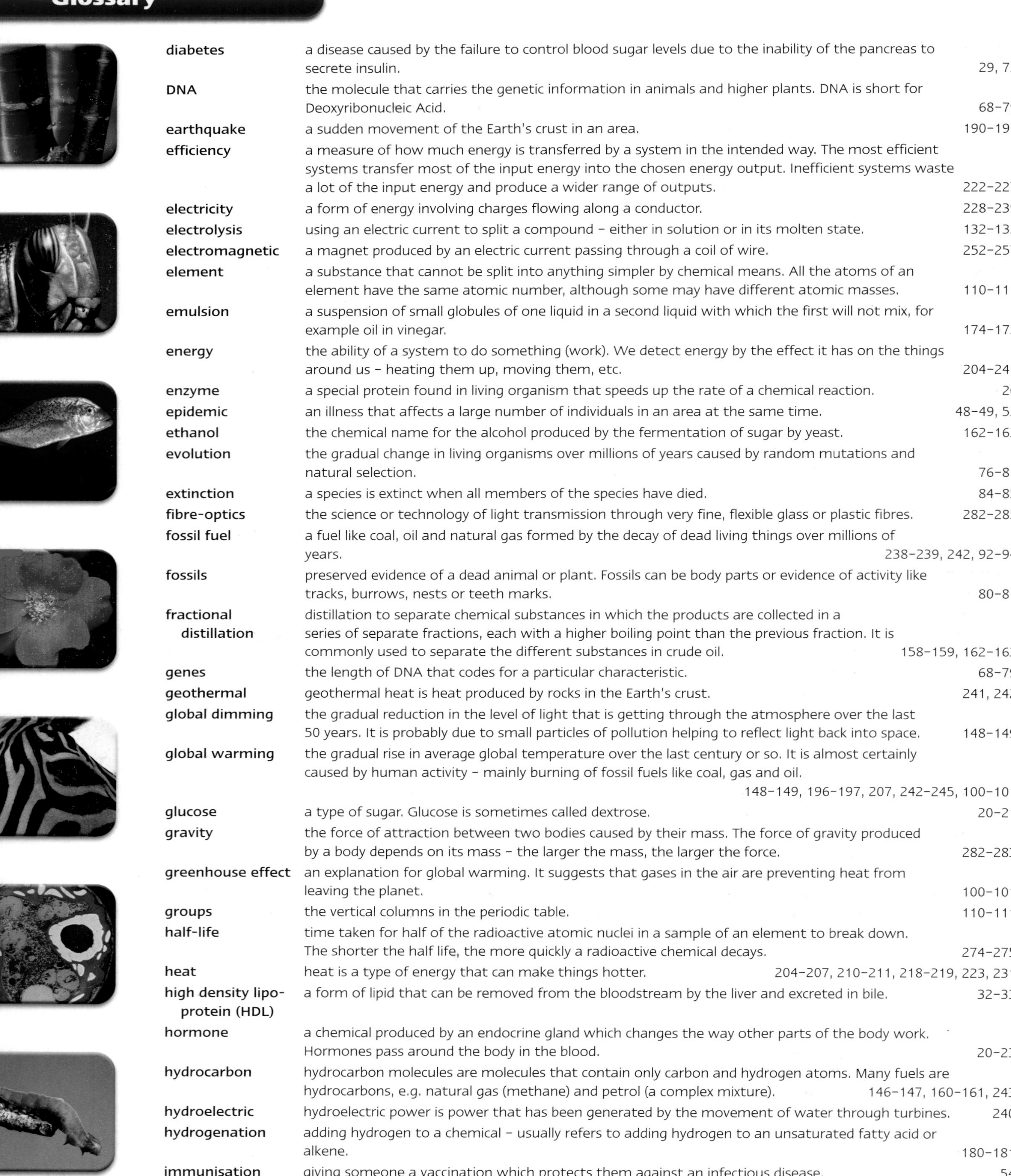

diabetes	a disease caused by the failure to control blood sugar levels due to the inability of the pancreas to secrete insulin.	29, 75
DNA	the molecule that carries the genetic information in animals and higher plants. DNA is short for Deoxyribonucleic Acid.	68–79
earthquake	a sudden movement of the Earth's crust in an area.	190–191
efficiency	a measure of how much energy is transferred by a system in the intended way. The most efficient systems transfer most of the input energy into the chosen energy output. Inefficient systems waste a lot of the input energy and produce a wider range of outputs.	222–227
electricity	a form of energy involving charges flowing along a conductor.	228–239
electrolysis	using an electric current to split a compound – either in solution or in its molten state.	132–133
electromagnetic	a magnet produced by an electric current passing through a coil of wire.	252–257
element	a substance that cannot be split into anything simpler by chemical means. All the atoms of an element have the same atomic number, although some may have different atomic masses.	110–111
emulsion	a suspension of small globules of one liquid in a second liquid with which the first will not mix, for example oil in vinegar.	174–175
energy	the ability of a system to do something (work). We detect energy by the effect it has on the things around us – heating them up, moving them, etc.	204–241
enzyme	a special protein found in living organism that speeds up the rate of a chemical reaction.	20
epidemic	an illness that affects a large number of individuals in an area at the same time.	48–49, 55
ethanol	the chemical name for the alcohol produced by the fermentation of sugar by yeast.	162–163
evolution	the gradual change in living organisms over millions of years caused by random mutations and natural selection.	76–81
extinction	a species is extinct when all members of the species have died.	84–85
fibre-optics	the science or technology of light transmission through very fine, flexible glass or plastic fibres.	282–285
fossil fuel	a fuel like coal, oil and natural gas formed by the decay of dead living things over millions of years.	238–239, 242, 92–94
fossils	preserved evidence of a dead animal or plant. Fossils can be body parts or evidence of activity like tracks, burrows, nests or teeth marks.	80–81
fractional distillation	distillation to separate chemical substances in which the products are collected in a series of separate fractions, each with a higher boiling point than the previous fraction. It is commonly used to separate the different substances in crude oil.	158–159, 162–163
genes	the length of DNA that codes for a particular characteristic.	68–79
geothermal	geothermal heat is heat produced by rocks in the Earth's crust.	241, 242
global dimming	the gradual reduction in the level of light that is getting through the atmosphere over the last 50 years. It is probably due to small particles of pollution helping to reflect light back into space.	148–149
global warming	the gradual rise in average global temperature over the last century or so. It is almost certainly caused by human activity – mainly burning of fossil fuels like coal, gas and oil.	148–149, 196–197, 207, 242–245, 100–101
glucose	a type of sugar. Glucose is sometimes called dextrose.	20–21
gravity	the force of attraction between two bodies caused by their mass. The force of gravity produced by a body depends on its mass – the larger the mass, the larger the force.	282–283
greenhouse effect	an explanation for global warming. It suggests that gases in the air are preventing heat from leaving the planet.	100–101
groups	the vertical columns in the periodic table.	110–111
half-life	time taken for half of the radioactive atomic nuclei in a sample of an element to break down. The shorter the half life, the more quickly a radioactive chemical decays.	274–275
heat	heat is a type of energy that can make things hotter.	204–207, 210–211, 218–219, 223, 231
high density lipo-protein (HDL)	a form of lipid that can be removed from the bloodstream by the liver and excreted in bile.	32–33
hormone	a chemical produced by an endocrine gland which changes the way other parts of the body work. Hormones pass around the body in the blood.	20–23
hydrocarbon	hydrocarbon molecules are molecules that contain only carbon and hydrogen atoms. Many fuels are hydrocarbons, e.g. natural gas (methane) and petrol (a complex mixture).	146–147, 160–161, 243
hydroelectric	hydroelectric power is power that has been generated by the movement of water through turbines.	240
hydrogenation	adding hydrogen to a chemical – usually refers to adding hydrogen to an unsaturated fatty acid or alkene.	180–181
immunisation	giving someone a vaccination which protects them against an infectious disease.	54
intensive farming	farming that uses fertilisers and high energy inputs to get the maximum production of food from an area of land.	89

ionic bond	the bond formed when an electron from one atom passes to travel around the nucleus of another, so creating two electrically charged ions. The different electrical charges attract the ions and hold them together.	114–115
ions	charged particles made when an atom, or group of atoms, gains or loses electrons.	114–115, 133
IVF	*In Vitro* Fertilisation: techniques which allow an egg and sperm to fuse outside the human body. The fertilised egg is then transplanted into a woman for a normal pregnancy.	25
joules	a unit of energy. It takes 4.2 J to raise the temperature of 1 g of water by 1° C.	220, 233
kwashiorkor	an illness caused by protein deficiency due to lack of food. Sufferers of kwashiorkor often have swollen bellies caused by retention of fluid in the abdomen.	30–31
limestone	a kind of rock made of the remains of shells and skeletons from living creatures. It is mainly calcium carbonate.	94, 116–123
lithosphere	the outer part of the earth, consisting of the crust and upper mantle, approximately 100 km thick.	188–189
low density lipoprotein (LDL)	a form of lipid that cannot be removed from the bloodstream by the liver and is deposited on the lining of blood vessels. High levels of LDL have been linked to heart attacks.	33
magnets	an object that is magnetic is attracted by a magnet.	237
malnutrition	poor nutrition because of an insufficient or poorly balanced diet or faulty digestion or utilisation of foods.	30–31
metabolic rate	the average speed of chemical reactions in an organism. Sometimes called the basal metabolic rate or BMR.	27
minerals	natural solid materials with a fixed chemical composition and structure. Rocks are made of collections of minerals. Mineral nutrients in our diet are things like calcium and iron. They are simple chemicals needed for health.	170–171
motor neurone	a nerve cell linking the central nervous system to a muscle fibre.	16–18
motor, electric	a device for converting electricity into circular movement.	236–237
national grid	the network of electricity cables that distribute electricity across the country.	234–235
natural selection	factors in the environment affect animals and plants so that some survive to reproduce successfully and pass on their good combinations of genes. Others survive less well and do not pass on their poor combinations of genes as often.	53, 78–79
nerve cells	cells that can carry messages.	15
neurone	a nerve cell.	17
nitrogen	a non-reactive gas that makes up most of the atmosphere.	192–193
nuclear energy	nuclear energy, or radiation, is the energy given out by a radioactive element as its nucleus decays. This radiation is in the form of sub-atomic particles.	267–269, 278–279
oestrogen	a female hormone produced by the ovaries. Oestrogen affects the menstrual cycle and a range of secondary sexual characteristics in females.	22–23
oils, natural	oils which occur naturally, such as those found in plants, nuts and seeds.	170–171
oxidation	a reaction which adds oxygen to a compound or element. Combustion and respiration are both oxidation reactions.	123, 133
oxygen	a colourless gas with no smell that makes up about 20% of the air.	192–193
pancreas	an organ in the abdomen that produces enzymes to break down food. It also contains the islets of Langerhans which are small groups of cells which produce the hormone insulin.	21
pandemic	something that affects the whole world, often used to describe an infection that affects the whole Earth.	48–49, 53
pathogen	an organism that causes a disease.	46
periodic table	a chart showing the relationships between the elements based on their atomic number.	110–111, 128–129
pituitary gland	a small gland found out the base of the brain. It links the endocrine system to the nervous system and secretes a range of hormones that affect other endocrine glands.	23
placebo	a treatment with no active ingredient used in drug trials.	38–41
pollution	chemicals made by human activity that are damaging to the environment.	90–97, 142–143, 148–151, 168–169, 242–243
polymer	a molecule made of many repeating subunits, for example polythene or starch	164–169
polyunsaturated	a hydrocarbon molecule that contains many double-carbon bonds and so less hydrogen than a saturated hydrocarbon. Polyunsaturated fats tend to have lower melting points and are regarded as healthier than saturated fats.	176–177
population	a group of organisms of the same type living in the same area.	86–87
power stations	buildings containing generators which produce electricity. Energy sources for power stations include burning of fossil fuels, nuclear radiation, sunlight, falling water and wind.	238–239, 244–245
proteins	a group of complex molecules that contain carbon, hydrogen, oxygen, nitrogen, and usually sulfur. They are made of one or more chains of amino acids. Proteins are important parts of all living cells and include enzymes, hormones, and antibodies. They are essential in the diet of animals for the growth and repair of tissue and can be obtained from foods such as meat, fish, eggs and milk.	26–27

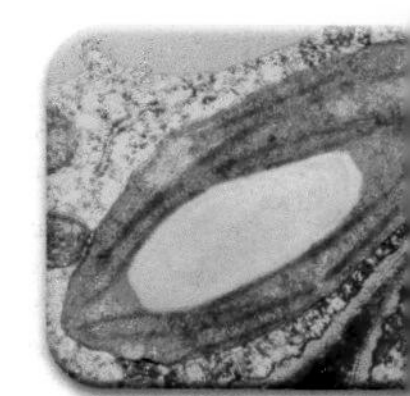

Glossary

Term	Definition	Pages
radiation	energy that travels as a wave and requires no physical medium to carry it, for example light, radio waves or infra-red radiation.	260–261, 266–271, 174–177
ray	a beam of light.	252–253, 268–271
recycle	to recover or reuse waste products.	134–135, 168–169, 102
reduction	a reaction in which oxygen is removed from a compound or hydrogen is added to it.	123, 133
reproduction	producing offspring. All living things must reproduce.	66–67
resistance	wires reduce the electricity flowing through them. This is called the resistance of the wire, it is a measure of how difficult it is to transfer energy through it as electricity.	231
respiration	the chemical process that makes energy from food in the cells in your body. All living things must respire.	27
saturated fats	the carbon atoms in the fatty acid part of the fat molecule are all linked to hydrogen atoms. They are more likely to be solid at higher temperatures than other fats and are linked to heart disease.	32–33
solar power	power generated from sunlight energy, usually used to describe electricity produced by photovoltaic cells.	244–245
solar system	the Sun and the planets orbiting it.	286–287
space	the area where the Sun, Earth and the stars exist, sometimes called the universe.	280–293
stars	huge balls of gas held together by their own gravitational field. Nuclear reactions in stars produce huge amounts of energy which leaves them as heat and light.	284–289
steel	an alloy of iron and carbon. Other metals are sometimes added to give steel special properties for particular uses. Steel is stronger than iron and does not rust so quickly.	126–127
sulfur	a yellow, crystalline non-metal.	150–151, 93
sustainability	development that does not make life more difficult for the generations that come after us.	102–103
synapse	the join between two nerve cells.	19
target organs	the organs which are affected by a particular hormone, e.g. the ovaries are the target organs for the hormone FSH which is secreted by the pituitary gland.	15
tectonic plates	sections of the Earth's crust that float on top of the mantle. Plates are hundreds of miles across and move relative to each other by a few inches a year.	188–189
telecommunications	devices which use electromagnetic waves to carry messages over long distances.	282–285
telescopes	a device which uses a combination of lenses and possibly mirrors to make a distant object look closer.	280–28
temperature	a measure of how hot something is.	62–63, 204–207, 210–211
Thermal decomposition	breaking down a compound by heating it, for example lead oxide is decomposed by heat to lead and oxygen.	118–119
thermal radiation	thermal radiation is electromagnetic radiation from an object caused by its temperature. It rapidly increases in power and frequency with increasing temperatures.	206–207
tidal power	electrical power generated from energy in moving waves	241
titanium	a strong, low-density silvery-grey metal that is used in aircraft and some laptop computer cases.	136–137
toxic	poisonous	39
total internal reflection	reflection of a ray of light back into a glass object as it hits the inner surface of the outside. Optical fibres rely on total internal reflection to keep the light within the fibre.	285
transition metal	a metal in the transition metal group in the periodic table. Transition metals are strong. They are good conductors of heat and electricity.	126, 129
unsaturated fats	a fat that contains many double-carbon bonds and so less hydrogen than a saturated fat Unsaturated fats are more common in plants than animals, tend to have lower melting points and are regarded as healthier than saturated fats.	32–33
virus	a tiny microorganism that lives inside other cells. Some viruses cause very serious diseases, such as smallpox.	46–47, 51, 53
volcanoes	an opening in the Earth's crust through which molten lava, ash, and gases are ejected.	190–191, 194
waves	energy travelling through a medium by moving individual particles short distances to-and-fro without causing any permanent movement of the medium itself.	252–259
weight	the force of gravity acting on a body on the Earth. Since weight is a force it is measured in newtons. People often use the word weight to mean mass but this is not strictly correct.	221
white blood cells	a group of blood cells produced by the bone marrow and lymph glands, which are involved in the immune response.	48–49
withdrawal symptoms	the combination of physical and psychological symptoms produced when an addictive drug is withheld for a period of time. The symptoms of withdrawal sickness fade after a while as the body adjusts to the absence of the drug.	37